The Enduring Vision

The Enduring Vision

SIXTH EDITION

A History of the American People
Volume I: To 1877

Paul S. Boyer
University of Wisconsin

Clifford E. Clark, Jr.
Carleton College

Joseph F. Kett
University of Virginia

Neal Salisbury
Smith College

Harvard Sitkoff
University of New Hampshire

Nancy Woloch
Barnard College

Houghton Mifflin Company   *Boston*   *New York*

Publisher: Suzanne Jeans
Marketing Manager: Katherine Bates
Marketing Assistant: Lauren Bussard
Senior Developmental Editor: Jennifer E. Sutherland
Senior Project Editor: Bob Greiner
Editorial Assistant: Emily Meyer
Senior Art and Design Manager: Jill Haber
Cover Design Director: Anthony L. Saizon
Senior Photo Editor: Jennifer Meyer Dare
Composition Buyer: Chuck Dutton
New Title Project Manager: James Lonergan

Cover Art: *View of the South East Prospect of the City of Philadelphia* by Peter Cooper on a signboard, 1720. Library Company of Philadelphia.

Printed in the U.S.A.

Library of Congress Catalog Number: 2006930132

Instructor's exam copy:
ISBN-10: 0-618-83405-2
ISBN-13: 978-0-618-83405-1

For orders, use student text ISBNs:
ISBN-10: 0-618-80161-8
ISBN-13: 978-0-618-80161-9

2   3   4   5   6   7   8   9-VH-10   09   08   07

Brief Contents

Contents

14 From Compromise to Secession, 1850–1861   *398*

15 Crucible of Freedom: Civil War, 1861–1865   *426*

16 The Crises of Reconstruction, 1865–1877   *466*

Special Features

Beyond America—Global Interactions

Technology and Culture

Maps, Figures, and Tables

Figures

Tables

Preface

Much has changed in America and the world since we began planning *The Enduring Vision* more than two decades ago. Some of these developments have been welcome and positive; others deeply unsettling. This new Sixth Edition fully documents all of these changes, as well as the continuities that offer reassurance for the future.

Although the United States of today differs in many ways from the nation of even a few decades ago, the will to live up to the values that give meaning to America—among them individual freedom, social justice, tolerance for diversity, and equality of opportunity—remains a guiding force in our life as a people. Our desire to convey the strength of this enduring vision in a world of change continues to guide our efforts in writing this book.

Since its inception *The Enduring Vision* has been one of the most widely used American history textbooks. The Sixth Edition builds on the underlying strategy that has guided us from the beginning. We want our history to be not only comprehensive and illuminating, but also lively, readable, and true to the lived experience of earlier generations of Americans. Within a clear political and chronological framework, we integrate the best recent scholarship in all areas of American history. Our interest in social and cultural history, which shapes our own teaching and scholarship, has suffused *The Enduring Vision* from the outset, and it remains central. We integrate the historical experience of women, African-Americans, Hispanic Americans, Asian-Americans, and American Indians—in short, of men and women of all regions, ethnic groups, and social classes who make up the American mosaic.

New Interpretations, Expanded Coverage

In each new edition of *The Enduring Vision* we carefully assess the coverage, interpretations, and analytic framework to incorporate the latest scholarship and emerging themes. In recent years, American historians have emphasized how deeply our history is embedded within a larger global context. In the Sixth Edition we have underscored the wider context of American history throughout the narrative. From the origins of agriculture two millennia ago to the impact of globalization today, we have emphasized how the social, economic, and political developments central to our historical experience emerge with fresh new clarity when viewed within a broader world framework. The global theme is also the focus of an innovative new feature, "Beyond America—Global Interactions" (see "Special Features," below).

As in earlier editions, coverage of environmental history, the land, and the West is fully integrated into the narrative, and treated analytically, not simply "tacked on" to a traditional account. We also incorporate the best of the new political history, stressing the social, cultural, and economic issues at stake in political decisions and debates.

This edition of *The Enduring Vision* continues to emphasize science and technology. From the hunting implements of the Paleo-Indians to the inventions and manufacturing innovations of the industrial age and today's breakthroughs in information processing and genetic engineering, the applications of science and technology are central throughout. We have included four new Technology and Culture boxed features, ranging from the telegraph to global warming (see "Revisions and Innovations in Each Chapter," below).

We again offer extensive coverage of medicine and disease, from the epidemics brought by European explorers and settlers to today's AIDS crisis, bioethics debates, and controversies over health-care financing. We also give careful attention to religious history, from the spiritual values of pre-Columbian communities to the political activism of contemporary conservative Christian groups.

Special Features

We are especially proud and excited to introduce a new feature, "Beyond America—Global Interactions," which highlights the Sixth Edition's intensified global emphasis. The fifteen illustrated essays explore the wider context of key developments in American history. The essays examine such topics as "Trade and Empire in the Pacific, to

1800," "Slave Emancipation in the Atlantic World," and "The Challenge of Globalization," underscoring how America's history takes on vivid new interest, and can be viewed in strikingly new ways, when seen in its global context. These new essays make clear that just as America has influenced the world, so has the world influenced America. Each essay is accompanied by a map of North America at the time, allowing students to trace the territorial expansion of the United States. A full list of the Beyond America and Technology and Culture essays appears on page xxi. (The "A Place in Time" essays in earlier editions may now be found on *The Enduring Vision* website.)

Every chapter now begins with the story of a representative individual, including Massachusetts Bay colonist Elizabeth Freake, black Revolutionary soldier Agrippa Hull, Tejano politician José Antonio Navarro, film star Rudolph Valentino, and Hmong immigrant Bao Xiong. These vignettes (each illustrated with an image of the person featured) introduce a central theme of the chapter and remind us that, in the last analysis, history involves the choices and actions of individual men and women.

Revisions and Innovations in Each Chapter

A chapter-by-chapter glimpse of some of the changes in this edition highlights its new content and up-to-the-minute scholarship.

Chapter 1 launches the Beyond America feature with a comparative essay on the origins and spread of agriculture, enabling students to view the development of farming America in a global context. The chapter also explicitly links some additional pre-contact cultures with Native American peoples important in later periods of American history.

Chapter 2 incorporates further detail on Spanish colonization in the Caribbean and on Anglo-Indian relations in early Virginia, including a clarification of the roles of John Smith and Pocahontas. The material in the former "Mediterranean Crossroads" section has been distributed among other sections. In Chapter 3, the discussion of the Chesapeake colonies now precedes that of New England.

Chapter 4 offers an expanded definition of mercantilism and added details on England's Navigation Acts, augmenting the new Beyond America essay on European maritime empires from 1450 to 1750. This chapter also draws a sharper contrast between the experiences of Europeans and Africans who arrived in the colonies in the first half of the eighteenth century. Chapter 5 includes a revised treatment of the Albany Congress and Plan of Union and of the Paxton Boys. This chapter also offers an expanded discussion of military maneuvering and fighting between the battles of Lexington and Concord and the Declaration of Independence.

The Beyond America essay in Chapter 6 presents a fresh perspective on the American Revolution as an international war and deepens the explanation for Britain's defeat in North America. The chapter offers new material on ordinary soldiers' experiences in the Continental Army, white women's political activities during the Revolution, and the Articles of Confederation.

Chapter 7 includes a Beyond America feature on trade and empire in the Pacific before 1800, providing a broader context for the discussion of Spanish and Russian colonization on the Pacific coast. This chapter also considers more fully the implementation of the new national government, the emergence of political parties, Spanish relations with Native Americans in Texas and New Mexico, and Federalist policy toward Native Americans.

Chapter 8 features a new opening vignette on Margaret Bayard Smith, an early chronicler of Washington society, and extends the account of Lewis and Clark's negotiations with the Indians. Chapter 9 expands and restructures the discussion of equality and inequality in the early Republic and blacks' efforts to secure education. Chapter 10, with a new opening vignette on the utopian and reformer Frances Wright, offers expanded coverage of the Shakers and features a Beyond America essay situating the Panic of 1837 in its transatlantic context.

Judicious cuts in Chapter 11 have resulted in an even more readable treatment of technology, culture, and everyday life in pre–Civil War America. An illuminating Beyond America essay in Chapter 12 examines slavery as a global phenomenon while noting how American slavery differed from that found elsewhere. A new Technology and Culture essay in Chapter 13 focuses on the invention of the telegraph and its transatlantic impact, while the Beyond America feature in Chapter 14 documents the rise of antislavery movements in the Atlantic world and their impact on the United States.

Chapter 15, on the Civil War, offers new insights and coverage. Chapter 16 begins with a new vignette about ex-slave Katie Rowe's memories of emancipation and includes a new Technology and Culture feature on the sewing machine, a key advance in domestic technology.

Chapter 17 opens with the story of Buffalo Bird Woman, a Plains Indian of North Dakota, and includes a new table on legislation relating to Indians, new material on the Mormons, and a Beyond America feature placing American cowboys in a global context. Chapter 18 adds a new Technology and Culture essay on electricity, a discussion of the South's economy in world perspective, and expanded coverage of black workers in the South and the labor activist Mary Harris ("Mother") Jones.

Chapter 19 includes new material on African-Americans, baseball, and the painter Mary Cassatt. A unique new map illustrates both the Asian and European sources of immigration to the Western Hemisphere in the late nineteenth century. Chapter 20 expands coverage of Clara Barton, founder of the army nursing corps, and Ida B. Wells, the African-American crusader against lynching. A new table lists and explains Gilded Age currency legislation.

Chapter 21's Beyond America essay offers a comparative overview of the reform spirit that gripped many Western countries in the early twentieth century, while a new "Racism and Progressivism" section underscores the pervasiveness of racism in this era, from lynch mobs to the White House. Chapter 22 offers new material on American overseas missionaries, the Mexican leader Pancho Villa, local vigilante movements during World War I, and the growth of the NAACP.

Chapter 23, with a new opening vignette on Rudolph Valentino, includes a Beyond America feature on the "New Woman" of the 1920s as a global phenomenon; expands coverage of the 1929 Gastonia textile strike, Hollywood sex scandals, and Herbert Hoover's conservationist policies; and discusses the composer Ruth Crawford Seeger and the African-American filmmaker Oscar Micheaux. The chapter also expands coverage of movies and the National Youth Administration, and offers a concise assessment of New Deal agricultural policies.

The five chapters covering the four decades from 1933 to 1974 offer three new Beyond America essays: on the intellectual migration from fascist regimes in Europe in the 1930s (Chapter 25); on the relationship between decolonization movements and U.S. foreign policy during the Cold War (Chapter 26); and on the "British invasion" of the Beatles and other bands in the 1960s (Chapter 29).

In addition, Chapter 25 includes more information on the causes and consequences of World War II and the impact of the war on American minorities and on U.S. society in general. Chapter 26, featuring a new opening vignette on baseball legend Jackie Robinson, includes a greater emphasis on the Cold War as a global phenomenon and on the early stirrings of postwar conservatism.

Chapter 27, with a new opening vignette on the comedians Lucille Ball and Desi Arnaz, gives greater attention to the shift in the Cold War from Europe to what was then called the Third World, and discusses in more depth the consequences of the rise in TV ownership and viewing. Chapter 28 offers additional background on the American war in Vietnam, environmental issues, and the significance of the 1964 Goldwater campaign in the emergence of postwar conservatism. This chapter also explores more fully the civil-rights struggles of African-Americans, especially the roles of CORE and SNCC, as well as the activism of American Indians, Hispanic Americans, and Asian-Americans.

Chapter 29 analyzes more fully the conservative resurgence of the 1970s as a reaction to the radicalism of the 1960s and the counterculture. This chapter also gives extensive attention to the rise of the Sunbelt, the Tet offensive as a turning point in the Vietnam War, and the importance of foreign affairs and energy issues in the Nixon administration.

The concluding three chapters, 30–32, incorporate new findings from recent scholarship. Chapter 30 expands coverage of popular culture; explores electronic-age privacy issues; and deepens the discussion of deindustrialization, labor activism, the Iran-Iraq War, violence associated with Islamic fundamentalism, and Soviet leader Mikhail Gorbachev's reasons for seeking better relations with the United States.

Chapter 31, extensively revised, now includes both terms of the Clinton administration and an expanded discussion of the stock-market boom, the influence of religious conservatives in the decade's culture wars, and bursts of domestic terrorist violence. This chapter also examines in more detail President George H. W. Bush's decision not to invade Iraq during the Persian Gulf War and updates the long-term effects of the Welfare Reform Act of 1996. A Beyond America essay weighs the cultural and economic impact of globalization.

Chapter 32, with an opening vignette on Hmong immigrant Bao Xiong, brings the story of American history down to the present, from George W. Bush's inauguration in 2001 to the 2006 elections. This chapter describes the Bush administration's response to the September 11, 2001, terrorist attacks, including the invasion of Iraq, new prisoner-detention policies, and domestic surveillance programs. The chapter also explores recent economic developments, social and demographic trends, and the ongoing debate over immigration policy. A new Technology and Culture essay examines the timely issue of global warming.

Visual Resources and Aids to the Student

Complementing the innovations in content is a fresh new design, giving the Sixth Edition a strikingly contemporary look. Scores of new photographs and other illustrations, many in color, not only add visual appeal but also enhance the book's instructional value.

To help students grasp the structure and purpose of each chapter, the Outlines at the beginning of each chapter now include the subheads as well as the major headings. The Focus Questions correspond to the major sections of the chapter and appear as running heads on the right-hand pages, helping students identify the key point in the section they are reading. The chapter Conclusion addresses and answers the Focus Questions in order. As a further pedagogical aid, each chapter now includes Key Terms that appear in boldface in the text and in a box at the end of the chapter. Key Terms are defined in an alphabetical glossary on *The Enduring Vision* website (see "Supplementary Resources" below).

Chronologies at the end of each chapter facilitate review. An annotated, up-to-date list of core readings at the end of each chapter offer guidance for those wishing to explore a particular topic in depth. More extensive chapter-by-chapter listings appear in the Additional Bibliographies section of *The Enduring Vision* website.

Understanding history requires a firm grasp of geography, and the Sixth Edition retains our unique Prologue on the American land. We have added eight entirely new maps. Maps on Protestant missionary activity in East Asia before World War I and on the current conflicts in Afghanistan and Iraq enhance the book's global coverage, while "Asian and European Immigrants Living in the Western Hemisphere and Hawaii in 1900," "The Growth of the Sunbelt, 1950–2000," "Voter Registration of African-Americans in the South, 1960–1968," and "The Hispanic Population of the United States, 2000," track important demographic changes.

New graphs compare the economic growth of the industrial powers in the late nineteenth century, track the foreign-born percentage of the U.S. population since 1900, and chart inflation from 1965 to the present, making these complex developments easier for students to see and understand.

Supplementary Resources

A wide array of supplements accompanies this text to help students master the material and guide instructors in teaching from *The Enduring Vision*, Sixth Edition. For details on viewing or ordering these materials, please consult your sales representative.

Online Study Center student website and Study Guide, including the Student Guide

Online Teaching Center instructor website, including Instructor's Resource Manual

HM Testing CD-ROM (powered by Diploma)

PowerPoint maps and images

PowerPoint questions for personal response systems

Blackboard™ Course Cartridges and WebCT™ e-packs

Eduspace™

Online multimedia eBook

Transparencies of Maps and Images

US History Atlas from Rand McNally

Enduring Voices Document Sets

For Students:

■ **The Online Study Center** is a companion website for students that features a wide array of resources to help them master the subject matter. It has been redesigned and expanded for the Sixth Edition. On the site, students will find ACE self-assessment quizzes; primary sources, including the Articles of Confederation; interactive maps; pre-class quizzes; downloadable audio summaries of chapter conclusions; vocabulary flashcards, and new to the Sixth Edition, an alphabetical list of all the Key Terms in the textbook, with full definitions, as well as additional bibliographies for each chapter. In addition, all of the "A Place in Time" features (from the fifth and previous editions) and some "Technology and Culture" features (from earlier editions) are posted on the site, along with questions to consider. Instructors and students can access the *Online Study Center* for this text by visiting **http://college.hmco.com/pic/boyer6e**.

■ **The Student Guide with Map Exercises,** by Barbara Blumberg at Pace University, available online, offers students chapter outlines and summaries, a glossary with definitions, identification questions, map exercises, skill-building activities, various historical sources for further research, and short-answer and essay questions.

For Instructors:

■ **The Online Teaching Center is a companion website for instructors.** It offers the *Instructor's Guide,* an online manual including Instructional Techniques and Resources, Historical Investigations for students, and for each chapter, chapter themes, lecture suggestions, print and nonprint resources, and a guide to using the Enduring Voices document sets. The *Online Teaching Center* also includes all of the material on the student site (including interactive maps and primary sources) to use as assignments, plus *PowerPoint* slides of maps, graphs, and images, and questions for use in personal response systems. Access the *Online Teaching Center* for this text by visiting **http://college.hmco.com/pic/boyer6e**.

■ **HM Testing.** The Test Item File, written by David Snead of Liberty University, is the complete testing resource for the book in CD-ROM format, with multiple-choice questions, map exercises, and essay questions. *HM Testing* (powered by *Diploma*) offers instructors a flexible and powerful tool for test generation and test management. Instructors can import questions from the test bank, create their own questions, or edit existing questions within the Diploma platform.

■ **Eduspace, Blackboard, and WebCT** A variety of assignable homework, study, and testing material for *The Enduring Vision* has been developed to work with the *Blackboard* and *WebCT* course management systems, as well as with *Eduspace*: Houghton Mifflin's Online Learning Tool. *Eduspace* is a web-based online learning environment that provides instructors with a gradebook and communication capabilities, such as synchronous and asynchronous chats and announcement postings. It offers access to assignments such as more than 400 gradeable homework questions, writing assignments, interactive maps with questions, primary sources, video resources with questions, questions for online discussion boards, and tests, incorporating the test item file described above, which all come ready-to-use and arranged by chapter of *The Enduring Vision*. Instructors can choose to use the content as is, modify it, or even add their own. *Eduspace* also contains an online multimedia e-Book, which contains in-text links to interactive maps, primary sources, and video resources, as well as review and self-testing material for students.

■ **The Houghton Mifflin U.S. History Transparency Set** offers approximately 150 full-color maps and graphs.

■ **US History Atlas** A US History Atlas, created by Rand McNally for Houghton Mifflin and newly revised, is available to be packaged with the text.

■ **Enduring Voices Document Set.** A two-volume document collection, *Enduring Voices*, can be packaged with the text.

Acknowledgments

In undertaking this major revision of our textbook, we have drawn on our own scholarly work and teaching experience. We have also kept abreast of new work of historical interpretation, as reported by our U.S. history colleagues in their books, scholarly articles, and papers at historical meetings. We list much of this new work in the books cited at the close of each chapter, and in the Additional Bibliographies on *The Enduring Vision* website.

We have also benefited from the comments and suggestions of instructors who have adopted *The Enduring Vision*; from students who have written us about specific details; and from the following scholars and teachers who offered systematic evaluations of specific chapters. Their perceptive comments have been most helpful in the revision process.

Jami McCoy Allen, *University of Louisville*

Debra Back, *Vanderbilt University*

Thomas Born, *Blinn College*

Diane F. Britton, *University of Toledo*

Lori Clune, *California State University at Fresno*

Stephanie Cole, *University of Texas at Arlington*

Rory T. Cornish, *Winthrop University*

Monica Cubberly, *Collin County Community College*

Krista Dornbush, *Marina High School, Huntington Beach, California*

C. Grady Eades, *Volunteer State Community College*

Keith Edgerton, *Montana State University*

Neil Foley, *University of Texas at Austin*

Yvonne Davis Frear, *Sam Houston State University*

Patricia Furnish, *Blue Ridge Community College*

Ben Gates, *Indiana University–Purdue University, Fort Wayne*

Paul S. George, *Miami Dade Community College*

George Gerdow, *Northeastern Illinois University*

Laura Graves, *South Plains College*

Larry Grubbs, *University of Georgia*

Howell H. Gwin, Jr., *Lamar University*

Peter L. Hahn, *Ohio State University*

Thomas M. Heaney, *Feather River College*

Dan Hicks, *Pennsylvania State University*

Andrew E. Kersten, *University of Wisconsin–Green Bay*

Tracy E. K'Meyer, *University of Louisville*

Janilyn Kocher, *Richland Community College*

Yawei Liu, *Georgia Perimeter College*

James J. Lorence, *Gainesville State College*

Jonathan Lurie, *Rutgers University*

Jennifer Mandel, *University of New Hampshire*

Gregory D. Massey, *Freed-Hardeman University*

Marko Maunula, *Clayton State University*

Stephen Middleton, *North Carolina State University*

Loyce B. Miles, *Hinds Community College*

John W. Miller, *University of Science and Arts of Oklahoma*

Anthony B. Miller, *The Bolles School*

Randall M. Miller, *Saint Joseph's University*

Earl F. Mulderink, *Southern Utah University*

Diane Mutti Burke, *University of Missouri at Kansas City*

Michael W. Nagle, *West Shore Community College*

Robert D. Parmet, *York College, City University of New York*

Richard Pells, *University of Texas at Austin*

Laura R. Prieto, *Simmons College*

Marc S. Rodriguez, *University of Notre Dame*

Connie Sexauer, *University of Wisconsin–Marathon County*

David Snead, *Liberty University*

Adam L. Tate, *Clayton State University*

Donald W. Trotter, Jr., *Johnson Bible College*

David J. Ulbrich, *Ball State University*

Faith Vautour, *Camden Hills Regional High School*

W. Michael Weis, *Illinois Wesleyan University*

In addition, Clifford Clark would like to thank his research assistant, Meredith Goddard, and his colleagues Martha Paas, Andrew Fisher, and Michael McNally.

Finally, we are delighted to salute the skilled professionals at Houghton Mifflin Company whose expertise and enthusiastic commitment to this new Sixth Edition guided us through every stage of the process and helped sustain our own determination to make this the best book we could possibly write. Our warmest thanks, then, go to Sponsoring Editor Sally Constable, who played a key role as we initially planned this new edition and offered support and wise advice at every stage; Jennifer Sutherland, Senior Developmental Editor, who with great skill and unfailing calm and good nature pushed us to do the tough work of rethinking each chapter and making our prose a model of clarity; Bob Greiner, Project Editor, who saw the work through the crucial production stages with careful attention to detail and supportive good humor; Emily Meyer, Editorial Assistant, who provided support at each stage during production; Penny Peters, who diligently supervised the art program; Marketing Manager Katherine Bates, who brings a wealth of experience to this crucial phase of the process; and Editorial Assistant Uzma Burney, who supervised the supplements program, worked with the scholars and instructors who reviewed our chapters, and helped in many other ways. Pembroke Herbert and Sandi Rygiel of Picture Research Consultants & Archives brought their creative skills to bear in seeking out fresh and powerful visual images for the work.

Paul S. Boyer
Clifford E. Clark, Jr.
Joseph F. Kett
Neal Salisbury
Harvard Sitkoff
Nancy Woloch

About the Authors

Paul S. Boyer, Merle Curti Professor of History emeritus at the University of Wisconsin, Madison, earned his Ph.D. from Harvard University. An editor of *Notable American Women, 1607–1950* (1971), he also coauthored *Salem Possessed: The Social Origins of Witchcraft* (1974), for which, with Stephen Nissenbaum, he received the John H. Dunning Prize of the American Historical Association. His other works include *Urban Masses and Moral Order in America, 1820–1920* (1978), *By the Bomb's Early Light: American Thought and Culture at the Dawn of the Atomic Age* (1985), *When Time Shall Be No More: Prophecy Belief in Modern American Culture* (1992), and *Promises to Keep: The United States since World War II,* 3rd ed. (2003). He is also editor-in-chief of the *Oxford Companion to United States History* (2001). His articles and essays have appeared in the *American Quarterly, New Republic,* and other journals. He has been a visiting professor at the University of California, Los Angeles; Northwestern University; and the College of William and Mary.

Clifford E. Clark, Jr., M.A. and A.D. Hulings Professor of American Studies and professor of history at Carleton College, earned his Ph.D. from Harvard University. He has served as both the chair of the History Department and director of the American Studies program at Carleton. Clark is the author of *Henry Ward Beecher: Spokesman for a Middle-Class America* (1978), *The American Family Home, 1800–1960* (1986), *The Intellectual and Cultural History of Anglo-America since 1789* in the *General History of the Americas,* and, with Carol Zellie, *Northfield: The History and Architecture of a Community* (1997). He also has edited and contributed to *Minnesota in a Century of Change: The State and Its People since 1900* (1989). A past member of the Council of the American Studies Association, Clark is active in the fields of material culture studies and historic preservation, and he serves on the Northfield, Minnesota, Historical Preservation Commission.

Joseph F. Kett, James Madison Professor of History at the University of Virginia, received his Ph.D. from Harvard University. His works include *The Formation of the American Medical Profession: The Role of Institutions, 1780–1860* (1968), *Rites of Passage: Adolescence in America, 1790–Present* (1977), *The Pursuit of Knowledge under Difficulties: From Self-Improvement to Adult Education in America, 1750–1990* (1994), and *The New Dictionary of Cultural Literacy* (2002), of which he is coauthor. A former History Department chair at Virginia, he also has participated on the Panel on Youth of the President's Science Advisory Committee, has served on the Board of Editors of the *History of Education Quarterly,* and is a past member of the Council of the American Studies Association.

Neal Salisbury, Barbara Richmond 1940 Professor in the Social Sciences and professor of history at Smith College, received his Ph.D. from the University of California, Los Angeles. He is the author of *Manitou and Providence: Indians, Europeans, and the Making of New England, 1500–1643* (1982), editor of *The Sovereignty and Goodness of God,* by Mary Rowlandson (1997), and coeditor, with Philip J. Deloria, of *The Companion to American Indian History* (2002). With R. David Edmunds and Frederick E. Hoxie, he has written *The People: A History of Native America* (2007), also published by Houghton Mifflin. He has contributed numerous articles to journals and edited collections, and coedits a book series, Cambridge Studies in North American Indian History. Formerly chair of the History Department at Smith, he has served as president of the American Society for Ethnohistory and is currently a member of the Council of the Omohundro Institute of Early American History and Culture.

Harvard Sitkoff, professor of history at the University of New Hampshire, earned his Ph.D. from Columbia University. He is the author of *A New Deal for Blacks* (1978), *The Struggle for Black Equality, 1954–1992* (1992), and *Postwar America: A Student Companion* (2000); coauthor of the National Park Service's *Racial Desegregation in Public Education in the United States* (2000) and *The*

World War II Homefront (2003); and editor of *Fifty Years Later: The New Deal Reevaluated* (1984), *A History of Our Time,* 6th ed. (2002), and *Perspectives on Modern America: Making Sense of the Twentieth Century* (2001). His articles have appeared in the *American Quarterly, Journal of American History,* and *Journal of Southern History,* among others. A frequent lecturer at universities abroad, he has been awarded the Fulbright Commission's John Adams Professorship of American Civilization in the Netherlands and the Mary Ball Washington Professorship of American History in Ireland.

Nancy Woloch received her Ph.D. from Indiana University. She is the author of *Women and the American Experience* (1984, 1994, 1996, 2000, 2002, 2006), editor of *Early American Women: A Documentary History, 1600–1900* (1992, 1997, 2002), and coauthor, with Walter LaFeber and Richard Polenberg, of *The American Century: A History of the United States since the 1890s* (1986, 1992, 1998). She is also the author of *Muller v. Oregon: A Brief History with Documents* (1996). She teaches American history and American Studies at Barnard College, Columbia University.

Prologue

Prologue

Enduring Vision, Enduring Land

This is the story of America and of a vision that Americans have shared. One part of that vision was of the American land. For the Native Americans who spread over the land thousands of years ago, for the Europeans who began to arrive in the sixteenth century, and for the later immigrants who poured in by the tens of millions from all parts of the world, North America was a haven for new beginnings. If life was hard elsewhere, it would be better here. Once here, the immigrants continued to be lured by the land. If times were tough in the East, they would be better in the West. New Englanders migrated to Ohio; Ohioans migrated to Kansas; Kansans migrated to California. For Africans the migration to America was forced and brutal. But after the Civil War, newly freed African-Americans embraced the vision and dreamed of traveling to a Promised Land of new opportunities. Interviewed in 1938, a former Texas slave recalled a popular verse that he and other blacks had sung when emancipated:

> *I got my ticket,*
> *Leaving the thicket,*
> *And I'm a-heading for the Golden Shore!*

For most of America's history, its peoples have celebrated the land—its beauty, its diversity, and its ability to provide sustenance and even wealth to those who tapped its resources. But within this shared vision have been deep-seated tensions. Even Native Americans—who regarded the land and other natural phenomena as spiritual forces to be feared and respected—sometimes depleted the resources on which they depended. Europeans tended to consider "nature" an alien force to be conquered and were even less restrained. The very abundance of America's natural resources led them to think of these resources as infinitely available and exploitable. In moving from one place to another, some sought to escape starvation or oppression, while others pursued wealth despite the environmental consequences. Regardless of their motives, migrants often left behind a land bereft of wild animals, its fertility depleted by intensive farming, its waters dammed and polluted or dried up altogether. If the land today remains part of Americans' vision, it is because they realize its vulnerability, rather than its immunity, to irreversible degradation at the hands of people and their technology.

To comprehend fully Americans' relationship with the land, we must know the land itself. The North American landscape, as encountered by its human inhabitants, took shape over at least 3 billion years, culminating in the last Ice Age (see Chapter 1). In turn, the continent's fundamental physical characteristics have shaped human events, from the earliest peopling to more recent waves of immigration; cycles of intensive agriculture and industrialization; the rise of cities; the course of politics; and even the basic themes of American literature, art, and music. Geology, geography, and environment are among the fundamental building blocks of human history.

Douglas Firs, Washington State
The impact of clear-cutting timber to meet worldwide demand for wood is made vividly clear in this photograph.

The Continent and Its Regions

Differences in climate, physical features, soils and minerals, and organic life are the basis of America's geographic diversity (see Maps P.1, P.2, and P.3). As each region's human inhabitants utilized available resources, geographic diversity contributed to a diversity of regional cultures, first among Native Americans and then among the immigrant peoples who spread across America after 1492. Taken together, the variety of these resources would also contribute to the rise to wealth and global preeminence of the United States.

The West

With its extreme climate and profuse wildlife, Alaska recalls the land that North America's earliest peoples encountered. Alaska's far north resembles a world formerly covered by ice caps—a treeless tundra of grasses, lichens, and stunted shrubs. This region, the Arctic, appears as a stark wilderness in winter and is reborn in fleeting summers of colorful flowers and returning birds. In contrast, the subarctic of central Alaska is a heavily forested country known as taiga. Here rises North America's highest peak, 20,320-foot Mt. McKinley. Average temperatures in the subarctic range from the fifties above zero Fahrenheit in summer to well below zero in the long, dark winters, and the soil is permanently frozen except during summer surface thaws and where, ominously, global warming is having an effect.

The Pacific coastal region is in some ways a world apart. Vegetation and animal life, isolated from the rest of the continent by mountains and deserts, include many species unfamiliar farther east. Warm, wet westerly winds blowing off the Pacific create a climate more uniformly temperate than anywhere else in North America. From Anchorage to south of San Francisco Bay, winters are cool, humid, and foggy, and the coast's dense forest cover includes the largest living organisms on Earth, the giant redwood trees. Along the southern California coast, winds and currents generate a warmer, Mediterranean climate, and vegetation includes a heavy growth of shrubs and short trees, scattered stands of oak, and grasses able to endure prolonged seasonal drought.

To the east of the coastal region, the rugged Sierra Nevada, Cascade, and coastal ranges stretch the length of Washington, Oregon, and California. Their majestic peaks trap abundant Pacific Ocean moisture that is carried eastward by gigantic clockwise air currents. Between the ranges nestle flat, fertile valleys that have been major agricultural centers in recent times.

Still farther east lies the Great Basin, encompassing Nevada, western Utah, southern Idaho, and eastern Oregon. The few streams here have no outlet to the ocean. A remnant of an inland sea that once held glacial meltwater survives in Utah's Great Salt Lake. Today, however, the Great Basin is dry and severely eroded, a cold

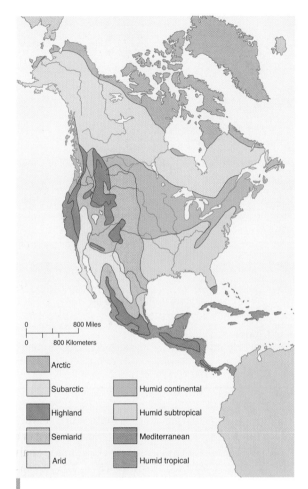

Map P.1 North American Climatic Regions
America's variety of mostly temperate climates is key to its environmental and economic diversity.

Legend:
- Arctic
- Subarctic
- Highland
- Semiarid
- Arid
- Humid continental
- Humid subtropical
- Mediterranean
- Humid tropical

0   800 Miles
0   800 Kilometers

environmental conditions, many plants and animals that thrive here could not survive elsewhere. Dust storms, cloudbursts, and flash floods have everywhere carved, abraded, and twisted the rocky landscape. Works of fantastic geological sculpture appear on the most monumental scale in the Grand Canyon, where the Colorado River has been cutting down to Precambrian bedrock for 20 million years. In the face of such tremendous natural forces, human activity might well seem paltry and transitory. Yet it was in the Southwest that Native Americans cultivated the first crops in what is now the continental United States.

The Heartland

North America's heartland comprises the area extending eastward from the Rockies to the Appalachians. This vast region forms one of the world's largest drainage systems. From it the Great Lakes empty into the North Atlantic through the St. Lawrence River, and the Mississippi-Missouri-Ohio river network flows southward into the Gulf of Mexico. By facilitating the transportation of peoples and goods, the heartland's network of waterways has supported commerce and communication among peoples for centuries—before the arrival of Europeans as well as since.

The mighty Mississippi—the "Father of Waters" to nearby Native Americans, and one of the world's longest rivers—has changed course many times. Southward from its junction with the Ohio River, the Mississippi meanders constantly, depositing rich sediments throughout its broad, ancient floodplain. It has carried so much silt over the millennia that in its lower stretches, the river flows above the surrounding valley, which it periodically floods when its high banks (levees) are breached. Over millions of years, such riverborne sediment covered what was once the westward extension of the Appalachians in northern Mississippi and eastern Arkansas. Only the Ozark Plateau and Ouachita Mountains remain exposed, forming the hill country of southern Missouri, north-central Arkansas, and eastern Oklahoma.

Below New Orleans the Mississippi empties into the Gulf of Mexico through an enormous delta with an intricate network of grassy swamps known as bayous. The Mississippi Delta offers rich farm soil capable of supporting a large population. Swarming with waterfowl, insects, alligators, and marine plants and animals, this environment has nurtured a distinctive way of life for the Native American, white, and black peoples who have inhabited it.

North of the Ohio and Missouri Rivers, themselves products of glacial runoff, Ice Age glaciation molded the American heartland. Because the local terrain was generally flat prior to glaciation, the ice sheets distributed glacial debris quite evenly. Spread even farther by wind and rivers,

desert rich in minerals and imposing in its austere grandeur and lonely emptiness. North of the basin, the Columbia and Snake Rivers, which drain the plateau country of Idaho and eastern Washington and Oregon, provide plentiful water for farming.

Western North America's "backbone" is the Rocky Mountains. The Rockies form part of the immense mountain system that reaches from Alaska to the Andes of South America. Beyond the front range of the Rockies lies the Continental Divide, the watershed separating the rivers flowing eastward into the Atlantic from those draining westward into the Pacific. The climate and vegetation of the Rocky Mountain high country resemble those of the Arctic and subarctic regions.

Arizona, southern Utah, western New Mexico, and southeastern California form America's southwestern desert. The climate is arid, searingly hot on summer days and cold on winter nights. Adapted to stringent

Map P.2 Land Use and Major Mineral Resources in the United States
The land has been central to America's industrial as well as agricultural productivity.

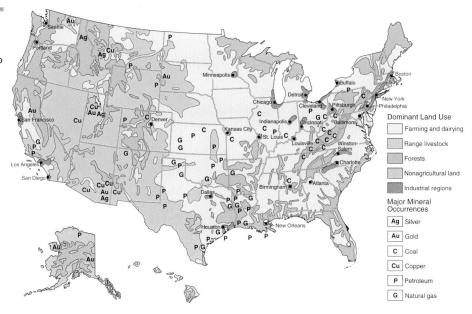

Dominant Land Use
- Farming and dairying
- Range livestock
- Forests
- Nonagricultural land
- Industrial regions

Major Mineral Occurrences
- Ag Silver
- Au Gold
- C   Coal
- Cu Copper
- P   Petroleum
- G   Natural gas

Map P.3 Natural Vegetation of the United States
The current distribution of plant life came about only after the last Ice Age ended, c. 10,000 BC, and Earth's climate warmed.

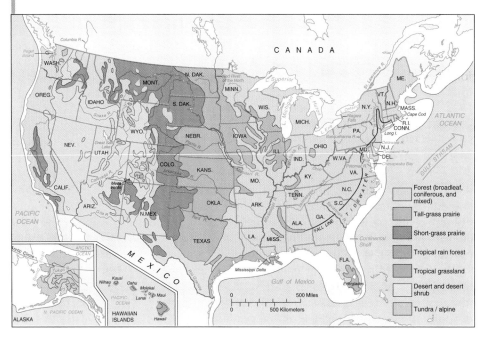

- Forest (broadleaf, coniferous, and mixed)
- Tall-grass prairie
- Short-grass prairie
- Tropical rain forest
- Tropical grassland
- Desert and desert shrub
- Tundra / alpine

this fine-ground glacial dust slowly created the fertile farm soil of the Midwest. Glaciers also dug out the five Great Lakes (Superior, Michigan, Huron, Erie, and Ontario), collectively the world's largest body of fresh water. Water flowing from Lake Erie to the lower elevation of Lake Ontario created Niagara Falls, a testimony like the Grand Canyon to the way that water can shape a beautiful landscape.

Most of the heartland's eastern and northern sectors were once heavily forested. To the west thick, tallgrass prairie covered Illinois, parts of adjoining states, and much of the Missouri River basin and the middle Arkansas River basin (Oklahoma and central Texas). Beyond the Missouri the prairie gave way to short-grass steppe—the Great Plains, cold in winter, blazing hot in

Devastation from Hurricane Katrina, 2005
Businesses destroyed by Katrina in Gulfport, Mississippi.

summer, and often dry. The great distances that separate the heartland's prairies and Great Plains from the moderating effects of the oceans continue to make this region's annual temperature range the most extreme in North America. As one moves westward, elevations rise gradually; trees grow only along streambeds; long droughts alternate with violent thunderstorms and tornadoes; and water and wood are ever scarcer.

During the nineteenth and twentieth centuries, much of this forested, grassy world became open farming country. Gone are the flocks of migratory birds that once darkened the daytime skies of the plains; gone are the free-roaming bison. Forests now only fringe the heartland: in the lake country of northern Minnesota and Wisconsin, on Michigan's upper peninsula, and across the hilly uplands of the Appalachians, southern Indiana, and the Ozarks. The settlers who largely displaced the region's Native Americans plowed up prairie grass and cut down trees. Destruction of the forest and grassy cover made the heartland both a "breadbasket" for the world market and, during intervals of drought, a bleak "dust bowl." With farming now in decline, the heartland's future is uncertain.

The Atlantic Seaboard

The eastern edge of the heartland is formed by the ancient Appalachian Mountain chain, which over the course of 210 million years has been ground down to gentle ridges paralleling one another southwest to northeast. Between the ridges lie fertile valleys such as Virginia's Shenandoah. The Appalachian hill country's wealth is in thick timber and mineral beds—particularly the Paleozoic coal deposits—whose heavy exploitation since the nineteenth century has accelerated destructive soil erosion in this softly beautiful, mountainous land.

Descending gently from the Appalachians' eastern slope is the Piedmont region. In this broad, rolling upland extending from Alabama to Maryland, the rich, red soil has been ravaged in modern times by excessive cotton and tobacco cultivation. The Piedmont's modern piney-woods cover constitutes "secondary growth," replacing the sturdy hardwood trees that Native Americans and pioneering whites and blacks once knew. The northward extension of the Piedmont from Pennsylvania to New England has more broadleaf vegetation and a harsher winter climate, and was shaped by glacial activity. The terrain in upstate New York and New England comprises hills contoured by advancing and retreating ice, and numerous lakes scoured out by glaciers. Belts of rocky debris remain, and in many places granite boulders shoulder their way up through the soil. Though picturesque, the land is the despair of anyone who has tried to plow it.

From southeastern Massachusetts and Rhode Island to south-central Alabama runs the fall line, at which rivers fall quickly to near sea level as they pass from the hard rock of the upland interior to the softer sediment of the coastal plain. Over time in many of the rivers, the abrupt fall has made rapids that block navigation upstream from the coast.

The character of the Atlantic coastal plain varies strikingly from south to north. At the tip of the Florida peninsula in the extreme south, the climate and vegetation are subtropical. The southern coastal lands running north from Florida to Chesapeake Bay and the mouth of the Delaware River compose the tidewater region. This is a wide, rather flat lowland, heavily wooded with a mixture of broadleaf and coniferous forests, ribboned with numerous small rivers, occasionally swampy, and often miserably hot and humid in summer. North of Delaware Bay, the coastal lowlands narrow and flatten to form the New Jersey pine barrens, Long Island, and Cape Cod—all created by the deposit of glacial debris. Here the climate is noticeably milder than in the interior. North of Massachusetts Bay, the land beyond the immediate shoreline becomes increasingly mountainous.

Many large rivers drain into the Atlantic—the Connecticut in New England; the Hudson, Delaware, Susquehanna, and Potomac in what are now the Middle Atlantic states; the Savannah in the South. Most of these originally carried glacial meltwater. The Susquehanna and the Potomac filled in the broad, shallow Chesapeake Bay, teeming with marine life and offering numerous anchorages for oceangoing ships.

North America's true eastern edge is not the coastline but the offshore continental shelf, whose relatively shallow waters extend as far as 250 miles into the Atlantic before plunging deeply. Along the rocky Canadian and Maine coasts, where at the end of the Ice Age the rising ocean half-covered glaciated mountains and valleys, oceangoing craft may find numerous small anchorages. South of Massachusetts Bay, the Atlantic shore and the Gulf of Mexico coastline form a shoreline of sandy beaches and long barrier islands paralleling the mainland. Tropical storms boiling up from the open seas regularly lash North America's Atlantic shores, and at all times brisk winds make coastal navigation treacherous.

For millions, the Atlantic coastal region of North America offered a welcome. Ancient Indian hunters and more recent European colonists alike found its climate and its abundance of food sources alluring. Offshore, well within their reach, lay such productive fishing grounds as the Grand Banks, off Newfoundland, and Cape Cod's coastal bays, where cool-water upwellings on the continental shelf had lured swarms of fish and crustaceans. "The abundance of sea-fish are almost beyond believing," wrote a breathless English settler in

Abandoned "Rust Belt" Factory
The American landscape is littered with reminders that large-scale factory production has ended or been diminished in many industries.

1630, "and sure I should scarce have believed it, except I had seen it with my own eyes."

A Legacy and a Challenge

North America's fertile soil, extensive forests, and rich mineral resources long nourished visions of limitless natural abundance that would yield limitless wealth to its human inhabitants. Such visions have contributed to the acceleration of population growth, intensive agriculture, industrialization, urbanization, and hunger for material goods—processes that are exhausting resources, polluting the environment, and raising temperatures to the point of endangering human health and well-being.

In searching for ways to avoid environmental catastrophe, Americans would do well to recall the Native American legacy. Although Indians often wasted, and occasionally exhausted, a region's resources to their detriment, their practices generally encouraged the renewal of plants, animals, and soil over time. Underlying these practices were Indians' beliefs that they were spiritually related to the land and all living beings that shared it. In recapturing the sense that they are intimately related to the land they inhabit, rather than alien to it, future American generations could revitalize the enduring vision of those who came before them.

The Enduring Vision

Chapter 1

Hohokam Ceramics, ca. A.D. 1000
These examples of Southwestern ceramic artistry were found at the Snaketown site in Arizona.

Native Peoples of America, to 1500

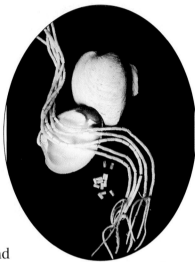

Wampum Strings

Hiawatha was in the depths of despair. For years his people, a group of five Native American nations known as the Iroquois, had engaged in a seemingly endless cycle of violence and revenge. Iroquois families, villages, and nations fought one another, and neighboring Indians attacked relentlessly. When Hiawatha tried to restore peace within his own Onondaga nation, an evil sorcerer caused the deaths of his seven beloved daughters. Grief-stricken, Hiawatha wandered alone into the forest. After several days, he experienced a series of visions. First, he saw a flock of wild ducks fly up from the lake, taking the water with them. Hiawatha walked onto the dry lakebed, gathering the beautiful purple-and-white shells that lay there. He saw the shells, called **wampum**, as symbolic "words" of condolence (sympathy). When properly presented, strings of wampum beads could soothe anyone's grief, no matter how deep. Then he met a holy man named Deganawidah (the Peacemaker), who presented him with thirteen strings of wampum and spoke the appropriate words—one to dry his weeping eyes, another to open his ears to words of peace and reason, still another to clear his throat so that he himself could once again speak peacefully and reasonably. Together the thirteen words restored Hiawatha's emotional balance. Then Deganawidah and Hiawatha took the wampum to the five Iroquois nations. (Besides the Onondaga, these were the Mohawk, the

Oneida, the Cayuga, and the Seneca.) To each they presented wampum words of condolence as a new message of peace. The Iroquois submerged their differences and created a council of chiefs and a confederacy based on the condolence ceremony. Thus was born the powerful **Iroquois Confederacy**.

Although an oral tradition retold through the generations and not written down until the late nineteenth century, the story of Hiawatha and Deganawidah depicts a concrete event in American history. Archaeological findings corroborate the sequence of bloody warfare followed by peace and date the confederacy's origins at about A.D. 1400. As with all events in American history before Europeans brought their system of writing, archaeological evidence, oral traditions, and cultural patterns—examined critically—are our principal sources of evidence.

The founding of the Iroquois Confederacy represents one moment in a long history that began more than ten thousand years before Christopher Columbus reached America in 1492. The earliest Native Americans lived in small, mobile bands of hunter-gatherers. They spread over the Americas during a period of global warming and adapted to a wide variety of regional environments. As a result, their cultures diverged and diversified. By the time Europeans arrived, Indians lived in communities numbering from a few dozen to several thousand. All residents were equal in most of these communities, but in some they were divided into social ranks. Some Native American societies obtained most of their food by farming, others by hunting, and still others by fishing, but most drew on a variety of food sources. Many of Indian peoples' customs and spiritual beliefs were equally varied. At the same time, through social and political interactions, peoples with different tribal, ethnic, and linguistic backgrounds often shared cultural characteristics.

Focus Questions

- How did environmental change shape the transition from Paleo-Indian to Archaic ways of life?

- What were the principal differences among the Native American cultures that emerged after 2500 B.C.?

- What significant values and practices did North American Indians share, despite their diversity?

The First Americans, c. 13,000–2500 B.C.

Precise details as to how and when the vast Western Hemisphere was first settled remains uncertain. Many Indians believe that their ancestors originated in the Americas, but most scientific findings point to the arrival of the first humans—ancestral Native Americans—from northeastern Asia sometime during the last Ice Age (c. 33,000–10,700 B.C.). These earliest Americans traveled by two different routes when land linked Siberia and Alaska (see Map 1.1). Thereafter, as the Ice Age waned and global temperatures rose, Native Americans dispersed throughout the hemisphere, adapting to environments ranging from tropical to frigid. Though divided into small, widely scattered groups, they interacted through trade and travel. Over several thousand years, Indians learned from one another and developed ways of life that had much in common despite their diverse backgrounds.

Peopling New Worlds

Most archaeologists agree that humans had begun to arrive in the Americas by 13,000 B.C. Traveling in small foraging bands in search of ample sources of food, the first Americans did not consciously move from one continent to another. Rather they apparently traveled by watercraft, following the then-continuous coastline from Siberia to Alaska and progressing southward along the Pacific coast. At various points along the way, groups stopped and either settled nearby or traveled inland to establish new homes. Coastal sites as far south as Monte Verde, in Chile, reveal evidence from about 12,000 B.C. of peoples who fed on marine life, birds, small mammals, and wild plants, as well as an occasional mastodon. (Archaeologists estimate dates by measuring the radioactive carbon 14 [radiocarbon] in organic materials such as food remains. They can extend their estimates when organic remains are clearly associated with nonorganic materials such as stone tools.) Some later groups of migrants reached North America by land. As the glaciers gradually melted, a corridor developed east of the Rocky Mountains through which these nomadic travelers passed before dispersing themselves over much of the Western Hemisphere.

Linguists, biological anthropologists, and archaeologists have determined that most Native Americans are descended from these early migrants. However, the ancestors of some native peoples came later, also from northeastern Asia, after the land connecting Siberia with Alaska had submerged. Speakers of a language known as

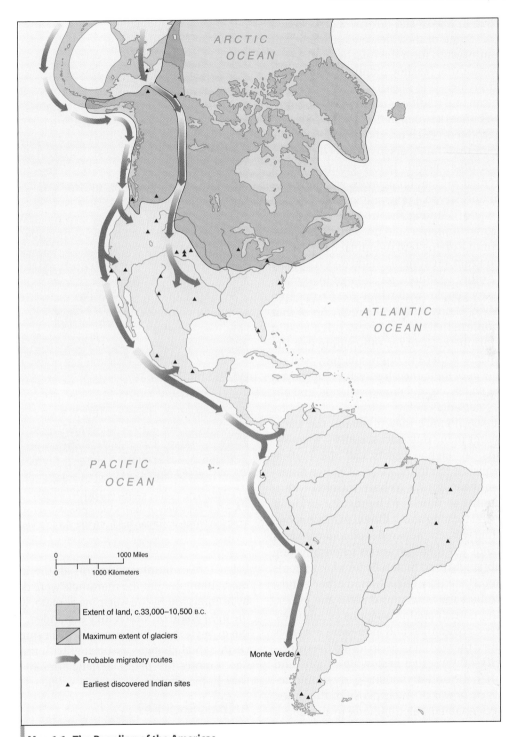

Map 1.1 The Peopling of the Americas
Scientists postulate two probable routes by which the earliest peoples reached America. By 9500 B.C.,
they had settled throughout the Western Hemisphere.

Athapaskan settled in Alaska and northwestern Canada in about 7000 B.C. Some of their descendants later migrated to the Southwest to form the Apaches and Navajos. After 3000 B.C., Inuits (Eskimos) and Aleuts crossed the Bering Sea from Siberia to Alaska.

Native American oral traditions offer conflicting support for scientists' theories, depending on how the traditions are interpreted. Pueblos and Navajos in the Southwest tell how their forebears experienced perilous journeys through other worlds before emerging from underground in their present homelands, while the Iroquois trace their ancestry to a pregnant woman who fell from the "sky world." Among the Iroquois and other peoples, the original humans could not settle the water-covered planet until a diving bird or animal brought soil from the ocean bottom, creating an island on which they could walk. Still other traditions recall large mammals, monsters, or "hairy people" with whom the first people shared Earth. Many Native Americans today insist that such accounts confirm that their ancestors originated in the Western Hemisphere. However, others note that the stories do not specify a place of origin and may well reflect the experiences of their ancestors as they journeyed from Asia, across water, ice, and unknown lands, and encountered large mammals before settling in their new homes. If not taken literally, they maintain, the traditions support rather than contradict scientists' theories.

Paleo-Indians, as archaeologists call the earliest Americans, established the foundations of Native American life. Paleo-Indians appear to have traveled within well-defined hunting territories in **bands** consisting of several families and totaling about fifteen to fifty people. Men hunted, while women prepared food and cared for the children. Bands left their territories when traveling to quarries to obtain favored materials for making tools and spear points. There they encountered other bands, with whose members they exchanged ideas and goods, intermarried, and participated in religious ceremonies. As in non-market economies and non-state societies throughout history, these exchanges followed the principle of **reciprocity**—the mutual bestowing of gifts and favors—rather than the notion that one party should accumulate profits or power at the expense of the other. These encounters enabled Paleo-Indians to develop a broad cultural life that transcended their small bands.

The earliest Paleo-Indians found a hunter's paradise in which large mammals—mammoths, mastodons, and giant species of horses, camels, bison, caribou, and moose—roamed America, innocent of the ways of human predators. Around 9000 B.C., the megafauna rather quickly became extinct. Although some scholars believe that

Sky Woman, **Ernest Smith (1936)**
A visual depiction of the Iroquois people's account of their origins, in which a woman fell from the sky to a watery world.

Paleo-Indian hunters killed off all the large mammals, most maintain that the mammals were doomed not just by humans but by the warming climate, which disrupted the food chain on which they depended. In other words, the extinction of the mammals was symptomatic of environmental changes associated with the end of the Ice Age. Among the major beneficiaries of these changes were human beings.

Archaic Societies

After about 8000 B.C., peoples throughout the Americas began modifying their Paleo-Indian ways of life. The warming of Earth's atmosphere continued until about 4000 B.C., with far-reaching global effects. Sea levels rose, flooding low-lying coastal areas, while glacial runoff filled interior waterways. As the glaciers receded northward, so did the arctic and subarctic environments that had previously extended into what are now the lower forty-eight states of the United States. Treeless plains and evergreen forests gave way to deciduous forests in the East, grassland prairies on the Plains, and desert in much of the West. The immense range of flora and fauna with which we are familiar today emerged during this period.

Archaic peoples, as archaeologists term Native Americans who flourished in these new environments, lived off the wider varieties of smaller mammals, fish, and wild plants that were now available. With more sources of food, communities required less land and could support larger populations. Some Indians in temperate regions began residing in year-round villages. From about 3900 to 2800 B.C., for example, the 100 to 150 residents of a community near Kampsville, Illinois, obtained ample supplies of fish, mussels, deer and other mammals, birds, nuts, and seeds without moving their homes.

Over time, Archaic Americans sharpened some distinctions between women's and men's roles. Men took responsibility for fishing as well as hunting, while women procured wild plant products. Gender roles are apparent in burials at Indian Knoll, in Kentucky, where tools relating to hunting, fishing, woodworking, and leatherworking were usually buried with men and those relating to cracking nuts and grinding seeds with women. Yet gender-specific distinctions did not apply to all activities, for objects used by religious healers were distributed equally between male and female graves.

Archaic Indians—women in most North American societies—honed their skills at harvesting wild plants. Through generations of close observation, they determined how to weed, prune, irrigate, transplant, burn, and otherwise manipulate their environments to favor plants that provided food and medicine. They also developed specialized tools for digging and grinding as well as more effective methods of drying and storing seeds. The most sophisticated early plant cultivators lived in **Mesoamerica** (central and southern Mexico and Central America), where maize agriculture was highly developed by 2500 B.C. (see Beyond America—Global Interactions: The Origins and Spread of Agriculture).

Cultural Diversity, c. 2500 B.C.–A.D. 1500

After about 2500 B.C., many Native Americans moved far beyond the ways of their Archaic forebears. The most far-reaching transformation occurred among peoples whose environments permitted them to produce food surpluses, by cultivating crops or other means. Some of these societies transformed trade networks into extensive religious and political systems linking several—sometimes dozens of—local communities. A few of these groupings evolved into formal confederacies and even states. In environments where food sources were few and widely scattered, mobile hunting-fishing-gathering bands persisted.

Mesoamerica and South America

As Mesoamerican farmers developed their methods, the quantity and quality of their crops increased. Farmers also planted beans alongside maize. The beans eaten released an amino acid, lysine, in the maize that further heightened its nutritional value. Higher yields and improved nutrition led some societies to center their lives around farming. Over the next eight centuries, maize-based farming societies spread throughout Mesoamerica.

After 2000 B.C., some Mesoamerican farming societies produced crop surpluses that they traded to less-populous, nonfarming neighbors. Expanding their trade contacts, a few of these societies established formal exchange networks that enabled them to enjoy more wealth and power than their partners. After 1200 B.C., a few communities, such as those of the Olmecs in Mesoamerica (see Map 1.2) and Chavín de Huántar in the Andes (see Map 1.3), developed into large urban centers, subordinating smaller neighbors. Unlike in earlier societies, Indian cities were highly unequal, with a few wealthy elites dominating thousands of residents and with hereditary rulers claiming kinship with religious deities. Laborers built elaborate religious temples and palaces, including the earliest American pyramids, and artisans created statues of the rulers and the gods.

Although the earliest hereditary rulers exercised absolute power, their realms were limited to a few closely clustered communities. Anthropologists term such political societies **chiefdoms**, as opposed to **states** in which a ruler or government exercises direct authority over many communities. Chiefdoms eventually emerged in several parts of the Americas, from the Mississippi valley to the Amazon valley and the Andes Mountains. A few states arose in Mesoamerica after A.D. 1 and in South America after A.D. 500. Although men ruled most chiefdoms and states, women served as chiefs in some Andean societies until the Spanish arrived.

From capital cities with thousands of inhabitants, states centered at Monte Alban and Teotihuacán in Mesoamerica (see Map 1.2) and at Wari in the Andes (see Map 1.3) drafted soldiers and waged bloody wars of conquest. Bureaucrats administered state territories, collected taxes, and managed huge public works projects. Priests conducted ceremonies in enormous temples and

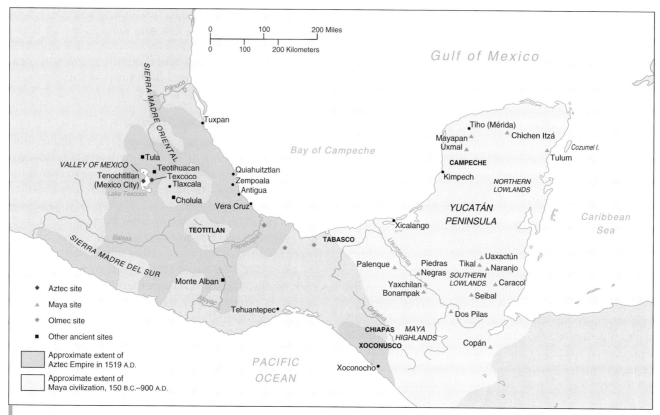

Map 1.2 Major Mesoamerican Cultures, c. 1000 B.C.–A.D. 1519
The Aztecs consolidated earlier Mesoamerican cultural traditions. They were still expanding when invaded by Spain in 1519.

presided over religious hierarchies extending throughout the states. The capital of the largest early state, Teotihuacán, was situated about fifty miles northeast of modern Mexico City and numbered about a hundred thousand people at the height of its power between the second and seventh centuries A.D. At its center was a complex of pyramids, the largest of which, the Sun Pyramid, was about 1 million cubic meters in volume. Teotihuacán dominated the peoples of the valley of Mexico, and its trade networks extended over much of modern-day Mexico. Although Teotihuacán declined in the eighth century, it exercised enormous influence on the religion, government, and culture of its neighbors.

Teotihuacán's greatest influence was on the Maya, whose kingdom-states flourished from southern Mexico to Honduras between the seventh and fifteenth centuries. The Maya moved far beyond their predecessors in developing a calendar, a numerical system (which included the concept of zero), and a system of phonetic, hieroglyphic writing. Maya scribes produced thousands of books on bark paper glued into long, folded strips. The books

Sun Pyramid, Teotihuacán
Built over several centuries, this pyramid remained the largest structure in the Americas until after the Spanish arrived.

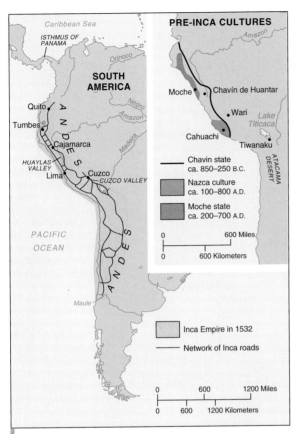

Map 1.3 Major Andean Cultures, 900 B.C.–A.D. 1432
Despite the challenges posed by the rugged Andes
Mountains, native peoples there developed several com-
plex societies and cultures, culminating in the Inca Empire.

recorded religious ceremonies, historical traditions, and
astronomical observations.

Other powerful states flourished in Mesoamerica and
South America until the fifteenth century, when two
mighty empires arose to challenge them. The first was the
empire of the **Aztecs** (known at the time as the Mexica),
who had migrated from the north during the thirteenth
century and settled on the shore of Lake Texcoco as subjects of the local inhabitants. Overthrowing their rulers in
1428, the Aztecs went on to conquer other cities around
the lake and extended their domain to the Gulf Coast (see
Map 1.2). Aztec expansion took a bloody turn in the 1450s
during a four-year drought, which the Aztecs interpreted
as a sign that the gods, like themselves, were hungry.
Aztec priests maintained that the only way to satisfy the
gods was to serve them human blood and hearts. From
then on, conquering Aztec warriors sought captives for
sacrifice in order, as they believed, to nourish the gods.

A massive temple complex at the capital of Tenochtitlán formed the sacred center of the Aztec empire. The

Great Temple consisted of two joined pyramids and was
surrounded by several smaller pyramids and other
buildings. Aztec culture reflected both Mesoamerican
tradition and the multicultural character of the state.
Most of the more than two hundred deities they honored originated with earlier and contemporary societies, including those they had subjugated. They based
their system of writing on the one developed centuries before at Teotihuacán and their calendar on
that of the Maya.

To support the nearly two hundred thousand people residing in and around Tenochtitlán, the Aztecs
maximized their production of food. They drained
swampy areas and added rich soil from the lake bottom
to artificial islands that formed. The highly fertile islands enabled Aztec farmers to supply the urban population with food. Aztec engineers devised an elaborate
irrigation system to provide fresh water for both people
and crops.

The Aztecs collected taxes from subjects living within
about a hundred miles of the capital. Conquered peoples farther away paid tribute, which replaced the free
exchanges of goods they had formerly carried on with
the Aztecs and other neighbors. Trade beyond the Aztec
domain was conducted by *pochteca*, traders who traveled in armed caravans. The pochteca sought salt, cacao,
jewelry, feathers, jaguar pelts, cotton, and precious
stones and metals, including gold and turquoise, the latter obtained from Indians in the American Southwest.

The Aztecs were still expanding in the early sixteenth
century, but rebellions constantly flared within their
realm. They had surrounded and weakened, but not subjugated, one neighboring rival, while another blocked
their westward expansion. Might the Aztecs have expanded still farther? We will never know because they were
violently crushed in the sixteenth century by another, even
more far-flung empire, the Spanish (see Chapter 2).

Meanwhile, a second empire, that of the **Incas**, had
arisen in the Western Hemisphere. From their sumptuous capital at Cuzco, the Incas conquered and subordinated societies over much of the Andes and adjacent
regions after 1438. One key to the Incas' expansion was
their ability to produce and distribute a wide range of
surplus crops, including maize, beans, potatoes, and
meats. They constructed terraced irrigation systems
for watering crops on uneven terrain, perfected freeze-
drying and other preservation techniques, built vast
storehouses, and constructed a vast network of roads
and bridges. The Incas were still expanding when they
too were overcome by Spanish invaders in the sixteenth century.

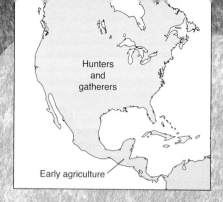
Hunters and gatherers

Early agriculture

The Origins and Spread of Agriculture

For most of their two and a half million years on Earth, human beings lived as hunter-gatherers or foragers, subsisting on wild plants and animals. It was only between ten thousand and four thousand years ago that scattered groups of people transformed a few dozen wild plant species into domesticated crops. The grain, pulse (peas and beans), root, and melon/squash crops they produced remain the principal sources of plant food for humans and their domestic animals today.

The transformation of wild plants into crops was a gradual process. Through careful observation, gatherers selected varieties of plants that produced the highest yields. After planting the largest seeds of these varieties, they eliminated nearby, competing plants and harvested the favored plants when the food was ripe. As crop production intensified, farmer-gatherers developed specialized tools, such as digging sticks and hoes, to facilitate the planting of seeds and elimination of weeds. Over time, the new foods replaced many wild sources of food in farming peoples' diets.

Gatherers domesticated plants in just a few, widely separate parts of the world. People began cultivating wild species of wheat, barley, and peas in the Middle East in about 8000 B.C. Within 500 years, similar processes had begun with rice in southern China; bananas and taro, a root crop, in New Guinea; and sorghum, a grain, in the eastern Sahara region of Africa. (Climatic warming would later turn the Sahara into a desert, ending farming there.) The origins of farming in the Western Hemisphere date to about 5000 B.C., in Mesoamerica. By around 3500 B.C., Native Americans had domesticated potatoes in the Andes Mountains and manioc—a starchy root crop—in the Amazon Basin. Within another one thousand years, women in the Mississippi and Ohio valleys of North America had begun cultivating favored varieties of squash, sunflowers, and grasses.

In domesticating wild plants, early farmers shaped the evolution of plant species. The most complex example of domestication occurred in the highland Mexican valley of Tehuacan, where Native Americans experimented with a lowland plant called *teosinte*. Through an intricate process of trial and error, they selected mutated seeds that flourished at higher elevations and yielded favorable characteristics such as larger cobs and kernels and better taste. By continuing to plant preferred seeds, the Indians eventually

emmer wheat

einkorn wheat

bread wheat

wild wheat   later domesticated varieties

Domesticating Wheat
Middle Eastern farmers planted the largest seeds of wild wheat, eventually producing varieties with larger kernels.

produced a new, much larger species—maize—with dozens of varieties. In so doing, geneticist Nina V. Federoff has written, they achieved "arguably man's first, and perhaps his greatest, feat of genetic engineering."

From its few points of origin, agriculture spread to other parts of the world. In some cases, nonfarming societies acquired seeds and agricultural know-how through trade or from immigrating farmers. Wheat and barley moved beyond the Middle East to Europe, reaching Greece by 6000 B.C., Central Europe by 5000 B.C., and parts of western Europe by 4000 B.C. Similarly, maize cultivation expanded in all directions from the Tehuacan Valley. By 2500 B.C., Indians were growing it elsewhere in Central America, in the Amazon River basin, and as far northward as what is now the American Southwest. In other cases, whole societies of farmers invaded new lands, subordinating or expelling hunter-gatherers. For example, southern Chinese rice farmers took over favorable lands in northern China and Southeast Asia. In a few places, such as the British Isles in c. 2500 B.C., arriving farmers were the first inhabitants.

As agriculture spread, farmers adapted plants to new environments. Maize arrived in eastern North America in about 300 B.C. but remained a minor crop for another thousand years, until women there developed a strain that produced high yields in climates with as few as one hundred frost-free days per year. Thereafter, it was a dietary mainstay for eastern North American Indians. Once they adopted crops originating elsewhere, some farmers then domesticated local plants, further diversifying their diets. For example, only after adopting wheat and barley from the Middle East did western Europeans discover how to cultivate indigenous oats and poppies.

Climate, topography, soil composition, and availability of water limited agricultural production to certain, mostly temperate areas. Within these areas, farming required that people have access to and knowledge of the select group of plants that could be effectively cultivated on a large scale. In the absence of these conditions, many people remained foragers and did not attempt to farm. Even where farming was a realistic option, its adoption was not inevitable. When members of a hunting-gathering band began to rely on crops, they had to remain in one place for longer periods of each year in order to tend the fields, thereby foregoing other food-gathering practices that had proven reliable. A decision to cultivate was often dictated by the shortage of a wild food source on which a group had depended, but in other cases people took a risk that unfamiliar crops would flourish and not succumb to fluctuations in climate or to blight. While evidence is hard to come by, a group's cultural values and beliefs about their place in nature undoubtedly influenced their decisions.

In many parts of the world, as people began cultivating plants, they also domesticated animals. Although hunters had long used dogs to track prey, it was only after 8000 B.C. that people in the Middle East began to tame wild sheep, goats, and cattle. Soon people in the Eastern Hemisphere domesticated other species, including water buffalo, donkeys, pigs, chickens, and—much later—horses and camels. Various sorts of animals supplied their keepers not only with meat but also with milk, eggs, wool, labor (including in agricultural fields), and transportation. Animal domestication was severely limited in the Western Hemisphere. Ancestral species of horses and camels flourished in the Americas when humans first arrived but soon became extinct. By the time Native Americans began farming, the only species suitable for taming were dogs, llamas, turkeys, and guinea pigs.

Until A.D. 1492, domesticated plants (and animals) spread strictly within either the Eastern Hemisphere or the Western Hemisphere. Thereafter a "Columbian exchange" would transform many species into global crops (see Chapter 2).

Questions for Analysis

- By what processes were plants first domesticated?

- Why were domesticated crops a primary source of food in some parts of the world and not in others?

Guale Indians Planting Crops, 1564
A French explorer sketched this scene on the Florida coast in which men are breaking up the soil while women sow corn, bean, and squash seeds.

The Southwest

The Southwest is a uniformly arid region with a variety of landscapes. Waters from rugged mountains and forested plateaus follow ancient channels through vast expanses of desert on their way to the gulfs of Mexico and California. The amount of water has fluctuated over time, depending on climatic conditions, but securing water has always been a challenge for southwestern peoples. Nevertheless, some of them augmented their supplies of water and became farmers.

Maize reached the Southwest via Mesoamerican trade links by about 2500 B.C. Yet full-time farming began only after 400 B.C., when the introduction of a more drought-resistant strain enabled some farmers to move from the highlands to drier lowlands. In the centuries that followed, southwestern populations rose, and Indian cultures were transformed. The two most influential new cultural traditions were the Hohokam and the Anasazi.

The **Hohokam culture** emerged during the third century B.C., when ancestors of the Akimel O'odham and Tohono O'odham Indians began farming in the Gila and Salt River valleys of southern Arizona. Hohokam peoples built irrigation canals that enabled them to harvest two crops a year, an unprecedented feat in the arid environment. To construct and maintain their canals, the Hohokam organized large, coordinated work forces. They built permanent towns, usually consisting of several hundred people. Although many towns remained independent, others joined confederations in which several towns were linked by canals. The central village in each confederation coordinated labor, trade, religion, and political life for all member communities.

Although a local creation, Hohokam culture drew extensively on Mesoamerican materials and ideas. From about the sixth century A.D., the large villages had ball courts and platform mounds similar to those in Mesoamerica at the time. Mesoamerican influence was also apparent in the creations of Hohokam artists, who worked in clay, stone, turquoise, and shell. Archaeologists have uncovered rubber balls, macaw feathers, cottonseeds, and copper bells from Mesoamerica at Hohokam sites.

The **Anasazi culture** originated during the first century B.C. in the Four Corners area where Arizona, New Mexico, Colorado, and Utah meet. By around A.D. 700, Anasazi people—ancestors of modern Pueblo Indians—were harvesting crops, living in permanent villages, and making pottery. Thereafter, they expanded over a wide area and became the most powerful people in the Southwest.

One distinguishing characteristic of Anasazi culture was its architecture. Anasazi villages consisted of extensive complexes of attached apartments and storage rooms, along with *kivas*—partly underground structures in which male religious leaders conducted ceremonies. To this day, Anasazi-style apartments and kivas are central features of Pueblo Indian architecture in the Southwest.

Pueblo Bonito, Chaco Canyon, New Mexico
Pueblo Bonito illustrates the richness and grand scale of Anasazi architecture.

Anasazi culture reached its height between about 900 and 1150, during an unusually wet period in the Southwest. In Chaco Canyon, a cluster of twelve large towns forged a powerful confederation numbering about fifteen thousand people. A system of roads radiated from the canyon to satellite towns as far as sixty-five miles away. The roads were perfectly straight; their builders even carved out stairs or footholds on the sides of steep cliffs rather than go around them. By controlling rainwater runoff through small dams and terraces, the towns fed themselves as well as the satellites. The largest of the towns, Pueblo Bonito, had about twelve hundred inhabitants and was the home of two Great Kivas, each about fifty feet in diameter. People traveled over the roads from the satellites to Chaco Canyon's large kivas for religious ceremonies. The canyon was also a major trade center, importing and exporting a wide range of materials from and to Mesoamerica, the Great Plains, the Mississippi valley, and California.

The classic Anasazi culture, as manifested at Chaco Canyon, Mesa Verde in southwestern Colorado, and other sites, came to an end in the twelfth and thirteenth centuries. Although other factors contributed, the overriding cause of the Anasazi demise was drought. As has often happened in human history, an era of especially abundant rainfall, which the Anasazi thought would last forever, abruptly ended. Without enough water, the highly concentrated inhabitants abandoned the great Anasazi centers, dispersing to form new, smaller communities. Their Pueblo Indian descendants would encounter Spanish colonizers three centuries later (see Chapter 2). Hohokam communities also dispersed when drought came. With farming peoples now clustered in the few areas with enough water, the drier lands of the Southwest attracted the nonfarming Apaches and Navajos, whose arrival at the end of the fourteenth century ended their long migration from the far north (mentioned above).

The Eastern Woodlands

In contrast to the Southwest, the Eastern Woodlands—the vast expanse stretching from the Mississippi valley to the Atlantic Ocean—had abundant water. Water and deciduous forests provided Woodlands Indians with a rich variety of food sources, while the region's extensive river systems facilitated long-distance communication and travel. As a result, many eastern Indians established populous villages and complex confederations well before adopting full-time, maize-based farming.

By 1200 B.C., about five thousand people lived at **Poverty Point** on the lower Mississippi River. The town featured earthworks consisting of two large mounds and six concentric embankments, the outermost of which spanned more than half a mile in diameter. During the spring and autumn equinoxes, a person standing on the larger mound could watch the sun rise directly over the village center. As in some Mesoamerican societies at the time, solar observations were the basis for religious beliefs and a calendar.

Poverty Point was the center of a much larger political and economic unit. The settlement imported large quantities of quartz, copper, obsidian, crystal, and other materials from long distances for redistribution to nearby communities. These communities almost certainly supplied some of the labor for the earthworks. Poverty Point's general design and organization indicate Olmec influence from Mesoamerica (see above). Poverty Point flourished for about three centuries and then declined, for reasons unknown. Nevertheless, it foreshadowed later developments in the Eastern Woodlands.

A different kind of mound-building culture, called **Adena**, emerged in the Ohio valley around 400 B.C. Adena villages were smaller than Poverty Point, rarely exceeding four hundred inhabitants. But Adena people spread over a wide area and built hundreds of mounds, most of them containing graves. The treatment of Adena dead varied according to social or political status. Some corpses were cremated; others were placed in round clay basins; and still others were given elaborate tombs.

After 100 B.C., Adena culture evolved into a more complex and widespread culture known as **Hopewell**, which spread from the Ohio valley to the Illinois River valley. Some Hopewell centers contained two or three dozen mounds within enclosures of several square miles. The variety and quantity of goods buried with members of the elite were also greater. Hopewell elites were buried with thousands of freshwater pearls or copper ornaments or with sheets of mica, quartz, or other sacred substances. Hopewell artisans fashioned fine ornaments and jewelry, which their owners wore in life and took to their graves. The raw materials for these objects originated in locales throughout America east of the Rockies. Through far-flung trade networks, Hopewell religious and technological influence spread to communities as far away as Wisconsin, Missouri, Florida, and New York. Although the great Hopewell centers were abandoned by about 600 (for reasons that are unclear), they had an enormous influence on subsequent developments in eastern North America.

The peoples of Poverty Point and the Adena and Hopewell cultures did little farming. Indian women in Kentucky and Missouri had cultivated small amounts of squash as early as 2500 B.C., and maize first appeared

Hopewell Mounds, Mound City, Ohio
Many Hopewell earthworks that served as temples remain visible today in the Ohio valley.

east of the Mississippi by 300 B.C. But agriculture did not become the primary food source for Woodlands people until between the seventh and twelfth centuries A.D., as women moved beyond gathering and minor cultivating activities to become the major producers of food.

The first full-time farmers in the East lived on the floodplains of the Mississippi River and its major tributaries. Beginning around A.D. 700, they developed a new culture, called **Mississippian**. The volume of Mississippian craft production and long-distance trade dwarfed that of the Adena and Hopewell peoples. As in Mesoamerica, Mississippian centers, numbering hundreds or even thousands of people, arose around open plazas. Large platform mounds adjoined the plazas, topped by sumptuous religious temples and the residences of chiefs and other elites. Religious ceremonies focused on the worship of the sun as the source of agricultural fertility. The people considered chiefs to be related to the sun. When a chief died, his wives and servants were killed so that they could accompany him in the afterlife. Largely in connection with their religious and funeral rituals, Mississippian artists produced highly sophisticated work in clay, stone, shell, copper, wood, and other materials.

After A.D. 900, Mississippian centers formed extensive networks based on river-borne trade and shared religious beliefs, each dominated by a single metropolis. The largest, most powerful such system centered on **Cahokia**,

located near modern St. Louis, Missouri, where about twenty thousand people inhabited a 125-square-mile metropolitan area.

For about two and a half centuries, Cahokia reigned supreme in the Mississippi valley. After A.D. 1200, however, Cahokia and other valley centers experienced shortages of food and other resources. As in the Southwest, densely concentrated societies had taxed a fragile environment with a fluctuating climate. One result was competition for suddenly scarce resources, which led to debilitating warfare and the undermining of Cahokia and its allies. The survivors fled to the surrounding prairies and, in some cases, westward to the lower valleys of the Plains. By the fifteenth century, their descendants were living in villages linked by reciprocity rather than coercion. Mississippian chiefdoms and temple mound centers persisted in the Southeast, where Spanish explorers would later encounter them as the forerunners of Cherokees, Creeks, and other southeastern Indian peoples (see Chapter 2).

Despite Cahokia's decline, Mississippian culture profoundly affected Native Americans in the Eastern Woodlands. Mississippians spread new strains of maize and beans, along with techniques and tools for cultivating these crops, enabling women to weave agriculture into the fabric of village life. Life for Indians as far north as the Great Lakes and southern New England revolved around village-based farming. Only in more northerly Woodlands areas was the growing season usually too

Cahokia Mounds
This contemporary painting conveys Cahokia's grand scale. Not until the late eighteenth century did another North American city (Philadelphia) surpass the population of Cahokia, c. 1200.

short for maize (which required one hundred or more frost-free days) to be a reliable crop.

Woodland peoples' method of land management was environmentally sound and economically productive. Indian men systematically burned hardwood forests, eliminating the underbrush and forming open, parklike expanses. Although they occasionally lost control of a fire, so that it burned beyond their hunting territory, the damage was not lasting. Burned-over tracts favored the growth of grass and berry bushes that attracted a profusion of deer and other game. They then cleared fields so that women could plant corn, beans, and squash in soil enriched by ash. After several years of abundant harvests, yields declined, and the Indians moved to another site to repeat the process. Ground cover eventually reclaimed the abandoned clearing, restoring fertility naturally, and the Indians could return.

Nonfarming Societies

Outside the Southwest and the Eastern Woodlands, farming north of Mesoamerica was either impossible because of inhospitable environments or impractical because native peoples could obtain enough food from wild sources with less work. On the Northwest coast, from the Alaskan panhandle to northern California, and in the Columbia Plateau, Native Americans devoted brief periods of each year to catching salmon and other spawning fish. After drying the fish, they stored it in quantities sufficient to last the year. As a result, their seasonal movements gave way to a settled lifestyle in permanent villages. For example, the Makah Indians of Ozette, on Washington's Olympic Peninsula, pursued fish and sea mammals, including whales, while procuring shellfish, salmon and other river fish, land mammals, and wild plants.

By A.D. 1, most Northwest coast villages numbered several hundred people who lived in multifamily houses built of cedar planks. Trade and warfare with interior groups strengthened the wealth and power of chiefs and other elites. Leading families displayed their power in the potlatch—a feast at which they gave away to guests or destroyed their material wealth. From the time of the earliest contacts, Europeans were amazed by the artistic and architectural achievements of the Northwest coast Indians. "What must astonish most," wrote a French explorer in 1791, "is to see painting everywhere, everywhere sculpture, among a nation of hunters."

At about the same time, Native Americans on the coast and in the valleys of what is now California were clustering in villages of about a hundred people to coordinate the processing of acorns. After gathering millions

Chumash Baskets
California Indians, including the Chumash, gathered, prepared, and stored acorns and other foods in baskets crafted by specialized weavers.

of acorns from California's extensive oak groves each fall, tribal peoples such as the Chumash and Ohlones ground the acorns into meal, leached them of their bitter tannic acid, and then roasted, boiled, or baked the nuts prior to eating or storing them. Facing intense competition for acorns, California Indians combined their villages into chiefdoms and defended their territories. Chiefs conducted trade, diplomacy, war, and religious ceremonies. Along with other wild species, acorns enabled the Indians of California to prosper. As a Spanish friar arriving in California from Mexico in 1770 wrote, "This land exceeds all the preceding territory in fertility and abundance of things necessary for sustenance."

Between the Eastern Woodlands and the Pacific coast, the Plains and deserts remained too dry to support large human settlements. Dividing the region are the Rocky Mountains, to the east of which lie the grasslands of the Great Plains, while to the west are several deserts of varying elevations that ecologists call the Great Basin. Except in the Southwest, Native Americans in this region remained in mobile hunting-gathering bands.

Plains Indian hunters pursued a variety of game animals, including antelope, deer, elk, and bear, but their favorite prey was buffalo, or bison, a smaller relative of the giant bison that had flourished before the arrival of humans. Buffalo provided Plains Indians with meat and with hides, from which they made clothing, bedding, portable houses (tipis), kettles, shields, and other items. They made tools from buffalo bones and containers and arrowheads from buffalo horns, and they used most

other buffalo parts as well. Limited to travel by foot, Plains hunters stampeded herds of bison into small box canyons, easily killing the trapped animals, or over cliffs. Dozens, or occasionally hundreds, of buffalo would be killed. Since a single buffalo could provide two hundred to four hundred pounds of meat and a band had no means of preserving and storing most of it, the latter practice was especially wasteful. On the other hand, humans were so few in number that they had no significant impact on the bison population before the arrival of Europeans. There are no reliable estimates of the number of buffalo then roaming the Plains, but the earliest European observers were flabbergasted. One Spanish colonist, for example, witnessed a "multitude so great that it might be considered a falsehood by one who had not seen them."

During and after the Mississippian era, groups of Eastern Woodlands Indians migrated to the lower river valleys of the Plains, where over time the rainfall had increased enough to support cultivated plants. In contrast to Native Americans already living on the Plains, such as the Blackfeet and the Crow, farming newcomers like the Mandans and Pawnees built year-round villages and permanent earth lodges. But they also hunted buffalo and other animals. (Many of the Plains Indians familiar today, such as the Sioux and Comanches, moved to the region only after Europeans had begun colonizing North America [see Chapter 4].)

As Indians elsewhere increased their food production, the Great Basin grew warmer and drier, further limiting already scarce sources of foods. Ducks and other waterfowl on which Native Americans formerly feasted disappeared as marshlands dried up after 1200 B.C., and the number of buffalo and other game animals also dwindled. Great Basin Indians such as the Shoshones and the Utes countered these trends by relying more heavily on piñon nuts, which they harvested, stored, and ate in winter camps. Hunting improved after about A.D. 500, when Indians in the region adopted the bow and arrow.

In western Alaska, where the first Americans had appeared thousands of years earlier, Aleuts, carrying highly sophisticated tools and weapons from their Siberian homeland, arrived after 3000 B.C. Combining ivory, bone, and other materials, they fashioned harpoons and spears for the pursuit of sea mammals and—in the case of the Aleut—caribou. Through continued contacts with Siberia, the Aleut introduced the bow and arrow in North America. As they perfected their ways of living in the cold tundra environment, many Aleut spread westward across upper Canada and to Greenland.

The very earliest contacts between Native Americans and Europeans occurred in about A.D. 980, five centuries before the arrival of Columbus, when Norse expansionists from Scandinavia colonized parts of Greenland. The Greenland Norse hunted furs, obtained timber, and traded with Aleut people on the eastern Canadian mainland. They also made several attempts, beginning in about 1000, to colonize Vinland, as they called Newfoundland. The Vinland Norse initially exchanged metal goods for ivory with the local Beothuk Indians, but peaceful trade gave way to hostile encounters. Within a century, Beothuk resistance led the Norse to withdraw from Vinland. As a Norse leader, dying after losing a battle with some natives, put it, "There is fat around my belly! We have won a fine and fruitful country, but will hardly be allowed to enjoy it." Although some Norse remained in Greenland as late as the 1480s, it was later Europeans who would enjoy, at the expense of native peoples, the fruits of a "New World."

North American Peoples on the Eve of European Contact

By A.D. 1500, native peoples had transformed the Americas into a dazzling array of cultures and societies (see Map 1.4). The Western Hemisphere numbered about 75 million people, most thickly clustered in urbanized areas of Mesoamerica and South America. But North America was no empty wasteland. Between 7 million and 10 million Indians lived north of Mesoamerica. They were unevenly distributed. As they had for thousands of years, small, mobile hunting bands peopled the Arctic, Subarctic, Great Basin, and much of the Plains. More sedentary societies based on fishing or gathering predominated along the Pacific coast, while village-based agriculture was typical in the Eastern Woodlands and the river valleys of the Southwest and Plains. Mississippian urban centers still prevailed in areas of the Southeast. All these peoples grouped themselves in several hundred nations and tribes, and spoke hundreds of languages and dialects.

Despite the vast differences among Native Americans, much bound them together. Rooted in common practices, Indian societies were based on kinship, the norms of reciprocity, and communal use and control of resources. Trade facilitated the exchange not only of goods but also of technologies and ideas. Thus, the bow and arrow, ceramic pottery, and certain religious values and practices characterized Indians everywhere.

Kinship and Gender

Like their Archaic forebears, Indian peoples north of the Mesoamerican states were bound together primarily by kinship. Ties among biological relatives created complex patterns of social obligation and interdependence, even in societies that did not expect spouses to be married forever. Customs regulating marriage varied considerably, but strict rules always prevailed. In most cultures, young people married in their teens, generally after engaging in numerous sexual relationships, both casual and long-term. Some male leaders had more than one wife, but **nuclear families** (a husband, a wife, and their biological children) never stood alone. Instead, they lived with one of the parents' relatives in what social scientists call **extended families**.

In some Native American societies, such as the Iroquois, the extended families of women took precedence over those of men. Upon marriage, a new husband moved in with his wife's extended family. The primary male authority figure in a child's life was the mother's oldest brother, not the father. In many respects, a husband and father was simply a guest of his wife's family. Other Indian societies recognized men's extended families as primary, and still others did not distinguish sharply between the status of female and male family lines.

Kinship was also the basis for armed conflict. Indian societies typically considered homicide a matter to be resolved by the extended families of the victim and the perpetrator. If the perpetrator's family offered a gift that the victim's family considered appropriate, the question was settled; if not, political leaders attempted to resolve the dispute. Otherwise, the victim's family members and their supporters might seek to avenge the killing by armed retaliation. Such feuds could escalate into wars between communities. The potential for war rose when densely populated societies competed for scarce resources, as on the Northwest and California coasts, and when centralized Mississippian societies used coercion to dominate trade networks. Yet Native American warfare generally remained minimal, with rivals seeking to humiliate one another and seize captives rather than inflict massive casualties or conquer land. A New England officer, writing in the seventeenth century, described a battle between two Indian groups as "more for pastime than to conquer and subdue enemies." He concluded that "they might fight seven years and not kill seven men."

Women did most of the cultivating in farming societies except in the Southwest (where women and men shared the responsibility). With women producing the greater share of the food supply, some societies accorded them more power than did Europeans. Among

Map 1.4 Locations of Selected Native American Peoples, A.D. 1500
Today's Indian nations were well established in homelands across the continent when Europeans first arrived. Many would combine with others or move in later centuries, either voluntarily or because they were forced.

the Iroquois, for example, women collectively owned the fields, distributed food, and played a decisive role in selecting chiefs. In New England, women often served as sachems, or political leaders.

Spiritual and Social Values

Native American religions revolved around the conviction that all nature was alive, pulsating with spiritual power—*manitou* in the Algonquian languages, *orenda* in the Iroquoian, and *wakan* in the Siouan. A mysterious, awe-inspiring force that could affect human life for both good and evil, such power united all nature in an unbroken web. *Manitou* encompassed "every thing which they cannot comprehend," reported Rhode Island's Roger Williams. Native Americans endeavored to conciliate the spiritual forces in their world—living things, rocks and water, sun and moon, even ghosts and witches. For example, Indian hunters prayed to the spirits of the animals they killed, thanking them for the gift of food.

Native Americans had several ways of gaining access to spiritual power. One was through dreams and visions, which most Native Americans interpreted as a form of spiritual instruction. Sometimes, as in Hiawatha's case, a dreamer received a message of importance for his or her people. Native people also sought power through difficult physical ordeals. Young men in many societies gained recognition as adults through a vision quest—a solitary venture that entailed fasting and awaiting the appearance of a spirit who would endow them with special powers. Some tribes initiated girls at the onset of menstruation into the spiritual world from which female reproductive power flowed. Entire communities often practiced collective power-seeking rituals such as the Sun Dance, performed by Indians of the Plains and Great Basin.

Native Americans who had gained special religious powers assisted others in communicating with unseen spirits. These medicine men and women were healers who used both medicinal plants and magical chants to cure illnesses. They also served as spiritual advisers and leaders, interpreting dreams, guiding vision quests, and conducting ceremonies.

Native American societies demanded a strong degree of cooperation. From early childhood, Indians in most cultures learned to be accommodating and reserved—slow to reveal their own feelings until they could sense the feelings of others. Using physical punishment sparingly, if at all, Indians punished children psychologically, by public shaming. Communities sought unity through consensus rather than tolerating lasting divisions. Political leaders articulated slowly emerging agreements in dramatic oratory. The English colonizer John Smith noted that the most effective Native American leaders spoke "with vehemency and so great passions that they sweat till they drop and are so out of breath they scarce can speak."

Native Americans reinforced cooperation with a strong sense of order. Custom, the demands of social conformity, and the rigors of nature strictly regulated life and people's everyday affairs. Exacting familial or community revenge was a ritualized way of restoring order that had broken down. On the other hand, the failure of measures to restore order could bring the fearful consequences experienced by Hiawatha's Iroquois—blind hatred, unending violence, and the most dreaded of evils, witchcraft. In fearing witchcraft, Native Americans resembled the Europeans and Africans they would encounter after 1492.

Huron War Leader
Warfare among the Iroquois and neighboring Hurons was intense by Hiawatha's time. Warriors wore wooden shields to protect themselves from enemy arrows.

The principle of reciprocity remained strong among Native Americans. Reciprocity involved mutual give-and-take, but its aim was not to ensure equality. Instead, societies based on reciprocity tried to maintain equilibrium and interdependence between individuals of unequal power and prestige. Even in the most complex societies, chiefs coordinated families' uses of land and other resources, but never awarded these outright.

Most Indian leaders' authority depended on the obligations they bestowed rather than on coercion. By distributing gifts, they obligated members of the community to support them and to accept their authority, however limited. The same principle applied to relations between societies. Powerful communities distributed gifts to weaker neighbors who reciprocated with tribute in the form of material goods and submission. A French observer in early seventeenth-century Canada clearly understood: "For the savages have that noble quality, that they give liberally, casting at the feet of him whom they will honor the present that they give him. But it is with hope to receive some reciprocal kindness, which is a kind of contract, which we call . . . 'I give thee, to the end thou shouldst give me.'"

Chronology 13,000 B.C.–A.D. 1500

c. 13,000 B.C.	People present in Americas.		c. 100 B.C.–A.D. 600	Hopewell culture thrives in Midwest.
c. 9000 B.C.	Paleo-Indians established throughout Western Hemisphere. Extinction of big-game mammals.		c. A.D. 1	Rise of chiefdoms on Northwest coast and in California.
c. 8000 B.C.	Earliest Archaic societies.		c. 700	Mississippian culture begins. Anasazi expansion begins.
c. 7000 B.C.	Athapaskan-speaking peoples enter North America.		c. 900	Urban center arises at Cahokia.
c. 5000 B.C.	First domesticated plants grown.		c. 1000	Norse attempt to colonize Vinland (Newfoundland).
c. 3000 B.C.	First maize grown in Mesoamerica.		c. 1200	Anasazi and Hohokam peoples disperse in Southwest.
c. 3000–2000 B.C.	Inuit and Aleut peoples enter North America from Siberia.		c. 1200–1400	Cahokia declines and inhabitants disperse.
c. 2500 B.C.	Archaic societies begin giving way to a more diverse range of cultures. First maize grown in North America.		c. 1400	Iroquois Confederacy formed.
c. 1200–900 B.C.	Poverty Point flourishes in Louisiana.		1428	Aztec empire expands.
c. 400–100 B.C.	Adena culture flourishes in Ohio valley.		1438	Inca empire expands.
c. 250 B.C.	Hohokam culture begins in Southwest.		1492	Christopher Columbus reaches Western Hemisphere.
c. 100 B.C.	Anasazi culture begins in Southwest.			

Conclusion

When Europeans "discovered" America in 1492, they did not, as they thought, enter an unchanging "wilderness" inhabited by "savages." American history had begun with the arrival of people in the Americas thousands of years earlier during an Ice Age, when Asia and North America were directly connected. As Earth's climate warmed, the earliest Paleo-Indians spread over the Americas, adapting to new, warmer environments by exploiting wider ranges of food sources that could support larger populations. They also learned from one another through inter-band exchanges. These developments eventually resulted in the emergence of new, regional cultures, termed Archaic. After 2500 B.C., Native Americans in several regions moved beyond Archaic cultures, clustering in seasonal or permanent villages where they produced food surpluses by growing crops, fishing for salmon, or processing acorns. Some built larger towns or cities. While people in the smallest bands were equal, political leaders in most societies came from prominent families. In a few, very large societies, hereditary chiefs, kings, and even emperors ruled far-flung peoples.

Key Terms

wampum	Incas
Iroquois Confederacy	Hohokam culture
Paleo-Indians	Anasazi culture
bands	Poverty Point
reciprocity	Adena
Archaic peoples	Hopewell
Mesoamerica	Mississippian
chiefdoms	Cahokia
states	nuclear families
Aztecs	extended families

Underlying their diversity, North American Indians had much in common. First, they usually identified themselves as members of multigenerational families rather than as individuals or political subjects. Second, most emphasized reciprocity rather than domination and submission as the underlying principle for relations within and between communities. Third, they perceived the entire universe, including nature, as sacred. These core values arrived with the earliest Americans and persisted beyond the invasions of Europeans and their sharply contrasting ideas. Throughout their long history, Native Americans reinforced shared beliefs and customs through exchanges of material goods, new technologies, and religious ideas.

Although they had much in common with one another, Native Americans had never thought of themselves as a single people. Only after Europeans arrived and emphasized the differences between themselves and indigenous peoples did the term "Indian" come into usage. (The term originated with Columbus, who thought in 1492 that he had landed in the Indies [see Chapter 2].) The new America in which people were categorized according to continental ancestry was radically different from the one that had flourished for thousands of years before 1492.

For Further Reference

The Cambridge History of the Native Peoples of the Americas (3 vols., 1996–2000). Volumes on North America, Mesoamerica, and South America, each containing authoritative essays by archaeologists and historians covering the entire expanse of Native American history.

Cheryl Claassen and Rosemary A. Joyce, eds., *Women in Prehistory: North America and Mesoamerica* (1997). Fourteen essays draw on and examine archaeological evidence of women's roles and gender identity in a range of Native American societies.

Jared Diamond, *Guns, Germs, and Steel: The Fates of Human Societies* (1997). A bold, sweeping inquiry into the reasons that human societies around the globe developed so differently from one another.

Thomas D. Dillehay, *The Settlement of the Americas: A New Prehistory* (2000). An excellent critical review of current scholarly debates on the earliest Americans.

Brian Fagan, *Ancient North America: The Archaeology of a Continent* (2005). A thorough, comprehensive introduction to the continent's history before the Europeans' arrival.

Alvin M. Josephy, Jr., *America in 1492: The World of the Indian Peoples Before the Arrival of Columbus* (1992). Highly readable regional and thematic essays on life in the Western Hemisphere on the eve of European contact.

Shepard Krech III, *The Ecological Indian: Myth and History* (1999). A controversial, well-informed critique of the idea that Native Americans invariably lived in harmony with nature before Europeans arrived.

Charles C. Mann, *1491: New Revelations of the Americas Before Columbus* (2005). A probing, well-written discussion of how recent archaeological scholarship undermines older conceptions of American history before Columbus.

Lynda Norene Shaffer, *Native Americans Before 1492: The Moundbuilding Centers of the Eastern Woodlands* (1992). A thoughtful, readable interpretation of eastern moundbuilders from Poverty Point through the Mississippians.

Lawrence E. Sullivan, ed., *Native American Religions: North America* (1989). Essays focusing on religious life and expression throughout the continent.

Chapter 2

Bartholomew Gosnold Trading with Wampanoag Indians at Martha's Vineyard (1602)
by Theodore de Bry, 1634
Exchanges between Native Americans and Europeans transformed the Atlantic Ocean from a barrier to a bridge between Earth's two hemispheres.

The Rise of the Atlantic World, 1400–1625

Christopher Columbus

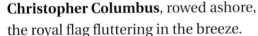

At ten o'clock on a moonlit night, the tense crew spotted a glimmering light. At two the next morning came the shout, "Land! Land!" At daybreak they entered a shallow lagoon. The captain, **Christopher Columbus**, rowed ashore, the royal flag fluttering in the breeze. "And, all having rendered thanks to the Lord, kneeling on the ground, embracing it with tears of joy for the immeasurable mercy of having reached it, [he] rose and gave this island the name San Salvador." At the same time, Columbus claimed the island for the king and queen of Spain. The date was October 12, 1492. The place was a tiny island in the Bahamas, less than four hundred miles from the North American mainland.

Columbus and his crew were not alone. Witnessing their landing were the local Taino Indians, who called their island Guanahaní. The first meeting between the two peoples went smoothly. The Spanish gave the Native Americans red caps, glass beads, and small bells. In return, the Tainos presented the visitors with "parrots, and cotton thread in balls, and spears and many other things." "In fact," Columbus continued, "they took all and gave all, such as they had, with good will." Without Columbus realizing it, Tainos were engaging in the kind of reciprocal exchange that Native Americans had conducted among themselves for thousands of years (see Chapter 1).

While the Tainos understood their encounter with Columbus in terms of reciprocity, he saw it differently. The authority he claimed for Spain over the island extended to its native inhabitants. "They should be good servants," he observed in his journal, " . . . and I believe that they would easily be made

Christians." As "a people very deficient in everything," the Tainos would now receive the benefits of Christianity, Spanish rule, and European "civilization," whether they wanted these things or not. The fact that some of their jewelry appeared to contain gold only heightened Columbus's determination to colonize the island.

Columbus's landfall at Guanahaní marked not only Europe's discovery of America but also a critical step in the formation of an Atlantic world. After 1492 peoples from Europe, Africa, and North and South America became intertwined in colonial societies, obligatory and forced labor relations, trade networks, religious missions, and wars. Whether traveling to new lands or experiencing the transformation of familiar homelands, they entered "new worlds" in which their customary ways of thinking and acting were repeatedly challenged. The massive "Columbian exchange" included not only people but also animals, plants, and germs whose transfer had far-reaching environmental and demographic consequences. The Columbian exchange was shaped by the efforts of several European nations to increase their wealth and power by controlling the land and labor of non-Europeans they considered uncivilized.

In much of what is now Latin America, the coming of Europeans quickly turned into conquest. In the future United States and Canada, European mastery would come more slowly. More than a hundred years would pass before truly self-sustaining colonies appeared. Nevertheless, from the moment of Columbus's landing, the American continents became the stage for the encounter of Native American, European, and African peoples in the new Atlantic world.

African and European Backgrounds

When the Atlantic world emerged in the fifteenth and sixteenth centuries, all the continents facing the Atlantic Ocean were undergoing internal change. In the Americas, some societies rose, others fell, and still others adapted to new circumstances (see Chapter 1). West Africa and western Europe were also being transformed; a market society emerged on each continent alongside older systems of barter and local exchange. Wealthy merchants financed dynastic rulers seeking to extend their domains.

Western Europe's transformation was thoroughgoing. Its population nearly doubled in size, the distribution of wealth and power shifted radically, and new modes of thought and spirituality undermined established beliefs and knowledge. The result was social, political, and religious upheaval alongside remarkable expressions of creativity and innovation.

West Africa: Tradition and Change

Before the advent of Atlantic travel, the broad belt of grassland, or savanna, separating the Sahara Desert from the forests to the south played a major role in long-distance trade between the Mediterranean Sea and West Africa (see Map 2.1). The trans-Saharan caravan trade stimulated the rise of grassland kingdoms and empires, whose size and wealth rivaled any in Europe at the time. The richest grassland states were in West Africa, with its ample stores of gold. During the fourteenth and early fifteenth centuries, the empire of **Mali** was the leading power in the West African savanna. Through ties with wealthy Muslim rulers and merchants in North Africa and the Middle East, Mali's Muslim rulers imported brass, copper, cloth, spices, manufactured goods, and Arabian horses. Among their leading exports were gold and slaves. Mali's best-known city, Timbuktu, was widely recognized for its intellectual and academic vitality and for its beautiful mosque, designed and built by a Spanish Muslim architect.

During the fifteenth century, divisions within Mali's royal family severely weakened the empire, leading

---

Focus Questions

- What forces were transforming West Africa before the advent of the Atlantic slave trade?

- How did European monarchs use commerce and religion to advance their nations' fortunes?

- What role did the Columbian exchange play in the formation of an Atlantic world?

- How did European relations with Native Americans affect the success of early European colonizing efforts?

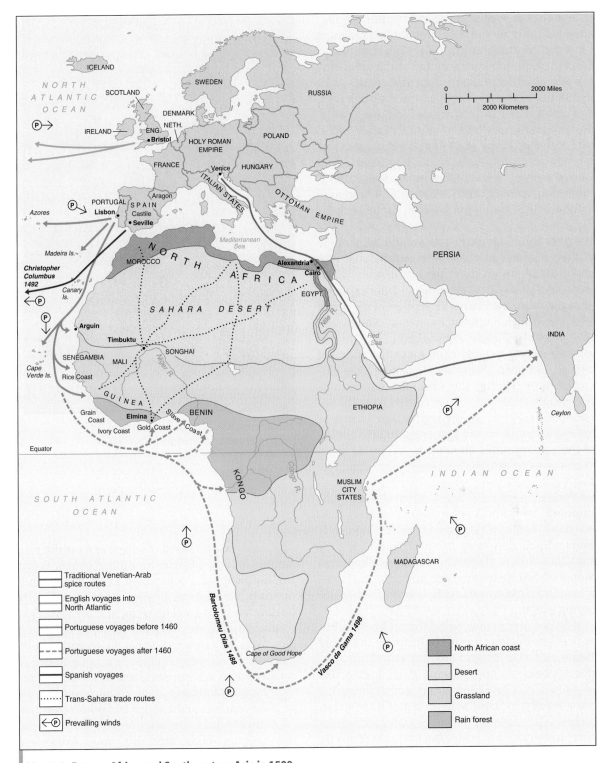

Map 2.1 Europe, Africa, and Southwestern Asia in 1500
During the fifteenth century, Portuguese voyages established trade links between Africa and Europe, circumventing older overland routes. Several voyages near the end of the century extended Europe's reach to India and the Americas.

several territories to secede. A successor empire, Songhai, expanded from the south and forcibly united most of the seceded territory. But in 1591 Moroccan troops from North Africa defeated Songhai and established Morocco's domination of the western grassland.

Immediately south of the grassland empires lay a region of small states and chiefdoms. In Senegambia, at Africa's westernmost bulge, several Islamic states took root. Infestation by the tsetse fly, the carrier of sleeping sickness, kept livestock-herding peoples out of Guinea's coastal forests, but many small states arose here, too. Among these was Benin, where artisans had been fashioning magnificent metalwork for centuries.

Still farther south, along the coast and inland on the Congo River, a welter of chiefdoms consolidated into four major kingdoms by the fifteenth century. Their kings were chiefs who, after defeating neighboring chiefdoms, installed their own kin as local rulers of the newly conquered territories. Of these kingdoms, **Kongo** was the most powerful and highly centralized.

With gold having recently been made the standard for nearly all European currencies, demand for the precious metal rose. During the fifteenth century, this demand brought thousands of newcomers from the savanna and Central Africa to the region later known as Africa's Gold Coast. New states emerged to take advantage of the opportunities afforded by exporting gold, though none was as extensive or powerful as Mali at its height.

West African political leaders differed sharply in the amounts and kinds of political power they wielded. Some kings and emperors enjoyed semigod-like status, which they only thinly disguised if they adopted Islam. Rulers of smaller kingdoms depended largely on their ability to persuade, to conform to prevailing customs, and to satisfy their people when redistributing wealth.

As did Native Americans, West Africans lived within a network of interlocking mutual obligations to kinfolk (see Chapter 1). Not just parents but also aunts, uncles, distant cousins, and persons sharing clan ties formed an African's extended family and claimed his or her first loyalty. Africans held their grandparents in high esteem and accorded village or clan elders great deference. In centuries to come, the tradition of strong extended families would help enslaved Africans in the Americas endure the forced breakup of nuclear families by sale.

Mali Horseman, c. 13th–14th century
This terra-cotta figure originated in Mali, one of several powerful empires in West Africa before the arrival of Europeans.

West Africans viewed marriage as a way for extended families to forge alliances for mutual benefit. A prospective husband made a payment to his bride's kin before marriage. He was not "buying" a wife; in effect, he was posting bond for good behavior and acknowledging the relative prestige of his own and his bride's extended families. West African wives generally maintained lifelong links with their own families. As among Native Americans, children in many societies traced descent through their mother's forebears, rather than their father's. These practices reinforced the status and power of women.

A driving force behind marriage in West Africa was the region's high mortality rate from frequent famines and tropical disease epidemics. The shortage of people placed a high premium on the production of children. Children contributed to a family's wealth by increasing its food production and the amount of land it could cultivate. Men of means frequently married more than one wife in order to produce children more frequently, and women generally married soon after reaching puberty.

West Africans depended on farming by both men and women for most of their food. The abundance of land relative to population enabled African farmers—like many Native Americans and unlike Europeans—to shift their fields periodically and thereby maintain high soil quality. Before planting new fields, men felled the trees and burned off the wild vegetation. After several years of intensive cultivation, largely by women, farmers shifted to a new location. After a few years, while the soil of the recently used fields was being replenished, they returned to repeat the cycle. In the coastal rain forests, West Africans grew such crops as yams, sugar cane, bananas, okra, and eggplant, among other foods, as well as cotton for weaving cloth. On the grasslands the staff of life was grain—millet, sorghum, and rice—supplemented by cattle raising and fishing.

By the fifteenth century, the market economy, stimulated by long-distance trade, extended to many small families. Farmers traded surplus crops at local marketplaces for other food or cloth. Artisans wove cotton or raffia palm leaves, made clothing and jewelry, and crafted tools and religious objects of iron and wood. While gold was the preferred currency among wealthy rulers and merchants, cowry shells served as the medium of exchange for most people.

Religion permeated African life. Like Native Americans and Europeans, Africans believed that another world lay beyond the one people perceived through their five senses. This other world was only rarely glimpsed by living persons besides priests, but the souls of most people passed there at death. Deities spoke to mortals through priests, dreams, religious "speaking shrines," and magical charms. Unlike Islam and Christianity, with their fixed dogmas, indigenous West African religions emphasized the importance of believers' continuous revelations as sources of spiritual truth. Like both Native Americans and Europeans, Africans explained misfortunes in terms of witchcraft. But African religion differed from other traditions by emphasizing ancestor worship, in which departed forebears were venerated as spiritual guardians.

Africa's magnificent artistic traditions were also steeped in religion. The ivory, cast iron, and wood sculptures of West Africa (whose bold designs would influence twentieth-century western art) were used in ceremonies reenacting creation myths and honoring spirits. A strong moralistic streak ran through African folk tales. Storytellers transmitted these tales in dramatic public presentations with ritual masks, dance, and music of a highly complex rhythmic structure, which is now appreciated as one of the foundations of jazz.

Among Africans, Islam appealed primarily to merchants trading with North Africa and the Middle East and to kings and emperors eager to consolidate their power. Some Muslim rulers modified Islam, retaining elements of traditional religion as a concession to popular opinion. By 1400, Islam was just beginning to affect the daily lives of some cultivators and artisans in the savanna.

European Culture and Society

When Columbus reached Guanahaní in 1492, western Europe was undergoing a cultural **Renaissance** (literally, rebirth). Intellectuals and poets celebrated Europe's descent from a classical tradition originating in ancient Greece and Rome but obscured for a thousand years during the "dark" or "middle" ages. Western European scholars discovered scores of forgotten ancient texts in philosophy, science, medicine, geography, and other subjects, and a rich tradition of commentary on them by Muslim, Eastern Orthodox, and Jewish scholars. Armed with the new learning, Renaissance scholars strove to reconcile ancient philosophy with Christian faith, to explore the mysteries of nature, to map the world, and to explain the motions of the heavens.

The Renaissance was also an era of intense artistic creativity. Wealthy Italian merchants and rulers—especially in the city-states of Florence and Venice, and in Rome (controlled by the papacy)—commissioned magnificent architecture, painting, and sculpture. Artists such as Leonardo da Vinci and Michelangelo created works that were rooted in classical tradition and were based on close observations of nature (including the human body) and attention to perspective. Europeans celebrated these artistic achievements, along with those of writers, philosophers, scientists, and explorers, as the height of "civilization" to which other cultures should aspire.

But European society was also quivering with tension. The era's artistic and intellectual creativity was partly inspired by intense social and spiritual stress as Renaissance Europeans groped for stability by glorifying order, hierarchy, and beauty. A concern for power and rank ("degree") dominated European life between the fifteenth and seventeenth centuries. Writing near the end of the Renaissance, William Shakespeare (1564–1616) expressed these values with eloquence:

The heavens themselves, the planets and this center [earth]
Observe degree, priority, and place . . .
Take but degree away, untune that string,
And hark, what discord follows!

Gender, wealth, inherited position, and political power affected every European's status, and few lived outside the reach of some political authority's taxes and laws. But this order was shaky. Conflicts between states, between religions, and between social classes constantly threatened the balance.

At the heart of these conflicts lay deep-seated forces of change. By the end of the fifteenth century, strong national monarchs in Spain, France, and England had consolidated royal authority at the expense of the Catholic Church and the nobility. The "new monarchs" cultivated powerful merchants by promoting their enterprises in exchange for financial support. On the Iberian Peninsula, King Ferdinand of Aragon had married Queen Isabella of Castile in 1479 to create the Spanish monarchy. France's boundaries expanded as a series of kings absorbed neighboring lands through interdynastic marriage and military conquest. England's Tudor dynasty gradually suppressed the aristocracy's ability to plunge the nation into deadly civil war.

Most Europeans—about 75 percent—were peasants, frequently driven to starvation by taxes, rents, and other dues owed to landlords and Catholic Church officials. Not surprisingly, peasant revolts were frequent, but the authorities mercilessly suppressed such uprisings.

Conditions among European peasants were made worse by a sharp rise in population, from about 55 million in 1450 to almost 100 million by 1600. Neighboring families often cooperated in plowing, sowing, and harvesting as well as in grazing their livestock on jointly owned "commons." But with new land at a premium, landlords, especially in England, wanted to "enclose" the commons—that is, convert the land to private property. Peasants who had no written title to their land were especially vulnerable to these pressures.

The environmental effects of land scarcity and population growth further exacerbated peasants' circumstances. Beginning in the fourteenth century, lower-than-average temperatures marked a "Little Ice Age" that lasted for more than four centuries. During this time, many European crops were less abundant or failed to grow. Hunger and malnutrition were widespread, and full-scale famine struck in some areas. Another consequence of population growth was deforestation resulting from increased human demand for wood to use as fuel and building materials. Deforestation also deprived peasants of wild foods and game (whose food sources disappeared with deforestation), accelerating the exodus of rural Europeans to towns and cities.

European towns were numerous but small, typically with several thousand inhabitants each. A great metropolis like London, whose population ballooned from fifty-five thousand in 1550 to two hundred thousand in 1600, was quite exceptional. But all towns were dirty and disease-ridden, and townspeople lived close-packed with their neighbors.

Unappealing as sixteenth-century towns might seem today, many men and women preferred them to the villages and tiny farms they left behind. Immigration from the countryside—rather than an excess of births over deaths—accounted for towns' expansion. Most people who flocked into towns remained at the bottom of the social order as servants or laborers and could not accumulate enough money to marry and live independently.

The consequences of rapid population growth were particularly acute in England, where the number of people doubled from about 2.5 million in 1500 to 5 million in 1620. As throughout western Europe, prices rose while wages fell during the sixteenth and early seventeenth centuries (see Figure 2.1), widening the gap between rich and poor. Although English entrepreneurs expanded textile production by assembling spinners and weavers in household workshops, the workers were competing for fewer jobs in the face of growing competition that was diminishing European markets for English cloth. Enclosures of common lands severely aggravated unemployment, forcing large numbers of people to wander the country in search of work. To the upper and middle classes, these poor vagabonds seemed to threaten law and order. To control them, Parliament passed Poor Laws that ordered vagrants whipped and sent home, but most offenders only moved on to other towns. Some English writers, such as two men (cousins) named Richard Hakluyt, viewed overseas colonies as places where the unemployed, landless poor could find

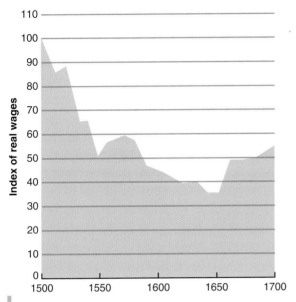

**Figure 2.1 Decline in Real Wages in England,
1500–1700**
This index measures the drop in purchasing power due to
inflation and declining wages. It indicates that by around
1630, living standards for English workers had declined by
about two-thirds since 1500.
Source: E. H. Phelps Brown and S. V. Hopkins, "Builders'
Wage-Rates, Prices and Population: Some Further
Evidence," *Economica*, XXVI (1959): 18–38; adapted from D. C.
North and R. P. Thomas, *The Rise of the Western World: A New
Economic History* (Cambridge: Cambridge University Press,
1973), 111.

that amassed capital through sales of stock to investors. Demand rose for capital investment, and so did the supply of accumulated wealth. A new economic outlook gradually took form that justified the unimpeded acquisition of wealth and insisted that individuals owed one another nothing but the money necessary to settle their transactions. This new outlook, the central value system of capitalism or the "market economy," rejected traditional demands that economic activity be regulated in order to ensure social reciprocity and maintain "just prices."

Sixteenth- and seventeenth-century Europeans therefore held conflicting attitudes toward economic enterprise and social change, and their ambivalence remained unresolved. A restless desire for fresh opportunity kept European life simmering with competitive tension. But those who prospered still sought the security and prestige provided by high social status, whereas the poor longed for the age-old values that would restrain irresponsible greed.

Perhaps the most sensitive barometer of social change was the family. Throughout Europe the typical household consisted of a small nuclear family—two parents and several children—in which the husband and father functioned as a head whose authority was not to be questioned. The role of the wife and mother was to bear and rear children as well as assist her husband in providing for the family's subsistence. Children were regarded as potential laborers who would assist in these tasks until they left home to start their own families. The household, then, was not only a family of intimately related people but also the principal economic unit in European society. Peasants on their tiny farms, artisans and merchants in their shops, and even nobles in their castles all lived and worked in households. People who did not live with their own families resided as dependents in the households of others as servants, apprentices, or relatives. Europeans regarded those who lived outside family-based households with extreme suspicion, often accusing them of crime or even witchcraft.

Europeans frequently characterized the nuclear family as a "little commonwealth." A father's authority over his family supposedly mirrored God's rule over Creation and the king's over his subjects. Even grown sons and daughters regularly knelt for their father's blessing. The ideal, according to a German writer, was that "wives should obey their husbands and not seek to dominate them; they must manage the home efficiently. Husbands . . . should treat their wives with consideration and occasionally close an eye to their

opportunity, thereby enriching their countries rather than draining resources.

As in America and Africa, traditional society in Europe rested on maintaining long-term, reciprocal relationships. European reciprocity required the upper classes to act with self-restraint and dignity, and the lower classes to show deference to their "betters." It also demanded strict economic regulation to ensure that no purchaser paid more than a "just price"—one that permitted a seller a "reasonable" profit but that barred him from taking advantage of buyers' and borrowers' misfortunes to make "excessive" profits.

Yet for several centuries Europeans had been compromising the ideals of traditional economic behavior. "In the Name of God and of Profit," thirteenth-century Italian merchants had written on their ledgers. By the sixteenth century, nothing could stop lenders' profiting from interest on borrowed money or sellers' raising prices in response to demand. New forms of business organization slowly spread in the commercial world—especially the **joint-stock company**, a business corporation

The Woman Spinning **by Geertruyd Roghman (c. 1650) (detail)**
In early modern Europe, mothers introduced their daughters to spinning at an early age. Roghmann, one of the few female engravers of her time, specialized in depicting the daily lives of women.

faults." In practice, the father's sovereignty often had to make room for the wife's responsibility in managing family affairs and helping to run the farm or the workshop. Repeated male complaints, such as that of an English author in 1622 about wives "who think themselves every way as good as their husbands, and no way inferior to them," suggest that male domination had its limits.

Religious Upheavals

Although Europe was predominantly Christian in 1400, it was also home to significant numbers of Muslims and Jews. Adherents to these three religious traditions worshiped a single supreme being, based on the God of the Hebrew Bible. While they often coexisted peacefully in lands bordering the Mediterranean, hatred and violence also marked their shared history. For more than three centuries, European Christians had conducted numerous Crusades against Muslims in Europe and the

Middle East, and Muslims retaliated with "holy war." Each side labeled the other "infidels." Eventually, the participation of rulers transformed the religious conflicts into wars of conquest. While the Islamic Ottoman Empire seized Christian strongholds in the eastern Mediterranean, the Catholic monarchies of Portugal and Spain undertook a "reconquest" of the Iberian Peninsula by conquering Muslim states and expelling or forcibly converting non-Christians. Portugal was entirely Christian by 1250. As part of its national consolidation (discussed above), Spain in 1492 drove the last Muslim rulers from Iberia and expelled all Jews who refused to convert to Catholicism.

Following the Spanish Reconquest, the Roman Catholic Church dominated western and central Europe. Nevertheless, older, non-Christian beliefs persisted. Many Europeans feared witches and thought that individuals could manipulate nature by invoking unseen spiritual powers—that is, by magic. Others looked to astrology, insisting that a person's fate depended on the conjunction of various planets and stars. Such beliefs in spiritual forces not originating with a supreme deity resembled those of Native Americans and non-Muslim Africans.

Like Orthodox Christians in eastern Europe and the Middle East, Catholics believed that Jesus Christ, God's Son, had redeemed sinners by suffering crucifixion and rising from the dead. Equally vivid was Catholics' belief in the devil, Satan, whom God had hurled from heaven soon after the Creation and who ceaselessly lured people to damnation by tempting them to do evil.

The Catholic Church taught that Christ's sacrifice was repeated every time a priest said Mass, and that divine grace flowed to sinners through the sacraments that priests alone could administer—above all, baptism, confession, and the Eucharist (communion). The Church was a vast network of clergymen and religious orders, male and female, set apart from laypeople by the fact that its members did not marry. At the top was the pope, the "vicar [representative] of Christ" on earth.

Besides conducting services, priests heard the confessions of repentant sinners and assigned them penance, most often in the form of devotional exercises and good works that would demonstrate repentance. During the Middle Ages, the Church gradually assumed the authority to grant extra blessings, or "indulgences," to repentant sinners. Indulgences promised cancellation both of penance and of time in purgatory, where the dead atoned for sins they had already confessed and been forgiven. (Hell, from which there was no escape, awaited those who died unforgiven.) Given Catholics' anxieties about sinful behavior, indulgences were enormously popular. By the early sixteenth century, many religious authorities granted them in return for such "good works" as donating money to the Church. The jingle of one enterprising German friar promised that

As soon as the coin in the cash box rings,
The soul from purgatory's fire springs.

The sale of indulgences provoked charges that the materialism and corruption infecting economic life had spread to the Church. In 1517 a German monk, Martin Luther (1483–1546), openly attacked the practice. When the pope censured him, Luther broadened his criticism to encompass the Mass, purgatory, priests, and the papacy. After Luther refused to recant, the Roman Church excommunicated him. Luther's revolt initiated what became known as the **Protestant Reformation**, which changed Christianity forever. (The word *Protestant* comes from the *protest* of Luther's princely supporters against the anti-Lutheran policies of Holy Roman Emperor Charles V.)

To Luther, indulgence selling and similar examples of clerical corruption were evil not just because they bilked people. The Church, he charged, gave people false confidence that they could earn salvation simply by doing good works. His own agonizing search for salvation had convinced Luther that God bestowed salvation not on the basis of worldly deeds, but solely to reward a believer's faith. "I did not love a just and angry God," recalled Luther, ". . . until I saw the connection between the justice of God and the [New Testament] statement that 'the just shall live [be saved] by faith.'. . . Thereupon I felt myself to be reborn." Luther's spiritual struggle and experience of being "reborn" constituted a classic conversion experience— the heart of Protestant Christianity.

Other Protestant reformers followed Luther in breaking from Catholicism, most notably John Calvin (1509–1564), who fled his native France for Geneva, Switzerland. Whereas Luther stressed faith in Christ as the key to salvation, Calvin insisted on the stark doctrine of **predestination**. Calvin asserted that an omnipotent God predestined most sinful humans to hell, saving only a few in order to demonstrate his power and grace. It was only these few, called the "elect," "godly," or "saints," who would have a true conversion experience. At this moment, said Calvin, a person confronted the horrifying truth of his or her unworthiness and felt God's transcend-

ing power. A good Christian, in Calvin's view, would never be absolutely certain that he or she was saved and could do nothing to affect the outcome. But good Christians would be pious and avoid sin because they knew that godly behavior was a sign (not a cause and not a guarantee) of salvation.

Calvinists and Lutherans, as the followers of the two Reformation leaders came to be called, were equally horrified by more radical Protestants such as the Anabaptists, who appealed strongly to women and common people with their criticisms of the rich and powerful and sought to restrict baptism to "converted" adults. Judging the Anabaptists a threat to the social order, governments and mainstream churches persecuted them.

But Protestants also shared much common ground. For one thing, they denied that God had endowed priests with special powers. The church, Luther claimed, was a "priesthood of all believers." Protestant reformers insisted that laypeople take responsibility for their own spiritual and moral conditions. Accordingly, they placed a high value on reading. Protestants demanded that the Bible be translated from Latin into spoken languages so that believers could read it for themselves. The new faith was spread by the recently invented printing press. Wherever Protestantism became established, basic education and religious indoctrination followed. Finally, Protestantism represented a yearning in many people for the simplicity and purity of the ancient Christian church. More forcefully than Catholicism, it (initially) condemned the replacement of traditional reciprocity by marketplace values. Protestantism's greatest appeal was to all those—ordinary individuals, merchants, and aristocrats alike—who brooded over their chances for salvation and valued the steady performance of duty.

In the face of the Protestant challenge, Rome was far from idle. Reformers like Teresa of Ávila (1515–1582), a Spanish nun from a *converso* (converted Jewish) family, urged members of Catholic holy orders to repudiate corruption and to lead the Church's renewal by living piously and austerely. Another reformer, Ignatius Loyola (1491–1556), founded a militant religious order, the Society of Jesus, whose members (Jesuits) would distinguish themselves in coming centuries as royal advisers and missionaries. The high point of Catholic reform came during the Council of Trent (1545–1563), convened by the pope. The council defended Catholic teachings and denounced those of the Protestants. But it also reformed Church administration in order to combat corruption and broaden public participation

Saint Teresa of Ávila
One of the leading Catholic reformers, Saint Teresa was a nun whose exemplary life and forceful views helped reshape the Roman church during the Catholic or Counter-Reformation.

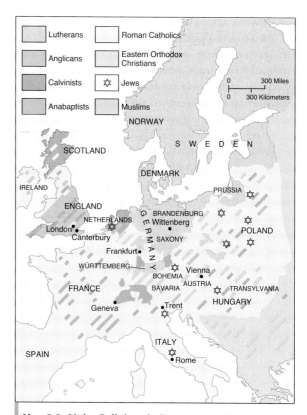

Map 2.2 Major Religions in Europe, c. 1560
By 1560, some European lands were solidly Catholic, Lutheran, or Calvinist. Others remained bitterly divided for another century or more.

in religious observances. This revival, the **Catholic** or **Counter-Reformation**, brought the modern Roman Catholic Church into existence.

The Protestant Reformation changed the religious map of Europe (see Map 2.2). Lutheranism became the state religion in the Scandinavian countries, while Calvinism made significant inroads in France, the Netherlands (which a royal marriage had brought under Spanish rule), England, and Scotland. The tiny states comprising the modern nations of Germany and Switzerland were divided among Catholics, Lutherans, and Calvinists.

The Reformation in England, 1533–1625

England's Reformation began not with the writings of a theologian or with cries of the people, but with the actions of a king and Parliament. King Henry VIII (ruled 1509–1547) wanted a male heir, but his queen, Catherine of Aragon, failed to bear a son. Henry asked the pope to annul his marriage, but the pope refused. Frustrated and determined, Henry persuaded Parliament to

pass a series of acts in 1533–1534 dissolving his marriage and proclaiming him supreme head of the **Church of England** (or Anglican Church). The move justified Henry's seizure of income-producing Catholic Church properties, further consolidating royal power and financial independence.

Religion remained a source of conflict in England for more than a century after Henry's break with Rome. Under Edward VI (ruled 1547–1553), Henry's son by the third of his six wives, the church veered sharply toward Calvinism. Edward's sister and successor, Mary I (ruled 1553–1558), tried to restore Catholicism, in part by burning several hundred Protestants at the stake.

The reign of Elizabeth I (ruled 1558–1603), a half-sister of Edward and Mary, marked a crucial turning point. After the reign of "Bloody Mary," most English people were ready to become Protestant; *how* Protestant was the divisive question. Elizabeth took a middle road by affirming the monarch's role as head of the Anglican hierarchy of archbishops, bishops, and parish priests while endorsing the Calvinist belief in predestination. She also allowed individuals and parish churches wide latitude in deciding which customs and practices to follow.

Militant Calvinists, whose opponents derisively called them "**Puritans**," demanded a more thorough purification of the Church of England from "popish [Catholic] abuses." Puritans insisted that membership in a congregation be limited to those who had had a conversion experience and that each congregation be independent of other congregations and of the Anglican hierarchy (body of ranked officials). Thus, they repudiated the Anglican (and Catholic) practices of extending membership to anyone who had been baptized and of subordinating congregations to the authority of priests, bishops, archbishops, and the head of the church (the monarch). Some "nonseparating" Puritans remained within the Church of England, hoping to reform it. Others, called Separatists, withdrew, insisting that a "pure" church had to be entirely free of Anglican "pollution."

The severe self-discipline and moral uprightness of Puritans appealed to few among the nobility and the poor. Puritanism appealed primarily to the small but growing number of people in the "middling" ranks of English society—landowning gentry, yeomen (small independent farmers), merchants, shopkeepers, artisans, and university-educated clergy and intellectuals. Self-discipline had become central to both the secular and spiritual dimensions of these people's lives. From their ranks, and particularly from among farmers, artisans, and clergy, would later come the settlers of New England (see Chapter 3).

Elizabeth distrusted Puritan militancy; but, after 1570 when the pope declared her a heretic and urged Catholics to overthrow her, she regarded English Catholics as even more dangerous. Thereafter, she courted influential Puritans and embraced militant anti-Catholicism.

Although opposed by Elizabeth, most Puritans still hoped to transform the Church of England into independent congregations of "saints." But her successor, James I (ruled 1603–1625), a distant cousin of Elizabeth who was king of Scotland, bitterly opposed Puritan calls to eliminate Anglican bishops. He made clear that he saw Puritan attacks on bishops as a threat to the throne when he snapped, "No bishop, no king." But while James insisted on outward conformity to Anglican practice, he tolerated Calvinists who did not publicly proclaim their dissent.

Europe and the Atlantic World, 1400–1600

The forces transforming Europe quickly reverberated beyond that continent. During the fifteenth and sixteenth centuries, the alliances of merchants and dynastic monarchs organized imperial ventures to Africa, Asia, and the Americas. Besides seeking wealth and power, expanding Europeans proclaimed it their mission to introduce Christianity and "civilization" to the "savages" and "pagans" of alien lands. Two prominent outcomes of the new imperialism were a transatlantic slave trade and the colonization of the Americas. The multiple exchanges that resulted gave rise to a new Atlantic world.

Portugal and the Atlantic, 1400–1500

During the fifteenth century, some European merchants recognized that they could enhance their profits by circumventing costly Mediterranean-overland trade routes to and from Asia and Africa. Instead they hoped to establish direct contacts with sources of prized imports via the seas. Tiny Portugal led the way in overcoming impediments to long-distance oceanic travel.

Important changes in maritime technology occurred in the early fifteenth century. Shipbuilders and mariners along Europe's stormy Atlantic coast added the triangular Arab sail to their heavy cargo ships. They created a more maneuverable vessel, the caravel, which sailed more easily against the wind. Sailors also mastered the compass and astrolabe, by which they got their bearings on the open sea. Without this maritime revolution, European exploration would have been impossible.

Renaissance scholars' readings of ancient texts enabled fifteenth-century Europeans to look at their world with new eyes. The great ancient Greek authority on geography was Ptolemy, but Renaissance cartographers corrected his data when they tried to draw accurate maps based on recent European and Arabic observations. Thus, Renaissance "new learning" helped sharpen Europeans' geographic sense.

Led by Prince Henry "the Navigator" (1394–1460), Portugal was the first nation to capitalize on these developments. Henry gained the support of merchants seeking to circumvent Moroccan control of the African-European gold trade and of religious zealots eager to confront Muslim power. Henry encouraged Portuguese seamen to pilot the new caravels southward along the African coast, mastering the Atlantic's currents while searching for opportunities to trade or raid profitably.

African View of Portuguese, c. 1650–1700
A carver in the kingdom of Benin, on Africa's west coast, created this salt holder depicting Portuguese officials and their ship.

Africans were enslaved because of indebtedness. Their debts were purchased by kings and emperors who made them servants or by families seeking additional laborers. They or their children were either absorbed into their new families over time or released from bondage when their debts were considered paid off through their work. But a long-distance commercial trade in slaves also flourished. For several centuries, Middle Eastern and North African traders had furnished local rulers with a range of fine, imported products in exchange for black laborers. Some of these slaves had been debtors, while others were captured in raids and wars.

One fifteenth-century Italian who witnessed Portuguese and Muslim slave trading noted that the Arabs "have many Berber horses, which they trade, and take to the Land of the Blacks, exchanging them with the rulers for slaves. Ten or fifteen slaves are given for one

Vasco da Gama
The first European to reach India by sea, da Gama established Portuguese naval and commercial power in the Indian Ocean.

By the time of Henry's death, Portugal was exporting substantial quantities of gold and slaves from south of the Sahara. By then they were also in a position to expand their vision of a trading empire beyond Africa. In 1488 Bartolomeu Días reached the Cape of Good Hope at Africa's southern tip. A decade later Vasco da Gama led a Portuguese fleet around the Cape of Good Hope and on to India (see Map 2.1).

Although the Portuguese did not destroy older Euro-Asian commercial links, they showed western Europeans a way around Africa to Asia. In the process, they brought Europeans face-to-face with West Africans and an already flourishing slave trade.

The "New Slavery" and Racism

Slavery was well established in fifteenth-century Africa. The institution took two basic forms. Many of these horses, according to their quality." Portuguese traders quickly realized how lucrative the trade in slaves could be for them, too. The same Italian observer continued, "Slaves are brought to the market town of Hoden; there they are divided. . . .[Some] are taken . . . and sold to the Portuguese leaseholders [in Arguin]. As a result every year the Portuguese carry away . . . a thousand slaves."

Although in 1482 the Portuguese built one outpost, Elmina, on West Africa's Gold Coast, they primarily traded through African-controlled commercial networks. Often Portuguese merchants traded slaves and local products to other Africans for gold. The local African kingdoms were too strong for the Portuguese to attack, and African rulers traded—or chose not to trade—according to their own self-interest.

Despite preventing the Portuguese from directly colonizing them, West African societies were profoundly affected by the new Atlantic slave trade. Portuguese traders enriched favored African rulers not only with luxury products but also with guns. As a result, they exacerbated conflicts among African communities and helped redraw the political map of West Africa. In Guinea and Senegambia, where most sixteenth-century slaves came from, small kingdoms expanded to "service" the trade. Some of their rulers became comparatively rich. Farther south, the kings of Kongo used the slave trade to expand their regional power and voluntarily adopted Christianity, just as rulers farther north had converted to Islam. Kongo flourished until the mid-sixteenth century, when a series of internal rebellions weakened it.

Although slavery had long been practiced in many parts of the Eastern Hemisphere, including in Europe, there were ominous differences between these older practices and the **"new slavery"** initiated by Portugal and later adopted by other western Europeans. First, the unprecedented magnitude of the trade resulted in a demographic catastrophe for West Africa and its peoples. Before the Atlantic slave trade finally ended in the nineteenth century, nearly 12 million Africans would be shipped in terrible conditions across the sea. Slavery on this scale had been unknown to Europeans since the collapse of the Roman Empire. Second, African slaves were subjected to new extremes of dehumanization. In medieval Europe and in West Africa itself, most slaves had lived in their masters' households and primarily performed domestic service. Africans shipped to Arab lands endured harsher conditions, but were nevertheless regarded as humans. But by 1450 the Portuguese and Spanish created large slave-labor plantations on their Atlantic and Mediterranean islands (see Technology and Culture: Sugar Production in the Americas). These plantations produced sugar for European markets, using capital supplied by Italian investors to buy African slaves who toiled until death. In short, Africans enslaved by Europeans were regarded as property rather than as persons of low status; as such, they were consigned to labor that was unending, exhausting, and mindless. By 1600 the "new slavery" had become a central, brutal component of the Atlantic world.

Finally, race became the ideological basis of the new slavery. Africans' blackness, along with their alien religions and customs, dehumanized them in European eyes. As their racial prejudice hardened, Europeans justified enslaving blacks as their Christian duty. From the fifteenth century onward, European Christianity made few attempts to soften slavery's rigors, and race defined a slave. Slavery became a lifelong, hereditary, and despised status.

To America and Beyond, 1492–1522

Europeans' varying motivations for expanding their horizons converged in the fascinating, contradictory figure of Christopher Columbus (1451–1506), the son of a weaver from the Italian port of Genoa. Columbus's maritime experience, self-taught geographical learning, and keen imagination led him to conclude that Europeans could reach Asia more directly by sailing westward across the Atlantic rather than around Africa and across the Indian Ocean. By the early 1480s, he was obsessed with this idea. Religious fervor led Columbus to dream of carrying Christianity around the globe and liberating Jerusalem from Muslim rule, but he also burned with ambition to win wealth and glory.

Columbus was not the first European to cross the Atlantic. Besides the early Norse (see Chapter 1), English fishermen in the North Atlantic may already have landed on the North American coast. But these efforts did not attract the attention of powerful rulers eager for wealth. Columbus was unique in the persistence with which he hawked his "enterprise of the Indies" around the royal courts of western Europe. John II of Portugal showed interest until Días's discovery of the Cape of Good Hope confirmed a sure way to the Indies. Finally, in 1492, hoping to break Portugal's threatened monopoly on direct trade with Asia, Queen Isabella and King Ferdinand of Spain accepted Columbus's offer. Picking up the westward-blowing trade winds at the Canary Islands, Columbus's three small ships reached Guanahaní within a

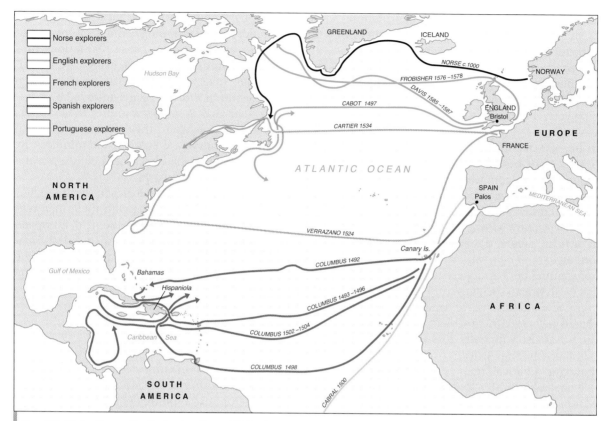

Map 2.3 Major Transatlantic Explorations, 1000–1587
Following Columbus's 1492 voyage, Spain's rivals soon began laying claim to parts of the New World based on the voyages of Cabot for England, Cabral for Portugal, and Verrazano for France. Later English and French exploration focused on finding a passage to Asia around or through Canada.

month. After his meeting with the Tainos there, he sailed on in search of gold, making additional contacts with Tainos in Cuba (which he thought was Japan) and Hispaniola, the Caribbean island today occupied by Haiti and the Dominican Republic (see Map 2.3). Finding gold on Hispaniola, he returned to Spain to tell Isabella and Ferdinand about his discovery.

Returning to Hispaniola to found a colony, Columbus proved to be a poor administrator. Although he made two more voyages (1498–1502), he was shunted aside and died an embittered man, convinced that he had reached the threshold of Asia only to be cheated of his rightful rewards.

Meanwhile, word of Columbus's discovery caught Europeans' imaginations. To forestall competition between them as well as potential rivals, Isabella and Portugal's King John II in 1494 signed the Treaty of Tordesillas (see Map 2.4). The treaty drew a line in the mid-Atlantic dividing all future discoveries between Spain and Portugal.

Ignoring the Treaty of Tordesillas, England attempted to join the race for Asia in 1497 when Henry VII (ruled 1485–1509), sent an Italian navigator, John Cabot, to explore the North Atlantic. Sailing past Nova Scotia, Newfoundland, and the rich Grand Banks fisheries, Cabot claimed everything he saw and the lands beyond them for England. But England failed to follow up on Cabot's voyage for another sixty years.

The more Europeans explored, the more apparent it became that a vast landmass blocked the route to Asia. In 1500, a Portuguese voyage headed for India accidentally stumbled on Brazil (much of which lay, unexpectedly, east of the line established in the Treaty of Tordesillas). Other voyages soon revealed a continuous coastline from the Caribbean to Brazil. In 1507, this landmass got its name when a publisher brought out a collection of voyagers' tales. One of the chroniclers was an Italian named Amerigo Vespucci. With a shrewd marketing touch, the publisher devised a catchy name for the new continent: America.

Getting past America and reaching Asia remained the early explorers' primary aim. In 1513, the Spaniard Vasco Núñez de Balboa came upon the Pacific Ocean when he crossed the narrow isthmus of Panama. Then in 1519 the Portuguese Ferdinand Magellan, sailing for Spain, began a voyage around the world by way of the stormy straits (later named for him) at South America's southern tip. In an incredible feat of endurance, he crossed the Pacific to the Philippines, only to die fighting with local natives. One of his five ships and fifteen emaciated sailors finally returned to Spain in 1522, the first people to have sailed around the world.

Spain's Conquistadors, 1492–1536

Columbus was America's first slave trader and the first Spanish conqueror, or conquistador. At his struggling colony on Hispaniola, he and the colonists who flocked there started the first American gold rush. Although fighting among themselves, they forced Native people to mine gold and supply the Spanish with food and other needs. After the crown took direct control of Hispaniola, Spain extended the search for gold to nearby islands, establishing new colonies at Puerto Rico (1508), Jamaica (1510), and Cuba (1511).

Tainos and other Native Americans in the Caribbean colonies died off in shockingly large numbers from smallpox, measles, and other imported diseases. To replace the perishing Indians, the colonists began importing enslaved Africans to perform labor. Spanish

Spanish Map of the Antilles, 1519
This map offers a rare glimpse of Spain's early colonies in the West Indies. It depicts African laborers, forcibly imported to replace Native Americans lost to disease and harsh treatment.

Sugar Production in the Americas

Beginning with Christopher Columbus's first expedition, organisms ranging from bacteria to human beings crossed the Atlantic in both directions. This Columbian exchange had wide-ranging ecological, economic, political, and cultural consequences for the lands and peoples of the Americas, Africa, and Europe. One significant set of consequences arose from the transfer of Mediterranean sugar production to the Americas. Out of this transfer came the single-crop plantation system, based on enslaved African labor, and a new consumer product that revolutionized diets and, quite literally, taste in Europe and its colonies.

Domesticated in New Guinea before 8000 B.C., sugar cane was one of the earliest wild plants harvested by human beings. By 350 B.C., sugar was an ingredient in several dishes favored by elites in India, from where it spread to the Mediterranean world. It became a significant commodity in the Mediterranean in the eight century A.D. when expanding Arabs carried it as far west as Spain and Morocco. The Mediterranean would remain the center of sugar production for Europe over the next seven centuries.

The basic process of making sugar from the sugar cane plant changed little over time. (Sugar made from sugar beets did not become widespread until the nineteenth century.) The earliest producers discovered that one of the six species of cane, *Saccharum officinarum*, produced the most sugar in the shortest span of time. The optimal time for harvesting was when the cane had grown twelve to fifteen feet in height, with stalks about two inches thick. At this point, it was necessary to extract the juice from the plant and then the sucrose (a carbohydrate) from the juice as quickly as possible or risk spoilage. Sugar makers crushed the cane fibers in order to extract the liquid, which they then heated so that it evaporated, leaving the sucrose—or sugar—in the form of crystals or molasses, depending on its temperature.

Sugar production was central to the emerging Atlantic world during the fifteenth century, after Spanish and Portuguese planters established large sugar plantations in the Madeira, Canary, and Cape Verde islands off Africa's Atlantic coast. Initially, the islands' labor force included some free Europeans, but enslaved Africans soon predominated. The islands were the birthplace of the European colonial plantation system. Planters focused entirely on the production of a single export crop and sought to maximize profits by minimizing labor costs. Although some planters used servants, the largest-scale, most profitable plantations imported slaves and

Sugar Making in the West Indies
This drawing, published in 1665, shows enslaved Africans feeding sugar cane into a three-roller mill, driven by cattle, that crushes the cane into juice. Other slaves then boil the juice.

Consuming Sugar in North America
The plantation system's low production costs made sugar affordable for many Europeans and colonists. In this painting, made in 1730, Susanna Truax, a New York colonist, adds sugar to her tea.

worked them as hard as possible until they died. Utilizing such methods, the island planters soon outstripped the production of older sugar makers in the Mediterranean. By 1500 the Spanish and Portuguese had successfully tapped new markets across Europe, especially among the wealthy classes.

On his second voyage in 1493, Columbus took a cargo of sugar from the Canaries to Hispaniola. Early efforts by Spanish colonists to produce sugar failed because they lacked efficient milling technology, because the Taino Indians were dying so quickly from epidemic diseases, and because most colonists concentrated on mining gold. But as miners quickly exhausted Hispaniola's limited gold, the enslaved Africans brought to work in the mines became available for sugar production. In 1515 a planter named Gonzalo de Vellosa hired some experienced sugar masters from the Canaries who urged him to import a more efficient type of mill. The mill featured two vertical rollers that could be powered by either animals or water, through which laborers passed the cane in order to crush it. With generous subsidies from the Spanish crown, the combination of vertical-roller mills and slave labor led to a rapid proliferation of sugar plantations in Spain's island colonies, with some using as many as five hundred slaves. But when Spain discovered gold and silver in Mexico and the Andes, its interest in sugar declined almost as rapidly as it had arisen.

Originally discovered by accident (see above), Portugal's colony of Brazil emerged as the major source of sugar in the sixteenth century. Here, too, planters established the system of large plantations and enslaved Africans. By 1526, Brazil was exporting shiploads of sugar annually, and before the end of the century it supplied most of the sugar consumed in Europe. Shortly after 1600 Brazilian planters either invented or imported a three-roller mill that increased production still further and became the Caribbean standard for several more centuries. Portugal's sugar monopoly proved short-lived. Between 1588 and 1591, English privateers captured and diverted thirty-four sugar-laden vessels during their nation's war with Spain and Portugal. In 1630 the Netherlands seized Brazil's prime sugar-producing region and increased annual production to a century-high 30,000 tons. Ten years later some Dutch sugar and slave traders, seeking to expand their activity, shared the technology of sugar production with English planters in Barbados, who were looking for a new crop following disappointing profits from tobacco and cotton. The combination of sugar and slaves took hold so quickly that, within three years, Barbados's annual output rose to 150 tons.

Sugar went on to become the economic heart of the Atlantic economy (see Chapter 3). Its price dropped so low that even many poor Europeans could afford it. As a result, sugar became central to European diets as they were revolutionized by the Columbian exchange. Like tobacco, coffee, and several other products of the exchange, sugar and such sugar products as rum, produced from molasses, proved habit-forming, making sugar even more attractive to profit-seeking planters and merchants.

More than any other single commodity, sugar sustained the early slave trade in the Americas, facilitating slavery's spread to tobacco, rice, indigo, and other plantation crops as well as to domestic service and other forms of labor. Competition between British and French sugar producers in the West Indies later fueled their nations' imperial rivalry (see Chapter 4) and eventually led New England's merchants to resist British imperial controls—a resistance that helped prepare the way for the American Revolution (see Chapter 5).

Questions for Analysis

- What role did Spain's and Portugal's island colonies play in revolutionizing sugar production?

- How did developments in mill technology interact with other factors to make sugar the most profitable crop in the Americas?

missionaries who came to Hispaniola to convert Native Americans had sent back grim reports of Spanish exploitation of Indians. But while the missionaries deemed Native Americans potential Christians, they joined most other colonizers in condemning Africans as less than fully human and thereby beyond hope of redemption. Blacks could therefore be exploited without limit. In Cuba, Puerto Rico, and other islands, they were forced to perform backbreaking work on Spanish sugar plantations (see Technology and Culture: Sugar Production in the Americas).

Meanwhile, Spanish colonists fanned out even farther in search of Indian slaves and gold. In 1519, a restless nobleman, Hernán Cortés (1485–1547), led six hundred troops to the Mexican coast. Destroying his boats, he enlisted the support of enemies and discontented subjects of the Aztecs (see Chapter 1) in a quest to conquer that empire. Besides military support, Cortés gained the services of Malintzin (or Malinche), later known as Doña Marina, an Aztec woman brought up among the Maya. Malintzin served as Cortés's interpreter, diplomatic broker, and mistress.

Upon reaching the Aztec capital of Tenochtitlán, the Spanish were stunned by its size and wealth. "We were amazed and said that it was like the enchantments they tell of [in stories], and some of our soldiers even asked whether the things that we saw were not a dream," recalled one soldier. Certainly, the golden gifts that the Aztec emperor, Moctezuma II (ruled 1502–1520), initially offered the invaders were no dream. "They picked up the gold and fingered it like monkeys," one Aztec recalled. "Their bodies swelled with greed, and their hunger was ravenous. They hungered like pigs for that gold."

The Spanish ignored Moctezuma's offer, raiding his palace and treasury, and melting down all the gold they could find. Despite their emperor's imprisonment, the Aztecs regrouped and drove the invaders from the city, killing three hundred Spanish and four thousand of their Indian allies before Spanish reinforcements arrived from Cuba. The Aztecs' defeat was ensured by a smallpox epidemic the Spanish brought with them, the same one that was killing large numbers of Indians on Hispaniola and the other islands. Lacking any previous contact with the disease, the Aztecs' and other Indians' immune systems were ill equipped to resist it. Just when the Aztecs took back Tenochtitlán, the epidemic struck. When the Spanish finally recaptured the city, wrote one Spanish chronicler, "the streets were so filled with dead and sick people that our men walked over nothing but bodies." In striking down other Indians, friends as well as foes, the epidemic enabled the Spanish to consolidate their control over

Cortés and Malintzin (Doña Marina)
The Spanish conqueror and his most important Indian collaborator meet with other Native allies on their march toward the Aztec capital of Tenochtitlán.

much of central Mexico. By 1521, Cortés had overthrown the Aztecs and began to build a Spanish capital, Mexico City, on the ruins of Tenochtitlán.

Over the remainder of the sixteenth century, other conquistadors and officials established a great Spanish empire stretching from New Spain (Mexico) southward to Chile (see Map 2.4). The most important of these later conquests was that of the Inca empire (see Chapter 1) between 1532 and 1536 by a second reckless conquistador, Francisco Pizarro (c. 1478–1541). As with the Aztecs, smallpox and native unfamiliarity with European ways and weapons enabled a small army to overpower a mighty emperor and his realm. The human cost of the Spanish conquest was enormous.

Broken spears lie in the roads;
We have torn our hair in our grief.
The houses are roofless now . . .
And the walls are splattered with gore . . .
We have pounded our hands in despair
Against the adobe walls.

When Cortés landed in 1519, central Mexico's population had been between 13 and 25 million. By 1600, it had shrunk to about seven hundred thousand. Peru and other

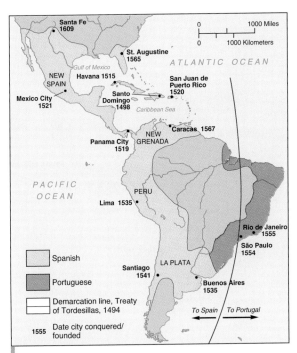

Map 2.4 The Spanish and Portuguese Empires, 1610
By 1610, Spain dominated Latin America, including
Portugal's possessions. Having devoted its energies to
exploiting Mexico and the Caribbean, Spain had not yet
expanded into what is now the United States, aside from
establishing outposts in Florida and New Mexico.

regions experienced similar devastation. America had witnessed the greatest demographic disaster in world history.

The Columbian Exchange

The emerging Atlantic world linked not only peoples but also animals, plants, and germs from Europe, Africa, and the Americas in a **Columbian exchange**. After 1492, vast numbers of Native Americans died because they lacked antibodies that could resist infectious diseases brought by Europeans and Africans—especially deadly, highly communicable smallpox. From the first years of contact, epidemics scourged defenseless Indian communities. A Spanish observer estimated that the indigenous population of the West Indies declined from about 1 million in 1492 to just five hundred a half century later. Whole villages perished at once, with no one left to bury the dead. Such devastation directly facilitated European colonization everywhere in the Americas, whether accompanied by a military effort or not.

The biological encounter of the Eastern and Western Hemispheres affected the everyday lives of peoples throughout the Atlantic world. Besides diseases,

sixteenth-century Europeans introduced horses, cattle, sheep, swine, chickens, wheat and other grains, coffee, sugar, numerous fruits and garden vegetables, and many species of weeds, insects, and rodents to America. In the next century, enslaved Africans carried rice and yams with them across the Atlantic. The list of American gifts to Europe and Africa was equally impressive: corn, many varieties of beans, white and sweet potatoes, tomatoes, squash, pumpkins, peanuts, vanilla, cacao (for making chocolate and cocoa), avocados, pineapples, chilis, tobacco, and turkeys. Often, several centuries passed before new plants became widely accepted. For example, many Europeans initially suspected that potatoes were aphrodisiacs and that tomatoes were poisonous.

European weeds and domestic animals drastically altered many American environments. Especially in temperate zones, livestock devoured indigenous plants, enabling hardier European weeds to take over. As a result, wild animals that had fed on the plants stayed away, depriving Indians of a critical source of food. Free-roaming livestock, especially hogs, also invaded Native Americans' cornfields. In this way, colonists' ways of life impinged directly on those of Native peoples. Settlers' crops, intensively cultivated on lands never replenished by lying fallow, often exhausted American soil. But the worldwide exchange of food products also enriched human diets and later made enormous population growth possible.

Another dimension of the Atlantic world was the mixing of peoples. During the sixteenth century, about three hundred thousand Spaniards immigrated, 90 percent of them male. Particularly in towns, a racially blended people emerged as these men married Indian women, giving rise to the large mestizo (mixed Spanish-Indian) population of Mexico and other Latin American countries. Lesser numbers of *métis*, as the French termed people of both Indian and European descent, would appear in the French and English colonies of North America. Throughout the Americas, particularly in plantation colonies, European men fathered mulatto children with enslaved African women, and African-Indian unions occurred in most regions. Colonial societies differed significantly in their official attitudes toward the different kinds of interracial unions and in their classifications of the children who resulted.

The Americas supplied seemingly limitless wealth for Spain. More important sources of wealth than Aztec and Inca gold and West Indian sugar plantations were the immense quantities of silver that crossed the Atlantic after rich mines in Mexico and Peru began producing in the 1540s. But Spanish kings squandered this wealth. Bent on dominating Europe, they needed ever more

American silver to finance a long series of wars there. Several times they went bankrupt, and in the 1560s their efforts to squeeze more taxes from their subjects helped provoke the revolt of Spain's rich Netherlands provinces (see below). In the end, American wealth proved to be a mixed blessing for Spain.

Footholds in North America, 1512–1625

Most European immigrants in the sixteenth century flocked to Mexico, the Caribbean, and points farther south. But a minority extended the Atlantic world to North America through exploratory voyages, fishing expeditions, trade with Native Americans, and piracy and smuggling. Except for a tiny Spanish base at St. Augustine, Florida, the earliest attempts to plant colonies failed, generally because they were predicated on unrealistic expectations of fabulous wealth and natives who would be easily conquered.

After 1600 the ravaging of Indian populations by disease and the rise of English, French, and Dutch power made colonization possible. By 1614, Spain, England, France, and the Netherlands had made often overlapping territorial claims and established North American footholds (see Maps 2.4 and 2.5). Within another decade, each colony developed a distinct economic orientation and its own approach to Native Americans.

Spain's Northern Frontier

The Spanish had built their American empire by subduing the Aztec, Inca, and other Indian states. The dream of more such finds drew would-be conquistadors northward to what would later be called Florida and New Mexico. "As it was his object to find another treasure like that . . . of Peru," a witness wrote of one such man, Hernando de Soto, he "would not be content with good lands nor pearls."

The earliest of these invaders was Juan Ponce de León, who had founded Puerto Rico. In 1513, he explored the coast of a peninsula he named "La Florida." Returning to Florida in 1521 to found a colony, Ponce de León's quest ended in death in a skirmish with Calusa Indians.

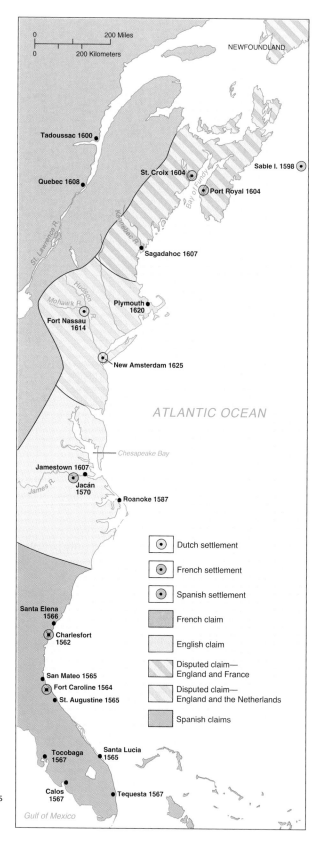

Map 2.5 European Imperial Claims and Settlements in Eastern North America, 1565–1625
By 1625, four European nations contended for territory on North America's Atlantic coast. Except for St. Augustine, Florida, all settlements established before 1607 had been abandoned by 1625.

The most astonishing early expedition began in Florida in 1527. After provoking several attacks by Apalachee Indians, the three hundred explorers were separated into several parties. All were thought to have perished until eight years later, when four survivors, led by Alvar Nuñez Cabeza de Vaca and including an African slave, Esteban, arrived in northern Mexico. Cabeza de Vaca's account of their long journey, living in dozens of Native American communities, is the most compelling European literary work on North America before permanent colonization.

Cabeza de Vaca provided direct inspiration for two more formidable attempts at Spanish conquest. De Soto and his party in 1539–1543 blundered from Tampa Bay to the Appalachians to the southern Plains, scouring the land for gold and alienating Native people wherever they went. "Think, then," one Indian chief appealed to him vainly,

what must be the effect on me and mine, of the sight of you and your people, whom we have at no time seen, astride the fierce brutes, your horses, entering with such speed and fury into my country, that we had no tidings of your coming—things so absolutely new, as to strike awe and terror into our hearts.

In 1540, a coalition of Native Americans gathered at the Mississippian city of Mábila to confront the invaders. Although victorious militarily, the expedition's own losses doomed the Spanish effort. Most of their horses died from arrow wounds while their livestock (their principal source of food aside from the corn they seized) scattered. Thereafter, the expedition floundered.

Although de Soto died without finding gold or extending Spanish rule, his and other expeditions spread epidemics that destroyed most of the remaining Mississippian societies (see Chapter 1). By the time Europeans returned to the southeastern interior late in the seventeenth century, only the Natchez on the lower Mississippi River still inhabited their sumptuous temple-mound center and remained under the rule of a Great Sun monarch. Depopulated groups like the Cherokees and Creeks had adopted the less-centralized village life of other eastern Indians.

Meanwhile Cabeza de Vaca had reported hearing of golden cities in the Southwest to Spanish officials in Mexico.

In 1540–1542 Francisco Vásquez de Coronado led a massive expedition bent on finding and conquering these cities. Coronado plundered several pueblos on the Rio Grande and wandered from the Grand Canyon to present-day Kansas before returning to Mexico, finding no gold but embittering many Native Americans toward the Spanish. Other expeditions along the California coast and up the Colorado River likewise proved fruitless.

For several decades after these failed ventures, Spain's principal interest north of Mexico and the Caribbean lay in establishing strategic bases to keep out French and English intruders. In 1565, Spain established the first lasting European post in North America, a fortress at **St. Augustine, Florida**. Despite plans to strengthen Florida and to build a road with presidios (military forts) at key locations from there to Mexico, St. Augustine remained a lone military stronghold. It also served as a base for a chain of Catholic missions on the Florida peninsula and Atlantic coast as far northward as Chesapeake Bay. Rejecting missionary efforts to reorder their lives, the Guale, Powhatan, and other Indians rebelled and forced the closing of all the missions before 1600. Franciscan missionaries renewed their efforts in Florida in the early seventeenth century and secured the nominal allegiance of about sixteen thousand Guale and Timucua Indians. But epidemics in the 1610s killed about half the converts.

Navajo View of Spanish Colonizers
This pictograph (a painting or drawing on rock) was sketched in the early colonial period in Cañón del Muerto, Arizona.

Meanwhile, in the 1580s, Spanish missionaries had returned to the Southwest, preaching Christianity and scouting the area's potential wealth. Encouraged by their reports, New Spain's viceroy in 1598 commissioned Juan de Oñate to lead five hundred Spaniards, mestizos, Mexican Indians, and African slaves into the upper Rio Grande Valley. They seized a pueblo of the Tewa Indians, renamed it San Juan, and proclaimed the royal colony of **New Mexico**.

The Spanish encountered swift resistance at the mesa-top pueblo of Ácoma in December 1598. When the Ácoma Indians refused Spanish demands for corn and other provisions, fifteen Spanish soldiers ascended the mesa to obtain the goods by force. But the natives resisted and killed most of the soldiers. Determined to make an example of Ácoma, Oñate ordered massive retaliation. In January, Spanish troops captured the pueblo, killing eight hundred inhabitants in the process. Oñate forced surviving men to have one foot cut off and, along with the women and children, to be servants of the soldiers and missionaries. Two prominent leaders also had their right hands amputated.

Despite having crushed Ácoma and imposed *encomiendas*—grants awarding Indian labor to wealthy colonists—on other Pueblo Indians, New Mexico barely survived. The Spanish government replaced Oñate in 1606 because of mismanagement and excessive brutality toward Native Americans, and seriously considered withdrawing from the Southwest altogether. Franciscan missionaries, aiming to save Pueblo Indian souls, persuaded the authorities to keep New Mexico alive. By 1630 Franciscans had been dispatched to more than fifty pueblos. Prompted by deadly epidemics and believing that Catholic rituals could be reconciled with traditional practices, a few thousand Indians accepted baptism. But resistance was common because, as the leading Franciscan summarized it, "the main and general answer given [by the Pueblos] for not becoming Christians is that when they do, . . . they are at once compelled to pay tribute and render personal service." New Mexico began, then, amidst uneasy tensions between colonists and natives.

France: Colonizing Canada

France entered the imperial competition in 1524 when King Francis I (ruled 1515–1547) dispatched an Italian navigator, Giovanni da Verrazano, to find a more direct "northwest passage" to the Pacific. Verrazano explored the North American coast from the Carolinas to Newfoundland. His several encounters with Native Americans ranged from violent to friendly. In 1534 and 1535–1536,

French explorer Jacques Cartier probed the coasts of Newfoundland, Quebec, and Nova Scotia and sailed up the St. Lawrence River as far as present-day Montreal. Although encountering large numbers of Native Americans (some of whom called the land "kanata," or Canada), Cartier found neither gold nor a northwest passage.

France made its first colonizing attempt in 1541 when Cartier returned to the St. Lawrence Valley with ten ships carrying four hundred soldiers, three hundred sailors, and a few women. Cartier had earned Native Americans' distrust during his previous expeditions, and his construction of a fortified settlement on Stadacona Indian land (near modern Quebec City) removed all possibility of friendly relations. Over the next two years, the French suffered heavy losses from Stadacona attacks and harsh winters before abandoning the colony.

The failed French expedition seemed to verify one Spaniard's opinion that "this whole coast as far [south] as Florida is utterly unproductive." The next French effort at colonization began in 1562 when French Huguenots (Calvinists) seeking religious freedom attempted to settle in Florida. In 1564, the Huguenots founded a settlement near present-day Jacksonville. Sensing a Protestant threat to their control of the Caribbean, Spanish forces destroyed the settlement a year later, executing all 132 male defenders. These failures, along with a civil war in France itself between Catholics and Huguenots, temporarily hindered France's colonizing efforts.

Meanwhile, French and other European fishermen were working the plenteous Grand Banks fisheries off the coast of Newfoundland. Going ashore to dry their fish, some sailors abused local Beothuk Indians, but others bartered with them for skins of beaver. By the late sixteenth century, European demand for beaver hats was skyrocketing, and a French-dominated fur trade blossomed. Before the end of the century, French traders were returning annually to sites from Newfoundland to New England and along the lower St. Lawrence.

Unlike explorers such as de Soto and colonizers such as those at Roanoke (see below), most fur traders recognized the importance of reciprocity in dealing with Native Americans. Consequently, they were generally more successful. In exchange for pelts, they traded axes, knives, copper kettles, cloth, and glass beads. Usually dismissed by Europeans as "trinkets," glass beads were valued by northeastern Indians for possessing spiritual power comparable to that of quartz, mica, and other sacred substances that they had long obtained via trade networks (see Chapter 1). By the next century, specialized factories in Europe would be producing both cloth and glass for the "Indian trade."

The Beaver as Worker and as Prey
This French engraving illustrates beavers' environmental impact and Indian methods of hunting them for commercial purposes.

Seeing the lucrative Canadian trade as a source of revenue, the French government dispatched the explorer Samuel de Champlain to establish the colony of **New France** at Quebec in 1608. The French concluded that a colony was the surest means of deterring English, Dutch, and independent French competitors. Having previously explored much of the Northeast and headed a small French settlement at Acadia (later Nova Scotia), Champlain was familiar with Indian politics and diplomacy in the region. Building on this understanding, he shrewdly allied with the Montagnais and Algonquins of the St. Lawrence and the Hurons of the lower Great Lakes. He agreed to help these allies defeat their enemies, the Mohawks of the Iroquois Confederacy, who sought direct access to European traders on the St. Lawrence. The Indians were equally shrewd in recognizing the advantage of having armed French allies when facing the dreaded Mohawks.

In July 1609 Champlain and two other Frenchmen accompanied sixty Montagnais and Huron warriors to Lake Champlain (which the explorer named for himself). Soon they encountered two hundred Mohawks at Point Ticonderoga near the lake's southern tip. After a night of mutual taunting, the two parties met on shore the following morning. As the main French-Indian column neared its opponents, Champlain stepped ahead and confronted the Mohawks' three spectacularly attired war leaders.

When I saw them make a move to draw their bows upon us, I took aim with my arquebus [a kind of gun] and shot *straight at one of the three chiefs, and with this same shot two fell to the ground, and one of their companions was wounded and died a little later. . . . As I was reloading my arquebus, one of my [French] companions fired a shot from within the woods, which astonished them again so much that, seeing their chiefs dead, they lost courage and took to flight.*

The French and their allies pursued the fleeing Mohawks, killing about fifty and capturing a dozen prisoners. A few pro-French Indians suffered minor arrow wounds.

The battle at Lake Champlain marked the end of an era in Indian-European relations in the Northeast. Except in a few isolated places, casual encounters between small parties gave way to trade, diplomacy, and warfare coordinated by Indian and European governments. Through their alliance with the powerful Hurons and other Native American groups, the French gained access to the thick beaver pelts of the Canadian interior while providing their Indian allies with European goods and armed protection from Iroquois attacks. These economic and diplomatic arrangements, and Iroquois reactions (see below), defined the course of New France's history for the rest of the seventeenth century.

England and the Atlantic World, 1558–1603

When Elizabeth I became queen in 1558, Spain and France were grappling for supremacy in Europe, and England was a minor power. But largely Protestant England worried about Spain's suppression of Calvinists in the Netherlands and about the pope's call for Elizabeth's overthrow. Elizabeth adopted a militantly anti-Spanish foreign policy, with Anglicans and Puritans alike hailing England as an "elect nation" whose mission was to elevate "true" Christianity and to overthrow Catholicism, represented by Spain. Secretly, she stepped up her aid to Dutch Calvinists and encouraged English privateers (armed private ships), commanded by "sea dogs" like John Hawkins and Francis Drake, to attack Spanish ships.

The Anglo-Spanish rivalry in the Atlantic extended to Ireland after 1565, when Spain and the pope began directly aiding Irish Catholics' longtime resistance to English rule. In a war that ground on to the early seventeenth century, the English drove the Irish clans off their lands, especially in northern Ireland, or Ulster, and established their own settlements ("plantations") of English and Scottish Protestants. The English practiced "scorched earth" warfare to break the rebellious population's spirit, inflicting starvation and mass slaughter by destroying villages in the winter.

Elizabeth's generals justified these atrocities by claiming that the Irish were "savages" and that Irish customs, religion, and methods of fighting absolved the English from guilt in waging exceptionally cruel warfare. Ireland thus furnished precedents for later English tactics and rationales for crushing Native Americans.

England had two objectives in the Western Hemisphere in the 1570s. The first was to find the northwest passage to Asia and discover gold on the way; the second, in Drake's words, was to "singe the king of Spain's beard" by raiding Spanish fleets and ports. The search for the northwest passage led only to such embarrassments as explorer Martin Frobisher's voyages to the Canadian Arctic. Frobisher returned with several thousand tons of an ore that looked like gold but proved worthless. However, privateering raids proved spectacularly successful and profitable for their financial backers, including merchants, gentry, government leaders, and Elizabeth herself. The most breathtaking enterprise was Drake's voyage around the world (1577–1580) in quest of sites for colonies. During this voyage, he sailed up the California coast and entered Drake's Bay, north of San Francisco, where he traded with Miwok Indians.

Now deadly rivals, Spain and England sought to outmaneuver one another in North America. In 1572, the Spanish tried to fortify a Jesuit mission on Chesapeake Bay. They failed, largely because Powhatan Indians resisted. In 1583, an English attempt to colonize Newfoundland (where Europeans from several nations fished annually) also failed. Sir Walter Raleigh obtained a royal patent (charter) in 1584 to start an English colony farther south, closer to the Spanish—a region the English soon named Virginia in honor of their virgin queen. Raleigh sent Arthur Barlowe to explore the region, and Barlowe returned singing the praises of Roanoke Island, its peaceable natives, and its ideal location as a base for anti-Spanish privateers. Raleigh then persuaded Elizabeth to dispatch an expedition to found Roanoke colony.

At first all went well, but by winter, the English had outlived the Roanoke Indians' welcome. Fearing that the natives were about to attack, English soldiers killed Wingina, the Roanoke leader, in June 1586. When Drake visited soon after on his way back to England, many colonists joined him.

Roanoke Indian Town of Secota
Based on a watercolor by John White, a member of the Roanoke expedition, this engraving celebrates the abundant crops and rich ceremonial life of the Roanoke Indians. Other English leaders took a dimmer view of the Native Americans.

Thereafter, the Anglo-Spanish conflict repeatedly prevented English ships from returning to Roanoke to supply those who remained. When a party finally arrived in 1590, it found only rusty armor, moldy books, and the word *CROATOAN* cut into a post. Although the stranded colonists were presumably living among the Croatoan Indians of Cape Hatteras, the exact fate of the "lost colony" remains a mystery to this day.

In 1588, while Roanoke struggled, England won a spectacular naval victory over the Armada, a huge invasion fleet sent into the English Channel by Spain's Philip II. This famous victory preserved England's independence and confirmed its status as a major power in the Atlantic.

Failure and Success in Virginia, 1603–1625

Anglo-Spanish relations took a new turn after 1603, when Elizabeth died and James I succeeded her. The cautious, peace-loving James signed a truce with Spain in 1604. Alarmed by Dutch naval victories (see below), the Spanish now considered England the lesser danger. Consequently, Spain's new king, Philip III (ruled 1598–1621), conceded what his predecessors had always refused: a free hand to another power in part of the Americas. Spain renounced its claims to Virginia, allowing England to colonize unmolested.

The question of how to finance English colonies remained. Neither the crown nor Parliament would agree to spend money on colonies, and Roanoke's failure had proved that private fortunes were inadequate to finance successful settlements. Political and financial leaders determined that joint-stock companies could raise enough funds for American settlement. Such stock offerings produced large sums with limited risk for each investor.

In 1606, James I granted a charter authorizing overlapping grants of land to two separate joint-stock companies. The Virginia Company of Plymouth received a grant extending south from modern Maine to the Potomac River, while the Virginia Company of London's lands ran north from Cape Fear, North Carolina, to the Hudson River. Both companies dispatched colonists in 1607.

The Virginia Company of Plymouth sent 120 men to Sagadahoc, on the Maine coast. After bickering among themselves, alienating nearby Abenaki Indians, and enduring a hard New England winter, the colonists returned to England and the company was disbanded.

The Virginia Company of London barely avoided a similar failure. Its first expedition included many gentlemen who, considering themselves above manual work, expected Native Americans to feed them and riches to fall into their laps. Choosing a site on the James River, they called it Jamestown and formally named their colony **Virginia**. Discipline quickly fell apart, and, as at Roanoke, the colonists neglected to plant crops. The local Powhatan Indians had sold them some corn but, with their own supplies running low, declined to offer more. By December, the English were running out of food. As with Roanoke and numerous Spanish ventures, Virginia's military leader, Captain John Smith, led some soldiers in an attempt to seize corn from the Powhatans. After capturing Smith, the Powhatan *weroance* (chief), also named Powhatan, released the captain but did share some of his people's remaining supplies with the English. (Many years later, Smith would claim that Powhatan's ten-year-old-daughter, Pocahontas, saved him at the last minute from execution. Because Smith claimed to have been rescued in similar fashion by females on two other occasions during his military adventures, the story's accuracy is doubtful.)

Powhatan's gesture was intended to remind the English that his people were the stronger force and that reciprocity was preferable to force in their dealings with one another. In releasing Smith and giving him more corn, he expected the English to support him in return. In particular he hoped the newcomers would ally with the Powhatans against local Indian enemies.

Powhatan recognized the early Virginians' weaknesses. When relief ships arrived in January 1608 with reinforcements, only 38 survivors remained out of 105 immigrants. Virginia also lacked effective leadership. The council's first president hoarded supplies, and its second was lazy and indecisive. By September 1608, three councilors had died, and three others had returned to England, leaving Smith in complete charge of the colony.

Twenty-eight years old and of yeoman origin, Smith had experience fighting Spaniards and Turks that prepared him for assuming control in Virginia. Organizing all but the sick in work gangs, he ensured sufficient food and housing for winter. Applying lessons learned in his soldiering days, he laid down rules for maintaining sanitation and hygiene to limit disease. Above all, he brought order through military discipline. During the next winter (1608–1609), Virginia lost just a dozen men out of two hundred.

Smith prevented Virginia from disintegrating as Sagadahoc had. But when he returned to England in 1609 after being wounded in a gunpowder explosion, discipline again crumbled. Expecting the Indians to provide them with corn, the colonists had not laid away sufficient food for the winter. A survivor wrote,

So lamentable was our scarcity, that we were constrained to eat dogs, cats, rats, snakes, toadstools, horsehides, and what not; one man out of the misery endured, killing his wife powdered her up [with flour] to eat her, for which he was burned. Many besides fed on the corpses of dead men.

Of the 500 residents at Jamestown in September 1609, about 400 died by May 1610. But an influx of new recruits, coupled with renewed military rule, enabled Virginia to recover and to assert its supremacy to the Powhatans. When Powhatan refused to submit to the new governor's authority, the colony waged the First Anglo-Powhatan War (1610–1614). After the English captured Powhatan's daughter, Pocahontas, and she converted to Christianity, the war ended when the aging weroance agreed that she could marry a colonist named John Rolfe. The English population remained small— just 380 in 1616—and had yet to produce anything of value for Virginia Company stockholders.

Tobacco emerged as Virginia's salvation. Rolfe spent several years adapting a salable variety of Caribbean tobacco to conditions in Virginia. In 1616, he and Pocahontas traveled to England, where his tobacco was received enthusiastically. (While there, Pocahontas contracted a respiratory disease and died.) By 1619, tobacco commanded high prices, and Virginia exported large amounts to a newly emergent European market.

To attract labor and capital to its suddenly profitable venture, the Virginia Company awarded a fifty-acre "headright" for each person ("head") entering the colony, to whoever paid that person's passage. By paying the passage of prospective laborers, some enterprising planters accumulated sizable tracts of land. Thousands of young men and a few hundred women calculated that uncertainty in Virginia was preferable to continued unemployment and poverty in England. In return for their passage and such basic needs as food, shelter, and clothing, they agreed to work as **indentured servants** for fixed terms, usually four to seven years.

The Virginia Company abandoned military rule in 1619 and provided for an assembly to be elected by the "inhabitants" (apparently meaning only the planters). Although the assembly's actions were subject to the company's veto, it was the first representative legislature in North America.

By 1622 Virginia faced three serious problems. First, local officials systematically defrauded the shareholders by embezzling treasury funds, overcharging for supplies, and using company laborers to work their own tobacco fields. They profited, but the company sank deep into debt. Second, the colony's population suffered from an appallingly high death rate. Most of the 3,500 immigrants entering Virginia from 1618 to 1622 died within three years, primarily from malnutrition or from salt poisoning, typhus, or dysentery contracted from drinking polluted water from the James River. Finally, relations with Native Americans steadily worsened after Pocahontas and then Powhatan died. Leadership passed to Powhatan's younger brother, Opechancanough, who at first sought to accommodate the English. But relentless English expansion provoked Indian discontent and the rise of a powerful religious leader, Nemattenew, who urged the Powhatans to resist the English. After some settlers killed Nemattenew, the Indians launched a surprise attack in 1622 that killed 347 of the 1,240 colonists. With much of their livestock destroyed, spring planting prevented, and disease spreading through cramped fortresses, hundreds more colonists died in the ensuing months.

After the Virginia Company sent more men, Governor Francis Wyatt reorganized the settlers and took the offensive during the Second Anglo-Powhatan War (1622–1632). Using tactics developed during the Irish war, Wyatt inflicted widespread starvation by destroying food supplies, conducted winter campaigns to drive Indians from their homes when they would suffer most, and fought (in John Smith's words) as if he had "just cause to destroy them by all means possible." By 1625 the English had effectively won the war, and the Powhatans had lost their best chance of driving out the intruders.

The clash left the Virginia Company bankrupt. After receiving a report critical of the company's management, James I revoked its charter in 1624 and made Virginia a royal colony. Only about five hundred colonists now lived there, including a handful of Africans who had been brought in since 1619. With its combination of fabulous profits, unfree labor, and massive mortality, Virginia was truly a land of contradictions.

New England Begins, 1614–1625

The next English colony, after Virginia, that proved permanent arose in New England. In 1614, the ever-enterprising John Smith, exploring its coast, gave New England its name. "Who," he asked, "can but approve this most excellent place, both for health and fertility?" Smith hoped to establish a colony there, but in 1616–1618 a terrible epidemic spread by fishermen or traders devastated New England's coastal Native American communities by about 90 percent. Later visitors found the ground littered with the "bones and skulls" of the unburied dead and acres of overgrown cornfields.

Against this tragic backdrop, the Virginia Company of London gave a patent to some London merchants headed by Thomas Weston for a settlement. In 1620, Weston sent over twenty-four families (a total of 102 people) in a small, leaky ship called the *Mayflower*. The colonists promised to send lumber, furs, and fish back to Weston in England for seven years, after which they would own the tract.

The expedition's leaders, but only half its members, were Separatist Puritans (see above) who had withdrawn from the Church of England and fled to the Netherlands to practice their religion freely. Fearing that their children were assimilating into Dutch culture, they decided to emigrate to America.

In November 1620 the *Mayflower* landed at Plymouth Bay in present-day Massachusetts, north of Virginia's boundary. Knowing that they had no legal right to be there, the expedition's leaders insisted that all adult males in the group (including non-Puritans) sign the Mayflower Compact before they landed. By this document, they constituted themselves a "civil body politic," or government, and claimed the land for King James, establishing **Plymouth** colony.

Weakened by their journey and unprepared for winter, half the Pilgrims, as the colonists later came to be known, died within four months of landing. Those still alive in the spring of 1621 owed much to the aid of two English-speaking Native Americans. One was Squanto, a Wampanoag Indian who had been taken to Spain as a slave in 1614 but was freed and then traveled to England. Returning home with a colonizing expedition, he learned that most of the two thousand people of his village had perished in the recent epidemic. The other Indian, an Abenaki from Maine named Samoset, had experience trading with the English. To prevent the colonists from stealing the natives' food, Squanto showed them how to grow corn, using fish as fertilizer. Plymouth's first harvest was marked by a festival, "at which time . . . we exercised our arms, many of the Indians coming amongst us, . . . some 90 men, whom for three days we entertained and feasted." This festival became the basis for Thanksgiving, a holiday established in the nineteenth century.

Plymouth's relations with the Native Americans soon worsened. The alliance that Squanto and Samoset had arranged between Plymouth and the Wampanoags, headed by Massasoit, had united two weak parties. But news of the Powhatan attack in 1622 hastened the colony's militarization under Miles Standish, chosen as military commander over John Smith. Standish threatened Plymouth's "allies" with the colony's monopoly of firepower. For although Massasoit remained loyal, other Indians were offended by the colonists' conduct.

Plymouth soon became economically self-sufficient. After the colony turned from communal farming to individually owned plots, its more prosperous farmers produced corn surpluses, which they traded to nonfarming Abenaki Indians in Maine for furs. Within a decade, Plymouth's elite had bought out the colony's London backers and several hundred colonists had arrived.

Although a tiny colony, Plymouth was significant as an outpost for Puritans dissenting from the Church of England and for proving that a self-governing society consisting mostly of farm families could flourish in New England. In these respects, it proved to be the vanguard of a massive migration of Puritans to New England in the 1630s (see Chapter 3).

A "New Netherland" on the Hudson, 1609–1625

Among the most fervently Calvinist regions of Europe were the Dutch-speaking provinces of the Netherlands. The provinces had come under Spanish rule during the sixteenth century, but Spain's religious intolerance and high taxes drove the Dutch to revolt, beginning in 1566. Exhausting its resources trying to quell the revolt, Spain finally recognized Dutch independence in 1609. By then, the Netherlands was a wealthy commercial power. The Dutch built an empire stretching from Brazil to South Africa to Indonesia, and played a key role in colonizing North America.

Just as the French were routing the Mohawk Iroquois at Lake Champlain in 1609, Henry Hudson sailed up the river later named for him, traded with Native Americans, and claimed the land for the Netherlands. When Dutch traders returned the following year, some of their most eager customers were—not surprisingly—Mohawks. Having established lucrative ties with Indians on the lower Hudson River, Dutch traders in 1614 built Fort Nassau near what would become Albany, and established the colony of **New Netherland**. In 1626 local Munsee Indians allowed the Dutch to settle on an island at the mouth of the Hudson. The Dutch named the island Manhattan and the settlement, New Amsterdam.

The earliest New Netherlanders lived by the fur trade. Through the Mohawks, they relied on the Five Nations Iroquois, much as the French depended on the Hurons, as commercial clients and military allies. In the 1620s, to stimulate a flow of furs to New Netherland, Dutch traders obtained from coastal Indians large quantities of wampum—sacred shells like those used by Deganawidah and Hiawatha to convey solemn "words" of condolence in rituals (see Chapter 1)—for trade with the Iroquois. The Dutch-Iroquois and French-Huron alliances became embroiled in an ever-deepening contest to control the movement of goods between Europeans and Indians (discussed in Chapter 3).

Conclusion

The sixteenth century marked the emergence of an Atlantic world linking Europe, Africa, and the Americas. Kings and emperors in West Africa were already competing ferociously for the wealth brought by long-distance trade, including trade in slaves. Western Europe entered a new era in which nation-states drew on Renaissance knowledge, merchants' capital, and religious zeal to advance national power and overseas expansion.

Chronology, 1400–1625

c. 1400–1600	European Renaissance.
c. 1400–1500	Coastal West African kingdoms rise and expand.
c. 1440	Portuguese slave trade in West Africa begins.
c. 1450	Songhai succeeds Mali as major power in West African grassland.
1492	Christian "reconquest" of Spain. Columbus lands at Guanahaní.
1498	Vasco da Gama rounds the Cape of Good Hope and reaches India.
1517	Protestant Reformation begins in Germany.
1519–1521	Cortés leads Spanish conquest of Aztec empire.
1519–1522	Magellan's expedition circumnavigates the globe.
1532–1536	Pizarro leads Spanish conquest of Inca empire.
1534	Church of England breaks from Roman Catholic Church.
1541–1542	Cartier attempts to colonize eastern Canada.
1539–1543	De Soto attempts conquests in southeastern United States.
1540–1542	Coronado attempts conquests in southwestern United States.
c. 1550	Kongo declines in West Africa.
1558	Elizabeth I becomes queen of England.
1565	St. Augustine founded by Spanish.
1585–1590	English colony of Roanoke established, then disappears.
1588	England defeats the Spanish Armada.
1591	Moroccan forces defeat Songhai in West Africa.
1598	Oñate founds New Mexico.
1603	James I becomes king of England.
1607	English found colonies at Jamestown and Sagadahoc.
1608	Champlain founds New France.
1609	Henry Hudson explores the Hudson River.
1610–1614	First Anglo-Powhatan War.
1614	New Netherland founded.
1619	Virginia begins exporting tobacco. First Africans arrive in Virginia.
1620	Plymouth colony founded.
1622–1632	Second Anglo-Powhatan War.
1624	James I revokes Virginia Company's charter.

The Atlantic world brought few benefits to West Africans and Native Americans. Proclaiming that civilization and Christianity rendered them superior, Europeans denigrated Native Americans and Africans as savages whose land and labor Europeans could seize and exploit. Initial Portuguese incursions promised to expand West Africa's trade ties with Europe. But Europe's overwhelming demand for slave labor depleted the region's population and accelerated the reshaping of trade, politics, warfare, and societies. Africa's notorious underdevelopment, which persists in our own time, had begun.

After 1492, the Atlantic world spread to the Americas. Indigenous peoples in the Caribbean, Mexico, Peru, and elsewhere in Central and

Key Terms

Christopher Columbus	"new slavery"
Mali	Columbian exchange
Kongo	St. Augustine, Florida
Renaissance	New Mexico
joint-stock company	*encomiendas*
Protestant Reformation	New France
predestination	Virginia
Catholic or Counter-Reformation	indentured servants
	Plymouth
Church of England	New Netherland
Puritans	

South America were the first to be ravaged by European epidemic diseases, leaving them vulnerable to violent conquest and exploitation. The forced and unforced movements of people, as well as of animals, plants, and disease-causing germs constituted a Columbian exchange that transformed environments throughout the Atlantic world.

Native peoples north of Mexico and the Caribbean held would-be conquerors and colonizers at bay until after 1600. Thereafter they too suffered the effects of European-borne diseases. Native North Americans cooperated with Europeans who practiced reciprocity while resisting those who tried to dominate them. By 1625, Spain had advanced only as far north as seemed worthwhile to protect its prized Mexican and Caribbean conquests. Meanwhile, French, English, and Dutch colonists focused on less spectacular resources. New France and New Netherland existed primarily to obtain furs from Indians, while the English in Virginia and Plymouth cultivated fields recently belonging to Native Americans. All these colonies depended for their success on maintaining stable relations with at least some Native Americans. The transplantation of Europeans into North America was hardly a story of inevitable triumph.

For Further Reference

Robert J. Berkhofer, Jr., *The White Man's Indian: Images of the American Indian from Columbus to the Present* (1978). A penetrating analysis of the shaping of European and American attitudes, ideologies, and policies toward Native Americans.

Nicholas Canny, ed., *The Origins of Empire* (*The Oxford History of the British Empire*, vol. 1; 1998). Essays by leading authorities offer a comprehensive treatment of the origins and early development of English imperialism.

Alfred W. Crosby, Jr., *Ecological Imperialism: The Biological Expansion of Europe, 900–1900* (1986). Accessible discussion of the environmental and medical history of European overseas colonization.

Philip Curtin et al., eds., *African History: From Earliest Times to Independence*, 2nd ed. (1995). Excellent essay overviews by leading historians in the field.

James Horn, *A Land as God Made It: Jamestown and the Birth of America* (2005). An authoritative account of colonization in the Chesapeake through the collapse of the Virginia Company.

Olwen Hufton, *The Prospect Before Her: A History of Women in Western Europe*, vol. 1: *1500–1800* (1996). An outstanding interpretive synthesis.

D. W. Meinig, *The Shaping of America*, vol. 1: *Atlantic America, 1492–1800* (1986). A geographer's engrossing study of Europeans' encounters with North America and the rise of colonial societies.

Sidney W. Mintz, *Sweetness and Power: The Place of Sugar in Modern History* (1985). The role of sugar as crop, commodity, food, and cultural artifact.

David B. Quinn, *North America from Earliest Discoveries to First Settlements: The Norse Voyages to 1612* (1977). A thorough, learned account of European exploration, based on a wide range of scholarship.

John Thornton, *Africa and Africans in the Making of the Atlantic World, 1400–1800*, 2nd ed. (1998). Insightful perspectives on the slave trade and on the role of West Africans in American colonization.

Chapter 3

George Calvert, Lord Baltimore
King Charles I awarded Baltimore, a Catholic aristocrat, the first proprietary grant for an English colony. After he died, his son, Cecilius, also Lord Baltimore, founded Maryland.

The Emergence of Colonial Societies, 1625–1700

Mary Freake

Although little is known today of her life, we can be certain that Elizabeth Clarke Freake was rarely alone with nothing to do. Born into one prominent merchant family in 1642, in Dorchester, Massachusetts, she joined another when she married John Freake in 1661. After they had eight children, John died when some cargo on one of his ships exploded. Elizabeth then married yet another wealthy merchant, Edward Hutchinson, and bore five more children. By the time she died in 1713, she had several dozen grandchildren. There is little doubt that in her roles as wife, mother, grandmother, manager of a prominent household, church member, and leader of Boston's female community, Freake was never idle. In all these capacities she contributed to the remarkable demographic and economic growth of colonial New England and to the shaping of a distinct regional society and culture there.

The colonial society that Freake helped to build in New England was but one of several that emerged in seventeenth-century North America. By 1700, almost 250,000 people of European birth or parentage lived within the modern-day United States and Canada. They made up North America's first large wave of immigrant settlers. But colonial North America was the work of more than its settlers. Nearly 30,000 enslaved Africans also resided in North America in 1700, most of them in the Chesapeake colonies and South Carolina. Whereas European immigrants could at least hope to realize economic opportunity or religious freedom, nearly all Africans and their children remained the property of others for as long as they lived.

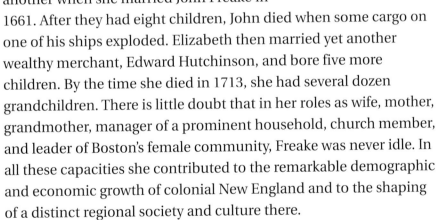

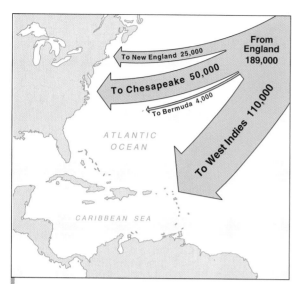

Map 3.1 English Migration, 1610–1660
During the first phase of English transatlantic migration, more than half of the colonists settled in the West Indies.

The movements of Europeans and Africans were possible only because of yet another demographic upheaval, the depopulation and uprooting of Native Americans. Having begun in the sixteenth century (see Chapter 2), the process expanded in the seventeenth, primarily as a result of epidemic diseases, but also because of warfare and other factors associated with Europeans' encroaching on Indian lands. Although many Native populations partly recovered, it is likely that about 1 million North American Indians died as a result of contact with Europeans before 1700. European colonists built their farms, plantations, towns, and cities not in wildernesses but on lands long inhabited and worked by Native Americans.

Patterns of Indian depopulation and of European and African immigration transformed North America during the seventeenth century. Although other parts of the Americas had been colonized for several decades or more, by 1625 Europeans had established just a few scattered outposts north of Mexico and the Caribbean. Thereafter, they expanded their territorial domains and by 1700 had begun colonies as far north as the St. Lawrence River and as far west as the Rio Grande.

The massive migration of people from England ensured that nation's domination of North America's eastern coast as well as the Caribbean (see Map 3.1). Before 1700, the English would force the Dutch out of mainland

North America and leave France and Spain with lands less attractive to colonists. Within England's mainland colonies, four distinct regions emerged: the Chesapeake, New England, Carolina, and the middle colonies. These regions varied in numerous ways, including their physical environments, patterns of population growth, economies, social structures, religious practices, modes of government, and ethnic and racial compositions. There were no "typical" colonists in the seventeenth century. Elizabeth Clarke Freake's life represented just one of the countless ways that women and men experienced colonial America.

Chesapeake Society

Building on the tobacco boom of the 1620s, the English colonies on the Chesapeake Bay—Virginia and its neighbor Maryland—were the first to prosper in North America. Despite differences between their political and religious institutions, Virginia and Maryland had similar economies, populations, and patterns of growth that gave them a distinct regional identity.

Chesapeake society was highly unequal and unstable. Life for most colonists was short, good health was rare, and the familiar comforts of family and community were missing. After a civil conflict, Bacon's Rebellion, the English seized yet more Native American land for growing tobacco and shifted from white indentured servitude to black slavery as the principal source of labor. On this foundation, white Virginians finally achieved stability,

Focus Questions

- Why did Chesapeake planters shift from using white indentured servants as laborers to black slaves?

- Why did colonial New Englanders abandon John Winthrop's vision of a "city upon a hill"?

- What factors facilitated the extension of slavery from the English Caribbean to Carolina?

- In what ways did the middle colonies differ from other English colonial regions?

- How did the French and Spanish colonies in mainland North America differ from those of England?

harmony, and at least minimal prosperity within their own ranks.

State and Church in Virginia

King James I had reorganized Virginia as a **royal colony**, to be administered by a crown-appointed governor, who would appoint and dismiss leading gentlemen in the colony to an advisory council. James did not reconvene Virginia's elected assembly. With civil war threatening, James's successor Charles I (ruled 1625–1649) in 1639 formally restored the assembly as a means of securing tobacco revenues and the support of Virginia's Anglican planters. The small number of elected representatives, or burgesses, initially met as a single body with the council to pass laws. During the 1650s, the legislature split into two chambers—the House of Burgesses and the Governor's Council, whose members held lifetime appointments.

Virginia adopted England's county-court system for local government. Justices of the peace served as judges but also set local tax rates, paid county officials, and oversaw the construction and maintenance of roads, bridges, and public buildings. Justices and sheriffs, who administered the counties during the courts' recesses, were chosen by the governor instead of by an electorate. Everywhere south of New England, unelected county courts became the basic unit of local government by 1710.

View of Jamestown, 1625
As Virginia's tobacco production boomed, the capital expanded beyond the fort that had originally confined it.

As in England, Virginia's established church was the Church of England. In each parish, six vestrymen managed church finances, determined who was deserving of poor relief, and prosecuted moral offenses such as fornication or drunkenness. Taxpayers, who were legally obliged to pay fixed rates to the Anglican Church, elected vestries until 1662, when the assembly made them self-perpetuating and independent of the voters.

Because the Anglican clergy could only be trained in England and could usually find pulpits there, few were attracted to Virginia. Consequently, Virginia experienced a chronic shortage of clergymen, and most ministers rotated among two or three parishes. But when a minister was conducting services in a parish, church attendance was required; violators were subject to fines payable in cash or labor on public works projects.

State and Church in Maryland

After 1632, the crown created new colonies by awarding portions of the Virginia Company's forfeited territory to wealthy, trusted English elites. One or more proprietors, as they were called, were responsible for peopling, governing, and defending each **proprietary colony**.

In 1632, Charles I awarded the first such grant to a Catholic nobleman, **Lord Baltimore**, for a large tract of land north of the Potomac River and east of Chesapeake Bay. The grant guaranteed Lord Baltimore freedom from royal taxation, the power to appoint all sheriffs and judges, and the privilege of creating a local nobility. The only checks on the proprietor's power were the crown's control of war and trade and the requirement that an elected assembly approve all laws.

Naming his colony Maryland, Lord Baltimore intended it as an overseas refuge for English Catholics, who constituted about 2 percent of England's population. Although many English Catholics were very wealthy and a few held political office, they could not worship in public and (like other dissenters) paid taxes to support the Anglican Church.

To avoid antagonizing English Protestants, Baltimore introduced the English institution of the manor—an estate on which a lord could maintain private law courts and employ a Catholic priest as his chaplain. Local Catholics could go to the manor to hear Mass and receive the sacraments privately. Baltimore adapted Virginia's headright system (see Chapter 2) by offering large land grants to English Catholic aristocrats on condition that they bring settlers at their own cost. Anyone transporting five adults (a requirement raised to twenty by 1640) received a two-thousand-acre manor. Baltimore hoped that this arrangement would allow Catholics to survive and prosper in Maryland while making it unnecessary to pass any special laws alarming to Protestants.

Maryland's colonization did not proceed as Baltimore envisioned. In 1634, the first two hundred immigrants landed. Maryland was the first colony spared a starving time, thanks to Baltimore's careful study of Virginia's early history. The new colony's success showed that English overseas expansion had come of age. Baltimore, however, stayed in England, governing as an absentee proprietor, and few Catholics went to Maryland. From the outset, Protestants formed the majority of the population. With land prices low, they purchased their own property, thereby avoiding becoming tenants on the manors. These conditions doomed Baltimore's dream of creating a manorial system of mostly Catholic lords collecting rents. By 1675, all of Maryland's sixty nonproprietary manors had evolved into plantations.

Religious tensions soon emerged. In 1642, Catholics and Protestants in the capital at St. Mary's argued over use of the city's chapel, which the two groups had shared until then. As antagonisms intensified, Baltimore drafted the **Act for Religious Toleration**, or Toleration Act, which the Protestant-dominated assembly passed in 1649. The act made Maryland the second colony (after Rhode Island) to affirm religious toleration. However, the act did not protect non-Christians, nor did it separate church and state, since it empowered the government to punish religious offenses such as blasphemy.

The Toleration Act also failed to secure religious peace. In 1654, the Protestant majority barred Catholics from voting, ousted Governor William Stone (a pro-tolerance Protestant), and repealed the Toleration Act. In 1655, Stone raised an army of both faiths to regain the government but was defeated at the Battle of the Severn River. The victors imprisoned Stone and hanged three Catholic leaders.

Lord Baltimore resumed control of Maryland in 1658, ironically by order of the Puritan authorities then ruling England. Even so, he and his descendants would encounter continued obstacles in governing Maryland because of Protestant resistance to Catholic rule.

Death, Gender, and Kinship

Tobacco sustained a sharp demand for labor that lured about 110,000 English to the Chesapeake from 1630 to 1700. Ninety percent of these immigrants were indentured servants, and, because men were more valued as field hands than women, 80 percent of arriving servants were males. So few women initially immigrated to the Chesapeake that only a third of male colonists found brides before 1650. Male servants married late because their indentures forbade them to wed before completing their term of labor. Their scarcity gave women a great advantage in negotiating favorable marriages. Female indentured servants often found prosperous planters to be their suitors and to buy their remaining time of service.

The high death rates that characterized early Virginia persisted after tobacco production became routine. The greatest killers were typhoid fever and, after 1650, malaria. Malaria became endemic as sailors and slaves arriving from Africa brought a particularly virulent form and carried it into marshy lowlands, where mosquitoes spread it rapidly. Life expectancy in the 1600s was about forty-eight for men and forty-four for women—slightly lower than in England and nearly twenty years lower than in New England. Servants died at horrifying rates, with perhaps 40 percent going to their graves within six years of arrival, and 70 percent by age forty-nine. Such high death rates severely crippled family life. Half of all people married in Charles County, Maryland, during the late 1600s became widows or widowers within seven years. The typical Maryland family saw half of its four children die in childhood.

Chesapeake widows tended to enjoy greater economic power than widowed women elsewhere. Instead of leaving widows the one-third of an estate required by English law, Chesapeake husbands were usually more generous and often gave their wives perpetual and complete control of their estates. A widow in such circumstances gained economic independence yet still needed to marry a man who could produce income by farming her fields. But because there were so many more men than women, she had a wider choice of husbands than widows in most societies.

The prevalence of early death produced complex households in which stepparents might raise children with two or three different surnames. Mary Keeble of Middlesex County, Virginia, bore seven children before being widowed at age twenty-nine, whereupon she married Robert Beverley, a prominent planter. Mary died in 1678 at age forty-one after having five children by Beverley, who then married Katherine Hone, a widow with one child. Upon Beverley's death in 1687, Katherine quickly wed Christopher Robinson, who had just lost his wife and needed a mother for his four children. Christopher

The forme of binding a servant.

This Indenture _made the_   _day of_
                   in the
yeere of our Soveraigne Lord King Charles, &c.
betweene   _of the one_
party, and   _on the_
other party, Witnesseth, _that the said_
                doth hereby covenant promise, and
grant, to and with the said
his Executors and Assignes, to serve him from
the day of the date hereof, vntill his first and
next arrivall in Maryland; _and after for and_
during the tearme of   _yeeres, in such_
service and imployment, as he the said
                or his assignes shall there im-
ploy him, according to the custome of the Countrey
in the like kind. In consideration whereof, the said
                         doth promise
and grant, to and with the said
                to pay for his passing, and to
find him with Meat, Drinke, Apparell and Lodg-
ing, with other necessaries during the said tearme;
and at the end of the said terme, to give him one
whole yeeres provision of Corne, and fifty acres of
Land, according to the order of the countrey. In
witnesse whereof, the said
hath hereunto put his hand and seale, the day and
yeere above written.
      Sealed and delivered in
         the presence of   **H**

The usuall terme of binding a servant, is for
five yeers; but for any artificer, or one that shall
deserve more then ordinary, the Adventurer
shall doe well to shorten that time, and adde
encouragements of another nature (as he shall
see cause) rather then to want such usefull men.

Blank Servant Indenture Form, 1635
The vast majority of Chesapeake colonists immigrated from England after signing contracts similar to this one.

resistance acquired from childhood immunities allowed native-born residents to survive into their fifties, ten years longer than immigrants. As a result, more laborers now lived beyond their terms of indenture instead of dying without tasting freedom.

Tobacco Shapes a Region, 1630–1675

Compared to colonists in New England's compact towns, Chesapeake residents had few neighbors. A typical community contained about two dozen families in an area of twenty-five square miles, or about six persons per square mile. Friendship networks typically extended for a two- to three-mile walk from one's farm and included about fifteen other families.

The isolated folk in Virginia and Maryland shared a way of life shaped by one overriding fact—their future depended on the price of tobacco. Tobacco had dominated Chesapeake agriculture since 1618, when demand for the crop exploded and prices spiraled to dizzying levels. The boom ended in 1629 when prices sank a stunning 97 percent (see Figure 3.1). After stabilizing, tobacco rarely again fetched more than 10 percent of its former price.

Figure 3.1 Tobacco Prices, 1618–1710
Even after the tobacco boom ended in 1629, tobacco remained profitable until about 1660, when its price fell below the break-even point—the income needed to support a family or pay off a farm mortgage.
Source: Russell R. Menard, "The Chesapeake Economy, 1618–1720: An Interpretation" (unpublished paper presented at the Johns Hopkins University Seminar on the Atlantic Community, November 20, 1973) and "Farm Prices of Maryland Tobacco, 1659–1710," _Maryland Historical Magazine_, LVIII (Spring 1973): 85.

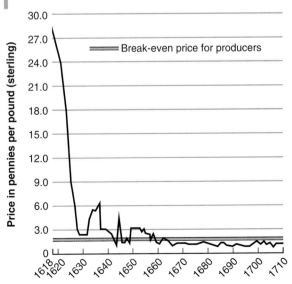

and Katherine's household included children named Keeble, Beverley, Hone, and Robinson. This tangled chain of six marriages among seven people eventually produced twenty-five children who lived at least part of their lives with one or more stepparents.

The combination of predominantly male immigration and devastating death rates sharply limited population growth. Although the Chesapeake had received perhaps one hundred thousand English immigrants by 1700, its white population stood at no more than seventy thousand that year. By contrast, a benign disease environment and a more balanced gender ratio among the twenty-eight thousand immigrants to New England during the 1600s allowed that region's white population to grow to ninety-one thousand by 1700.

The Chesapeake's dismal demographic history began improving in the late seventeenth century. By then,

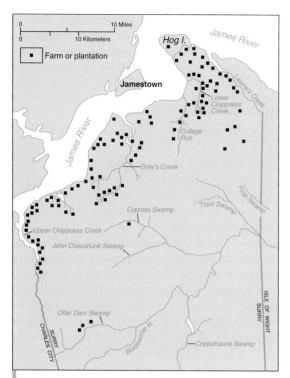

Map 3.2 Pattern of Settlement in Surry County, Virginia, 1620–1660
In contrast to New Englanders (see Map 3.4), Chesapeake colonists spread out along the banks of rivers and creeks in order to facilitate the exporting of tobacco.
Source: Thad W. Tate and David Ammerman, eds., *The Chesapeake in the Seventeenth Century* (Chapel Hill: University of North Carolina Press, 1979). Copyright © 1979 by the University of North Carolina Press. Used by permission of the publisher.

capital like Maryland's St. Mary's, which as late as 1678 had just thirty scattered houses.

Taking advantage of the headright system, a few planters built up large landholdings and grew wealthy from their servants' labor. The servants' lot was harsh. Most were poorly fed, clothed, and housed. The exploitation of labor in the Chesapeake was unequaled anywhere in the English-speaking world outside the West Indies, and the gap between rich and poor whites far exceeded that of New England.

Although servants after 1650 increasingly lived to complete their terms, their futures remained bleak. Having received no pay, they entered into freedom impoverished. Virginia obliged masters to provide a new suit of clothes and a year's supply of corn to a freed servant. Maryland required these items plus a hoe and an ax and gave the right to claim fifty acres—if an individual paid to have the land surveyed and deeded. Thus, Maryland's policy enabled many of its freedmen to become landowners. Two-thirds of all Chesapeake servants lived in Virginia, however, where no such entitlement existed. Moreover, large planters and absentee English speculators monopolized most land in Virginia that was suitable for cultivating tobacco.

After 1660, the possibility of upward mobility almost vanished from the Chesapeake as the price of tobacco fell far below profitable levels, to a penny a pound (see Figure 3.1). Large planters offset their tobacco losses through income from rents, trade, interest on loans to small planters, and fees earned as government officials. They also cut labor costs by extending servants' terms as penalties for even minor infractions. Lacking capital, many freedmen worked as tenants or wage laborers on large plantations at wages well below the level needed to accumulate savings.

Freedmen who managed to obtain land nevertheless remained poor. A typical family inhabited a shack barely twenty feet by sixteen feet and owned no more property than Adam Head of Maryland possessed when he died in 1698: three mattresses without bedsteads, a chest and barrel that served as table and chair, two pots, a kettle, "a parcell of old pewter," a gun, and some books. Most tobacco farmers lacked furniture, lived on mush or stew because they had just one pot, and slept on the ground—often on a pile of rags. Having fled poverty in England for the promise of a better life, they found utter destitution in the Chesapeake.

Bacon's Rebellion, 1676

By the 1670s whites in Virginia seeking land turned their attention to nearby Native Americans. Virginia had been free of serious conflict with Indians since the **Third**

Despite the plunge, tobacco stayed profitable as long as it sold for more than two pence per pound and was cultivated on fertile soil near navigable water. The plant grew best on level ground with good internal drainage, so-called light soil, which was usually found beside rivers. Locating a farm along Chesapeake Bay or one of its tributary rivers also minimized transportation costs by permitting tobacco to be loaded on ships at wharves near one's home. Perhaps 80 percent of early Chesapeake homes lay within a half-mile of a riverbank, and most were within just six hundred feet of the shoreline (see Map 3.2).

From such waterfront bases, wealthy planters built wharves that served not only as depots for tobacco exports but also as distribution centers for imported goods. Planters' control of commerce stunted the growth of towns and the emergence of a merchant class. Urbanization proceeded slowly in the Chesapeake, even in a

Anglo-Powhatan War (1644–1646). Resentful of tobacco planters' continued encroachments on their land, a coalition of Native Americans led by Opechancanough, then nearly a century old but able to direct battles from a litter, killed five hundred of the colony's eight thousand whites before being defeated. By 1653, tribes encircled by English settlement began agreeing to remain within boundaries set by the government—in effect, on reservations. Thereafter white settlement expanded north to the Potomac River, and by 1675 Virginia's four thousand Indians were greatly outnumbered by forty thousand whites.

Tensions flared between Native Americans struggling to retain land and independence and expanding settlers, especially white freedmen who often squatted illegally on tribal lands. The conflict also divided white society because both Governor Berkeley and Lord Baltimore, along with a few wealthy cronies, held fur-trade monopolies that profited from friendly relations with some Indians. The monopolies alienated not only freedmen but also wealthier planters who were excluded from them and who wished to expand further their own landholdings. As a result, colonists' resentments against the governor and proprietor became fused with those against Native Americans. In June 1675, a dispute between some Doeg Indians and a Virginia farmer escalated until a force of Virginia and Maryland militia pursuing the Doegs instead murdered fourteen friendly Susquehannocks and then assassinated the Susquehannocks' leaders during a peace conference. The Susquehannocks retaliated by killing an equal number of settlers and then offered to make peace. But with most colonists refusing to trust any Indians, the violence was now unstoppable.

Tensions were especially acute in Virginia, reflecting the greater disparities among whites there. Governor Berkeley proposed defending the panic-stricken frontier with a chain of forts linked by patrols. Stung by low tobacco prices and taxes that took almost a quarter of their yearly incomes, small farmers preferred the less costly solution of waging a war of extermination. Nathaniel Bacon, a newly arrived, wealthy planter and Berkeley's distant relative, inspired them. Defying the governor's orders, three hundred colonists elected Bacon to lead them against nearby Indians in April 1676, thereby initiating **Bacon's Rebellion**. Bacon's expedition found only peaceful Indians but massacred them anyway.

When he returned in June 1676, Bacon demanded authority to wage war "against all Indians in generall," which an intimidated Berkeley granted. The assembly defined as enemies any Indians who left their villages without English permission (even if they did so out of fear of attack by Bacon), and declared their lands forfeited. Bacon's troops were free to plunder all "enemies" of their furs, guns, wampum, and corn harvests and also to keep Indian prisoners as slaves. The assembly's incentives for enlisting were directed at men eager to get rich quickly by seizing land and enslaving any Indians who fell into their clutches.

Berkeley soon had second thoughts about letting Bacon's thirteen hundred men continue their frontier slaughter and called them back. The rebels returned with their guns pointed toward Jamestown. Forcing Berkeley to flee across Chesapeake Bay, the rebels burned the capital, offered freedom to any Berkeley supporters' servants or slaves who joined the uprising, and looted their enemies' plantations. But at the very moment of triumph in late 1676, Bacon died of dysentery and his followers dispersed.

A royal commission dispatched from England in 1677 found that Berkeley had mismanaged the crisis but also that some of the Indian lands seized by Bacon's followers had been guaranteed to the tribes by previous treaties. Under the Treaty of Middle Plantation (1677), the tribes and the colony pledged peace toward one another, English-held captives were freed, and the tribes' lands were guaranteed in perpetuity. (Several more tribes joined the pact in 1680.) The leading tribe, the Pamunkeys, agreed to present the governor of Virginia with three arrowheads and twenty beaver pelts annually, a provision they honor to this day.

Most Indian-held land seized during Bacon's Rebellion was not protected by formal treaties. The colony retained most of this land and made it available to settlers (see Map 3.3).

The tortured course of Bacon's Rebellion revealed a society under stress. It was an outburst of long pent-up frustrations by marginal taxpayers and former servants seeking land, but also by wealthier planters. Although sheer economic opportunism was one motive for the uprising, the willingness of whites to murder, enslave, or expel all Native Americans, no matter how loyal, made clear that racial hostility also played a major role.

From Servitude to Slavery

Race was also fundamental in the reshaping of Chesapeake society that followed Bacon's Rebellion. Even before the uprising, planters had begun substituting black slaves for white servants.

Racial slavery had developed in three stages in the Chesapeake since 1619. Until about 1640, colonists carefully distinguished between blacks and whites in official documents, but did not assume that every African sold was a slave for life. The same was true for Native Americans

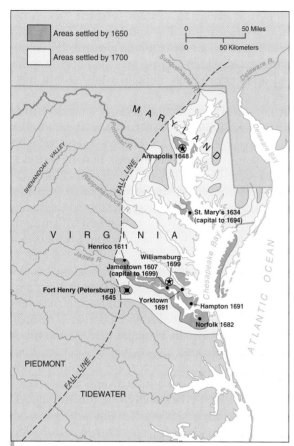

Map 3.3 Chesapeake Expansion, 1607–1700
The Chesapeake colonies expanded slowly before midcentury. By 1700, Anglo-Indian wars, a rising English population, and an influx of enslaved Africans permitted settlers to spread throughout the tidewater.

arms consisted entirely of slaves and servants. By 1705, strict legal codes defined the place of slaves in society and set standards of racial etiquette. By then, free blacks had all but disappeared from the Chesapeake. Although this period saw racial slavery become fully legalized, many of the specific practices enacted into law had evolved into custom earlier.

Emerging gradually in the Chesapeake, slavery was formally codified by planter elites attempting to stabilize Chesapeake society and defuse the resentment of whites. In deeming nonwhites unfit for freedom, the elites created a common, exclusive identity for whites as free or potentially free persons.

Chesapeake planters began formulating this racial caste system before slavery itself became economically significant. As late as 1660, fewer than a thousand slaves lived in Virginia and Maryland. The number in bondage first became truly significant in the 1680s when the Chesapeake's slave population (by now almost entirely black, owing to Indian decline) almost tripled, rising from forty-five hundred to about twelve thousand. By 1700, slaves made up 22 percent of the inhabitants and over 80 percent of all unfree laborers.

Having developed as a labor system reserved for blacks, slavery replaced indentured servitude for economic reasons. First, it became more difficult for planters to import white laborers as the seventeenth century advanced. Between 1650 and 1700, wages rose in England by 50 percent, removing poor people's incentive to move to the Chesapeake. Second, before 1690 the Royal African Company, which held a monopoly on selling slaves to the English colonies, shipped most its cargoes to the West Indies. Some of these slaves were then transported to the Chesapeake and other mainland regions of English America. During the 1690s, this monopoly was broken, and rival companies began shipping large numbers of Africans directly to the Chesapeake.

The rise of a direct trade in slaves between the Chesapeake and West Africa exacerbated the growing gap between whites and blacks in another way. Until 1690, most blacks in the Chesapeake had either been born, or spent many years, in West African ports or in other American colonies. As a consequence, they were familiar with Europeans and European ways and, in many cases, spoke English. Such familiarity had enabled some blacks to carve out space for themselves as free landowners, and had facilitated marriages and acts of resistance across racial lines among laborers. But after 1690, far larger numbers of slaves poured into Virginia and Maryland, arriving directly from the West African interior. Language and culture now became barriers rather than

captured in the colony's early wars. Some Africans gained their freedom during this period, and a few owned their own tobacco farms.

During the second phase, from 1640 to 1660, growing numbers of blacks and some Indians were treated as slaves for life, in contrast to white indentured servants who had fixed terms of service. Slaves' children inherited their parents' status. At the same time, evidence from this period shows that white and black laborers often ran away or rebelled against a master together, and occasionally married one another.

Apparently in reaction to such incidents, the colonies officially recognized and regulated slavery after 1660. Maryland first defined slavery as a lifelong, inheritable racial status in 1661. Virginia followed suit in 1670. This hardening of status lines did not prevent some black and white laborers from joining Bacon's Rebellion together. Indeed, the last contingent of rebels to lay down their

Preparing a Slave Voyage
Africans weep as relatives or friends are taken to a slave vessel.

bridges to mutual understanding among blacks as well as between blacks and whites, reinforcing the overt racism arising among whites.

The changing composition of the white population also contributed to the emergence of race as the foundation of Chesapeake society. As increasing numbers of immigrants lived long enough to marry and form their own families, the number of such families slowly rose, and the ratio of men to women became more equal, since half of all children were girls. By 1690, an almost even division existed between males and females. Thereafter, the white population grew primarily through an excess of births over deaths rather than through immigration, so that by 1720 most Chesapeake colonists were native-born. Whites' shared attachments to the colony heightened their sense of a common racial identity vis-à-vis an increasingly fragmented and seemingly alien black population.

From its beginnings as a region where profits were high but life expectancy was low, the Chesapeake had transformed by 1700. As nonwhites' conditions deteriorated, Virginia and Maryland expanded their territories, and their white colonists flourished.

Puritanism in New England

After the Chesapeake, New England was the next colonial region to prosper in North America. Separatist Puritans had established Plymouth in 1620 (see Chapter 2), which grew slowly but thrived over the next decade. Plymouth was dwarfed after 1630, when a massive Puritan-led "Great Migration" to New England began. By the time England's civil war halted the migration in 1642, about twenty-one thousand settlers had arrived. The newcomers established the colonies of Massachusetts Bay, Connecticut, New Haven (absorbed by Connecticut in 1662), and Rhode Island. New England's leaders endeavored to build colonies based on religious and social ideals. Although internal divisions and social-economic change undermined these ideals, Puritanism gave New England a distinctive regional identity.

New England offered a sharp contrast to the Chesapeake colonies. The religious foundations, economies, class structure, local communities, families, and living standards in the two regions could not have been more different. The Chesapeake and New England colonists did, however, share English nationality and a determination to expand at Native Americans' expense.

A City upon a Hill

After becoming king in 1625, Charles I reversed James's policy of tolerating Puritans (see Chapter 2). Beginning a systematic campaign to eliminate Puritan influence within the Church of England, Anglican authorities insisted that services be conducted according to the Book of Common Prayer, which prescribed rituals similar to Catholic practices. Bishops dismissed Puritan ministers who refused to perform these "High Church" rites, and church courts fined or excommunicated Puritan laypersons who protested.

In the face of such harassment, a group of wealthy Puritans successfully petitioned the crown for a charter to colonize at Massachusetts Bay, north of Plymouth, in March 1629. Organizing as the Massachusetts Bay Company, they took advantage of a gap in their charter and later that year moved the seat of their colony's government, along with four hundred colonists, to Salem, Massachusetts. Like Plymouth, Massachusetts Bay would be a Puritan-dominated, self-governing colony rather than one controlled from England by stockholders, proprietors, or the crown. In 1630, the company sent out eleven ships and seven hundred passengers under Governor **John Winthrop**. Upon arriving at the new capital of Boston, Winthrop distributed an essay (perhaps already delivered as a shipboard address) titled **"A Model of Christian Charity,"** spelling out the new colony's social and political ideals. In it, he boldly declared that Massachusetts "shall be as a city upon a hill, the eyes of all people are upon us." The settlers would build a harmonious, godly community in which individuals would subordinate their personal interests to a higher purpose. The result would be an example for all the world and would particularly inspire England to live up to its role as God's "elect nation."

In outlining this ideal society, Winthrop denounced the economic jealousy that bred class hatred. God intended that "in all times some must be rich and some poor," he asserted. The rich had an obligation to show charity and mercy toward the poor, who should meekly accept rule by their social superiors as God's will. God expected the state to keep the greedy among the rich from exploiting the needy and to prevent the lazy among the poor from burdening their fellow citizens. In outlining a divine plan in which all people, rich and poor, served one another, Winthrop expressed a conservative European's understanding of social hierarchy (see Chapter 2) and voiced Puritans' dismay at the forces of individualism and class warfare that were battering—and changing—English society.

By fall 1630, six towns had sprung up around Boston. During the unusually severe first winter, 30 percent of Winthrop's party died, and another 10 percent went home in the spring. By mid-1631, however, thirteen hundred new settlers had landed, and more were on the way. The worst was over. The colony would never suffer another starving time. Like Plymouth, Massachusetts Bay primarily attracted landowning farm families of modest means, most of them receptive if not actively committed to Calvinism. Compared to the Chesapeake in 1630, there were few indentured servants and almost no slaves. New Englanders quickly established a healthier, more stable colonial region than did their Chesapeake contemporaries. By 1642, more than fifteen thousand colonists had settled in New England.

Political participation was more broadly based in New England than elsewhere in Europe and its colonies. Instead of requiring voters or officeholders to own property, Massachusetts permitted voting by every adult male church member. By 1641, about 55 percent of the colony's twenty-three hundred men could vote. (The other Puritan colonies based male voting on property ownership.) But since most white men owned property, the suffrage was similarly broad. By contrast, English property requirements allowed fewer than 30 percent of adult males to vote.

In 1634, after protests that the governor (Winthrop) and council held too much power, the General Court (legislature) allowed each town to send two delegates. Initially resisting this effort, Winthrop was defeated for reelection and did not return to the governorship for three years. In 1644, the General Court became a bicameral (two-chamber) lawmaking body when the towns' deputies separated from the appointed Governor's Council.

New England Ways

Although most New Englanders nominally belonged to the Church of England, their self-governing congregations, like those in Separatist Plymouth, ignored Anglican bishops' authority. Control of each congregation lay squarely in the hands of its male "saints," as Puritans termed those who had been saved. By majority vote, these men chose their minister, elected a board of elders to handle finances, and decided who else deserved recognition as saints. Compared to Anglican parishes in England and Virginia, where a few powerful landowners selected priests (subject to a bishop's formal approval) and made other major decisions, control of New England churches was broadly based.

Although congregations were largely independent of one another and controlled by their male members, the clergy quickly asserted its power in New England's religious life. As members of a popular religious movement in England, Puritans had emphasized broad Calvinist principles and their common opposition to Anglican practices. But upon arriving in New England, many ministers feared that complete congregational independence would undermine Puritan unity and lead to religious disorder. Religious disharmony would as effectively undermine "the city upon a hill" as would the social disharmony feared by Winthrop. Accordingly, the ministers established a set of official practices—the **"New England Way"**—that strengthened their authority at the expense of that of laypersons (nonclergy) within their congregations.

In its church membership requirements, the New England Way diverged from other Puritans' practices. English Puritans accepted as saints any adult who correctly professed the Calvinist faith, repented his or her sins, and lived free of scandal. Massachusetts Puritans, however, insisted that candidates for membership stand before their congregation and provide a convincing, soul-baring "relation," or account, of their conversion experience (see Chapter 2). Many colonists shared the reluctance of Jonathan Fairbanks, who refused for several years to give a public profession of grace before the church in Dedham, Massachusetts, until the faithful persuaded him with many "loving conferences." The conversion relation would prove to be the New England Way's most vulnerable feature.

One means of ensuring orthodoxy was through education. Like most European Protestants, Puritans insisted that conversion required familiarity with the Bible and, therefore, literacy. Education, they believed, should begin in childhood and should be promoted by each colony. In 1647, Massachusetts Bay ordered every town of fifty or more households to appoint a teacher to whom all children could come for instruction, and every town of at least one hundred households to maintain a grammar school. This and similar laws in other Puritan colonies represented New England's first steps toward public education. But none of these laws required school attendance, and boys were more likely to be taught reading and especially writing than were girls.

To ensure a supply of ministers trained in the New England Way, Massachusetts founded Harvard College in 1636. From 1642 to 1671, the college produced 201 graduates, including 111 ministers. As a result, New England was the only part of English America to produce its own clergy and college-educated elite before 1700.

Puritans agreed that the church must be free of state control, and they opposed theocracy (government by clergy). But Winthrop and other Massachusetts Bay leaders insisted that a holy commonwealth required cooperation between church and state. The colony obliged all adults to attend services and levied taxes to support local churches. Thus Massachusetts, like England and Anglican Virginia, had an established church.

Driving the clergy's efforts to define orthodox practices was the arrival in New England of Puritans whose views threatened to divide Puritans along theological lines. Roger Williams and Anne Hutchinson led movements considered by political as well as religious authorities to be especially dangerous because they attracted popular followings.

Roger Williams, a Separatist minister who arrived in 1631, aroused elite anxieties by advocating the complete separation of church and state and religious toleration. He argued that civil government should play no role in regulating religious matters, whether blasphemy (cursing God), failure to pay tithes, refusal to attend worship, or swearing oaths on the Bible in court. Williams also opposed any kind of compulsory church service or government interference with religious practice, not because all religions deserved equal respect but because the state (a creation of sinful human beings) would corrupt the church.

As Williams's popularity grew, Winthrop and other authorities declared his opinions subversive and banished him in 1635. Williams moved south to a place that he called Providence, which he purchased from the Narragansett Indians. At Williams's invitation, a steady stream of dissenters drifted to the group of settlements near Providence, which in 1647 joined to form Rhode Island colony. (Other Puritans scorned the place as "Rogues Island.") True to Williams's ideals, Rhode Island was the only New England colony to practice religious toleration. Growing slowly, the colony's four towns had eight hundred settlers by 1650.

A second major challenge to the New England Way began when **Anne Hutchinson**, a deeply religious member of the Boston congregation, publicly criticized the clergy for judging prospective church members on the basis of "good works"—the Catholic standard for salvation that Protestants had criticized since the Reformation (see Chapter 2). Supposedly, Puritans followed John Calvin in maintaining that God had "predestined" all persons for either salvation or damnation. But Hutchinson argued that ministers who scrutinized a person's outward behavior for "signs" of salvation, especially when that person was relating his or her conversion experience, were discarding God's judgment in favor of their own. Only by looking inward and ignoring such false prophets could individuals hope to find salvation. Hutchinson charged that only two of the colony's ministers had been saved; the rest lacked authority over the elect.

By casting doubt on the clergy's spiritual state, Hutchinson undermined its authority over laypersons. Critics charged that her beliefs would delude individuals into imagining that they were accountable to no one but themselves. Winthrop branded her followers Antinomians, meaning those opposed to the rule of law.

Hutchinson bore the additional liability of violating gender norms. As a woman steeped in Scripture, Hutchinson had led other women in discussions of ministers' sermons. But she went beyond that prescribed role by asserting her own opinions and by including men at the meetings. As one of her accusers put it, "You have stepped out of your place; you [would] have rather been a husband than a wife, a preacher than a hearer; and a magistrate than a subject."

By 1637, Massachusetts Bay had split into two camps. Hutchinson's supporters, primarily Bostonians, included merchants (like her husband) who disliked the government's economic restrictions on their businesses, young men chafing against the rigid control of church elders, and women impatient with their second-class status in church affairs. Even the colony's governor, Henry Vane, was an Antinomian. But most colonists outside Boston were alarmed by what they regarded as religious extremism. In the election of 1637 they rejected Vane and returned Winthrop to the governorship.

The victorious Winthrop brought Hutchinson to trial for heresy before the General Court, whose members peppered her with questions. Hutchinson's knowledge of Scripture was so superior to that of her interrogators, however, that she would have been acquitted had she not claimed to be converted through a direct revelation from God. Like most Christians, Puritans believed that God had ceased to make known matters of faith by personal revelation after New Testament times. Thus, Hutchinson's own words condemned her.

The General Court banished the leading Antinomians from the colony, and others voluntarily followed them to Rhode Island, New Hampshire, or back to England. The largest group, led by Hutchinson, settled in Rhode Island. Some Rhode Island Antinomians later converted to Quakerism (see below), returning to Massachusetts and again defying political and religious authorities.

Antinomianism's defeat was followed by new restrictions on women's independence and religious expression. Increasingly, women were prohibited from assuming the kind of public religious roles claimed by Hutchinson. To minimize their influence, they were required to relate their conversion experiences privately to ministers rather than publicly before their congregations.

Towns, Families, and Farm Life

To ensure that colonists would settle in communities with congregations, all New England colonies, including Rhode Island, provided for the establishment of towns, which would distribute land. Legislatures authorized a town by awarding a grant of land to several dozen landowning church members. These men then laid out the settlement, organized its church, distributed land among themselves, and established a town meeting—a distinctly New England institution. At the center of each town lay the meetinghouse, which served as both church and town hall.

Whereas justices of the peace in England and Virginia administered local government through county courts, New England's county courts served strictly as courts of law, and local administration was conducted by the town meeting. Town meetings decentralized authority over political and economic decisions to a degree unknown in England and its other colonies. Each town determined its own qualifications for voting and holding office in the town meeting, although most allowed all male taxpayers (including nonsaints) to participate. The meeting could exclude anyone from settling in town, and it could grant the right of sharing in any future land distributions to male newcomers, whose sons would inherit this privilege.

Few aspects of early New England life are more revealing than the first generation's attempt in many towns to promote communalism by keeping settlement tightly clustered (see Map 3.4). They did so by granting house lots near the town center and by granting families no more land than they needed to support themselves. Dedham's forty-six founders, for example, received 128,000 acres from Massachusetts Bay in 1636 yet gave themselves just 3,000 acres by 1656, or about 65 acres per family. The rest remained in trust for future generations.

With families clustered within a mile of one another, the physical settings of New England towns were conducive to traditional reciprocity. They also fostered an atmosphere of mutual watchfulness that Puritans hoped would promote godly order. For the enforcement of such order, they relied on the women of each town as well as male magistrates.

Although women's public roles had been sharply curtailed following the Antinomian crisis, women—especially female saints—remained a social force in their communities. With their husbands and older sons attending the family's fields and business, women remained at home in the tightly knit neighborhoods at the center of each town. Neighboring women exchanged not only goods—say, a pound of butter for a section of spun wool—but advice and news of other neighbors as well. They also gathered at the bedside when one of them gave birth, an occasion supervised by a midwife and entirely closed to men. In these settings, women confided in one another, creating a "community of women" within each town that helped enforce morals and protect the poor and vulnerable. In 1663, Mary Rolfe of Newbury, Massachusetts, was being sexually harassed by a high-ranking gentleman while her fisherman husband was at sea. Rolfe confided in her mother, who in turn consulted with a neighboring woman of influence before filing formal charges. Clearly influenced by the town's women, a male jury convicted the gentleman of attempted adultery. When a gentlewoman, Patience

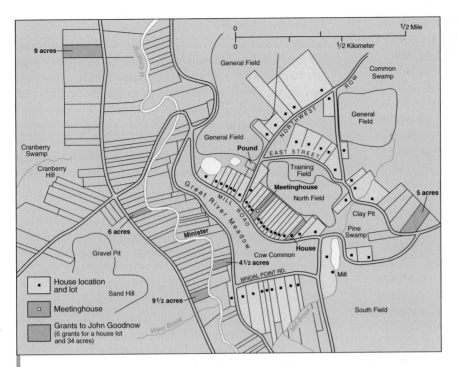

Map 3.4 Land Divisions in Sudbury, Massachusetts, 1639–1656
Most early New England towns clustered homes around a meetinghouse and a town commons, used for grazing. Sudbury, like many towns, followed an English practice of distributing croplands in scattered strips. John Goodnow, for example, grew crops in five fields at varying distances from his house.
Source: Puritan Village: The Formation of a New England Town. Copyright © 1963 by Sumner Chilton Powell and reprinted by permission of Wesleyan University Press.

Dennison, charged her maidservant with repeatedly stealing food and clothing, a fourth woman testified that the maid had given the provisions to a poor young wife, whose family was thereby saved from perishing. The servant was cleared while her mistress gained a lifelong reputation for stinginess.

Puritans defined matrimony as a contract rather than a religious sacrament, and justices of the peace rather than ministers married New England couples. As a civil institution, a marriage could be dissolved by the courts in cases of desertion, bigamy, adultery, or physical cruelty. By permitting divorce, the colonies diverged radically from practices in England, where Anglican authorities rarely annulled marriages and civil divorces required a special act of Parliament. Still, New Englanders saw divorce as a remedy fit only for extremely wronged spouses, such as the Plymouth woman who discovered that her husband was also married to women in Boston, Barbados, and England. Massachusetts courts allowed just twenty-seven divorces before 1692.

New England wives enjoyed significant legal protections against spousal violence and nonsupport and also had more opportunity than other European women to escape failed marriages. But they also suffered the same legal disabilities as all Englishwomen. An English wife had no property rights independent of her husband unless he consented to a prenuptial agreement leaving her in control of property she already owned. Only if a husband had no other heirs or so stipulated in a will could a widow claim more than the third of the estate reserved by law for her lifetime use.

In contrast to the Chesapeake, New England benefited from a remarkably benign disease environment. Most families owned farms and produced an ample amount and variety of foods to ensure an adequate diet, which improved resistance to disease and lowered death rates associated with childbirth. Malaria and other tropical diseases did not thrive in New England's frozen winters. And while settlements were compact, New Englanders rarely traveled outside their own towns. Thus while travelers brought communicable diseases to Boston and other ports, such diseases rarely spread inland.

Consequently, New Englanders lived longer and raised larger families than their contemporaries in England and other colonial regions. Life expectancy for men reached sixty-five, and women lived nearly that long. More than 80 percent of all infants survived long enough to get married. The 58 men and women who founded Andover, Massachusetts, for example, had 247 children; by the fourth generation, the families of their descendants numbered 2,000 (including spouses who married in from other families). Because most settlers came as members of family groups, the population was evenly divided between males and females from the beginning. This balance permitted rapid population growth without heavy immigration.

Most colonists had little or no cash, relying instead on the labor of their large, healthy families to sustain them and secure their futures. Male household heads managed the family's crops and livestock, conducted most of its business transactions, and represented it in town government. Their wives bore, nursed, and reared their children. Women were

Mary Hollingsworth Embroidered Sampler Many women found in embroidery a creative outlet that was compatible with their domestic duties.

Economic and Religious Tensions

Saddled with the burdens of a short growing season, rocky soil salted with gravel, and (in most towns) a system of land distribution in which farmers cultivated widely scattered parcels, the colonists managed to feed large families and keep ahead of their debts, but few became wealthy from farming. Seeking greater fortunes than agriculture offered, some seventeenth-century New Englanders turned lumbering, fishing, fur trading, shipbuilding, and rum distilling into major industries. As its economy became more diversified, New England prospered. But the colonists grew more worldly and their values began to shift.

The most fundamental threat to Winthrop's city upon a hill was that colonists would abandon the ideal of a close-knit community to pursue self-interest. Other colonies—most pointedly, Virginia—displayed the acquisitive impulses transforming England, but in New England, as one minister put it, "religion and profit jump together." While hoping for prosperity, Puritans believed that there were limits to legitimate commercial behavior. Government leaders tried to regulate prices so that consumers would not suffer from the chronic shortage of manufactured goods that afflicted New England. In 1635, when the Massachusetts General Court forbade pricing any item more than 5 percent above its cost, Robert Keayne of Boston and other merchants objected. These men argued that they had to sell some goods at higher rates in order to offset their losses from other sales, shipwrecked cargoes, and inflation. In 1639, after selling nails at 25 percent to 33 percent above cost, Keayne was fined heavily in court and was forced to make a humiliating apology before his congregation.

Controversies between the Puritan clergy and farming elites on one hand, and merchants on the other, were part of a struggle for New England's soul. On various occasions, Elizabeth Clark Freake's father and each of her husbands (all wealthy merchants) clashed with colony leaders who sought to limit mercantile interests. Some merchants were attracted to less rigid variants of Calvinism. Merchants were prominent among the followers of both Roger Williams and Anne Hutchinson. William Pynchon of Springfield was banished from Massachusetts in 1652, after publishing a tract that authorities considered heretical. In all these conflicts, political and religious leaders sought to insulate their city upon a hill from the competitiveness and pursuit of self-interest basic to a market economy.

Other social and economic changes further undermined Winthrop's vision. After about 1660, farmers eager to expand their agricultural output and provide land for their sons voted themselves larger amounts of land after 1660 and insisted that their scattered parcels be

in charge of work in the house, barn, and garden, including the making of food and clothing. Women also did charitable work and played other roles in their communities (see above).

More than in England and the other colonies, the sons of New England's founding generation depended on their parents to provide them with acreage for farming. With eventual landownership guaranteed and few other opportunities available, sons delayed marriage and worked in their fathers' fields until finally receiving their own land, usually after age twenty-five. Because the average family raised three or four boys to adulthood, parents could depend on thirty to forty years of sons' labor.

While daughters performed equally vital labor, their future lay with another family—the one into which they would marry. Being young, with many childbearing years ahead of them, enhanced their value to that family. Thus first-generation women, on average, were only twenty-one when they married.

consolidated. For example, Dedham, Massachusetts, which distributed only three thousand acres from 1636 to 1656, allocated five times as much in the next dozen years. Rather than continue living closely together, many farmers built homes on their outlying tracts. The dispersal of settlers away from town centers generated friction between townspeople settled near the meetinghouse and "outlivers," whose distance from the town center limited their influence over town affairs. Although groups of outlivers often formed new towns (see Map 3.5), John Winthrop's vision of a society sustained by reciprocity was slowly giving way to the materialistic, acquisitive society that the original immigrants had fled in England.

As New England slowly prospered, England fell into chaos. The efforts of Charles I to impose taxes without Parliament's consent sparked a civil war in 1642. Alienated by years of religious harassment, Puritans gained control of the successful revolt and beheaded Charles in 1649. Puritan Oliver Cromwell's consolidation of power raised orthodox New Englanders' hopes that England would finally heed their example and establish a truly reformed church. But Cromwell preferred Rhode Island's Roger Williams to other New Englanders and developed England's commercial empire. After Cromwell died, chaos returned to England until a provisional government "restored" the monarchy and crowned King Charles II (ruled 1660–1685). The **Restoration** left New England Puritans without a mission. Contrary to Winthrop's vision, "the eyes of all people" were no longer, if ever they had been, fixed on New England.

The erosion of Winthrop's social vision was accompanied by the decline of the religious vision embodied in the New England Way. This decline was reflected most vividly in a crisis over church membership. The crisis arose because many Puritans' children were not joining the elect. By 1650, for example, fewer than half the adults in the Boston congregation were saints. The principal reason was the children's reluctance to undergo public grilling on their conversion experience. Most children must have witnessed at least one ordeal like Sarah Fiske's. For more than a year, Fiske answered petty charges of speaking uncharitably about her relatives—especially her husband—and then was admitted to the Wenham, Massachusetts, congregation only after publicly denouncing herself as worse "than any toad."

Because Puritan ministers baptized only babies born to saints, the unwillingness of the second generation to provide a conversion relation meant that most third-generation children would remain unbaptized. Unless a solution were found, saints' numbers would dwindle and Puritan rule would end. In 1662 a synod of clergy proposed a compromise known as the Halfway Covenant, which would permit the children of baptized adults, including nonsaints, to receive baptism. Derisively termed the "halfway" covenant by its opponents, the proposal would allow the founders' descendants to transmit potential church membership to their grandchildren, leaving their adult children "halfway" members who could not take communion or vote in church affairs. Congregations divided bitterly over limiting membership to pure saints or compromising purity in order to maintain Puritan power in New England. In the end, they opted for worldly power over spiritual purity.

The crisis in church membership signaled a weakening of the old orthodoxy. Most

Map 3.5 New England Expansion, 1620–1674
Before 1660, religious dissent and land-hunger drove whites' expansion. Thereafter, a second, larger generation, eager to consolidate its landholdings, established many new towns. The resulting pressures on Native Americans and their land was a major cause of King Philip's War (1675–1676).
Source: Frederick Merk, *History of the Westward Movement.* Copyright © 1979 by Lois Bannister Merk. Used by permission of Alfred A. Knopf, a division of Random House, Inc.

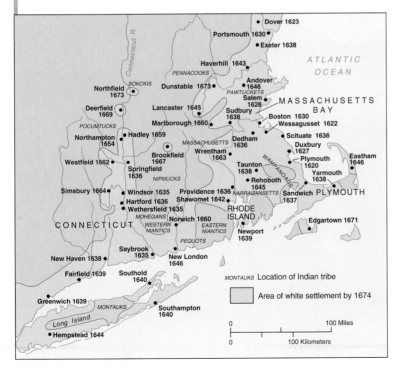

second-generation adults remained in "halfway" status for life, and the saints became a shrinking minority as the third and fourth generations matured. Sainthood tended to flow in certain families, and soon there were more women than men among the elect. But because women could not vote in church affairs, religious authority stayed in male hands. Nevertheless, ministers publicly recognized women's role in upholding piety and the church itself.

Expansion and Native Americans

New England's first colonists met with little sustained resistance from Native Americans, whose numbers were drastically reduced by the ravages of disease. After one epidemic killed about 90 percent of New England's coastal Indians (see Chapter 2), smallpox inflicted comparable casualties on Indians throughout the Northeast in 1633–1634. Having dwindled from twenty thousand in 1600 to a few dozen survivors by the mid-1630s, the coastal Massachusett and Pawtucket Indians were pressed to sell most of their land to the English. During the 1640s, Massachusetts Bay passed laws prohibiting them from practicing their own religion and encouraging missionaries to convert them to Christianity. Thereafter, they ceded more land to the colonists and moved into "praying towns" like Natick, a reservation established by the colony. In the praying towns, Puritan missionary John Eliot hoped to teach the Native Americans Christianity and English "civilization."

On the other hand, English expansion farther inland aroused Native American resistance. Beginning in 1633, settlers moved into the Connecticut River Valley and in 1635 organized the new colony of Connecticut. Friction quickly developed with the Pequot Indians, who controlled the trade in furs and wampum with New Netherland. After tensions escalated into violence, Massachusetts and Connecticut took coordinated military action in 1637, thereby beginning the **Pequot War**. Having gained the support of the Mohegan and Narragansett Indians, they waged a ruthless campaign, using tactics similar to those devised by the English to break Irish resistance during the 1570s (see Chapter 2). In a predawn attack, English troops surrounded and set fire to a Pequot village at Mystic, Connecticut, and then cut down all who tried to escape. Several hundred Pequots, mostly women and children, were killed. Although their Narragansett allies protested that "it is too furious, and slays too many men," the English found a cause for celebration in the grisly massacre. Wrote Plymouth's Governor William Bradford,

It was a fearful sight to see them [the Pequots] thus frying in the fire and the streams of blood quenching the same, and horrible was the stink and scent thereof; but the victory seemed a sweet sacrifice, and they [the English] gave the praise to God, who had wrought so wonderfully for them, thus to enclose their enemies in their hands and give them so speedy a victory over so proud and insulting an enemy.

By late 1637, Pequot resistance was crushed, with the survivors taken by pro-English Indians as captives or by the English as slaves. The Pequots' lands were awarded to the colonists of Connecticut and New Haven.

As settlements grew and colonists prospered, the numbers and conditions of Native Americans in New England declined. Although Indians began to recover from the initial epidemics by midcentury, the settlers brought new diseases such as diphtheria, measles, and tuberculosis as well as new outbreaks of smallpox, which

Attack on Mystic Fort, Pequot War
This print, published in an English participant's account of the war, shows English troops, backed by allied Indians, surrounding the Pequot village while soldiers prepare to burn it.

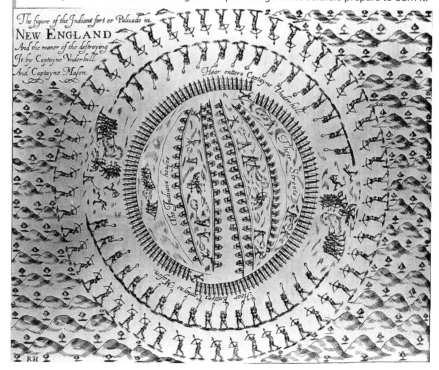

took heavy tolls. New England's Indian population fell from 125,000 in 1600 to 10,000 in 1675.

Native Americans felt the English presence in other ways. The fur trade, which initially benefited interior Natives, became a liability after midcentury. Once Indians began hunting for trade instead of just for their own subsistence needs, they quickly depleted the region's beavers and other fur-bearing animals. Because English traders shrewdly advanced trade goods on credit to Indian hunters before the hunting season, the lack of pelts pushed many Natives into debt. Traders such as John Pynchon of Springfield, Massachusetts, began taking Indian land as collateral and selling it to settlers. The expansion of English settlement often separated Native villages from one another and from hunting, gathering, and fishing areas.

English expansion put new pressures on Native peoples and the land. As early as 1642, Miantonomi, a Narragansett sachem (chief), warned neighboring Indians,

These English having gotten our land, they with scythes cut down the grass, and with axes fell the trees; their cows and horses eat the grass, and their hogs spoil our clam banks, and we shall all be starved.

Within a generation, Miantonomi's fears were being borne out. By clearing away extensive stands of trees for fields and for use as fuel and building material, colonial farmers altered an entire ecosystem. Deer were no longer attracted, and the wild plants upon which Native Americans depended for food and medicine could not grow. The soil became drier and flooding more frequent in the face of this deforestation. The settlers also introduced domestic livestock, which, according to English custom, ranged freely. Pigs damaged Indian cornfields (until the Natives adopted the alien practice of fencing their fields) and shellfish-gathering sites. English cattle and horses quickly devoured native grasses, which the settlers then replaced with English varieties.

With their leaders powerless to halt the alarming decline of their population, land, and food sources, many Indians became demoralized. In their despair, some turned to alcohol, increasingly available during the 1660s despite colonial efforts to suppress its sale to Native Americans. Interpreting the crisis as one of belief, other Natives responded to an expanded initiative by John Eliot and other Puritan missionaries to convert them to Christianity. By 1675, about 2,300 Indians inhabited thirty praying towns in eastern Massachusetts, Plymouth, and offshore islands. Regularly visited by supervising missionaries, each praying town had its own Native American magistrate, usually a sachem, and many congregations had Indian preachers.

Although the missionaries struggled to convert the Indians to "civilization" (meaning English culture and lifestyles) as well as Christianity, most praying Indians integrated the new faith with their native cultural identities.

Anglo-Indian conflict became acute during the 1670s because of pressures imposed on unwilling Indians to sell their land and to accept missionaries and the legal authority of colonial courts. Tension ran especially high in Plymouth colony where Metacom, or "King Philip," the son of the colony's onetime ally Massasoit (see Chapter 2), was now the leading Wampanoag sachem. The English had engulfed the Wampanoags, persuaded many of them to renounce their loyalty to Metacom, and forced several humiliating concessions on the sachem.

In 1675, Plymouth hanged three Wampanoags for killing a Christian Indian and threatened to arrest Metacom. A minor incident, in which several Wampanoags were shot while burglarizing a farmhouse, ignited the conflict known as **King Philip's War**.

Eventually, two-thirds of the colonies' Native Americans, including some Christians, rallied around Metacom. Unlike Indians in the Pequot War, they were familiar with guns and were as well armed as the colonists. Indian raiders attacked fifty-two of New England's ninety towns (entirely destroying twelve), burned twelve hundred houses, slaughtered eight thousand head of cattle, and killed twenty-five hundred colonists (5 percent).

The tide turned against Metacom in 1676 after the Mohawk Indians of New York and many Christian Indians joined the English against him. The colonists and their Native American allies scattered their enemies and destroyed their food supplies. About five thousand Indians starved or fell in battle, including Metacom himself, and others fled to New York and Canada. After crushing the uprising, the English sold hundreds of captives into slavery, including Metacom's wife and child.

King Philip's War reduced southern New England's Indian population by about 40 percent and eliminated overt resistance to white expansion. It also deepened English hostility toward all Native Americans, even the Christian and other Indians who had supported the colonies. In Massachusetts, ten praying towns were disbanded, and Native peoples restricted to the remaining four; all Indian courts were dismantled; and English "guardians" were appointed to supervise the reservations. "There is a cloud, a dark cloud upon the work of the Gospel among the poor Indians," mourned John Eliot. In the face of poverty and discrimination, remaining Indians struggled to survive and maintain their communities.

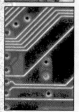

Technology (and) *Culture*

Native American Baskets and Textiles in New England

For thousands of years before 1492, peoples of the Eastern and Western Hemispheres exchanged materials and techniques for making things with their neighbors. After Columbus broke the Atlantic barrier in 1492, they were able to broaden those exchanges across the hemispheres. Such exchanges rarely resulted in one group's wholesale adoption of another's technology. Instead, each group selected materials and techniques from the other group, incorporating what it selected into customary practices. Such was the case with Native Americans living near New England colonists in the seventeenth century.

Among the Wampanoags, Narragansetts, Mohegans, Pequots, and other Native peoples of southern New England, men and women each specialized in crafting objects for everyday use. Men made tobacco pipes from stone, ornaments from copper, and bows from wood. Women used the wild and domestic plants they harvested not only for preparing food but also to make baskets and other containers, fish traps, and mats to cover wigwams and line graves. English observers admired the scale and variety of women's products. One described an underground storage container that held sixty gallons of maize. Another saw baskets of "rushes; ... others of maize husks; others of a kind of silk grass; others of a wild hemp; and some of barks of trees, ... very neat and artificial, with the portraitures of birds, beasts, fishes, and flowers upon them in colors."

Indian women employed a variety of techniques in crafting these objects. One author told how Massachusett Indian women made mats by stitching together long strips of sedge, a marsh grass, with "needles made of the splinter bones of a cranes leg, with threads made of ... hemp." Another described Abenaki women's "dishes ... of birch bark sewed with threads drawn from spruce and white cedar roots, and garnished on ... the brims with glistening quills taken from the porcupine and dyed, some black, others red." Others elaborated on the several varieties of bark and plant fibers that women interwove to make wigwams. The combination of fibers ensured that a house kept its occupants warm and dry while remaining light and flexible enough to be carried from place to place.

When English colonists arrived in New England beginning in 1620, they brought the practices and products of their own textile traditions. Many colonial families raised

Native American Basket, Rhode Island, 1675
This basket stands about four and a half inches tall and is four inches in diameter. It is similar to baskets described by English writers in which Indians carried *yoheage*, a parched corn meal, and the shell beads known as wampum.

sheep for wool while others harvested flax, a plant used to make linen. Englishwomen used spinning wheels to make woolen yarn and linen thread, and both men and women operated looms to weave yarn and thread into cloth.

Over time, Native American women incorporated these English materials into their traditional baskets. A few such baskets survive today in museums. For one, the weaver used long strips of bark as the warp, or long thread, which she stitched together with two different "wefts," one of red and blue wool and the second probably from cornhusks (see photo). The basic technique of "twining" the warp and wefts is found in New England baskets dating to a thousand years earlier; the use of wool, however, was new. The basket came into English hands during King Philip's War (1675–1676). A Native woman whose community was at peace with the colonists entered the English garrison town at what is now Cranston, Rhode Island, and asked a woman there for some milk. In return, the Indian woman gave her English benefactor the basket.

The story behind a second twined basket made of bark and wool has been lost. But it is clear that someone worked the wool into this basket after it was originally made. Archaeological evidence suggests that the addition of new materials to existing baskets was not exceptional. One Rhode Island site yielded seventy-three pieces of European cloth among the remains of sixty-six Indian baskets.

Besides incorporating European yarn and thread into familiar objects, Native Americans obtained finished European cloth, especially duffel, a woolen fabric that manufacturers dyed red or blue to suit Indian tastes. European traders furnished Native American customers with cloth as well as iron scissors, needles, and pins for shaping and sewing the cloth. In return, the traders obtained the material from which Indians made their own garments—beaver pelts. In these two-way exchanges of textiles, the English realized profits while Native Americans broadened ties of reciprocity (see Chapter 1) with the colonists.

English colonists and Indians shaped their newly acquired materials to their own tastes. The traders sold the pelts to European hatters, who cut and reworked them into beaver hats, a fashion rage in Europe. Native women used cloth in ways that were just as unfamiliar to Europeans. Mary Rowlandson, an Englishwoman captured by enemy Indians during King Philip's War, wrote a vivid description of what Americans would later call "the Indian fashion." As her captors danced during a ceremony, Rowlandson described the garb of her Narragansett "master" and Wampanoag "mistress":

He was dressed in his holland shirt [a common English shirt], with great laces sewed at the tail of it. His garters were hung round with shillings, and he had girdles of wampum upon his head and shoulders. She had a kersey [coarse wool] coat covered with girdles of wampum from the loins upward. Her arms from her elbows to her hands were covered with bracelets. There were handfuls of necklaces about her neck and several sorts of jewels in her ears. She had fine red stockings and white shoes, [and] her hair [was] powdered and face painted red.

In combining indigenous materials in distinctive styles, the dancers—like Native basket makers and textile artisans—

Ninigret, Niantic Sachem, c. 1684
Ninigret was a powerful sachem who traded with both English and Dutch. His outfit in this portrait artfully combines indigenous and European materials and objects in a way that is unmistakably Native American.

acknowledged the colonists' presence while resisting assimilation to English culture. They affirmed the new, multicultural reality of New England life but defied colonial efforts to suppress their culture and their communities. Once again technological exchange had led people to change without abandoning familiar ways of making things and expressing cultural identity.

Questions for Analysis

- How did Native American women in New England use English materials and techniques to modify traditional ways of making baskets and textiles during the seventeenth century?

- How did the new products Indians made reflect their attitudes about the colonists and about English culture?

Salem Witchcraft, 1691–1693

Nowhere in New England did the conflicts dividing white New Englanders converge more forcefully than in Salem, Massachusetts, the region's second largest port. Trade made Salem prosperous but also destroyed the relatively equal society of first-generation fishermen and farmers. Salem's divisions were especially sharp in the precinct of Salem Village (now Danvers), an economically stagnant district located north of Salem Town. Residents of the village's eastern section farmed richer soils and benefited from Salem Town's commercial expansion, whereas those in the less fertile western half did not share in this prosperity and had lost the political influence that they once held in Salem.

In late 1691 several Salem Village girls encouraged an African slave woman, Tituba, to tell them their fortunes and talk about sorcery. When the girls later began behaving strangely, villagers assumed that they were victims of witchcraft. Pressed to identify their tormenters, the girls named two local white women and Tituba.

So far, the incident was not unusual. Witchcraft beliefs remained strong in seventeenth-century Europe and its colonies. Witches were people (nearly always women) whose pride, envy, discontent, or greed supposedly led them to sign a pact with the devil. Thereafter, they allegedly used *maleficium* (the devil's supernatural power of evil) to torment neighbors and others by causing illness, destroying property, or—as with the girls in Salem Village—inhabiting or "possessing" their victims' bodies and minds. Witnesses usually also claimed that witches displayed aggressive, unfeminine behavior. In most earlier witchcraft accusations in New England, there was only one defendant and the case never went to trial. The few exceptions to this rule were tried with little fanfare. Events in Salem Village, on the other hand, led to a colony-wide panic.

By April 1692, the girls had denounced two locally prominent women and had identified the village's former minister as a wizard (male witch). Fears of witchcraft soon overrode doubts about the girls' credibility and led local judges to sweep aside normal procedural safeguards. Specifically, the judges ignored the law's ban on "spectral evidence"—testimony that a spirit resembling the accused had been seen tormenting a victim. Thereafter, accusations multiplied until the jails overflowed with 342 accused witches.

The pattern of hysteria in Salem Village reflected that community's internal divisions. Most accusations originated in the village's poorer western division, and were directed at wealthier families in the eastern village or in Salem Town (see Map 3.6).

Images of Witchcraft
Most seventeenth-century Europeans and colonists feared that, at any time, Satan and those in his grip (witches) could attack and harm them with the power of evil.

Other patterns were also apparent. Two-thirds of all "possessed" accusers were females aged eleven to twenty, and more than half had lost one or both parents in Anglo-Indian conflicts in Maine. They and other survivors had fled to Massachusetts, where most were now servants in other families' households. These young women gained momentary power and prominence by voicing the anxieties and hostilities of others in their community and by virtually dictating the course of events in and around Salem for several months.

Accusers and witnesses most frequently named as witches middle-aged wives and widows—women who had avoided the poverty and uncertainty they themselves faced. A disproportionate number of accused women had inherited, or stood to inherit, property beyond the one-third of a husband's estate normally bequeathed to

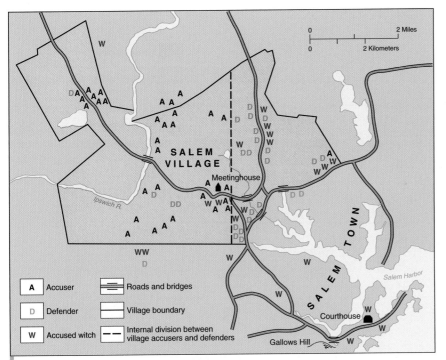

Map 3.6 The Geography of Witchcraft: Salem Village, 1692
Geographic patterns of witchcraft testimony mirrored social-economic tensions within
Salem Village and between the village and Salem Town.
Source: Adapted from Paul Boyer and Stephen Nissenbaum, *Salem Possessed: The Social
Origins of Witchcraft* (Cambridge, Mass.: Harvard University Press, 1974).

widows. In other words, the accused tended to be women
who had or soon might have more economic power and
independence than many men. For New Englanders
who felt the need to limit both female independence
and economic individualism, witches symbolized the
dangers awaiting those who disregarded such limits.

The number of persons facing trial multiplied
quickly. Those found guilty desperately tried to stave off
death by implicating others. As the pandemonium
spread beyond Salem, fear dissolved ties of friendship
and family. A minister heard himself condemned by his
own granddaughter. A seven-year-old girl helped send
her mother to the gallows. Fifty persons saved themselves by confessing. Twenty others who refused to disgrace their own names or betray other innocents went to
their graves. Shortly before she was hanged, a victim
named Mary Easty begged the court to come to its
senses: "I petition your honors not for my own life, for I
know I must die . . . [but] if it be possible, that no more
innocent blood be shed."

By late 1692, most Massachusetts ministers came to
doubt that justice was being done. They objected that
spectral evidence, crucial in most convictions, lacked
legal credibility because the devil could manipulate

it. New Englanders, concluded Increase Mather, a leading clergyman,
had fallen victim to a deadly game
of "blind man's bluff" set up by
Satan and were "hotly and madly,
mauling one another in the dark."
Backed by the clergy (and alarmed
by an accusation against his wife),
Governor William Phips forbade
further imprisonments for witchcraft in October—by which time
over a hundred individuals were in
jail and twice that many stood accused. Shortly thereafter, he suspended all trials, and in early 1693
he pardoned all those convicted or
suspected of witchcraft.

The witchcraft hysteria marked
the end of Puritan New England.
Colonists reaching maturity after
1692 would reject the ideals of earlier
generations and become "Yankees"
who shrewdly pursued material gain.
True to their Puritan roots, they would
retain their forceful convictions and
self-discipline, giving New England
a distinctive regional identity that
would endure.

The Spread of Slavery: The Caribbean and Carolina

As the Chesapeake and New England flourished, an
even larger wave of settlement swept the West Indies
(see Maps 3.1 and 3.7). Between 1630 and 1642, almost
60 percent of the seventy thousand English who emi-
grated to the Americas went to the Caribbean. Beginning
in the 1640s, some English planters began using slave
labor to produce sugar on large plantations. After 1670,
many English islanders moved to the new mainland
colony of Carolina, thereby facilitating the spread of large-
scale plantation slavery to the North American mainland.

Sugar and Slaves: The West Indies

As on the North American mainland, the Netherlands,
France, and England entered the colonial race in the West
Indies during the early seventeenth century and expanded thereafter. Challenging Spain's monopoly in the
region, each nation seized islands in the region. Most notably, the Dutch took over Curaçao, the French claimed

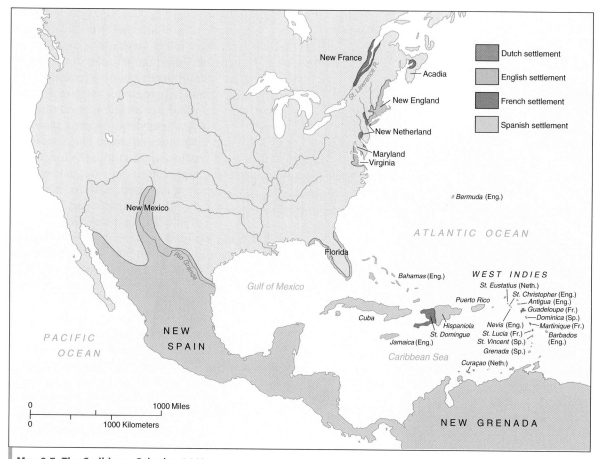

Map 3.7 The Caribbean Colonies, 1660
By 1660 nearly every West Indian island had been colonized by Europeans and was producing sugar with slave labor.

St. Domingue, the western half of Hispaniola, and the English established Barbados and seized Jamaica from Spain.

The tobacco boom that powered Virginia's economy until 1630 led early English settlers to cultivate that plant in the Caribbean. But with most colonists arriving after 1630, few realized spectacular profits. Through the 1630s, the English West Indies remained a society with a large percentage of independent landowners, an overwhelmingly white population, and a relative equality of wealth.

During the early 1640s an alternative to tobacco rapidly revolutionized the islands' economy and society. Dutch merchants familiar with Portuguese methods of sugar production in Brazil began encouraging West Indian planters to raise and process sugar cane, which the Dutch would then market (see Technology and Culture, Chapter 2).

Because planters needed three times as many workers per acre to produce sugar as tobacco, rising production greatly multiplied the demand for labor. As in the Chesapeake, planters in the English West Indies initially imported white indentured servants. After 1640, however, sugar planters increasingly purchased enslaved Africans from Dutch traders to do common fieldwork and used their indentured servants as overseers or skilled artisans.

Sugar planters preferred black slaves to white servants because slaves could be driven harder and cost less to maintain. Whereas most servants ended their indentures after four years, slaves toiled until death. Although slaves initially cost two to four times more than servants, they proved a more economical long-term investment. In this way, the profit motive and the racism that emerged with the "new slavery" (see Chapter 2) reinforced one another.

By 1670, the sugar revolution had transformed the British West Indies into a predominantly slave society. Thereafter the number of blacks shot up from approximately 40,000 to 130,000 in 1713. Meanwhile, the white population remained stable at about 33,000 because the planters' preference for slave labor greatly reduced the importation of indentured servants after 1670.

Three victorious wars with the Dutch and enactment of the Navigation Acts (see Chapter 4) enabled English merchants and shippers to monopolize the trade in sugar and slaves (and other commodities) of England's colonies. The profits from its Caribbean colonies were a principal factor in England's becoming the wealthiest nation in the Atlantic world by 1700.

Declining demand for white labor in the West Indies diverted the flow of English immigration from the islands to mainland North America and so contributed to population growth there. Furthermore, because the expansion of West Indian sugar plantations priced land beyond the reach of most whites, perhaps thirty thousand people left the islands from 1655 to 1700. Most whites who quit the West Indies migrated to the mainland colonies, especially Carolina.

Rice and Slaves: Carolina

In 1663, King Charles II bestowed the swampy coast between Virginia and Spanish Florida on several English supporters, making it the first of several Restoration colonies. The grateful proprietors named their colony Carolina in honor of Charles (*Carolus* in Latin).

One of the proprietors, Anthony Ashley Cooper, and his young secretary, John Locke—later acclaimed as one of the great philosophers of the age (see Chapter 4)—drew up a plan for Carolina's settlement and government. Their Fundamental Constitutions provided for a three-tiered nobility that would hold two-fifths of all land, make laws through a Council of Nobles, and dispense justice through manorial law courts. Ordinary Carolinians with smaller landholdings were expected to defer to this nobility, although they would enjoy religious toleration and English common law, and could elect an assembly. To induce settlement, the proprietors offered a headright of one hundred fifty acres to planters for each arriving family member or slave as well as one hundred acres to each servant who completed a term of indenture.

Uninterested in moving themselves, the proprietors arranged for settlers from the West Indian island of Barbados, where the largest sugar planters had bought up most of the land, to get their colony started. Accordingly, in 1670, two hundred white Barbadians and their slaves landed near modern-day Charleston, "in the very chops of the Spanish." The settlement called Charles Town formed the colony's nucleus.

Until the 1680s, most settlers were from Barbados, with smaller numbers from mainland colonies and some French Huguenots. Obtaining all the land they needed, the colonists saw little reason to obey absentee lords and ignored most of the plans drawn up for them across the Atlantic. Southern Carolinians raised livestock and exported Indian slaves (see below), while colonists in northern Carolina produced tobacco, lumber, and pitch, giving local people the name "tarheels." At first these activities did not produce enough profit to warrant maintaining many slaves, so self-sufficient white families predominated in the area.

Map of Barbados, c. 1650
Drawn only a decade after the introduction of sugar planting and slave labor in Barbados, this English map shows how far the new economy and society had already spread.

But some southern Carolinians, particularly wealthier settlers from Barbados, sought a staple crop that could make them rich. By the early eighteenth century, they found it in rice. Because rice, like sugar, enormously enriched a few men with capital to invest in costly dams, dikes, and slaves, it remade southern Carolina into a society resembling the one from which they came. By earning annual profits of 25 percent, rice planters within a generation became the one mainland colonial elite whose wealth rivaled that of the Caribbean sugar planters.

Even when treated humanely, indentured English servants simply did not survive in humid rice paddies swarming with malaria-bearing mosquitoes. The planters' solution was to import an ever-growing force of enslaved Africans who, they calculated, possessed two major advantages. First, perhaps 15 percent of the Africans taken to Carolina had cultivated rice in their homelands in Senegambia, and their expertise was vital in teaching whites how to raise the unfamiliar crop. Second, many Africans had developed immunities to malaria and yellow fever, infectious and deadly diseases transmitted by mosquito bites, which were endemic to coastal regions of West Africa. Enslaved Africans, along with infected slave ships' crews, carried both diseases to North America. (Tragically, the antibody that helps ward off malaria also tends to produce the sickle-cell trait, a genetic condition often fatal to the children who inherit it.) These two advantages made commercial rice production possible in Carolina. Because a typical rice planter farming 130 acres needed sixty-five slaves, a great demand for black slave labor resulted. The proportion of slaves in southern Carolina's population rose from just 17 percent in 1680 to about half by 1700. Thereafter, Carolina would have a black majority.

Rice thrived only within a forty-mile-wide coastal strip extending from Cape Fear to present-day Georgia. Carolinians grimly joked that the malaria-infested rice belt was a paradise in spring, an inferno in summer, and a hospital in the wet, chilly fall. In the worst months, planters' families usually escaped to the relatively cool and more healthful climate of Charles Town and let overseers supervise their slaves during harvests.

Enslavement in Carolina was by no means confined to Africans. In the 1670s, traders in southern Carolina armed nearby Native Americans and encouraged them to raid rival tribes for slaves. After local supplies of Indian slaves were exhausted, the English-allied Indians captured unarmed Guale, Apalachee, and Timucua Indians at Spanish missions in Florida and traded them to the Carolinians for guns and other European goods. The English in turn sold the enslaved Indians, mostly to planters in the West Indies but also in the mainland colonies as far north as New England. By the mid-1680s, the Carolinians had extended the trade through alliances with the Yamasees and the Creeks, a powerful confederacy centered in what is now western Georgia and northern Alabama. For three decades, these Indian allies of the English terrorized Catholic mission Indians in Spanish Florida with their slave raids. No statistical records of Carolina's Indian slave trade survive, but the most recent study estimates that thirty to fifty thousand Native Americans were enslaved between 1670 and 1715. Most of those shipped to the West Indies died quickly because they lacked immunities to both European and tropical diseases.

The Middle Colonies

Between the Chesapeake and New England, two non-English nations established colonies (see Map 3.8). New Netherland and New Sweden were small commercial outposts, although the Dutch colony eventually flourished and took over New Sweden. But England seized New Netherland from the Dutch in 1664, and carved New York, New Jersey, and Pennsylvania out of the former Dutch territory. These actions together created a fourth English colonial region, the middle colonies.

Precursors: New Netherland and New Sweden

New Netherland was North America's first multiethnic colony. Barely half its colonists were Dutch; most of the rest were Germans, French, Scandinavians, and Africans, free as well as enslaved. In 1643, the population included Protestants, Catholics, Jews, and Muslims; and eighteen European and African languages were spoken. But religion counted for little (in 1642 the colony had seventeen taverns but not one place of worship), and the colonists' get-rich-quick attitude had fostered New Amsterdam's growth as a thriving port. The same attitude sapped company profits as private individuals persisted in illegally trading furs. In 1639, the company bowed to mounting pressure and legalized private fur trading.

Privatization led to a rapid rise in the number of guns reaching New Netherland's Iroquois allies, giving them a distinct advantage over rival Natives. As overhunting depleted local supplies of beaver skins and as smallpox epidemics took their toll, the Iroquois encroached on pro-French Indians in a quest for pelts and for captives who could be adopted into Iroquois families to replace the dead. Between 1648 and 1657, the Iroquois, in a series of bloody **"beaver wars,"** dispersed the Hurons and other French allies, incorporating many members of these nations into their own ranks. Then they attacked

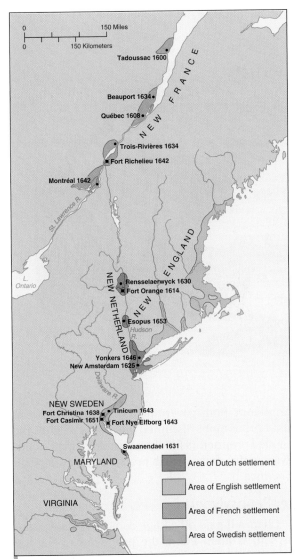

**Map 3.8 European Colonization in the Middle and
North Atlantic, c. 1650**
North of Spanish Florida, four European powers competed
for territory and trade with Native Americans in the early
seventeenth century. Swedish and Dutch colonization was
the foundation upon which England's middle colonies
were built.

Indians who were protesting settler encroachments on
Long Island. By 1645, the Dutch prevailed over these Indians and their allies only with English help and by inflicting additional atrocities. But the fighting, known as
Kieft's War for the governor who ordered the massacre,
helped reduce New Netherland's Indian population
from sixteen hundred to seven hundred.

Another European challenger distracted the Dutch as
they sought to suppress neighboring Native Americans.
In 1638, Sweden had planted a small fur-trading colony
in the lower Delaware Valley. Trading with the Delaware
(or Lenni Lenape) and Susquehannock Indians, New
Sweden diverted many furs from New Netherland. An-
noyed, the Dutch colony's governor, Peter Stuyvesant,
led seven warships and three hundred troops into New
Sweden in 1655. The four hundred residents of the rival
colony peacefully accepted Dutch annexation.

Tiny though they were, the Dutch and Swedish
colonies were historically significant. New Netherland
had attained a population of nine thousand and featured a wealthy, thriving port city by the time it came
under English rule in 1664. Even short-lived New Sweden
left a mark—the log cabin, that durable symbol of the
American frontier, which Finnish settlers in the Swedish
colony first introduced to the continent. Above all, the
two colonies bequeathed a social environment characterized by ethnic and religious diversity that would continue in England's middle colonies.

English Conquests: New York and New Jersey

Like Carolina, New York and New Jersey originated as proprietary colonies, awarded by King Charles II to favored
upper-class supporters. Here, too, proprietors hoped to
create hierarchical societies in which they would profit
from settlers' rents. These plans failed in New Jersey, as in
Carolina. Only in New York did they achieve some success.

In 1664, waging war against the Dutch Republic, Charles
II dispatched a naval force to conquer New Netherland. Weakened by additional wars with Indians as New Netherland sought to expand northward on the Hudson River,
Dutch governor Peter Stuyvesant and four hundred poorly
armed civilians surrendered peacefully. Most of the Dutch
remained in the colony on generous terms.

Charles II made his brother James, Duke of York, proprietor of the new province and renamed it New York.
When the duke became King James II in 1685, he proclaimed New York a royal colony. Immigration from New
England, Britain, and France boosted the population
from nine thousand in 1664 to twenty thousand in 1700,
of whom just 44 percent were of Dutch descent.

Following Dutch precedent, New York's governors rewarded their wealthiest political supporters, both Dutch

the French settlements along the St. Lawrence. "They
come like foxes, they attack like lions, they disappear like
birds," wrote a French Jesuit of the Iroquois.

Although the Dutch allied successfully with the inland Iroquois, their relations with nearby coastal Native
Americans paralleled white-Indian relations in England's seaboard colonies. With its greedy settlers and
military weakness, New Netherland had largely itself to
blame. In 1643, all-out war erupted when the colony's
governor ordered the massacre of previously friendly

Dutch Couple at New Amsterdam
Dutch wealth and enslaved African labor contributed to New Amsterdam's early prosperity.

and English, with large land grants. By 1703, five families held approximately 1.75 million acres in the Hudson River Valley (see Map 3.9), which they withheld from sale in hope of creating manors with numerous rent-paying tenants. Earning an enormous income from their rents over the next half-century, the New York **patroons** (the Dutch name for manor lords) formed a landed elite second in wealth only to the Carolina rice planters.

Ambitious plans collided with American realities in New Jersey, which also was carved out of New Netherland. Immediately after the Dutch province's conquest in 1664, the Duke of York awarded New Jersey to a group of proprietors headed by William Penn, John Lord Berkeley, and Sir Philip Carteret. About four thousand Delaware Indians and a few hundred Dutch and Swedes inhabited the area at the time. From the beginning New Jersey's proprietors had difficulty controlling their province. By 1672, several thousand New Englanders had settled along the Atlantic shore. After the quarrelsome Puritans renounced allegiance to them, Berkeley and Carteret sold the region to a group of even more contentious religious dissenters called Quakers, who split the territory into the two colonies of West Jersey (1676) and East Jersey (1682).

The Jerseys' Quakers, Anglicans, Puritans, Scottish Presbyterians, Dutch Calvinists, and Swedish Lutherans got along poorly with one another and even worse with the proprietors. Both governments collapsed between 1698 and 1701 as mobs disrupted the courts. In 1702, the disillusioned proprietors finally surrendered their political powers to the crown, which proclaimed New Jersey a royal province.

Quaker Pennsylvania

In 1681 Charles II paid off a huge debt by making a supporter's son, **William Penn**, the proprietor of the last unallocated tract of American territory at the king's disposal. Perhaps the most distinctive of all English colonial founders, Penn (1644–1718) had two aims in developing Pennsylvania (Penn's Woods). First, he was a Quaker and wanted to launch a "holy experiment" based on the teachings of the radical English preacher George Fox. Second, "though I desire to extend religious freedom," he explained, "yet I want some recompense for my trouble."

Quakers in late-seventeenth-century England stood well beyond the fringe of respectability. Quakerism appealed strongly to men and women at the bottom of the economic ladder, and its adherents challenged the conventional foundation of the social order. George Fox, the movement's originator, had received his inspiration while wandering civil war–torn England's byways and searching for spiritual meaning among distressed common people. Tried on one occasion for blasphemy, he warned the judge to "tremble at

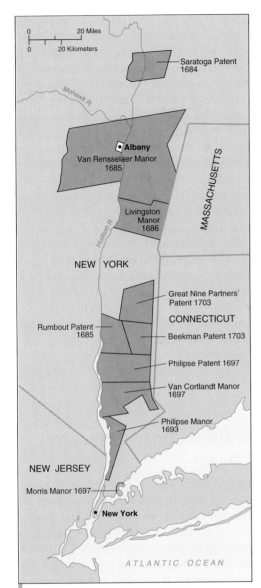

Map 3.9 New York Manors and Land Grants
Between 1684 and 1703, English governors
awarded most of the best land east of the
Hudson River as manors to prominent supporters, thereby closing it off to ordinary settlers
seeking land of their own.

revealed. Although trusting direct inspiration and disavow-
ing the need for a clergy, Friends also took great pains to ensure that individual opinions would not be mistaken for
God's will. They felt confident that they understood the
Inner Light only after having reached near-unanimous
agreement through intensive and searching discussion led
by "Public Friends"—ordinary laypeople. In their simple religious services ("meetings"), Quakers sat silently until the
Inner Light prompted one of them to speak.

Some of the Friends' beliefs led them to behave in
ways that aroused fierce hostility for being disrespectful
to authorities and their social superiors. For example, insisting that individuals deserved recognition for their
spiritual state rather than their wealth or status, Quakers
refused to tip their hats to their social betters. They likewise flouted convention by not using the formal pronoun
"you" when speaking to members of the gentry, instead
addressing everyone with the informal "thee" and "thou"
as a token of equality. By wearing their hats in court,
moreover, Quakers appeared to mock the state's authority; and by taking literally Scripture's ban on swearing
oaths, they seemed to place themselves above the law.
The Friends' refusal to bear arms appeared unpatriotic
and cowardly to many. Finally, Quakers accorded women
unprecedented equality. The Inner Light, Fox insisted,
could "speak in the female as well as the male." Acting on
these beliefs, Quakers suffered persecution and occasionally death in England, Massachusetts, and Virginia.

Not all Quakers came from the bottom of society. The
movement's emphasis on quiet introspection and its refusal to adopt a formal creed also attracted some well-
educated and prosperous individuals disillusioned by the
quarreling of rival faiths. The possessor of a great fortune,
William Penn was hardly a typical Friend, but there were
significant numbers of merchants among the estimated
sixty thousand Quakers in the British Isles in the early
1680s. Moreover, the industriousness that the Society of
Friends encouraged in its members ensured that many
humble Quakers accumulated money and property.

Much care lay behind the Quaker migration to Pennsylvania that began in 1681, and it resulted in the most
successful beginning of any European colony in North
America. Penn sent an advance party to the Delaware Valley, where about five thousand Delaware Indians and one
thousand Swedes and Dutch already lived. After an agonizing voyage in which one-third of the passengers died,
Penn arrived in 1682. Choosing a site for the capital, he
named it Philadelphia—the "City of Brotherly Love." By
1687, some eight thousand settlers had joined Penn across
the Atlantic. Most were Quakers from the British Isles, but
they also included Presbyterians, Baptists, Anglicans, and
Catholics, as well as Lutherans and radical sectarians from

the word of the Lord" and was ridiculed as a "quaker."
Fox's followers called themselves the Society of
Friends, but the name Quaker stuck. They were the
most successful of the many radical religious sects
born in England during the 1640s and 1650s.

The core of Fox's theology was his belief that the Holy
Spirit or "Inner Light" could inspire every soul. Mainstream
Christians, by contrast, found any such claim of direct, per-
sonal communication with God highly dangerous, as Anne
Hutchinson's banishment from Massachusetts Bay in 1637

Germany—most of them attracted by Pennsylvania's religious toleration as well as its economic promise. As in New England, most immigrants arrived in family groups rather than as single males, so that the population grew rapidly. In 1698, one Quaker reported that in Pennsylvania one seldom met "any young Married Woman but hath a Child in her belly, or one upon her lap."

After wavering between authoritarian and more democratic plans, Penn finally gave Pennsylvania a government with a strong executive branch (a governor and governor's council) and granted the lower legislative chamber (the assembly) only limited powers. Friends, forming the majority of the colony's population, dominated this elected assembly. Penn named Quakers and their supporters as governor, judges, and sheriffs. Like most elites of the time, he feared "the ambitions of the populace which shakes the Constitution," and he intended to check "the rabble" as much as possible. Because he also insisted on the orderly disposition of property and hoped to avoid unseemly wrangling, he carefully oversaw land sales in the colony. To prevent haphazard growth and social turmoil in Philadelphia, Penn designed the city with a grid plan, laying out the streets at right angles and reserving small areas for parks.

Unlike most seaboard colonies, Pennsylvania avoided early hostilities with Native Americans. This was partly a result of the reduced Native population in the Delaware Valley. But it was also a testament to Penn's Quaker tolerance. To the Delaware Indians Penn expressed a wish "to live together as Neighbours and Friends," and he made it the colony's policy to buy land it wanted for settlement from them.

Land was a key to Pennsylvania's early prosperity. Rich, level lands and a lengthy growing season enabled immigrants to produce bumper crops. West Indian demand for the colony's grain rose sharply and by 1700 made Philadelphia a major port.

Like other attempts to base new American societies on preconceived plans or lofty ideals, Penn's "peaceable kingdom" soon bogged down in human bickering. After the founder returned to England in 1684, the settlers quarreled incessantly. An opposition party attacked Penn's efforts to monopolize foreign trade and to make each landowner pay him a small annual fee. Bitter struggles between Penn's supporters in the governor's council and opponents in the assembly deadlocked the government. From 1686 to 1688, the legislature passed no laws, and the council once ordered the lower house's speaker arrested. Penn's brief return to Pennsylvania from 1699 to 1701 helped little. Just before he sailed home, he made the legislature a unicameral (one-chamber) assembly and allowed it to initiate measures.

Religious conflict shook Pennsylvania during the 1690s, when George Keith, a college-educated Public Friend, urged Quakers to adopt a formal creed and train ministers. This would have changed the democratically functioning Quaker movement—in which the humblest member had equal authority in interpreting the Inner Light—into a hierarchical church dominated by a clergy. The majority of Friends rejected Keith's views in 1692, whereupon he joined the Church of England, taking some Quakers with him. Keith's departure began a major decline in the Quaker share of Pennsylvania's population. The proportion fell further once Quakers ceased immigrating in large numbers after 1710.

William Penn met his strongest opposition in the counties on the lower Delaware River, where Swedes and Dutch had taken up the best lands. In 1704, these counties became the separate colony of Delaware, but Penn continued to name their governors.

The middle colonies demonstrated that British America could benefit by encouraging religious toleration and ethnic pluralism. New York and New Jersey successfully integrated New Netherland's Swedish and Dutch population; and neither Pennsylvania, New Jersey, nor Delaware required taxpayers to support an established church.

Rivals for North America: France and Spain

In marked contrast to England's compact, densely populated settlements on the Atlantic, France and Spain established far-flung inland networks of fortified trading posts and missions. Unable to attract large numbers of colonists, they enlisted Native Americans as trading partners and military allies, and the two Catholic nations had far more success than English Protestants in converting Indians to Christianity. By 1700, French and Spanish missionaries, traders, and soldiers—and relatively few farmers and ranchers—were spreading European influence well beyond the range of England's colonies, to much of Canada and to what is now the American Midwest, Southeast, and Southwest.

France Claims a Continent

After briefly losing Canada to England (1629–1632), France resumed and extended its colonization there. Paralleling the early English and Dutch colonies, a privately held company initially assumed responsibility for settling New France. The Company of New France granted extensive tracts, called *seigneuries*, to large landlords (*seigneurs*), who could either import indentured servants or rent out small tracts within their holdings to prospective farmers. Although some farmers and other colonists spread along the St. Lawrence River as far inland as Montreal (see Map 3.8), Canada's harsh winters and short growing season sharply limited their numbers.

More successful in New France were commercial traders and missionaries who spread beyond the settlements and relied on stable relations with Indians to succeed. Despite the defeat of some of France's Native American allies in the beaver wars (see above), French-Indian trade prospered. Indeed, the more lucrative opportunities offered by trade diverted many French men who had initially arrived to take up farming.

The colony also benefited from the substantial efforts of Catholic religious workers, especially Jesuit missionaries and Ursuline nuns. Given a virtual monopoly on missions to Native Americans in 1633, the Jesuits followed the fur trade into the North American interior. Although the missionaries often feuded with the traders, whose morality they condemned, the two groups together spread French influence westward to the Great Lakes, securing the loyalty of the region's Indians in their struggles with the Iroquois. The Ursulines ministered particularly to Native American women and girls nearer Quebec, ensuring that Catholic piety and morality directly reached all members of Indian families.

The chief minister of France's King Louis XIV (reigned 1661–1715), Jean-Baptiste Colbert, was a forceful proponent of the doctrine of mercantilism (see Chapter 4), which held that colonies should provide their home country with raw materials for manufacturing and markets for manufactured goods. Ideally, the nation would not have to depend on rival countries for trade. Accordingly, Colbert hoped that New France could increase its output of furs, ship agricultural surpluses to France's new sugar-producing colonies in the West Indies, and export timber to those colonies and for the French navy. To begin realizing these goals, France revoked the charter of the Company of New France in 1663 and placed the colony under royal direction.

With the colony under its direct control, the French government sought to stifle the Iroquois threat to New France's economy. For more than half a century, and especially since the beaver wars, the Iroquois had limited New France's productivity by intercepting convoys of beaver pelts from the interior and taking them to Dutch merchants in New Netherland. (The Dutch maintained their ties to the Iroquois after the English takeover in 1664.) In 1666, France sent fifteen hundred soldiers to stop Iroquois interference with the fur trade. In that year, the troops sacked and burned four Mohawk villages that were well stocked with winter food. After the alarmed Iroquois made a peace that lasted until 1680, New France enormously expanded its North American fur exports.

Meanwhile, Colbert encouraged French immigration to Canada. Within a decade of the royal takeover, the number of whites rose from twenty-five hundred to eighty-five hundred. The vast majority consisted of indentured servants who were paid wages and given land after three years' work. Others were former soldiers and their officers who were given land grants and other incentives to remain in New France and farm while strengthening the colony's defenses. The officers were encouraged to marry among the "king's girls," female orphans shipped over with dowries.

The upsurge in French immigration petered out after 1673. Tales of disease and other hazards of the transatlantic voyage, of Canada's hard winters, and of wars with the "savage" Iroquois were spread by the two-thirds of French immigrants who returned to their native land. New France would grow slowly, relying on the natural increase of its small population rather than on newcomers from Europe.

Colbert had encouraged immigration in order to enhance New France's agricultural productivity. But as in earlier years, many French men who remained spurned farming in the St. Lawrence Valley, instead swarming westward in search of furs. By 1670, one-fifth of them were *voyageurs*, or *coureurs de bois*—independent traders unconstrained by government authority. Living in Indian villages and often marrying Native women, the *coureurs* built an empire for France. From Canadian and Great Lakes Indians they obtained furs in exchange for European goods, including guns to use against the Iroquois and other rivals. In their commercial interactions, the French and Indians observed Native American norms of reciprocity (see Chapter 1). Their exchanges of goods sealed bonds of friendship and alliance, which served their mutual interests in trade and in war against common enemies.

Alarmed by the rapid expansion of England's colonies and by Spanish plans to link Florida with New Mexico (see below), France boldly sought to dominate the North American heartland. As early as 1672, fur trader Louis Jolliet and Jesuit missionary Jacques Marquette became the first Europeans known to have reached the upper Mississippi River (near modern Prairie du Chien, Wisconsin); they later paddled twelve hundred miles downstream to the Mississippi's junction with the Arkansas River. Ten years later, **Robert Cavelier de La Salle**, an ambitious upper-class adventurer, descended the entire Mississippi to the Gulf of Mexico. When he reached the delta, La Salle formally claimed the entire Mississippi basin—half the territory of the present-day continental United States—for Louis XIV, in whose honor he named the territory Louisiana.

Having asserted title to this vast empire, the French began settling the southern gateway into it. In 1698, the first colonizers arrived on the Gulf of Mexico coast. A year

View of Quebec, 1699
New France's modest prosperity was built on its rising commercial economy and its close ties to Native Americans.

later the French erected a fort near present-day Biloxi, Mississippi. In 1702, they occupied the former Mississippian city of Mábila, where De Soto's expedition had faltered a century and a half earlier (see Chapter 2), founding a trading post, and calling it Mobile. But Louisiana's growth would stall for another decade.

New Mexico: The Pueblo Revolt

Spanish colonization in North America after 1625 expanded upon the two bases established earlier in New Mexico and Florida (see Chapter 2). Lying at the northerly margin of Spain's empire, both colonies remained small and weak through the seventeenth century. With few settlers, they needed ties with friendly Native Americans in order to obtain land, labor, and security. But Spanish policies made friendly relations hard to come by in both places.

From the beginning, the Spanish sought to rule New Mexico by subordinating the Pueblo Indians to their

authority in several ways. First, Franciscan missionaries supervised the Indians' spiritual lives by establishing churches in most of the Indian communities (pueblos) and attempting to force the natives to attend mass and observe Catholic rituals and morality. Second, Spanish landowners were awarded *encomiendas* (see Chapter 2), which allowed them to exploit Indian labor and productivity for personal profits. Finally, the Spanish drove a wedge between the Pueblo Indians and their nonfarming neighbors, the Apaches and Navajos. Because the Spanish collected corn as tribute, the Pueblo Indians could no longer trade their surplus crops with the Apaches and Navajos. Having incorporated corn into their diets, the Apaches and Navajos raided the pueblos for the grain. They also raided the colonists to retaliate for Spanish slave traders having captured and sold some of their people to work in Mexican silver mines. A few outlying pueblos made common cause with the Apaches, but most Pueblo Indians relied on the Spanish for protection from the raids.

Although local rebellions erupted sporadically over the first six decades of Spanish rule, most Pueblo Indians initially accepted Spanish rule and tried to reconcile Catholicism with their own religious traditions. Beginning in the 1660s, however, many Natives grew disillusioned. For several consecutive years their crops withered under the effects of sustained drought. Drought-induced starvation plus deadly epidemic diseases sent the Pueblo population plummeting from about eighty thousand in 1598 to just seventeen thousand in the 1670s. In response, many Christian Indians openly resumed traditional Pueblo ceremonies, hoping to restore the spiritual balance that had brought ample rainfall, good health, and peace before the Spanish arrived. Seeking to suppress this religious revival as "witchcraft" and "idolatry," the Franciscan missionaries entered sacred kivas (underground ceremonial centers), destroyed religious objects, and publicly whipped Native religious leaders and their followers.

Matters came to a head in 1675 when Governor Juan Francisco Treviño ordered soldiers to sack the kivas and arrest Pueblo religious leaders. Three leaders were sentenced to the gallows; a fourth hanged himself; and forty-three others were jailed, whipped, and sold as slaves. In response, armed warriors from several pueblos converged on Santa Fe and demanded the prisoners' release. With most of his soldiers off fighting the Apaches, Governor Treviño complied.

Despite this concession, there was now no cooling of Pueblo resentment against the Spanish. Pueblo leaders began gathering secretly to plan the overthrow of Spanish rule. At the head of this effort was Popé, one of those who had been arrested in 1675. Besides Popé and one El Saca, the leaders included men such as Luis Tupatú, Antonio Malacate, and others whose Christian names signified that they had once been baptized. They and many of their followers had attempted to reconcile conversion to Christianity and subjection to Spanish rule with their identities as Indians. But deteriorating conditions and the cruel intolerance of the Spanish had turned them against Catholicism.

In August 1680 Popé and his cohorts were ready to act. On the morning of August 10, some Indians from the pueblo of Taos and their Apache allies attacked the homes of the seventy Spanish colonists residing near Taos and killed all but two. Then, with Indians from neighboring pueblos, they proceeded south and joined a massive siege of New Mexico's capital, Santa Fe. Thus began the **Pueblo Revolt** of 1680, the most successful Indian uprising in American history.

At each pueblo, rebels destroyed the churches and religious paraphernalia and killed those missionaries who did not escape. All told, about four hundred colonists were slain. Then they "plunge[d] into the rivers and wash[ed] themselves with amole," a native root, in order to undo their baptisms. As a follower later testified, Popé also called on the Indians "to break and enlarge their cultivated fields, saying now they were as they had been in ancient times, free from the labor they had performed for the religious and the Spaniards."

The siege of Santa Fe led to the expulsion of the Spanish from New Mexico for twelve years. Only in 1692 did a new governor, Diego de Vargas, arrive to "reconquer" New Mexico. Exploiting divisions that had emerged among the Pueblos in the colonists' absence, Vargas used violence and threats of violence to reestablish Spanish rule. Even then, Spain did not effectively quash Pueblo resistance until 1700, and thereafter its control of the province was more limited than before. To appease the Pueblos, on whom they depended for defense against the Apaches and other Indians, Spanish authorities abolished the hated *encomienda*. They also ordered the Franciscans not to disturb the Pueblos in their traditional religious practices and to cease inflicting corporal punishment on the Indians.

Pueblos' suspicions of the Spanish lingered after 1700, but they did not again attempt to overthrow them. With the missions and *encomienda* less intrusive, they sustained their cultural identities within, rather than outside, the bounds of colonial rule.

Florida and Texas

The Spanish fared no better in Florida, an even older colony than New Mexico. For most of the seventeenth century, Florida's colonial population numbered only in the hundreds, primarily Spanish soldiers and Franciscan missionaries. Before 1680, the colony faced periodic rebellions from Guale, Timucua, and Apalachee Indians protesting forced labor and Franciscan attempts to impose religious conformity. Thereafter Creek and other Indian slave raiders allied to the English in Carolina added to the Florida Indians' miseries. While the Spanish, with their small numbers of soldiers and arms looked on helplessly, the invading Indians killed and captured thousands of Florida's Natives and sold them to English slave traders in Carolina (see above). Even before a new round of warfare erupted in Europe at the turn of the century, Spain was ill prepared to defend its beleaguered North American colonies.

English expansion threatened Florida, while the French establishment of Louisiana defied Spain's hope of one day linking that colony with New Mexico. To counter the French, Spanish authorities in Mexico proclaimed the province of Texas (Tejas) in 1691. But no permanent Spanish settlements appeared there until 1716 (see Chapter 4).

Diego de Vargas
As the newly appointed governor of New Mexico, Vargas led Spain's reoccupation of New Mexico, beginning in 1692.

Chronology, 1625–1700

1629	Massachusetts Bay colony founded.
1630–1642	"Great Migration" to New England.
1633	First English settlements in Connecticut.
1634	Lord Baltimore establishes Maryland.
1636	Roger Williams founds Providence. Harvard College established.
1636–1637	Antinomian crisis in Massachusetts Bay.
1637	Pequot War in Connecticut.
1638	New Sweden established.
1642–1649	English Civil War.
1643–1645	Kieft's War in New Netherland.
1644–1646	Third Anglo-Powhatan War in Virginia.
1647	Rhode Island established.
1648–1657	Iroquois "beaver wars."
1649	Maryland's Act for Religious Toleration. King Charles I executed in England.
1655	New Netherland annexes New Sweden.
1660	Restoration in England; Charles II crowned king.
1661	Maryland defines slavery as a lifelong, inheritable racial status.
1662	Halfway Covenant debated in New England.
1664	English conquer New Netherland; establish New York and New Jersey.
1670	Charles Town, Carolina, founded. Virginia defines slavery as a lifelong, inheritable racial status.
1675–1676	King Philip's War in New England.
1676	Bacon's Rebellion in Virginia.
1680	Pueblo Revolt begins in New Mexico.
1681	William Penn founds Pennsylvania.
1682	La Salle claims Louisiana for France.
1690s	End of Royal African Company's monopoly on English slave trade.
1691	Spain establishes Texas.
1692–1700	Spain "reconquers" New Mexico.
1692–1693	Salem witchcraft trials.
1698	First French settlements in Louisiana.

Conclusion

In less than a century, from 1625 to 1700, the movements of peoples and goods, across the Atlantic and within the continent, transformed the map of North America. Immigrants and slaves spread far and wide among colonial regions in the Americas. Depending on their circumstances, Native Americans resisted or accommodated the newcomers.

The English colonies were by far the most populous. By 1700 the combined number of whites and blacks in England's mainland North American colonies was about 250,000, compared with 15,000 for those of France and 4,500 for those of Spain.

Within the English colonies, four distinct regions emerged. After beginning with a labor force

Key Terms

royal colony	Anne Hutchinson
proprietary colony	Restoration
Lord Baltimore	Pequot War
Act for Religious Toleration	King Philip's War
Third Anglo-Powhatan War	beaver wars
Bacon's Rebellion	patroons
John Winthrop	William Penn
"A Model of Christian Charity"	Quakers
"New England Way"	Robert Cavelier de la Salle
Roger Williams	Pueblo Revolt

consisting primarily of white indentured servants, the tobacco planters of the Chesapeake region replaced them with enslaved Africans. New England's Puritanism grew less utopian and more worldly as the inhabitants gradually reconciled their religious views with the realities of a commercial economy. Slavery had been instituted among the English by sugar planters in the West Indies, some of whom introduced it in the third North American region, Carolina. Between the Chesapeake and New England, a fourth region, the middle colonies, continued the ethnic pluralism and religious toleration of their Swedish and Dutch predecessors. Middle colonists, including the Quakers, embraced the market economy with far less hesitation than their Puritan neighbors in New England. While planters or merchants rose to prominence in each English region, most whites continued to live on family farms.

With far fewer colonists, French and Spanish colonists depended more on friendly relations with Native Americans for their livelihoods and security than did the English. Before 1700 most French North Americans lived in the St. Lawrence Valley, where a lively commercial-agrarian economy was emerging, though on a far smaller scale than in New England and the middle colonies. Most Spanish colonists not connected to the government, military, or a missionary order resided in the Rio Grande valley in New Mexico. But smaller numbers and geographic isolation would prevent the Southwest from becoming a major center of colonization.

By 1700 there were clear differences between the societies and economies of the three colonial powers in North America. These differences would prove decisive in shaping American history during the century that followed.

For Further Reference

Ira Berlin, *Many Thousands Gone: The First Two Centuries of Slavery in North America* (1998). A major study comparing the experiences and cultures of three distinct cohorts of mainland slaves, from the earliest arrivals through the age of the American Revolution.

Paul Boyer and Stephen Nissenbaum, *Salem Possessed: The Social Origins of Witchcraft* (1974). A study of the witchcraft episode as the expression of social conflict in one New England community.

Kathleen M. Brown, *Good Wives, Nasty Wenches, and Anxious Patriarchs: Gender, Race, and Power in Colonial Virginia* (1996). A significant work, demonstrating how gender and race shaped slavery and the social order in Virginia.

William Cronon, *Changes in the Land: Indians, Colonists, and the Ecology of New England* (1983). A pioneering study of the interactions of Native Americans and European settlers with the New England environment.

Alan Gallay, *The Indian Slave Trade: The Rise of the English Empire in the American South, 1670–1717* (2002). A major study that has broadened historians' understanding of the enslavement of Native Americans.

Allison Games, *Migration and the Origins of the English Atlantic World* (1999). An in-depth study of English emigrants to the Chesapeake, New England, and the Caribbean in the second quarter of the seventeenth century.

Jack P. Greene, *Pursuits of Happiness: The Social Development of Early Modern British Colonies and the Formation of American Culture* (1988). A brilliant synthesis that takes a regional approach in discussing England's mainland and island colonies.

Allan Greer, *The People of New France* (1997). An excellent brief introduction to the social history of French North America.

Andrew L. Knaut, *The Pueblo Revolt of 1680: Conquest and Resistance in Seventeenth-Century New Mexico* (1995). A comprehensive, insightful account of Pueblo-Spanish relations during the seventeenth century.

Edmund S. Morgan, *American Slavery, American Freedom: The Ordeal of Colonial Virginia* (1975). A classic analysis of the origins of southern slavery and race relations.

Chapter 4

Mrs. Harme Gansevoort (Magdalena Bouw) by Pieter Vanderlyn, c. 1740
This New York "lady" personified the ideal of gentility, developed in the eighteenth century, as affluent colonists consciously emulated the lifestyles of English elites.

The Bonds of Empire, 1660–1750

George Whitefield

Alexander Garden, the Church of England's commissary (representative) in the southern colonies, was furious. George Whitefield, a young Anglican minister just over from England, was preaching that Garden's ministers were unsaved and were endangering their parishioners' souls. Asserting his authority, Garden summoned Whitefield to Charles Town and demanded a retraction. But Whitefield brushed off the demand, claiming that Garden "was as ignorant as the rest" of the local clergy for failing to teach the central Calvinist doctrine of salvation by predestination (see Chapter 2). Whitefield threatened to widen his attacks if Garden refused to condemn dancing and other "sinful" entertainments. Garden shot back that Whitefield would be suspended if he preached in any church in the province, to which Whitefield retorted that he would treat such an action as he would an order from the pope. The meeting ended with Garden shouting, "Get out of my house!"

Garden got Whitefield out of his house but not out of his hair. The two men continued their dispute in public. Garden accused Whitefield of threatening social order, while Whitefield charged that the Anglican clergy valued human reason over religious piety. An extraordinary orator, Whitefield was the first intercolonial celebrity, traveling thousands of miles to spread his critique of the established form of Protestantism. Everywhere he went, people from all walks of life poured out by the thousands to experience the overwhelming power of a direct connection with God.

Whitefield represented one of two European cultural currents that crossed the Atlantic during the middle decades of the eighteenth century. He was the greatest English-speaking prophet of a powerful revival of religious piety sweeping the Protestant world. The second current was the Enlightenment—a faith in reason rooted in natural science—which found its earliest and foremost American exponent in Benjamin Franklin. Franklin's emphasis on reason might seem at odds with Whitefield's deliberately tapping his audience's deepest emotions. But both men had left behind provincial upbringings in favor of careers that brought them fame throughout the British mainland colonies and on both sides of the Atlantic Ocean.

Whitefield, an Englishman in America, and Franklin, a colonist who traveled frequently to England, also signaled the close ties that increasingly bound Britain and America. Beginning in the late seventeenth century, England tightened the political and economic bonds linking the colonies' fortunes with its own. Coupled with the astonishing growth of its population, slave as well as free, the new imperial relationship enabled British North America to achieve a level of growth and collective prosperity unknown elsewhere in the Americas.

Focus Questions

- How did the Glorious Revolution shape relations between England and its North American colonies?

- What were the most important consequences of British mercantilism for the mainland colonies?

- What factors explain the relative strengths of the British, French, and Spanish empires in North America?

- What were the most significant results of the Enlightenment and Great Awakening in the British colonies?

Rebellion and War, 1660–1713

The Restoration (1660) of the monarchy in England did not resolve the nation's deep-seated political antagonisms. Charles II and James II (ruled 1685–1688) attempted to strengthen the crown at Parliament's expense and abolished locally elected offices and legislatures in several colonies. After England in 1689 overthrew

James and replaced him with his daughter, Mary, and her husband, William, Massachusetts, New York, and Maryland carried out their own revolts. The outcome was a strengthening of both royal authority and representative legislatures in the colonies.

The overthrow of James, a pro-French Catholic, led directly to a period of warfare between England and France. By the time peace was restored in 1713, the colonists had become closely tied to a new, powerful British empire.

Royal Centralization, 1660–1688

The Restoration monarchs had little use for representative government. Charles II rarely called Parliament into session after 1674, and not at all after 1681. James II, Charles's younger brother, hoped to reign as an "absolute" monarch like France's Louis XIV, who never faced an elected legislature. Not surprisingly, the two English kings had little sympathy for American colonial assemblies.

Royal intentions of extending direct political control to North America first became evident in New York. The proprietor, the future James II, considered elected assemblies "of dangerous consequence" and forbade them to meet, except briefly between 1682 and 1686. Meanwhile, Charles II appointed former army officers to about 90 percent of all royal governorships, thereby compromising the time-honored English tradition of separating military from civilian authority. By 1680 such "governors general" ruled 60 percent of all American colonists. James II continued this policy.

Established by Puritan dissenters, Massachusetts proved most stubborn in defending self-government and resisting English authority. The crown insisted that the colony base voting rights on property ownership rather than church membership, that it tolerate Anglicans and Quakers, and that it observe the Navigation Acts (see below). As early as 1661, the General Court defiantly declared Massachusetts colonists exempt from all parliamentary laws and royal decrees except declarations of war. Charles II moved to break the Puritan establishment's power. In 1679, he carved a new royal colony, New Hampshire, out of its territory. Then, in 1684, he declared Massachusetts a royal colony and revoked its charter, the very foundation of the Puritan city upon a hill. Puritan leaders repudiated the king's actions, calling on colonists to resist even to the point of martyrdom.

Royal centralization accelerated after James II ascended to the throne. In 1686, the new king consolidated Massachusetts, New Hampshire, Connecticut, Rhode Island, and Plymouth into a single administrative unit, the **Dominion of New England**, with its capital at Boston. He added New York and the Jerseys to the dominion in

1688. With these bold strokes, the legislatures in these colonies ceased to exist, and still another former army officer, Sir Edmund Andros, became governor of the new supercolony.

Massachusetts burned with hatred for the dominion and its governor. By "Exercise of an arbitrary Government," preached Salem's minister, "ye wicked walked on Every Side & ye Vilest of men ware [sic] exalted." Andros was indeed arbitrary. He limited towns to a single annual meeting, and strictly enforced religious toleration and the Navigation Acts. "You have no more privileges left you," Andros reportedly told a group of outraged colonists, "than not to be sold for slaves."

Tensions also ran high in New York, where Catholics held prominent political and military posts under James, himself a Catholic. By 1688, colonists feared that these Catholic officials would betray New York to France, England's chief imperial rival. When Andros's local deputy allowed the harbor's forts to deteriorate and downplayed rumors that Native Americans would attack, New Yorkers suspected the worst.

The Glorious Revolution, 1688–1689

Not only colonists but also most English people were alarmed by the religious, political, and diplomatic directions in which the monarchy was taking the nation. Charles II (who had secretly converted to Catholicism) and James II ignored Parliament and violated its laws, issuing decrees allowing Catholics to hold high office and worship openly. English Protestants' fears that they would have to accept Catholicism intensified after both kings expressed their friendship with France's King Louis XIV, just as the French monarch launched new persecutions of his country's Protestant Huguenots in 1685.

The English tolerated James's Catholicism only because the potential heirs to the throne, his daughters Mary and Anne, remained Anglican. But in 1688, James's wife bore a son who would be raised a Catholic and, as a male, precede his sisters in the line of succession to the throne. Aghast at the thought of another Catholic monarch, several leading political and religious figures invited Mary and her husband, William of Orange (head of state in the Protestant Netherlands), to intervene. When William led a small Dutch army to England in November 1688, most royal troops defected to them, and James II fled to France.

This revolution of 1688, called the **Glorious Revolution**, created a "limited monarchy" as defined by the **English Bill of Rights** (1689). The crown was required to summon Parliament annually, sign all its bills, and respect traditional civil liberties. This circumscribing of monarchial power and vindication of limited representative government burned deeply into the English political consciousness, and Anglo-Americans never forgot it.

News that England's Protestant leaders had overthrown James II electrified New Englanders. On April 18, 1689, well before confirmation of the English revolt's success, Boston's militia arrested Andros and his councilors. (The governor tried to flee in women's clothing but was caught after an alert guard spotted a "lady" in army boots.) The Massachusetts political leaders acted in the name of William and Mary, risking their necks should James return to power in England.

Although William, now King William III, dismantled the Dominion of New England and restored the power to elect their own governors to Connecticut and Rhode Island, he used the opportunity to rein in Massachusetts's leanings toward independence of imperial authority. He issued a new charter for the colony in 1691, stipulating that the crown would continue to choose the governor. In addition, property ownership, not church membership, became the criterion for voting. Finally, the new charter required Massachusetts to tolerate all Protestants, especially the rising numbers of Anglicans, Baptists, and Quakers (although non-Puritans' taxes would continue to support the established Congregational church). While Plymouth and Maine remained within Massachusetts, New Hampshire became a separate royal colony. For Puritans already demoralized by the demise of the "New England Way" (see Chapter 3), this was indeed bitter medicine.

New York's counterpart of the anti-Stuart uprising was **Leisler's Rebellion**. Emboldened by news of Boston's coup, the city's militia—consisting mainly of Dutch and other non-English artisans and shopkeepers—seized the harbor's main fort on May 31, 1689. Captain Jacob Leisler of the militia took command of the colony, repaired its rundown defenses, and called elections for an assembly. When English troops arrived at New York in 1691, Leisler, fearing (wrongly) that their commander was loyal to James II, denied them entry to key forts. A skirmish resulted, and Leisler was arrested.

"Hott brain'd" Leisler unwittingly had set his own downfall in motion. He had jailed many elite New Yorkers for questioning his authority, only to find that his former enemies had persuaded the new governor to charge Leisler with treason for firing on royal troops. In the face of popular outrage, a packed jury found Leisler and his son-in-law, Jacob Milborne, guilty. Both men went to the gallows insisting that they were dying "for the king and queen and the Protestant religion."

News of England's Glorious Revolution heartened Maryland's Protestant majority, which had long chafed

Sir Edmund Andros and Boston Broadside Urging Him to Surrender, 1689
News of the Glorious Revolution in England quickly undermined Andros's authority within the Dominion of New England. Shortly after town authorities issued this public warning to Andros, Boston's militia arrested him.

under Catholic rule. Hoping to prevent a repetition of religion-tinged uprisings that had flared in 1676 and 1681, Lord Baltimore sent a messenger from England in early 1689, ordering colonists to obey William and Mary. But the courier died en route, leaving Maryland's unknowing Protestants in fear that their Catholic proprietor still supported James II.

Acting on this fear, John Coode and three others organized the **Protestant Association** to secure Maryland for William and Mary. These conspirators may have been motivated more by their exclusion from high public office than by religious zeal, for three of them had Catholic wives. Coode's group seized the capital in July 1689, removed all Catholics from office, and requested a royal governor. They got their wish in 1691, and the Church

of England became the established religion in 1692. Catholics, who composed less than one-fourth of the population, lost the right to vote and thereafter could worship only in private. Maryland stayed in royal hands until 1715, when the fourth Lord Baltimore joined the Church of England and regained his proprietorship.

The revolutionary events of 1688–1689 decisively changed the colonies' political climate by reestablishing representative government and ensuring religious freedom for Protestants. Dismantling the Dominion of New England and directing governors to call annual assemblies, William allowed colonial elites to reassert control over local affairs. By encouraging the assemblies to work with royal and proprietary governors, he expected colonial elites to identify their interests with those of England. A foundation was thus laid for an empire based on voluntary allegiance rather than submission to raw power imposed from faraway London. The crowning of William and Mary opened a new era in which Americans drew rising confidence from their relationship to the English throne. "As long as they reign," wrote a Bostonian who helped topple Andros, "New England is secure."

A Generation of War, 1689–1713

The Glorious Revolution ushered in a quarter-century of warfare, convulsing both Europe and North America. In 1689, England joined a general European coalition against France's Louis XIV, who supported James's claim to the English crown. The resulting War of the League of Augsburg, which Anglo-Americans called **King William's War**, would prove to be the first in a series of European wars that would be fought in part on North American soil.

With the outbreak of King William's War, New Yorkers and New Englanders launched a two-pronged invasion of New France in 1690, with one prong aimed at Montreal and the other at Quebec. After both invasions failed, the war took the form of cruel but inconclusive border raids against civilians carried out by both English and French troops, and their respective Indian allies.

Already weary from a new wave of wars with pro-French Indians, the Five Nations Iroquois Confederacy bore the bloodiest fighting. Standing almost alone against their foes, the Iroquois faced overwhelming odds. While their English allies failed to intercept most enemy war parties, they faced an alliance of the French and virtually all other Indians from Maine to the Great Lakes. In 1691, every Mohawk and Oneida war chief died in battle; by 1696 French armies had destroyed the villages and crops of every Iroquois nation, except the Cayugas.

Although King William's War ended in 1697, the Five Nations staggered until 1700 under invasions by pro-French Indians (including Iroquois who had become Catholic and moved to Canada). By then one-quarter of the Confederacy's two thousand warriors had been killed or taken prisoner or had fled to Canada. The total Iroquois population declined 20 percent over twelve years, from eighty-six hundred to fewer than seven thousand. (By comparison, the war cost about thirteen hundred English, Dutch, and French lives.)

By 1700, the Confederacy was divided into pro-English, pro-French, and neutralist factions. Under the impact of war, the neutralists set a new direction for Iroquois diplomacy. In two separate treaties, together called the **Grand Settlement of 1701**, the Five Nations made peace with France and its Indian allies in exchange for access to western furs, and redefined their alliance with Britain to exclude military cooperation. Skillful negotiations brought the exhausted Iroquois far more success than had war by allowing them to keep control of their lands, rebuild their decimated population, and avoid more losses in Europe's destructive wars.

In 1702 European war again erupted when England fought France and Spain in the War of the Spanish Succession, called **Queen Anne's War** by England's American colonists. This conflict reinforced Anglo-Americans' awareness of their military weakness. French and Indian raiders from Canada destroyed several towns in Massachusetts and Maine that expanding colonists had recently established on the Indians' homelands. In the Southeast, the Spanish invaded Carolina and nearly took Charles Town in 1706. Enemy warships captured many English colonial vessels and landed looting parties along the Atlantic coast. Meanwhile, English colonists' sieges of Quebec and St. Augustine ended as expensive failures.

England's own forces had more success than those of the colonies, seizing Hudson Bay and Acadia (renamed Nova Scotia) and kept these gains in the Treaty of Utrecht (1713).

The most important consequence of the imperial wars for Anglo-Americans was political, not military. The conflicts with France reinforced colonists' identity with post-1689 England as a bastion of Protestantism and political liberty. Recognizing their own military weakness and the extent to which the Royal Navy had protected their shipping, colonists acknowledged their dependence on the newly formed United Kingdom of Great Britain (created by the formal union of England and Scotland in 1707). As a new generation of English colonists matured, war buttressed their loyalty to the crown and reinforced their identity as Britons.

Colonial Economies and Societies, 1660–1750

The achievement of peace in 1713 enabled Britain, France, and Spain to concentrate on competing economically rather than militarily. Over several decades, England and France had developed maritime empires that successfully seized control of Atlantic commerce from the Dutch (see Beyond America—Global Interactions: European

Maritime Empires, 1440–1740). Thereafter, all three powers hoped to expand their American colonies and integrate them into single imperial economies. Spain and France gained territory but realized few benefits from their mainland colonies north of Mexico. Meanwhile, British North America thrived.

Mercantilist Empires in America

The imperial practices of Britain, France, and Spain were rooted in a set of political-economic assumptions known as **mercantilism**. Mercantilist theory held that each nation's power was measured by its wealth, especially in gold. To secure wealth, a country needed to maximize its sale of goods abroad in exchange for gold while minimizing foreign purchases paid for in gold. In pursuit of this goal, mercantilist nations—especially France and England—sought to produce everything they needed without relying on other nations, while obliging other nations to buy from them. Although the home country would do most manufacturing, colonies would supply vital raw materials. If needed, a country would go to war, financed by gold, in order to gain raw materials or markets, or to prevent a rival from doing the same.

Britain's mercantilist policies were articulated above all in a series of **Navigation Acts** governing commerce between England and its colonies. Parliament enacted the first Navigation Act in 1651, requiring that colonial trade be carried on in English, including colonial-owned, vessels in order to replace Dutch shippers with English. After the Restoration, Parliament enacted the Navigation Act of 1660, requiring that certain "enumerated" commodities (see below) be exported via England or Scotland, and barring imports from arriving in non-English ships. The Navigation Act of 1663 stipulated that imports to the colonies arrive via England rather than directly from another country. Later, the Molasses Act (1733) taxed all foreign molasses (produced from sugar cane and imported primarily for distilling rum) entering the mainland colonies at sixpence per gallon. This act was intended less to raise revenue than to serve as a tariff that would protect British West Indian sugar producers at the expense of French rivals on neighboring islands.

The Navigation Acts affected the British colonial economy in four major ways. First, they limited all imperial trade to British-owned ships whose crews were at least three-quarters British. The acts classified all colonists as British, including slaves (many of whom served as seamen). This restriction not only contributed to Britain's rise as Europe's foremost shipping nation but also laid the foundations of an American shipbuilding industry and merchant marine. By the 1750s, one-third of all "British" vessels were American-owned, mostly by merchants in New England and the middle colonies. The swift growth of this merchant marine diversified the northern colonial economy and made it more commercial. The expansion of colonial shipping also hastened urbanization by creating a need for centralized docks, warehouses, and repair shops in the colonies. By mid-century Philadelphia, New York City, Boston, and Charles Town had emerged as major transatlantic ports.

The second major way in which the Navigation Acts affected the colonies lay in their stipulating that "enumerated" exports pass through England or Scotland. The colonies' major "enumerated" exports were sugar (by far the most profitable commodity), tobacco, rice, furs, indigo (a Carolina plant that produced a blue dye), and naval stores (masts, hemp, tar, and turpentine). Parliament never restricted grain, livestock, fish, lumber, or rum, which together made up 60 percent of colonial exports. Parliament further reduced the burdens on exporters of tobacco and rice—the chief mainland

Tobacco Production in Virginia
Slaves performed virtually every task in the production of tobacco on plantations as well as on many smaller farms in the Chesapeake colonies.

commodities affected—with two significant concessions. First, it gave tobacco growers a monopoly over the British market by excluding foreign tobacco, even though this hurt British consumers. (Rice planters enjoyed a natural monopoly because they had no competitors.) Second, it minimized the added cost of landing tobacco and rice in Britain by refunding customs duties when those products were later shipped to other countries. With about 85 percent of all American tobacco and rice eventually being sold outside the British Empire, the acts reduced planters' profits by less than 3 percent.

The navigation system's third effect on the colonies was to encourage economic diversification. Parliament used British tax revenues to pay modest bounties to Americans producing such items as silk, iron, dyes, hemp, and lumber, which Britain would otherwise have had to import from other countries, and it raised the price of commercial rivals' imports by imposing protective tariffs on them. The trade laws did prohibit Anglo-Americans from competing with British manufacturing of certain products, most notably clothing. However, colonial tailors, hatters, and housewives could continue to make any item of dress in their households or small shops. Manufactured by low-paid labor, British clothing imports generally undersold whatever the colonists could have exported. The colonists were also free to produce iron, and by 1770 they had built 250 ironworks employing thirty thousand men, a work force larger than the entire population of Georgia or of any provincial city.

Finally, the Navigation Acts made the colonies a protected market for low-priced consumer goods and other exports from Britain. Steady overseas demand for colonial products spawned a prosperity that enabled white colonists to purchase ever larger amounts not only of clothing but also of dishware, furniture, tea, and a range of other imports from British and overseas sources. Shops sprang up in cities and rural crossroads throughout the colonies, and itinerant peddlers took imported wares into more remote areas of the countryside. One such peddler arrived in Berwick, Maine, in 1721 and sold several kinds of cloth, a "pair of garters," and various "small trifles" before local authorities confiscated his goods because he had failed to purchase a license. Other traders traveled to Native American communities where they exchanged cloth and other commodities for furs. As a result of colonial consumption, the share of British exports bound for North America spurted from just 5 percent in 1700 to almost 40 percent by 1760. Mercantilism had given rise to a "consumer revolution" in British America.

The economic development of the French and Spanish colonies in North America paled beside that of the British. Although France's most forceful proponent of mercantilism, Colbert (see Chapter 3), and his successors had great difficulty implementing mercantilist policies, New France became agriculturally self-sufficient and exported some wheat to the French West Indies. It also exported small amounts of fish and timber to the Caribbean and to France. Canada's chief imports were wine and brandy, its chief export, furs. Although European demand for furs had flattened, the French government expanded the fur trade, even losing money, in order to retain Native Americans as military allies against Britain. Moreover, France maintained a sizable army in its Canadian colony that, like the trade with Native Americans, was a drain on the royal treasury. Meanwhile, Canada attracted little private investment from France or from within the colony. French Canadians enjoyed a comfortable if modest standard of living but lacked the private investment, extensive commercial infrastructure, vast consumer market, and manufacturing capacity of their British neighbors.

France's wealthiest colonies were in the West Indies, where French planters, like their English neighbors, imported large numbers of enslaved Africans to produce sugar under appalling conditions. Ironically, French sugar planters' success was partly a result of their defying mercantilist policies. In St. Domingue, Martinique, and Guadeloupe, many planters built their own sugar refineries and made molasses instead of shipping their raw sugar to refineries in France, as French regulations prescribed. They then sold much of their molasses to merchants in Britain's mainland colonies, especially Massachusetts, which similarly ignored British mercantilist laws.

Although Spain had squandered the wealth from gold and silver extracted by the conquistadors and early colonists (see Chapter 2), its economy and that of Latin America revived during the eighteenth century. That revival did not extend to New Mexico, Texas, and Florida, where colonists conducted little overseas commerce.

At bottom, Britain's colonies differed from those of France and Spain in their respective economies and societies. While mercantilist principles governed all three nations, the monarchy, the nobility, and the Catholic Church controlled most wealth in France and Spain. Most private wealth was inherited and took the form of land. England, on the other hand, had become a mercantile-commercial economy, and a significant portion of the nation's wealth was in the form of capital held by merchants who

European Maritime Empires, 1440–1740

The fifteenth century saw the emergence of a new phenomenon in world history—maritime empires. The Roman, Mongol, and other earlier empires had been land empires, built by armies that marched on foot or rode on horseback. Maritime empires were created by sailors who crossed the Atlantic and Pacific in new kinds of oceangoing ships armed with cannons. First Portugal, followed quickly by Spain, and then the Netherlands, France, and England projected their power around the world. The new seaborne empires promoted trade and settlement, transforming lands and peoples in Europe, Africa, Asia, and the Americas.

The impetus for maritime expansion came from the ruling families of Portugal and Spain, who sought direct trade routes to the riches of Asia and Africa. Although both countries were familiar with the North African coast, Portugal began exploring south of the Sahara during the 1430s, reaching the Senegal River ("River of Gold") in 1440. By 1500, Portuguese mariners had rounded the Cape of Good Hope. Thereafter, the Portuguese bombarded and seized several Indian Ocean ports in East Africa, India, and the East Indies. From there, they expanded into the Pacific and, with Chinese permission, established a port at Macao in 1557. Meanwhile, Portugal had also claimed Brazil in 1500. Spain, having followed Portugal into West Africa, attempted to outflank its rival. In 1492, Columbus sailed westward to what he thought was East Asia. Magellan's expedition finished Columbus's journey to Asia in the course of circumnavigating the globe (1519–1522). These discoveries led to the creation of Spain's maritime empire, which by 1600 included the Philippines in Asia as well as most of the Americas from Mexico and the Caribbean southward.

Although an accidental discovery, the Americas became the driving force behind a new form of maritime imperialism during the sixteenth century. Portugal and Spain's empires in the Indian and Pacific Oceans were based on trade ties (voluntary or forced) with native rulers rather than on colonization by Europeans. In the

Portuguese in India
A Portuguese man and two Indian women converse in this drawing from about 1540.

Americas, by contrast, European powers exploited the massive depopulation of Native Americans due to imported epidemic diseases and established territorial colonies. Small numbers of European colonists used the forced labor of Native Americans and enslaved Africans to derive wealth from the land. For Spain, wealth came from the rich silver and gold mines in present-day Mexico and Bolivia, which brought it unprecedented power in Europe. But Spain's descent was as sudden as its rise. With an inflated, uncompetitive economy and a series of disastrous wars, its riches flowed to bankers and merchants, who financed its European rivals. Among the chief beneficiaries were England, France, and (after securing its independence in 1609) the Netherlands, which established maritime empires of their own.

During the first half of the seventeenth century, the Netherlands took over Portugal's Indian Ocean ports and extended its commercial activity to the Pacific, becoming the leading European power in South and East Asia. In the Atlantic, the Dutch seized control of the trade linking West Africa, the Americas, and Europe, frequently capturing Spanish treasure ships. They established settler colonies in New Netherland (1614), Brazil (1624–1630), Curaçao (1634), and Cape Colony (later South Africa, 1652). At the same time, France planted fur-trading colonies in Canada and tobacco plantations on several West Indian islands. In a series of different ventures, the English established a long string of colonies, from Newfoundland in the north to Barbados in the south. Together these colonies in the Americas attracted nearly 200,000 English settlers by 1660. The most lucrative products were tobacco from the Chesapeake Bay and West Indies, and fish from the North Atlantic, but Dutch merchants dominated commerce in the Chesapeake and Caribbean.

As with Spain, the preeminence of the Dutch among European maritime powers proved to be brief. The Dutch were unable to prevent England from aggressively expanding in India, where by the mid-seventeenth century it had initiated trade ties with several powerful coastal princes. After France joined the competition for trade and influence near the end of the century, the Dutch were excluded from trade with India.

The rise of England and France at Dutch expense was even more pronounced in the Atlantic world. The number and population of English mainland and Caribbean colonies multiplied, and the volume of English trade expanded exponentially, especially after the islands shifted from tobacco to sugar production in the 1640s. In keeping with the principles of mercantilism, England sought to gain control of its own colonies' commerce from the Dutch and give it to English merchants and shippers, including those in its colonies. To this end, Parliament enacted a series of mercantilist Navigation Acts. In three Anglo-Dutch wars (1652–1674), England drove the Dutch from New Netherland and largely ended Dutch trade with mainland North America. Likewise expanding its sugar-producing colonies in the Caribbean, France quietly took advantage of the wars to shift control of its trade from Dutch to French merchants. Meanwhile, an uprising by Portuguese planters expelled the Dutch from Brazil by 1654. By 1700, the Netherlands was a secondary commercial and naval power.

Having successfully integrated their maritime empires on firm mercantilist principles, France and England now faced one another as rivals for dominance of the seas as well as within Europe. The sequence of wars waged from 1689 to 1713 between France (supported by Spain) and England (supported by the Netherlands) resulted in a decisive advantage for Great Britain (as the union of England and Scotland was called). Britain further consolidated its position during the long interval of peace (to 1740) that followed. British supremacy made possible the diversification and maturation of the mainland North American colonial economy and the astonishing rise in colonists' living standards. By 1750, the heavily populated colonies possessed the material prerequisites for independent nationhood.

reinvested it in commercial and shipping enterprises. For its part, the British government used much of its considerable income from duties, tariffs, and other taxes to enhance commerce. For example, the government strengthened Britain's powerful navy to protect the empire's trade and created the Bank of England in 1694 to ensure a stable money supply and lay the foundation for a network of lending institutions. These benefits extended not only to Britain but also to colonial entrepreneurs and consumers. Indeed the colonies' per capita income rose 0.6 percent annually from 1650 to 1770, a pace twice that of Britain.

Population Growth and Diversity

Britain's economic advantage over its rivals in North America was reinforced by its sharp demographic edge. In 1700, approximately 250,000 non-Indians resided in English America, compared to only 15,000 French colonists and 4,500 Spanish north of the Rio Grande. During the first half of the eighteenth century, all three colonial populations at least quadrupled in size—the British to 1,170,000, the French to 60,000, and the Spanish to 19,000—but this only magnified Britain's advantage.

Spanish emigrants could choose from among that nation's many Latin American colonies, most of which offered more opportunities than remote, poorly developed Florida, Texas, and New Mexico. Reports of Canada's harsh winters and Louisiana's poor economy deterred most potential French colonists. France and Spain made few attempts to attract immigrants to North America from outside their own empires. And both limited immigration to Roman Catholics, a restriction that diverted French Huguenots to the English colonies instead. The English colonies, for their part, boasted good farmlands, healthy economies, and a willingness to absorb Europeans of most Protestant denominations. While anti-Catholicism remained strong, small Jewish communities also formed in several Anglo-American cities.

Spain regarded its northernmost colonies less as centers of population than as buffers against French and English penetration of their more valued colonies to the south. While hoping to lure civilian settlers, the Spanish relied heavily on soldiers stationed in *presidios* (forts) for defense plus missionaries who would, they hoped, attract loyal Native Americans to strategically placed missions. Most colonists in Spanish North America came not from Spain itself but from Mexico and other Spanish colonies.

Although boasting more people than the Spanish colonies, New France and Louisiana were comparably limited. There too the military played a strong role, while missionaries and traders worked to enhance the colony's relations with Native Americans. New France's population growth in the eighteenth century resulted largely from natural increase rather than immigration. Some rural Canadians established new settlements along the Mississippi River in Upper Louisiana, in what are now Illinois and Missouri. On the lower Mississippi, Louisiana acquired a foul reputation, and few French went there willingly. To boost its population, the government sent paupers and criminals, recruited some German refugees, and encouraged large-scale slave imports. By 1732, two-thirds of lower Louisiana's 5,800 people were black and enslaved.

The British colonies outpaced the population growth of not only their French and Spanish rivals but of Britain itself. White women in the colonies had an average of eight children and forty-two grandchildren, compared to five children and fifteen grandchildren for women in Britain. The ratio of England's population to that of the mainland colonies plummeted from 20 to 1 in 1700 to 3 to 1 in 1775.

Although immigration contributed less to eighteenth-century population growth than did natural increase, it remained important. In the forty years after Queen Anne's War, the British colonies absorbed 350,000 newcomers, approximately 210,000 of them from Europe. A rising proportion of these white immigrants came from outside of England (see Figure 4.1). Whereas between 1630 and 1700 an average of 2,000 English settlers landed annually, only about 500 English arrived each year after 1713. Rising employment and higher wages in England made voluntary immigration to America less attractive than before. But economic hardship elsewhere in the British Isles and northern Europe supplied a steady stream of immigrants, who contributed to greater ethnic diversity among white North Americans.

One of the largest contingents was made up of 100,000 newcomers from Ireland, two-thirds of them "Scots-Irish" descendants of Scottish Presbyterians who had previously sought economic opportunity in northern Ireland. After 1718, Scots-Irish fled to America to escape rack renting (frequent sharp increases in farm rents), usually moving as complete families. In contrast, most of the smaller number of Irish Catholics were unmarried males who arrived as indentured servants. Rarely able to find Catholic wives, they often abandoned their faith to marry Protestant women.

Meanwhile, from German-speaking regions in central Europe came 125,000 settlers, most of them fleeing terrible economic conditions in the Rhine Valley. Wartime devastation had compounded the misery of Rhineland peasants, many of whom were squeezed onto plots of

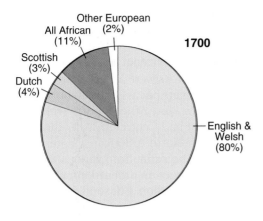

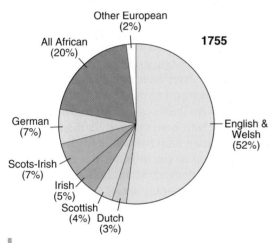

**Figure 4.1 Distribution of Europeans and Africans Within
the British Mainland Colonies, 1700–1755**
The impact of heavy immigration from 1720 to 1755 can be seen
in the reduction of the English and Welsh from four-fifths of the
colonial population to a slight majority; in the sudden influx of
Germans and Irish (who together comprised a fifth of white
colonists by 1755); and in the doubling of the African population.
For a more detailed breakdown of African origins see Map 4.2.
Source: Thomas L. Purvis, "The European Ancestry of the United
States Population," *William & Mary Quarterly*, LXI (1984): 85–101.

land too small to feed a family. One-third of German immigrants financed their voyage by indenturing themselves or their children as servants. Most Germans were
either Lutherans or Calvinists. But a significant minority
belonged to small, pacifist religious sects that desired
above all to be left alone.

Overwhelmingly, the eighteenth-century immigrants
were poor. Those who were indentured servants worked
from one to four years for an urban or rural master. Servants could be sold or rented out, beaten, granted minimal legal protection, kept from marrying, and sexually

harassed. Attempted escape usually meant an extension
of their service. But at the end of their terms, most managed to collect "freedom dues," which could help them
marry and acquire land.

Few immigrants settled in New England, New Jersey,
lower New York, and the southern tidewater, where land
was most scarce and expensive. Philadelphia became
immigrants' primary port of entry. So many foreigners
went to Pennsylvania that by 1755 the English accounted for only one-third of that colony's population;
the rest came mostly from elsewhere in the British Isles
and from Germany.

Rising numbers of immigrants also traveled to the
Piedmont region, stretching along the eastern slope of
the Appalachians. A significant German community developed in upper New York, and thousands of other Germans as well as Scots-Irish fanned southward from
Pennsylvania into western Maryland. Many more from
Germany and Ireland arrived in the second-most popular American gateway, Charles Town. Most moved on to
the Carolina Piedmont, where they raised grain, livestock, and tobacco, generally without slaves. After 1750,
both streams of immigration merged with an outpouring of Anglo-Americans from the Chesapeake in the
rolling, fertile hills of western North Carolina. In 1713,
few Anglo-Americans had lived more than fifty miles
from the sea, but by 1750 one-third of all colonists
resided in the Piedmont (see Map 4.1).

The least-free white immigrants were convict laborers. England had deported some convicts to America in
the seventeenth century, but between 1718 and 1783
about thirty thousand condemned prisoners arrived,
mostly in the Chesapeake colonies. A few of the convicts
were murderers; most were guilty of more trivial offenses, like a young Londoner who "got intoxicated with
liquor, and in that condition attempted to snatch a
handkerchief from the body of a person in the street to
him unknown." (English law authorized the death
penalty for 160 offenses, including what today would be
considered petty theft.) Convicts were sold as servants
on arrival. Relatively few committed crimes in America,
and some eventually managed to establish themselves
as backcountry farmers.

Affluent English-descended colonists did not relish
the influx of so many people different from themselves.
"These confounded Irish will eat us all up," snorted one
Bostonian. Benjamin Franklin spoke for many when he
asked in a 1751 essay on population,

*Why should Pennsylvania, founded by the English, become
a colony of aliens, who will shortly be so numerous as to*

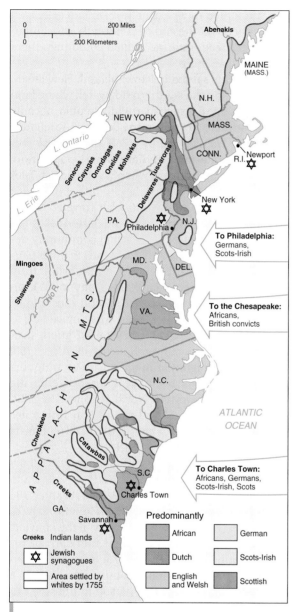

Map 4.1 Immigration and British Colonial Expansion, to 1755

Black majorities emerged in much of the Chesapeake tidewater and the Carolina-Georgia low country. Immigrants from Germany, Ireland, and Scotland predominated among the settlers in the Piedmont. A significant Jewish population emerged in the seaports.

Germanize us instead of us Anglicizing them, and will never adopt our language or customs any more than they can acquire our complexion?

In the same ungenerous spirit, Franklin objected to the slave trade because it would increase America's black population at the expense of industrious whites, and suggested that the colonists send rattlesnakes to Britain in return for its convict laborers.

About 40 percent (140,000) of newcomers to the British mainland colonies were African-born slaves who arrived not as passengers but as cargo. All but a few slave ships departed from West African ports with captives from dozens of West and Central African ethnic groups (see Map 4.2). Most North American planters deliberately mixed slaves who came from various regions and spoke different languages, in order to minimize the potential for collective rebellion. But some in Carolina and Georgia expressly sought slaves from Gambia and nearby regions for their rice-growing experience.

Conditions aboard slave ships during the **Middle Passage**, from Africa to America, were appalling by any standard. Africans were crammed into tight quarters with inadequate sanitary facilities, and many died from disease. A Guinea-born slave, later named Venture Smith, was one of 260 who were on a voyage out of a Gold Coast port in 1735. But "smallpox . . . broke out on board," Smith recalled, and "when we reached [Barbados], there were found . . . not more than two hundred alive."

Slaves who refused to eat or otherwise defied shipboard authority were flogged. Some hurled themselves overboard in a last, desperate act of defiance against those who would profit from their misery. When possible, others acted in groups. Rebellions on one scale or another erupted on about one in ten slave voyages. The rebellions forced shippers to hire full-time guards and install barricades to confine slaves. Shippers then passed the cost on to American buyers.

From 1713 to 1754, five times as many slaves poured onto mainland North America as in all the preceding years. The proportion of blacks in the colonies doubled, rising from 11 percent at the beginning of the century to 20 percent by midcentury. Slavery was primarily a southern institution, but 15 percent of its victims lived north of Maryland, mostly in New York and New Jersey. By 1750, every seventh New Yorker was a slave.

Because West Indian and Brazilian slave owners outbid those on the mainland, a mere 5 percent of enslaved Africans were transported to the present-day United States. Unable to buy as many male field hands as they wanted, rice and tobacco planters purchased African women and protected their investments by minimally maintaining slaves' health. These factors promoted family formation and increased life expectancy far beyond the Caribbean's low levels (see Chapter 3). By 1750 the rate of natural increase for mainland blacks almost

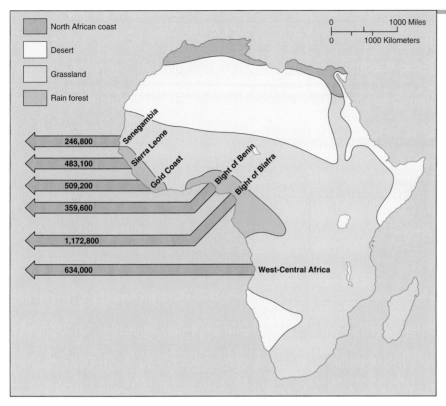

North African coast

Desert

Grassland

Rain forest

0   1000 Miles

0   1000 Kilometers

Senegambia   246,800

Sierra Leone   483,100

Gold Coast   509,200

Bight of Benin   359,600

Bight of Biafra   1,172,800

West-Central Africa   634,000

Map 4.2 African Origins of Slaves Shipped by British, 1692–1807
Virtually all slaves brought to English North America came from West Africa, between Senegambia and West-Central Africa. Most were captured or bought inland and marched to the coast, where they were sold to African merchants who in turn sold them to European slave traders.

equaled that for whites. Meanwhile, distinct cultural differences arose between African-born slaves and creoles born in America (see below).

Rural White Men and Women

Although most whites benefited from rising living standards in the British colonies, they enjoyed these advantages unevenly. Except for Benjamin Franklin (who was born neither rich nor poor) and a few others, true affluence was reserved for those who inherited their wealth. For other whites, personal success was limited and came through hard work, if at all.

Because most farm families owned just enough acreage for a working farm, they could not provide all their children with land of their own when they married. A young male had to build savings to buy farm equipment by working (from about age sixteen to twenty-three) as a field hand for his father or neighbors. After marrying, he normally supported his growing family by renting a farm from a more prosperous landowner until his early or mid-thirties. In some areas, especially the oldest colonized areas of New England, the continued high birthrates of rural families combined with a shortage of productive land to close off farming opportunities altogether. As a result, many young men turned elsewhere to make their livings—the frontier, the port cities, or the high seas.

Families who did acquire land worked off mortgages slowly because the long-term cash income from a farm (6 percent) about equaled the interest on borrowed money (5 to 8 percent). After making a down payment of one-third, a husband and wife generally satisfied the next third upon inheriting shares of their deceased parents' estates. They paid off the final third when their children reached their teens and the family could expand farm output with two or three full-time workers. Only by their late fifties, just as their youngest offspring got ready to leave home, did most colonial parents free themselves of debt.

In general, the more isolated a community or the less productive its farmland, the more self-sufficiency and bartering its people practiced. Remote or poor rural families depended heavily on wives' and daughters'

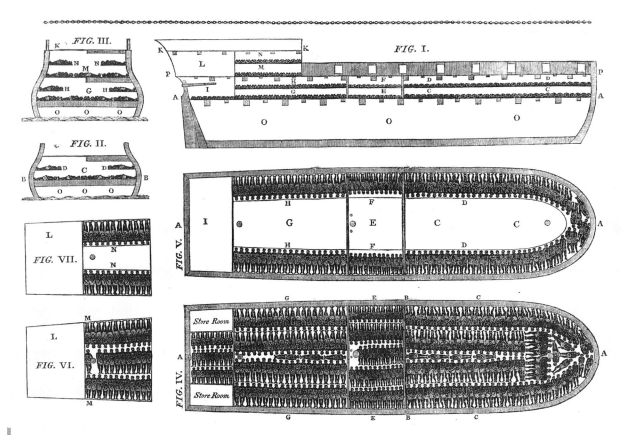

Architect's Plan of a Slave Ship
This plan graphically depicts the crowded, unsanitary conditions under which enslaved Africans were packed like cargo and transported across the Atlantic.

making items that the family would otherwise have had to purchase. Besides cooking, cleaning, and washing, wives preserved food, boiled soap, made clothing, and tended the garden, dairy, orchard, poultry house, and pigsty. They also sold dairy products to neighbors or merchants, spun yarn into cloth for tailors, knitted garments for sale, and even sold their own hair for wigs. A farm family's ability to feed itself and its animals was worth about half of its cash income (a luxury that few European peasants enjoyed), and women worked as much as men did in meeting this end.

Legally, however, white women in the British colonies were constrained (see Chapter 3). A woman's single most autonomous decision was her choice of a husband. Once married, she lost control of her dowry, unless she was a New Yorker subject to Dutch custom, which allowed her somewhat more authority. Women in the French and Spanish colonies retained ownership of, and often augmented, the property they brought to a marriage.

Widows did control between 8 and 10 percent of all property in eighteenth-century Anglo-America, and a few—among them Eliza Pinckney of South Carolina, from a prominent planter family—owned and managed large estates.

Colonial Farmers and the Environment

The rapid expansion of Britain's colonies hastened environmental change east of the Appalachians. Whereas the earliest colonists farmed land already cleared and cultivated by Native Americans, eighteenth-century settlers usually removed trees before beginning their plots. Despite the labor involved, farmers and planters, especially those using slave labor, preferred heavily forested areas where the soil was most fertile. New England farmers had to clear innumerable heavy rocks—debris from the last Ice Age—with which they built walls around their fields. Colonists everywhere used timber to construct their houses, barns, and fences and to provide fuel for

Poor Farmer's House
Many poor Chesapeake farmers lived in a single room with a dirt floor, no interior walls, an unglazed window, and minimal furnishings.

A New England Woman's Cupboard
Modest prosperity enabled some married women to exercise power as consumers and even to express their individuality. Hannah Barnard, a Hadley, Massachusetts, farm woman, commissioned this cupboard for storing linens and other fine textiles, in about 1720.

heating and cooking. Farmers and planters also sold firewood to the inhabitants of cities and towns. Only six years after Georgia's founding, a colonist noted, there was "no more firewood in Savannah; . . . it must be bought from the plantations for which reason firewood is already right expensive."

In removing the trees (deforestation), farmers drove away bears, panthers, wild turkeys, and other forest animals while attracting grass- and seed-eating rabbits, mice, and possums. By removing protection from winds and, in summer, from the sun, deforestation also brought warmer summers and colder winters, further increasing colonists' demand for firewood. By hastening the runoff of spring waters, it led both to heavier flooding and drier streambeds in most areas and, where water could not escape, to more extensive swamps. In turn, less stable temperatures and water levels, along with impediments created by mills and by the floating of timbers

downstream, rapidly reduced the number of fish in colonial waters. Writing in 1766, naturalist John Bartram noted that fish "abounded formerly when the Indians lived much on them & was very numerous," but that "now there is not the 100th or perhaps the 1000th [portion of] fish to be found."

Deforestation dried and hardened the soil, but colonists' crops had even more drastic effects. Native Americans, recognizing the soil-depleting effects of intensive cultivation, rotated their crops regularly so that fields could lie fallow (unplanted) for several years and thereby be replenished with vital nutrients (see Chapter 1). But many colonial farmers either did not have enough land to leave some unplanted or were unwilling to sacrifice short-term profits for potential long-term benefits.

As early as 1637, one New England farmer discovered that his soil "after five or six years [of planting corn] grows barren beyond belief and puts on the face of winter in the

Figure 4.2 Populations of Boston, New York, and Philadelphia, 1690–1776
Transatlantic commerce contributed to the rapid growth of the three northern seaports. But Boston's growth leveled off in 1740, while New York and Philadelphia continued to flourish.
Source: Gary B. Nash, *The Urban Crucible: Social Change, Political Consciousness, and the Origins of the American Revolution* (Cambridge: Harvard University Press, 1979), p. 409.

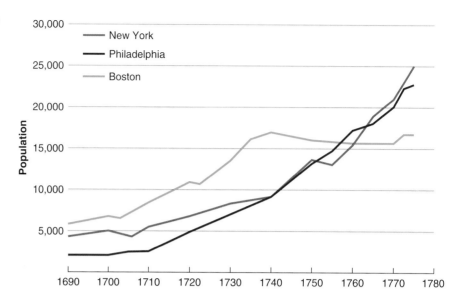

time of summer." Chesapeake planters' tobacco yields declined after only three or four years in the same plot. Like farmers elsewhere, they used animal manure to fertilize their food crops but not their tobacco, fearing that manure would spoil the taste for consumers. As Chesapeake tobacco growers moved inland to hillier areas, away from rivers and streams, they also contributed to increased soil erosion.

Confronting a more serious shortage of land and resources, Europe's well-to-do farmers were already turning their attention to conservation and "scientific" farming. But most colonists ignored such techniques, either because they could not afford to implement them or because they believed that American land, including that still held by Indians, would sustain them and future generations indefinitely.

The Urban Paradox

The cities were British North America's economic paradox. As major ports of entry and exit, they were keys to the colonies' rising prosperity; yet they held only 4 percent of the colonies' population, and a growing percentage of city-dwellers were caught in a downward spiral of declining opportunity.

As colonial prosperity reached new heights after 1740, poverty spread among residents of the three major seaports—Philadelphia, New York, and, especially, Boston. The cities' poor rolls bulged as poor white men, women (often widowed), and children arrived from Europe and the colonial countryside. High

population density and poor sanitation allowed contagious diseases to run rampant, so that half of all city children died before age twenty-one and urban adults lived ten years less on average than country folk.

Changing labor practices also contributed to poverty. Early-eighteenth-century urban artisans typically trained apprentices and employed them as journeymen for many years until they could open their own shops. By midcentury, however, more and more employers kept laborers only as long as business was brisk, releasing them when sales slowed. In 1751, a shrewd Benjamin Franklin recommended this practice to employers as a way to reduce labor costs. Recessions hit more frequently after 1720 and created longer spells of unemployment, making it increasingly difficult for many to afford rents, food, and firewood.

Insignificant before 1700, urban poverty became a major problem. By 1730, Boston ceased providing shelter for its growing number of homeless residents. The proportion of residents considered too poor to pay taxes climbed even as the total population leveled (see Figure 4.2). Not until 1736 did New York build a poorhouse (for forty people), but by 1772, 4 percent of its residents (over eight hundred) required public assistance to survive. The number of Philadelphia families listed as poor on tax rolls jumped from 3 percent in 1720 to 11 percent by 1760.

Wealth, on the other hand, remained highly concentrated. For example, New York's wealthiest 10 percent (mostly merchants) owned about 45 percent of the property throughout the eighteenth century. Similar patterns existed in Boston and Philadelphia. Set alongside the growth of a poor underclass in these cities, such statistics underscored the polarization of status and wealth in urban America.

Most southern cities were little more than large towns. Charles Town, however, became North America's fourth-largest city. South Carolina's capital offered gracious living to the wealthy planters who flocked from their plantations to townhouses during the months of the worst heat and insect infestation. Shanties on the city's outskirts sheltered a growing crowd of destitute whites. The colony encouraged whites to immigrate in hopes of reducing blacks' numerical preponderance, but most European newcomers could not establish farms or find any work except as ill-paid temporary laborers. Like their counterparts in northern ports, Charles Town's poor whites competed for work with urban slaves whose masters rented out their labor.

Although middle-class women in cities and large towns performed somewhat less manual drudgery than farm women, they nonetheless managed complex households that often included servants, slaves, and apprentices. While raising poultry and vegetables as well as sewing and knitting, urban wives purchased their cloth and most of their food in daily trips to public markets. Many had one or more household servants, usually young single women or widows, to help with cooking, cleaning, and laundering—tasks that required more attention than in the country because of higher urban standards of cleanliness and appearance. Wives also worked in family businesses or their own shops, which were located in owners' homes.

Less affluent wives and widows had the fewest opportunities of all. They housed boarders rather than servants, and many spun and wove cloth in their homes for local merchants. Poor widows with children looked to the community for relief. Whereas John Winthrop and other Puritan forebears had deemed it a Christian's duty to care for poor dependents (see Chapter 3), affluent Bostonians in the eighteenth century scorned the needy. Preaching in 1752, the city's leading minister, Charles Chauncy, lamented "the swarms of children, of both sexes, that are continually strolling and playing about the streets of our metropolis, clothed in rags, and brought up in idleness and ignorance." Another clergyman warned that charity for widows and their children was money "worse than lost."

Slavery

For slaves, the economic progress achieved in colonial America meant only that most masters could afford to keep them healthy. Rarely did masters choose to make their human property comfortable. A visitor to a Virginia plantation from Poland (where peasants lived in dire poverty) recorded this impression of slaves' quality of life:

We entered some Negroes huts—for their habitations cannot be called houses. They are far more miserable than the poorest of the cottages of our peasants. The husband and wife sleep on a miserable bed, the children on the floor . . . a little kitchen furniture amid this misery . . . a teakettle and cups . . . five or six hens, each with ten or fifteen chickens, walked there. That is the only pleasure allowed to the negroes.

Women Entrepreneurs
Women shopkeepers were common in the cities, especially in trades that required only a small investment. These Boston women advertised imported garden seeds in a city newspaper.

Juſt imported in Capt. *Part-i-lge* from LONDON and to be Sold by

Suſanna Renken,

At her Shop in Fore-Street near the Draw-Bridge, BOSTON, *Viz.*

EARLY Charlton, Hotſpur, Marrowfat, Golden Hotſpur, and blue Marrowfat Peas; Large Windſor, early Hotſpur, early yellow Kidney, early Spaniſh Beans:——Early *Yorkſhire*, Dutch, Batterſea, Red, and large Winter Cabbage: yellow and green Savoy; Purple and Colliflower Brocoli; white Goſs-Cabbage, Marble, white Sileſia, green Sileſia, and ſcarlet Lettice, green and yellow Hyſſop; Turkey Melons; and Winter Savory; with all ſorts of other Garden Seeds, among which are a great Variety of Flower-Seeds:——Red and white Clover, Herd Graſs and Trefoile.

Juſt Imported from LONDON, and to be Sold

By Sarah DeCoſter,

At the Sign of the Walnut-Tree in Milk-Street in *Boſton,* a little below the Rev. Dr. *Sewall's* Meeting-House,

WINDSOR Beans; Early Peas of ſeveral Sorts; Early Cabbage-Seeds, and other Sorts of Garden-Seeds; too many to enumerate: All at reaſonable Rates.

To maintain slaves, masters normally spent just 40 percent of the amount paid for the upkeep of indentured servants. Whereas white servants ate two hundred pounds of meat yearly, black slaves consumed fifty pounds. The value of the beer and hard cider given to a typical servant alone equaled the expense of feeding and clothing the average slave. Masters usually provided adult slaves with eight quarts of corn and a pound of pork each week but expected them to grow their own vegetables, forage for wild fruits, and perhaps raise poultry.

Blacks worked for a far longer portion of their lives than whites. Slave children entered the fields as part-time helpers soon after reaching seven and began working full-time between eleven and fourteen. Whereas most white women worked in their homes, barns, and gardens, black females routinely tended tobacco or rice crops, even when pregnant, and often worked outdoors in the winter. Most slaves toiled until they died, although most who survived to their sixties were spared hard labor.

As the numbers of American-born creole slaves grew, sharp differences emerged between them and African-born blacks in the southern colonies. Unlike African-born slaves, creoles spoke a single language, English, and were familiar from birth with their environment and with the ways of their masters. These advantages occasionally translated into more autonomy for creoles. Until the 1770s, planters continued to import African-born slaves to labor in their fields, especially on more remote lands recently gained from Native Americans. But as wealthier, more long-established planters diversified economically and developed more elaborate lifestyles (see below), they diverted favored creoles toward such services as shoeing horses, repairing and driving carriages, preparing and serving meals, sewing and mending clothing, and caring for planters' children.

Africans and creoles proved resourceful at maximizing opportunities within this harsh, confining system. House slaves aggressively demanded that guests tip them for shining shoes and stabling horses. They also sought presents on holidays, as a startled New Jersey visitor to a Virginia plantation discovered early one Christmas morning when slaves demanding gifts of cash roused him from bed.

In the Carolina-Georgia rice country, slaves working under the task system gained control of about half their waking hours. Under tasking, each slave spent some hours caring for a quarter-acre, after which his or her duties ended for the day. This system permitted a few slaves to keep hogs and sell surplus vegetables on their own.

In 1728, an exceptional slave, Sampson, earned enough money in his off-hours to buy another slave, whom he then sold to his master in exchange for his own freedom.

The gang system used on tobacco plantations afforded Chesapeake slaves less free time than those in Carolina. As one white observer noted, Chesapeake blacks labored "from daylight until the dusk of evening and some part of the night, by moon or candlelight, during the winter."

Despite Carolina slaves' greater autonomy, racial tensions ran high in the colony. As long as Europeans outnumbered Africans, race relations in Carolina remained relaxed. But as a black majority emerged, whites increasingly used force and fear to control "their" blacks. For example, a 1735 law, noting that many Africans wore "clothes much above the condition of slaves," imposed a dress code limiting slaves' apparel to fabrics worth less than ten shillings per yard and even prohibited their wearing their owners' cast-off clothes. Of even greater concern were large gatherings of blacks uncontrolled by whites. In 1721, Charles Town enacted a 9:00 P.M. curfew for blacks, while Carolina's assembly placed all local slave patrols under the colonial militia. Slaves responded to

Asante Drum
Enslaved Africans carried their cultures with them to the Americas. This drum, made from African wood, was found in Virginia.

the colony's vigilance and harsher punishments with increased instances of arson, theft, flight, and violence.

Despite these measures, South Carolina (separated from North Carolina in 1729) was rocked in 1739 by a powerful slave uprising, the **Stono Rebellion**. It began when twenty Africans seized guns and ammunition from a store at the Stono River Bridge, outside Charles Town. Marching under a makeshift flag and crying "Liberty!" they collected eighty men and headed south toward Spanish Florida, a well-known refuge for escapees (see below). Along the way they burned seven plantations and killed twenty whites, but they spared a Scottish innkeeper known for being "a good Man and kind to his slaves." Within a day, mounted militia surrounded the slaves near a riverbank, cut them down mercilessly, and spiked a rebel head on every milepost between that spot and Charles Town. Uprisings elsewhere in the colony required more than a month to suppress, with insurgents generally "put to the most cruel Death." Thereafter, whites enacted a new slave code, essentially in force until the Civil War, which kept South Carolina slaves under constant surveillance. Furthermore, it threatened masters with fines for not disciplining slaves and required legislative approval for manumission (freeing of individual slaves). The Stono Rebellion and its cruel aftermath thus reinforced South Carolina's emergence as a rigid, racist, and fear-ridden society.

Slavery and racial tensions were by no means confined to plantations. By midcentury, slaves made up 20 percent of New York City's population and formed a majority in Charles Town and Savannah. Southern urban slave owners augmented their incomes by renting out the labor of their slaves, who were cheaper to employ than white workers. Slave artisans—usually creoles—worked as coopers, shipwrights, rope makers, and, in a few cases, goldsmiths and cabinetmakers. Some artisans supplemented their work as slaves by earning income of their own. Slaves in northern cities were more often unskilled. Urban slaves in both North and South typically lived apart from their masters in rented quarters alongside free blacks.

Although city life afforded slaves greater freedom of association than did plantations, urban blacks remained the property of others and chafed at racist restrictions. In 1712, rebellious slaves in New York City killed nine whites in a calculated attack. As a result, eighteen slaves were hanged or tortured to death, and six others committed suicide to avoid similar treatment. In 1741, a wave of thefts and fires was attributed on dubious testimony to conspiring New York slaves. Of the one hundred fifty-two blacks who were arrested, thirteen were burned at the stake, seventeen were hanged (along with four whites), and seventy were sent to the West Indies.

The Rise of Colonial Elites

A few colonists benefited disproportionately from the growing wealth of Britain and its colonies. Most of these elite colonists inherited their advantages at birth and

John Potter and His Family
The Potters of Matunuck, Rhode Island, relax at tea. In commissioning a portrait depicting themselves at leisure and attended by a black slave, the Potters proclaimed their elite status.

men augmented them by producing plantation crops, buying and selling commodities across the Atlantic or transporting them, or serving as attorneys for other elite colonists. They constituted British America's upper class, or gentry.

A gentleman was expected by his contemporaries to behave with an appropriate degree of responsibility, to display dignity and generosity, and to be a community leader. His wife, a "lady," was to be a skillful household manager and, in the presence of men, a refined yet deferring hostess.

Before 1700, the colonies' class structure was less apparent because elites spent their limited resources buying land, servants, and slaves rather than luxuries. As late as 1715, a traveler noticed that one of Virginia's richest planters, Robert Beverley, owned "nothing in or about his house but just what is necessary, . . . [such as] good beds but no curtains and instead of cane chairs he hath stools made of wood."

As British mercantilist trade flourished, higher incomes enabled elite colonists to display their wealth more openly, particularly in their housing. The greater gentry—the richest 2 percent, owning about 15 percent of all property—constructed elaborate showcase mansions that broadcast their elite status. The lesser gentry, or second wealthiest 2 to 10 percent holding about 25 percent of all property, lived in more modest two-story dwellings. In contrast, middle-class farmers commonly inhabited one-story wooden buildings with four small rooms and a loft.

Colonial gentlemen and ladies also exhibited their status by imitating the "refinement" of upper-class Europeans. They wore costly English fashions, drove carriages instead of wagons, and bought expensive chinaware, books, furniture, and musical instruments. They pursued a gracious life by studying foreign languages, learning formal dances, and cultivating polite manners. Whereas ordinary men bet on cockfighting, considered a vulgar sport, gentlemen preferred horse races, a form of recreation which they alone could afford. A few young gentlemen even traveled abroad to get an English education. Thus, elites led colonists' growing taste for British fashions and consumer goods.

Competing for a Continent, 1713–1750

After a generation of war, Europe's return to peace in 1713 only heightened British, French, and Spanish imperial ambitions in North America. Europeans expanded their territorial claims, intensifying both trade and warfare with Native Americans, and carving out new settlements. Native Americans welcomed some of these developments and resisted others, depending on how they expected their sovereignty and livelihoods to be affected.

France and the American Heartland

France focused its imperial efforts on Louisiana. In 1718, Louisiana officials established New Orleans as the colony's capital and port. Louisiana's staunchest Indian allies were the Choctaws, through whom the French hoped to counter both the expanding influence of Carolina's traders and the Spanish presence in Florida. But by the 1730s inroads by the persistent Carolinians led the Choctaws to become bitterly divided into pro-English and pro-French factions.

Life was dismal in Louisiana for whites as well as blacks. A thoroughly corrupt government ran the colony. With Louisiana's sluggish export economy failing to sustain them, settlers and slaves found other means of survival. Like the Native Americans, they hunted, fished, gathered wild plants, and cultivated gardens. In 1727 a priest described how some whites eventually prospered: "A man with his wife or partner clears a little ground, builds himself a house on four piles, covers it with sheets of bark, and plants corn and rice for his provisions; the next year he raises a little more for food, and has also a field of tobacco; if at last he succeeds in having three or four Negroes, then he is out of difficulties."

But many red, white, and black Louisianans depended on exchanges with one another in order to stay "out of difficulties." Nearby Native Americans provided corn, bear oil, tallow (for candles), and above all deerskins to French merchants in return for blankets, kettles, axes, chickens, hogs, guns, and alcohol. Indian and Spanish traders from west of the Mississippi brought horses and cattle. Familiar with cattle from their homelands, enslaved Africans managed many of Louisiana's herds, and some became rustlers and illicit traders of beef.

French settlers in Upper Louisiana, or Illinois, were somewhat better off, but more than a third of the colony's twenty-six hundred inhabitants were enslaved in 1752. Illinois's principal export was wheat, a more reliably profitable crop than the plantation commodities grown farther south. In exporting wheat, the French colony resembled Pennsylvania to the east; but Illinois's remote location limited such exports and attracted few whites, obliging it to depend on France's Native American allies to defend it from Indian enemies.

With Canada and the Mississippi Valley secure from European rivals, France sought to counter growing British influence in the Ohio Valley. The "Ohio country" was at peace after the Iroquois declared their neutrality in 1701 (see above), encouraging Indian refugees to settle there. Former inhabitants such as the Kickapoos and Shawnees returned from elsewhere to reoccupy homelands. Other arrivals were newcomers, such as Delawares escaping English encroachments in the East and Seneca Iroquois seeking improved hunting territories. Hoping to secure commercial and diplomatic ties with these Natives, the French expanded their trade activities. Several French posts ballooned into sizable villages housing Indians, French, and mixed-ancestry *métis*. But English traders were arriving with better goods at lower prices, and most Indians steered a more independent course.

Although generally more effective in Indian diplomacy than the English, the French were not always successful and could be equally oppressive. The Carolina-supported Chickasaws frequently attacked the French and their Native allies on the Mississippi River, while the French fought a long war against the Mesquakie (or Fox) Indians in the upper Midwest and brutally suppressed the Natchez in

Huron (Wyandotte) Woman
Her cloth dress, glass beads, and iron hoe reflect the influence of French trade on this woman and other Indians of the Great Lakes–Ohio region in the eighteenth century.

Louisiana. The French captured Native Americans in these wars and sold them as slaves in Louisiana, Illinois, Canada, and the West Indies.

By 1744, French traders were traveling as far west as North Dakota and Colorado, and were buying beaver pelts and Indian slaves on the Great Plains. These traders and their British competitors spread trade goods, including guns, to Native Americans throughout central Canada and the Plains. Meanwhile, Indians in the Great Basin and southern Plains were acquiring horses, thousands of which had been left behind by the Spanish when they fled New Mexico during the Pueblo Revolt of 1680. Adopting the horse and gun, Indians such as the Lakota Sioux and Comanches moved to the Plains and built a new, highly mobile way of life based on the pursuit of buffalo. By 1750, France had an immense domain, but one that depended on often-precarious relations with Native Americans.

Native Americans and British Expansion

As in the seventeenth century, British colonial expansion was made possible by the depopulation and dislocation of Native Americans. Epidemic diseases, environmental changes, war, and political pressures on Indians to cede land and to emigrate all combined to make new lands available to white immigrants.

Conflict came early to Carolina, where a trade in Indian slaves (see Chapter 3) and imperial war had already produced violence. The **Tuscarora War** (1711–1713) began when Iroquoian-speaking Tuscaroras, provoked by encroaching whites who enslaved some of their people, destroyed New Bern, a nearby settlement of seven hundred Swiss immigrants. To retaliate, northern Carolina enlisted the aid of southern Carolina and its well-armed Indian allies. By 1713, after about a thousand Tuscaroras (one-fifth of the total population) had been killed or enslaved, the nation surrendered. Most Tuscarora survivors migrated northward to what is now upstate New York and in 1722 became the sixth nation of the Iroquois Confederacy.

After helping defeat the Tuscaroras, Carolina's Indian allies experienced a growing number of abuses, including cheating, violence, and enslavement by English traders and encroachments on their land by settlers. The Yamasees were the most seriously affected. In the **Yamasee War** (1715–1716), they led a coordinated series of attacks by Catawbas, Creeks, and other allies on English trading houses and settlements. Only by enlisting the aid of the Cherokee Indians, and allowing four hundred slaves to bear arms, did the colony crush the uprising. Yamasees

Tuscarora Resistance, 1711
Defending their homeland against an influx of settlers, the Tuscaroras captured Baron Christopher von Graffenried, leader of the Swiss community at New Bern. Graffenried drew this sketch, which depicts him being held along with an English trader, John Lawson, and an African slave. Lawson was later executed.

not killed or captured fled to Florida or to Creek towns in the interior.

The defeat of the Yamasees left their Catawba supporters vulnerable to pressures from English on one side and Iroquois on the other. As Carolina settlers moved uncomfortably close to some Catawba villages, the inhabitants abandoned these villages. Having escaped the settlers, however, the Catawbas faced rising conflict with the Iroquois. After making peace with the Indian allies of New France in 1701 (see above), the Iroquois looked south when launching raids for captives to adopt into their ranks. To counter the well-armed Iroquois, the Catawbas turned back to Carolina. By ceding land and helping defend Carolina against outside Indians, the Catawbas received guns, food, and clothing. Their relationship with the English allowed the Catawbas the security they needed to strengthen their traditional institutions. However, the growing gap in numbers between Catawbas and colonists greatly favored the English in the two peoples' competition for resources.

To the north, the Iroquois Confederacy accommodated English expansion while consolidating its own power among Native Americans. Late in the seventeenth century, the Iroquois and several colonies forged a series of treaties known as the **Covenant Chain**. Under these treaties the Confederacy helped the colonies subjugate Indians whose lands the English wanted. Under one such agreement, the Iroquois assisted Massachusetts in subjugating that colony's Natives following King Philip's War in New England (see Chapter 3). Under another, the Susquehannock Indians, after being crushed in Bacon's Rebellion, moved northward from Maryland to a new homeland adjacent to the Iroquois' own. By relocating

non-Iroquois on their periphery as well as by inviting the Tuscaroras into their Confederacy, the Iroquois controlled a center of Native American power that was distinct from, but cooperative with, the British. At the same time, the Iroquois established buffers against, and deflected, potential English expansion to their own lands.

Although it did not formally belong to the Covenant Chain, Pennsylvania maintained a similar relationship with the Iroquois. With immigration and commercial success, William Penn's early idealism waned in Pennsylvania, along with his warm ties with the Delaware Indians. Between 1729 and 1734, Penn's sons, now the colony's proprietors, and his former secretary coerced the Delawares into selling more than fifty thousand acres. Then the Penn brothers produced a patently fraudulent "deed," which alleged that the Delawares had agreed in 1686 to sell their land as far westward as a man could walk in a day and a half. After selling much of the land to settlers and speculators in a lottery and hiring two men to rehearse the walk, the Penns in 1737 sent the two men on an "official" walk. The men covered sixty-four miles, meaning that the Delawares, in what became known as the **Walking Purchase**, had to hand over an additional twelve hundred square miles of land. Despite the protests of Delaware elders who had been alive in 1686 and remembered no such treaty, the Delawares were forced to move under Iroquois supervision. Settlers began pouring in and, within a generation, the Delawares' former lands were among the most productive in the British Empire.

British Expansion in the South: Georgia

Britain moved to expand southward toward Spanish Florida in 1732 when Parliament authorized a new colony,

Georgia. Charitable idealism and profits, as well as imperial strategizing, lay behind Georgia's founding. Although expecting Georgia to export such expensive commodities as wine and silk, the colony's sponsors intended that it be a refuge for bankrupt but honest debtors. A board of trustees was formed to oversee the colony for twenty-one years before turning it over to the crown. During that time, the trustees decreed, Georgia would do without slavery, alcohol, landholdings of more than five hundred acres, and representative government.

One of the trustees, **James Oglethorpe**, moved to Georgia and dominated it for a decade. Ignoring Spain's claims, Oglethorpe purchased the land for the colony from Creek Indians, with whom he cultivated close ties. Oglethorpe founded the port of Savannah in 1733, and by 1740 twenty-eight hundred colonists had arrived. Almost half the immigrants came from Germany, Switzerland, and Scotland, and most had their overseas passage paid by the government. A small number of Jews were among the early colonists. Along with Pennsylvania, early Georgia was the most inclusive of the British colonies.

Oglethorpe was determined to keep slavery out of Georgia. "They live like cattle," he wrote to the trustees after viewing Charles Town's slave market. "If we allow slaves, we act against the very principles by which we associated together, which was to relieve the distressed." Slavery, he thought, degraded blacks, made whites lazy, and presented a terrible risk. Oglethorpe worried that wherever whites relied on a slave labor force, they courted slave revolts, which the Spanish could then exploit. But most of all, he recognized that slavery undermined the economic position of poor whites like those he sought to settle in Georgia.

Oglethorpe's well-intentioned plans failed completely. Few debtors arrived because Parliament set impossibly stringent conditions for their release from prison. Limitations on settlers' rights to sell or enlarge their holdings, as well as the ban on slavery, also discouraged immigration. Raising exotic export crops proved impractical. Looking to neighboring South Carolina, some Georgians recognized that rice, which required large estates, substantial capital, and many cheap laborers, could flourish in Georgia's lowlands. Under pressure from colonists, the trustees lifted limits on the size of landholdings in 1744 and the ban on slavery in 1750. The trustees also authorized a representative assembly in 1750, just two years before turning the colony over to the crown. By 1760, 6,000 whites and 3,500 enslaved blacks were making Georgia profitable.

Spain's Borderlands

While endeavoring to maintain its empire in the face of Native American, French, and British adversaries, Spain spread its language and culture over much of North America. Seeking to recolonize New Mexico after the Pueblo Revolt (see Chapter 3), Spain awarded grants of approximately twenty-six square miles wherever ten or more families founded a town. Soldiers erected strong fortifications to protect against Indian attacks, now coming primarily from mounted Apaches. As in early New England, settlers built homes on small lots around the church plaza, farmed separate fields nearby, grazed livestock at a distance, and shared a community wood lot and pasture.

The livestock-raising ranchos, radiating out for many miles from little clusters of houses, monopolized vast tracts along the Rio Grande and blocked further town settlement. On the ranchos, mounted cattle herders created the way of life later associated with the American cowboy, featuring lariat and roping skills, cattle drives, roundups (rodeos), and livestock branding.

By 1750 New Mexico numbered about 14,000, more than half of them Pueblo Indians. Most Pueblos now cooperated with the Spanish, and although many had converted to Catholicism, they also practiced their traditional religion. Like the colonists, the Pueblos were village-dwellers who grew crops and raised livestock,

Slave-Raiding Expedition in New Mexico
This surviving portion of a painting on buffalo hide, dating to the 1720s, depicts a Spanish soldier and allied Pueblo Indians as they attack an encampment, probably of Apaches. Women and children look on from behind a palisade surrounding the encampment.

making them equally vulnerable to horse-mounted raiders. Apache raids were now augmented by those of armed and mounted Comanches from the north and east. The raiders sought livestock and European goods as well as captives, often to replace those of their own people who had been enslaved by Spanish raiders and sent to mine silver in Mexico.

Spain had established Texas in order to counter growing French influence among the Comanches and other Native Americans on the southern Plains. Colonization began after 1716, when Spaniards established several outposts on the San Antonio and Guadalupe Rivers. The most prominent center was at San Antonio de Béxar, where two towns, a presidio, and a mission (later known as the Alamo) were clustered. But most Indians in Texas preferred trading with the French to farming, Christianity, and the ineffective protection of the Spanish. Lack of security also deterred Hispanic settlement, so that by 1760 only twelve hundred Spaniards inhabited Texas.

Spain's position in Florida was only somewhat less precarious. As early as 1700, there were already thirty-eight hundred English in recently founded Carolina, compared to just fifteen hundred Spanish in Florida. This disparity widened thereafter.

Florida found ways to offset its small number of colonists. After the Yamasee War (see above), the Creeks broke off their alliance with Carolina in favor of a policy of neutrality. The Creeks' neutrality enabled some Spaniards to trade with them for deerskins, and to sponsor Creek raids into Carolina. But Florida's trade profits remained limited because it lacked ample supplies of cheap, desirable trade goods, compared to its British and French neighbors.

Florida gained more at English expense through its effective recruitment of escaped slaves from Carolina. From the time of Carolina's founding, some enslaved blacks had found their way to the Spanish colony. In 1693, Spain's King Charles II ruled that any English-owned slaves arriving in Florida would be freed upon converting to Catholicism. Word of the ruling spread back to Carolina, prompting more slaves to flee to Florida, especially while planters were distracted during the Yamasee War. In 1726, Spanish authorities created an all-black militia unit under the command of Francisco Menéndez, a former South Carolina slave, to help defend Florida. In 1738, the colony built a fortified village, Mose, for Menéndez's men and their families adjacent to the capital at St. Augustine. The unit would prove critical after England and Spain went to war the next year (see below).

By 1750, Spain controlled much of the Southeast and Southwest, while France exercised influence in the Mississippi, Ohio, and Missouri River valleys, as well as around the Great Lakes and in Canada (see Map 4.3). Both empires were spread thin and depended on the support or acquiescence of non-Europeans. In contrast, British North America was compact, wealthy, densely populated by whites, and aggressively expansionist.

Fort Mose
This artist's reconstruction of the free black community at St. Augustine is based on archaeological and documentary evidence.

The Return of War, 1739–1748

After a generation of war ended in 1713, the American colonies enjoyed a generation of peace as well as prosperity. But in 1739, British launched a war against Spain, using as a pretext Spain's cutting off the ear of a British smuggler named Jenkins. (Thus, the British termed the conflict the "War of Jenkins' Ear.") In 1740, James Oglethorpe led a

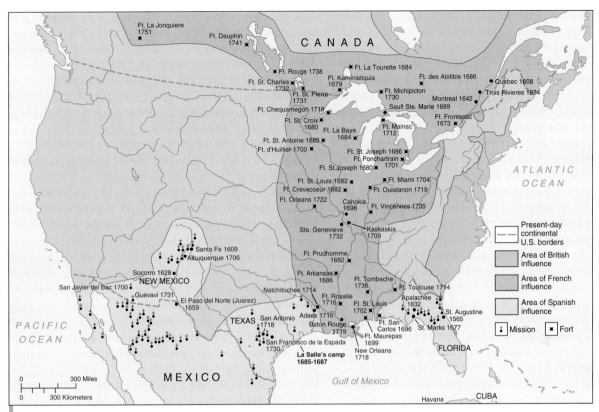

Map 4.3 European Occupation of North America, to 1750
Spanish and French occupation depended on ties with Native Americans. By contrast, British colonists had dispossessed Native peoples and densely settled the eastern seaboard.

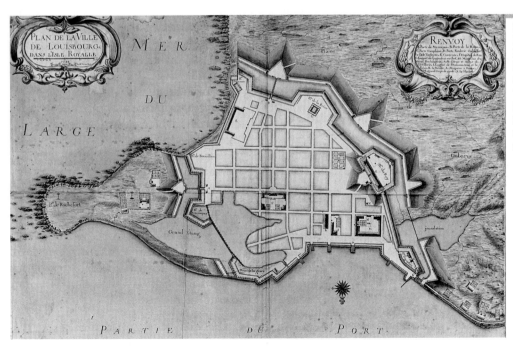

Plan of Louisbourg, 1744
Built to defend New France, Louisbourg fell to New Englanders in 1745, but was returned to France by the Treaty of Aix-la-Chapelle (1748). France would lose the fortress for good when British troops seized it in 1758 (see Chapter 5).

massive British assault on Florida. The English captured Mose, but after Francisco Menéndez's black militia and other troops recaptured the town, Oglethorpe withdrew. Two years later, Oglethorpe led 650 men in repelling 3,000 Spanish troops who counterattacked Georgia.

The Anglo-Spanish War quickly merged with a larger one in Europe, the War of the Austrian Succession, called **King George's War** in British America (1740–1748). King George's War followed the pattern of earlier imperial conflicts. Few battles involved more than six hundred men, and most were attacks and counterattacks on civilians in the Northeast in which many noncombatants were killed and others captured. Most captives were New Englanders seized by French and Indians from isolated towns. Although prisoners were exchanged at the end of the war, some English captives, particularly women and children, elected to remain with the French or Indians.

King George's War produced just one major engagement in North America. In 1745, almost four thousand New Englanders under William Pepperell of Maine besieged and, after seven weeks of intense fighting, captured the French bastion of Louisbourg, which guarded the entrance to the St. Lawrence River. After three more years of inconclusive warfare, Britain signed the Treaty of Aix-la-Chapelle (1748), exchanging Louisbourg for a British outpost in India that the French had seized.

Public Life in British America, 1689–1750

During the early and middle eighteenth century, the ties linking Britain and its colonies consisted of much more than the movements of goods and peoples. England's new Bill of Rights was the foundation of government and politics in the colonies. The ideas of English thinkers initially inspired the intellectual movement known as the Enlightenment, while the English preacher George Whitefield sparked a generation of colonists to transform the practice of Protestantism in British America. While reinforcing the colonies' links with Britain, these developments were also significant because they involved many more colonists than before as active participants in politics, in intellectual discussions, and in new religious movements. Taken as a whole, this wider participation signaled the emergence of a broad Anglo-American "public."

Colonial Politics

The most significant political result of the Glorious Revolution was the rise of colonial legislatures, or assemblies,

as a major political force. Except in Connecticut and Rhode Island, the crown or a proprietor in England chose each colony's governor. In most colonies the governor named a council, or upper house of the legislature. The assembly was therefore the only political body subject to control by colonists rather than by English officials. Before 1689, governors and councils took the initiative in drafting laws, and the assemblies followed their lead; but thereafter the assemblies assumed a more central role in politics.

Colonial leaders argued that their legislatures should exercise the same rights as those won by Parliament in its seventeenth-century struggle with royal authority. Indeed, Anglo-Americans saw their assemblies as comparable to England's House of Commons, which represented the people and defended their liberty against centralized authority, particularly through its exclusive power to originate revenue-raising measures. After Parliament won supremacy over the monarchy through the Bill of Rights in 1689, assemblymen insisted that their governors' powers were similarly limited.

The lower houses steadily asserted their prestige and authority by refusing to permit outside meddling in their proceedings, by taking firm control over taxes and budgets, and especially by keeping a tight rein on executive salaries. Although governors had considerable powers (including the right to veto acts, call and dismiss assembly sessions, and schedule elections), they were vulnerable to legislatures' financial pressure because they received no salary from British sources and relied on the assemblies for income. This "power of the purse" sometimes enabled assemblies to force governors to sign laws opposed by the crown.

The assemblies' growing importance was reinforced by British policy. The Board of Trade, established in 1696 to monitor American developments, could have weakened the assemblies by persuading the crown to disallow objectionable colonial laws signed by the governors. But it rarely exercised this power before midcentury. The resulting political vacuum allowed the colonies to become self-governing in most respects except for trade regulation, restrictions on printing money, and declaring war. Representative government in the colonies originated and was nurtured within the protective environment of the British Empire.

The elite planters, merchants, and attorneys who monopolized colonial wealth also dominated politics. Most assemblymen ranked among the wealthiest 2 percent of colonists. To placate them, governors invariably appointed other members of the greater gentry to sit on their councils and as judges on the highest courts. Although members of the lesser gentry sat less often in the legislature, they commonly served as justices of the peace.

Outside New England (where any voter was eligible for office), legal requirements barred 80 percent of white men from running for the assembly, most often by specifying that a candidate own a minimum of a thousand acres. (Farms then averaged 180 acres in the South and 120 acres in the middle colonies.) Even without such property qualifications, few ordinary colonists could have afforded to hold elective office. Assemblymen received only living expenses, which might not fully cover the cost of staying at their province's capital, much less compensate a farmer or an artisan for his absence from farm or shop for six to ten weeks a year. As a result, a few wealthy families in each colony dominated the highest political offices. Nine families, for example, provided one-third of Virginia's councilors after 1680. John Adams, a rising young Massachusetts politician, estimated that most towns in his colony chose their legislators from among just three or four families.

By eighteenth-century standards, the colonies set liberal qualifications for male voters, but all provinces barred women and nonwhites from voting. In seven colonies, voters had to own land (usually forty to fifty acres), and the rest demanded that an elector have enough property to furnish a house and work a farm with his own tools. About 40 percent of free white men—mostly indentured servants and young men still living with parents or just beginning family life—could not meet these requirements. Still, most white males in British North America could vote by age forty, whereas two-thirds of all men in England and nine-tenths in Ireland were never eligible.

In rural areas, voter participation was low unless a vital issue was at stake. The difficulties of voting limited the average rural turnout to about 45 percent (a rate of participation higher, however, than in typical U.S. elections today, apart from those for president). Most governors called elections when they saw fit, so that elections might lapse for years and suddenly be held on very short notice. Thus voters in isolated areas often had no knowledge of upcoming contests. The fact that polling took place at the county seat discouraged many electors from traveling long distances over poor roads to vote. In several colonies, voters stated their choices orally and publicly, often with the candidates present. This procedure inhibited the participation of humbler men whose views differed from those of elites, especially those who also depended on elites for credit, shipping privileges, or other favors. Finally, most rural elections before 1750 were uncontested. Local elites decided in advance which of them would "stand" for office. Regarding officeholding as a gentleman's public duty, they considered it demeaning to appear interested in being chosen, much less to compete or "run" for a position.

Given all these factors, many rural voters were indifferent about politics at the colony level. For example, to avoid paying legislators' expenses at the capital, many smaller Massachusetts towns refused to elect assemblymen. Thirty percent of men elected to South Carolina's assembly neglected to take their seats from 1731 to 1760, including a majority of those chosen in 1747 and 1749.

Despite these limitations, rural elections slowly emerged as community events in which many nonelite white men participated. In time, rural voters would follow urban colonists and express themselves more forcefully.

Competitive politics first developed in the northern seaports. Depending on their economic interests and family ties, wealthy colonists aligned themselves with or against royal and proprietary governors. To gain advantage over rivals, some factions courted artisans and small shopkeepers whose fortunes had stagnated or declined as the distribution of urban wealth tilted increasingly toward the rich. In actively courting nonelite voters, they scandalized rival elites who feared that an unleashing of popular passions could disturb the social order.

New York was the site of the bitterest factional conflicts. In one episode in 1733, Governor William Cosby suspended his principal rival, Chief Justice Lewis Morris, after Morris ruled against the governor. To mobilize popular support for Morris, his faction established the *New-York*

Hanover County Courthouse, Virginia
The county courthouse was the seat of local government and the center of political and social life in the Chesapeake colonies.

Weekly Journal, which repeatedly accused Cosby and his associates of rampant corruption. In 1734, the governor's supporters engineered the arrest of the *Weekly Journal's* printer, John Peter Zenger, on charges that he had seditiously libeled Cosby. Following a celebrated trial in August 1735, Zenger was acquitted.

Although it neither led to a change in New York's libel law nor significantly enhanced freedom of the press at the time, the Zenger verdict was significant for several reasons. In New York and elsewhere, it encouraged the broadening of political discussion and participation beyond a small circle of elites. Equally significant were its legal implications. Zenger's brilliant attorney, Andrew Hamilton, effectively employed the growing practice among colonial attorneys of speaking directly to a jury on behalf of a defendant. He persuaded the jury that it alone, without the judge's advice, could reject a charge of libel "if you should be of the opinion that there is no falsehood in [Zenger's] papers." Until then, truth alone was not a sufficient defense against a charge of libel in British and colonial courts of law. By empowering nonelites as voters, readers, and jurors, the Morris-Cosby rivalry and the Zenger trial encouraged broader participation in New York's public life.

The Enlightenment

If property and wealth were keys to political participation and officeholding, literacy and education permitted Anglo-Americans to participate in the transatlantic world of ideas and beliefs. Perhaps 90 percent of New England's adult white men and 40 percent of white women could write well enough to sign documents, thanks to the region's traditional support for primary education. Among white males elsewhere in the colonies, the literacy rate varied from about 35 percent to more than 50 percent. (In England, by contrast, no more than one-third of all males could read and write.) How readily most of these people read a book or wrote a letter was another matter.

The best-educated colonists—members of the gentry, well-to-do merchants, educated ministers, and growing numbers of artisans and farmers—embraced a wider world of ideas and information. Though costly, books, newspapers, and writing paper could open up eighteenth-century European civilization to reading men and women. A rich, exciting world it was. Scientific advances seemed to explain the laws of nature; human intelligence appeared poised to triumph over ignorance, prejudice, superstition, and irrational tradition. For those who had the time to read and to ponder ideas, an age of optimism and boundless progress was dawning, an age known as the Enlightenment.

Enlightenment ideals combined confidence in human reason with skepticism toward beliefs not founded on science or strict logic. A major source of Enlightenment thought was English physicist Sir Isaac Newton (1642–1727), who in 1687 explained how gravitation ruled the universe. Newton's work appealed to educated Europeans by demonstrating the harmony of natural laws and stimulated others to search for rational principles in medicine, law, psychology, and government.

Before 1750, no American more fully embodied the Enlightenment spirit than **Benjamin Franklin**. Born in Boston in 1706, Franklin migrated to Philadelphia at age seventeen. He brought skill as a printer, considerable ambition, and insatiable intellectual curiosity. In moving to Philadelphia, Franklin put himself in the right place at the right time, for the city was growing much more rapidly than Boston and was attracting merchants and artisans who shared Franklin's zest for learning and new ideas. Franklin organized some of these men into a reading-discussion group called the Junto, and they helped him secure printing contracts. In 1732 he first published

Benjamin Franklin
This earliest known portrait of Franklin dates to about 1740, when he was a rising leader in bustling Philadelphia.

Poor Richard's Almanack, a collection of maxims and proverbs that made him famous. By age forty-two Franklin had earned enough money to retire and devote himself to science and public service.

These dual goals—science and public benefit—were intimately related in Franklin's mind, for he believed that all true science would be useful, in the sense of making everyone's life more comfortable. For example, experimenting with a kite, Franklin demonstrated in 1752 that lightning was electricity, a discovery that led to the lightning rod.

Although some southern planters, such as Thomas Jefferson, later championed progress through science, the Enlightenment's earliest and primary American centers were cities, where the latest European books and ideas circulated and where gentlemen and self-improving artisans met to investigate nature and conduct experiments. Franklin organized one such group, the American Philosophical Society, in 1743 to encourage "all philosophical experiments that let light into the nature of things, tend to increase the power of man over matter, and multiply the conveniences and pleasures of life." By 1769, this society had blossomed into an intercolonial network of amateur scientists. The societies emulated the Royal Society in London, the foremost learned society in the English-speaking world. In this respect, the Enlightenment initially strengthened the ties between colonial and British elites.

Just as Newton inspired the scientific bent of Enlightenment intellectuals, English philosopher John Locke, in his *Essay Concerning Human Understanding* (1690), led many to embrace "reasonable" or "rational" religion. Locke contended that ideas, including religion, are not inborn but are acquired by toilsome investigation of and reflection upon experience. To most Enlightenment intellectuals, the best argument for the existence of God was the harmony and order of nature, which pointed to a rational Creator. Some individuals, including Franklin and, later, Jefferson and Thomas Paine, carried this argument a step farther by insisting that where the Bible conflicted with reason, one should follow the dictates of reason. Called Deists, they concluded that God, having created a perfect universe, did not thereafter intervene in its workings but rather left it alone to operate according to natural laws.

Most colonists influenced by the Enlightenment described themselves as Christians and attended church. But they feared Christianity's excesses, particularly as indulged in by those who persecuted others in religion's name and by "enthusiasts" who emphasized emotion rather than reason in the practice of piety. Above all, they distrusted zealots and sectarians. Typically, Franklin contributed money to most of the churches in Philadelphia but thought that religion's value lay in its encouragement of virtue and morality rather than in theological hair splitting.

In 1750, the Enlightenment's greatest contributions to American life still lay in the future. A quarter-century later, Anglo-Americans drew on the Enlightenment's revolutionary ideas as they declared their independence from Britain and created the foundations of a new nation (see Chapters 5 and 6). Meanwhile, a series of religious revivals known as the Great Awakening challenged the Enlightenment's most basic assumptions.

The Great Awakening

Viewing the world as orderly and predictable, rationalists were inclined to a sense of smug self-satisfaction. Writing his will in 1750, Franklin thanked God for giving him "such a mind, with moderate passions" and "such a competency of this world's goods as might make a reasonable mind easy." But many Americans lacked such a comfortable competency of goods and lived neither orderly nor predictable lives. Earlier generations of young people coming of age had relied on established authority figures—parents, local leaders, clergy—for wisdom and guidance as they faced the future. But the world had changed by the middle decades of the eighteenth century. Older authorities were of little help when one's economic future was uncertain, when established elites seemed to act out of self-interest, and when one encountered more strangers than familiar faces on a daily basis. The result was a widespread spiritual hunger that neither traditional religion nor Enlightenment philosophy could satisfy.

Throughout the colonial period, religious fervor periodically surged within a denomination or region and then receded. But in 1739 an outpouring of European Protestant revivalism spread to British North America. This "Great Awakening," as colonial promoters termed it, cut across lines of class, gender, and even race. Above all, the revivals represented an unleashing of anxiety and longing among ordinary people—anxiety about sin, and longing for assurances of salvation. The answers they received were conveyed through the powerful preaching of charismatic ministers who appealed to their audiences' emotions rather than to their intellects. Some revivalists were themselves intellectuals, comfortable amid the books and ideas of the Enlightenment. But for all, religion was primarily a matter of emotional commitment.

In contrast to rationalists, who stressed the potential for human improvement, revivalist ministers aroused their audiences by depicting the emptiness of material comfort, the utter corruption of human nature, the fury of divine wrath, and the need for immediate repentance. Although well read in Enlightenment philosophy and science, the Congregationalist Jonathan Edwards, who led a revival at Northampton, Massachusetts, in 1735, drove home this message with breathtaking clarity. "The God that holds you over the pit of Hell, much as one holds a spider or other loathsome insect over the fire, abhors you," Edwards intoned in a famous sermon, "Sinners in the Hands of an Angry God." "His wrath toward you burns like fire; He looks upon you as worthy of nothing else but to be cast into the fire."

Even before Edwards's Northampton revival, two New Jersey ministers, Presbyterian William Tennent and Theodore Frelinghuysen of the Dutch Reformed Church, had stimulated conversions in prayer meetings called Refreshings. But the event that brought these threads of revival together was the arrival from Britain in 1739 of **George Whitefield** (see above). So overpowering was Whitefield that some joked that he could make crowds swoon simply by uttering "Mesopotamia." In an age without microphones, crowds exceeding twenty thousand could hear his booming voice clearly, and many wept at his eloquence.

Whitefield's American tour inspired thousands to seek salvation. Most converts were young adults in their late twenties. In Connecticut alone, church membership jumped from 630 in 1740 to 3,217 after Whitefield toured in 1741. Within two more years, every fifth Connecticut resident under forty-five had reportedly been saved by God's grace. Whitefield's allure was so mighty that he even awed potential critics. Hearing him preach in Philadelphia, Benjamin Franklin first vowed to contribute nothing to the collection. But so admirably did Whitefield conclude his sermon, Franklin recalled, "that I empty'd my Pocket wholly into the Collector's Dish, Gold and all." Divisions over the revivals quickly developed and were often exacerbated by social and economic tensions. For example, after leaving Boston in October 1740, Whitefield invited Gilbert Tennent (William's son) to follow "in order to blow up the divine flame lately kindled there." Denouncing Boston's established clergymen as "dead Drones" and lashing out at aristocratic fashion, Tennent built a following among the city's poor and downtrodden. So did another preacher, James Davenport, who spoke daily on the Boston Commons and then frightened polite Bostonians by leading processions of "idle or ignorant persons, and those of the lowest Rank" through the streets. Brought before a grand jury, Davenport was expelled for asserting "that Boston's ministers were leading the people blindfolded to hell."

Exposing colonial society's divisions, Tennent and Davenport sparked opposition to the revivals among established ministers and officials. As Whitefield's exchange with Alexander Garden showed, the lines hardened between the revivalists, known as New Lights, and the rationalist clergy, or Old Lights, who dominated the Anglican, Presbyterian, and Congregational churches. In 1740, Gilbert Tennent published *The Danger of an Unconverted Ministry*, which hinted that most Presbyterian ministers lacked saving grace and hence were bound for hell, and urged parishioners to abandon them for the New Lights. By thus sowing the seeds of doubt about individual ministers, Tennent undermined one of the foundations of social order. For if the people could not trust their own ministers, whom would they trust?

Old Light rationalists fired back. In 1742, Charles Chauncy, Boston's leading Congregationalist minister, condemned the revival as an epidemic of the "enthusiasm" that enlightened intellectuals loathed. Chauncy particularly blasted those who mistook the ravings of their overheated imaginations for the experience of divine grace. He even provided a kind of checklist for spotting enthusiasts: look for "a certain wildness" in their eyes, the "quakings and tremblings" of their limbs, and foaming at the mouth. Put simply, the revival had unleashed "a sort of madness."

The Great Awakening opened unprecedented splits in American Protestantism. In 1741, New and Old Light Presbyterians formed rival branches that did not reunite until 1758, when the revivalists emerged victorious. The Anglicans lost many members to New Light congregations, especially Baptist and New Light Presbyterian. Congregationalists splintered so badly that by 1760, New Lights had seceded from one-third of New England's churches and formed New Light congregations or joined the Baptists.

The secession of New Lights was especially bitter in Massachusetts and Connecticut, where the Congregational church was established by law. Old Lights repeatedly denied new churches legal status, meaning that New Lights' taxes would go to their former churches. Connecticut passed repressive laws forbidding revivalists to preach or perform marriages, and the colony expelled New Lights from the legislature. In Connecticut's Windham County, an extra story was added to the jail to hold all the New Lights arrested for not paying church taxes (tithes). Elisha Paine, a revivalist imprisoned there for illegal preaching, gave sermons from his cell and drew such crowds that his followers built bleachers nearby to hear him. Paine and his fellow victims generated widespread sympathy for the New Lights, who finally won control of Connecticut's assembly in 1759.

Although New Lights made steady gains until the 1770s, the Great Awakening peaked in New England in 1742. The revival then crested everywhere but in Virginia, where its high point came after 1755 with an upsurge of conversions by Baptists, who also suffered legal harassment.

For all the commotion it raised at the time, the Great Awakening's long-term effects exceeded its immediate impact. First, the revival marked a decline in the influence of Quakers (who were not significantly affected by revivalism), Anglicans, and Congregationalists. In undermining Anglicans and Congregationalists, the Great Awakening contributed to the weakening of officially established denominations. As these churches' importance waned after 1740, the number of Presbyterians and Baptists increased.

The Great Awakening also stimulated the founding of new colleges as both Old and New Lights sought institutions free of one another's influence. In 1746, New Light Presbyterians established the College of New Jersey (Princeton). Then followed King's College (Columbia) for Anglicans in 1754, the College of Rhode Island (Brown) for Baptists in 1764, Queen's College (Rutgers) for Dutch Reformed in 1766, and Dartmouth College for Congregationalists in 1769.

The revivals were also significant because they spread beyond the ranks of white society. The emphasis on piety over intellectual learning as the key to God's grace led some Africans and Native Americans to combine aspects of their traditional cultures with Christianity. The Great Awakening marked the beginnings of black Protestantism after New Lights reached out to slaves, some of whom joined white churches and even preached at revival meetings. Meanwhile, a few New Light preachers became missionaries to Native Americans residing within the colonies. A few Christian Indians trained in a special school to become missionaries to other Native Americans, and one, Samson Occom, a Mohegan born in Connecticut, became widely known among whites. Despite these breakthroughs, blacks and Indians still faced considerable religious discrimination, even among New Lights.

The Great Awakening also added to white women's religious prominence. For several decades non-Anglican ministers had singled out women—who constituted the majority of church members—as embodying the Christian ideal of piety. Now some New Light churches, mostly Baptist and Congregationalist, granted women the right to speak and vote in church meetings. Like Anne Hutchinson a century earlier (see Chapter 3), some women moved from leading women's prayer and discussion groups to presiding over meetings that included men. One such woman, Sarah Osborn of Newport, Rhode Island, conducted "private praying Societies Male and female" that included black slaves in her home. In

Reverend Samson Occom, Mohegan Indian Preacher Born in a wigwam in Connecticut, Occom converted to Christianity under the influence of the Great Awakening and preached to other Native Americans. But he grew disillusioned with the treatment of his people by whites and, after the American Revolution, joined an exodus of Indians from New England to upstate New York.

1770, Osborn and her followers won a bitter fight over their congregation's choice of a new minister. While most assertive women were prevented from exercising as much power as Osborn, none was persecuted as Hutchinson had been in Puritan New England.

Finally the revivals blurred denominational differences among Protestants. Although George Whitefield was an Anglican who defied his superior, Garden, and later helped found Methodism, he preached with Presbyterians such as Gilbert Tennent and Congregationalists like Jonathan Edwards. By emphasizing the need for salvation over details of doctrine and church governance, revivalism emphasized Protestants' common experiences and promoted the coexistence of denominations.

Historians have disagreed over whether the Great Awakening had political as well as religious effects. Although Tennent and Davenport called the poor "God's people" and flayed the wealthy, they never advocated revolution, and the Awakening did not produce a distinct political ideology. Yet by empowering ordinary people to assert and act openly on beliefs that countered those in authority, the revivals laid some of the groundwork for political revolutionaries a generation later.

Chronology, 1660–1750

1651–1663	England enacts first three Navigation Acts.	1716	San Antonio de Béxar founded.
1660	Restoration of the English monarchy.	1718	New Orleans founded.
1686–1689	Dominion of New England.	1729–1730	French war on Natchez Indians in Louisiana.
1688–1689	Glorious Revolution in England.	1733	Georgia founded. Molasses Act.
1689	English Bill of Rights.	1735	John Peter Zenger acquitted of seditious libel in New York.
1689–1691	Uprisings in Massachusetts, New York, and Maryland.		Jonathan Edwards leads revival in Northampton, Massachusetts.
1689–1697	King William's War (in Europe, War of the League of Augsburg).	1737	Walking Purchase of Delaware Indian lands in Pennsylvania.
1690	John Locke, *Essay Concerning Human Understanding*.	1739	Great Awakening begins with George Whitefield's arrival in British colonies. Stono Rebellion in South Carolina.
1693	Spain begins offering freedom to English-owned slaves escaping to Florida.	1739–1740	Anglo-Spanish "War of Jenkins' Ear."
1701	Iroquois Confederacy's Grand Settlement with England and France.	1740–1748	King George's War (in Europe, the War of the Austrian Succession).
1702–1713	Queen Anne's War (in Europe, War of the Spanish Succession).	1743	Benjamin Franklin founds American Philosophical Society.
1711–1713	Tuscarora War in Carolina.	1750	Slavery legalized in Georgia.
1715–1716	Yamasee War in Carolina.		

Conclusion

By 1750, Britain's mainland colonies barely resembled those of a century earlier. Mercantilist policies bound an expanded number of colonies to the rising prosperity of the British Empire. A healthy environment for whites, along with encroachments on Native Americans' land, enabled the combined white and black population to grow by more than twenty times—from about fifty thousand to over one million. The political settlement that followed England's Glorious Revolution further bound the colonies to the empire and—at the same time—provided the foundation for representative government in the colonies. Educated Anglo-Americans joined the European intellectual ferment known as the Enlightenment. The Great Awakening, with its European origins and its intercolonial appeal, further signaled the colonies' emergence from provincial isolation. All these developments made British Americans more conscious of their ties to other colonies, to Great Britain, and to the broader Atlantic world.

Key Terms

Dominion of New England	Middle Passage
Glorious Revolution	Stono Rebellion
English Bill of Rights	Tuscarora War
Leisler's Rebellion	Yamasee War
Protestant Association	Covenant Chain
King William's War	Walking Purchase
Grand Settlement of 1701	James Oglethorpe
Queen Anne's War	King George's War
mercantilism	Benjamin Franklin
Navigation Acts	George Whitefield

The achievements of France and Spain on the North American mainland contrasted starkly with those of Britain. More lightly populated by Europeans, their colonies were more dependent on Native Americans for their survival. Despite their mercantilist orientations, neither France nor Spain profited significantly by colonizing mainland North America.

For all of its evident wealth and progress, British America was rife with tensions. In some areas, vast discrepancies in the distribution of wealth and opportunities fostered a rebellious spirit among whites who were less well off. The Enlightenment and the Great Awakening revealed deep-seated religious and ideological divisions. Slave resistance and Anglo-Indian warfare demonstrated the depths of racial antagonisms. The revived imperial warfare of 1739–1748 signaled that the peace that had nurtured prosperity was over and that an Anglo-French showdown was imminent.

For Further Reference

Bernard Bailyn and Philip D. Morgan, eds., *Strangers Within the Realm: Cultural Margins of the First British Empire* (1991). Leading historians examine the interplay of race, ethnicity, and empire in North America, the Caribbean, and the British Isles.

Jon Butler, *Becoming America: The Revolution Before 1776* (2000). A provocative discussion of the British colonies, arguing that they became a distinctive modern society between 1680 and 1770.

W. J. Eccles, *France in America*, rev. ed. (1991). An interpretive overview of French colonization in North America and the Caribbean by a distinguished scholar.

P. J. Marshall, ed. *The Oxford History of the British Empire*, vol. 2: *The Eighteenth Century* (1998). Authoritative essays on political and economic developments in North America and elsewhere in the British Empire.

John J. McCusker and Russell R. Menard, *The Economy of British America, 1607–1789*, rev. ed. (1991). A comprehensive discussion of the colonial economy, drawing on a wide range of scholarship.

James H. Merrell, *Into the Woods: Negotiators on the Pennsylvania Frontier* (1999). A brilliant, innovative study of intercultural diplomacy as practiced by Indians and colonists.

Philip D. Morgan, *Slave Counterpoint: Black Culture in the Eighteenth-Century Chesapeake and Lowcountry* (1998). The definitive study of African-American life in Britain's southern colonies.

Daniel K. Richter, *Facing East from Indian Country: A Native History of Early America* (2001). A highly original, stimulating perspective on Native Americans' interactions with Europeans.

Laurel Thatcher Ulrich, *The Age of Homespun: Objects and Stories in the Creation of an American Myth* (2001). A pathbreaking study that uses New England women's work with textiles as a window into economic, gender, and cultural history.

David J. Weber, *The Spanish Frontier in North America* (1992). A masterful synthesis of Spanish colonial history north of the Caribbean and Mexico.

Chapter 5

The Boston Massacre, 1770, Engraving by Paul Revere
After this incident, a Bostonian observed, "unless there is some great alteration in the state of things, the era of the independence of the colonies is much nearer than I once thought it, or now wish it."

Roads to Revolution, 1750–1776

George Robert Twelves Hewes

On the evening of March 5, 1770, an angry crowd of poor and working-class Bostonians gathered in front of the guard post outside the Boston customs house. The crowd was protesting a British soldier's abusive treatment a few hours earlier of a Boston apprentice who was trying to collect a debt from a British officer. Suddenly, shots rang out. When the smoke had cleared, four Bostonians lay dead, and seven more were wounded, one mortally.

Among those in the crowd was an impoverished twenty-eight-year-old shoemaker named George Robert Twelves Hewes. Hewes had already witnessed, and once experienced, abuses by British troops, but the appalling violence of the **Boston Massacre**, as the shooting became known, led Hewes to political activism. Four of the five who died were personal friends, and he himself received a serious blow to the shoulder from a soldier's rifle butt. Over the next several days, Hewes attended meetings and signed petitions denouncing British conduct in the shooting, and he later testified against the soldiers. Thereafter, he participated prominently in such anti-British actions as the Boston Tea Party.

How was it that four thousand British troops were stationed on the streets of Boston—a city of sixteen thousand—in 1770? What had brought those troops and the city's residents to the verge of war? What led obscure, humble people like George Robert Twelves Hewes to become angry political activists in an age when the lowborn were expected to leave politics to their social superiors? The Boston Massacre was one of a long chain of events that finally resulted in a complete break between Britain and its American colonies.

The seeds of conflict between Britain and the colonies were planted during the **Seven Years' War** (1756–1763), known to Anglo-Americans as the French and Indian War, when Britain and the colonies together defeated France. As a result, Britain gained most of France's former territory in eastern North America. Thereafter Parliament attempted to reorganize its suddenly enlarged empire by tightening control over economic and political affairs in the colonies. Long accustomed to benefiting economically from the empire while conducting provincial and local affairs on their own (see Technology and Culture), colonists resisted this effort to centralize decision making in London. Many colonial leaders, such as Benjamin Franklin, interpreted Britain's clampdown as calculated antagonism intended to deprive the colonists of their prosperity and their relative independence. Others, such as Massachusetts Lieutenant Governor and Chief Justice Thomas Hutchinson, stressed the importance of maintaining order and authority.

For many ordinary colonists like Hewes, however, the conflict was more than a constitutional crisis. In the port cities, crowds of poor and working people engaged in direct, often violent demonstrations against British authority. Sometimes, they acted in support of elite radicals, and other times in defiance of them. Settlers in the remote backcountry of several colonies invoked the language and ideas of urban radicals when resisting large landowners and distant colonial governments dominated by seaboard elites. These movements reflected political and economic tensions within the colonies as well as the growing defiance of elites by ordinary colonists. By the same token, the growing participation of white women in colonial resistance reflected their impatience with the restraints imposed by traditional gender norms. Nonwhite African-Americans and Native Americans had varying views, but many in each group perceived the colonists as greater threats to their liberty than Britain. Moreover, colonial protests were inspired by ideas and opposition movements in Britain and elsewhere in Europe.

Taken as a whole, colonial resistance involved many kinds of people with many outlooks. It arose most immediately from a constitutional crisis within the British Empire, but it also reflected deep democratic stirrings in America and in the Atlantic world generally. These stirrings would erupt in the American Revolution in 1776, then in the French Revolution in 1789, and subsequently spread over much of Europe and the Americas.

Most colonists expressed their opposition peacefully before 1775, through such tactics as legislative resolutions and commercial boycotts, and they did not foresee the revolutionary outcome of their protests. Despite eruptions of violence, relatively few Anglo-Americans and no royal officials or soldiers lost their lives during the twelve years prior to the battles at Lexington and Concord. Even after fighting broke out, colonists agonized for more than a year about whether to sever their political relationship with England, which even some native-born colonists referred to affectionately as "home." Anglo-Americans were the most reluctant of revolutionaries in 1776.

Focus Questions

- How did Britain and its colonies view their joint victory over France in the Seven Years' War?

- How did colonial resistance to the Stamp Act differ from earlier opposition to British imperial measures?

- In what ways did resistance to the Townshend duties differ from earlier colonial resistance efforts?

- In what ways did colonists' views of parliamentary authority change after 1770?

- What led most colonists in 1776 to abandon their loyalty to Britain and choose national independence?

Triumph and Tensions: The British Empire, 1750–1763

King George's War (see Chapter 4) ended in 1748 with Britain and France still intent on defeating one another. After a "diplomatic revolution" in which Austria shifted its allegiance from Britain to France, and Britain aligned with Prussia, the conflict resumed. Known as the Seven Years' War, it pitted British and French forces against one another in every continent except Australia. The war resulted in the expulsion of France from mainland North America, leaving the region to a triumphant British Empire. Yet even as war wound down, tensions developed within the victorious coalition of Britons, colonists, and Native Americans.

A Fragile Peace, 1750–1754

Soon after King George's War, Britain and France began preparations for another war, this time in the North American interior. The tinderbox for conflict was the Ohio valley, the subject of competing claims by Virginia, Pennsylvania, France, and the Six Nations Iroquois, as well as by the Native Americans who actually lived there.

Traders from Virginia and Pennsylvania were strengthening British influence among Indians in the Ohio valley. Seeking to drive out the traders, the French began building a chain of forts in the Ohio country in 1753. Virginia retaliated by sending a twenty-one-year-old surveyor and speculator, **George Washington**, to persuade or force the French to leave. Fearing that Washington had designs on their land, Native Americans refused to support him, and in 1754 French troops drove the Virginians back to their homes.

Chief Hendrick (Theyanoguin) of the Mohawk Iroquois
A longtime ally of the British, Hendrick led a Mohawk delegation to the Albany Congress (1754).

While Washington was still in Ohio, British officials called a meeting in mid-1754 of delegates from Virginia and colonies to the north to negotiate a treaty with the Six Nations Iroquois. Iroquois support would be vital in any effort to drive the French from the Ohio valley. Seven colonies (but neither Virginia nor New Jersey) sent delegates to the **Albany Congress** in Albany, New York. Long allied with Britain in the Covenant Chain, the Iroquois were also bound by the Grand Settlement of 1701 to remain neutral in any Anglo-French war (see Chapter 4). Moreover, the easternmost Mohawk Iroquois were angry because New York settlers were encroaching on their land. Despite these circumstances, the delegates obtained expressions of friendship from the Six Nations, but Iroquois suspicions of Britain persisted.

The delegates also endorsed a proposal for a colonial confederation, the Albany Plan of Union, largely based on the ideas of Pennsylvania's Franklin and Massachusetts's Thomas Hutchinson. The plan called for a Grand Council representing all the colonial assemblies, with a crown-appointed president general as its executive officer. The Grand Council would develop coordinated policies regarding military defense and Indian affairs, which the colonies would fund according to an agreed-upon formula. Although later regarded as a precedent for American unity, the Albany Plan in fact came to nothing, primarily because no colonial legislature approved it.

The Seven Years' War in America, 1754–1760

Although France and Britain remained at peace in Europe until 1756, Washington's 1754 clash with French troops began the war in North America. In response, the British dispatched General Edward Braddock and a thousand regular troops to North America to seize Fort Duquesne at the headwaters of the Ohio.

Scornful of colonial soldiers and refusing Delaware Indians' offers of assistance, Braddock expected his disciplined British regulars to make short work of the enemy. On July 9, 1755, about 600 Native Americans and 250 French and Canadians ambushed Braddock's force of 2,200 Britons and Virginians nine miles east of Fort Duquesne. Riddled by three hours of steady fire from an unseen foe, Braddock's troops retreated. Nine hundred British and provincial soldiers died in Braddock's defeat, including the general himself, compared to just twenty-three French and Indians.

As British colonists absorbed the shock of Braddock's disastrous loss, French-armed Shawnees, Delawares, and Mingos from the upper Ohio valley struck hard at encroaching settlers in western Pennsylvania, Maryland, and Virginia. For three years, these attacks halted English expansion and prevented the three colonies from joining the British war against France.

Confronted by the numerically superior but disorganized Anglo-Americans, the French and their Native American allies—now including the Iroquois—captured Fort Oswego on Lake Ontario in 1756 and Fort William Henry on Lake George in 1757. The French now threatened central New York and western New England. In Europe, too, the war began badly for Britain, which by 1757 seemed to be facing defeat on all fronts (see Map 5.1).

In this dark hour, two developments turned the tide for the British. First, the Iroquois and most Ohio Indians, angered at French treatment of them and sensing that the French were gaining too decisive an advantage, agreed at a treaty conference at Easton, Pennsylvania, in 1758 to abandon the French. Their subsequent withdrawal from Fort Duquesne enabled the British to capture it and other French forts. Many Native Americans simply withdrew from the fighting, while others actively joined Britain's cause.

The second decisive development occurred when William Pitt took control of military affairs in the British cabinet and reversed the downward course. Pitt saw himself as the man of the hour. "I know," he declared, "that I can save this country and that no one else can."

Map 5.1 The Seven Years' War in North America, 1754–1760
After experiencing major defeats early in the war, Anglo-American forces turned the tide against the French in 1758 by taking Fort Duquesne and Louisbourg. After Canada fell in 1760, the fighting shifted to Spain's Caribbean colonies.

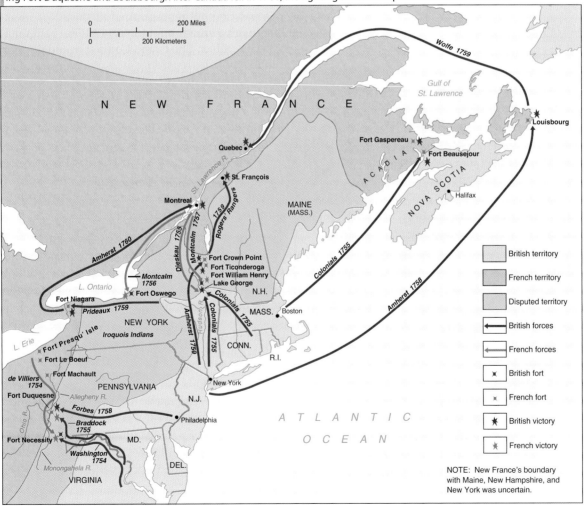

Destruction of Quebec, 1759
After the fall of Quebec to British forces, France's defeat in North America was virtually certain.

True to his word, Pitt reinvigorated British patriotism throughout the empire. By the war's end, he was the colonists' most popular hero, the symbol of what Americans and the English could accomplish when united.

Hard-pressed in Europe by France and its allies (which included Spain after 1761), Pitt chose not to send large numbers of additional troops to America. He believed that the key to crushing New France lay in the mobilization of colonial soldiers. To encourage the colonies to assume the military burden, he promised that if they raised the necessary men, Parliament would bear most of the cost of fighting the war.

Pitt's offer to free Anglo-Americans from the war's financial burdens generated unprecedented support. The colonies organized more than forty thousand troops in 1758–1759, far more soldiers than the crown sent to the mainland during the entire war.

The impact of Pitt's decision was immediate. Anglo-American troops under General Jeffery Amherst captured Fort Duquesne and Louisbourg in 1758 and drove the French from northern New York the next year. In September 1759, Quebec fell after General James Wolfe defeated the French commander-in-chief, Louis Joseph Montcalm, on the Plains of Abraham, where both commanders died in battle. French resistance ended in 1760 when Montreal surrendered.

The End of French North America, 1760–1763

Although the fall of Montreal effectively dashed French hopes of victory in North America, the war continued in Europe and elsewhere, and France made one last desperate attempt to capture Newfoundland in June 1762. Thereafter, with defeat inevitable, France entered into negotiations with its enemies. The Seven Years' War officially ended in both America and Europe with the signing of the Treaty of Paris in 1763.

Under terms of the treaty, France gave up all its lands and claims east of the Mississippi (except New Orleans) to Britain. In return for Cuba, which a British expedition had seized in 1762, Spain ceded Florida to Britain. Neither France nor Britain wanted the other to control Louisiana, so in the Treaty of San Ildefonso (1762), France ceded the vast territory to Spain. Thus, France's once mighty North American empire was reduced to a few tiny fishing islands off Newfoundland and several prosperous sugar islands in the West Indies. Britain reigned supreme in eastern North America while Spain now claimed the west below Canada (see Map 5.2).

Several thousand French colonists in an area stretching from Quebec to Illinois to Louisiana were suddenly British and Spanish subjects. The most adversely affected Franco-Americans were the Acadians, who had been

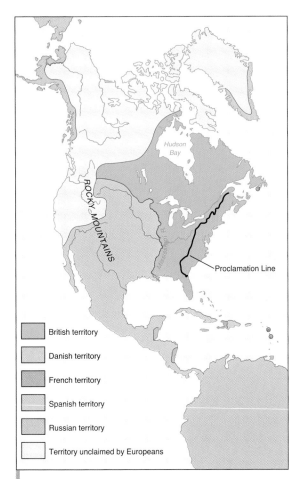

Map 5.2 European Territorial Claims, 1763
The treaties of San Ildefonso (1762) and Paris (1763) divided France's North American empire between Britain and Spain. Britain in 1763 established direct imperial authority west of the Proclamation Line.

nominal British subjects since England took over Acadia in 1713 and renamed it Nova Scotia. In 1755, Nova Scotia's government ordered all Acadians to swear loyalty to Britain and not to bear arms for France. After most refused to take the oath, British soldiers drove them from their homes and attempted to disperse them among Britain's other colonies. About 7,000 of the 18,000 Acadians were forcibly deported in this way, while others were sent to France or French colonies. Facing poverty and intense anti-French, anti-Catholic prejudice in the British colonies and seeking to remain together, a majority of the exiles and refugees eventually moved to Louisiana, where their descendants became known as Cajuns.

King George's War and the Seven Years' War produced ironically mixed effects. On one hand, they fused the

bonds between the British and the Anglo-Americans. Fighting side by side against the French Catholic enemy, the British and the American colonists came to rely on each other as rarely before and celebrated their common identity. But each war also planted seeds of mutual misunderstanding and suspicion.

Anglo-American Friction

During the Seven Years' War, British officers regularly complained about the quality of colonial troops, not only their inability to fight but also their tendency to return home—even in the midst of campaigns—when their terms were up or when they were not paid on time. For their part, colonial soldiers complained of British officers who, as one put it, treated their troops "but little better than slaves."

Tensions between British officers and colonial civilians also flared. Officers complained about colonists being unwilling to provide food and shelter while colonists resented the officers' arrogant manners. One general groused that South Carolina planters were "extremely pleased to have Soldiers to protect their Plantations but will feel no inconveniences for them." Quakers in the Pennsylvania assembly, acting from pacifist convictions, refused to vote funds to support the war effort, while assemblies in New York and Massachusetts opposed the quartering of British troops on their soil as an encroachment on their English liberties. English authorities regarded such actions as affronts to the king's prerogative and as undermining Britain's efforts to defend its territories.

Pitt's promise to reimburse the colonial assemblies for their military expenses angered many in Britain, who concluded that the colonists were escaping scot-free from the war's financial burden. The colonies had already profited enormously from the war, as military contracts and spending by British troops brought an influx of British currency into the hands of farmers, artisans, and merchants. Some merchants had even traded illicitly with the French enemy during wartime (see below). Meanwhile, Britain's national debt nearly doubled during the war, from £72 million to over £132 million. Whereas in 1763 the total debt of all the colonies collectively amounted to £2 million, the interest charges alone on the British debt came to more than £4 million a year. This debt was assumed by British landowners through a land tax and, increasingly, by ordinary consumers through excise duties on a wide variety of items, including beer, tea, salt, and bread.

Colonists felt equally burdened. Those who profited during the war spent their additional income on goods

George III, Studio of A. Ramsay, c. 1767
Although unsure of himself and emotionally little more than a boy upon his accession to the English throne, George III possessed a deep moral sense and a fierce determination to rule as well as to reign.

imported from Britain, the annual value of which doubled during the war's brief duration. Thus, the effect of the war was to accelerate the Anglo-American "consumer revolution" in which colonists' purchases of British goods fueled Britain's economy, particularly its manufacturing sector. But when peace returned in 1760, the wartime boom in the colonies ended as abruptly as it had begun. To maintain their lifestyles, many colonists went into debt. British creditors obliged their American merchant customers by extending the usual period for remitting payments from six months to a year. Nevertheless, many recently prosperous colonists suddenly found themselves overloaded with debts and, in some cases, bankrupt. As colonial indebtedness to Britain grew, some Americans began to suspect the British of deliberately plotting to "enslave" the colonies.

The ascension to the British throne of King **George III** (ruled 1760–1820) at age twenty-two reinforced Anglo-American tensions. The new king was determined

to have a strong influence on government policy, but neither his experience, his temperament, nor his philosophy suited him to the formidable task of building political coalitions and pursuing consistent policies. Until 1774, George III made frequent abrupt changes in government leadership that destabilized politics in Britain and exacerbated relations with the colonies.

Frontier Tensions

Victory over the French spurred new Anglo-Indian conflicts that drove the British debt even higher. With the French gone, Ohio and Great Lakes Indians recognized that they could no longer play the two imperial rivals off against each other. Their fears that the British would treat them as subjects rather than as allies were confirmed when General Jeffery Amherst, Britain's commander in North America, decided to cut expenses by refusing to distribute food, ammunition (needed for hunting), and other gifts. Moreover, squatters from the colonies were moving westward onto Indian lands and harassing the occupants, and many Native Americans feared that the British occupation was intended to support these incursions.

As tensions mounted, a Delaware Indian religious prophet named Neolin reported a vision in which the "Master of Life," or Great Spirit, instructed him to urge Native Americans of all tribes to unify and to repudiate European culture, material goods, and alliances. Meanwhile, other Native Americans hoped that the French would return so Indians could once again manipulate an imperial balance of power. Indian political leaders, including Pontiac, an Ottawa, drew on these sentiments to forge an explicitly anti-British movement, misleadingly called "Pontiac's Rebellion." During the spring and summer of 1763, they and their followers sacked eight British forts near the Great Lakes and besieged those at Pittsburgh and Detroit. But over the next three years, shortages of food and ammunition, a smallpox epidemic at Fort Pitt (triggered when British officers deliberately distributed infected blankets at a peace parley), and a recognition that the French would not return led the Indians to make peace with Britain. Although word of the uprising spread to Native Americans in the Southeast and Mississippi valley, British diplomacy prevented violence from erupting there.

Despite the uprising's failure, the Native Americans had not been decisively defeated. Hoping to conciliate the Indians and end the fighting, George III issued the **Proclamation of 1763**, asserting direct British control of land transactions, settlement, trade, and other activities of non-Indians west of a Proclamation Line along

Technology and Culture

Public Sanitation in Philadelphia

Even as the imperial crisis intruded on their lives, city-dwellers confronted long-standing problems occasioned by rapid growth. The fastest-growing city in eighteenth-century America was Philadelphia, whose population approached seventeen thousand in 1760 (see Figure 4.2 in Chapter 4). One key to Philadelphia's rise was its location as both a major Atlantic port and the gateway to Pennsylvania's farmlands and the Appalachian backcountry. Local geography also contributed to its success. Choosing a site where the Delaware and Schuylkill Rivers met, William Penn had built Philadelphia along a system of streams and the tidal cove on the Delaware into which they flowed. Philadelphians referred to the principal stream and cove together as "the Dock," for one of their principal functions. The Dock's shores were the setting for the early city's mansions and public gathering spaces. As some residents pointed out in 1700, the Dock was the city's heart and "the Inducing Reason . . . to Settle the Town where it now is."

Over time, the growth that made Philadelphia so successful rendered its environment, especially its water, dangerous to inhabitants' health. Several leading industries used water for transforming animals and grains into consumer products. Tanneries made leather by soaking cowhides several times in mixtures of water and acidic liquids, including sour milk and fermented rye, and with an alkaline solution of buttermilk and dung. When cleaning their vats, tanners dumped residues from these processes into the streets or into underground pits from which they seeped into wells and streams. Breweries and distilleries also used water-based procedures and similarly discarded their waste, while slaughterhouses put dung, grease, fat, and other unwanted byproducts into streets and streams. Individual residents exacerbated the problems by tossing garbage into streets, using privies that polluted wells, and leaving animal carcasses to rot in the open air. Most of the city's sewers were open channels that frequently backed up, diverting the sewage to the streets. Buildings and other obstructions caused stagnant pools to form in streets, and when the polluted water did drain freely, it flowed into the Dock.

Almost from the city's founding, residents had complained about the stench arising from waste and stagnant water left by the tanneries and other large industries. Many attributed the city's frequent disease epidemics to these practices. In 1739, a residents' petition complained of "the great Annoyance arising from the Slaughter-Houses, Tanyards, . . . etc. erected on the publick Dock, and Streets, adjacent." It called for prohibiting new tanneries and for eventually removing existing ones. Such efforts made little headway at first. Tanners, brewers, and other manufacturers were among the city's wealthiest residents and dissuaded their fellow elites from regulating their industries.

A turning point came in 1748 when, after another epidemic, the Pennsylvania Assembly appointed an ad hoc committee to recommend improvements in Philadelphia's sanitation. One member, Benjamin Franklin, was already known both for his innovative approaches to urban issues, as when he organized Philadelphia's first fire company in 1736, and for his interest in the practical applications of technology. Combining these interests, Franklin advocated applying new findings in hydrology (the study of water and its distribution) and water-pumping technology to public sanitation. Accordingly, the committee recommended building a wall to keep the high tides of the Delaware River out of the Dock, widening the stream's channel, and covering over a tributary that had become a "common sewer." The plan was innovative not only because it was based on hydrology but also because it acknowledged the need for a public approach to sanitation problems. But once again, neither the city, the colony, nor private entrepreneurs would pay for the proposal. Many elites declined to assume the sense of civic responsibility that Franklin and his fellow advocates of Enlightenment sought to inculcate.

Only in the 1760s, after both growth and pollution had accelerated, did Philadelphia begin to address the Dock's problems effectively. In 1762, the Pennsylvania Assembly appointed a board to oversee the "Pitching [sloping], Paving and Cleansing" of streets and walkways, and the design, construction, and maintenance of sewers and storm drains—all intended to prevent waste and stagnant water from accumulating on land. In the next year, residents petitioned that the Dock itself be "cleared out, planked at the bottom, and walled on each side" to maximize its flow and prevent it from flooding. The Pennsylvania Assembly responded by requiring adjoining property owners to build "a good, strong, substantial wall of good, flat stone from the bottom of the said Dock," and remove

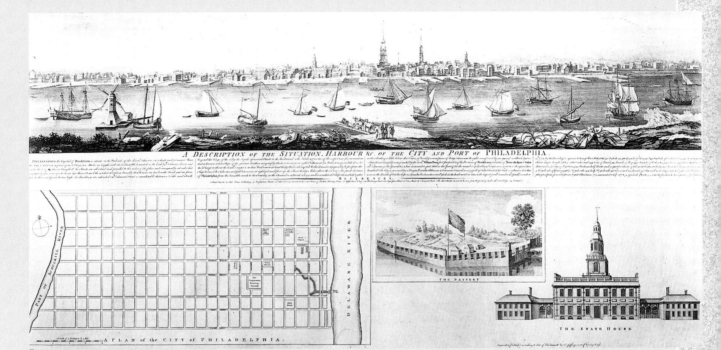

"An East Prospect of the City of Philadelphia" (1756)
The converging streams flowing into the Delaware River in the map (lower left) constitute the Dock. The engraving at the top illustrates Philadelphia's dynamism as a port city at the time of the Seven Years' War.

any "encroachments" that blocked drainage into or on the streams. Finally, legislators had implemented the kind of public, engineering-based solution that Franklin had advocated two decades earlier.

While some owners evaded their responsibility, others went even further by also building an arch over the principal stretch of the Dock. Then they installed market stalls on the newly available surface. Once an open waterway used for transport and valued as a central landmark, the Dock was now a completely enclosed, engineered sewer. A new generation of entrepreneurs dominated the neighborhood, catering to consumers who preferred a clean, attractive environment.

By 1763, however, Philadelphia's problem with sanitation had grown well beyond the Dock. Thereafter, the growing controversy over British imperial policies diverted official attention from public health problems. Yet by empowering poor and working people, that very controversy encouraged some to point out that improvements at the Dock had changed nothing in their own neighborhoods. Writing in a city newspaper in 1769, "Tom Trudge" lamented the lot of

"such poor fellows as I, who sup on a cup of skim milk, etc., have a parcel of half naked children about our doors, . . . whose wives must, at many seasons of the Year, wade to the knees in carrying a loaf of bread to bake, and near whose penurious doors the dung-cart never comes, nor the sound of the paver will be heard for many ages." Both public and private solutions, Trudge and others asserted, favored the wealthy and ignored the less fortunate. Environmental controversy had once again shifted with the course of politics. But the Revolution would postpone the search for solutions. Philadelphia's problems with polluted water persisted until 1799, when the city undertook construction of the United States' first municipal water system.

Questions for Analysis

- How did early manufacturing contribute to pollution in Philadelphia?

- How did engineering provide a successful resolution of sanitary problems at the Dock?

Fort Pitt
The key to British control of the Ohio valley and its Native Americans, Fort Pitt replaced France's Fort Dusquesne and was the site of the future city of Pittsburgh.

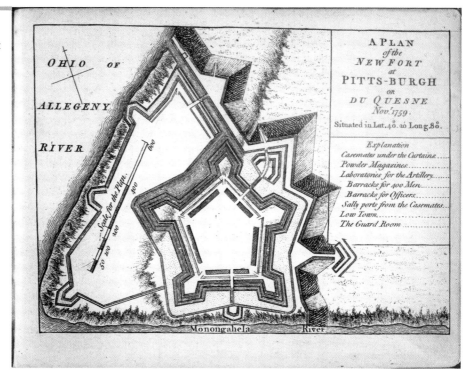

the Appalachian crest (see Map 5.2). The government's goal was to restore order to the process of colonial expansion by replacing the authority of the various (and often competing) colonies with that of the crown. The proclamation recognized existing Indian land titles everywhere west of the "proclamation line" until such time as tribal governments agreed to cede their land through treaties. Although calming Indian fears, the proclamation angered the colonies by subordinating their western claims to imperial authority and by slowing expansion.

The uprising was also a factor in the British government's decision to leave ten thousand soldiers in France's former forts on the Great Lakes and in the Ohio valley. The burden of maintaining control over the western territories would reach almost a half million pounds a year, fully 6 percent of Britain's peacetime budget. Britons considered it perfectly reasonable for the colonists to help offset this expense. Although the troops would help offset the colonies' unfavorable balance of payments with Britain, many Anglo-Americans regarded them as a peacetime "standing army" that threatened their liberty. With the French

menace to their security removed, they saw westward expansion onto Indian lands as a way to prosperity, and they viewed British troops enforcing the Proclamation of 1763 as hindering rather than enhancing that expansion.

Imperial Authority, Colonial Opposition, 1760–1766

After the Seven Years' War, Anglo-American tensions centered on British efforts to finance its suddenly enlarged empire through a series of revenue measures and to enforce these and other measures directly rather than relying on local authorities. Following passage of the Stamp Act, opposition movements arose in the mainland colonies to protest not only the new measures' costs but also what many people considered a dangerous extension of Parliament's power. Their success revealed a widening gulf between British and colonial perceptions of the proper relationship between the empire and its colonies.

Writs of Assistance, 1760–1761

Even before the Seven Years' War ended, British authorities attempted to halt American merchants' trade with the French enemy in the West Indies. In 1760, the royal governor of Massachusetts authorized revenue officers to employ a document called a writ of assistance to seize illegally imported goods. The writ was a general search warrant that permitted customs officials to enter any ship or building where smuggled goods might be hidden. Because the document required no evidence of probable cause for suspicion, many critics considered it unconstitutional. The writ of assistance also threatened the traditional privacy of a family's home, since most merchants conducted business from home.

Writs of assistance proved effective against smuggling. In quick reaction to the writs, merchants in Boston, virtually the smuggling capital of the colonies, hired lawyer James Otis to challenge the constitutionality of these warrants. Arguing his case before the Massachusetts Supreme Court in 1761, Otis proclaimed that "an act against the Constitution is void"—even one passed by Parliament. But the court, influenced by Chief Justice Thomas Hutchinson, who noted the use of identical writs in England, ruled against the Boston merchants.

Despite losing the case, Otis expressed the fundamental conception of many, both in Britain and in the colonies, of Parliament's role under the British constitution. The British constitution was not a written document but instead a collection of customs and accepted principles that guaranteed certain rights to all citizens. Most British politicians assumed that Parliament's laws were themselves part of the constitution and hence that Parliament could alter the constitution at will. But Otis contended that Parliament possessed no authority to violate the "rights of Englishmen," and he asserted that there were limits "beyond which if Parliaments go, their Acts bind not." Such challenges to parliamentary authority would be renewed once peace was restored.

The Sugar Act, 1764

In 1764, just three years after Otis challenged the writs of assistance, Parliament passed the **Sugar Act**. The measure's goal was to raise revenues to help offset Britain's military expenses in North America, and thus end Britain's longstanding policy of exempting colonial trade from revenue-raising measures. The Navigation Acts had not been designed to bring money into the British treasury but rather to benefit the imperial economy indirectly by stimulating trade and protecting English manufacturers from foreign competition. English importers, not American producers, paid the taxes that Parliament levied on colonial products entering Britain, and then passed the cost on to consumers. So little revenue did the Navigation Acts bring in (just £1,800 in 1763) that they did not even pay the cost of their own enforcement.

The Sugar Act amended the Molasses Act of 1733 (see Chapter 4), the last of the Navigation Acts, which amounted to a tariff on French West Indian molasses entering British North America. But colonists had simply continued to import the cheaper French molasses after 1733, bribing customs officials into taking $1\frac{1}{2}$ pence per gallon to look the other way when it was unloaded. Aware of the widespread bribery, Parliament assumed that colonial rum drinkers would accept a three-pence per gallon duty.

New taxes were not the only feature of the Sugar Act that American merchants found objectionable. The act also stipulated that colonists could export lumber, iron, furs, and many other commodities to foreign countries only if the shipments first landed in Britain. Previously, American ships had taken these products directly to Dutch and German ports and returned with goods to sell to colonists. By channeling this trade through Britain, Parliament hoped that colonial shippers would purchase more British goods, buy fewer goods from foreign competitors, and provide jobs for Englishmen.

The Sugar Act also vastly complicated the requirements for shipping colonial goods. A captain now had to fill out a confusing series of documents to certify his trade as legal, and the absence of any of them left his entire cargo liable to seizure. The law's petty regulations made it virtually impossible for many colonial shippers to avoid committing technical violations.

Finally, the Sugar Act disregarded many traditional English protections for a fair trial. First, the law allowed customs officials to transfer smuggling cases from the colonial courts, in which juries decided the outcome, to vice-admiralty courts, where a British-appointed judge gave the verdict. Because the Sugar Act (until 1768) awarded vice-admiralty judges 5 percent of any confiscated cargo, judges had a financial incentive to find defendants guilty. Second, until 1767 the law did not permit defendants to be tried where their offense allegedly had taken place (usually their home province) but required all cases to be heard in the vice-admiralty court at Halifax, Nova Scotia. Third, the law reversed normal courtroom procedures, which presumed innocence until guilt was proved, by requiring the defendant to disprove the prosecution's charge.

The Sugar Act was no idle threat. British prime minister George Grenville ordered the navy to enforce the measure, and it did so vigorously. A Boston resident complained in 1764 that "no vessel hardly comes in or goes out but they find some pretense to seize and detain her." That same year, Pennsylvania's chief justice reported that customs officers were extorting fees from small boats carrying lumber across the Delaware River to Philadelphia from New Jersey and seemed likely "to destroy this little River-trade."

Rather than pay the three-pence tax, Americans continued smuggling molasses until 1766. Then, to discourage smuggling, Britain lowered the duty to a penny—less than the customary bribe American shippers paid to get their cargoes past inspectors. The law thereafter raised about £30,000 annually in revenue.

Opposition to the Sugar Act remained fragmented and ineffective. The law's burden fell overwhelmingly on Massachusetts, New York, and Pennsylvania; other provinces had little interest in resisting a measure that did not affect them directly. The Sugar Act's immediate effect was minor, but it heightened some colonists' awareness of the new direction of imperial policies and their implications.

The Stamp Act Crisis, 1765–1766

The revenue raised by the Sugar Act did little to ease Britain's financial crisis. The national debt continued to rise, and the British public groaned under the weight of the second-highest tax rates in Europe. Particularly irritating to Britons was the fact that by 1765 their rates averaged 26 shillings per person, whereas the colonial tax burden varied from $\frac{1}{2}$ to $1\frac{1}{2}$ shillings per inhabitant, or barely 2 to 6 percent of the British rate. Well aware of how lightly the colonists were taxed, Grenville thought that they should make a larger contribution to the empire's American expenses.

To raise such revenues, Parliament passed the **Stamp Act** in March 1765. The law obliged colonists to purchase and use special stamped (watermarked) paper for newspapers, customs documents, various licenses, college diplomas, and legal forms used for recovering debts, buying land, and making wills. As with the Sugar Act, violators would face prosecution in vice-admiralty courts, without juries. The prime minister projected yearly revenues of £60,000 to £100,000, which would offset 12 to 20 percent of North American military expenses.

Unlike the Sugar Act, which was an external tax levied on imports as they entered the colonies, the Stamp Act was an internal tax, or a duty levied directly on property, goods, and government services in the colonies. Whereas external taxes were intended to regulate trade and fell mainly on merchants and ship captains, internal taxes were designed to raise revenue for the crown and affected many more people. In the case of the Stamp Act, anyone who made a will, transferred property, borrowed money, or bought playing cards or newspapers would pay the tax.

To Grenville and his supporters, the new tax seemed a small price for the benefits of the empire, especially since Britons had been paying a similar tax since 1695. Nevertheless, some in England, most notably William Pitt, objected in principle to Britain's levying an internal tax on the colonies. They emphasized that the colonists had never been subject to British revenue bills and noted that they already taxed themselves through their own elected assemblies.

Grenville and his followers agreed that Parliament could not tax any British subjects unless they enjoyed representation in that body. But they contended that Americans shared the same status as the majority of British adult males who either lacked sufficient property to vote or lived in large cities that had no seats in Parliament. Such people, they maintained, were "virtually" represented in Parliament. The principle of virtual representation held that every member of Parliament stood above the narrow interests of his constituents and considered the welfare of all subjects when deciding issues. By definition, then, British subjects, including colonists, were not represented by particular individuals but by all members of Parliament.

Grenville and his supporters also denied that the colonists were entitled to any exemption from British taxation because they elected their own assemblies. These legislative bodies, they alleged, were no different from British local governments, whose powers to pass laws and taxes did not nullify Parliament's authority over them. Accordingly, colonial assemblies were an adaptation to unique American circumstances and possessed no more power than Parliament allowed them to exercise. But Grenville's position clashed directly with the stance of many colonists who had been arguing for several decades that their assemblies exercised legislative powers equivalent to those of the House of Commons in Great Britain (see Chapter 4).

Many colonists felt that the Stamp Act forced them either to confront the issue of parliamentary taxation head-on or to surrender any claim to meaningful rights of self-government. However much they might admire and respect Parliament, few colonists imagined that it represented them. They accepted the validity of virtual representation for England and Scotland but denied that it could be extended to the colonies. Instead, they argued, they enjoyed a substantial measure of self-governance similar to that of Ireland, whose Parliament alone could tax its people but could not interfere with laws, like the Navigation Acts, passed by the British Parliament. In a speech before the Boston town meeting opposing the Sugar Act, James Otis expressed Americans' basic argument: "that by [the British] Constitution, every man in the dominions is a free man: that no parts of His Majesty's dominions can be taxed without consent: that every part has a right to be represented in the supreme or some subordinate legislature." In essence, the colonists assumed that the empire was a loose federation in which their legislatures possessed considerable autonomy, rather than an extended nation governed directly from London.

To many colonists passage of the Stamp Act demonstrated both Parliament's indifference to their interests and the shallowness of the theory of virtual representation. Colonial agents in London had lobbied against passage of the law, and provincial legislatures had sent petitions warning against passage. But Parliament had dismissed the petitions without a hearing. Parliament "must have thought us Americans all a parcel of Apes and very tame Apes too," concluded Christopher Gadsden of South Carolina, "or they would have never ventured on such a hateful, baneful experiment."

In late May 1765, Patrick Henry, a twenty-nine-year-old Virginia lawyer and planter with a talent for fiery oratory, dramatically conveyed the rising spirit of resistance. Henry urged the Virginia House of Burgesses to adopt several strongly worded resolutions denying Parliament's power to tax the colonies. In the debate over the resolutions, Henry reportedly stated that "he did not doubt but some good American would stand up in favor of his country." Viewing such language as treasonous, the Assembly passed only the weakest four of Henry's seven resolutions. Garbled newspaper accounts of Henry's resolutions and the debates were published in other colonies, and by year's end seven other assemblies had passed resolutions against the act. As in Virginia, the resolutions were grounded in constitutional arguments and avoided Henry's inflammatory language.

Henry's words resonated more loudly outside elite political circles, particularly in Boston. There, in late summer, a group of mostly middle-class artisans and small business owners joined together as the Loyal Nine to fight the Stamp Act. They recognized that the stamp distributors, who alone could accept money for watermarked paper, were the law's weak link. If the public could pressure them into resigning before taxes became due on November 1, the Stamp Act would become inoperable.

It was no accident that Boston set the pace in opposing Parliament. A large proportion of Bostonians lived by shipbuilding, maritime trade, and distilling, and in 1765 they were not living well. In part, they could blame British policies for their misfortune. No other port suffered so much from the Sugar Act's trade restrictions. The law burdened rum producers with a heavy tax on molasses, dried up a flourishing import trade in Portuguese wines, and prohibited the direct export of many New England products to profitable overseas markets.

New Hampshire Stamp Act Protest
In order to frighten stamp tax collectors into resigning their posts, crowds in colonial cities and towns would parade an agent's effigy through the streets.

But Boston's misery was rooted in older problems. Even before the Seven Years' War, its shipbuilding industry had lost significant ground to New York and Philadelphia, and the output of its rum and sugar producers had fallen by half in just a decade. British impressment (forced recruitment) of Massachusetts fishermen for naval service had undermined the fishing industry. The resulting unemployment led to increased taxes for poor-relief. The taxes, along with a shrinking number of customers, drove many marginal artisans out of business and into the ranks of the poor. Other Bostonians, while remaining employed or in business, struggled in the face of rising prices for basic necessities as well as taxes. To compound its misery, the city still struggled to recover from a great fire in 1760 that had burned 176 warehouses and left every tenth family homeless.

Widespread economic distress produced an explosive situation in Boston. Already resentful of an elite whose fortunes had risen spectacularly while they suffered, many poor and working-class Bostonians blamed British officials and policies for the town's hard times. The crisis was sharpened because they were accustomed to gathering in large crowds that engaged in pointed political expression, both satirical and serious and usually directed against the "better sort."

In the aftermath of the Stamp Act, Boston's crowds aimed their traditional forms of protest more directly and forcefully at imperial officials. The morning of August 14 found a likeness of Boston's stamp distributor, Andrew Oliver, swinging from a tree guarded by a menacing crowd. Oliver apparently did not realize that the Loyal Nine were warning him to resign immediately, so at dusk several hundred Bostonians, led by a South End shoemaker named Ebenezer MacIntosh, demolished a new building of Oliver's at the dock. Thereafter, the Loyal Nine withdrew, and the crowd continued on its own. The men surged toward Oliver's house, where they beheaded his effigy and "stamped" it to pieces. The crowd then shattered the windows of his home, smashed his furniture, and even tore out the paneling. When Lieutenant Governor Hutchinson and the sheriff tried to disperse the crowd, they were driven off under a barrage of rocks. Surveying his devastated home the next morning, Oliver announced his resignation.

Bitterness against the Stamp Act unleashed spontaneous, contagious violence. Twelve days after the first Boston riot, Bostonians demolished the elegant home of Thomas Hutchinson. This attack occurred in part because smugglers held grudges against Hutchinson for certain of his decisions as chief justice and also because many financially pinched citizens saw him as a symbol of the royal policies crippling Boston's already troubled economy and their own livelihoods. In their view, wealthy officials "rioted in luxury," with homes and fancy furnishings that cost hundreds of times the annual incomes of most Boston workingmen. They were also reacting to Hutchinson's efforts to stop the destruction of his brother-in-law Andrew Oliver's house. Ironically, Hutchinson privately opposed the Stamp Act.

Meanwhile, groups similar to the Loyal Nine calling themselves Sons of Liberty were forming throughout the colonies. After the assault on Hutchinson's mansion and

Thomas Hutchinson
As lieutenant governor and, later, governor of Massachusetts, Hutchinson believed that social and political order under British authority must be maintained at all costs.

an even more violent incident in Newport, Rhode Island, the leaders of the **Sons of Liberty** sought to prevent more such outbreaks. They recognized that people in the crowds were casting aside their customary deference toward their social "superiors," a development that could broaden to include all elites if not carefully contained. Fearful of alienating wealthy opponents of the Stamp Act, the Sons of Liberty focused their actions strictly against property and invariably left avenues of escape for their victims. Especially fearful that a royal soldier or revenue officer might be shot or killed, they forbade their followers to carry weapons, even when facing armed adversaries. Realizing the value of martyrs, they resolved that the only lives lost over the issue of British taxation would come from their own ranks.

In October 1765, representatives of nine colonial assemblies met in New York City in the so-called Stamp Act Congress. The session was remarkable for the colonies' agreement on and bold articulation of the general principle that Parliament lacked authority to levy taxes outside Great Britain and to deny any person a jury trial. "The Ministry never imagined we could or would so generally unite in opposition to their measures," wrote a Connecticut delegate to the congress, "nor I confess till I saw the Experiment made did I."

By late 1765, most stamp distributors had resigned or fled, and without the watermarked paper required by law, most royal customs officials and court officers were refusing to perform their duties. In response, legislators compelled the reluctant officials to resume operation by threatening to withhold their pay. At the same time, merchants obtained sailing clearances by insisting that they would sue if cargoes spoiled while delayed in port. By late December, the courts and harbors of almost every colony were again functioning.

Thus colonial elites moved to keep an explosive situation from getting out of hand by taking over leadership of local Sons of Liberty groups, by coordinating protest through the Stamp Act Congress, and by having colonial legislatures restore normal business. Elite leaders feared that chaos could break out, particularly if British troops landed to enforce the Stamp Act. An influential Pennsylvanian, John Dickinson, summed up how respectable gentlemen envisioned the dire consequences of revolutionary turmoil: "a multitude of Commonwealths, Crimes, and Calamities, Centuries of mutual jealousies, Hatreds, Wars of Devastation, till at last the exhausted provinces shall sink into savagery under the yoke of some fortunate Conqueror."

To force the Stamp Act's repeal, New York's merchants agreed on October 31, 1765, to boycott all British goods, and businessmen in other cities soon followed their example. Because American colonists purchased about 40 percent of England's manufactures, this nonimportation strategy put the English economy in danger of recession. The colonial boycotts consequently triggered panic within England's business community, whose members descended on Parliament to warn that continuation of the Stamp Act would stimulate a wave of bankruptcies, massive unemployment, and political unrest.

The Marquis of Rockingham, who had succeeded Grenville as prime minister in mid-1765, hesitated to advocate repeal because the overwhelming majority within Parliament was outraged at colonial defiance of the law. Then in January 1766 William Pitt, a steadfast opponent of the Stamp Act, boldly denounced all efforts to tax the colonies, declaring, "I rejoice that America has resisted." Parliamentary support for repeal thereafter grew, though only as a matter of practicality, not as a surrender of principle. In March 1766, Parliament revoked the Stamp Act, but only in conjunction with passage of the **Declaratory Act**, which affirmed parliamentary power to legislate for the colonies "in all cases whatsoever."

Because the Declaratory Act was written in general language, Americans interpreted its meaning to their own advantage. Most colonial political leaders recognized that the law was modeled after an earlier statute of 1719 regarding Ireland, which was considered exempt from British taxation. The measure therefore seemed no more than a parliamentary exercise in saving face to compensate for the Stamp Act's repeal, and Americans ignored it. The House of Commons, however, intended that the colonists take the Declaratory Act literally to mean that they could not claim exemption from any parliamentary statute, including a tax law. The Stamp Act crisis thus ended in a fundamental disagreement between Britain and America over Parliament's authority in the colonies.

Although the Stamp Act crisis had not resolved the underlying philosophical differences between Britain and America, most colonists eagerly put the events of 1765 behind them, and they showered both king and Parliament with loyal statements of gratitude for the Stamp Act's repeal. The Sons of Liberty disbanded. Still possessing a deep emotional loyalty to "Old England," Anglo-Americans concluded with relief that their active resistance to the law had slapped Britain's leaders back to their senses. Nevertheless, the crisis led many to ponder British policies and actions more deeply than ever before.

Ideology, Religion, and Resistance

The Stamp Act and the conflicts that arose around it revealed a chasm between Britain and its colonies that startled Anglo-Americans. For the first time, some of them critically reconsidered the imperial relationship that they always thought of as beneficial to the colonies. In order to put their concerns into perspective, educated colonists turned to the works of philosophers, historians, and political writers. Many more, both educated and uneducated, looked to religion.

By the 1760s, the colonists were already widely familiar with the political writings of European Enlightenment thinkers, particularly John Locke (see Chapter 4). Locke argued that humans originated in a "state of nature" in which each man enjoyed the "natural rights" of life, liberty, and property. Thereafter, groups of men entered into a "social contract," under which they formed governments for the sole purpose of protecting those individual rights. A government that encroached on natural rights, then, broke its contract with the people. In such cases, people could resist their government, although Locke cautioned against outright rebellion except in the most extreme cases. To many colonial readers, Locke's concept of natural rights appeared to justify opposition to arbitrary legislation by Parliament.

Colonists also read European writers who emphasized excessive concentrations of executive power as threats to the liberty of the people. Some of them balanced Locke's emphasis on the rights of individuals with an emphasis on subordinating individual interests to the greater good of the people as a whole. Looking to the ancient Greeks and Romans as well as to more recent European theorists, these writers developed a set of ideas termed "republican." "Republicans" especially admired the sense of civic duty that motivated citizens of the Roman republic. Like the early Romans, they maintained that a free people had to avoid moral and political corruption, and practice a disinterested "public virtue." An elected leader of a republic, one author noted, would command obedience "more by the virtue of the people, than by the terror of his power."

Among those influenced by republican ideas were a widely read group of English political writers known as oppositionists. According to John Trenchard, Thomas Gordon, and others belonging to this group, Parliament—consisting of the freely elected representatives of the people—formed the foundation of England's unique political liberties and protected those liberties against the inherent corruption and tyranny of executive power. But since 1720, the oppositionists argued, prime ministers had exploited the treasury's vast resources to provide pensions, contracts, and profitable offices to politicians or had bought elections by bribing voters. Most members of Parliament, in their view, no longer represented the true

interests of their constituents; rather, they had created self-interested "factions" and joined in a "conspiracy against liberty." Often referring to themselves as the "country party," these oppositionists feared that a power-hungry "court party" of unelected officials close to the king was using a corrupted Parliament to gain absolute power for themselves.

Influenced by such ideas, a number of colonists pointed to a diabolical conspiracy behind British policy during the Stamp Act crisis. James Otis characterized a group of pro-British Rhode Islanders as a "little, dirty, drinking, drabbing, contaminated knot of thieves, beggars, and transports . . . made up of Turks, Jews, and other infidels, with a few renegade Christians and Catholics." Joseph Warren of Massachusetts noted that the act "induced some to imagine that the minister designed by this to force the colonies into a rebellion, and from thence to take occasion to treat them with severity, and, by military power, to reduce them to servitude." Over the next decade, a proliferation of pamphlets denounced British efforts to "enslave" the colonies through excessive taxation and the imposition of officials, judges, and a standing army directed from London. In such assaults on liberty and natural rights, some Americans found principled reasons for opposing British policies and actions.

Beginning with the Stamp Act protest, many Protestant clergymen, both Old Lights and New Lights (see Chapter 4), wove resistance to British authority into their sermons, summoning their congregations to protect their God-given liberty. "A just regard to our liberties . . . is so far from being displeasing to God that it would be ingratitude to him who has given them to us to . . . tamely give them up," exhorted one New England minister. Most Anglican ministers, whose church was headed by the king, tried to stay neutral or opposed the protest; and pacifist Quakers kept out of the fray. But to large numbers of Congregationalist, Presbyterian, and Baptist clergymen, battling for the Lord and defending liberty were one and the same.

Voicing such a message, clergymen exerted an enormous influence on public opinion. Far more Americans heard sermons than had access to newspapers or pamphlets, and ministers always got a respectful hearing at town meetings. Community leaders' proclamations of days of "fasting and public humiliation"—a traditional means of focusing public attention on an issue and invoking divine aid—inspired sermons on the theme of God's sending the people woes only to strengthen and sustain them until victory. Even Virginia gentlemen (not usually known for their piety) felt moved by such proclamations. Moreover, protest leaders' calls for boycotting

British luxuries meshed neatly with traditional pulpit warnings against self-indulgence and wastefulness. Few ordinary Americans escaped the unceasing public reminders that community solidarity against British tyranny and "corruption" meant rejecting sin and obeying God.

Resistance Resumes, 1766–1770

Although Parliament's repeal of the Stamp Act momentarily quieted colonial protests, its search for new sources of revenue soon revived them. While British leaders condemned the colonists for evading their financial responsibilities and for insubordination, growing numbers of Anglo-Americans became convinced that the Stamp Act had not been an isolated mistake but rather part of a deliberate design to undermine colonial self-governance. In this, they were joined by many in Britain who opposed policies that seemed to threaten Britons and colonists alike.

Opposing the Quartering Act, 1766–1767

In August 1766, George III dismissed the Rockingham government and summoned William Pitt to form a cabinet. Opposed to taxing the colonies, Pitt might have repaired the Stamp Act's damage, for no man was more respected in America. But after Pitt's health collapsed in March 1767, effective leadership passed to his Chancellor of the Exchequer (treasurer) Charles Townshend.

Just as Townshend took office, a conflict arose with the New York legislature over the Quartering Act, enacted in 1765. This law ordered colonial legislatures to pay for certain goods needed by soldiers stationed within their respective borders. The necessary items were relatively inexpensive barracks supplies such as candles, windowpanes, mattress straw, polish, and a small liquor ration.

Despite its seemingly petty stipulations, the Quartering Act aroused resentment, for it constituted an indirect tax; that is, although it did not (like the Stamp Act) empower royal officials to collect money directly from the colonists, it obligated assemblies to raise a stated amount of revenue. Such obligations clashed with the assemblies' claimed power to initiate all revenue-raising measures. Likewise, by reinforcing the presence of a standing army, the Quartering Act further reinforced tyranny in the eyes of many colonists. The law fell lightly or not at all on most colonies; but New York, where more soldiers were stationed than in any other province, found compliance very burdensome and refused to grant any supplies.

New York's resistance to the Quartering Act produced a torrent of anti-American feeling in the House of Commons, whose members remained bitter at having had to withdraw the Stamp Act. Townshend responded by drafting the New York Suspending Act, which threatened to nullify all laws passed by the colony if the assembly refused to vote the supplies. By the time George III signed the measure, however, New York had appropriated the necessary funds.

Although New York's retreat averted further confrontation, the conflict over the Quartering Act demonstrated that British leaders would not hesitate to defend Parliament's authority through the most drastic of all steps: by interfering with American claims to self-governance.

Crisis over the Townshend Duties, 1767–1770

Parliamentary resentment toward the colonies expressed widespread British frustration over the government's failure to cut taxes from wartime levels. Dominating the House of Commons, members of the landed gentry slashed their own taxes by 25 percent in 1767. This move cost the government £500,000 and prompted Townshend to propose laws that would tax imports entering America from Britain and increase colonial customs revenue.

Townshend sought to tax the colonists by exploiting an oversight in their arguments against the Stamp Act. In confronting the Stamp Act, Americans had emphasized their opposition to internal taxes, but had said little about Parliament's right to tax imports as they entered the colonies. Townshend and other British leaders chose to interpret this silence as evidence that the colonists accepted Britain's right to tax their trade—to impose external taxes. Yet not all British politicians were so mistaken. "They will laugh at you," predicted a now wiser George Grenville, "for your distinctions about regulations of trade." Brushing aside Grenville's warnings, Parliament passed Townshend's **Revenue Act** (popularly called the Townshend duties) in June and July 1767. The new law taxed glass, paint, lead, paper, and tea imported to the colonies from England.

The Revenue Act differed significantly from what Americans had long seen as a legitimate way of regulating trade through taxation. To the colonists, charging a duty was a lawful way for British authorities to control trade only if that duty excluded foreign goods by making them prohibitively expensive to consumers. The Revenue Act, however, set moderate rates that did not price goods out of the colonial market; clearly, its purpose was to collect money for the treasury. Thus from the colonial standpoint, Townshend's duties were taxes just like the Stamp Act duties.

Although Townshend had introduced the Revenue Act in response to the government's budgetary problems, he had an ulterior motive for establishing an American source of revenue. Traditionally, royal governors had depended on colonial legislatures to vote their salaries; for their part, the legislatures had often refused to allocate these salaries until governors signed certain bills they themselves opposed. Through the Revenue Act, Townshend hoped to establish a fund that would pay the salaries of governors and other royal officials in America, thus freeing them from the assemblies' control. In effect, by stripping the assemblies of their most potent weapon, the power of the purse, the Revenue Act threatened to tip the balance of constitutional power away from elected colonial representatives and toward unelected royal officials.

In reality, the Revenue Act would never yield anything like the income that Townshend anticipated. Of the various items taxed, only tea produced any significant revenue—£20,000 of the £37,000 that the law was expected to yield. And because the measure would serve its purpose only if British tea were affordable to colonial consumers, Townshend eliminated £60,000 worth of import fees paid on tea entering Britain from India before transshipment to America. On balance, the Revenue Act worsened the British treasury's deficit by £23,000. By 1767, Britain's financial difficulties were more an excuse for, than the driving force behind, political demands to tax the colonies. From Parliament's standpoint, the conflict with America was becoming a test of national will over the principle of taxation.

Colonial resistance to the Revenue Act remained weak until December 1767, when John Dickinson published twelve essays entitled *Letters from a Farmer in Pennsylvania.* (Dickinson was actually a lawyer.) Appearing in nearly every colonial newspaper, the essays argued that although Parliament could regulate trade by imposing duties that produced small amounts of "incidental revenue," it had no right to tax commerce for the single purpose of raising revenue. In other words, the legality of any external tax depended on its intent. No tax designed to produce revenue could be considered constitutional unless a people's elected representatives voted for it. Dickinson said nothing that others had not stated or implied during the Stamp Act crisis. Rather, his contribution lay in persuading many Americans that the arguments they had marshaled against the Stamp Act also applied to the Revenue Act.

In early 1768, the Massachusetts assembly condemned the Townshend duties and called on Samuel Adams to draft a "circular letter" calling on other colonial legislatures to join it. Adams's letter forthrightly condemned both taxation without representation and the threat to self-governance posed by Parliament's making governors and other royal officials financially independent of the legislatures. But it acknowledged Parliament as the "supreme legislative Power over the whole Empire," and it advocated no illegal activities. Virginia's assembly warmly approved Adams's message and sent out a more strongly worded circular letter of its own, urging all colonies to oppose imperial policies that would "have an immediate tendency to enslave them." But most colonial legislatures reacted indifferently. In fact, resistance to the Revenue Act might have disintegrated had the British government not overreacted to the circular letters.

Parliamentary leaders regarded even the mild Massachusetts letter as "little better than an incentive to Rebellion." Disorganized by Townshend's sudden death in 1767, the king's Privy Council directed Lord Hillsborough, first appointee to the new post of secretary of state for the colonies, to express the government's displeasure. Hillsborough flatly told the Massachusetts assembly to disown its letter, forbade all colonial assemblies to endorse it, and commanded royal governors to dissolve any legislature that violated his instructions. George III later commented that he never met "a man of less judgment than Lord Hillsborough." A wiser man might have tried to divide the colonists by appealing to their sense of British patriotism, but Hillsborough had chosen to challenge their elected representatives directly, guaranteeing a unified, angry response.

To protest Hillsborough's crude bullying, many legislatures previously indifferent to the Massachusetts circular letter now adopted it enthusiastically. The Massachusetts House of Representatives voted 92 to 17 not to recall its letter. The number 92 immediately acquired symbolic significance for Americans; colonial politicians on more than one occasion drank 92 toasts in tipsy salutes to Massachusetts's action. In obedience to Hillsborough, royal governors responded by dismissing legislatures in Massachusetts and elsewhere. These moves played directly into the hands of Samuel Adams, James Otis, and John Dickinson, who wanted nothing more than to ignite widespread public opposition to the Townshend duties.

Although increasingly outraged over the Revenue Act, the colonists still needed some effective means of pressuring Parliament for its repeal. One approach, nonimportation, seemed especially promising because it offered an alternative to violence and would distress Britain's economy. In August 1768, Boston's merchants therefore adopted a nonimportation agreement, and the tactic slowly spread southward. "Save your money, and you save your country!" became the watchword of the Sons of Liberty, who began reorganizing after two years of inactivity. Not all colonists supported nonimportation, however. Its effectiveness ultimately depended on the compliance of merchants whose livelihood relied on buying and selling imports. In several major communities, including Philadelphia, Baltimore, and Charles Town, South Carolina, merchants continued buying British goods until 1769. Nevertheless, the boycott was significant not only because it limited British imports but also because it mobilized colonists into more actively resisting British policies.

By 1770, a new British prime minister, Lord North, favored eliminating most of the Townshend duties to prevent the American commercial boycott from widening. But to underscore British authority, he insisted on retaining the tax on tea. Parliament agreed, and in April 1770, giving in for the second time in three years to colonial pressure, it repealed most of the Townshend duties.

Parliament's partial repeal produced a dilemma for American politicians. They considered it intolerable that taxes remained on tea, the most profitable item for the royal treasury. Colonial leaders were unsure whether they should press on with the nonimportation agreement until they achieved total victory, or whether it would suffice to maintain a selective boycott of tea. When the nonimportation movement collapsed in July 1770, colonists resisted external taxation by voluntary agreements not to drink British tea. Through nonconsumption, they succeeded in limiting revenue from tea to about one-sixth the level originally expected. This amount was far too little to pay the salaries of royal governors as Townshend had intended. Yet colonial resistance leaders took little satisfaction in having forced Parliament to compromise. The tea duty remained a galling reminder that Parliament refused to retreat from the broadest possible interpretation of the Declaratory Act.

Women and Colonial Resistance

The boycotts of British goods provided a unique opportunity for white women to join the defense of Anglo-American liberties. White women's participation in public affairs had been widening slowly and unevenly in the colonies for several decades. By the 1760s, when colonial protests against British policies began, colonial women such as Sarah Osborn (see Chapter 4) had become well-known religious activists. Calling themselves the Daughters of Liberty, a contingent of upper-class female patriots had played a part in defeating the Stamp Act. Some had attended political rallies during the Stamp Act crisis, and many more had expressed their opposition in discussions and correspondence with family and friends.

Just two years later, women assumed an even more visible role during the Townshend crisis. To protest the Revenue Act's tax on tea, more than three hundred "mistresses of families" in Boston denounced consumption of the beverage in early 1770. In some ways, the threat of nonconsumption was even more effective than that of nonimportation, for women served and drank most of the tea consumed by colonists.

Nonconsumption agreements soon became popular and were extended to include English manufactures, especially clothing. Again women played a vital role, both because they made most decisions about consumption in colonial households and because it was they who could replace British imports with apparel of their own making. Responding to leaders' pleas that they expand domestic cloth production, women of all social ranks, even those who customarily did not weave their own fabric or sew their own clothing, organized spinning bees. These events attracted intense publicity as evidence of American determination to forgo luxury and idleness for the common defense of liberty. One historian calculates that more than sixteen hundred women participated in spinning bees in New England alone from 1768 to 1770. The colonial cause, noted a New York woman, had enlisted "a fighting army of amazons . . . armed with spinning wheels."

Spinning bees not only helped undermine the notion that women had no place in public life but also endowed spinning and weaving, previously considered routine household tasks, with special political virtue. "Women might recover to this country the full and free enjoyment of all our rights, properties and privileges," exclaimed the Reverend John Cleaveland of Ipswich, Massachusetts, in 1769, adding that this "is more than the men have been able to do." For many colonists, such logic enlarged the arena of supposed feminine virtues from strictly religious matters to include political issues.

Spinning bees, combined with female support for boycotting tea, dramatically demonstrated that American

Mercy Otis Warren, by John Singleton Copley, 1763
An essayist and playwright, Warren was the most prominent woman intellectual of the Revolutionary era.

Smuggling cases were heard in vice-admiralty courts, moreover, where the probability of conviction was extremely high.

In the face of lax enforcement, including widespread bribery of customs officials by colonial shippers and merchants, Townshend wanted the board to bring honesty, efficiency, and more revenue to overseas customs operations. But the law quickly drew protests because of the way it was enforced and because it assumed those accused to be guilty until or unless they could prove otherwise.

Under the new provisions, revenue agents commonly filed charges for technical violations of the Sugar Act, even when no evidence existed of intent to conduct illegal trade. They most often exploited the provision that declared any cargo illegal unless it had been loaded or unloaded with a customs officer's written authorization. Customs commissioners also fanned angry passions by invading the traditional rights of sailors. Long-standing maritime custom allowed a ship's crew to supplement their incomes by making small sales between ports. Anything stored in a sailor's chest was considered private property that did not have to be listed as cargo on the captain's manifest. After 1767, however, revenue agents began treating such belongings as cargo, thus establishing an excuse to seize the entire ship. Under this new policy, crewmen saw their trunks ruthlessly broken open by arrogant inspectors who confiscated trading stock worth several months' wages because it was not listed on the captain's loading papers.

To merchants and seamen alike, the commissioners had embarked on a program of "customs racketeering" that constituted little more than a system of legalized piracy. The board's program fed an upsurge in popular violence. Above all, customs commissioners' use of informers provoked retaliation. In 1769, the *Pennsylvania Journal* scorned these agents as "dogs of prey, thirsting after the fortunes of worthy and wealthy men." By betraying the trust of employers, and sometimes of friends, informers aroused hatred in their victims and were roughly handled whenever found.

Nowhere were customs agents and informers more detested than in Boston, where in June 1768 citizens finally retaliated against their tormentors. The occasion was the seizure, on a technicality, of colonial merchant John Hancock's sloop *Liberty*. Hancock, reportedly North America's richest merchant and a leading opponent of British taxation, had become a chief target of the customs commissioners. Now they fined him £9,000, an amount almost thirteen times greater than the taxes he

resistance ran far deeper than the protests of a few male merchants and the largely male crowds in American seaports. Women's participation showed that colonial protests extended into the heart of American households and congregations, and were leading to broader popular participation in politics.

Customs "Racketeering," 1767–1770

Besides taxing colonial imports, Townshend sought to increase revenues through stricter enforcement of the Navigation Acts. While submitting the Revenue Act of 1767, he also introduced legislation creating the American Board of Customs Commissioners. This law raised the number of port officials, funded the construction of a colonial coast guard, and provided money for secret informers. It also awarded an informer one-third of the value of all goods and ships appropriated through a conviction of smuggling. The fact that fines could be tripled under certain circumstances provided an even greater incentive to seize illegal cargoes.

supposedly evaded on a shipment of Madeira wine. A crowd, "chiefly sturdy boys and Negroes," in Thomas Hutchinson's words, tried to prevent the towing of Hancock's ship and then began assaulting customs agents. Growing to several hundred as it surged through the streets, the mob drove all revenue inspectors from Boston.

Under Lord North, the British government, aware of officers' excesses, took steps to rein in the powers of the American Board of Customs Commissioners. The smuggling charges against Hancock were dropped because the prosecution feared that Hancock would appeal a conviction to England, where honest officials might take action against the commissioners responsible for violating his rights. But British officials were conceding nothing to the colonists. For at the same time, they dispatched four thousand troops to Boston, making clear that they would not tolerate further violent defiance of their authority.

"Wilkes and Liberty," 1768–1770

Although most Britons blamed the colonists for their own high taxes, a minority found common cause with the Americans. They formed a movement that arose during the 1760s to oppose the domestic and foreign policies of George III and a Parliament dominated by wealthy landowners. Their leader was John Wilkes, a fiery London editor and member of Parliament who first gained notoriety in 1763 when his newspaper regularly and irreverently denounced George III's policies. The government finally arrested Wilkes for seditious libel, but to great popular acclaim, he won his case in court. The government, however, succeeded in shutting down his newspaper and in persuading a majority in the House of Commons to deny Wilkes his seat. After again offending the government with a publication, Wilkes fled to Paris.

Wilkes returned to England in 1768, defying a warrant for his arrest, and again ran for Parliament. By this time, the Townshend acts and other government policies were stirring up widespread protests. Merchants and artisans in London, Bristol, and other cities demanded the dismissal of the "obnoxious" ministers who were "ruining our manufactories by invidiously imposing and establishing the most impolitic and unconstitutional taxations and regulations on your Majesty's colonies." They were joined by (nonvoting) weavers, coal heavers, seamen, and other workers who protested low wages and high prices that stemmed in part from government policies. All these people rallied around the cry "Wilkes and liberty!"

After he was again elected to Parliament, Wilkes was arrested. The next day, twenty to forty thousand angry "Wilkesites" massed on St. George's Fields, outside the prison where he was being held. When members of the crowd began throwing stones, soldiers and police responded with gunfire, killing eleven protesters. The "massacre of St. George's Fields" had given the movement some martyrs. Wilkes and an associate were elected twice more and were both times denied their seats by other legislators. Meanwhile, the imprisoned Wilkes was besieged by outpourings of popular support from the colonies as well as from Britain. Some Virginians sent him tobacco, and the South Carolina assembly voted to contribute £1,500 to help defray his debts. He maintained a regular correspondence with the Boston Sons of Liberty and, upon his release in April 1770, was

John Wilkes, by William Hogarth, 1763
Detesting Wilkes and all he stood for, Hogarth depicted the radical leader as menacing and untrustworthy.

hailed in a massive Boston celebration as "the illustrious martyr to Liberty."

Wilkes's cause sharpened the political thinking of government opponents in Britain and the colonies alike. Thousands of voters in English cities and towns signed petitions to Parliament protesting its refusal to seat Wilkes as an affront to the electorate's will. Like the colonists, they regarded the theory of "virtual representation" in Parliament as a sham. Fearing arbitrary government actions, some of them formed a Society of the Supporters of the Bill of Rights "to defend and maintain the legal, constitutional liberty of the subject." And while more "respectable" opponents of the government such as William Pitt and Edmund Burke disdained Wilkes for courting the "mob," his movement emboldened them to speak more forcefully against the government, especially on its policies toward the colonies. For the colonists themselves, Wilkes and his following made clear that Parliament and the government represented a small if powerful minority whose authority could be legitimately questioned.

The Deepening Crisis, 1770–1774

After 1770, the imperial crisis took on some ominous new dimensions. Colonists and British troops clashed on the streets of Boston. Resistance leaders in the colonies developed means of systematically coordinating their actions and policies. After Bostonians defied a new act of Parliament, the Tea Act, Britain was determined to subordinate the colonies once and for all. Adding to the general tensions of the period were several violent conflicts that erupted in the western backcountry.

The Boston Massacre, 1770

Responding to the violence provoked by Hancock's case, British authorities had dispatched four thousand British troops to Boston in the summer and fall of 1768 (see above). Regarding the redcoats as a standing army that threatened their liberty as well as a financial burden, Bostonians resented the military presence.

In the presence of so many soldiers, Boston took on the atmosphere of an occupied city and crackled with tension. Armed sentries and resentful civilians traded insults. The mainly Protestant townspeople found it especially galling that many soldiers were Irish Catholics. The poorly paid enlisted men, moreover, were free to seek employment following the morning muster. Often

agreeing to work for less than local laborers, they generated fierce hostility in a community that was plagued by persistently high unemployment.

Poor Bostonians' deep-seated resentment against all who upheld British authority suddenly boiled over on February 22, 1770, when a customs informer shot into a crowd picketing the home of a customs-paying merchant, killing an eleven-year-old boy. While elite Bostonians had disdained the unruly exchanges between soldiers and crowds, the horror at a child's death momentarily united the community. "My Eyes never beheld such a funeral," wrote John Adams. "A vast Number of Boys walked before the Coffin, a vast Number of Women and Men after it. . . . This Shews there are many more Lives to spend if wanted in the Service of their country."

Although the army had played no part in the shooting, it became a natural target for popular frustration and rage. A week after the boy's funeral, tensions between troops and a crowd led by Crispus Attucks, a seaman of African and Native American descent, and including George Robert Twelves Hewes, erupted at the guard post protecting the customs office. When an officer tried to disperse the civilians, his men endured a steady barrage of flying objects and dares to shoot. A private finally did fire, after having been knocked down by a block of ice, and then shouted, "Fire! Fire!" to his fellow soldiers. The soldiers' volley hit eleven persons, five of whom, including Attucks, died.

The shock that followed the March 5 bloodshed marked the emotional high point of the Townshend crisis. Royal authorities in Massachusetts tried to defuse the situation by isolating all British soldiers on a fortified island in the harbor, and Governor Thomas Hutchinson promised that the soldiers who had fired would be tried. Patriot leader John Adams, an opponent of crowd actions, served as their attorney. Adams appealed to the Boston jury by claiming that the soldiers had been provoked by a "motley rabble of saucy boys, negroes and mulattoes, Irish teagues, and outlandish jack tarres," in other words, people not considered "respectable" by the city's elites and middle class. All but two of the soldiers were acquitted, and the ones found guilty suffered only a branding on their thumbs.

Burning hatreds produced by an intolerable situation underlay the Boston Massacre, as it came to be called in conscious recollection of the St. George's Fields Massacre in London two years earlier. The shooting of unarmed American civilians by British soldiers and the light punishment given the soldiers forced the colonists to confront the stark possibility that the British government was bent on coercing and suppressing them through naked force. In a play written by Mercy Otis Warren, a character predicted that soon "Murders, blood and carnage/Shall crimson all these streets" as patriots rose to defend their republican liberty against tyrannical authority.

The Committees of Correspondence, 1772–1773

In the fall of 1772, Lord North's ministry was preparing to implement Townshend's goal of paying the royal governors' salaries out of customs revenue. The colonists had always viewed efforts to free the governors from financial dependence on the legislatures as a threat to representative government. In response, Samuel Adams persuaded Boston's town meeting to request that every Massachusetts community appoint a committee whose members would be responsible for exchanging information and coordinating measures to defend colonial rights. Of approximately 260 towns, about half immediately established "**committees of correspondence**," and most others did so within a year. The idea soon spread throughout New England.

The committees of correspondence were the colonists' first attempt to maintain close and continuing political cooperation over a wide area. By linking almost every interior community to Boston through a network of dedicated activists, the system enabled Adams to send out messages for each local committee to read at its own town meeting, which would then debate the issues and adopt a formal resolution. Involving tens of thousands of colonists to consider evidence that their rights were in danger, the system committed them to take a personal stand by voting.

Adams's most successful effort to mobilize popular sentiment came in June 1773, when he publicized certain letters of Massachusetts Governor Thomas Hutchinson that Benjamin Franklin had obtained. Massachusetts town meetings discovered through the letters that their own chief executive had advocated "an abridgment of what are called English liberties" and "a great restraint of natural liberty." The publication of the Hutchinson correspondence confirmed many colonists' suspicions of a plot to destroy basic freedoms.

In March 1773, Patrick Henry, Thomas Jefferson, and Richard Henry Lee proposed that Virginia establish colony-level committees of correspondence. Within a year, every province but Pennsylvania had followed its example. By early 1774, a communications web linked colonial leaders for the first time since 1766.

Conflicts in the Backcountry

Although most of the turbulence between 1763 and 1775 swirled in the eastern seaports, various combinations of protagonists also clashed in the West—Native Americans, various groups of colonists, colonial governments, and imperial authorities. These conflicts were rooted in the rapid population growth that had spurred the migration of whites to the Appalachian backcountry.

Backcountry tensions surfaced soon after the Seven Years' War in western Pennsylvania, where Scots-Irish Presbyterian settlers had fought repeatedly with Native Americans. Settlers in and around the town of Paxton resented Pennsylvania's Quaker-dominated assembly for failing to provide them with adequate military protection and for denying them equal representation in the legislature. They also concluded that all Native Americans, regardless of wartime conduct, were their racial enemies. In December 1763, armed settlers attacked two villages of peaceful Conestoga Indians, killing and scalping men, women, and children. In February 1764, about 200 "Paxton Boys," as they were called, set out for Philadelphia, with plans to kill Christian Indian refugees there. A government delegation headed by Benjamin Franklin met the armed, mounted mob on the outskirts of the city. After Franklin promised that the assembly would consider their grievances, the Paxton Boys returned home.

Land pressures and the lack of adequate revenue from the colonies left the British government utterly helpless in enforcing the Proclamation of 1763. Speculators such as George Washington sought western land because "any person who . . . neglects the present opportunity of hunting out good Lands will never regain it." Settlers, traders, hunters, and thieves also trespassed on Indian land, and a growing number of instances of violence by colonists toward Native Americans were going unpunished. In the meantime, the British government was unable to maintain garrisons at many of its forts, to enforce violations of laws and treaties, or to provide gifts to its Native allies. Under such pressure, Britain and its Six Nations Iroquois allies agreed in the Treaty of Fort Stanwix (1768) to grant land along the Ohio River that was occupied and claimed by the Shawnees, Delawares, and Cherokees to the governments of Pennsylvania and Virginia. The Shawnees

Paxton Boys Expedition
Philadelphia militiamen prepare to march against the Paxton Boys while voters file into the courthouse (upper center) to cast their ballots.

now assumed leadership of the Ohio Indians who, along with the Cherokees, sensed that no policy of appeasement could stop colonial expansion.

The treaty served to heighten rather than ease western tensions, especially in the Ohio country, where settlers agitated to establish a new colony, Kentucky. Growing violence culminated in 1774 in the unprovoked slaughter by colonists of thirteen Shawnees and Mingos, including eight members of the family of Logan, until then a moderate Mingo leader. The outraged Logan led a force of Shawnees and Mingos who retaliated by killing an equal number of white Virginians. Virginia in turn opened a campaign against the Indians known as **Lord Dunmore's War** (1774), for the colony's governor. The two forces met at Point Pleasant on the Virginia side of the Ohio River, where the English soundly defeated Logan's people. During the peace conference that followed, Virginia gained uncontested rights to lands south of the Ohio in exchange for its claims on the northern side. But Anglo-Indian resentments remained strong, and fighting would resume once Britain and its colonies went to war.

The Treaty of Fort Stanwix resolved the conflicting claims of Pennsylvania and Virginia in Ohio at the Indians' expense. But other western disputes led to conflict among the colonists themselves. Settlers moving west in Massachusetts in the early 1760s found their titles challenged by some of New York's powerful landlords. When two landlords threatened to evict tenants in 1766, the New Englanders joined the tenants in an armed uprising, calling themselves Sons of Liberty

after the Stamp Act protesters. In 1769, in what is now Vermont, settlers from New Hampshire also came into conflict with New York. After four years of guerrilla warfare, the New Hampshire settlers, calling themselves the Green Mountain Boys, established an independent government. Unrecognized at the time, it eventually became the government of Vermont. A third group of New England settlers from Connecticut settled in the Wyoming valley of Pennsylvania, where they clashed in 1774 with Pennsylvanians claiming title to the same land.

Expansion also provoked conflicts between back-country settlers and their colonial governments. In North Carolina, a group known as the Regulators aimed to redress the grievances of westerners who, underrepresented in the colonial assembly, found themselves exploited by dishonest eastern officeholders. The Regulator movement climaxed on May 16, 1771, at the battle of Alamance Creek. Leading an army of perhaps thirteen hundred eastern militiamen, North Carolina's royal governor defeated about twenty-five hundred Regulators in a clash that produced almost three hundred casualties. Although the Regulator uprising then disintegrated, it crippled the colony's subsequent ability to resist British authority.

An armed Regulator movement also arose in South Carolina, in this case to counter the government's unwillingness to prosecute bandits who were terrorizing settlers. But the South Carolina government did not dispatch its militia to the backcountry for fear that the colony's restive slave population might use the occasion to revolt. Instead, it conceded to the principal demands of the Regulators by establishing four new judicial circuits and allowing jury trials in the newly settled areas.

Although not directly interrelated, these episodes all reflected the tensions generated by a increasing land-hungry white population and its willingness to resort to violence against Native Americans, other colonists, and British officials. As Anglo-American tensions mounted in older settled areas, the western settlers' anxious mood spread.

The Tea Act, 1773

Colonial smuggling and nonconsumption had taken a heavy toll on the British East India Company, which enjoyed a legal monopoly on the sale of tea within Britain's empire. By 1773, with tons of tea rotting in its warehouses, the company was teetering on the brink of bankruptcy. Lord North could not afford to let the company fail. Not only did it pay substantial duties on the tea it shipped to Britain, but it also provided huge indirect savings for the government by subsidizing British authority in India (see chapter 6, Beyond America—Global Interactions).

If the East India Company could only control the colonial market, North reasoned, its chances for returning to profitability would greatly increase. Americans supposedly consumed more than a million pounds of tea each year, but by 1773 they were purchasing just one-quarter of it from the company. In May 1773, to save the beleaguered company from financial ruin, Parliament passed the **Tea Act**, which eliminated all remaining import duties on tea entering England and thus lowered the selling price to consumers. (Ironically, the same saving could have been accomplished by repealing the Townshend tax, which would have ended colonial objections to the company's tea and produced enormous goodwill toward the British government.) To lower the price further, the Tea Act also permitted the East India Company to sell its tea directly to consumers rather than through wholesalers. These two concessions reduced the cost of company tea in the colonies well below the price of all smuggled competition. Parliament expected simple economic self-interest to overcome Anglo-American scruples about buying taxed tea.

But the Tea Act alarmed many Americans, above all because they saw in it a menace to liberty and virtue as well as to colonial representative government. By making taxed tea competitive in price with smuggled tea, the law would raise revenue, which the British government would use to pay royal governors. The law thus threatened to corrupt Americans into accepting the principle of parliamentary taxation by taking advantage of their weakness for a frivolous luxury. Quickly, therefore, the committees of correspondence decided to resist the importation of tea, though without violence and without destroying private property. Either by pressuring the company's agents to refuse acceptance or by intercepting the ships at sea and ordering them home, the committees would keep East India Company cargoes from being landed. In Philadelphia, an anonymous "Committee for Tarring and Feathering" warned harbor pilots not to guide any ships carrying tea into port.

Edenton Ladies' Tea Party
In October 1774, fifty-one women gathered at Edenton, North Carolina, and declared it their "duty" to boycott British imports. Nevertheless, the British man who drew this cartoon chose to satirize the event as an unruly "tea party."

In Boston, however, this strategy failed. On November 28, 1773, the first ship came under the jurisdiction of the customshouse, where duties would have to be paid on its cargo within twenty days. Otherwise, the cargo would be seized from the captain and the tea claimed by the company's agents and placed on sale. When Samuel Adams, John Hancock, and other popular leaders repeatedly asked the customs officers to issue a special clearance for the ship's departure, they were blocked by Thomas Hutchinson's refusal to compromise.

On the evening of December 16, five thousand Bostonians gathered at Old South Church. Samuel Adams informed the citizens of Hutchinson's insistence upon landing the tea and proclaimed that "this meeting can do no more to save the country." About fifty young men, including George Robert Twelves Hewes, stepped forward and disguised themselves as Mohawk Indians—symbolizing a virtuous, proud, and assertive American identity distinct from that of corrupt Britain. Armed with "tomahawks," they headed for the wharf, followed by most of the crowd.

The disciplined band assaulted no one and damaged nothing but the hated cargo. Thousands lined the waterfront to see them heave forty-five tons of tea overboard. For almost an hour, the onlookers stood silently transfixed, as if at a religious service, while they peered through the crisp, cold air of a moonlit night. The only sounds were the steady chop of hatchets breaking open wooden chests and the soft splash of tea on the water. When Boston's "Tea Party," as it was later called, was finished, the participants left quietly, and the town lapsed into a profound hush—"never more still and calm," according to one observer.

Toward Independence, 1774–1776

The calm that followed the Boston Tea Party proved to be a calm before the storm. The incident inflamed the British government and Parliament, which now determined once and for all to quash colonial insubordination. Colonial political leaders responded with equal determination to defend self-government and liberty. The empire and its American colonies were on a collision course, leading by spring 1775 to armed clashes. Yet even after blood was shed, colonists hesitated before declaring their complete independence from Britain. In the meantime, free and enslaved African-Americans pondered how best to realize their own freedom.

Liberty for African-Americans

Throughout the imperial crisis, African-American slaves, as a deeply alienated group within society, quickly responded to calls for liberty and equality. In January 1766, when a group of blacks, inspired by the protests against the Stamp Act, had marched through Charles Town, South Carolina, shouting "Liberty!" they had faced arrest for inciting a rebellion. Thereafter, unrest among slaves—usually in the form of violence or escape—kept pace with that among white rebels. Then in 1772, a court decision in England electrified much of the black population. A Massachusetts slave, James Somerset, had accompanied his master to England, where he ran away but was recaptured. Imprisoned on a ship bound for Jamaica, Somerset sued for his freedom. Writing for the King's Court, Lord Chief Justice William Mansfield ruled that because Parliament had never explicitly established slavery in England, a master could not send a slave outside the country against his will.

Although the Somerset decision applied only to slaves being sent out of England, rumors spread that it abolished slavery there. In January 1773, some of Somerset's fellow Massachusetts blacks filed the first of three petitions to the legislature, arguing that the decision should be extended to the colony. In Virginia and Maryland, dozens of slaves ran away from their masters and sought passage aboard ships bound for England. As Anglo-American tensions mounted in 1774, many slaves, especially in the Chesapeake colonies, looked for war and the arrival of British troops as a means to their liberation. The young Virginia planter James Madison remarked that "if America and Britain come to a hostile rupture, I am afraid an insurrection among the slaves may and will be promoted" by England.

Madison's fears were borne out in November 1775 when Virginia's governor, Lord Dunmore, promised freedom to any able-bodied male slave who enlisted in the cause of restoring royal authority. Similarly to Florida when it provided a refuge for escaping South Carolina slaves (see Chapter 4), **Lord Dunmore's Proclamation** appealed to slaves' longings for freedom in order to undermine a planter-dominated society. Ignoring Dunmore's restrictions, about one thousand Virginia blacks joined Dunmore. Those who fought donned uniforms proclaiming "Liberty to Slaves." Dunmore's proclamation associated British forces with slave liberation in the minds of both blacks and whites in the southern

"List of Negroes that went off to Dunmore" (1775)
As this list shows, African-Americans of all ages and both genders sought freedom by responding to Lord Dunmore's Proclamation.

colonies, an association that continued during the war that followed.

The "Intolerable Acts"

Following the Boston Tea Party, Lord North fumed that only "New England fanatics" could imagine themselves oppressed by inexpensive tea. A Welsh member of Parliament drew wild applause by declaring that "the town of Boston ought to be knocked about by the ears, and destroy'd." In vain did the great parliamentary orator Edmund Burke plead for the one action that could end the crisis. "Leave America . . . to tax herself. . . . Leave the Americans as they anciently stood." The British government, however, swiftly asserted its authority by enacting four "Coercive Acts" that, together with the unrelated Quebec Act, became known to colonists as the "Intolerable Acts."

The first of the Coercive Acts, the Boston Port Bill, became law on April 1, 1774. It ordered the navy to close Boston harbor unless the Privy Council certified by June 1 that the town had arranged to pay for the ruined tea. Lord North's cabinet deliberately imposed this impossibly short deadline in order to ensure the harbor's closing, which would lead to serious economic distress.

The second Coercive Act, the Massachusetts Government Act, revoked the Massachusetts charter and restructured the government to make it less democratic. The colony's upper house would no longer be elected annually by the assembly but instead be appointed for life by the crown. The governor gained absolute control over the naming of all judges and sheriffs. Jurymen, previously elected, were now appointed by sheriffs. Finally, the new charter forbade communities to hold more than one town meeting a year without the governor's permission. These changes simply brought Massachusetts into line with other royal colonies, but the colonists interpreted them as evidence of hostility toward representative government and liberty.

The third of the new acts, the Administration of Justice Act, which some colonists cynically called the Murder Act, permitted any person charged with murder while enforcing royal authority in Massachusetts (such as the British soldiers indicted for the Boston Massacre) to be tried in England or in other colonies.

Finally, a new Quartering Act went beyond the earlier act of 1765 by allowing the governor to requisition empty private buildings for housing troops. These measures, along with the appointment of General Thomas Gage, Britain's military commander in North America, as the new governor of Massachusetts, struck New Englanders as proof of a plan to place them under a military tyranny.

Americans learned of the Quebec Act along with the previous four statutes and associated it with them. Intended to cement loyalty to Britain among conquered French-Canadian Catholics, the law established Roman Catholicism as Quebec's official religion. This provision alarmed Protestant Anglo-Americans who widely believed that Catholicism went hand in hand with despotism. Furthermore, the Quebec Act gave Canada's governors sweeping powers but established no legislature. It also permitted property disputes (but not criminal cases) to be decided by French law, which did not use juries. Additionally, the law extended Quebec's territorial claims south to the Ohio River and west to the Mississippi, a vast area populated by Native Americans and some French. Although designated off-limits by the Proclamation of 1763, several colonies continued to claim portions of the region.

The "**Intolerable Acts**" convinced Anglo-Americans that Britain was plotting to abolish traditional English liberties throughout North America. Rebel pamphlets fed fears that the governor of Massachusetts would starve Boston into submission and appoint corrupt sheriffs and judges to crush political dissent through rigged trials. By this reasoning, the new Quartering Act would repress any resistance by forcing troops on an unwilling population, and the "Murder Act" would encourage massacres by preventing local juries from convicting soldiers who killed civilians. Once resistance in Massachusetts had been smashed, the Quebec Act would serve as a blueprint for extinguishing representative government throughout the colonies. Parliament would revoke every colony's charter and introduce a government like Quebec's. Elected assemblies, freedom of religion for Protestants, and jury trials would all disappear.

Intended by Parliament simply to punish Massachusetts—and particularly that rotten apple in the barrel, Boston—the acts instead pushed most colonies to the brink of rebellion. Repeal of these laws became, in effect, the colonists' nonnegotiable demand. Of the twenty-seven reasons justifying the break with Britain that Americans later cited in the Declaration of Independence, six concerned these statutes.

The First Continental Congress

In response to the "Intolerable Acts," the extralegal committees of correspondence of every colony but Georgia sent delegates to a **Continental Congress** in Philadelphia. Among those in attendance when the Congress assembled on September 5, 1774, were many of the colonies' most prominent politicians: Samuel and John Adams of Massachusetts; John Jay of New York; Joseph Galloway and John Dickinson of Pennsylvania; and Patrick Henry, Richard Henry Lee, and George Washington of Virginia. The fifty-six delegates had come together to find a way of defending the colonies' rights in common, and in interminable dinner parties and cloakroom chatter, they took one another's measure.

The First Continental Congress opened by endorsing a set of statements of principle called the Suffolk Resolves that recently had placed Massachusetts in a state of passive rebellion. Adopted by delegates at a convention of Massachusetts towns just as the Continental Congress was getting under way, the resolves declared that the colonies owed no obedience to any of the Coercive Acts, that a provisional government should collect all taxes until the former Massachusetts charter was restored, and that defensive measures should be taken in the event of an attack by royal troops. The Continental Congress also voted to boycott all British goods after December 1 and to cease exporting almost all goods to Britain and its West Indian possessions after September 1775 unless a reconciliation had been accomplished.

This agreement, the Continental Association, would be enforced by locally elected committees of "observation" or "safety," whose members in effect would be usurping control of American trade from the royal customs service.

Such bold defiance was not to the liking of all delegates. Jay, Dickinson, Galloway, and other moderates who dominated the middle-colony contingent most feared the internal turmoil that would surely accompany a head-on confrontation with Britain. These "trimmers" (John Adams's scornful phrase) vainly opposed nonimportation and tried unsuccessfully to win endorsement of Galloway's plan for a "Grand Council," an American legislature that would share the authority to tax and govern the colonies with Parliament.

Finally, however, the delegates summarized their principles and demands in a petition to the king. This document affirmed Parliament's power to regulate imperial commerce, but it argued that all previous parliamentary efforts to impose taxes, enforce laws through admiralty courts, suspend assemblies, and unilaterally revoke charters were unconstitutional. By addressing the king rather than Parliament, Congress was imploring George III to end the crisis by dismissing those ministers responsible for passing the Coercive Acts.

From Resistance to Rebellion

Most Americans hoped that their resistance would jolt Parliament into renouncing all authority over the colonies except trade regulation. But tensions between moderates and radicals ran high, and bonds between men formerly united in outlook sometimes snapped. John Adams's onetime friend Jonathan Sewall, for example, charged that the Congress had made the "breach with the parent state a thousand times more irreparable than it was before." Fearing that Congress was enthroning "their High Mightinesses, the MOB," he and like-minded Americans refused to defy the king.

To solidify their defiance, colonial resistance leaders coerced those colonists who refused to support them. Thus the elected committees that Congress had created to enforce the Continental Association often turned themselves into vigilantes, compelling merchants who still traded with Britain to burn their imports and make public apologies, browbeating clergymen who preached pro-British sermons, and pressuring Americans to adopt simpler diets and dress in order to relieve their dependence on British imports. Additionally, in colony after colony, the committees took on government functions by organizing volunteer military companies and extralegal legislatures. By the spring of 1775, colonial patriots had established provincial "congresses" that paralleled and rivaled the existing colonial assemblies headed by royal governors.

There as elsewhere, colonists had prepared for the worst by collecting arms and organizing extralegal militia units (locally known as minutemen) whose members could respond instantly to an emergency. The British government ordered Massachusetts's Governor Gage to quell the "rude rabble" by arresting the principal patriot leaders. On April 19, 1775, aware that most of these leaders had already fled Boston, Gage instead sent seven hundred British soldiers to seize military supplies that the colonists had stored at Concord. Two couriers, William Dawes and Paul Revere, rode out to warn nearby towns of the British troop movements and target. At Lexington, about seventy minutemen confronted the soldiers. After a confused skirmish in which eight minutemen died and a single redcoat was wounded, the British pushed on to Concord. There they found few munitions but encountered a growing swarm of armed Yankees. When some minutemen mistakenly became convinced that the town was being burned, they exchanged fire with the British regulars and touched off a running battle that continued for most of the sixteen miles back to Boston. By day's end, the redcoats had suffered 273 casualties, compared to only 92 for the colonists, and they had gained some respect for Yankee courage. These engagements awakened the countryside, and by the evening of April 20, some twenty thousand New Englanders were besieging the British garrison in Boston.

Three weeks later, the Second Continental Congress convened in Philadelphia. Most delegates still opposed independence and at Dickinson's urging agreed to send a "loyal message" to George III. Dickinson composed what became known as the **Olive Branch Petition**. Excessively polite, it nonetheless presented three demands: a cease-fire at Boston, repeal of the Coercive Acts, and negotiations to establish guarantees of American rights. Yet while pleading for peace, the delegates also passed measures that Britain could only construe as rebellious. In particular, they voted in May 1775 to establish an "American continental army" and appointed George Washington its commander.

The Olive Branch Petition reached London along with news of the Continental Army's formation and of a battle fought just outside Boston on June 17. In this engagement, British troops attacked colonists entrenched on Breed's

A View of the Town of Concord, 1775, by Ralph Earl
British troops enter Concord to search for armaments. A few hours later, hostilities with the townspeople would erupt.

Hill and Bunker Hill. Although successfully dislodging the Americans, the British suffered 1,154 casualties out of 2,200 men, compared to a loss of 311 patriots.

After Bunker Hill, many Britons wanted retaliation, not reconciliation. On August 23, George III proclaimed New England in a state of rebellion, and in October he extended that pronouncement to include all the colonies. In December, Parliament likewise declared all the colonies rebellious, outlawing all British trade with them and subjecting their ships to seizure.

Common Sense

Despite the turn of events, many colonists clung to hopes of reconciliation. Even John Adams, who believed in the inevitability of separation, described himself as "fond of reconciliation, if we could reasonably entertain Hopes of it on a constitutional basis." Like many elites, Adams recognized that a war for independence would entail arming common people, many of whom reviled all men of wealth regardless of political allegiance. Such an outcome would threaten elite rule and social order as well as British rule.

Through 1775, many colonists, not only elites, clung to the notion that evil ministers rather than the king were forcing unconstitutional measures on them and that saner heads would rise to power in Britain. On both counts they were wrong. The Americans exaggerated the influence of Pitt, Burke, Wilkes (who finally took his seat in Parliament in 1774), and their other friends in Britain. And once George III himself declared the colonies to be in "open and avowed rebellion . . . for the purpose of establishing an independent empire," Anglo-Americans had no choice but either to submit or to acknowledge their goal of national independence.

Most colonists' sentimental attachment to the king, the last emotional barrier to their accepting independence, finally crumbled in January 1776 with the publication of Thomas Paine's **Common Sense**. A failed corset maker and schoolmaster, Paine immigrated to the colonies from England late in 1774 with a letter of introduction from Benjamin Franklin, a penchant for radical politics, and a gift for writing plain and pungent prose that anyone could understand.

Paine told Americans what they had been unable to bring themselves to say: monarchy was an institution rooted in superstition, dangerous to liberty, and inappropriate to Americans. The king was "the royal brute" and a "hardened, sullen-tempered Pharaoh." Whereas previous writers had maintained that certain corrupt politicians were directing an English conspiracy against American liberty, Paine argued that such a conspiracy was rooted in the very institutions of monarchy and empire. Moreover, he argued, America had no economic need for the British connection. As he put it, "The commerce by which she [America] hath enriched herself are the necessaries of life, and will always have a market while eating is the custom in Europe." In addition, he pointed out, the events of the preceding six months had made independence a reality. Finally, Paine linked America's awakening nationalism with the sense of religious mission felt by many in New England and elsewhere when he proclaimed, "We have it in our power to begin the world over again. A situation, similar to the present, hath not happened since the days of Noah until now." America, in Paine's view, would be not only a new nation but a new kind of nation, a model society founded on republican principles and unburdened by the oppressive beliefs and corrupt institutions of the European past.

Printed in both English and German, *Common Sense* sold more than one hundred thousand copies within three months, equal to one for every fourth or fifth adult male, making it a best seller. Readers passed copies from hand to hand and read passages aloud in public gatherings. The *Connecticut Gazette* described Paine's pamphlet as "a landflood that sweeps all before it." *Common Sense* had dissolved lingering allegiance to George III and Great Britain, removing the last psychological barrier to American independence.

Declaring Independence

As colonists absorbed Paine's views, the military conflict between Britain and the colonies escalated, making the possibility of reconciliation even less likely. In May 1775

irregular troops from Vermont and Massachusetts had captured Fort Ticonderoga and Crown Point on the key route connecting New York and Canada. Six months later Washington ordered Colonel Henry Knox, a Boston bookseller and the army's senior artillerist, to bring the British artillery seized at Ticonderoga to reinforce the siege of Boston. Knox and his men built crude sleds to haul their fifty-nine cannons through dense forest and rugged mountains covered by two feet of snow. Forty days and three hundred miles after leaving Ticonderoga, Knox and his exhausted New Yorkers reported to Washington in late January 1776. They had accomplished one of the Revolution's great feats of endurance. The guns from Ticonderoga placed the outnumbered British in a hopeless position and forced them to evacuate Boston on March 17, 1776.

As Britain regrouped and added to its forces gathered at Halifax, Nova Scotia, it planned an assault on New York in order to drive a wedge between rebellious New England and the other colonies. Recognizing New York's

Thomas Paine
Having arrived in the colonies less than two years earlier, Paine became a best-selling author with the publication of *Common Sense* (1776).

strategic importance, Washington led most of his troops there in April 1776.

Other military moves reinforced the drift toward all-out war. In June Congress ordered a two-pronged assault on Canada in which forces under General Philip Schuyler would move northward via Fort Ticonderoga to Montreal while Benedict Arnold would lead a march through the Maine forest to Quebec. Schuyler succeeded but Arnold failed. As Britain poured troops into Canada, the Americans prudently withdrew. At the same time, a British offensive in the southern colonies failed after an unsuccessful attempt to seize Charles Town.

By spring 1776 Paine's pamphlet, reinforced by the growing reality of war, had stimulated dozens of local gatherings—artisan guilds, town meetings, county conventions, and militia musters—to pass resolutions favoring American independence. The groundswell quickly spread to the colonies' extralegal legislatures. New England was already in rebellion, and Rhode Island declared itself independent in May 1776. The middle colonies hesitated to support independence because they feared, correctly, that any war would largely be fought over control of Philadelphia and New York. Following the news in April that North Carolina's congressional delegates were authorized to vote for independence, several southern colonies pressed for separation. Virginia's legislature instructed its delegates at the Second Continental Congress to propose independence, which Richard Henry Lee did on June 7. Formally adopting Lee's resolution on July 2, Congress created the United States of America.

The task of drafting a statement to justify the colonies' separation from England fell to a committee of five, including John Adams, Benjamin Franklin, and Thomas Jefferson, with Jefferson as the principal author. Among Congress's revisions to Jefferson's first draft were its insertion of the phrase "pursuit of happiness" in place of "property" in the Declaration's most famous sentence, and its deletion of a statement blaming George III for foisting the slave trade on unwilling colonists. The **Declaration of Independence** (see Appendix) never mentioned Parliament by name, for Congress had moved beyond arguments over legislative representation and now wanted to separate America altogether from Britain and its head of state, the king. Jefferson listed twenty-seven "injuries and usurpations" committed by George III against the colonies. And he drew on a familiar line of radical thinking when he added that the king's actions had as their "direct object the establishment of an absolute tyranny over these states."

Like Paine, Jefferson elevated the colonists' grievances from a dispute over English freedoms to a struggle of universal dimensions. In the tradition of Locke and other Enlightenment figures, Jefferson argued that the English government had violated its contract with the colonists, thereby giving them the right to replace it with a government of their own design. And his eloquent emphasis on the equality of all individuals and their natural entitlement to justice, liberty, and self-fulfillment expressed republicans' deepest longing for a government that would rest on neither legal privilege nor exploitation of the majority by the few.

Jefferson addressed the Declaration of Independence as much to Americans uncertain about the wisdom of independence as to world opinion, for even at this late date a significant minority opposed independence or were uncertain whether to endorse it. Above all he wanted to convince his fellow citizens that social and political progress could no longer be accomplished within the British Empire. But he left unanswered just which Americans were and were not equal to one another and entitled to liberty. All the colonies endorsing the Declaration countenanced, on grounds of racial inequality, the enslavement of blacks and severe restrictions on the freedoms of those blacks who were not enslaved. Moreover, all had property qualifications that also prevented many white men from voting. The proclamation that "all men" were created equal accorded with the Anglo-American assumption that women could not and should not function politically or legally as autonomous individuals. And Jefferson's accusation that George III had unleashed "the merciless Indian savages" on innocent colonists seemed to place Native Americans outside the bounds of humanity.

Was the Declaration of Independence a statement that expressed the sentiments of all but a minority of colonists? In a very narrow sense it was, but by framing the Declaration in universal terms, Jefferson and the Continental Congress made it something much greater. The ideas motivating Jefferson and his fellow delegates had moved thousands of ordinary colonists to political action over the preceding eleven years, both on their own behalf and on behalf of the colonies in their quarrel with Britain. For better or worse, the struggle for national independence had hastened, and become intertwined with, a quest for equality and personal independence that, for many Americans, transcended boundaries of class, race, or gender. In their reading, the Declaration never claimed that perfect justice and equal opportunity existed in the United States; rather, it challenged the Revolutionary generation and all who later inherited the nation to bring this ideal closer to reality.

Chronology, 1750–1776

1744–1748	King George's War (in Europe, the War of Austrian Succession, 1740–1748).
1754	Albany Congress.
1754–1761	Seven Years' War (in Europe, 1756–1763).
1755	British expel Acadians from Nova Scotia.
1760	George III becomes king of Great Britain. Writs of assistance.
1762	Treaty of San Ildefonso.
1763	Treaty of Paris. Indian uprising in Ohio valley and Great Lakes. Proclamation of 1763.
1763–1764	Paxton Boys uprising in Pennsylvania.
1764	Sugar Act.
1765	Stamp Act. African-Americans demand liberty in Charles Town. First Quartering Act.
1766	Stamp Act repealed. Declaratory Act.
1767	Revenue Act (Townshend duties). American Board of Customs Commissioners created.
1768	Massachusetts "circular letters." John Hancock's ship Liberty seized by Boston customs commissioner. First Treaty of Fort Stanwix. St. George's Fields Massacre in London.
1770	Townshend duties, except tea tax, repealed. Boston Massacre.
1771	Battle of Alamance Creek in North Carolina.
1772–1774	Committees of correspondence formed.
1772	Somerset decision in England.
1773	Tea Act and Boston Tea Party.
1774	Lord Dunmore's War. Coercive Acts and Quebec Act. First Continental Congress.
1775	Battles of Lexington and Concord. Lord Dunmore's Proclamation. Olive Branch Petition. Battles at Breed's Hill and Bunker Hill. George III and Parliament declare colonies to be in rebellion.
1776	Thomas Paine, Common Sense. Declaration of Independence.

Conclusion

In 1763, Britain and its North American colonies concluded a stunning victory over France, entirely eliminating that nation's formidable mainland American empire. Colonists proudly joined in hailing Britain as the world's most powerful nation, and they fully expected to reap territorial and economic benefits from the victory. Yet by 1775, colonists and Britons were fighting with one another. The war had exhausted Britain's treasury and led the government to look to the colonies for help in defraying the costs of maintaining its enlarged empire. In attempting to collect more revenue and to centralize imperial authority, English officials confronted the ambitions and attitudes of Americans who felt themselves to be in every way equal to Britons.

The differences between British and American viewpoints sharpened slowly and unevenly between 1760 and 1776. One major turning point was the Stamp Act crisis (1765–1766), when many Americans began questioning Parliament's authority, as opposed to that of their own elected legislatures, to levy taxes in the colonies. Colonists also broadened their protests during the Stamp Act crisis, moving beyond carefully worded petitions to fiery resolutions, crowd actions, an intercolonial congress, and a nonimportation movement. Colonial resistance became even more effective during the crisis over the Townshend duties (1767–1770) because of increased intercolonial cooperation and support from Britain. Thereafter, growing numbers of colonists moved from simply denying Parliament's authority to tax them to rejecting virtually any British authority over them.

After 1774, independence was virtually inevitable. Yet Americans were the most reluctant of revolutionaries—even after their own state and national legislatures were functioning, their troops had clashed with Britain's, and George III had declared them to be in rebellion. Tom Paine's prose finally persuaded them that they could stand on their own, without the support of Britain's markets, manufactures, or monarch. Thereafter, a grass-roots independence movement began, leading Congress in July 1776 to proclaim American independence.

Americans by no means followed a single path to the point of advocating independence. Ambitious elites resented British efforts to curtail colonial autonomy as exercised almost exclusively by members of their own class in the assemblies. They and many more in the middle classes were angered by British policies that made commerce less profitable as an occupation and more costly to consumers. But others, including both western settlers and poor and working urban people like George Robert Twelves Hewes, defied conventions demanding that humble people defer to the authority of their social superiors. Sometimes resorting to violence, they directed their wrath toward British officials and colonial elites alike. Many African-Americans, on the other hand, considered Britain as more likely than white colonists, especially slaveholders, to liberate them. And Native Americans recognized that British authority, however limited, provided a measure of protection from land-hungry colonists.

Key Terms

Boston Massacre	committees of
Seven Years' War	correspondence
George Washington	Lord Dunmore's War
Albany Congress	Tea Act
George III	Lord Dunmore's
Proclamation of 1763	Proclamation
Sugar Act	"Intolerable Acts"
Stamp Act	Continental Congress
Sons of Liberty	Olive Branch Petition
Declaratory Act	*Common Sense*
Revenue Act	Declaration of Independence

For Further Reference

Fred Anderson, *Crucible of War: The Seven Years' War and the Fate of Empire in British North America, 1754–1766* (2000). A meticulous, engaging study of the war as a critical turning point in the history of British North America.

Bernard Bailyn, *The Ideological Origins of the American Revolution* (1967). A probing discussion of the ideologies that shaped colonial resistance to British authority.

T. H. Breen, *The Marketplace of Revolution: How Consumer Politics Shaped American Independence* (2004). A wide-ranging account of the role of consumption and boycotts in colonists' resistance to British rule.

Eliga Gould, *The Persistence of Empire: British Political Culture in the Age of the American Revolution* (2000). An examination of British popular support for George III's policies in the American colonies.

Eric Hinderaker, *Elusive Empires: Constructing Colonialism in the Ohio Valley, 1673–1800* (1997). A study of the multifaceted competition among Native Americans, Europeans, and European Americans for control of a critical American region.

Woody Holton, *Forced Founders: Indians, Debtors, Slaves, and the Making of the American Revolution* (1999). A major reinterpretation of the causes of the Revolution in Virginia, emphasizing the role of internal conflicts across lines of class, race, and economic interest in propelling secession from Britain.

Pauline Maier, *American Scripture: Making the Declaration of Independence* (1997). A fine study of the immediate context in which independence was conceived and the Declaration was drafted and received.

Mary Beth Norton, *Liberty's Daughters: The Revolutionary Experience of American Women, 1750–1800* (1980). A wide-ranging discussion of the experiences and roles of women in eighteenth-century colonial society and the American Revolution.

Gordon S. Wood, *The American Revolution: A History* (2002). A concise interpretive overview of the Revolutionary-constitutional period by one of its leading historians.

Alfred F. Young, *The Shoemaker and the Revolution: Memory and the American Revolution* (1999). A fascinating study of the participation of ordinary people—particularly George Robert Twelves Hewes—in the Revolution, and of how later generations of Americans interpreted and memorialized their role.

Chapter 6

George Washington, by John Trumbull, 1780
Washington posed for this portrait at the height of the Revolutionary War, accompanied by his personal servant, William Lee. Lee was a slave whom Washington had purchased in 1768.

Securing Independence, Defining Nationhood,

1776–1788

Agrippa Hull

O n May 1, 1777, eighteen-
year-old Agrippa Hull, a
free African-American man
from Stockbridge, Massachusetts,
enlisted in the Continental Army. Like
most black recruits but relatively few
whites, Hull enlisted not for a limited
period but for the duration of the
Revolutionary War.

Although his motives went unrecorded, Hull probably agreed to serve indefinitely because, lacking family and property, there was nothing certain in
his postwar future. His military service changed all that. After two years as
an orderly for one general, he spent four more years in that capacity for General Thaddeus Kosciuszko, a Polish republican and abolitionist who had
volunteered for the American cause. Upon being discharged, Hull declined
Kosciuszko's invitation to join him in Poland, returning instead to Stockbridge,
where he was welcomed as a hero and became a New England celebrity until
his death at age eighty-nine. A gifted storyteller, Hull regaled locals and visitors
with accounts of his wartime experiences—of horrors such as his assisting
surgeons performing amputations, of such glorious American victories as
Saratoga and Monmouth Court House (see below), and of lighter moments
such as Kosciuszko's finding him entertaining his black friends in the general's
uniform. When Kosciuszko made a triumphant return visit to the United
States in 1797, Hull and the Polish patriot reunited in New York to much public
acclaim.

As with thousands of other Americans, Hull's participation in the Revolution
combined practicality and principle. Monetary reward, the pressures of family
and community, and the respective appeals of each cause led men to decide
whether to enlist as patriots or loyalists. For victorious patriots like Hull, military service strengthened a new national identity as American. Until the end of
his life, one of Hull's most prized possessions was the order discharging him

from service in the Continental Army, personally signed by George Washington.

For the new nation itself as well as for individuals like Hull, a distinctive identity as American emerged only gradually over the course of the war. In July 1776, the thirteen colonies had jointly declared their independence from Britain and formed a loosely knit confederation of states. Shaped by the collective hardships experienced during eight years of terrible fighting, the former colonists shifted from seeing themselves primarily as military allies to accepting one another as fellow citizens.

Americans were also divided over some basic political questions relating to the distribution of power and authority within the new nation. While the war was still under way, the United States of America was formalized with the adoption of the Articles of Confederation. But divisions remained, erupting in some states' struggles to adopt constitutions and, even more forcefully, in the national contest over replacing the Articles. The ratification of the Constitution in 1787 marked the passing of America's short-lived Confederation and a triumph for those favoring more centralization of power at the national level. It also left most of Agrippa Hull's fellow blacks in slavery.

Focus Questions

- What factors enabled the Americans to defeat the British in the American Revolution?

- How did the Revolution affect relationships among Americans of different classes, races, and genders?

- What older political ideals did the first state constitutions and Articles of Confederation reflect?

- What were the principal issues dividing proponents and opponents of the new federal Constitution?

The Prospects of War

The Revolution was both a collective struggle that pitted the independent states against Britain and a civil war between American peoples. Americans opposed to the colonies' independence constituted one of several factors working in Britain's favor as war began. Others included Britain's larger population and its superior military resources and preparation. America, on the other hand,

was located far from Britain and enjoyed the intense commitment to independence of patriots and the Continental Army, led by the formidable George Washington.

Loyalists and Other British Sympathizers

As late as January 1776, most colonists still hoped that declaring independence from Britain would not be necessary. Not surprisingly, when separation came six months later, some Americans remained unconvinced that it was justified. About 20 percent of all whites either opposed the rebellion actively or refused to support the Confederation until threatened with fines or imprisonment. Although these internal enemies of the Revolution called themselves **loyalists,** they were "Tories" to their patriot, or Whig, opponents. Whigs remarked, only half in jest, that "a tory was a thing with a head in England, a body in America, and a neck that needed stretching."

Loyalists shared many political beliefs with patriots. Like the rebels, they usually opposed Parliament's claim to tax the colonies. Many loyalists thus found themselves fighting for a cause with which they did not entirely agree, and as a result many would change sides during the war. Most probably shared the worry expressed in 1775 by the Reverend Jonathan Boucher, a well-known Maryland loyalist, who preached with two loaded pistols lying on his pulpit cushion: "For my part I equally dread a Victory by either side."

Loyalists disagreed, however, with the patriots' insistence that independence was the only way to preserve the colonists' constitutional rights. The loyalists denounced separation as an illegal act certain to ignite an unnecessary war. Above all, they retained a profound reverence for the crown and believed that if they failed to defend their king, they would sacrifice their personal honor.

The mutual hatred between Whigs and Tories exceeded that of patriots and the British. Each side saw its cause as so sacred that opposition by a fellow American was an unforgivable act of betrayal. Americans inflicted the worst atrocities committed during the war upon each other.

The most important factor in determining loyalist strength in any area was the degree to which local Whigs exerted political authority and successfully convinced their neighbors that the king and Parliament threatened their liberty. New England town leaders, the Virginia gentry, and the rice planters of South Carolina's seacoast had vigorously pursued a program of political education and popular mobilization from 1772 to 1776. Repeatedly explaining the issues at public meetings, these elites persuaded the overwhelming majority to favor resistance. As a result, probably no more than 5 percent of whites in these areas were committed loyalists in 1776. Where leading families acted indecisively, however, their communities remained divided when the fighting began. The proportion of loyalists was highest in New York and New Jersey, where elites were especially reluctant to declare their allegiance to either side. Those two states eventually furnished about half of the twenty-one thousand Americans who fought as loyalists.

The next most significant factor influencing loyalist military strength was the geographic distribution of recent British immigrants, who remained closely identified with their homeland. Among these newcomers were thousands of British soldiers who had served in the Seven Years' War and stayed on in the colonies, usually in New York, where they could obtain land grants of two hundred acres. An additional 125,000 English, Scots, and Irish landed from 1763 to 1775—the greatest number of Britons to arrive during any dozen years of the colonial era. In New York, Georgia, and the backcountry of North and South Carolina, where native-born Britons were heavily concentrated, the proportion of loyalists among whites probably ranged from 25 percent to 40 percent in 1776. During the war, immigrants from the British Isles would form many Tory units, including the Loyal Highland Emigrants, the North Carolina Highlanders, and the Volunteers of Ireland. After the Revolution, foreign-born loyalists were a majority of those whom the British compensated for wartime property losses—including three-quarters of all such claimants from the Carolinas and Georgia.

Canada's religious and secular elites comprised another significant white minority to hold pro-British sympathies. After the British had conquered New France in the Seven Years' War, the Quebec Act of 1774 (see Chapter 5) retained Catholicism as the established religion in Quebec and continued partial use of French civil law, measures that reconciled Quebec's elites to British rule. When Continental forces invaded Quebec in 1775–1776, they found widespread support among non-elite French as well as English Canadians. Although British forces repulsed the invasion, many Canadians continued to hope for an American victory. But Britain's military kept a firm hold on the region throughout the war.

Other North Americans supported the British cause not out of loyalty to the crown but from a perception that an independent America would pose the greater threat to their own liberty and independence. For example, recent settlers in the Ohio valley disagreed among themselves about which course would guarantee the personal independence they valued above all. A few German, Dutch, and French religious congregations doubted that their rights would be as safe in an independent nation dominated by Anglo-Americans. Yet most non-British whites

TEUCRO DUCE NIL DESPERANDUM.

Firſt Battalion of PENNSYLVANIA LOYALISTS, commanded by His Excellency Sir WILLIAM HOWE, K.B.

ALL INTREPID ABLE-BODIED

HEROES,

WHO are willing to ſerve His MAJESTY KING GEORGE the Third, in Defence of their Country, Laws and Conſtitution, againſt the arbitrary Uſurpations of a tyrannical Congreſs, have now not only an Opportunity of manifeſting their Spirit, by aſſiſting in reducing to Obedience their too-long deluded Countrymen, but alſo of acquiring the polite Accompliſhments of a Soldier, by ſerving only two Years, or during the preſent Rebellion in America.

Such ſpirited Fellows, who are willing to engage, will be rewarded at the End of the War, beſides their Laurels, with 50 Acres of Land, where every gallant Hero may retire, and enjoy his Bottle and Laſs.

Each Volunteer will receive, as a Bounty, FIVE DOLLARS, beſides Arms, Cloathing and Accoutrements, and every other Requiſite proper to accommodate a Gentleman Soldier, by applying to Lieutenant Colonel ALLEN, or at Captain KEARNY's Rendezvous, at PATRICK TONRY's, three Doors above Market-ſtreet, in Second-ſtreet.

Loyalist Recruitment Broadside
Loyalists attempted to recruit troops by appealing to Americans' distaste for arbitrary government (applied in this case to the Continental Congress) as well as by offering material rewards.

in the thirteen colonies supported the Revolution. The great majority of German colonists, for example, had embraced republicanism by 1776 and would overwhelmingly support the cause of American independence.

The rebels never attempted to win over three other mainland colonies—Nova Scotia and East and West Florida—whose small British populations consisted of recent immigrants and British troops. Nor was independence seriously considered in Britain's thirteen West Indian colonies, which were dominated by absentee plantation owners who lived in England and depended on selling their sugar exports in the protected British market.

The British cause would draw significant wartime support from nonwhites. Prior to the outbreak of fighting, African-Americans made clear that they considered their own liberation from slavery a higher priority than the colonies' independence from Britain. While Virginia slaves flocked to Lord Dunmore's ranks (see Chapter 5), hundreds of South Carolina slaves had escaped and had taken refuge on British ships in Charles Town's harbor. During the war about twenty thousand enslaved African-Americans, mostly from the southern colonies, escaped their owners. Although many were recaptured or died, especially from epidemics, about nine thousand achieved freedom, often after serving as laborers or soldiers in the Royal Army. Among the slaveholders whose slaves escaped to British protection was Thomas Jefferson. On the other hand, most African-Americans in the northern colonies calculated that supporting the rebels would hasten their own liberation.

Although Native Americans were deeply divided, most supported the British, either from the beginning or after being pressured by one side or the other to abandon neutrality. In the Ohio country, most Shawnees, Delawares, Mingos, and other Indians continued to bristle at settlers' incursions, but some sought to remain neutral and a few Delaware and Shawnee towns initially supported the Americans. After the uprising of 1763 (see Chapter 5), Native Americans in the Upper Great Lakes had developed good relations with British agents in the former French forts and were solidly in the British camp.

The most powerful Native American confederacies—the Six Nations Iroquois, the Creeks, and the Cherokees—were badly divided when the war broke out. Among the Six Nations, the central council fire at Onondaga, a symbol of unity since Hiawatha's time (see Chapter 1), died out. Most Iroquois followed the lead of the Mohawk chief **Joseph Brant** (Thayendagea) in supporting Britain. But the Oneidas and Tuscaroras, influenced by Congregationalist missionary Samuel Kirkland, actively sided with the rebels against other Iroquois. Creeks' allegiances reflected each village's earlier trade ties with either Britain or Spain (the latter leaned toward the colonists). Cherokee ranks were split between anti-American militants who saw an opportunity to drive back settlers and those who thought that Cherokees' best hope was to steer clear of the Anglo-American conflict.

The patriots also had other sources of Indian support. Native Americans in upper New England, easternmost Canada, and the Illinois and Wabash valleys initially took an anti-British stand because of earlier ties with the French, though many of them became alienated from the colonists during the war. In eastern areas long dominated by colonial governments, there were fewer Indians, most of whom actively and effectively supported the American war effort.

The Opposing Sides

Britain entered the war with two major advantages. First, in 1776 the 11 million inhabitants of the British Isles greatly outnumbered the 2.5 million colonists, one-third of whom were either slaves or loyalists. Second, Britain possessed the world's largest navy and one of its best professional armies. Even so, the royal military establishment grew during the war years to a degree that strained Britain's resources. The number of soldiers stationed in North America, the British Isles, and the West Indies more than doubled from 48,000 to 111,000 men, especially after the war became an international conflict (see Beyond America—Global Interactions). To meet its manpower needs, the British government hired 30,000 German mercenaries known as Hessians and enlisted 21,000 loyalists.

Britain's ability to crush the rebellion was further weakened by the decline in its sea power, a result of budget cuts after 1763. Midway through the war, half of the Royal Navy's ships sat in dry dock awaiting major repairs. Although the navy expanded rapidly from 18,000 to 111,000 sailors, it lost 42,000 men to desertion and 20,000 to disease or wounds. In addition, Britain's merchant marine suffered from raids by American privateers. During the war rebel privateers and the fledgling U.S. navy would capture over two thousand British merchant vessels and sixteen thousand crewmen.

Britain could ill afford these losses, for it faced a colossal task in trying to supply its troops in America. In fact, it had to import from Britain most of the food consumed by its army, a third of a ton per soldier per year. Seriously overextended, the navy barely kept the army supplied and never effectively blockaded American ports.

Mindful of the enormous strain that the war imposed, British leaders faced serious problems maintaining their people's support for the conflict. The war more than doubled the national debt, thereby adding to the burdens of a people already paying record taxes. The politically influential landed gentry could not be expected to vote against their pocketbooks forever.

The United States faced different but no less severe wartime problems. Besides the fact that many colonists and Native Americans favored the British, the patriots faced a formidable military challenge. Americans were accustomed to serving as citizen-soldiers in colonial (now state) militias. Although militias sometimes performed well in hit-and-run guerrilla skirmishes, they lacked the training to fight pitched battles against professional armies like Britain's. Congress recognized that independence would never be secured if the new nation relied on guerrilla tactics, avoided major battles, and allowed the British to occupy all major population centers. Moreover, European powers would recognize that dependence on guerrilla warfare meant that the rebels could not drive out the British army, thereby dooming American hopes of gaining foreign loans, diplomatic recognition, and military allies. Finally, citizen-soldiers were accustomed to serving for a few weeks or months alongside neighbors and relatives and then returning home.

For the United States to succeed, the Continental Army would have to supersede the state militias and would need to fight in the standard European fashion. Professional eighteenth-century armies relied on the precisely executed movements of mass formations. Victory often depended on rapid maneuvers to crush an enemy's undefended flank or rear. Attackers needed exceptional skill in close-order drill in order to fall on an enemy before the enemy could re-form and return fire. Because muskets had a range of less than one hundred yards, armies in battle were never far apart. The troops advanced within musket range of each other, stood upright without cover, and fired volleys at one another until one line weakened from its casualties. Discipline, training, and nerve were essential if soldiers were to stay in ranks while comrades fell beside them. The stronger side then attacked at a quick walk with bayonets drawn and drove off its opponents.

In 1775, Britain possessed a well-trained army with a strong tradition of discipline and bravery under fire. In contrast, the Continental Army lacked an inspirational heritage as well as a deep pool of experienced officers and sergeants who could turn raw recruits into crack units. European officers such as Kosciuszko, Lafayette, and von Steuben (see below) helped make up for the shortage of leaders. Although the United States mobilized about 220,000 troops, compared to the 162,000 who served in the British army, most (unlike Agrippa Hull) served short terms. Even with bounties (signing bonuses), promises of land after service, and other incentives, the army had difficulty attracting men for the long term. Most whites and blacks who did sign up for multiyear or indefinite lengths of time were poor and landless. Such men joined not out of patriotism but because, as one of them, a jailed debtor named Ezekiel Brown, put it, they had "little or nothing to lose."

The Americans experienced a succession of heartbreaking defeats in the war's early years, and the new nation would have been hard-pressed had it not been for the military contributions of France and Spain in the war's later stages. Yet, to win the war, the Continentals did not have to destroy the British army but only prolong the rebellion until Britain's taxpayers lost patience with the struggle. Until then, American victory would depend on the ability of one man to keep his army fighting despite defeat. That man was George Washington.

The young Washington's mistakes and defeats in the Ohio valley (see Chapter 5) taught him lessons that he

Thaddeus Kosciuszko, engraving by Gabriel Fiesinger, 1798 A Polish military engineer, Kosciuszko was one of numerous foreign officers who contributed significantly to the American cause during the Revolution.

might not have learned from easy, glorious victories. He discovered the dangers of overconfidence and the need for determination in the face of defeat. He also learned much about American soldiers, especially that they performed best when led by example and treated with respect.

After resigning his commission in 1758, Washington had sat in the Virginia House of Burgesses, where his influence grew, not because he thrust himself into every issue but because others respected him and sought his opinion. Having emerged as an early, though not outspoken, opponent of parliamentary taxation, he also sat in the Continental Congress. In the eyes of the many who valued his advice and remembered his military experience, Washington was the logical choice to head the Continental Army.

War and Peace, 1776–1783

The Revolutionary War had begun more than a year before Congress declared American independence in July 1776 (see Chapter 5). Until mid-1778 it remained centered in the North, where each side won some important victories. Meanwhile, American forces prevailed over British troops and their Native American allies to gain control of the trans-Appalachian West. The war was finally decided in the South when American and French forces won a stunning victory at Yorktown, Virginia, in 1781. In the peace treaty that followed, Britain finally acknowledged American independence.

Shifting Fortunes in the North, 1776–1778

During the second half of 1776, the two sides focused on New York. Under two brothers—General William Howe and Admiral Richard, Lord Howe—130 British warships carrying thirty-two thousand royal troops landed near New York harbor in the summer of 1776 (see Map 6.1).

Defending New York, America's second-largest city, were eighteen thousand poorly trained soldiers under George Washington.

By the end of the year, William Howe's men had killed or captured one-quarter of Washington's troops and had forced the survivors to retreat from New York across New Jersey and the Delaware River into Pennsylvania. Thomas Paine aptly described these demoralizing days as "the times that try men's souls."

With the British within striking distance of Philadelphia, Washington decided to seize the offensive before

Map 6.1 The War in the North, 1775–1778
During the early years of the war, most of the fighting took place from Philadelphia northward.

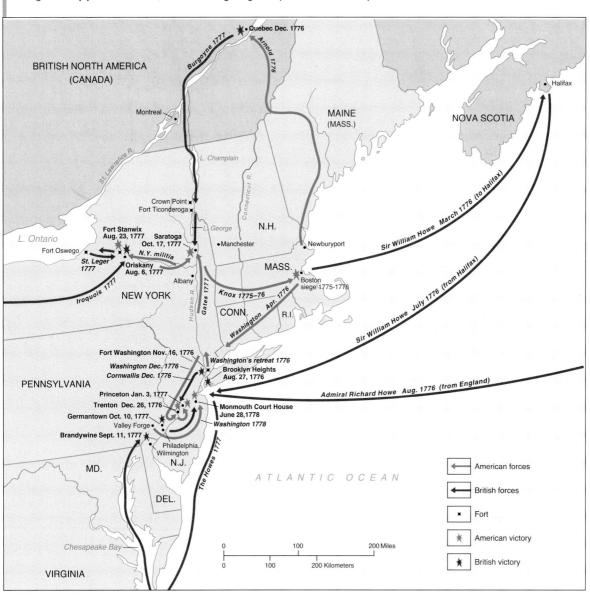

the morale of his army and country collapsed completely. On Christmas night 1776 he led his troops back into New Jersey and attacked a Hessian garrison at Trenton, where he captured 918 Germans and lost only 4 Continentals. Washington then attacked 1,200 British at Princeton on January 3, 1777, and killed or captured one-third of them while sustaining only 40 casualties.

These American victories at Trenton and Princeton had several important consequences. At a moment when defeat seemed inevitable, they boosted civilian and military morale. In addition, they drove a wedge between New Jersey's five thousand loyalists and the British army. Washington's victories forced the British to remove virtually all their New Jersey garrisons to New York early in 1777, while Washington established winter quarters at Morristown, New Jersey, only twenty-five miles from New York City.

New Jersey loyalism never recovered after the British evacuated the state. Even before the Battle of Trenton, British troops had alienated the state's five thousand loyalists by indiscriminately looting loyalist and patriot civilians. Once the British were gone, New Jersey's militia disarmed known loyalists, jailed their leaders, and kept a constant watch on suspected Tories. Bowing to the inevitable, most loyalists who remained in the state swore allegiance to the Continental Congress. Some even enlisted in the rebel militia.

After the Battle of Princeton, the Marquis de Lafayette, a young French aristocrat, joined Washington's staff. The twenty-year-old Lafayette was brave, idealistic, and optimistic. Given Lafayette's close connections with the French court, his presence in America indicated that the French king, Louis XVI, might recognize American independence and declare war on Britain. Before recognizing the new nation, however, Louis wanted proof that the Americans could win a major battle, a feat they had not yet accomplished.

Louis did not have to wait long. In the summer of 1777, the British planned a two-pronged assault intended to crush American resistance in New York State and thereby isolate New England. Pushing off from Montreal, a force of regulars and their Iroquois allies under Lieutenant Colonel Barry St. Leger would march south along Lake Ontario and invade central New York from Fort Oswego in the west. At the same time General John Burgoyne would lead the main British force south from Quebec through eastern New York and link up with St. Leger near Albany.

Nothing went according to British plans. St. Leger's force of 1,900 British and Iroquois advanced one hundred miles and halted to besiege 750 New York Continentals at

British Defeat at Saratoga, 1777
A British cartoonist expresses his disgust for Britain's surrender by depicting General Burgoyne, surrendering on his knees, and a sleeping General Howe.

Fort Stanwix. Unable to take the post after three weeks, St. Leger retreated in late August 1777.

Burgoyne's campaign appeared more promising after his force of 8,300 British and Hessians recaptured Fort Ticonderoga. But Burgoyne ran short of supplies as General Horatio Gates gathered nearly 17,000 American troops for an attack. Gates fought two indecisive battles near Saratoga in the fall, inflicting another 1,200 casualties on Burgoyne. Surrounded and hopelessly outnumbered, Burgoyne's 5,800 troops honorably laid down their arms on October 17, 1777.

The diplomatic impact of the **Battle of Saratoga** equaled its military significance and would prove to be the war's turning point. The victory convinced France that the Americans could win the war. In February 1778 France formally recognized the United States. Four months later, it went to war with Britain. Spain declared war on Britain in 1779, but as an ally of France, not the United States, and the Dutch Republic joined them in the last days of 1780 (see Beyond America—Global Interactions). Britain faced a coalition of enemies, without allies of its own.

Meanwhile, as Gates and Burgoyne maneuvered in upstate New York, Britain's General Howe landed eighteen thousand troops near Philadelphia. With Washington at their head and Lafayette at his side, sixteen thousand Continentals occupied the imperiled city in late August 1777.

The two armies collided on September 11, 1777, at Brandywine Creek, Pennsylvania. In the face of superior British discipline, most Continental units crumbled, and Congress fled Philadelphia in panic, enabling Howe to occupy the city. Howe again defeated Washington at Germantown on October 4. In one month's bloody fighting, 20 percent of the Continentals were killed, wounded, or captured.

The American Revolution as an International War

Originating as a conflict between Britain and its colonies in mainland North America, the American Revolution turned into an international war that extended to Europe, the West Indies, South America, Africa, and Asia. The widening of the war contributed directly to America's struggle for independence from Britain.

Britain and France had emerged as rival maritime empires nearly a century earlier (see Chapter 4, Beyond America—Global Interactions: European Maritime Empires, 1440–1740), and had fought four major wars. Most recently, in the Seven Years' War (1754–1763), the balance of power between them shifted dramatically when France lost all its possessions in mainland North America and India.

The war left both nations facing enormous debts and populations that were heavily but inequitably taxed, especially in France. Britain also sought to finance and administer its suddenly enlarged empire. The East India Company, which functioned as both colonial government in India and monopolistic trade company throughout Asia, was financially troubled. Its local officials in India pursued personal profits, it had accumulated an enormous surplus of tea from China, and American colonists refused to buy its tea. To enhance Company revenues, Parliament passed the Tea Act (1773), which lowered the price of tea by lifting import duties and by allowing Company agents to sell directly to colonial consumers, bypassing American merchants. When, in the Boston Tea Party, radical protesters destroyed Company tea to prevent its unloading, British officials no longer doubted that Americans were disloyal to the empire (see Chapter 5).

The outbreak of Anglo-American conflict in 1775 provided France with an opportunity to avenge its defeat in the Seven Years' War. France borrowed even more money to supply funds and arms to the rebels and welcomed American ships at its ports. French military volunteers, most notably the Marquis de Lafayette, joined the American cause. France also sped up the rebuilding of its army and navy, achieving naval equality with Britain by 1778. Spain, an ally of France and rival of Britain for nearly a century, also contributed arms and other supplies to the rebels. Imported weapons and ammunition were a critical factor in the American victory at Saratoga in October 1777.

As a result of Saratoga, France in February 1778 formally recognized American independence, allied with the United States against Britain, and renounced all territorial claims in mainland North America. After declaring war on Britain in June, France dispatched warships and troops to the West Indies, forcing Britain to evacuate Philadelphia and divert 5,000 troops from North America to defend its wealthy colonies there. Over the next year, British troops seized France's military stronghold at St. Lucia while French forces captured the British colonies of St. Vincent, Grenada, and Dominica.

Spain, eager to reclaim Gibraltar from Britain, joined the war in 1779 as an ally of France but not of the Americans. (Spain feared that an independent United States

Catherine the Great
The formidable tsarina (empress) of Russia led the neutral nations of Europe in defying British naval power during the American Revolution.

would threaten Louisiana.) Spain and France then planned a massive invasion of England. Although they failed to launch the invasion, Britain as a precaution kept half its war fleet nearby and five thousand troops in Ireland, thereby spreading its forces even more thinly.

The Americans gained another ally when the Netherlands abandoned its alliance with Britain. Since the outbreak of the Revolution, Dutch merchants and Dutch West Indian planters had traded with the Americans. Many Dutch also linked their republican aspirations with those of the United States while resenting British domination of its trade and foreign policy. After the British in 1780 seized a Dutch convoy bound for France, the Netherlands declared war on Britain. British forces in 1781 captured most Dutch possessions in the West Indies and adjacent South American mainland.

Like the Netherlands, most European countries bristled under British naval domination and feared that the war would lead Britain to interfere with their trade. To prevent such an outcome, Empress Catherine II ("the Great") in 1780 declared Russia's "armed neutrality." She asserted Russia's right as a neutral country to trade commodities with any nation, threatened to retaliate against any belligerent attempting to search Russian ships, and called on other countries to join a League of Armed Neutrality. Sweden, Denmark, the Netherlands, Prussia, Portugal, Turkey, and several smaller nations joined the League. Recognizing its diplomatic isolation, Britain left League members alone (except the Netherlands) lest it find itself fighting even more enemies.

In 1781 a formidable French fleet commanded by Admiral François de Grasse sailed from France via the West Indies to Chesapeake Bay. Arriving in August, the fleet landed several thousand French troops. The French troops joined Continental forces under George Washington in besieging Lord Cornwallis's base at Yorktown while the fleet prevented any British from slipping out. The Franco-American trap forced Cornwallis to surrender in October.

Although the outcome at Yorktown ensured America's independence, it did not end the international war. In 1782 Spain attempted, unsuccessfully, to seize Gibraltar. Meanwhile, de Grasse had returned to the Caribbean.

Although failing to recapture St. Lucia, he seized St. Kitts after five weeks of fierce British resistance. He was preparing a massive French-Spanish invasion of Jamaica when British forces cornered his fleet in an inter-island passage called the Saintes and captured four ships and de Grasse himself. Elsewhere France sought to regain territory that it had lost to Britain in the Seven Years' War. In 1779 its forces seized Senegal in West Africa. The most powerful state in India, Mysore, had long resisted the British East India Company and, before 1763, had favored France. In 1780, the ruler of Mysore, Hyder Ali, joined four other Indian rulers (usually political and religious rivals of one another) in calling for "the expulsion of the English nation from India." Although the alliance failed to act, Hyder Ali led Mysore's forces in a standoff with British troops for two years. In 1782, a French naval fleet arrived to aid Mysore, threatening Britain's presence in South India.

By then, however, the war's protagonists were discussing terms of peace. The result of their negotiations was the Treaty of Paris (1783), under which America became independent; Britain and France returned all territories seized from one another in the Caribbean (except for the French-held island of Tobago), India, and Senegal; and Britain returned an Indian Ocean port on Ceylon to the Netherlands.

The American Revolution left a volatile mix in the North Atlantic. In achieving independence, the United States accelerated the appeal of republican ideals that were fomenting popular discontent with monarchies across Europe. Ironically, by supporting the birth of a revolutionary republic, the French monarchy added to the nation's already crushing debts, thereby hastening its own downfall and the advent of an even more radical revolution in its own "country. Beginning in 1789, that" revolution would in turn generate a new cycle of global warfare lasting until 1815.

Questions for Analysis

- What impact did other countries have on the struggle between Britian and its American colonies?

- How did the results of the war in mainland North America compare with the outcome elsewhere?

While the British army wintered comfortably eighteen miles away in Philadelphia, the Continentals huddled in the bleak hills of Valley Forge. Joseph Plumb Martin, a seventeen-year-old Massachusetts recruit, recorded the troops' condition in his diary: "The greatest part were not only shirtless and barefoot but destitute of all other clothing, especially blankets." However, he concluded, there was no alternative but desertion, and no one seriously entertained that idea. "We had engaged in the defense of our injured country and were willing nay, we were determined, to persevere as long as such hardships were not altogether intolerable." Shortages of provisions, especially food, would continue to undermine morale and, on some occasions, discipline among American forces.

The army also lacked training. At Saratoga, the Americans' overwhelming numbers more than their skill had forced Burgoyne to surrender. Indeed, when Washington's men had met Howe's forces on equal terms, they lost badly. The Continentals mainly lacked the ability to march as compact units and maneuver quickly. Regiments often straggled single-file into battle and then wasted precious time forming to attack, and few troops were expert in bayonet drill.

The Continental Army received a desperately needed boost in February 1778, when a German soldier of fortune, Friedrich von Steuben, arrived at Valley Forge. The short, squat Steuben did not look like a soldier, but this earthy German instinctively liked Americans and became immensely popular. He had a talent for motivating men (sometimes by staging humorous tantrums featuring a barrage of German, English, and French swearing); but more important, he possessed administrative genius. In a mere four months, General Steuben almost single-handedly turned the army into a formidable fighting force.

British officials decided to evacuate Philadelphia in June 1778 so as to free up several thousand troops for action in the West Indies. General Henry Clinton, the new commander-in-chief in North America, led the troops northward for New York. The Continental Army got its first opportunity to demonstrate Steuben's training when it caught up with Clinton's rear guard at Monmouth Court House, New Jersey, on June 28, 1778. The battle raged for six hours in one-hundred-degree heat until Clinton broke off contact. Expecting to renew the fight at daybreak, the Americans slept on their arms, but Clinton's army slipped away before then. The British would never again win easily, except when they faced more militiamen than Continentals.

The Battle of Monmouth Court House ended the contest for the North. Clinton occupied New York, which the Royal Navy made safe from attack. Washington kept his army nearby to watch Clinton, while the Whig militia hunted down the last few Tory guerrillas and extinguished loyalism.

The War in the West, 1776–1782

A different kind of war developed west of the Appalachians and along the western borders of New York and Pennsylvania, where the fighting consisted of small-scale skirmishes rather than major battles involving thousands of troops. Native Americans and Anglo-Americans had alternately traded, negotiated, and fought in this region for several decades. But long-standing tensions between Native peoples and land-hungry settlers continued to simmer. In one sense, then, the warfare between Indians and white Americans only continued an older frontier struggle. Despite its smaller scale, the war in the West was fierce, and the stakes—for the new nation, for the British, and for Indians in the region—could not have been higher.

The war in the West erupted in 1776 when Cherokees began attacking settlers from North Carolina and other southern colonies who had moved onto or near their homelands (see Map 6.2). After suffering heavy losses, the colonies recovered and organized retaliatory expeditions. Within a year these expeditions had burned most Cherokee towns, forcing the Cherokees to sign treaties that ceded most of their land in South Carolina and substantial tracts in North Carolina and Tennessee.

The intense fighting lasted longer in the Northwest. Largely independent of American and British coordination, Ohio Indians and white settlers fought for two years in Kentucky, with neither side gaining a clear advantage. But after British troops occupied French settlements in the area that is now Illinois and Indiana, Colonel George Rogers Clark led 175 Kentucky militiamen north of the Ohio River. After capturing and losing the French community of Vincennes on the Wabash River, Clark retook the settlement for good in February 1779. With the British unable to offer assistance, their Native American allies were vulnerable. In May, John Bowman led a second Kentucky unit in a campaign that destroyed most Shawnee villages, and in August a move northward from Pittsburgh by Daniel Brodhead inflicted similar damage on the Delawares and the Seneca Iroquois. Although these raids depleted their populations and food supplies, most Ohio Indians resisted the Americans until the war's end.

Meanwhile, pro-British Iroquois, led by the gifted Mohawk leader Joseph Brant, devastated the Pennsylvania and New York frontiers in 1778. They killed 340

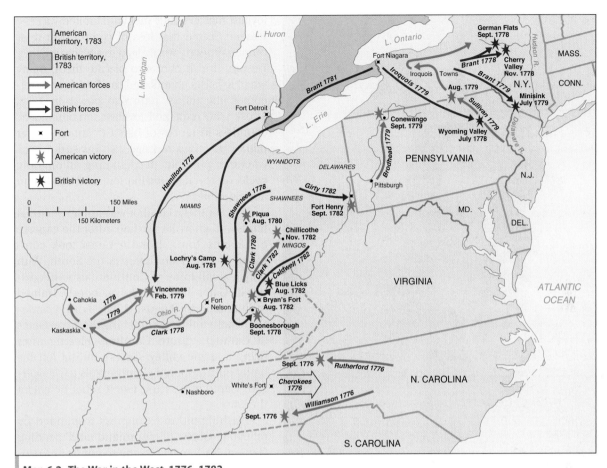

Map 6.2 The War in the West, 1776–1782
The war's western front was closely tied to Native Americans' defense of their homelands against expansionist settlers.

Pennsylvania militiamen at Wyoming, Pennsylvania, and as many more in other raids. In 1779 American General John Sullivan retaliated by invading Iroquois country with 3,700 Continental troops, along with several hundred Tuscaroras and Oneidas who had broken with the other Iroquois nations. Sullivan fought just one battle, near present-day Elmira, New York, in which his artillery routed Brant's warriors. Then he burned two dozen Iroquois villages and destroyed a million bushels of corn, causing most Iroquois to flee without food into Canada. Untold hundreds starved during the next winter, when more than sixty inches of snow fell.

In 1780, Brant's thousand warriors fell upon their fellow Iroquois, the Tuscaroras and Oneidas, and then laid waste to Pennsylvania and New York for two years. But this final whirlwind masked reality: Sullivan's campaign had devastated the pro-British Iroquois.

Fighting continued in the West until 1782. Despite their intensity, the western campaigns did not determine the outcome of the war itself. Nevertheless, they had a significant impact on the future shape of the United States, as discussed later.

Victory in the South, 1778–1781

In 1778, the war's focus shifted to the South. By securing southern ports, Britain expected to acquire the flexibility needed to move its forces back and forth between the West Indies—where they faced French and Spanish opposition—and the mainland, as necessity dictated. In addition, the South looked like a relatively easy target. General Henry Clinton was certain that a renewed invasion there would tap a huge reservoir of loyalist support. In sum, the British plan was to seize key southern ports and, with the aid of loyalist militiamen, move back toward the North, pacifying one region after another.

The plan unfolded smoothly at first. In the spring of 1778, British troops from East Florida took control of Georgia. After a two-year delay caused by political

Joseph Brant, by Gilbert Stuart, 1786
The youthful Mohawk leader was a staunch ally of the British during the Revolutionary War, and thereafter resisted U.S. expansion in the Northwest.

loyalist masters, they met with limited success. Planters feared that loss of control over their human property would lead to a black uprising. Despite British efforts to placate them, many white loyalists abandoned the British and welcomed the rebels' return to power in 1782. Those who remained loyalists, embittered by countless instances of harsh treatment under patriot rule, took revenge. Patriots struck back whenever possible, perpetuating an ongoing cycle of revenge, retribution, and retaliation among whites.

The southern conflict was not all personal feuds and guerrilla warfare. After the capture of Charles Town, Horatio Gates took command of American forces in the South. With only a small force of Continentals at his disposal, Gates had to rely on poorly trained militiamen. In August 1780, Lord Charles Cornwallis inflicted a crushing defeat on Gates at Camden, South Carolina. Fleeing after firing a single volley, Gates's militia left his badly outnumbered Continentals to be overrun. Camden was the worst rebel defeat of the war.

Washington and Congress responded by relieving Gates of command and sending General Nathanael Greene to confront Cornwallis. Greene subsequently fought three major battles between March and September 1781, and he lost all of them. "We fight, get beat, rise, and fight again," he wrote back to Washington. Still, Greene won the campaign, for he gave the Whig militia the protection they needed to hunt down loyalists, stretched British supply lines until they began to snap, and sapped Cornwallis's strength by inflicting much heavier casualties than the British general could afford. Greene's dogged resistance forced Cornwallis to leave the Carolina backcountry in American hands and to lead his battered troops into Virginia.

Cornwallis established a base at Yorktown, Virginia. Britain's undoing began on August 30, 1781, when a French fleet dropped anchor off the Virginia coast and landed troops near Yorktown. Lafayette and a small force of Continentals from nearby joined the French while Washington arrived with his army from New York. In the **Battle of Yorktown**, six thousand trapped British troops stood off eighty-eight hundred Americans and seventy-eight hundred French for three weeks before surrendering with military honors on October 19, 1781.

bickering at home, Clinton sailed from New York with nine thousand troops and forced the surrender of Charles Town, South Carolina, and its thirty-four-hundred-man garrison on May 12, 1780 (see Map 6.3). However, the British quickly found that there were fewer loyalists than they had expected.

Southern loyalism had suffered several serious blows since the war began. When the Cherokees had attacked the Carolina frontier in 1776, they killed whites indiscriminately. Numerous Tories had switched sides, joining the rebel militia to defend their homes. The arrival of British troops sparked a renewed exodus of enslaved Africans from their plantations. About one-third of Georgia's blacks and one-fourth of South Carolina's fled to British lines or to British-held Florida in quest of freedom. Although British officials attempted to return runaway slaves to

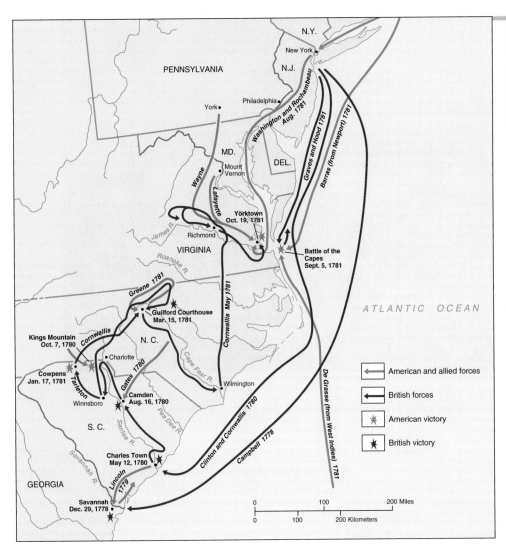

Map 6.3 The War in the South, 1778–1781
The South was the setting for the final and decisive phase of the war, culminating in the British surrender at Yorktown in October 1781.

Peace at Last, 1782–1783

"Oh God!" Lord North exclaimed upon hearing the news from Yorktown. "It's all over." Cornwallis's surrender drained the will of England's overtaxed people to continue fighting and forced Britain to negotiate for peace. John Adams, Benjamin Franklin, and John Jay were America's principal delegates to the peace talks in Paris, which began in June 1782.

Military realities largely influenced the terms of the **Treaty of Paris** (1783). Britain recognized American independence and agreed to withdraw all royal troops from the new nation's soil. The British had little choice but to award the Confederation all lands east of the Mississippi. Although the vast majority of Americans lived in the thirteen states clustered near the eastern seaboard, twenty

thousand Anglo-Americans now lived west of the Appalachians. Moreover, Clark's victories had given Americans control of the Northwest, while Spain had kept Britain out of the Southwest. The treaty also gave the new nation important fishing rights off the Grand Banks of Canada.

On the whole, the settlement was highly favorable to the United States, but it left some disputes unresolved. Under a separate treaty, Britain returned East and West Florida to Spain, but the boundaries designated by this treaty were ambiguous. Spain interpreted the treaty to mean that it regained the same Florida territory that it had ceded to Britain in 1763 (see Chapter 5). But the Treaty of Paris named the thirty-first parallel as the Floridas' northern border, well south of the area claimed by Spain. Spain and the United States would dispute the

Reddition de L'Armée Angloise Commandée par Mylord Comte de Cornwallis aux Armées Combinées des Etats unis de L'Amerique et de France aux ordres des Generaux Washington et de Rochambeau a Yorck town

Surrender of the British at Yorktown, 1781
French naval power combined with American military savvy to produce the decisive defeat of the British.

northern boundary of Florida until 1795 (see below and Chapter 7).

The Treaty of Paris failed to prevent several future disputes between Britain and America. Not bound by the treaty, which extended only to national governments, state governments refused to compensate loyalists for their property losses and erected barriers against British creditors' attempts to collect prewar debts. In retaliation, Britain refused to honor treaty pledges to abandon forts in the Northwest and to return American-owned slaves under their control.

Notably missing in the Treaty of Paris was any reference to Native Americans, most of whom had supported the British in order to avert the alternative—an independent American nation that would be no friend to Indian interests. In effect, the treaty left the Native peoples to deal with the Confederation on their own, without any provision for their status or treatment. Joseph Brant and other Native American leaders were outraged. Not surprisingly, many Indians did not acknowledge the new nation's claims to sovereignty over their territory.

The Treaty of Paris ratified American independence, but winning independence had exacted a heavy price. At least 5 percent of all free males between the ages of sixteen and forty-five—white, black, and Native American—died fighting the British. Only the Civil War produced a higher ratio of casualties to the nation's population. Furthermore, the war drove perhaps one of every six loyalists, several thousand slaves, and several thousand Native Americans into exile. Whites, blacks, and Indians moved to Canada, and whites moved to Britain and the West Indies. After finding that both the land and inhabitants in Nova Scotia were inhospitable, many blacks moved from there to the new British colony of Sierra Leone in West Africa. Perhaps as much as 20 percent of New York's white population fled. When the British evacuated Savannah in 1782, 15 percent of Georgia's whites accompanied them. Most whites who departed were recent British immigrants. Finally, although the war secured American independence, it did not address two important issues: what kind of society America was to become and what sort of government the new nation would possess. But the war had a profound effect on both questions.

The Revolution and Social Change

Two factors—the principles articulated in the Declaration of Independence and dislocations caused by the war itself—forced questions of class, gender, and race into public discussion during the Revolutionary era. As a result, popular attitudes regarding the rights of non-elite white men and of white women, and the future of slavery, shifted somewhat. Except for slaves in the northern states, however, there was little prospect of substantive change in status. Nevertheless, the discussions ensured that these issues would be debated again in the future. For Native Americans, however, the Revolution was a definite step backward.

Egalitarianism Among White Men

For much of the eighteenth century, social relations between elites and other white colonists became more formal, distant, and restrained (see Chapter 4). Members of the colonial gentry emphasized their social position by living far beyond the means of ordinary families. By the late 1760s, however, many elite politicians began wearing homespun rather than imported English clothes in order to win popular political approval during the colonial boycott of British goods. When Virginia planters organized minutemen companies in 1775, they put aside their expensive officers' uniforms and dressed in buckskin or homespun hunting shirts of a sort that even the poorest farmer could afford. By 1776, the anti-British movement had persuaded many elites to maintain the appearance, if not the substance, of equality with common people.

Then came war, which accelerated the trend by pressuring the gentry, who held officers' rank, to show respect to the ordinary men serving under them. Indeed, the soldiers demanded to be treated with consideration, especially in light of the ringing words of the Declaration of Independence, "All men are created equal." The soldiers would follow commands, but not if they were addressed as inferiors.

A few officers realized this fact immediately. Some, among them General Israel Putnam of Connecticut, went out of their way to show that they felt no superiority to their troops. While inspecting a regiment digging fortifications around Boston in 1776, Putnam saw a large stone nearby and told a soldier to throw it onto the outer wall. The individual protested, "Sir, I am a corporal." "Oh," replied Putnam, "I ask your pardon, sir." The general then dismounted his horse and hurled the rock himself, to the immense delight of the troops working there.

Unlike Putnam, many officers insisted that soldiers remain disciplined and subordinate under all circumstances. In May 1780—more than two years after the terrible winter at Valley Forge—Continental Army troops in New Jersey were again, in Joseph Plumb Martin's words, "starved and naked." "The men were now exasperated beyond endurance," Martin continued, "they could not stand it any longer." After a day of exercising with their arms, Martin's regiment defied orders to disarm and return to their quarters, instead urging two nearby regiments to join them in protesting their lack of provisions. A colonel, who "considered himself the soldier's friend," was wounded when trying to prevent his men from getting their weapons. After several officers seized one defiant soldier, his comrades pointed their rifles at the officers until they released the soldier. Other officers tried without success to order the men to disarm and finally gave up. The soldiers' willingness to defy their superiors paid off. Within a few days, more provisions arrived and, as Martin put it, "we had no great cause for complaint for some time."

After returning to civilian life, the soldiers retained their sense of self-esteem and insisted on respectful treatment by elites. As these feelings of personal pride gradually translated into political behavior and beliefs, many candidates took care not to scorn the common people. The war thus subtly but fundamentally democratized Americans' political assumptions.

The gentry's sense of superiority also diminished as elites met men who rose through ability rather than through advantages of wealth or family. The war produced numerous examples like James Purvis, the illiterate son of a nonslaveholding Virginia farmer, who joined the First Virginia Regiment as a private in 1775, soon rose to sergeant, and then taught himself to read and write so that he could perform an officer's duties. Captain Purvis fought through the entire war and impressed his well-born officers as "an uneducated man, but of sterling worth." As elites saw more and more men like Purvis performing responsibilities previously thought to be above their station in life, some came to recognize that a person's merit was not always related to his inherited wealth.

Many who considered themselves republicans did not welcome the apparent trend toward democracy. Especially among elites, they continued to insist that each social class had its own particular virtues and that a chief virtue of the lower classes was deference to those possessing the wealth and education necessary to govern. Writing to a friend in 1776, John Adams expressed alarm that "a jealousy or an Envy taking Place among the Multitude" would exclude "Men of Learning . . . from the public Councils and from Military Command." "A popular government is the worse Curse," he concluded, "despotism is better."

Nevertheless, most Revolutionary-generation Americans came to insist that virtue and sacrifice defined a citizen's worth independently of his wealth. Voters began to view members of the "natural aristocracy"—those who had demonstrated fitness for government service by personal accomplishments—as the ideal candidates for political office. This natural aristocracy had room for a few self-made men such as Benjamin Franklin, as well as for those, like Thomas Jefferson and John Hancock, who were born into wealth. Voters still elected the wealthy to office, but not if they flaunted their money or were condescending toward common people. The new emphasis on equality did not extend to propertyless males, women, and nonwhites, but it undermined the tendency to believe that wealth or distinguished family background conferred a special claim to public office.

Although many whites became more egalitarian in their attitudes, the Revolution left the actual distribution of wealth in the nation unchanged. The war had been directed at British imperial rule and not at the structure of American society. The exodus of loyalists did not affect the class structure because the 3 percent who fled the United States represented a cross-section of society and equally well-to-do Whig gentlemen usually bought up their confiscated estates. Overall, the American upper class seems to have owned about as much of the national wealth in 1783 as it did in 1776.

White Women in Wartime

White women's support of colonial resistance before the Revolution (see Chapter 5) broadened into an even wider range of activities during the war. Female "camp followers," many of them soldiers' wives, served military units on both sides by cooking, laundering, and nursing the wounded. A few female patriots, such as Massachusetts's Deborah Sampson, even disguised themselves as men and joined in the fighting. But most women remained at home, where they managed families, households, farms, and businesses on their own.

Even the most traditional female roles took on new meaning in the absence of male household heads. After her civilian husband was seized by loyalists and turned over to the British on Long Island, Mary Silliman of Fairfield, Connecticut, tended to her four children (and bore a fifth), oversaw several servants and slaves, ran a commercial farm that had to be evacuated when the British attacked Fairfield, and launched repeated appeals for her husband's release. Despite often enormous struggles, such experiences boosted white women's confidence in their abilities to think and act on matters traditionally reserved for men. "I have the vanity," wrote another Connecticut woman, Mary Fish, to a female friend, "to think I have in some measure acted the *heroine* as well as my dear Husband the Hero."

As in all wars, women's public roles and visibility were heightened during the Revolution. Some women interpreted their public activities in militant terms. In 1779, as the Continental Army struggled to feed and clothe itself, Esther de Berdte Reed and Sally Franklin Bache (Benjamin Franklin's daughter) organized a campaign among Philadelphia women to raise money for the troops. Not content to see their movement's role as secondary, they compared it to those of Joan of Arc and other female heroes who had saved their people, and proclaimed that American women were "born for liberty" and would never "bear the irons of a tyrannic Government."

The most direct wartime challenge to established gender relations came from **Abigail Adams**. "In the new Code of Laws which I suppose it will be necessary for you to make," Adams wrote to her husband John in 1776, "I desire that you would Remember the Ladies." Otherwise, she continued, "we are determined to foment a Rebellion and will not hold ourselves bound by any Laws in which we have no voice, or Representation." Abigail made clear that, besides participating in boycotts and spinning bees, women recognized that colonists' arguments against arbitrary British rule also applied to gender relations. Despite his high regard for his wife's intellect, John dismissed her plea as yet another effort to extend rights and power to those who were unworthy. The assumption that women were naturally dependent—either as children subordinate to their parents or as wives to their husbands—continued to dominate discussions of the female role. For that reason, married women's property remained, in Abigail's bitter words, "subject to the control and disposal of our partners, to whom the law have given a sovereign authority."

Although the war ended in 1783, discussions of women's roles in the new republic would continue (see Chapter 7).

A Revolution for Black Americans

The wartime situation of African-Americans contradicted the ideals of equality and justice for which Americans were fighting. About five hundred thousand black persons—20 percent of the total population—inhabited the United States in 1776, all but about twenty-five thousand of whom were enslaved. Even those who were free could not vote, lived under curfews and other galling restrictions, and lacked the guarantees of equal justice held by the poorest white criminal. Free blacks could

Abigail Adams
Painted by the famed artist Gilbert Stuart, this portrait conveys Adams's personal power and intellectual depth.

expect no more than grudging toleration, and few slaves ever gained their freedom.

Although the United States was a "white man's country" in 1776, the war opened some opportunities for African-Americans. Amid the confusion of war, some slaves, among them Jehu Grant of Rhode Island, ran off and posed as free persons. Grant later recalled his excitement "when I saw liberty poles and the people all engaged for the support of freedom, and I could not but like and be pleased with such a thing."

In contrast to the nine thousand who joined or supported British forces, approximately five thousand African-Americans, most of them (like Agrippa Hull) from the North, served in the Continental forces. Even though the army forbade enlistment by African-Americans in 1775, black soldiers were already fighting in units during the siege of Boston, and the ban on black enlistments started to collapse in 1777. The majority were free blacks, but some were slaves serving with their masters' consent.

For the most part, these wartime opportunities for African-American men grew out of the army's need for personnel rather than a white commitment to equal justice. In fact, until the mid-eighteenth century, few Europeans and white Americans had criticized slavery at all. Like disease and sin, slavery was considered part of the natural order. But in the decade before the Revolution, American opposition to slavery had swelled, especially as resistance leaders increasingly compared the colonies' relationship with Britain to that between slaves and a master.

Recognizing that slavery violated Quaker views on human equality, the earliest American initiatives against slavery originated within the Quaker religion. The yearly meeting of the New England Quakers abolished slavery among its members in 1770, and the yearly meetings of New York and Philadelphia Quakers followed suit in 1776. By 1779, Quaker slave owners had freed 80 percent of their slaves.

Although the Quakers aimed mainly to abolish slaveholding within their own ranks, some of them, most notably Anthony Benezet and John Woolman, broadened their condemnations to include slavery everywhere. Discussions of liberty, equality, and natural rights, particularly in the Declaration of Independence, also spurred antislavery sentiments. Between 1777 and 1784 Vermont, Pennsylvania, Massachusetts, Rhode Island, and Connecticut began phasing out slavery. New York did not do so until 1799, and New Jersey until 1804. New Hampshire, unmoved by petitions like that written in 1779 by Portsmouth slaves demanding liberty "to dispose of our lives, freedom, and property," never freed its slaves; but by 1810 none remained in the state.

The Revolutionary generation, rather than immediately abolishing slavery, took steps that would weaken the institution and in this way bring about its eventual demise. Most state abolition laws provided for gradual emancipation, typically declaring all children born of a slave woman after a certain date—often July 4—free. (They still had to work, without pay, for their mother's master for up to twenty-eight years.) Furthermore, the Revolution's leaders did not press for decisive action against slavery in the South out of fear that widespread southern emancipation would either bankrupt or break up the Union. They argued that the Confederation, already deeply in debt as a result of the war, could not finance immediate abolition in the South, and any attempt to do so without compensation would drive that region into secession.

Yet even in the South, where it was most firmly entrenched, slavery troubled some whites. When one of his slaves ran off to join the British and later was recaptured, James Madison of Virginia concluded that it would be hypocritical to punish the runaway "merely for coveting that liberty for which we have paid the price of so much blood." Still, Madison did not free the slave, and no state south of Pennsylvania abolished slavery. Nevertheless, all states except South Carolina and Georgia ended slave imports and all but North Carolina passed laws making it easy for masters to manumit (set free) slaves. The number of free blacks in Virginia and Maryland had risen from about four thousand in 1775 to nearly twenty-one thousand, or about 5 percent of all African-Americans there, by 1790.

These "free persons of color" faced the future as destitute, second-class citizens. Most had purchased their freedom by spending small cash savings earned in off-hours and were past their physical prime. Once free, they found whites reluctant to hire them or to pay equal wages. Black ship carpenters in Charleston (formerly Charles Town), South Carolina, for example, earned one-third less than their white coworkers in 1783. Under such circumstances, most free blacks remained poor laborers, domestic servants, and tenant farmers.

One of the most prominent free blacks to emerge during the Revolutionary period was Boston's **Prince Hall**. Born a slave, Hall received his freedom in 1770 and immediately took a leading role among Boston blacks protesting slavery. During the war he formed a separate African-American Masonic lodge, beginning a movement that spread to other northern communities and became an important source of community support for black Americans. In 1786 Hall petitioned the Massachusetts legislature for support of a plan that would enable interested blacks "to return to Africa, our native country . . . where we shall live among our equals and be more comfortable and happy than we can be in our present situation." Hall's request was unsuccessful, but later activists would revive his call for blacks to "return to Africa."

An African-American who was more widely recognized among whites was the Boston poet and slave Phillis Wheatley. Wheatley drew on Revolutionary ideals in considering her people's status. Several of her poems explicitly linked the liberty sought by white Americans with a plea for the liberty of slaves, including one that was autobiographical:

I, young in life, by seeming cruel fate
Was snatch'd from Afric's fancy'ed happy seat:

     . . . . .

Such, such my case. And can I then but pray
Others may never feel tyrannic sway?

Phillis Wheatley, African-American Poet
Wheatley was America's best-known poet at the time of the Revolution. Despite her fame, she remained a slave and died in poverty in 1784.

Most states granted some civil rights to free blacks during and after the Revolution. Free blacks had not participated in colonial elections, but those who were male and met the property qualification gained this privilege in a few states during the 1780s. Most northern states repealed or stopped enforcing curfews and other colonial laws restricting free African-Americans' freedom of movement. These same states generally changed their laws to guarantee free blacks equal treatment in court hearings.

The Revolution neither ended slavery nor brought equality to free blacks, but it did begin a process by which slavery eventually might have been extinguished. In half the nation, the end of human bondage seemed to be in sight. White southerners increasingly viewed slavery as a necessary evil rather than as a positive good. Slavery had begun to crack, and free blacks had made some gains. But events in the 1790s would reverse the move toward egalitarianism (see Chapter 7).

Native Americans and the Revolution

Whereas Revolutionary ideology held out at least an abstract hope for white women, blacks, and others seeking liberty and equal rights within American society, it made no provision for Native Americans wishing to remain politically and culturally independent of Europeans and European-Americans. Regardless of which side they had fought on—or whether they had fought at all—Native Americans suffered worse than any group during the war. During the three decades encompassed by the Seven Years' War and the Revolution (1754–1783), the Native population east of the Mississippi had declined by about half, and many Indian communities had been uprooted. Moreover, in an overwhelmingly agrarian society like the United States, the Revolution's implicit promise of equal economic opportunity for all male citizens set the stage for territorial expansion onto Native American landholdings. Even where Indians remained on their land, the influx of settlers posed dangers in the form of deadly diseases, farming practices inimical to Indian subsistence (see Chapter 3), and alcohol.

In the face of these uncertainties, most Native Americans continued to incorporate useful aspects of European culture into their own. From the beginning of contact with Europeans, Indians had selectively adopted European-made goods of cloth, metal, glass, and other materials into their lives. But Native Americans did not give up their older ways altogether; rather, their clothing, tools, weapons, utensils, and other material goods combined elements of the old and the new. Many Indians, especially those no longer resisting American expansion, also participated in the American economy by working for wages or by selling food, crafts, or other products. This interweaving of the new with the traditional characterized Indian communities throughout eastern North America.

Native Americans, then, did not remain stubbornly rooted in traditional ways or resist participation in a larger world dominated by whites. But they did insist on retaining control of their homelands and their ways of life. In this spirit, the Chickasaws of the Mississippi valley addressed Congress in 1783. While asking "from whare and whome we are to be supplied with necessaries," they also requested that the Confederation "put a stop to any encroachments on our lands, without our consent, and silence those [white] People who . . . inflame and exasperate our Young Men."

In the Revolution's aftermath, it appeared doubtful that the new nation would concede even this much to Native Americans.

Forging New Governments, 1776–1787

Even as they joined in resisting Britain's authority, white mainland colonists differed sharply among themselves over basic questions of social and political order. Many elite republicans welcomed hierarchical rule, so long as it was not based on heredity, and feared democracy as "mob rule." Working and poor people, especially in cities, worried that propertied elites profited at their expense. Rural colonists emphasized decentralizing power and authority as much as possible. These conflicts were reflected in the independent United States' first experiments in government at the state and national levels.

From Colonies to States

Political conflicts within the new states during and after the Revolution magnified the prewar struggle between more radical democratic elements and elites who would minimize popular participation. While the new state constitutions retained colonial precedents that favored the wealthiest elites, they laid the foundations for republican government in America.

In keeping with colonial practice, eleven of the thirteen states maintained bicameral (two-chamber) legislatures. Colonial legislatures had consisted of an elected lower chamber (or assembly) and an upper chamber (or council) appointed by the governor or chosen by the assembly (see Chapter 4). These two-part legislatures mirrored Parliament's division into the House of Commons and House of Lords, symbolizing the assumption that a government should have separate representation by the upper class and the common people.

Despite participation by people from all classes in the struggle against Britain, few questioned the long-standing practice of setting property requirements for voters and elected officials. In the prevailing view, the ownership of property, especially land, gave voters a direct stake in the outcome of elections. Whereas poor, uneducated tenant farmers and hired laborers might vote to please their landlords or employers, sell their votes, or be fooled by a demagogue, property holders supposedly had the financial means and the education to express their political preferences freely and responsibly. The association between property and citizenship was so deeply ingrained that even radicals such as Samuel Adams opposed allowing all males—much less women—to vote and hold office.

Americans also retained the notion that "virtuous" elected representatives should exercise independent judgment in leading the people rather than simply carry out the popular will. Although Americans today take political parties for granted, the idea of parties as groups organized to mobilize public opinion in favor of a political agenda was alien to eighteenth-century Anglo-Americans. Following England's "country party" (see Chapter 5), Revolutionary Americans equated parties with "factions"—selfish groups that advanced their own interests at the expense of liberty or the public good. Most candidates for office did not present voters with a clear choice between policies calculated to benefit rival interest groups; instead, they campaigned on the basis of their personal reputations and fitness for office. As a result, voters often did not know where office seekers stood on specific issues and hence found it hard to influence government actions.

Another colonial practice that persisted into the 1770s and 1780s was the equal (or nearly equal) division of legislative seats among all counties or towns, regardless of differences in population. Inasmuch as representation had never before been apportioned according to population, a minority of voters normally elected a majority of assemblymen. Only the most radical constitution, Pennsylvania's, sought to avoid such outcomes by attempting to ensure that election districts would be roughly equal in population. Nine of the thirteen states slightly reduced property requirements for voting, but none abolished such qualifications entirely.

Despite the holdover of certain colonial-era practices, the state constitutions in other respects departed radically from the past. Above all, they were written documents that usually required popular ratification and could be changed only if voters chose to amend them. In short, Americans jettisoned the British conception of a constitution as a body of customary arrangements and practices, insisting instead that constitutions were written compacts that defined and limited the powers of rulers. Moreover, as a final check on government power, the Revolutionary constitutions spelled out citizens' fundamental rights. By 1784, all state constitutions included explicit bills of rights that outlined certain freedoms that lay beyond the control of any government.

Without intending to extend political participation, elites had found themselves pulled in a democratic direction by the logic of the imperial crisis of the 1760s and 1770s. Elite-dominated but popularly elected assemblies had led the fight against royal governors and their appointees—the executive branch of colonial governments—who had enforced laws and policies deemed dangerous to liberty. Colonists entered the Revolution dreading executive officeholders and convinced that even elected governors could no more be trusted with power than could monarchs. Recent history seemed to confirm British "country party" thinking that those in power tended to become either corrupt or dictatorial. Consequently, Revolutionary statesmen proclaimed the need to strengthen legislatures at the governors' expense.

Accordingly, the earliest state constitutions severely limited executive power. In most states, the governor became an elected official, and elections themselves occurred far more frequently. (Pennsylvania actually eliminated the office of governor altogether.) Whereas most colonial elections had been called at the governor's pleasure, after 1776 all states scheduled annual elections except South Carolina, which held them every two years. In most states, the power of appointments was transferred from the governor to the legislature. Legislatures usually appointed judges and could reduce their salaries or impeach them (try them for wrongdoing). By relieving governors of most appointive powers, denying them the right to veto laws, and making them subject to impeachment, the constitutions turned governors into figureheads who simply chaired executive councils that made militia appointments and supervised financial business.

As the new state constitutions weakened the executive branch and vested more power in the legislatures, they also made the legislatures more responsive to the will of the people. Nowhere could the governor appoint the upper chamber. Eight constitutions written before 1780 allowed voters to select both houses of the legislature; one (Maryland) used a popularly chosen "electoral college" for its upper house; and the remaining "senates" were filled by vote of their assemblies. Pennsylvania and Georgia abolished the upper house and substituted a unicameral (single-chamber) legislature. American assaults on the executive branch and enhancement of legislative authority reflected bitter memories of royal governors who had acted arbitrarily to dismiss assemblies and control government through their power of appointment, and fear that republics' undoing began with executive usurpation of authority.

Despite their high regard for popularly elected legislatures, Revolutionary leaders described themselves as republicans rather than democrats. Although used interchangeably today, these words had different connotations in the eighteenth century. To many elites, democracy suggested mob rule; at best, it implied the concentration of power in the hands of an uneducated multitude. In contrast, republicanism presumed that government would be entrusted to virtuous leaders elected for their superior talents and commitment to the public good. For most republicans, the ideal government would delicately balance the interests of different classes to prevent any one group from gaining absolute power. Some, including John Adams, thought that a republic could include a hereditary aristocracy or even a monarchy if needed to counterbalance democratic tendencies, but most thought otherwise. Having blasted one king in the Declaration of Independence, most elites had no desire to enthrone another.

In the first flush of revolutionary enthusiasm, elites had to content themselves with state governments dominated by popularly elected legislatures. Gradually, however, wealthier landowners, bankers, merchants, and lawyers reasserted their desires for centralized authority and the political prerogatives of wealth. In Massachusetts, an elite-dominated convention in 1780 pushed through a constitution stipulating stiff property qualifications for voting and holding office, state senate districts that were apportioned according to property values, and a governor with considerable powers in making appointments and vetoing legislative measures. The Massachusetts constitution signaled a general trend. Georgia and Pennsylvania substituted bicameral for unicameral legislatures by 1790. Other states raised property qualifications for members of the upper chamber in a bid to encourage the "senatorial element" and to make room for men of "Wisdom, remarkable integrity, or that Weight which arises from property."

Even many republican elites believed that social divisions, if deep-seated and permanent, could jeopardize liberty, and attempted to prevent such an outcome through legislation. In 1776 in Virginia, for example, Thomas Jefferson persuaded the legislature to abolish entails, legal requirements that prevented an heir and all his descendants from selling or dividing an estate. Although entails were easy to break through special laws—Jefferson himself had escaped the constraints of one—he hoped that their elimination would strip wealthy families of the opportunity to amass land continuously and become an overbearing aristocracy. Through Jefferson's efforts, Virginia also ended primogeniture, the legal requirement that the eldest son inherit all of a family's property in the absence of a will. Jefferson argued that these laws would ensure a continuous division of wealth. By 1791, no state provided for primogeniture, and only two still allowed entails.

The first years of independence also witnessed the end of established churches in most states. The exceptions were New Hampshire, Connecticut, and Massachusetts, where the Congregational church continued to collect tithes (church taxes) from citizens not belonging to recognized Christian denominations into the nineteenth century. Wherever colonial taxpayers had supported the Church of England, independent states abolished such support by 1786. Thomas Jefferson best expressed the ideal behind disestablishment in his Statute for Religious Freedom (1786), whose preamble resounded with a defense of religious freedom at all times and places. "Truth is great," proclaimed Jefferson, "and will prevail if left to itself."

The American Revolution, wrote Thomas Paine in 1782, was intended to ring in "a new era and give a new turn to human affairs." Paine was celebrating America's rejection of hereditary rule and adoption of republican principles. All political institutions, new and old alike, now were being judged by the standard of whether they served the public good rather than the interests of the powerful few. More than any single innovation of the era, it was this new way of thinking that made American politics revolutionary.

Formalizing a Confederation, 1776–1781

As in their revolt against Britain and their early state constitutions, Americans' first national government reflected widespread fears of centralized authority and its potential for corruption. It also reflected their strong attachments to their states, most of which were about a century or more old, as opposed to the newly declared nation. In 1776, John Dickinson, who had stayed in Congress despite having refused to sign the Declaration of Independence, drafted a proposal for a national constitution. Congress adopted a weakened version of Dickinson's proposal, called the **Articles of Confederation**, and sent it to the states for ratification in 1777.

The Articles of Confederation explicitly reserved to each state—and not to the national government—"its sovereignty, freedom and independence." The "United States of America" was no more than "a firm league of friendship" among sovereign states, much like today's European Union. As John Adams later explained, the Whigs of 1776 never thought of "consolidating this vast Continent under one national Government" but instead erected "a Confederacy of States, each of which must have a separate government."

Under the Articles, the national government consisted of a single-chamber Congress, elected by the state legislatures, in which each state had one vote. Congress could request funds from the states but could not enact any tax without every state's approval, and could not regulate interstate or overseas commerce. The approval of seven states was required to pass minor legislation; nine states had to approve declarations of war, treaties, and the coining and borrowing of money. Besides for taxes, unanimous approval was required in order to ratify and amend the Articles. The Articles did not provide for an independent executive branch. Rather, congressional committees oversaw financial, diplomatic, military, and Indian affairs, and resolved interstate disputes. Nor was there a judicial system by which the national government could compel allegiance to its laws. The Articles did eliminate all interstate travel and trade barriers, and guaranteed that all states would recognize one another's judicial decisions.

Because of disputes among the states, especially over their claims to western lands, their contributions to Congress, and their representation in Congress, four years passed before all thirteen legislatures ratified the Articles. Only in February 1781—six months before the American victory at Yorktown—did the last state, Maryland, agree to ratification.

Finance, Trade, and the Economy, 1781–1786

Aside from finishing the war on the battlefield, the greatest challenge facing the Confederation was putting the nation on a sound financial footing. The war cost the nation's six hundred thousand taxpayers a staggering $160 million, a sum that exceeded by 2,400 percent the taxes raised to pay for the Seven Years' War. Yet even this was not enough; to finance the war fully, the government borrowed funds from abroad and printed its own paper money, called Continentals. Lack of public faith in the government destroyed 98 percent of the value of the Continentals from 1776 to 1781, an inflationary disaster that gave rise to the expression "not worth a Continental."

Seeking to overcome the national government's financial weakness, Congress in 1781 appointed a wealthy Philadelphia merchant, Robert Morris, as Superintendent of Finance. Morris proposed that the states authorize the collection of a national import duty of 5 percent, which would finance the congressional budget and guarantee interest payments on the war debt. Because the Articles required that every state approve a national tax, the import duty failed because Rhode Island alone rejected it.

Meanwhile, seeing themselves as sovereign, most states had assumed some responsibility for the war debt and begun compensating veterans and creditors within their borders. But Morris and other nationally minded elites insisted that the United States needed sources of revenue independent of the states in order to establish its creditworthiness, enabling it to attract capital, and to establish a strong national government. Hoping to panic the country into seeing things their way, Morris and New York congressman Alexander Hamilton engineered a

dangerous gamble known later as the Newburgh Conspiracy. In 1783, the two men secretly persuaded some army officers, then encamped at Newburgh, New York, to threaten a coup d'état unless the treasury obtained the taxation authority needed to raise their pay, which was months in arrears. But George Washington, learning of the conspiracy before it was carried out, ended the plot by delivering a speech that appealed to his officers' honor and left them unwilling to proceed. Although Morris may not have intended for a coup to actually occur, his willingness to take such a risk demonstrated the new nation's perilous financial straits and the vulnerability of its political institutions.

When peace came in 1783, Congress sent another tax measure to the states, but once again a single legislature, this time New York's, blocked it. From then on, the states steadily decreased their contributions to Congress. By the late 1780s, the states had fallen behind nearly 80 percent in providing the funds that Congress requested to operate the government and honor the national debt.

Nor did the Confederation succeed in prying trade concessions from Britain. After declaring the colonies in rebellion, Britain had virtually halted American trade with its Caribbean colonies and Great Britain itself (see Chapter 5). The continuation after the war of British trade prohibitions contributed to an economic depression that gripped New England beginning in 1784. A short growing season and poor soil kept yields so low, even in the best of times, that farmers barely produced enough grain for local consumption. New Englanders also faced both high taxes to repay the money borrowed to finance the Revolution and a tightening of credit that spawned countless lawsuits against debtors. Economic depression only aggravated the region's chronic overpopulation.

Resourceful New England captains took cargoes to the French West Indies, Scandinavia, and China (see Chapter 7, Beyond America—Global Interactions). Some even smuggled foodstuffs to the British West Indies under the nose of the Royal Navy. Nevertheless, by 1791 discriminatory British treatment had reduced the number of fishers and whalers in Massachusetts by 42 percent compared to the 1770s.

The mid-Atlantic states, on the other hand, were less dependent on British-controlled markets for their exports. As famine stalked Europe, farmers in Pennsylvania and New York prospered from climbing export prices—much as Thomas Paine had predicted (see Chapter 5). By 1788, the region had largely recovered from the Revolution's ravages.

Southern planters faced frustration at the failure of their principal crops, tobacco and rice, to return to prewar export levels. Whereas nearly two-thirds of American exports originated in the South in 1770, less than half were produced by southern states in 1790. In an effort to stay afloat, many Chesapeake tobacco growers shifted to wheat, and others expanded their production of hemp. But these changes had little effect on the region's exports and, because wheat and hemp required fewer laborers than tobacco, left slave owners with a large amount of underemployed, restless "human property." These factors, along with Native American and Spanish resistance to westward expansion, reinforced nagging uncertainties about the South's future.

The Confederation and the West, 1785–1787

After winning the war against Britain, one of the most formidable challenges confronting the Confederation was the postwar settlement and administration of American territory outside the boundaries of the states. White American settlers and speculators were determined to possess these lands, and Native Americans were just as determined to keep them out. At the same time, Britain and Spain supported the Indian nations in the hope of strengthening their own positions between the Appalachians and the Mississippi.

After the states surrendered claims to more than 160 million acres north of the Ohio River, forming the Northwest Territory (see Map 6.4), Congress established uniform procedures for surveying this land in the **Ordinance of 1785** (see Map 6.5). The law established a township six miles square as the basic unit of settlement. Every township would be subdivided into thirty-six sections of 640 acres each, one of which would be reserved as a source of income for schools. The Ordinance imposed an arbitrary grid of straight lines and right angles across the landscape that conformed to European-American notions of private property while utterly ignoring the land's natural features. Subsequently, in the **Northwest Ordinance** (1787), Congress defined the steps for the creation and admission of new states. This law designated the area north of the Ohio River as the Northwest Territory and provided for its later division into states. It forbade slavery while the region remained a territory, although the citizens could legalize the institution after statehood.

Map 6.4 State Claims to Western Lands, and State Cessions to the Federal Government, 1782–1802 Eastern states' surrender of land claims paved the way for new state governments in the West.

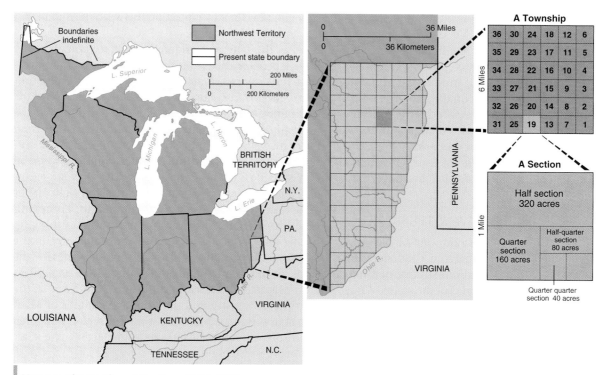

Map 6.5   The Northwest Territory, 1785–1787
The Ordinance of 1785 provided for surveying land into townships of thirty-six sections, each supporting four families on 160-acre plots. In 1787, the Northwest Ordinance stipulated that states ultimately be created in the region.

The Northwest Ordinance outlined three stages for admitting states into the Union. First, during the initial years of settlement, Congress would appoint a territorial governor and judges. Second, as soon as five thousand adult males lived in a territory, voters would approve a temporary constitution and elect a legislature that would pass the territory's laws. Third, when the total population reached sixty thousand, voters would ratify a state constitution, which Congress would have to approve before granting statehood.

The Ordinance of 1785 and the Northwest Ordinance had a lasting effect on later American history. Besides laying out procedures for settling and establishing governments in the Northwest, they later served as models for organizing territories farther west. The Northwest Ordinance also established a significant precedent for banning slavery from certain territories. But because Native Americans, who were determined to keep out settlers, controlled virtually the entire region north of the Ohio River, the ordinances could not be implemented immediately.

The Northwest Territory seemed to offer enough land to guarantee property to American citizens for centuries.

This fact satisfied republicans like Thomas Jefferson who feared that the rapidly growing white population would quickly exhaust available land east of the Appalachians and so create a large class of tenants and poor laborers who could not vote. Such a development would undermine the equality among whites that expansionist republicans thought essential for a healthy nation.

The realization of these expansionist dreams was by no means inevitable. Most "available" territory from the Appalachians to the Mississippi River belonged to those peoples whom the Declaration of Independence had condemned as "merciless Indian savages." Divided into more than eighty tribes and numbering perhaps 150,000 people in 1789, these Native Americans were struggling to preserve their own independence. At postwar treaty negotiations, they repeatedly heard Confederation commissioners scornfully declare, "You are a subdued people . . . we claim the country by conquest."

Under threats of continued warfare with the United States, some northwestern Indian leaders gave in to American pressure. The Iroquois, who had suffered heavily during the war, lost about half their land in New York and Pennsylvania in the second Treaty of Fort Stanwix

(1784). In the treaties of Fort McIntosh (1785) and Fort Finney (1786), Delaware and Shawnee leaders, respectively, were obliged to recognize American sovereignty over their lands. But upon hearing of the treaties, most Indians angrily repudiated them on the grounds that tribal members had never authorized their negotiators to give up territory.

Native Americans' resistance to Confederation encroachments also stemmed from their confidence that the British—still a presence in the West—would provide the arms and ammunition they needed to defy the United States. Contrary to the Treaty of Paris, Britain had refused to abandon seven northwestern forts within the new nation's boundaries, citing certain states' failure to compensate loyalists for confiscated property and to honor prewar debts owed by citizens. With Indian support, Britain hoped eventually to reclaim lands that lay within the Northwest Territory. The British strengthened their presence in the region by encouraging Canadian traders to exchange cloth, tools, and arms with Native peoples for furs.

The Mohawk Joseph Brant emerged as the initial inspiration behind Indian resistance in the Northwest. Courageous in battle, skillful in diplomacy, and highly educated (he had translated an Anglican prayer book and the Gospel of Mark into Mohawk), Brant became a minor celebrity when he visited King George in London in 1785. At British-held Fort Detroit in 1786, he helped organize some northwestern Indians into a military alliance to exclude Confederation citizens north of the Ohio River. But Brant and his Mohawks, who had relocated beyond American reach in Canada, could not win support from Senecas and other Iroquois who had chosen to remain in New York, where they now lived in peace with their white neighbors. Nor could he count on the support of the Ohio Indians, whom the Iroquois had betrayed on numerous occasions in the past (see Chapters 4 and 5).

Seizing on disunity within Indian ranks, Kentuckians and others organized militia raids into the Northwest Territory. These raids gradually forced the Miamis, Shawnees, and Delawares to evacuate southern Indiana and Ohio. The Indians' withdrawal northward, toward the Great Lakes, soon tempted whites to make their first settlements in what is now Ohio. In spring 1788, about fifty New Englanders sailed down the Ohio River in a bulletproof barge named the *Mayflower* and founded the town of Marietta. That same year some Pennsylvanians and New Jerseyites established a second community north of the Ohio on the site of modern-day Cincinnati. By then, another phase in the long-running contest for the Ohio valley was nearing a decisive stage.

The Confederation confronted similar challenges in the Southeast, where Spain and its Indian allies took steps to prevent American settlers from occupying their lands. The Spanish found a brilliant ally in the Creek leader **Alexander McGillivray**. In some fraudulent treaties, two Creeks had surrendered extensive territory to Georgia that McGillivray intended to regain. Patiently holding back his followers for three years, McGillivray negotiated a secret treaty in which Spain promised weapons so that the Creeks could protect themselves "from the Bears and other fierce Animals." When the Creeks finally attacked in 1786, they shrewdly expelled only those whites occupying disputed lands and then offered Georgia a cease-fire. Eager to avoid approving taxes for a costly war, Georgia politicians let the Creeks keep the land.

Spain also sought to prevent American infiltration by denying western settlers permission to ship their crops down the Mississippi River to New Orleans. Having negotiated a separate treaty with Britain (see above), Spain had not signed the Peace of Paris, by which Britain promised the United States export rights down the Mississippi, and in 1784 the Spanish closed New Orleans to Anglo-American commerce. Spain and the United States negotiated a treaty in 1786 that opened Spanish markets to American merchants and renounced Spanish claims to disputed southwestern lands—at the cost, however, of postponing American exporters' access to New Orleans for another twenty years. Westerners and southerners charged that this Jay-Gardoqui Treaty sacrificed their interests to benefit northern commerce, and Congress rejected it.

Unable to prevent American settlers from occupying territory it claimed in the Southeast (see Map 7.2), Spain sought to win the newcomers' allegiance by offering them citizenship. Noting that Congress seemed ready to accept the permanent closing of New Orleans in return for Spanish concessions elsewhere, many westerners began talking openly of secession. Most westerners who accepted Spanish favors and gold meant only to pocket badly needed cash in return for vague promises of goodwill. The episode showed, however, that leading citizens were susceptible to foreign manipulation. As young Andrew Jackson (the future U.S. general and president) concluded in 1789, making some arrangements with the Spanish seemed "the only immediate way to obtain peace with the Savage [Indians]."

Toward a New Constitution, 1786–1788

Under the Articles of Confederation, the United States made enormous strides in establishing itself as an independent nation. But impatience with the national government's limitations persisted among those seeking to establish the United States on a more solid financial and military footing. Impatience turned to anxiety in 1786 after Massachusetts farmers defied local authorities in protesting measures that would worsen their already severe economic circumstances. A national convention called to consider amendments to the Articles instead proposed a radical new frame of government, the Constitution. In 1788, the states ratified the Constitution, setting a new course for America.

Shays's Rebellion, 1786–1787

The Jay-Gardoqui Treaty revealed deep-seated tensions beneath the surface appearance of American national unity. The depression that had begun in 1784 persisted in New England, which had never recovered from the loss of its prime export market in the British West Indies. With farmers already squeezed financially, the state legislature, dominated by commercially minded elites, voted early in 1786 to pay off its Revolutionary debt in three years. This ill-considered policy necessitated a huge tax hike. Meanwhile, the state's unfavorable balance of payments with Britain had produced a shortage of specie (gold and silver coin) because British creditors refused any other currency. Fearing a flood of worthless paper notes, Massachusetts bankers and merchants insisted that they, too, be paid in specie, while the state mandated the same for payment of taxes. Lowest in this cycle of debt were thousands of small family farmers.

In contrast, the mid-Atlantic and southern states were emerging from the depression, thanks to rising tobacco and food exports to Europe. Taxpayers in these sections, moreover, were paying off war debts easily, and most were indifferent to national politics.

Despite the nation's prosperity outside New England, a growing minority was dissatisfied with the Confederation for various reasons. Merchants and shippers wanted a central government powerful enough to secure trading privileges for them abroad, and to ensure economic stability and America's standing in the Atlantic economy, still dominated by Britain. Land speculators and western settlers sought a government that would pursue a more activist policy against Spain, Britain, and Native Americans in the West. Meanwhile, urban artisans hoped for a stronger national government that would impose a uniformly high tariff and thereby protect them from foreign competition.

The spark that ignited this tinderbox originated in Massachusetts. The plight of that state's farmers was especially severe in the western part of the state, where agriculture was least profitable. Facing demands that they pay their debts and taxes in hard currency, which few of them had in abundance if at all, farmers held public meetings. As in similar meetings more than a decade earlier, the farmers—most of whom were Revolutionary War veterans—discussed "the Suppressing of tyrannical government," referring this time to the Massachusetts government rather than the British. In 1786, in a move reminiscent of pre-Revolutionary backcountry dissidents (see Chapter 5), farmer and former officer Daniel Shays led two thousand angry men in an attempt to shut down the courts in three western counties. The Shaysites hoped thereby to stop sheriffs' auctions for unpaid taxes and prevent foreclosures on farm mortgages. Although routed by state troops after several skirmishes, sympathizers of Shays won control of the Massachusetts legislature in 1787, cut taxes, and secured a pardon for their leader.

The Shaysites had limited objectives, were dispersed with relatively little bloodshed, and never seriously threatened anarchy. But their uprising, and similar but less militant movements in other states, became the rallying cry for advocates of a stronger central government. By threatening to seize weapons from a federal arsenal at Springfield, Massachusetts, the farmers' movement unintentionally enabled nationalists to argue that the United States had become vulnerable to "mobocracy." Writing to a fellow wartime general, Henry Knox, for news from Massachusetts, an anxious George Washington worried that "there are combustibles in every state, which a spark might set fire to," destroying the Republic. Meanwhile, rumors were flying that the Spanish had offered export rights at New Orleans to westerners if they would secede from the Union. Nationalists sowed fears that the United States was on the verge of coming apart.

Instead of igniting a popular uprising, as Washington feared, Shays's Rebellion sparked aggressive nationalists into pushing for a wholesale reform of the Republic's legal and institutional structure. Shortly before the outbreak of the rebellion, delegates from five states had assembled at Annapolis, Maryland. They had intended to discuss means of promoting interstate commerce but instead called for a general convention to propose amendments to the Articles of Confederation. Accepting their suggestion, Congress asked the states to appoint delegations to meet in Philadelphia.

The Philadelphia Convention, 1787

In May 1787, fifty-five delegates from every state but Rhode Island began gathering at the Pennsylvania State

House in Philadelphia, later known as Independence Hall. Among them were established figures like George Washington and Benjamin Franklin, as well as talented newcomers such as Alexander Hamilton and James Madison. Most were wealthy and in their thirties or forties, and nineteen owned slaves. More than half had legal training.

The convention immediately closed its sessions to the press and the public, kept no official journal, and even appointed chaperones to accompany the aged and talkative Franklin to dinner parties lest he disclose details of what was happening. Although these measures opened the members of the convention to the charge of acting undemocratically and conspiratorially, the delegates thought secrecy essential to ensure freedom of debate without fear of criticism from home.

The delegates shared a "continental" or "nationalist" perspective, instilled through their extended involvement with the national government. Thirty-nine had sat in Congress, where they had seen the Confederation's limitations firsthand. In the postwar years, they had become convinced that unless the national government was freed from the control of more popularly and locally oriented state legislatures, the country would fall victim to internal strife or foreign aggression.

The convention faced two basic issues. The first was whether to tinker with the Articles of Confederation, as the state legislatures had formally instructed the delegates to do, or to replace the Articles altogether with a new constitution that gave more power to the national government. The second fundamental question was how to balance the conflicting interests of large and small states. **James Madison** of Virginia, who had entered Congress in 1780 at twenty-nine, proposed an answer to each issue. Despite his youth and frail build, Madison commanded enormous respect for his profound knowledge of history and the passionate intensity he brought to debates.

Madison's **Virginia Plan**, introduced in late May, boldly called for the establishment of a strong central government rather than a federation of states. Madison's blueprint gave Congress virtually unrestricted rights of legislation and taxation, the power to veto any state law, and authority to use military force against the states. As one delegate immediately saw, the Virginia Plan was designed "to abolish the State Govern[men]ts altogether." The Virginia Plan specified a bicameral legislature and fixed representation in both houses of Congress proportionally to each state's population. The voters would elect the lower house, which would then choose delegates to the upper chamber from nominations submitted by the legislatures. Both houses would jointly name the country's president and judges.

Madison's scheme aroused immediate opposition, however, especially his call for state representation according to population—a provision highly favorable to his own Virginia. On June 15 William Paterson of New Jersey offered a counterproposal, the so-called **New Jersey Plan**, which recommended a single-chamber congress in which each state had an equal vote, just as under the Articles.

The two plans exposed the convention's great stumbling block: the question of representation. The Virginia Plan would have given the four largest states a majority in both houses. The New Jersey Plan would have allowed the seven smallest states, which included just 25 percent of all Americans, to control Congress. By July 2, the convention had arrived "at a full stop," as one delegate put it. To end the impasse, the delegates assigned a member from each state to a "grand committee" dedicated to compromise. The panel adopted a proposal offered earlier by the Connecticut delegation: an equal vote for each state in the upper house and proportional voting in the lower house. Although Madison and the Virginians doggedly opposed this compromise, it passed on July 17.

James Madison
Although one of the Philadelphia convention's youngest delegates, Madison of Virginia was among its most articulate and politically astute. He played a central role in the Constitution's adoption.

Despite their differences over representation, Paterson's and Madison's proposals alike would have strengthened the national government at the states' expense. No less than Madison, Paterson wished to empower Congress to raise taxes, regulate interstate commerce, and use military force against the states. The New Jersey Plan, in fact, defined congressional laws and treaties as the "supreme law of the land" and would also have established courts to force reluctant states to accept these measures. But other delegates were wary of undermining the sovereignty of the states altogether. Out of hard bargaining emerged the Constitution's delicate balance between the desire of nearly all delegates for a stronger national government and their fear that governments tended to grow despotic.

As finally approved on September 17, 1787, the **Constitution of the United States** (see Appendix) was an extraordinary document, and not merely because it reconciled the conflicting interests of the large and small states. The new frame of government augmented national authority in several ways. Although it did not incorporate Madison's proposal to give Congress a veto over state laws, it vested in Congress the authority to lay and collect taxes, to regulate interstate commerce, and to conduct diplomacy. States could no longer coin money, interfere with contracts and debts, or tax interstate commerce. Following the New Jersey Plan, all acts and treaties of the United States became "the supreme law of the land." All state officials had to swear to uphold the Constitution, even against acts of their own states. The national government could use military force against any state. These provisions added up to a complete abandonment of the principle on which the Articles of Confederation had rested: that the United States was a federation of sovereign states, with ultimate authority concentrated in their legislatures.

To allay the concerns of more moderate delegates, the Constitution's Framers devised two means of restraining the power of the new central government. First, in keeping with republican political theory, they established a **separation of powers** among the national government's three distinct branches—executive, legislative, and judicial; and second, they designed a system of **checks and balances** to prevent any one branch from dominating the other two. In the bicameral Congress, states' equal representation in the Senate was offset by the proportional representation, by population, in the House; and each chamber could block measures approved by the other. Furthermore, where the state constitutions had deliberately weakened the executive,

the Constitution gave the president the power to veto acts of Congress; but to prevent abuse of the veto, Congress could override the president by a two-thirds majority in each house. The president could conduct diplomacy, but the Senate had to ratify treaties. The president appointed a cabinet, but only with Senate approval. The president and any presidential appointee could be removed from office by a joint vote of Congress, but only for "high crimes," not for political disagreements.

To further ensure the independence of each branch, the Constitution provided that the members of one branch would not choose those of another, except for judges, whose independence would be protected because they were appointed for life by the president with the "advice and consent" of the Senate. For example, the president was to be selected by an Electoral College, whose members the states would select as their legislatures saw fit. The number of electors in each state would equal the number of its senators and representatives. In the event of a deadlock in the Electoral College, the House of Representatives, with one vote per state, would choose the president. The state legislatures also elected the members of the Senate, whereas the election of delegates to the House of Representatives was achieved by direct popular vote.

In addition to checks and balances, the founders devised a system of shared power and dual lawmaking by the national and state governments—"**federalism**"—in order to place limits on central authority. Not only did the state legislatures have a key role in electing the president and senators, but the Constitution could be amended by the votes of three-fourths of the states. Thus, the convention departed sharply from Madison's plan to establish a "consolidated" national government entirely independent of, and superior to, the states.

A key assumption behind federalism was that the national government would limit its activities to foreign affairs, national defense, regulating interstate commerce, and coining money. Most other political matters were left to the states. Regarding slavery in particular, each state retained full authority.

The dilemma confronting the Philadelphia convention centered not on whether slavery should be allowed in the new Republic but only on the much narrower question of whether slaves could be counted as persons when it came to determining a state's representation at the national level. For most legal purposes, slaves were regarded not as persons but rather as the chattel property of their owners, meaning that they were on a par with other living property such as horses and cattle. But southern states saw their large numbers of slaves as a means of augmenting their numbers in the House of Representatives and in the electoral colleges that would elect the nation's presidents every four years. So strengthened, they could prevent northerners from ever abolishing slavery.

Representing states that had begun ending slavery, northern delegates opposed giving southern states a political advantage by allowing them to count people who had no civil or political rights. As Madison—himself a slave owner—observed, "it seemed now to be pretty well understood that the real difference of interests lay, not between the large & small [states] but between the N. & South." But after Georgia and South Carolina threatened to secede if their demands were not met, northerners agreed to the "**three-fifths clause**," allowing three-fifths of all slaves to be counted for congressional representation and, thereby, in the Electoral College that selected the president.

The Constitution also reinforced slavery in other ways. Most notably, it forbade citizens of any state, even those that had abolished slavery, to prevent the return of escaped slaves to another state. The Constitution limited slavery only to the extent of prohibiting Congress from banning the importation of slaves before 1808, and by not repudiating Congress's earlier ban on slavery in the Northwest Territory.

Although leaving much authority to the states, the Constitution established a national government whose sovereignty, unlike under the Articles of Confederation, clearly superseded that of the states. Having thus strengthened national authority, the convention had to face the issue of ratification. For two reasons, it seemed unwise to submit the Constitution to state legislatures for ratification. First, the Framers realized that the state legislatures would reject the Constitution, which shrank their power relative to the national government. Second, most of the Framers repudiated the idea—implicit in ratification by state legislatures—that the states were the foundation of the new government. The opening words of the Constitution, "We the People of the United States," underlined the delegates' conviction that the government had to be based on the consent of the American people themselves, "the fountain of all power" in Madison's words, and not of the states.

In the end, the Philadelphia convention provided for the Constitution's ratification by special state conventions composed of delegates elected by the voters. Approval by nine such conventions would put the new government in operation. Because any state refusing to ratify the Constitution would legally remain under the Articles, the possibility existed that the country might divide into two nations.

Under the Constitution, the Framers expected the nation's elites to continue exercising political leadership, and took steps to rein in the democratic currents set in motion by the Revolution. Accordingly, they curtailed what they considered the excessive power of popularly elected state legislatures. And while they located sovereignty in the people rather than in the states, they provided for an Electoral College that would actually elect the president. The Framers did provide for one crucial democratic element in the new government, the House of Representatives. Moreover, by making the Constitution flexible and amendable (though not easily amendable), and by dividing political power among competing branches of government, the Framers made it possible for the national government to be slowly democratized, in ways unforeseen in 1787.

The Struggle over Ratification, 1787–1788

The Constitution's supporters began the campaign for ratification without significant popular support. Expecting the Philadelphia convention to offer some amendments to the Articles of Confederation, most Americans hesitated to restructure the entire system of government. Undaunted, the Constitution's friends moved decisively to marshal political support. In a clever stroke, they called themselves "Federalists," a term implying that the Constitution would more nearly balance the relationship between the national and state governments, and thereby undermined the arguments of those hostile to a centralization of national authority.

The Constitution's opponents became known as "Antifederalists." This negative-sounding title probably hurt them, for it did not convey the crux of their argument against the Constitution—that it was not "federalist" at all since it failed to balance the power of the national and state governments. By augmenting national authority, Antifederalists maintained, the Constitution would ultimately doom the states.

The Antifederalist arguments reflected Anglo-Americans' long-standing suspicion of concentrated power, reiterated by Americans from the time of the Stamp Act crisis, through the War of Independence, to the framing of the first state constitutions and the Articles of Confederation. Unquestionably, the Constitution gave the national government unprecedented authority in an age when most political thinkers argued that the best way to preserve liberty was to limit executive power. Compared to a distant national government, Antifederalists argued, state governments were far more responsive to the popular will. They acknowledged that the Framers had guarded against tyranny by preserving limited state powers and devising a system of checks and balances, but doubted that these devices would succeed. The proposed constitution, concluded one Antifederalist, "nullified and declared void" the constitutions and laws of the states except where they did not contradict federal mandates. Moreover, for all its checks and balances, opponents noted, the Constitution provided no guarantees that the new government would protect the liberties of individuals. The absence of a bill of rights made an Antifederalist of Madison's nationalist ally and fellow Virginian, George Mason, the author of the first such state bill in 1776.

Although the Antifederalists advanced some formidable arguments, they confronted a number of disadvantages in publicizing their cause. While Antifederalist ranks included some prominent figures, none had the stature of George Washington or Benjamin Franklin. As state and local leaders, the Antifederalists lacked their opponents' contacts and experience at the national level, acquired through service as Continental Army officers, diplomats, or members of Congress. Moreover, most American newspapers were pro-Constitution and did not hesitate to bias their reporting in favor of the Federalist cause.

The Federalists' advantages in funds and political organizing proved decisive. The Antifederalists failed to create a sense of urgency among their supporters, assuming incorrectly that a large majority would rally to them. Only one-quarter of the voters turned out to elect delegates to the state ratifying conventions, and most had been mobilized by Federalists.

The Constitution became the law of the land on June 21, 1788, when the ninth state, New Hampshire, ratified by the close vote of 57 to 47. Federalist delegates prevailed in seven of the first nine state conventions by margins of at least two-thirds. Such lopsided votes reflected the Federalists' organizational skills and aggressiveness rather than the degree of popular support for the Constitution. The Constitution's advocates rammed through approval in some states "before it can be digested or deliberately considered," in the words of a Pennsylvania Antifederalist.

But unless Virginia and New York—two of the largest states—ratified, the new government would be fatally weakened. In both states (and elsewhere) Antifederalist sentiment ran high among small farmers, who saw the Constitution as a scheme favoring city dwellers and moneyed interests (see Map 6.6). Prominent political leaders in these two states who called for

refusing ratification included New York governor George Clinton and Virginia's Richard Henry Lee, George Mason, Patrick Henry, and future president James Monroe.

At Virginia's convention, Federalists won crucial support from the representatives of the Allegheny counties—modern West Virginia—who wanted a strong national government capable of ending Indian raids from north of the Ohio River. Western Virginians' votes, combined with James Madison's leadership among tidewater planters, proved too much for Henry's spellbinding oratory. On June 25, the Virginia delegates ratified by a narrow 53 percent majority.

The struggle was even closer and more hotly contested in New York. Antifederalists had solid control of the state convention and would probably have voted down the Constitution, but then news arrived that New Hampshire (the ninth state) and powerful Virginia had approved. Federalist forces, led by Alexander Hamilton and John Jay, spread rumors that if the convention voted to reject, pro-Federalist New York City and adjacent counties would secede from the state and join the Union alone, leaving upstate New York a landlocked enclave. When several Antifederalist delegates took alarm at this threat and switched sides, New York ratified on July 26 by a 30 to 27 vote.

So the Antifederalists went down in defeat, and they did not survive as a political movement. Yet they left an important legacy. At their insistence, the Virginia, New York, and Massachusetts conventions ratified the Constitution with the accompanying request that the new charter be amended to include a bill of rights protecting Americans' basic freedoms. So widespread was the public demand for a bill of rights that it became a high priority on the new government's agenda (see Chapter 7).

Antifederalists' objections in New York also stimulated a response in the form of one of the great classics of political thought, *The Federalist*, a series of eighty-five newspaper essays penned by Alexander Hamilton, James Madison, and John Jay. The Federalist Papers, as they are commonly termed, had little influence on voting in the New York State convention. Rather, their importance lay in articulating arguments for the Constitution that addressed Americans' wide-ranging concerns about the powers and limits of the new federal government, thereby shaping a new philosophy of government. The Constitution, insisted *The Federalist*'s authors, had a twofold purpose: first, to defend the rights of political minorities

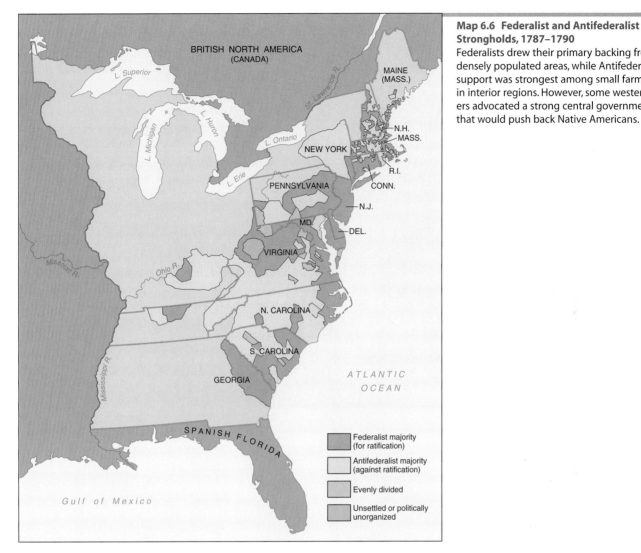

**Map 6.6 Federalist and Antifederalist
Strongholds, 1787–1790**
Federalists drew their primary backing from
densely populated areas, while Antifederalist
support was strongest among small farmers
in interior regions. However, some westerners advocated a strong central government
that would push back Native Americans.

Federalist majority
(for ratification)

Antifederalist majority
(against ratification)

Evenly divided

Unsettled or politically
unorganized

against majority tyranny; and second, to prevent a stubborn minority from blocking well-considered measures
that the majority believed necessary for the national interest. Critics, argued *The Federalist,* had no reason to
fear that the Constitution would allow a single economic
or regional interest to dominate. In the most profound
essay in the series, *Federalist* No. 10, Madison rejected
the Antifederalist argument that establishing a republic
for a nation as large as the United States would unleash a
chaotic contest for power and ultimately leave the majority exploited by a minority. "Extend the sphere," Madison
insisted, "and . . . you make it less probable that a major-

ity of the whole will have a common motive to invade
the rights of other citizens, . . . [or will be able to] act in
unison with each other." The country's very size and diversity would neutralize the attempts of factions to push
unwise laws through Congress.

Madison's analysis was far too optimistic, however.
As the Antifederalists predicted, the Constitution afforded enormous scope for special interests to influence
the government. The great challenge for Madison's generation would be how to maintain a government that
would provide equal benefits to all and at the same time
accord special privileges to none.

Chronology, 1776–1788

1776	British force American troops from New York City.
1777	Congress approves Articles of Confederation. American victory at Saratoga. British troops seize Philadelphia.
1778	France formally recognizes the United States; declares war on Britain. American victory in Battle of Monmouth Court House.
1779	Spain declares war on Britain. George Rogers Clark recaptures Vincennes. John Sullivan leads American raids in Iroquois country.
1780	British seize Charles Town.
1781	Articles of Confederation become law. Battle of Yorktown; British General Cornwallis surrenders.

1783	Peace of Paris.
1784	Spain closes New Orleans to American trade. Economic depression begins in New England. Second Treaty of Fort Stanwix.
1785	Ordinance of 1785. Treaty of Fort McIntosh.
1786	Congress rejects Jay-Gardoqui Treaty. Treaty of Fort Finney. Joseph Brant organizes Indian resistance to U.S. expansion.
1786–1787	Shays's Rebellion in Massachusetts.
1787	Northwest Ordinance. Philadelphia convention frames federal Constitution.
1787–1788	Alexander Hamilton, James Madison, and John Jay, The Federalist.
1788	Federal Constitution ratified.

Conclusion

The entry of North Carolina into the Union in late 1789 and of Rhode Island in May 1790 marked the final triumph of an uncertain nationalism. Among whites, blacks, and Native Americans alike, the American Revolution was a civil war as well as a war of national independence. So long as the war involved only Britain and America, it cost both sides heavily in casualties and finances without producing a conclusive result. Once other nations joined the anti-British cause, making the Revolution an international war, the tide turned. Now fatally overextended, Britain was defeated by American-French forces at Yorktown and obliged to surrender.

Key Terms

loyalists
Joseph Brant
Battle of Saratoga
Battle of Yorktown
Treaty of Paris
Abigail Adams
Prince Hall
Articles of Confederation
Ordinance of 1785
Northwest Ordinance
Alexander McGillivray

James Madison
Virginia Plan
New Jersey Plan
Constitution of the United States
separation of powers
checks and balances
federalism
"three-fifths clause"
The Federalist

Winning the war proved to be only the first step in establishing a new American nation. Forming new governments at the state and national levels was just as challenging, for most white Americans inherited older, Anglo-American suspicions of concentrated political power. As a result, they were deeply divided over how to strike proper balances between power and liberty and between national and state sovereignty. For a decade, conflicts between competing political visions were played out in the protracted debates over several state constitutions, the Articles of Confederation, and, most decisively, the new federal Constitution. The Constitution struck careful balances on these and many other questions and definitely limited democracy; but by locating sovereignty in the people it created a legal and institutional framework within which Americans could struggle to attain democracy. In that way its conception was a fundamental moment in the history of America's enduring vision.

For Further Reference

Colin G. Calloway, *The American Revolution in Indian Country: Crisis and Diversity in Native American Communities* (1995). A powerful set of case studies examining eight Indian communities from Canada to Florida and showing the variety of Native American experiences during and immediately after the Revolution.

Stephen Conway, *The British Isles and the War for American Independence* (2000). A thorough study of the effect on Britain and Ireland of the war in America.

Saul Cornell, *The Other Founders: Anti-Federalism and the Dissenting Tradition in America, 1788–1828* (1999). The definitive study of opponents to ratification of the Constitution and their continuing influence on politics during the early Republic.

Elizabeth A. Fenn, *Pox Americana: The Great Smallpox Epidemic of 1775–82* (2001). A pathbreaking study arguing for the importance of smallpox in shaping the Revolutionary War as well as Native American–European conflicts across the continent.

Linda K. Kerber, *Women of the Republic: Intellect and Ideology in Revolutionary America* (1980). A pathbreaking discussion of women and of ideologies of gender during the Revolutionary and early republican eras.

Robert Middlekauff, *The Glorious Cause: The American Revolution, 1763–1789* (1982). A narrative of military and political developments through the ratification of the Constitution.

Gary B. Nash, *The Unknown American Revolution: The Unruly Birth of Democracy and the Struggle to Create America* (2005). An eye-opening account of the Revolutionary experiences of non-elite Americans, cutting across boundaries of class, race, ethnicity, and gender.

Jack N. Rakove, *Original Meanings: Politics and Ideas in the Making of the Constitution* (1996). A thorough study of the Constitution's framing, rooted in historical context.

Charles Royster, *A Revolutionary People at War: The Continental Army and American Character* (1980). An illuminating analysis of how Revolutionary Americans created and fought in an army.

Gordon S. Wood, *The Radicalism of the American Revolution* (1991). A sweeping interpretation of the Revolution and its long-range effects on American society.

Chapter 7

Judith Sargent Stevens (Murray) by John Singleton Copley, c. 1770
Drawing on a movement developing in Europe, Judith Sargent Murray was the foremost
American advocate of women's rights at the end of the eighteenth century.

Launching the New Republic,
1788–1800

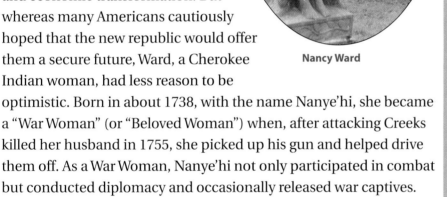

Nancy Ward

For Nancy Ward, as for all Americans, the 1790s was a decade marked by political and economic transformation. But whereas many Americans cautiously hoped that the new republic would offer them a secure future, Ward, a Cherokee Indian woman, had less reason to be optimistic. Born in about 1738, with the name Nanye'hi, she became a "War Woman" (or "Beloved Woman") when, after attacking Creeks killed her husband in 1755, she picked up his gun and helped drive them off. As a War Woman, Nanye'hi not only participated in combat but conducted diplomacy and occasionally released war captives. She changed her name when remarrying a British trader, Bryant Ward, and retained it after he left her and their daughter.

When the American Revolution broke out, the Cherokees were hopelessly divided. Ward and other prominent leaders urged the Cherokees to avoid war and negotiate with the winning side to achieve their goals. They argued that the Cherokees could not afford another bloodbath such as they had suffered when opposing Britain and the colonies during the Seven Years' War. But more militant Cherokees favored allying with Britain and Ohio valley tribes against the colonies as the best means of preserving their land and independence. They noted that negotiations by Ward's uncle and others had recently resulted in losses of about 50,000 square miles of Cherokee land. Unable to reconcile their differences, the two sides parted ways.

During the war, peaceful Cherokees, including Ward, sought an agreement with the newly independent United States. At a treaty conference in 1781, she and other speakers persuaded the Americans not to take additional Cherokee land. But after the war ended, U.S. treaty commissioners pressured the Cherokees in 1783 and 1785 to cede another eight thousand square miles. Thereafter, Ward urged those

Cherokees still resisting the Americans to make peace. Only in 1794, after their Shawnee allies were crushed at the Battle of Fallen Timbers (see below), did the last Cherokees submit to U.S. rule.

Ward advocated peace with the United States, not because she embraced the new republic and its values, but because she recognized that resistance to its military power was futile. Since the time when Ward became a War Woman in the 1750s, the Cherokees had lost nearly half of their population and more than half of their land. Whether pro-British, pro-American, or neutral, most other Native American tribes suffered comparable losses. During the same period, the former British colonies had grown from just under 2 million people to over 5 million, 90 percent of whom lived and worked on the land. Moreover, most white planters and farmers equated the ownership of land with liberty and political rights, and considered Native Americans like Ward an obstacle to those goals. Whether accommodating the expansionist republic would actually improve prospects for Ward and the 125,000 other Native Americans east of the Mississippi was questionable at best.

Besides holding common attitudes toward Native Americans and their lands, whites in 1789 successfully launched a new constitutional republic. But over the next decade, they became increasingly divided over the political and diplomatic course the United States should take. By 1798, voters had formed two parties, each of which accused the other of threatening republican liberty. Only when the election of 1800 had been settled—by the narrowest of margins—could it be said that the United States had managed to avoid dissolution.

Focus Questions

- Which points in Hamilton's economic program were most controversial and why?

- What was the impact of the French Revolution on American politics?

- What principal issues divided Federalists and Republicans in the election of 1800?

- On what basis were some Americans denied full equality by 1800?

Constitutional Government Takes Shape, 1788–1796

Although the Constitution had replaced the Articles of Confederation as the law of the land, the first test of its effectiveness was yet to come. Given the social and political divisions among Americans, and particularly their persistent fears of centralized authority, the successful establishing of a government at the national level was by no means inevitable. Would the American people accept the results of a national election? Would the legislative, executive, and judicial branches of the new government be organized so as to function effectively? Would Congress and the states amend the Constitution with a Bill of Rights, which several states had made a condition when voting to ratify?

Implementing Government

The first step in implementing the new government was the election of a president and Congress. The first elections under the Constitution, in fall 1788, resulted in a Federalist sweep in Congress. Antifederalists won just two of twenty seats in the Senate and five of fifty-nine in the House of Representatives. An electoral college met in each state on February 9, 1789, with each elector voting for two presidential candidates. Although unaware of deliberations in other states, every elector in every state designated George Washington as one of their choices. Having gotten the second most votes, John Adams became the vice president. (The Twelfth Amendment would later supersede this Electoral College procedure for choosing the president and vice president; see Chapter 8).

There was nothing surprising about the unanimity of Washington's victory. His leadership during the Revolutionary War and the Constitutional Convention earned him a reputation as a national hero whose abilities and integrity far surpassed those of his peers. Because of his exalted stature, Washington was able to calm Americans' fears of unlimited executive power.

Traveling slowly over the nation's miserable roads, the men entrusted with launching the federal experiment began assembling in New York, the new national capital, in March 1789. Because so few members were on hand, Congress opened its session a month late. George Washington did not arrive until April 23 and took his oath of office a week later.

The Constitution mentioned the executive departments only in passing, required the president to obtain the Senate's "advice and consent" to his nominees to head these bureaus, and made all executive personnel liable to impeachment. Otherwise, Congress was free to

George Washington's Inaugural Journey Through Trenton, 1789
Washington received a warm welcome in Trenton, site of his first victory during the Revolutionary War.

determine the organization and accountability of what became known as the cabinet. The first cabinet, established by Congress, consisted of five departments, headed by the secretaries of state, treasury, and war and by the attorney general and postmaster general. Vice President John Adams's tie-breaking vote defeated a proposal that would have forbidden the president from dismissing cabinet officers without Senate approval. This outcome reinforced the president's authority to make and carry out policy; it also separated the powers of the executive and legislative branches beyond what the Constitution required, and so made the president a more equal partner with Congress.

The Federal Judiciary and the Bill of Rights

The Constitution authorized Congress to establish federal courts below the level of the Supreme Court, but it offered no guidance in structuring a judicial system. Many citizens feared that the new federal courts would ride roughshod over local customs. Every state had gradually devised its own time-honored blend of judicial procedures. Any attempt to force states to abandon their

legal heritages would have produced strong counterdemands that federal justice be narrowly restricted.

In passing the **Judiciary Act** of 1789, Congress managed to quiet popular apprehensions by establishing in each state a federal district court that operated according to local procedures. As the Constitution stipulated, the Supreme Court exercised final jurisdiction. Congress had struck a compromise between nationalists and states' rights advocates, one that respected state traditions while offering wide access to federal justice.

The Constitution offered some protection of citizens' individual rights. It barred Congress from passing ex post facto laws (criminalizing previously legal actions and then punishing those who had engaged in them) and bills of attainder (proclaiming a person's guilt and stipulating punishment without a trial). Nevertheless, the absence of a comprehensive bill of rights had led several delegates at Philadelphia to refuse to sign the Constitution and had been a condition of several states' ratification of the new frame of government. James Madison, who had been elected to the House of Representatives, played the leading role in drafting the ten amendments that became known as the **Bill of Rights** (see Appendix).

The First Amendment guaranteed the most fundamental freedoms of expression—religion, speech, press, and political activity—against federal interference. The Second Amendment ensured that "a well-regulated militia" would preserve the nation's security by guaranteeing "the right of the people to bear arms." Along with the Third Amendment, it sought to protect citizens from what eighteenth-century Britons and Americans alike considered the most sinister embodiment of tyrannical power: standing armies. The Fourth through Eighth Amendments limited the police powers of the state by guaranteeing individuals' fair treatment in legal and judicial proceedings. The Ninth and Tenth Amendments reserved to the people or to the states powers not allocated to the federal government under the Constitution, but Madison headed off proposals to limit federal power more explicitly. In general, the Bill of Rights imposed no serious check on the Framers' nationalist objectives. The ten amendments were submitted to the states and ratified by December 1791.

Hamilton's Domestic Policies, 1789–1794

President Washington left his secretary of the treasury, **Alexander Hamilton**, in charge of setting the administration's domestic priorities. Hamilton quickly emerged as an imaginative and dynamic statesman with a sweeping program for strengthening the federal government and promoting economic development. While Hamilton succeeded in pushing his program through Congress, the controversies surrounding his program undermined popular support for Federalist policies.

Hamilton and His Objectives

Even more than most Federalists, Hamilton was an extreme nationalist. Born on the British Caribbean island of Nevis in 1755, Hamilton arrived in New York in 1772. Serving on Washington's staff during the Revolutionary War, the brilliant Hamilton gained extraordinary influence over the future president. During the Annapolis and Philadelphia conventions, and while writing many of the Federalist Papers (see Chapter 6), he forcefully advocated creating a strong national government and an economic environment attractive to investment.

In Hamilton's mind, the most immediate danger facing the United States concerned the possibility of war with Britain, Spain, or both. The Republic could finance a major war only by borrowing heavily, but because Congress under the Confederation had not assumed responsibility for the Revolutionary debt, the nation's credit was weakened abroad and at home.

Hamilton also feared that the Union might disintegrate because Americans tended to think first of state and local loyalties and private interests. For him, the Constitution's adoption had been a close victory of national over state authority. Now he worried that the states might reassert power over the new government. If this happened, he doubted whether the nation could prevent ruinous trade discrimination between states, deter foreign aggression, and avoid civil war. Hamilton concluded that the federal government's survival depended not on building popular support but on cultivating politically influential citizens through a straightforward appeal to their financial interests. Private ambitions would then serve the national welfare.

Establishing the Nation's Credit

Finding the nation's Revolutionary war debts in disarray, the First Congress requested that Hamilton's Treasury Department investigate the war debt. Hamilton responded in January 1790 with the first of two **Reports on the Public Credit**, containing recommendations that would at once strengthen the country's credit, enable it to defer paying its debt, and entice wealthy investors to place their capital at its service. The report listed $54 million in U.S. debt, $42 million of which was owed to Americans, and the rest to Europeans. Hamilton estimated that on top of the national debt, the states had debts of $25 million, some of which the United States had promised to reimburse.

Hamilton's first major recommendation was that the federal government support the national debt by "funding" it—that is, raise the $54 million needed to honor the debt by selling an equal sum in new government bonds. Purchasers of these securities would choose from several combinations of federal "stock" and western lands. Those who wished could retain their original bonds and earn 4 percent interest. All of the options would reduce interest payments on the debt from the full 6 percent set by the Confederation Congress. Hamilton knew that creditors would not object to this reduction because their investments would now be more valuable and more secure.

Second, the report proposed that the federal government pay off the $25 million in state debts remaining from the Revolution. This "assumption" of state debts would be funded along with the national debt in the manner described above.

Hamilton exhorted the government to use the money earned by selling federal lands in the West to pay off the

Alexander Hamilton, by John Trumbull, 1792
Hamilton's self-confident pride clearly shines through in this portrait, painted at the height of his influence in the Washington administration.

Hamilton advocated a perpetual debt as a lasting means of uniting the economic fortunes of the nation's creditors to the United States. In an age when financial investments were notoriously risky, the federal government would protect the savings of wealthy bondholders through conservative policies while offering an interest rate competitive with the Bank of England's. The guarantee of future interest payments would unite the interests of the moneyed class with those of the government. Few other investments would entail so little risk.

Hamilton's recommendations provoked immediate controversy. Although no one in Congress doubted that they would greatly enhance the country's fiscal reputation, many objected that those least deserving of reward would gain the most. The original owners of more than three-fifths of the debt certificates issued by the Continental Congress were Revolutionary patriots of modest means who had long before sold their certificates for a fraction of their promised value, usually out of dire financial need. Foreseeing that the government would fund the debt, wealthy speculators had bought the certificates and now stood to reap huge gains at the expense of the original owners, even collecting interest that had accrued before they purchased the certificates. "That the case of those who parted with their securities from necessity is a hard one, cannot be denied," Hamilton admitted. But making exceptions would be even worse.

Hamilton's plan to fund the debt generated widespread resentment because it would reward rich profiteers while ignoring the wartime sacrifices of soldiers and other ordinary citizens. To Hamilton's surprise, Madison—his longtime colleague—emerged as one of the chief opponents of funding. Facing opposition to the plan in his home state of Virginia, Madison tried but failed to obtain compensation for original owners who had sold their certificates. Congress rejected his proposal primarily on the grounds that it would weaken the nation's credit.

Opposition to Hamilton's proposal that the federal government assume states' war debts also ran high. Only Massachusetts, Connecticut, and South Carolina had failed to make effective provisions for satisfying their creditors. Understandably, the issue stirred the fiercest indignation in the South, which except for South Carolina had paid off 83 percent of its debt. Madison and others maintained that to allow residents of the laggard states to escape heavy taxes while others had liquidated theirs at great expense was to reward irresponsibility.

Southern hostility almost defeated assumption. In the end, however, Hamilton managed to save his proposal by enlisting Secretary of State Thomas Jefferson's help. Jefferson and other Virginians expected that moving the

$12 million owed to Europeans as quickly as possible. In a Second Report on the Public Credit, submitted to Congress in December 1790, he argued that the Treasury could easily accumulate the interest owed on the remaining $42 million by collecting customs duties on imports and an excise tax (a tax on domestic products transported within a nation's borders) on whiskey. In addition, Hamilton proposed that money owed to American citizens should be made a permanent debt. That is, he urged that the government not attempt to repay the $42 million principal but instead keep paying interest to bondholders. Under Hamilton's plan, the only burden on taxpayers would be the small annual cost of interest. The government could uphold the national credit at minimal expense, without ever paying off the debt itself.

capital to the Potomac River would make their state a national crossroads and thus help preserve its position as the largest, most influential state. In return for the northern votes necessary to transfer the capital, Hamilton secured enough Virginians' support to win the battle for assumption. The capital would move in the following year to Philadelphia and remain there until a new capital city was built. Despite this concession, the debate over state debts confirmed many white southerners' suspicions that northern financial and commercial interests would benefit from Hamilton's policies at their expense.

Congressional enactment in 1790 of Hamilton's recommendations dramatically reversed the nation's fiscal standing. Thereafter, European investors grew so enthusiastic about U.S. bonds that by 1792 some securities were selling at 10 percent above face value.

Creating a National Bank

Having significantly expanded the stock of capital available for investment, Hamilton intended to direct that money toward projects that would diversify the national economy through a federally chartered bank. Accordingly, in December 1790 he presented Congress with the **Report on a National Bank**.

The proposed bank would raise $10 million through a public stock offering. Private investors could purchase shares by paying for three-quarters of their value in government bonds. In this way, the bank would capture a significant portion of the recently funded debt and make it available for loans; it would also receive a substantial and steady flow of interest payments from the Treasury. Anyone buying shares under these circumstances had little chance of losing money and was positioned to profit handsomely.

Hamilton argued that the Bank of the United States would cost the taxpayers nothing and greatly benefit the nation. It would provide a safe place for the federal government to deposit tax revenues, make inexpensive loans to the government when taxes fell short, and help relieve the scarcity of hard cash by issuing paper notes that would circulate as money. Furthermore, it would possess authority to regulate the business practices of state banks. Above all, the bank would provide much needed credit to expand the economy.

Hamilton's critics denounced his proposal for a national bank, interpreting it as a dangerous scheme that would give a small, elite group special power to influence the government. These critics believed that the Bank of England had undermined the integrity of government in Britain. Shareholders of the new Bank of the United States could just as easily become the tools of unscrupulous

politicians. If significant numbers in Congress owned bank stock, they would likely support the bank even at the cost of the national good. Jefferson openly opposed Hamilton, claiming that the bank would be "a machine for the corruption of the legislature [Congress]." Another Virginian, John Taylor, predicted that the bank would take over the country, which would thereafter, he quipped, be known as the United States of the Bank.

Madison led the opposition to the bank in Congress, arguing that it was unconstitutional. He pointed out that the Philadelphia convention had rejected a proposal giving Congress just such power. Unless Congress closely followed the Constitution, he and other critics argued, the central government might oppress the states and trample individual liberties, just as Parliament had done to the colonies. Strictly limiting federal power seemed the surest way of preventing the United States from degenerating into a corrupt despotism.

Congress approved the bank by only a thin margin. Uncertain of the bank's constitutionality, Washington turned to both Jefferson and Hamilton for advice before signing the measure into law. Like many southern planters whose investments in slaves left them short of capital and often in debt, Jefferson distrusted banking. Moreover, his fear of excessively concentrated economic and political power led him, like Madison, to favor a "strict interpretation" of the Constitution. "To take a single step beyond the boundaries thus specifically drawn around the powers of Congress is to take possession of a boundless field of power no longer susceptible of any definition," warned Jefferson.

Hamilton fought back, urging Washington to sign the bill. Because the Constitution authorized Congress to enact all measures "necessary and proper" (Article I, Section 8), Hamilton contended, it could execute such measures. The only unconstitutional activities of the national government, he concluded, were those expressly prohibited. In the end, the president accepted Hamilton's argument for a "loose interpretation" of the Constitution. In February 1791 the Bank of the United States obtained a charter guaranteeing its existence for twenty years. Washington's acceptance of the principle of loose interpretation was an important victory for those advocating an active, assertive national government. But the split between Jefferson and Hamilton, and Washington's siding with the latter, signaled a deepening political divide within the administration.

Emerging Partisanship

Hamilton's attempt to build political support for Federalist policies by appealing to economic self-interest proved highly successful but also divisive. His arrangements for rescuing the nation's credit provided enormous gains for the speculators, merchants, and other "monied men" of the port cities who by 1790 held most of the Revolutionary debt. As holders of bank stock, these same groups had yet another reason to favor centralized national authority. Assumption of the state debts liberated New England, New Jersey, and South Carolina taxpayers from a crushing burden. Hamilton's efforts to promote industry, commerce, and shipping also struck a responsive chord among entrepreneurs in the Northeast (see below). Federalists dominated politics in New England, New Jersey, and South Carolina, and had considerable strength in Pennsylvania and New York.

Opposition to Hamilton's program was strongest in sections of the country where it offered few benefits. Southern reaction to Hamilton's program, for example, was overwhelmingly negative. Outside of Charleston, South Carolina, few southerners retained Revolutionary certificates in 1790. The Bank of the United States attracted few southern stockholders, and it allocated very little capital for loans there.

Hamilton's plans offered little to the West, where agriculture remained unprofitable without the right to export through New Orleans. In Pennsylvania and New York, too, the uneven effect of Hamiltonian policies generated dissatisfaction. Resentment against a national economic program whose main beneficiaries seemed to be eastern "monied men" and New Englanders who refused to pay their debts gradually united westerners, southerners, and some mid-Atlantic citizens into a political coalition that challenged the Federalists and called for a return to the "true principles" of republicanism.

With Hamilton having presented his measures as "Federalist," Jefferson, Madison, and their supporters began referring to themselves as "republicans." In this way, they implied that Hamilton's schemes to centralize the national government would threaten liberty. Besides appealing to Federalist opponents of Hamilton's policies, Jefferson and Madison reached out to former Antifederalists whose ranks had been fatally weakened after the election of 1788. In 1791, they supported the establishment in Philadelphia of an opposition newspaper, *The National Gazette,* whose editor, Philip Freneau, had been an ardent Antifederalist. For the year preceding the election of 1792, Freneau attacked Hamilton relentlessly, accusing him of trying to create an aristocracy and a monarchy in America. Hamilton responded vigorously to the attacks through his own column in Philadelphia's Federalist newspaper, *The Gazette of the United States.* Using pseudonyms, he also wrote columns in which he attacked Jefferson as an enemy of President Washington and revealed that he had lured Freneau to the capital by hiring him as a translator in the State Department.

Although political partisanship intensified as the election approached, there was no organized political campaigning. For one thing, most voters believed that organized factions or parties were inherently corrupt and were threats to liberty. The Constitution's Framers had neither wanted nor planned for political parties. Indeed, in *Federalist* No. 10, James Madison had argued that the Constitution would prevent the rise of national political factions. For another thing, George Washington, by appearing to be above the partisan disputes, remained supremely popular.

Meeting in 1792, the electoral college was again unanimous in choosing Washington to be president. John Adams was reelected vice president but by a far closer vote than in 1788, receiving 77 votes compared to 50 for George Clinton, the Antifederalist governor of New York.

The Whiskey Rebellion

Hamilton's program not only sparked an angry debate in Congress but also helped ignite a civil insurrection in 1794 called the **Whiskey Rebellion**. Reflecting serious regional and class tensions, this popular uprising was the young republic's first serious crisis.

As part of his financial program, Hamilton had recommended an excise tax on domestically produced whiskey (see above). He insisted that such a tax would not only help in financing the national debt but would improve morals by inducing Americans to drink less liquor. Though Congress enacted the tax, many members doubted that Americans (who on average annually consumed six gallons of hard liquor per adult) would submit tamely to limitations on their drinking. James Jackson of Georgia, for example, warned the administration that his constituents "have long been in the habit of getting drunk and that they will get drunk in defiance of . . . all the excise duties which Congress might be weak or wicked enough to pass."

The validity of such doubts became apparent in September 1791 when a crowd tarred and feathered an excise agent near Pittsburgh. Western Pennsylvanians found the new tax especially burdensome. Unable to ship their crops to world markets through New Orleans, most farmers had grown accustomed to distilling their rye or corn into alcohol, which could be carried across the Appalachians at a fraction of the price charged for bulkier grain. Hamilton's excise equaled 25 percent of whiskey's retail value, enough to wipe out a farmer's profit.

The law also stipulated that trials for evading the tax be conducted in federal courts. Any western Pennsylvanian indicted for noncompliance thus had to travel three hundred miles to Philadelphia. Not only would the accused face a jury of unsympathetic easterners, but he would also have to bear the cost of the long journey and lost earnings while at court, in addition to fines and other court penalties if found guilty. Moreover, Treasury officials rarely enforced the law rigorously outside western Pennsylvania. For all these reasons, western Pennsylvanians complained that the whiskey excise was excessively burdensome.

In a scene reminiscent of pre- and post-Revolutionary popular protests, large-scale resistance erupted in July 1794. One hundred men attacked a U.S. marshal serving sixty delinquent taxpayers with summonses to appear in court at Philadelphia. A crowd of five hundred burned the chief revenue officer's house after a shootout with federal soldiers assigned to protect him. Roving bands torched buildings, assaulted tax collectors, chased government supporters from the region, and flew a flag symbolizing an independent country that they hoped to create from six western counties.

Echoing elites' denunciations of earlier protests, Hamilton condemned the rebellion as simple lawlessness. He pointed out that Congress had reduced the tax rate per gallon in 1792 and had recently voted to allow state judges in western Pennsylvania to hear trials. Showing the same anxiety he had expressed six years earlier during Shays's Rebellion (see Chapter 6), Washington concluded that failure to respond strongly to the uprising would encourage outbreaks in other western areas where distillers were avoiding the tax.

Washington accordingly mustered nearly thirteen thousand militiamen from Pennsylvania and neighboring states to march west under his command. Opposition evaporated once the troops reached the Appalachians, and the president left Hamilton in charge of making arrests. Of about 150 suspects seized, Hamilton sent twenty in irons to Philadelphia. Two men received death sentences, but Washington eventually pardoned them both, noting that one was a "simpleton" and the other "insane."

The Whiskey Rebellion set severe limits on public opposition to federal policies. In the early 1790s, many Americans—including the whiskey rebels—still assumed that it was legitimate to protest unpopular laws using the same tactics with which they had blocked parliamentary measures like the Stamp Act. Indeed, western Pennsylvanians had justified their resistance with exactly such reasoning. By firmly suppressing the first major challenge to national authority, Washington served notice that citizens who resorted to violent or other extralegal means of political action would feel the full force of federal authority. In this way, he gave voice and substance to elites' fears of "mobocracy," now resurfacing in reaction to the French Revolution (see below).

The United States in a Wider World, 1789–1796

By 1793, disagreements over foreign affairs had emerged as the primary source of friction in American public life. The political divisions created by Hamilton's financial program hardened into ideologically oriented factions that argued vehemently over whether the country's foreign policy should favor industrial and overseas mercantile interests or those of farmers, planters, small businesses, and artisans. Moreover, having ratified its Constitution in the year that the French Revolution began (1789), the new government entered the international arena as European tensions were once again exploding. The rapid spread of pro-French revolutionary ideas and organizations alarmed Europe's monarchs and aristocrats. Perceiving a threat to their social orders as well as their territorial interests, most European nations declared war on France by early 1793. For most of the next twenty-two years—until Napoleon's final defeat in 1815—Europe and the Atlantic world remained in a state of war.

Whiskey Rebellion, 1794
Rebels in Washington County, Pennsylvania, tar and feather a federal tax collector.

While most Americans hoped that their nation could avoid this latest European conflict, the fact was that the interests and ambitions of many citizens collided at critical points with those of Britain, France, and Spain. Thus, differences over foreign policy fused with differences over domestic affairs, further intensifying partisanship in American politics.

Spanish Power in Western North America

Stimulated by its winning Louisiana from France in 1762 (see Chapter 5), Spain enjoyed a limited revival of its North American fortunes in the late eighteenth century. In what is now northern Mexico, New Mexico, and Texas, Spain built new presidios, at which it stationed more troops, and coordinated the actions of military and civilian officials. North of the Rio Grande, Spain sought to force nomadic Apaches, Navajos, and Comanches to end their damaging raids on Spanish colonists and their Pueblo Indian allies and to submit to Spanish authority. This effort succeeded, but only up to a point. The Apaches and Navajos moved farther from Spanish settlements, but primarily to avoid Indian enemies rather than Spanish attacks. Ironically, Spanish colonists remained dependent on the Comanches as sources of European goods, which the Comanches obtained through trade networks extending to Louisiana and to American territory east of the Mississippi. By 1800, nomadic Indians had agreed to cease their raids in New Mexico and Texas although parties of warriors sometimes acted on their own. Whether the truce would become a permanent peace depended on whether Spain could strengthen and broaden its imperial position in North America.

Spain's efforts in New Mexico and Texas were part of its larger effort to counter European rivals for North American territory and influence. The first challenge arose in the northern Pacific Ocean, where Spain had enjoyed an unchallenged monopoly for more than two centuries (see Beyond America—Global Interactions: Trade and Empire in the Pacific, to 1800). Russian traders in Siberia made inroads into North America during the 1740s by crossing the Bering Sea and brutally forcing the indigenous Aleut peoples to supply them with sea otter pelts, spreading deadly diseases in the process. As commercial overhunting exterminated the sea otter in the westernmost Aleutians, the traders moved eastward to mainland Alaska, where they would establish a colony in 1799.

Perceiving Russia's move into Alaska as a threat, Spain responded by expanding northward on the Pacific coast

Map 7.1 Spanish Settlements in Alta California, 1784 While the United States was struggling to establish its independence, Spain was establishing a new colony on the Pacific coast.

from Mexico. In 1769, it established the province of **Alta California** (the present American state of California) (see Map 7.1). Efforts to encourage large-scale Mexican immigration to Alta California failed, leaving the colony to be sustained by a chain of religious missions, several presidios, and a few large ranchos (ranches). Seeking support against inland adversaries, coastal Indians welcomed the Spanish at first. But the Franciscan missionaries sought to convert them to Catholicism and "civilize" them by imposing harsh disciplinary measures and putting them to work in vineyards and in other enterprises. Meanwhile, Spanish colonists' spreading of epidemic and venereal diseases among natives precipitated a decline in the Native American population from about seventy-two thousand in 1770 to about eighteen thousand by 1830.

Having gained Louisiana and strengthened its positions in Texas, New Mexico, and California, Spain attempted to make alliances with Indians in the area later known as Arizona. In this way Spain hoped to dominate the colonization of North America between the Pacific and the Mississippi River. But resistance from the Hopi, Quechan (Yuma), and other Native Americans thwarted these hopes. Fortunately for Spain, Arizona had not yet attracted the interest of other imperial powers.

BEYOND AMERICA—GLOBAL INTERACTIONS

Trade and Empire in the Pacific, to 1800

For more than two and a half centuries, no European nation challenged Spain's monopoly on transpacific commerce (see Beyond America—Global Interactions—European Maritime Empires, Chapter 4). Then in the late eighteenth century, peoples from several parts of the world began traveling, fighting, and trading in the Pacific. By 1800, the Pacific Ocean had become an avenue rather than a barrier to global interaction.

After Spain, the next European nation to link Asia and America was Russia. Russian traders in Siberia reached the Pacific in 1639, and in 1689 found a lucrative market for sea otter pelts among the Chinese from whom they obtained silk, porcelain, and tea. Later the Russians expanded into Alaska.

Meanwhile, Britain in 1768 appointed Captain James Cook to explore the entire Pacific Ocean. In two voyages (1768–1771, 1772–1775), Cook explored and mapped the South Pacific and the Antarctic coast. To pre-empt Russia and Britain, Spain in 1769 extended its empire on the Pacific coast to Alta California. In 1774, a Spanish expedition sailed to Nootka Sound at Vancouver Island and proclaimed Spanish sovereignty on the Northwest Coast.

Beginning in 1776, Cook led a third expedition north of the equator. Cook charted the American coast from the Aleutians to northern Califiornia and, ignoring Spain's claim, spent a month at Nootka Sound, trading with the Nootka Indians for provisions and 1,500 sea otter pelts. The expedition then sailed to Hawaii, where

Nootka Indians Greet Spanish Expedition, 1791

Cook was killed in a dispute with Natives. Despite his death, the British concluded that most Hawaiians were willing and able to provide ample supplies of food and hospitality to visitors.

Paralleling Magellan's voyage two and half centuries earlier (see Chapter 2), Cook's crew continued circling the globe after its leader died fighting with Native peoples in the Pacific. At the Portuguese port of Macao, they were pleasantly astonished to discover the large quantities of fine goods that Chinese traders offered for the sea otter pelts from Nootka Bay.

The combination of Chinese demand for sea otter pelts, European demand for Chinese goods at affordable prices, and Hawaii's prime location in the mid-Pacific proved irresistible to merchants from several North Atlantic nations. By the end of the decade, dozens of ships, mostly British and American, regularly traveled first to the Northwest Coast to trade cloth and metal goods to Native Americans for sea otter pelts, then to Hawaii to trade more goods with Native Hawaiians for provisions, and finally to the Chinese port of Canton to unload the pelts in return for Chinese goods. Back in their home countries, they found ready markets among middle-class consumers who craved Chinese tea, spices, porcelain, jewelry, painted fans, silk, and the newest craze, wallpaper.

Seeking to protect Spain's monopoly, a Spanish expedition in 1789 banned foreigners from the Northwest Coast and arrested a British trader at Nootka Sound. But Britain defied the challenge, turning it into an international incident. With its French ally engulfed in revolution, a humiliated Spain in 1795 formally acknowledged British rights to trade at Nootka Sound. Spain soon thereafter abandoned efforts to colonize north of San Francisco Bay.

Commercial and imperial expansion in the North Pacific affected Europeans, Americans, and Chinese, but its deepest impact was on indigenous peoples. European-borne diseases inflicted massive mortality on Inuits, Aleuts, Northwest Coast and California Indians, and Native Hawaiians. Many Natives also perished through the harsh practices of Russian traders and Spanish missionaries in California. British officials armed the chief of the island of Hawaii, enabling him to conquer the entire archipelago and proclaim himself its king. Even where Native peoples were not coerced, their cultures changed as they altered their work patterns to produce skins and incorporated objects of metal, cloth, and other new materials into their daily lives and their religious ceremonies. Some indigenous peoples, particularly Aleuts and Hawaiians, had even more novel experiences, hiring themselves out to Russians, Britons, and Americans as sailors and, occasionally, as hunters and traders in North America. (Defying Chinese imperial restrictions, a few dozen Chinese men also sailed with Europeans before 1800, becoming the first Asian immigrants to North America.) Although most such laborers were men, a few women, particularly Hawaiian, joined their ranks.

By the end of the eighteenth century, the Pacific was an arena for global commerce, imperial competition, and multicultural interaction. Although these developments had a relatively minor impact on the United States at the time, they fueled American dreams of expanding westward to the Pacific.

Questions for Analysis

- Which European rivals first challenged Spain's monopoly on transpacific commerce and by what means?

- How did the China trade affect the nations and peoples who participated in it?

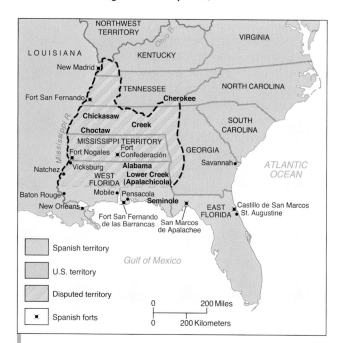

Map 7.2 Disputed Territorial Claims, Spain and the United States, 1783–1796
The two nations' claims to lands east of the Mississippi and north of the thirty-first parallel were a principal point of contention until the Treaty of San Lorenzo was ratified in 1796.

Challenging American Expansion, 1789–1792

Between the Appalachians and the Mississippi River, Spain, Britain, the United States, and numerous Indian nations jockeyed for advantage in a region that all considered central to their interests and that Native Americans regarded as homelands.

Realizing that the United States was in no position to dictate developments immediately in the West, President Washington pursued a course of patient diplomacy that was intended "to preserve the country in peace if I can, and to be prepared for war if I cannot." The prospect of peace improved in 1789 when Spain unexpectedly opened New Orleans to American commerce, although exports remained subject to a 15 percent duty.

Thereafter, Spanish officials continued to bribe well-known political figures in Tennessee and Kentucky, among them a former general on Washington's staff, James Wilkinson. Thomas Scott, a congressman from western Pennsylvania, meanwhile schemed with the British. Between 1791 and 1796, the federal government anxiously admitted Vermont, Kentucky, and Tennessee to the Union, partly in the hope of strengthening their residents' flickering loyalty to the United States.

Washington also tried to weaken Spanish influence by neutralizing Spain's most important ally, the Creek Indians.

The Creeks numbered more than twenty thousand, including perhaps five thousand warriors, and they bore a fierce hostility toward Georgian settlers, whom they called Ecunnaunuxulgee, or "the greedy people who want our lands." In 1790, the Creek leader Alexander McGillivray signed the Treaty of New York with the United States. The treaty permitted American settlers to remain on lands in the Georgia Piedmont fought over since 1786 (see Chapter 6), but in other respects preserved Creek territory against U.S. expansion. Washington insisted that Georgia restore to the Creeks' allies, the Chickasaws and Choctaws, the vast area along the Mississippi River known as the Yazoo Tract, which Georgia claimed and had begun selling off to white land speculators (see Chapter 8).

Washington and his secretary of war, Henry Knox, adopted a harsher policy toward Native Americans who resisted efforts by settlers and other whites to occupy the Ohio valley. In 1790, their first military effort collapsed when a coalition of tribes chased General Josiah Harmar and 1,500 troops from the Maumee River. A second campaign failed in November 1791, when one thousand Shawnee warriors surrounded an encampment of fourteen hundred soldiers led by General Arthur St. Clair. More than six hundred soldiers were killed and several hundred wounded before the survivors could flee for safety.

With Native Americans having twice humiliated U.S. forces in the Northwest Territory, Washington's western policy was in shambles. Matters worsened in 1792 when Spain persuaded the Creeks to renounce the Treaty of New York and resume hostilities. Ultimately, the damage done to U.S. prestige by these setbacks convinced many Americans that the combined strength of Britain, Spain, and the Native Americans could be counterbalanced only by an alliance with France.

France and Factional Politics, 1793

One of the most momentous events in world history, the French Revolution began in 1789. The French were inspired by America's Revolution, and Americans were initially sympathetic as France abolished nobles' privileges, wrote a constitution, bravely repelled invading armies from Austria and Prussia, and proclaimed itself a republic. But the Revolution took a radical turn in 1793 when France declared an international revolutionary war of all peoples against all kings and began a "Reign of Terror," executing not only the king but dissenting revolutionaries.

Americans grew bitterly divided in their attitudes toward the French Revolution and over how the United States should respond to it. While republicans such as Jefferson supported it as an assault on monarchy and tyranny, Federalists like Hamilton denounced France as a "mobocracy" and supported Great Britain in resisting its efforts to sow revolution abroad.

White southern slave owners were among France's fiercest supporters. In 1793, a slave uprising in the Caribbean colony of Saint Domingue became a revolution against French rule. Thousands of terrified French planters fled to the United States, recounting how British invaders had supported the uprising. Inspired by the American and French Revolutions, blacks had fought with determination and inflicted heavy casualties on French colonists. Recalling British courting of their own slaves during the Revolution, southern whites concluded that the British had intentionally sparked the bloodbath and would do the same in the South. Anti-British hysteria even eroded South Carolina's loyalty to Federalist policies.

Many northerners, on the other hand, were more repelled by the blood being shed in revolutionary France. The revolution was an abomination—"an open hell," thundered Massachusetts's Fisher Ames, "still ringing with agonies and blasphemies, still smoking with sufferings and crimes." Middle-class and elite Protestants in New England detested the French for worshiping Reason instead of God. Middle Atlantic Federalists, while perhaps less religious than New Englanders, condemned French leaders as evil radicals who incited the poor against the rich.

Northern and southern reactions to the French Revolution also diverged for economic reasons. In the North, merchants' growing antagonism toward France reflected the facts that virtually all the nation's merchant marine operated from northern ports and that most of the country's foreign trade was with Great Britain. Merchants, shippers, and ordinary sailors in New England, Philadelphia, and New York feared that an alliance with France would provoke British retaliation against this valuable commerce, and they argued that the United States could win valuable concessions by demonstrating friendly intentions toward Britain. Indeed, some influential members of Parliament now seemed to favor liberalizing trade with the United States.

Southerners had no such reasons to favor Britain. Southern spokesmen viewed Americans' reliance on British commerce as a menace to national self-determination and wished to divert most U.S. trade to France. Jefferson and Madison repeatedly demanded that British imports be reduced through the imposition of steep discriminatory duties on cargoes shipped from England and Scotland in British vessels. Federalist opponents warned that Britain, which sold more manufactured goods to the United States than to any other country, would not stand by while a weak French ally pushed it into depression. If Congress adopted a discriminatory tariff, Hamilton predicted in 1792, "there would be, in less than six months, an open war between the United States and Great Britain."

Enthusiasm for a pro-French foreign policy intensified in the southern and western states after France went to war against Spain and Great Britain in 1793. Increasingly, western settlers and speculators hoped for a decisive French victory that, they reasoned, would induce Britain and Spain to cease blocking U.S. expansion. The United States could then insist on free navigation of the Mississippi, force the evacuation of British garrisons, and end both nations' support of Native American resistance.

After declaring war on Britain and Spain, France actively tried to embroil the United States in the conflict. The French dispatched Edmond Genet as minister to the United States with orders to mobilize republican sentiment in support of France, enlist American mercenaries to conquer Spanish territories and attack British shipping, and strengthen the French-American alliance. Much to the French government's dislike, however, President Washington issued a proclamation of American neutrality on April 22, 1793.

Undeterred by Washington's proclamation, **Citizen Genet** (as he was known in French Revolutionary style) found no shortage of southern volunteers for his American Foreign Legion. Making generals of George Rogers Clark of Kentucky and Elisha Clarke of Georgia, Genet directed them to seize Spanish garrisons at New Orleans and St. Augustine. Clark defied Washington's Neutrality Proclamation by advertising for recruits for his mission in Kentucky newspapers, and Clarke began drilling three hundred troops on the Florida border. But the French failed to provide adequate funds for either campaign. Although the American recruits were willing to fight for France, few were willing to fight for free, so both expeditions eventually dispersed.

However, Genet did not need funds to outfit privateers, who financed themselves with captured plunder. By the summer of 1793, almost a thousand Americans were at sea in a dozen ships flying the French flag. These privateers seized more than eighty British vessels and towed them to U.S. ports, where French consuls sold the ships and cargoes at auction.

Diplomacy and War, 1793–1796

Although the Washington administration swiftly closed U.S. harbors to Genet's buccaneers and requested that France recall him, Genet's exploits provoked an Anglo-American crisis. George III's ministers decided that only a massive show of force would deter American support for France. Accordingly, on November 6, 1793, the Privy Council issued secret orders confiscating any foreign ships trading with the

French in the West Indies. The council purposely delayed publishing these instructions until after most American ships carrying winter provisions to the Caribbean left port, so that their captains would not know that they were sailing into a war zone. The Royal Navy then seized more than 250 American vessels.

Meanwhile, the Royal Navy inflicted a second galling indignity—the impressment (forced enlistment) of crewmen from U.S. ships. Thousands of British sailors had previously fled to the U.S. merchant marine, where they hoped to find an easier life than under the tough, poorly paying British system. In late 1793, British naval officers began routinely inspecting American crews for British subjects, whom they then impressed as the king's sailors. Overzealous commanders sometimes broke royal orders by taking U.S. citizens, and in any case the British did not recognize former subjects' right to adopt American citizenship. Impressment scratched a raw nerve in most Americans, who argued that their government's willingness to defend its citizens from such abuse was a critical test of national character.

Meanwhile, Britain, Spain, and many Native Americans continued to challenge the United States for control of territory west of the Appalachians. During a large intertribal council in February 1794, the Shawnees and other Ohio Indians welcomed an inflammatory speech by Canada's royal governor denying U.S. claims north of the Ohio River and urging destruction of every white settlement in the Northwest. Soon British troops were building an eighth garrison on U.S. soil, Fort Miami, near present-day Toledo. Meanwhile, the Spanish encroached on territory claimed by the United States by building Fort San Fernando in 1794 at what is now Memphis, Tennessee.

Hoping to halt the drift toward war, Washington launched three desperate initiatives in 1794. He authorized General Anthony Wayne to negotiate a treaty with the Shawnees and their Ohio valley allies, sent Chief Justice John Jay to Great Britain, and dispatched Thomas Pinckney to Spain.

Having twice defeated federal armies, the Shawnees and their allies scoffed at Washington's peace offer. "Mad Anthony" Wayne then led thirty-five hundred U.S. troops deep into Shawnee homelands, building forts and ruthlessly burning every village within his reach. On August 20, 1794, his troops routed four hundred Shawnees at the Battle of Fallen Timbers just two miles from British Fort Miami. (The British closed the fort's gates, denying entry to their fleeing allies.) Wayne's army then built an imposing stronghold to challenge British authority in the Northwest, appropriately named Fort

Negotiating the Treaty of Greenville, 1795
In this detail of a contemporary painting believed to have been done by a member of General Wayne's staff, Chief Little Turtle of the Miamis speaks to Wayne, who stands with one hand behind his back.

Defiance. Indian morale plummeted, not only because of the American victory and their own losses but also because of Britain's betrayal.

In August 1795, Wayne compelled the Shawnees and eleven other tribes to sign the **Treaty of Greenville**, which opened most of modern-day Ohio and a portion of Indiana to white settlement and ended U.S.-Indian hostilities in the region for sixteen years. But aside from the older leaders who were pressured to sign the treaty, most Shawnees knew that American designs on Indian land in the Northwest had not been satisfied and would soon resurface. Among them was a rising young warrior named Tecumseh (see Chapter 8).

Wayne's victory at Fallen Timbers helped John Jay win a British promise to withdraw troops from American soil by June 1796. Jay also managed to gain access to West Indian markets for small American ships, but only by bargaining away other American complaints as well as U.S. rights to load cargoes of sugar, molasses, and coffee from French colonies during wartime. Aside from fellow Federalists, few Americans interpreted **Jay's Treaty** as preserving peace with honor.

Jay's Treaty left Britain free not only to violate American neutrality but also to undermine profits by restricting U.S. trade with France. Opponents condemned the treaty's failure to end impressment and predicted that Great Britain would thereafter force even more Americans into the Royal Navy. Slave owners were resentful that Jay had not obtained compensation for slaves taken away by the British army during the Revolution. After the Senate ratified the treaty by just one vote in 1795, Jay nervously joked that he could find his way across the country at night by the fires of rallies burning him in effigy.

Despite its unpopularity, Jay's Treaty defused an explosive crisis with Great Britain before war became inevitable and finally ended Britain's post-Revolutionary occupation of U.S. territory. The treaty also helped stimulate an enormous expansion of American trade. Upon its ratification, British governors in the West Indies opened their harbors to U.S. ships. Other British officials permitted Americans to trade with India, even though such trade infringed on the East India Company's monopoly. Within a few years, American exports to the British Empire shot up 300 percent.

On the heels of Jay's controversial treaty came an unqualified diplomatic triumph engineered by Thomas Pinckney. Ratified in 1796, the **Treaty of San Lorenzo** with Spain (also called Pinckney's Treaty) won westerners the right of unrestricted, duty-free access to world markets via the Mississippi River. Spain also promised to recognize the thirty-first parallel as the United States' southern boundary, to dismantle its fortifications on American soil, and to discourage Native American attacks against western settlers.

By 1796, the Washington administration could claim to have successfully extended American authority throughout the trans-Appalachian West, opened the Mississippi for western exports, enabled northeastern shippers to regain British markets, and kept the nation out of a dangerous European war. As the popular outcry over Jay's Treaty demonstrated, however, the nation's foreign policy left Americans much more deeply divided in 1796 than they had been in 1789.

Parties and Politics, 1793–1800

By the time Washington was reelected, the controversies over domestic and foreign policy had led to the formation of two distinct political factions. During the president's second term, these factions became formal political parties, Federalists and Republicans, which advanced their members' interests, ambitions, and ideals. Thereafter, the two parties waged a bitter battle, culminating in the election of 1800.

Ideological Confrontation, 1793–1794

American attitudes about events in France accelerated the polarization of American politics. Linking the French Revolution and the Whiskey Rebellion, Federalists trembled at the thought of guillotines and "mob rule." They were also horrified by the sight of artisans in Philadelphia and New York bandying the French revolutionary slogan "Liberty, Equality, Fraternity" and rallying around pro-French politicians such as Jefferson. Citizen Genet had openly encouraged opposition to the Washington administration, and had found hundreds of Americans willing to fight for France. Federalists worried that all of this was just the tip of a revolutionary iceberg.

By the mid-1790s Federalists' worst fears of democracy seemed to have been confirmed. The people, they believed, were not evil-minded but simply undependable and vulnerable to rabble rousers such as Genet. As Senator George Cabot of Massachusetts put it, "the many do not think at all." For Federalists, democracy meant "government by the passions of the multitude." They argued that, as in colonial times, ordinary voters should not be presented with choices over policy, but should vote simply on the basis of the personal merits of elite candidates. Elected officials, they maintained, should rule in the people's name but be independent of direct popular influence.

Republicans offered a very different perspective on government and politics. They stressed the corruption inherent in a powerful government dominated by a highly visible few, and insisted that liberty would be safe only if power were widely diffused among white male property holders.

It might at first glance seem contradictory for southern slave owners to support a radical ideology like republicanism, with its emphasis on liberty and equality. Although a few southern republicans advocated abolishing slavery gradually, most did not trouble themselves over their ownership of human beings. Although expressed in universal terms, the liberty and equality they advocated were intended for white men only.

Political ambition drove men like Jefferson and Madison to rouse ordinary voters' concerns about civic affairs. The widespread awe in which Washington was held inhibited open criticism of him, his policies, and his fellow Federalists. If, however, the Federalists could be held accountable to the public, they would think twice before enacting measures opposed by the majority; or if they persisted in advocating misguided policies, they would ultimately be removed from office. Such reasoning led Jefferson, a wealthy landowner and large slaveholder, to say, "I am not among those who fear the people; they and not the rich, are our dependence for continued freedom."

Jefferson's frustration at being overruled at every turn by Hamilton and Washington finally prompted his resignation from the cabinet in 1793, and thereafter not even the president could halt the widening political split. Each side portrayed itself as the guardian of republican virtue and attacked the other as an illegitimate "cabal" or "faction."

In 1793–1794, opponents of Federalist policies began organizing Democratic (or Republican) societies. The societies formed primarily in seaboard cities but also in the rural South and West. Their members included planters, small farmers and merchants, artisans, distillers, and sailors; conspicuously absent were the clergy, the poor, nonwhites, and women.

The Republican Party, 1794–1796

Neither Jefferson nor Madison belonged to a Democratic society. However, these private clubs helped publicize their views, and they initiated into political activity numerous voters who would later support a new Republican Party.

In 1794, party development reached a decisive stage after Washington openly identified himself with Federalist policies. Republicans attacked the Federalists' pro-British leanings in many local elections and won a slight majority in the House of Representatives. The election signaled the Republicans' transformation from a coalition of officeholders and local societies to a broad-based party capable of coordinating local political campaigns throughout the nation.

Federalists and Republicans alike used the press to mold public opinion. In the 1790s, American journalism came of age as the number of newspapers rose from 92 to 242, mostly in New England and the mid-Atlantic states. By 1800, newspapers had about 140,000 paid subscribers (roughly one-fifth of the eligible voters), and their secondhand readership probably exceeded 300,000. Newspapers of both camps did not hesitate to engage in fear-mongering and character assassination. Federalists accused Republicans of plotting a reign of terror and of conspiring to turn the nation over to France. Republicans charged Federalists with favoring a hereditary aristocracy and even a royal dynasty that would form when John Adams's daughter married George III. Despite the extreme rhetoric, newspaper warfare stimulated many citizens to become politically active.

Washington grew impatient with the nation's growing polarization into openly hostile parties, and he deeply resented Republican charges that he secretly supported alleged Federalist plots to establish a monarchy. "By God," Jefferson reported him swearing, "he [Washington] would rather be in his grave than in his present situation . . . he had rather be on his farm than to be made emperor of the world." Lonely and surrounded by mediocre advisers after Hamilton returned to private life, Washington decided in the spring of 1796 to retire after two terms. Washington recalled Hamilton to give a sharp political twist to his Farewell Address.

The heart of Washington's message was a vigorous condemnation of political parties. Partisan alignments, he insisted, endangered the Republic's survival, especially if they became entangled in disputes over foreign policy. Washington warned that the country's safety depended on citizens' avoiding "excessive partiality for one nation and excessive dislike of another." Otherwise, "real patriots" would be overwhelmed by demagogues championing foreign causes and paid by foreign governments. Aside from scrupulously fulfilling its existing treaty obligations and maintaining its foreign commerce, the United States must avoid "political connection" with Europe and its wars. If the United States gathered its strength under "an efficient government," it could defy any foreign challenge; but if it became sucked into Europe's quarrels, violence, and corruption, the republican experiment was doomed. Washington and Hamilton had skillfully turned republicanism's fear of corruption against their Republican critics. They had also evoked a vision of an America virtuously isolated from foreign intrigue and power politics, which would remain a potent inspiration for long afterward.

Washington left the presidency in 1797 and died in 1799. Like many later presidents, he went out amid a barrage of partisan criticism.

The Election of 1796

With the **election of 1796** approaching, the Republicans cultivated a large, loyal body of voters. Their efforts to marshal popular support marked the first time since the Revolution that political elites had effectively mobilized non-elites to participate in public affairs. The Republicans' constituency included the Democratic societies, workingmen's clubs, and immigrant-aid associations.

Immigrants became prime targets for Republican recruiters. During the 1790s, the United States absorbed about twenty thousand French refugees from Saint Domingue and more than sixty thousand Irish, many of whom had been exiled for opposing British rule. Although potential immigrant voters were few—comprising less than 2 percent of the electorate—the Irish could make a difference in Pennsylvania and New York, where public opinion was closely divided and a few hundred immigrant voters could tip the balance toward the Republicans.

In 1796, the presidential candidates were the Federalist vice president John Adams and the Republicans' Jefferson. Republicans expected to win as many southern electoral votes and congressional seats as the Federalists counted on in New England, New Jersey, and South Carolina. The crucial "swing" states were Pennsylvania and New York, where the Republicans fought hard to win the large immigrant vote with their pro-French and anti-British rhetoric. In the end, the Republicans took Pennsylvania but not New York, so that Jefferson lost the presidency by just three electoral votes. As the second-highest vote-getter in the electoral college, he became vice president. The Federalists narrowly regained control of the House and maintained their firm grip on the Senate.

Adams's intellect and devotion to principle have rarely been equaled among American presidents. But the new president was more comfortable with ideas than with people, more theoretical than practical. He inspired trust and often admiration but could not command personal loyalty or inspire the public. Adams's reserved and often stubborn personality likewise left him ill suited to govern, and he ultimately proved unable to unify the country.

The French Crisis, 1798–1799

Even before the election, the French had recognized that Jay's Treaty was a Federalist-sponsored attempt to assist

John Adams
Adams presided over—and contributed to—the division of American voters into two political parties during the late 1790s.

Britain in its war against France. On learning of Jefferson's defeat, France began seizing American ships carrying goods to British ports, and within a year had plundered more than three hundred vessels. The French rubbed in their contempt for the United States by directing that every American captured on a British naval ship (even those involuntarily impressed) should be hanged.

Hoping to avoid war, Adams sent a peace commission to Paris. But the French foreign minister, Charles de Talleyrand, refused to meet the delegation, instead promising through three unnamed agents ("X, Y, and Z") that talks could begin after he received $250,000 and France obtained a loan of $12 million. This barefaced demand for a bribe became known as the XYZ Affair. Americans reacted to it with outrage. "Millions for defense, not one cent for tribute" became the nation's battle cry as the 1798 congressional elections began.

The XYZ Affair discredited the Republicans' foreign policy views, but the party's leaders compounded the damage by refusing to condemn French aggression and opposing Adams's call for military preparations. The

Republicans tried to excuse French behavior, whereas the Federalists rode a wave of militant patriotism. In the 1798 elections, Jefferson's supporters were routed almost everywhere, even in the South.

Congress responded to the XYZ Affair by arming fifty-four ships to protect American commerce. During an undeclared Franco-American naval conflict in the Caribbean known as the **Quasi-War** (1798–1800), U.S. forces seized ninety-three French privateers while losing just one vessel. The British navy meanwhile extended the protection of its convoys to America's merchant marine. By early 1799, the French remained a nuisance but were no longer a serious threat at sea.

Meanwhile, the Federalist-dominated Congress tripled the size of the regular army to ten thousand men in 1798, with an automatic expansion to fifty thousand in case of war. Yet the risk of a land war with France was minimal. In reality, the Federalists wanted a military force ready in the event of a civil war, for the crisis had produced near-hysteria about conspiracies being hatched by French and Irish revolutionaries flooding into the United States.

The Alien and Sedition Acts, 1798

The most heated controversies of the late 1790s arose from the Federalists' insistence that the threat of war with France required strict laws to protect national security. In 1798, the Federalist-dominated Congress accordingly passed four measures known collectively as the **Alien and Sedition Acts**. Adams neither requested nor particularly wanted these laws, but he deferred to Federalist congressional leaders and signed them.

The least controversial of the laws, the Alien Enemies Act, outlined procedures for determining whether citizens of a hostile country posed a threat to the United States as spies or saboteurs. If so, they were to be deported or jailed. The law established fundamental principles for protecting national security and respecting the rights of enemy citizens. It was to operate only if Congress declared war and thus was not used until the War of 1812 (see Chapter 8).

Second, the Alien Friends Act, a temporary statute, authorized the president to expel any foreign residents whose activities he considered dangerous. The law did not require proof of guilt, on the assumption that spies would hide or destroy evidence of their crime. Republicans maintained that the law's real purpose was to deport immigrants critical of Federalist policies.

Republicans also denounced the third law, the Naturalization Act. This measure increased the residency requirement for U.S. citizenship from five to fourteen years (the last five continuously in one state), with the purpose of reducing Irish voting.

Finally came the Sedition Act, the only one of these measures enforceable against U.S. citizens. Its alleged purpose was to distinguish between free speech and attempts at encouraging others to violate federal laws or to overthrow the government. But the act defined criminal activity so broadly that it blurred any real distinction between sedition and legitimate political discussion. For example, it prohibited an individual or group from opposing "any measure or measures of the United States"—wording that could be interpreted to ban any criticism of the party in power. Another clause made it illegal to speak, write, or print any statement about the president that would bring him "into contempt or disrepute." Under such restrictions, for example, a newspaper editor might face imprisonment for criticizing an action by Adams or his cabinet members. The Federalist *Gazette of the United States* expressed the twisted logic of the Sedition Act perfectly: "It is patriotism to write in favor of our government—it is sedition to write against it." However one looked at it, the Sedition Act interfered with free speech. Ingeniously, the Federalists wrote the law to expire in 1801 (so that it could not be turned against them if they lost the next election) and to leave them free meanwhile to heap abuse on Vice President Jefferson (who did not participate in the making of government policy).

The principal target of Federalist repression was the opposition press. Four of the five largest Republican newspapers were charged with sedition just as the election campaign of 1800 was getting under way. The attorney general used the Alien Friends Act to threaten Irish journalist John Daly Burk with expulsion (Burk went underground instead). Scottish editor Thomas Callender was being deported when he suddenly qualified for citizenship. Unable to expel Callender, the government tried him for sedition before an all-Federalist jury, which sent him to prison for criticizing the president.

Federalist leaders never intended to fill the jails with Republican martyrs. Rather, they hoped to use a small number of highly visible prosecutions to silence Republican journalists and candidates during the election of 1800. The attorney general charged seventeen persons with sedition and won ten convictions. Among the victims was Republican congressman Matthew Lyon of Vermont ("Ragged Matt, the democrat," to the Federalists), who spent four months in prison for publishing a blast against Adams.

Vocal criticism of Federalist repression erupted during the summer of 1798 in Virginia and Kentucky. Militia commanders in these states mustered their regiments not to drill but to hear speeches demanding that the federal government respect the Bill of Rights. Entire units then signed petitions denouncing the Alien and Sedition Acts.

He in a trice struck Lyon thrice Upon his head, enrag'd, sir.

Who seiz'd the tongs to ease his wrongs, And Griswold thus engag'd, sir.

Congress Hall, in Philad.ᵃ Feb. 15. 1798. S. E. Cor. 6.ᵗʰ & Chesnut S.

Violence in the House of Representatives, 1798
Partisan bitterness turned violent when Republican Matthew Lyon (with tongs) and Federalist Roger Griswold fought on the House floor.

The symbolic implications of these protests were sobering. Young men stepped forward to sign petitions on drumheads with a pen in one hand and a gun in the other, as older officers who had fought in the Continental Army looked on approvingly. It was not hard to imagine Kentucky rifles being substituted for quill pens as the men who had joined one revolution took up arms again.

Ten years earlier, opponents of the Constitution had warned that giving the national government extensive powers would eventually endanger freedom. By 1798, their prediction seemed to have come true. Shocked Republicans realized that because the Federalists controlled all three branches of the government, neither the Bill of Rights nor the system of checks and balances protected individual liberties. In this context, they advanced the doctrine of states' rights as a means of preventing the national government from violating basic freedoms.

Recognizing that opponents of federal power would never prevail in the Supreme Court, which was still dominated by Federalists, Madison and Jefferson anonymously wrote manifestos on states' rights known as the **Virginia and Kentucky Resolutions**, adopted respectively by the legislatures of those states in 1798. Madison's Virginia Resolutions declared that state legislatures had never surrendered their right to judge the constitutionality of federal actions and that they retained an authority

called *interposition,* which enabled them to protect the liberties of their citizens. Jefferson's resolution for Kentucky went further by declaring that ultimate sovereignty rested with the states, which empowered them to "nullify" federal laws to which they objected. Although Kentucky's legislature deleted the term "nullify" before approving the resolution in 1799, the intention of both resolutions was to invalidate any federal law in a state that had deemed the law unconstitutional. Although the resolutions were intended as nonviolent protests, they challenged the jurisdiction of federal courts and could have enabled state militias to march into a federal courtroom to halt proceedings at bayonet point.

Although no other state endorsed these resolutions (ten expressed disapproval), their passage demonstrated the great potential for disunion in the late 1790s. So did a minor insurrection called the Fries Rebellion, which broke out in 1799 when crowds of Pennsylvania German farmers released prisoners jailed for refusing to pay taxes needed to fund the national army's expansion. But the disturbance collapsed when federal troops intervened.

The nation's leaders increasingly acted as if a crisis were imminent. Vice President Jefferson hinted that events might push the southern states into secession from the Union, while President Adams hid guns in his home. After passing through Richmond and learning that state officials were purchasing thousands of muskets for the militia, an alarmed Supreme Court justice wrote in January 1799 that "the General Assembly of Virginia are pursuing steps which will lead directly to civil war." A tense atmosphere hung over the Republic as the election of 1800 neared.

The Election of 1800

In the election campaign, the two parties once again rallied around the Federalist Adams and the Republican Jefferson. The leadership of moderates in both parties helped to ensure that the nation survived the **election of 1800** without a civil war. Thus Jefferson and Madison discouraged radical activity that might provoke intervention by the national army, while Adams rejected demands by extreme "High Federalists" that he ensure victory by deliberately sparking an insurrection or asking Congress to declare war on France.

"Nothing but an open war can save us," argued one High Federalist cabinet officer. But when Adams suddenly learned in 1799 that France wanted peace, he proposed a special diplomatic mission. "Surprise, indignation, grief & disgust followed each other in quick succession," said a Federalist senator on hearing the news. Adams obtained Senate approval for his envoys only by threatening to resign and so make Jefferson president. Outraged High Federalists tried unsuccessfully to dump Adams, but their ill-considered maneuver rallied most New Englanders around the stubborn, upright president.

Adams's negotiations with France did not achieve a settlement until 1801, but the expectation that normal—perhaps even friendly—relations with France would resume prevented the Federalists from exploiting charges of Republican sympathy for the enemy. Without the immediate threat of war, moreover, voters grew resentful that in merely two years, taxes had soared 33 percent to support an army that had done nothing except chase terrified Pennsylvania farmers. As the danger of war receded, voters gave the Federalists less credit for standing up to France and more blame for adding $10 million to the national debt.

While High Federalists spitefully withheld the backing that Adams needed to win, Republicans redoubled their efforts to elect Jefferson. They were especially successful in mobilizing voters in Philadelphia and New York, where artisans, farmers, and some entrepreneurs were ready to abandon the Federalists, whom they saw as defenders of privilege and wealth. As a result of Republican efforts, popular interest in politics rose sharply. Voter turnout in 1800 leaped to more than double that of 1788, rising from about 15 percent to almost 40 percent;

in hotly contested Pennsylvania and New York, more than half the eligible voters participated.

Adams lost the presidency by just 8 electoral votes out of 138. He would have won if his party had not lost control of New York's state senate, which chose the electors, after a narrow defeat in New York City. Jefferson and his running mate, New York's Aaron Burr, also carried South Carolina after their backers made lavish promises of political favors to that state's legislators.

Although Adams lost, Jefferson's election was not assured. Because all 73 Republican electors voted for both of their party's nominees, the electoral college deadlocked in a Jefferson-Burr tie. Even more seriously than in 1796, the Constitution's failure to anticipate organized, rival parties affected the outcome of the electoral college's vote. The choice of president devolved upon the House of Representatives, where thirty-five ballots over six days produced no result. Aware that Republican voters and electors wanted Jefferson to be president, the wily Burr cast about for Federalist support. But after Hamilton—Burr's bitter rival in New York politics—declared his preference for Jefferson as "by far not so dangerous a man," a Federalist representative abandoned Burr and gave Jefferson the presidency by history's narrowest margin.

Economic and Social Change

During the nation's first twelve years under the Constitution, the spread of economic production for markets, even by households, transformed the lives of many Americans. For some people the changes were for the better and for others for the worse, but for most the ultimate outcome remained uncertain in 1800. At the same time, many Americans were rethinking questions of gender and race in American society.

The fierce political struggles that took place during the same period primarily involved white males, in other words those who had the right to vote and the guarantee of at least minimal civil rights. For those who were not both white and male, the struggle was to achieve those minimal rights or at the very least to survive.

Producing for Markets

For centuries the backbone of European societies and their colonial offshoots had been economies in which most production took place in household settings. At the core of each household was a patriarchal family—the male head, his wife, and their unmarried children. Beyond these family members, most households included other people. Some outsiders were relatives, but most were either boarders or workers—apprentices and journeymen in artisan shops, servants and slaves in well-off urban households, and slaves, "hired hands," and tenant farmers in rural settings. (Even slaves living in separate "quarters" on large plantations labored in an enterprise centered on their owners' households.) Unlike in our modern world, before the nineteenth century nearly everyone worked at what was temporarily or permanently "home." The notion of "going to work" would have struck them as odd.

Although households varied in size and economic orientation, in the late eighteenth century most were on small farms and consisted of only an owner and his family. By 1800, such farm families typically included seven children whose labor contributed to production. While husbands and older sons worked in fields away from the house, wives, daughters, and young sons maintained the barns and gardens near the house. Wives, of course, bore and reared the children as well. As in the colonial period, most farm families produced food and other products largely for their own consumption, adding small surpluses for bartering with neighbors or local merchants.

In the aftermath of the American Revolution, households in the most heavily populated regions of the Northeast began to change. Relatively prosperous farm families, particularly in the mid-Atlantic states, increasingly directed their surplus production to meet the growing demands of urban customers for produce, meat, and dairy products. These families often turned to agricultural experts, whose advice their parents and grandparents had usually, and proudly, spurned. Many

farm men introduced clover into the pastures they tended, following the suggestion of one author who maintained that clover "flushes [a cow] to milk." Men also recognized that while milk production was lower during winter, when most cattle remained outdoors, protecting their herds then would improve milk production year-round. Accordingly, they expanded acreage devoted to hay and built barns to shelter the cows in cold weather and to store the hay. A federal census in 1798 revealed that about half the farms in eastern Pennsylvania had barns, usually of logs or framed but occasionally of stone. After the turn of the century, men would also begin to shop for particular breeds of cattle that produced more milk for more months of each year.

Farmwomen of the period—often referred to as "dairymaids"—likewise sought to improve cows' productivity. The milking process itself changed little. Mid-Atlantic women milked an average of six animals twice a day, with each "milch cow" producing about two gallons per day during the summer. Most of women's efforts to increase production had to do with making butter, the dairy product in greatest demand among urban consumers.

Poorer farm families, especially in New England, found less lucrative ways to produce for commercial markets. Small plots of land on New England's thin, rocky soil no longer supported large families, leading young people to look beyond their immediate locales for means of support. While many young men and young couples moved west, unmarried daughters more frequently remained at

Churning Butter
During the late eighteenth century, farmwomen shifted from the plunger churn (background) to the more efficient barrel churn in order to increase their production of butter.

home, where they could help satisfy a growing demand for manufactured cloth. Before the Revolution, affluent colonists had imported cloth as well as finished clothing, but the boycott of British goods led many women to either spin their own or purchase it from other women (see Chapter 5). After the Revolution, enterprising merchants began catering to urban consumers as well as southern slave owners seeking to clothe their slaves as cheaply as possible. Making regular circuits through rural areas, the merchants supplied cloth to mothers and daughters in farm households. A few weeks later they would return and pay the women in cash for their handiwork.

A comparable transition began in some artisans' households. The shoemakers of Lynn, Massachusetts, had expanded their production during the Revolution when filling orders from the Continental Army. After the war, some more successful artisans began supplying leather to other shoemakers, paying them for the finished product. By 1800, these merchants were taking leather to farm families beyond Lynn in order to fill an annual demand that had risen from 189,000 pairs in 1789 to 400,000.

Numerous other enterprises likewise emerged, employing men as well as women to satisfy demands that self-contained households could never have met on their own. For example, a traveler passing through Middleborough, Massachusetts, observed,

In the winter season, the inhabitants . . . are principally employed in making nails, of which they send large quantities to market. This business is a profitable addition to their husbandry; and fills up a part of the year, in which, otherwise, many of them would find little employment.

Behind the new industries was an ambitious, aggressive class of businessmen, most of whom had begun as merchants and now invested their profits in factories, ships, government bonds, and banks. Such entrepreneurs stimulated a flurry of innovative business ventures that pointed toward the future. The country's first private banks were founded in the 1780s in Philadelphia, Boston, and New York. Philadelphia merchants created the Pennsylvania Society for the Encouragement of Manufactures and the Useful Arts in 1787. This organization promoted the immigration of English artisans familiar with the latest industrial technology, including Samuel Slater, a pioneer of American industrialization who helped establish a cotton-spinning mill at Pawtucket, Rhode Island, in 1790 (see Chapter 9). In 1791 investors from New York and Philadelphia, with Hamilton's enthusiastic endorsement, started the Society for the Encouragement of Useful Manufactures, which attempted to demonstrate the potential of large-scale industrial enterprises by building a factory town at Paterson, New Jersey. That same year, New York

merchants and insurance underwriters organized America's first formal association for trading government bonds, out of which the New York Stock Exchange evolved.

For many Americans, the choice between manufacturing and farming was moral as well as economic. Hamilton's aggressive support of entrepreneurship and industrialization was consistent with his larger vision for America and contradicted that of Jefferson. As outlined in his Report on the Subject of Manufactures (1791), Hamilton admired efficiently run factories in which a few managers supervised large numbers of workers. Manufacturing would provide employment opportunities, promote emigration, and expand the applications of technology. It would also offer "greater scope for the talents and dispositions [of] men," afford "a more ample and various field for enterprise," and create "a more certain and steady demand for the surplus produce of the soil." Jefferson, on the other hand, idealized white, landowning family farmers as bulwarks of republican liberty and virtue. "Those who labour in the earth are the chosen people," he wrote in 1784, whereas the dependency of European factory workers "begets subservience and venality, suffocates the germ of virtue, and prepares fit tools for the designs of ambition." For Hamilton, capital, technology, and managerial discipline were the surest roads to national order and wealth. Jefferson, putting more trust in white male citizens, envisioned land as the key to prosperity and liberty for all. The argument over the relative merits of these two ideals would remain a constant in American politics and culture for at least another two centuries.

White Women in the Republic

Alongside the growing importance of women's economic roles, whites' discussions of republicanism raised questions of women's rights and equality. The Revolution and the adoption of republican constitutions had not significantly affected the legal position of white women, although some states eased women's difficulties in obtaining divorces. Nor did women gain new political rights, except in New Jersey. That state's 1776 constitution, by not specifying gender and race, left a loophole that enabled white female and black property holders to vote, which many began to do. During the 1790s, New Jersey explicitly permitted otherwise qualified women to vote by adopting laws that stipulated "he or she" when referring to voters. In a hotly contested state election in 1797, seventy-five women voters nearly gave the victory to a Federalist candidate. His victorious Republican opponent, John Condict, would get his revenge in 1807 by successfully advocating a bill to disenfranchise women (along with free blacks).

In other areas of American life, social change and republican ideology together fostered more formidable challenges to traditional attitudes toward women's rights. American republicans increasingly recognized the right of a woman to choose her husband—a striking departure from the continued practice among some elites whereby fathers approved or even arranged marriages. Thus in 1790, on the occasion of his daughter Martha's marriage, Jefferson wrote to a friend that, following "the usage of my country, I scrupulously suppressed my wishes, [so] that my daughter might indulge her sentiments freely."

Outside elite circles, such independence was even more apparent. Especially in the Northeast, daughters increasingly got pregnant by preferred partners, thus forcing their fathers to consent to their marrying in order to avoid a public scandal. In Hallowell, Maine, in May 1792, for example, Mary Brown's father objected to her marrying John Chamberlain. In December, he finally consented and the couple wed—just two days before Mary Chamberlain gave birth. By becoming pregnant, northeastern women secured economic support in a region where an exodus of young, unmarried men was leaving a growing number of women single.

White women also had fewer children overall than had their mothers and grandmothers. In Sturbridge, Massachusetts, women in the mid-eighteenth century averaged nearly nine children per marriage, compared with six in the first decade of the nineteenth century. Whereas 40 percent of Quaker women had nine or more children before 1770, only 14 percent bore that many thereafter. Such statistics testify to declining farm sizes and urbanization, both of which were incentives for having fewer children. But they also indicate that some women were finding relief from the near-constant state of pregnancy and nursing that had consumed their grandmothers.

As white women's roles expanded, so too did republican notions of male-female relations. "I object to the word 'obey' in the marriage-service," wrote a female author calling herself Matrimonial Republican, "because it is a general word, without limitations or definition. . . . The obedience between man and wife is, or ought to be mutual." Lack of mutuality was one reason for a rising number of divorce petitions from women, from fewer than fourteen per year in Connecticut before the Revolution, to forty-five in 1795.

A few women also challenged the sexual double standard that allowed men to indulge in extramarital affairs while their female partners, single or married, were condemned. Writing in 1784, an author calling herself "Daphne" pointed out how a woman whose illicit affair was exposed was "forever deprive[d] . . . of all that renders life valuable," while "the base [male] betrayer is suffered to triumph in the success of his unmanly arts, and to pass unpunished even by a frown."

FRONTISPIECE.

Advocating Women's Rights, 1792
In this illustration from an American magazine for women, the "Genius of the Ladies Magazine" and the "Genius of Emulation" present Liberty with a petition based on British feminist Mary Wollstonecraft's *Vindication of the Rights of Woman.*

Daphne called on her "sister Americans" to "stand by and support the dignity of our own sex" by publicly condemning seducers rather than their victims.

Gradually, the subordination of women, which once was taken for granted among most whites, became the subject of debate. In "On the Equality of the Sexes" (1790), essayist and poet Judith Sargent Murray contended that the genders had equal intellectual ability and deserved equal education. "We can only reason from what we know," she wrote, "and if an opportunity of acquiring knowledge hath been denied us, the inferiority of our sex cannot fairly be deduced from there." Murray hoped that "sensible and informed" women would improve their minds rather than rush into marriage (as she had at eighteen), enabling them to instill republican ideals in their children.

Like many of her contemporaries, Murray supported the idea of "**republican motherhood.**" Advocates of republican motherhood emphasized the importance of educating white women in the values of liberty and independence in order to strengthen virtue in the new nation. It was the republican duty of mothers to inculcate these values in their sons—the nation's future leaders—as well as their daughters. John Adams reminded his daughter that she was part of "a young generation, coming up in America . . . [and] will be responsible for a great share of the duty and opportunity of educating a rising family, from whom much will be expected." Before the 1780s, only a few women had acquired an advanced education through private tutors. Thereafter, urban elites broadened such opportunities by founding numerous private schools, or academies, for girls. Massachusetts also established an important precedent in 1789 when it forbade any town to exclude girls from its elementary schools.

By itself, the expansion of educational opportunities for white women would have a limited effect. "I acknowledge we have an equal share of curiosity with the other sex," wrote Mercy Otis Warren to Abigail Adams, but men "have the opportunities of gratifying their inquisitive humour to the utmost, in the great school of the world, while we are confined to the narrow circle of domesticity." Although the great struggle for female political equality would not begin until the next century, republican assertions that women were intellectually and morally men's peers and played a vital public role provoked additional calls for political equality beyond those voiced by Abigail Adams and a few other women during the Revolution (see Chapter 6). In 1793, Priscilla Mason, a young woman graduating from a female academy, blamed "*Man, despotic man*" for shutting women out of the church, the courts, and government. In her salutatory oration, she urged that a women's senate be established by Congress to evoke "all that is human—all that is *divine* in the soul of woman." Warren and Mason had pointed out a fundamental limitation to republican egalitarianism in the America of the 1790s: while women could be virtuous wives and mothers, the world outside their homes still offered them few opportunities to apply their education.

Land and Culture: Native Americans

Perhaps the people in the most tenuous position in American society were Native Americans. By 1800, Indians east of the Mississippi had suffered severe losses of population, territory (see Map 7.3), and political and cultural self-determination. Thousands of deaths had resulted from battle, famine, and disease during the successive wars since the 1750s and from poverty, losses of land, and discrimination during peacetime as well. From 1775 to 1800, the Cherokee population declined from sixteen thousand to ten thousand, and Iroquois numbers fell from about nine thousand to four thousand. During the same period, Native Americans lost more land than the area inhabited by whites in 1775. Settlers, liquor dealers, and criminals trespassed on Indian lands, often stealing or inflicting violence on Native Americans and provoking them to retaliate. Indians who sold land or worked for whites were often paid in the unfamiliar medium of cash and then found little to spend it on in their isolated communities except alcohol.

While employing military force against Native Americans who resisted U.S. authority (see above), Washington and Secretary of War Knox recognized that actions by American citizens often contributed to Indians' resentment. Accordingly, they pursued a policy similar to Britain's under the Proclamation of 1763 (see Chapter 5) in which the government regulated relations between Indians and non-Indians. Congress enacted the new policy gradually in a series of **Indian Trade and Intercourse Acts** (1790–1796). (Thereafter, Congress periodically renewed and amended the legislation until making it permanent in 1834.) To halt fraudulent land cessions, the acts prohibited transfers of tribal lands to outsiders except as authorized in formal treaties or by Congress. Other provisions regulated the conduct of non-Indians on lands still under tribal control. To regulate intercultural trade and reduce abuses, the acts required that traders be licensed by the federal government. (But until 1802, the law did not prohibit the sale of liquor on Indian lands.) The law also defined murder and other abuses committed by non-Indians as federal offenses. Finally, the legislation authorized the federal government to establish programs that would "promote civilization" among Native Americans as a replacement for traditional culture. By "civilization," Knox and his supporters meant Anglo-American culture, particularly private property and a strictly agricultural way of life, with men replacing women in the fields. By abandoning communal landownership and seasonal migrations for hunting, gathering, and fishing, they argued, Indians would no longer need most of the land they were trying to protect, thereby making it available for whites.

Before 1800, the "civilization" program was offered to relatively few Native Americans. Although some Cherokees who were familiar with Anglo-American ways welcomed it, Nancy Ward was not one of them. She eventually discovered that "civilization" included male property ownership and political leadership and that Indian women were being urged to leave farming to men while taking up strictly domestic tasks like their white contemporaries. When she and twelve other War Women in 1817 protested a treaty that would give most Cherokee

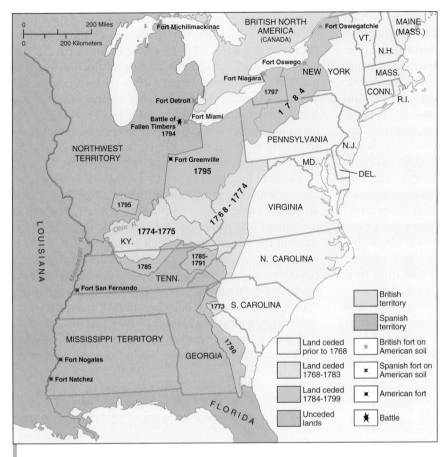

Map 7.3 Indian Land Cessions, 1768–1799
During the last third of the eighteenth century, Native Americans were forced to give up extensive homelands throughout the eastern backcountry and farther west in the Ohio and Tennessee River valleys.

land in Georgia to the United States, they were ignored—not by the U.S. government but by their own male leaders. Women in general, and War Women in particular, no longer wielded power in Cherokee society.

Among the most devastated Native Americans in the 1790s were the Seneca Iroquois. A majority of surviving Iroquois had moved to Canada after the Revolution, and those who stayed behind were pressured to sell, or were simply defrauded of, most of their land, leaving them isolated from one another on tiny reservations. Unable to practice any of their traditional occupations, Seneca men frequently resorted to heavy drinking, often becoming violent. All too typical were the tragedies that beset Mary Jemison, born a half-century earlier to white settlers but a Seneca since her wartime capture and adoption at age ten. Jemison saw one of her sons murder his two brothers in alcohol-related episodes before meeting a similar fate himself.

In 1799, a Seneca prophet, Handsome Lake, emerged and led his people in a remarkable spiritual revival. Severely ill, alcoholic, and

Creek House, 1791
By the end of the eighteenth century, most eastern Native Americans combined traditional and European ideas and materials in their everyday lives.

near death, he experienced a series of visions, which Iroquois and many other Native American societies interpreted as prophetic messages. As in the visions of the Iroquois prophet Hiawatha in the fourteenth century (see Chapter 1), spiritual guides appeared to Handsome Lake and instructed him first in his own recovery and then in that of his people. Invoking Iroquois religious traditions, Handsome Lake preached against alcoholism and sought to revive unity and self-confidence among the Seneca. But whereas many Indian visionary prophets rejected all white ways, Handsome Lake welcomed civilization, as introduced by Quaker missionaries (who did not attempt to convert Native Americans) supported by federal aid. In particular, he urged a radical shift in gender roles, with Seneca men displacing women not only in farming but also as heads of their families. At the same time, he insisted that men treat their wives respectfully and without violence.

The most traditional Senecas rejected the notion that Native men should work like white farmers. But many Seneca men welcomed the change. It was women who resisted most, because like Cherokee women they stood to lose their collective ownership of farmland, their control of the food supply, and their considerable political influence. Other Senecas accused women who rejected Handsome Lake's teachings of witchcraft, and even killed a few of them. The violence soon ceased and Handsome Lake's followers formed their own church, complete with traditional Iroquois religious ceremonies. The Seneca case would prove to be unique; after 1800, missionaries would usually introduce civilization to Native Americans and expect them to convert to Christianity as well as adopt the new ways of living.

African-American Struggles

The Republic's first years marked the high tide of African-Americans' Revolutionary era success in bettering their lot. Blacks and even many whites recognized that the ideals of liberty and equality were inconsistent with slavery. By 1790, 8 percent of all African-Americans had been freed from slavery, many having purchased their liberty or earned it through wartime service. Ten years later 11 percent

were free (see Figure 7.1). Various state reforms meanwhile attempted to improve the conditions of those who remained in slavery. In 1791, for example, the North Carolina legislature declared that the former "distinction of criminality between the murder of a white person and one who is equally an human creature, but merely of a different complexion, is disgraceful to humanity" and authorized the execution of whites who murdered slaves. Although for economic as much as for humanitarian reasons, by 1794 most states had outlawed the Atlantic slave trade.

Hesitant measures to ensure free blacks' legal equality also appeared in the 1780s and early 1790s. Most states dropped restrictions on African-Americans' freedom of movement and protected their property. By 1796, all but three of the sixteen states either permitted free blacks to vote or did not specifically exclude them. But by then a countertrend was reversing many of the Revolutionary-era advances. Before the 1790s ended, abolitionist sentiment ebbed, slavery became more entrenched, and whites resisted accepting even free blacks as fellow citizens.

Federal law led the way in restricting the rights of blacks and other nonwhites. When Congress passed the

State	Total Number of Free Blacks	Free Blacks as a Percentage of Total Black Population
Massachusetts	7,378	100%
Vermont	557	100%
New Hampshire	855	99%
Rhode Island	3,304	90%
Pennsylvania	14,564	89%
Connecticut	5,300	85%
Delaware	8,268	57%
New York	10,374	33%
New Jersey	4,402	26%
Maryland	19,587	16%
Virginia	20,124	6%
North Carolina	7,043	5%
South Carolina	3,185	2%
Georgia	1,019	2%
Kentucky	741	2%
Tennessee	309	2%
UNITED STATES	108,395*	11%

* Total includes figures from the District of Columbia, Mississippi Territory, and Northwest Territory. These areas are not shown on the chart.

Figure 7.1 Number and Percentage of Free Blacks, by State, 1800
Within a generation of the Declaration of Independence, a large free black population emerged that included every ninth African-American. In the North, only in New Jersey and New York did most blacks remain slaves. Almost half of all free blacks lived in the South. Every sixth black in Maryland was free by 1800. *Source:* U.S. Bureau of the Census.

Naturalization Act (1790), it limited eligibility for U.S. citizenship to "free white aliens." The federal militia law of 1792 required whites to enroll in local units but allowed states to exclude free blacks, an option that state governments increasingly chose. The navy and the marine corps forbade nonwhite enlistments in 1798. Delaware stripped free, property-owning black males of the vote in 1792, and by 1807 Maryland, Kentucky, and New Jersey had followed suit. Free black men continued to vote and to serve in some integrated militia organizations after 1800 (including in the slave states of North Carolina and Tennessee), but the number of settings in which they were treated as the equals of whites dropped sharply.

Even with these disadvantages, some free blacks became landowners or skilled artisans, and a few gained recognition among whites. One of the best known was Benjamin Banneker of Maryland, a self-taught mathematician and astronomer. In 1789, Banneker was one of three surveyors who laid out the new national capital in Washington, D.C., and after 1791 he published a series of widely read almanacs. Sending a copy of one to Thomas Jefferson, Banneker chided the future president for holding views of black inferiority that contradicted his own words in the Declaration of Independence.

In the face of growing constrictions on their freedom and opportunities, free African-Americans in the North turned to one another for support. Self-help among African-Americans flowed especially through religious channels. During the 1780s two free black Christians, Richard Allen and Absalom Jones, formed the Free African Society of Philadelphia, a community organization whose members pooled their scarce resources to assist one another and other blacks in need. After the white-dominated Methodist church they attended tried to restrict black worshipers to the gallery, Allen, Jones, and most of the black membership withdrew and formed a separate congregation. Comparable developments in other northern communities eventually resulted in the formation of a new denomination, the African Methodist Episcopal Church (see Chapter 9).

In 1793, Philadelphia experienced a yellow fever epidemic in which about four thousand residents eventually died. As most affluent whites fled, Allen and Jones organized a relief effort in which African-Americans, at great personal risk, tended to the sick and buried the dead of both races. But their only reward was a vicious publicity campaign wrongly accusing blacks from profiting at whites' expense. Allen and Jones vigorously defended the black community against these charges while condemning slavery and racism.

Another revealing indication of whites' changing racial attitudes also occurred in 1793, when Congress passed, and President Washington signed, the **Fugitive Slave Law**. This law required judges to award possession of an escaped slave upon any formal request by a master or his representative. Accused runaways not only were denied a jury trial but also were sometimes refused permission to present evidence of their freedom. Slaves' legal status as property disqualified them from claiming these constitutional privileges, but the Fugitive Slave Law denied free blacks the legal protections that the Bill of Rights guaranteed them as citizens. Congress nevertheless passed this measure without serious opposition. The law marked a striking departure from the atmosphere of the 1780s, when state governments had moved toward granting free blacks legal equality with whites.

The slave revolution on Saint Domingue (which victorious blacks would rename Haiti in 1802) heightened slave owners' fears of violent retaliation by blacks. In August 1800, such fears were kindled when a slave insurrection broke out near Richmond, Virginia's capital. Amid the election campaign that year, in which Federalists and Republicans accused one another of endangering liberty and hinted at violence, a slave named Gabriel calculated that the split among whites afforded blacks an opportunity to gain their freedom. Having secretly assembled weapons,

Absalom Jones, by Raphael Peale, 1810
Born a slave, Jones was allowed to study and work for pay; eventually he bought his freedom. He became a businessman, a cofounder of the African Methodist Episcopal Church, and a stalwart in Philadelphia's free black community.

Chronology, 1788–1800

1788	First election under the Constitution.
1789	First Congress convenes in New York. George Washington elected and inaugurated as first president. Judiciary Act. French Revolution begins.
1790	Alexander Hamilton submits Reports on Public Credit and National Bank to Congress. Treaty of New York. Judith Sargent Murray, "On the Equality of the Sexes." First Indian Trade and Intercourse Act.
1791	Bank of the United States established with twenty-year charter. Bill of Rights ratified. *National Gazette* established. Slave uprising begins in French colony of Saint Domingue. Society for the Encouragement of Useful Manufactures founded.
1792	Washington reelected president.
1793	Fugitive Slave Law. *Chisholm* v. *Georgia*. France at war with Britain and Spain.

	Washington's Neutrality Proclamation. Citizen Genet arrives in United States. First Democratic societies established.
1794	Whiskey Rebellion. Battle of Fallen Timbers.
1795	Treaty of Greenville. Jay's Treaty.
1796	Treaty of San Lorenzo. Washington's Farewell Address. John Adams elected president.
1798	XYZ Affair. Alien and Sedition Acts. Eleventh Amendment to the Constitution ratified.
1798–1799	Virginia and Kentucky Resolutions.
1798–1800	Quasi-War between United States and France.
1799	Russia establishes colony in Alaska. Fries Rebellion in Pennsylvania. Handsome Lake begins reform movement among Senecas.
1800	Gabriel's Rebellion in Virginia. Thomas Jefferson elected president.

he and several other blacks organized a march on Richmond by more than a thousand slaves. The plot of **Gabriel's Rebellion** was leaked on the eve of the march. Obtaining confessions from some participants, the authorities rounded up the rest and executed thirty-five of them, including Gabriel. "I have nothing more to offer than what General Washington would have had to offer, had he been taken by the British officers and put to trial by them," said one rebel before his execution. "I have ventured my life in endeavoring to obtain the liberty of my countrymen, and I am a willing sacrifice to their cause." In the end, Gabriel's Rebellion only confirmed whites' anxieties that Haiti's revolution could be replayed on American soil.

A technological development also strengthened slavery. During the 1790s, demand in the British textile industry stimulated the cultivation of cotton in coastal South Carolina and Georgia. The soil and climate were ideal for growing long-staple cotton, a variety whose fibers could be separated easily from its seed by squeezing it through rollers. In the South's upland and interior regions, however, the only cotton that would thrive was the short-staple variety, whose seed stuck so tenaciously to the fibers that rollers crushed the seeds and ruined the fibers. It was as if growers had discovered gold only to find that they could not mine it. But in 1793, a New Englander, Eli Whitney, invented a cotton gin that successfully separated the fibers of short-staple cotton from the seed. Quickly copied and improved upon by others, Whitney's invention removed a major obstacle to the spread of cotton cultivation. It gave a new lease on life to plantation slavery and undermined the doubts of those who considered slavery economically outmoded.

By 1800, free blacks had suffered noticeable erosion of their post-Revolutionary gains, and southern slaves were farther from freedom than a decade earlier. Two vignettes poignantly communicate the plight of African-Americans. By arrangement with her late husband, Martha Washington freed the family's slaves a year after George died. But many of the freed blacks remained impoverished and dependent on the Washington estate because Virginia law prohibited the education of blacks and otherwise denied them opportunities to realize their freedom. Meanwhile, across the Potomac at the site surveyed by Benjamin Banneker, enslaved blacks were performing most of the labor on the new national capital that would bear the first president's name. African-Americans were manifestly losing ground.

Conclusion

Although American voters were largely united when Washington took office in 1789, they soon became divided along lines of region, economic interest, and ideology. Hamilton pushed through a series of controversial measures that strengthened federal and executive authority as well as northeastern commercial interests. Jefferson, Madison, and many others opposed these measures, arguing that they favored a few Americans at the expense of the rest and that they threatened liberty. At the same time, Spain and Britain resisted U.S. expansion west of the Appalachians, and the French Revolution sharply polarized voters between those who favored and those who opposed it. During the mid-1790s, elites formed two rival political parties—the Federalists and the Republicans. Only with the peaceful transfer of power from Federalists to Republicans in 1800 could the nation's long-term political stability be taken for granted.

Key Terms

Judiciary Act
Bill of Rights
Alexander Hamilton
Reports on the Public Credit
Report on a National Bank
Whiskey Rebellion
Alta California
Citizen Genet
Treaty of Greenville
Jay's Treaty
Treaty of San Lorenzo
election of 1796
Quasi-War
Alien and Sedition Acts
Virginia and Kentucky Resolutions
election of 1800
republican motherhood
Indian Trade and Intercourse Acts
Fugitive Slave Law
Gabriel's Rebellion

The election of 1800 ensured that white male property owners would enjoy basic legal and political rights. But other Americans remained without such rights, especially on the basis of their gender or race.

For Further Reference

Douglas R. Egerton, *Gabriel's Rebellion: The Virginia Slave Conspiracies of 1800 and 1802* (1993). A thorough, well-written narrative that presents slave resistance against the backdrop of post-Revolutionary society and politics.

Stanley Elkins and Eric McKitrick, *The Age of Federalism: The Early American Republic, 1788–1800* (1993). A magisterial account of politics and diplomacy through the election of 1800.

Ron Chernow, *Alexander Hamilton* (2004). A thorough, original biography.

Joanne B. Freeman, *Affairs of Honor: National Politics in the New Republic* (2001). An insightful discussion of politics in the 1790s and the passions that underlay them.

Ramón A. Gutiérrez and Richard J. Orsi (eds.), *Contested Eden: California Before the Gold Rush* (1998). A strong, diverse collection of essays, introducing the history of the Pacific colony under Spanish and Mexican rule.

Joan M. Jensen, *Loosening the Bonds: Mid-Atlantic Farm Women, 1750–1850* (1986). A study of the interplay of women's roles and commercialization in what was then America's most dynamic agricultural region.

Gary B. Nash, *Forging Freedom: The Formation of Philadelphia's Black Community, 1720–1840* (1988). A landmark study of how North America's largest African-American community formed and survived in the face of racism and poverty.

Theda Perdue, *Cherokee Women: Gender and Culture Change, 1700–1835* (1998). The leading study of Native American women during the eighteenth and early nineteenth centuries.

Alan Taylor, *The Divided Ground: Indians, Settlers, and the Northern Borderland of the American Revolution* (2006). A compelling account of how the struggle among Native Americans, Britons, and Americans shaped the United States and Canada.

Laurel Thatcher Ulrich, *A Midwife's Tale: The Life of Martha Ballard, Based on Her Diary, 1785–1812* (1990). A Pulitzer Prize–winning study of a rural woman's life in northern New England.

Chapter 8

War of 1812 Scene
Captain Thomas Macdonough and his crew celebrate their victory over the British in the Battle of Lake Champlain, August 24, 1812.

Jeffersonianism and the Era of Good Feelings,

1801–1824

Margaret Bayard Smith

Born into a prominent Philadelphia family (her father had served in the Continental Congress and with George Washington at Valley Forge) and newly wed, the twenty-two-year-old Margaret Bayard Smith arrived in Washington with her husband, the editor Samuel Harrison Smith, in 1800. She would reside there for over four decades, establishing a reputation, mainly through her private letters, as an acute observer of the political stage and as a remarkably literate person.

With its transient population of politicians, most of whom lived in boardinghouses; with only two public buildings of note, the president's mansion and the unfinished Capitol; with avenues that were just paths cut through swamps and woods so dense that congressmen got lost in them, the new capital lacked nearly all refinements. But Margaret Bayard Smith quickly recognized that the crudeness of the capital worked to the advantage of elite women like herself. Craving interesting conversation and a wider social circle, politicians sought out vivacious and articulate women. In other cities, she observed, a lady attending a reception was expected to sit and wait for a gentleman to approach her to start a conversation. But in the cramped quarters of the capital's boardinghouses, there scarcely was room to sit. Men and women walked about the rooms in "mingled groups, which certainly produces more ease, freedom and equality." The House of Representatives became "the lounging place for both sexes, where acquaintance is as easily made as at public amusements." "The women here are taking over society," she wrote, "which is not known elsewhere. On every public occasion, a launch, an oration, an inauguration, in the court, in the representative hall, as well as in the drawing room, they are treated with mark'd distinction."

Between her arrival in 1800 and her death in 1844, Mrs. Smith came to know nearly everyone worth knowing in Washington, but the statesman who most impressed her was the first one she met, Thomas Jefferson. Raised a Federalist, she had heard Jefferson described as "the violent democrat, the vulgar demagogue, the bold atheist." But the Jefferson who visited her husband on a December morning in 1800 spoke gently and expressed the view, which she quickly embraced, that governments would win the affection of the people by governing lightly. She admired the way Jefferson sought to bring harmony to the young republic, whose survival seemed jeopardized by the intensity of its political divisions. She followed closely his purchase in 1803 of the vast Louisiana territory, which nearly doubled the size of the United States, and she shed no tears as the Federalists gradually disintegrated and then collapsed as a national force by 1820.

Yet the harmony for which Jefferson longed proved elusive. Contrary to Jefferson's expectation, events in Europe continued to agitate American politics. In 1807, the United States moved to end trade with Europe to avoid being sucked into the war between Britain and France. The failure of this policy led to war with Britain in 1812.

Foreign policy was not the only source of discord. The Federalist decline opened the way for intensified factionalism in the Republican Party during Jefferson's second term (1805–1809) and again during the misleadingly named Era of Good Feelings (1817–1824). Republican factionalism often arose when Jefferson's followers arrived at conflicting assessments of his philosophy. Some, like the eccentric John Randolph, argued that, as president, Jefferson was deserting his own principles. Other Republicans interpreted the often inept performance of the American government and army during

the War of 1812 as proving the need for a stronger centralized government than Jefferson had desired. Most ominously, in 1819 and 1820 northern and southern Republicans divided along sectional lines over the extension of slavery into Missouri.

The Age of Jefferson

Narrowly elected in 1800, Jefferson saw his popularity rise during his first term, when he moved quickly to scale down government expenditures. Increasingly confident of popular support, he worked to loosen the Federalists' grip on appointive federal offices, especially in the judiciary. His purchase of Louisiana against Federalist opposition added to his popularity. In all of these moves, Jefferson was guided not merely by political calculation but also by his philosophy of government, eventually known as Jeffersonianism.

Jefferson and Jeffersonianism

A man of extraordinary attainments, Jefferson was fluent in French, read Latin and Greek, and studied several Native American languages. He served for more than twenty years as president of America's foremost scientific association, the American Philosophical Society. A student of architecture, he designed his own mansion in Virginia, Monticello. Gadgets fascinated him. He invented a device for duplicating his letters, of which he wrote over twenty thousand, and he improved the design for a revolving book stand, which enabled him to consult up to five books at once. His public career was luminous: principal author of the Declaration of Independence, governor of Virginia, ambassador to France, secretary of state under Washington, and vice president under John Adams.

Yet he was, and remains, a controversial figure. His critics, pointing to his doubts about some Christian doctrines and his early support for the French Revolution, portrayed him as an infidel and radical. During the election campaign of 1800, Federalists alleged that he kept a slave mistress. In 1802 James Callender, a former supporter furious about not receiving a government job he wanted, wrote a newspaper account naming Sally Hemings, a house slave at Monticello, as the mistress. Drawing on the DNA of Sally's male heirs and linking the timing of Jefferson's visits to Monticello with the start of Sally's pregnancies, most scholars now view it as very likely that Jefferson, a widower, was the father of at least one of her four surviving children.

Callender's story did Jefferson little damage in Virginia, because Jefferson had acted according to the rules

Focus Questions

- How did Jefferson's philosophy shape policy toward public expenditures, the judiciary, and Louisiana?

- What led James Madison to go to war with Britain in 1812?

- How did the War of 1812 influence American domestic politics?

- To what extent did Jefferson's legacy persist into the Era of Good Feelings?

Man of the People
Foreign diplomats were often shocked when Jefferson
greeted them dressed in everyday clothes and carpet
slippers. But Jefferson thought of himself as a working
politician and man of the people, not as an aristocratic
figurehead.

of white Virginia gentlemen by never acknowledging any
of Sally's children as his own. Although he freed two of
her children (the other two ran away), he never freed
Sally, the daughter of Jefferson's own father-in-law and
so light-skinned that she could pass for white, nor did he
ever mention her in his vast correspondence. Yet the
story of Sally fed the charge that Jefferson was a hyp-
ocrite, for throughout his career he condemned the very
"race-mixing" to which he appears to have contributed.

Jefferson did not believe that blacks and whites
could live permanently side by side in American society.
As the black population grew, he feared a race war so vicious that it could be suppressed only by a dictator. This
view was consistent with his conviction that the real

threat to republics rose less from hostile neighbors than
from within. He believed that the French had turned to
a dictator, Napoleon Bonaparte, to save them from the
chaos of their own revolution. Only by colonizing blacks
in Africa, an idea embodied in the American Colonization Society (1816), could America avert a similar fate,
he believed.

Jefferson worried that high taxes, standing armies,
and corruption could destroy American liberty by turning government into the master rather than servant of
the people. To prevent tyranny, he advocated that state
governments retain considerable authority. In a vast republic, he reasoned, state governments would be more
responsive to the popular will than would the government in Washington.

He also believed that popular liberty required popular virtue. For republican theorists like Jefferson, virtue
consisted of a decision to place the public good ahead of
one's private interests and to exercise vigilance to keep
governments from growing out of control. To Jefferson,
the most vigilant and virtuous people were educated
farmers, who were accustomed to act and think with
sturdy independence. The least vigilant were the inhabitants of cities. Jefferson regarded cities as breeding
grounds for mobs and as menaces to liberty. Men who
relied on merchants or factory owners for their jobs
could have their votes influenced, unlike farmers who
worked their own land. When the people "get piled upon
one another in large cities, as in Europe," he wrote, "they
will become corrupt as in Europe."

Jefferson's "Revolution"

Jefferson described his election as a revolution. But the
revolution he sought was to restore the liberty and tranquillity that (he thought) the United States had enjoyed
in its early years and to reverse what he saw as a drift
into despotism. The $10 million growth in the national
debt under the Federalists alarmed Jefferson and his
secretary of the treasury, Albert Gallatin. They rejected
Hamilton's idea that a national debt would strengthen
the government by giving creditors a stake in its health.
Just paying the interest on the debt would require taxes,
which would suck money from industrious farmers, the
backbone of the Republic. The money would then fall
into the hands of creditors—leeches who lived off interest payments. Increased tax revenues might also tempt
the government to establish a standing army, always a
threat to liberty.

Jefferson and Gallatin secured the repeal of many
taxes, and they slashed expenditures by closing some em-
bassies overseas and reducing the army, which declined

Explosion of the *Intrepid*
In September 1804 the American fireship *Intrepid*, loaded with gunpowder and intending to penetrate Tripoli harbor in present-day Libya, blew up before reaching its target, killing Captain Richard Somers and his crew. Seven months earlier, commanded by Lieutenant Stephen Decatur, the *Intrepid* had destroyed the American frigate *Philadelphia*, which had fallen into Tripolitan hands. Britain's Lord Nelson reportedly described Decatur's exploit as "the most bold and daring act of the age."

from an authorized strength of over 14,000 in 1798 to 3,287 in 1802. They placed economy ahead of military preparedness. Gallatin calculated that the nation could be freed of debt in sixteen years if administrations held the line on expenditures. In Europe, the Peace of Amiens (1802) brought a temporary halt to the hostilities between Britain and France that had threatened American shipping, which buoyed Jefferson's confidence that minimal military preparedness was a sound policy. The Peace of Amiens, he wrote, "removes the only danger we have to fear. We can now proceed without risks in demolishing useless structures of expense, lightening the burdens of our constituents, and fortifying the principles of free government." This may have been wishful thinking, but it rested on a sound economic calculation, for the vast territory of the United States could not be secured from attack without astronomical expense.

While cutting back expenditures on the army, Jefferson was ready to use the navy to gain respect for the American flag. In 1801, he ordered a naval squadron into action in the Mediterranean against the so-called Tripolitan (or Barbary) pirates of North Africa. For centuries, the rulers of Tripoli, Morocco, Tunis, and Algiers had solved their budgetary problems by engaging in piracy and extorting tribute in exchange for protection; captured seamen were held for ransom or sold into slavery. Jefferson calculated that going to war would be cheaper than paying high tribute to maintain peace. Although suffering its share of reverses during the ensuing fighting, the United States did not come away empty-handed. In 1805, it was able to conclude a peace treaty with Tripoli. The war cost roughly half of what the United States had been paying annually for protection.

Jefferson and the Judiciary

In his first inaugural address Jefferson reminded Americans that their agreements were more basic than their disagreements. "We are all republicans," he proclaimed, "we are all federalists." He hoped to conciliate the moderate Federalists, but conflicts over the judiciary derailed this objective. Washington and Adams had appointed only Federalists to the bench, including the new chief justice, **John Marshall**. Not a single Republican was sitting on the federal judiciary when Jefferson came to office. Still bitter about the zeal of federal courts in enforcing the Alien and Sedition Acts, Jefferson saw the Federalist-sponsored Judiciary Act of 1801 as the last straw. By reducing the number of Supreme Court justices from six to five, the act threatened to strip him of an early opportunity to appoint a justice. At the same time, the act created sixteen new federal judgeships, which outgoing president John Adams had filled by last-minute ("midnight") appointments of Federalists. To Jefferson, this was proof that the Federalists intended to use the judiciary as a stronghold from which "all the works of Republicanism are to be beaten down and erased." In 1802, he won congressional repeal of the Judiciary Act of 1801.

Jefferson's troubles with the judiciary were not over. On his last day in office, Adams had appointed a Federalist, William Marbury, as justice of the peace in the District of Columbia but failed to deliver Marbury's commission before midnight. When Jefferson's secretary of state, James Madison, refused to send him notice of the appointment, Marbury petitioned the Supreme Court to issue a writ compelling delivery. In ***Marbury v. Madison*** (1803), Chief Justice John Marshall wrote the unanimous opinion. Marshall ruled that, although Madison should have delivered Marbury's commission, he was under no legal obligation to do so because part of the Judiciary Act of 1789 that had granted the Court the authority to issue such a writ, was unconstitutional.

For the first time, the Supreme Court had asserted its authority to void an act of Congress on the grounds that it was "repugnant" to the Constitution. Jefferson did not reject this principle, known as the doctrine of judicial review and destined to become highly influential, but he was enraged that Marshall had used part of his decision to lecture Madison on his moral duty (as opposed to his legal obligation) to deliver Marbury's commission. This gratuitous lecture, which was really directed at Jefferson as Madison's superior, struck Jefferson as another example of Federalist partisanship.

While the *Marbury* decision was brewing, the Republicans took the offensive against the judiciary by moving to impeach (charge with wrongdoing) two Federalist judges. One, John Pickering, was an insane alcoholic; the other, Supreme Court justice Samuel Chase, was a partisan Federalist notorious for jailing several Republican editors under the Sedition Act of 1798. These cases raised the same issue: Was impeachment, which the Constitution restricted to cases of treason, bribery, and

"high Crimes and Misdemeanors," an appropriate remedy for judges who were insane or excessively partisan? Pickering was removed from office, but the Senate narrowly failed to convict Chase, in part because moderate Republicans were coming to doubt whether impeachment was a solution to judicial partisanship.

Chase's acquittal ended Jefferson's skirmishes with the judiciary as Jefferson and the Federalist judges reached an uneasy truce. The Federalists did not attempt to use their control of the federal judiciary to undo Jefferson's "revolution" of 1800. The Marshall court, for example, upheld the constitutionality of the repeal of the Judiciary Act of 1801. For his part, Jefferson never proposed to impeach Marshall. No federal judge would be impeached for more than fifty years.

The Louisiana Purchase, 1803

When Jefferson was elected president, European powers had large landholdings in North America. Spain, a declining power, controlled East and West Florida as well as the vast Louisiana Territory. The latter was equal in size to the United States at that time. In 1800, Spain ceded the Louisiana Territory to France, which was fast emerging under Napoleon Bonaparte as the world's foremost military power. It took six months for news of the treaty to reach Jefferson and Madison but only a few minutes for them to grasp its significance.

Jefferson had long dreamed of an "empire of liberty" extending across North America and even into South America. He saw this empire being gained not by military conquest but by the inevitable expansion of the free and virtuous American people. An enfeebled Spain constituted no real obstacle to this expansion. But Bonaparte's capacity for mischief was boundless. If Bonaparte gave Britain a free hand in the Mediterranean in exchange for a license for French expansion in North America, the United States could be sandwiched between British Canada and French Louisiana. And if Britain refused to cooperate with France, the British might seize Louisiana, trapping the United States between two large British territories.

Although Americans feared these two possibilities, Bonaparte actually had a different goal. He dreamed of a new French empire bordering the Caribbean and the Gulf of Mexico, centering on the Caribbean colony of Saint Domingue (modern Haiti). He wanted to use Louisiana not as a base from which to threaten the United States but as a breadbasket for an essentially Caribbean empire. His immediate task was to subdue Saint Domingue, where by 1800 a bloody slave revolution had resulted in a takeover of the government by the former slave Toussaint L'Ouverture (see Chapter 7). Bonaparte dispatched an army to reassert French control and reestablish slavery, but the army was destroyed by a combination of an epidemic of yellow fever and fierce resistance by former slaves.

In the short run, Jefferson worried most about New Orleans. Because no rivers, roads, or canals connected the American territories of Ohio, Indiana, and Mississippi with the eastern ports, farmers in the interior had to ship their cash crops, worth $3 million annually, down the Ohio and Mississippi Rivers to New Orleans, a port that did not belong to the United States. The Spanish had temporarily granted Americans the right to park their produce there while awaiting transfer to seagoing vessels. But in 1802, the Spanish colonial administrator in New Orleans issued an order revoking this right. The

order had originated in Spain, but most Americans assumed that it had come from Bonaparte, who, although he now owned Louisiana, had yet to take possession of it. An alarmed Jefferson described New Orleans as the "one single spot" on the globe whose possessor "is our natural and habitual enemy." "The day that France takes possession of N. Orleans," he added, "we must marry ourselves to the British fleet and nation."

The combination of France's failure to subdue Saint Domingue and the termination of American rights to deposit produce in New Orleans stimulated two crucial decisions—one by Jefferson and the other by Bonaparte—that ultimately resulted in the purchase of Louisiana by the United States. First, Jefferson nominated James Monroe and Robert R. Livingston to negotiate with France for the purchase of New Orleans and as

Map 8.1 The Louisiana Purchase and the Exploration of the West
The explorations of Lewis and Clark demonstrated the vast extent of the area purchased from France.

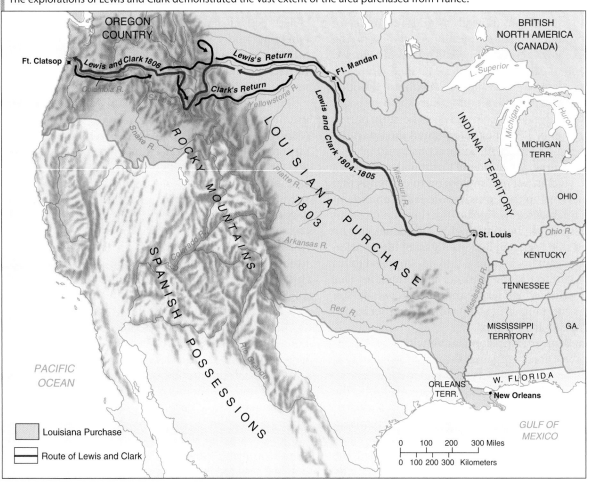

much of the Floridas as possible. (Because West Florida had repeatedly changed hands among France, Britain, and Spain, no one was sure who owned it.) Meanwhile, Bonaparte, mindful of his military failure in Saint Domingue and of American opposition to French control of Louisiana, had concluded that his projected Caribbean empire was not worth the cost. In addition, he planned to resume war in Europe and needed cash. So he decided to sell all of Louisiana. After some haggling between the American commissioners and Bonaparte's minister, Talleyrand, a price of $15 million for the **Louisiana Purchase** was settled on. (One-fourth of the total represented an agreement by the United States to pay French debts owed to American citizens.) For this sum, the United States gained an immense, uncharted territory between the Mississippi River and the Rocky Mountains (see Map 8.1). No one knew its exact size; Talleyrand merely observed that the bargain was noble. But the purchase virtually doubled the area of the United States at a cost, omitting interest, of thirteen and one-half cents an acre.

As a believer in a strict interpretation of the Constitution, the president had doubts about the constitutionality of the purchase. No provision of the Constitution explicitly gave the government authority to acquire new territory. Jefferson therefore drafted a constitutional amendment that authorized the acquisition of territory and prohibited the American settlement of Louisiana for an indefinite period. Fearing that an immediate and headlong rush to settle the area would lead to the destruction of the Native Americans and an orgy of land speculation, Jefferson wanted to control development so that Americans could advance "compactly as we multiply." But few Republicans shared his reservations, and Jefferson soon began to worry that the long process of ratifying an amendment might give Napoleon time to change his mind. He quietly dropped the amendment and submitted the treaty to the Senate, where it was quickly ratified.

Believing in strict construction—the doctrine that the Constitution should be interpreted ("constructed") according to its letter—Jefferson was also committed to the principle of establishing an "empire of liberty." Doubling the size of the Republic would guarantee land for American farmers, the backbone of the nation and the true guardians of liberty. Strict construction was not an end in itself but a means to promote republican liberty. If that end could be achieved in some way other than by strict construction, so be it. Jefferson was also alert to practical considerations. Most Federalists opposed the Louisiana Purchase because it would decrease the relative importance of their strongholds on the eastern seaboard. As the leader of the Republican Party, Jefferson saw no reason to hand the Federalists an issue by dallying over ratification of the treaty.

The Election of 1804

Jefferson's acquisition of Louisiana left the Federalists dispirited and without a popular national issue. As the election of 1804 approached, the main threat to Jefferson was not the Federalist Party but his own vice president, Aaron Burr. In 1800, Burr had tried to take advantage of a tie in the Electoral College to gain the presidency, a betrayal in the eyes of most Republicans, who assumed that he had been nominated for the vice presidency. The adoption in 1804 of the Twelfth Amendment, which required separate and distinct ballots in the Electoral College for the presidential and the vice-presidential candidates, put an end to the possibility of an electoral tie for the chief executive. Burr continued to cause trouble. Between 1801 and 1804, he entered into enough intrigues with the Federalists to convince the Republicans that it would be unsafe to renominate him for the vice presidency. The Republicans in Congress rudely dumped Burr in favor of George Clinton.

Without a hope of success, the Federalists nominated Charles C. Pinckney and Rufus King, and then watched their candidates go down to an overwhelming defeat in the election. The Federalists carried only two states, failing to hold even Massachusetts. Jefferson's overwhelming victory brought his first term to a fitting close. Between 1801 and 1804, the United States had doubled its territory, taken steps to pay off its debt, and remained at peace.

The Lewis and Clark Expedition

Louisiana dazzled Jefferson. Here was an immense territory about which American citizens knew virtually nothing. No one was sure of its western boundary. A case could be made for the Pacific Ocean, but Spain claimed part of the Pacific coast. Jefferson was content to claim that Louisiana extended at least to the mountains west of the Mississippi, which few citizens of the United States had ever seen. Jefferson himself had never been more than fifty miles west of his home in Virginia. Thus the Louisiana Purchase was both a bargain and a surprise package.

Even before the acquisition of Louisiana, Jefferson had planned an exploratory expedition; picked its leader, his personal secretary and fellow Virginian Lieutenant

Bull Dance, Mandan Okipa Ceremony
Among the Plains tribes encountered by Lewis and Clark were the Mandans. With the arrival of white men, the Mandans often acted as intermediaries between whites and tribes farther to the west. Their villages became trading centers where hide shirts and buffalo robes were exchanged for European cloth. Unfortunately, the whites also brought smallpox, against which the Mandans had no immunities. By the late 1830s their numbers had dwindled to 125.

Meriwether Lewis; and sent him to Philadelphia for a crash course in sciences such as zoology, astronomy, and botany that were relevant to exploration. Jefferson instructed Lewis to trace the Missouri River to its source, cross the western highlands, and follow the best water route to the Pacific. Jefferson was genuinely interested in the scientific information that could be collected on the expedition. His instructions to Lewis cited the need to learn about Indian languages and customs, climate, plants, birds, reptiles, and insects. But, above all, Jefferson hoped that the **Lewis and Clark expedition** would find a water route across the continent (see Technology and Culture: Mapping America). The potential economic benefits from such a route included diverting the lucrative fur trade from Canadian to American hands and boosting trade with China.

Setting forth from St. Louis in May 1804, Lewis, his second-in-command William Clark, and about fifty others followed the Missouri River and then the Snake and Columbia Rivers. In the Dakota country, Lewis and Clark hired a French-Canadian fur trader, Toussaint Charbonneau, as a guide and interpreter. Slow-witted and inclined to panic in crises, Charbonneau proved to be a mixed blessing, but his wife, **Sacajawea**, who accompanied him on the trip, made up for his failings. A Shoshone and probably no more than sixteen years old in 1804, Sacajawea had been stolen by a rival tribe and then claimed by Charbonneau. When first encountered by Lewis and Clark, she had just given birth to a son; indeed, the infant's presence helped reassure Native American tribes of the expedition's peaceful intent.

Even with their peaceful intent established, Lewis and Clark faced obstacles. The expedition brought them in contact with numerous tribes, most importantly the powerful Sioux but also Mandans, Hidatsas, and Arikaras. Each tribe had a history of warring on other tribes and of carrying on its own internal clans and feuds. Reliant on Indians for guides, packers, and interpreters, Lewis and Clark had to become instant diplomats. Jefferson had told them to assert American sovereignty over the Purchase. This objective led them to distribute medals and uniforms to chiefs ready to support American authority and to stage periodic military parades and displays of their weapons, which included cannons. But no tribe had a single chief; rather, different tribal villages had different chiefs. At times, Lewis and Clark miscalculated, for example when they treated an Arikara chief as the "grand chief" to the outrage of his rivals. Yet their diplomacy was generally successful, less because they were sophisticated ethnographers than because they avoided violence.

The group finally reached the Pacific Ocean in November 1805 and then returned to St. Louis, but not before collecting a mass of scientific information, including the disturbing fact that more than three hundred miles of mountains separated the Missouri from the Columbia. The expedition also produced a sprinkling of tall tales, many of which Jefferson believed, about gigantic Indians, soil too rich to grow trees, and a mountain composed of salt. Jefferson's political opponents railed that he would soon be reporting the discovery of a molasses-filled lake. For all the ridicule, the expedition's drawings of the geography of the region led to more accurate maps and heightened interest in the West.

The Gathering Storm

In gaining control of Louisiana, the United States had benefited from the preoccupation of European powers with their own struggles. But between 1803 and 1814, the renewal of the Napoleonic Wars in Europe turned the United States into a pawn in a chess game played by others and helped make Jefferson's second term far less successful than his first.

Europe was not Jefferson's only problem. He had to deal with a conspiracy to dismantle the United States, the product of the inventive and perverse mind of Aaron Burr, and to face down challenges within his own party, led by John Randolph.

Plains Pipe Bowl
Instructed by Jefferson to acquaint themselves with the Indians' "ordinary occupations in the arts," Lewis and Clark collected this Lakota sacred pipe, whose red stone symbolized the flesh and blood of all people and whose smoke represented the breath that carries prayers to the Creator. Considering pipes sacred objects, Indians used them to seal contracts and treaties, and to perform ceremonial healing.

Challenges on the Home Front

Aaron Burr suffered a string of reverses in 1804. After being denied renomination as vice president, he entered into a series of intrigues with a faction of despairing and extreme (or "High") Federalists in New England. Led by Senator Timothy Pickering of Massachusetts, these High Federalists plotted to sever the Union by forming a pro-British Northern Confederacy composed of Nova Scotia (part of British-owned Canada), New England, New York, and even Pennsylvania. Although most Federalists disdained the plot, Pickering and others settled on Burr as their leader and helped him gain the Federalist nomination for the governorship of New York. Alexander Hamilton, who had thwarted Burr's grab for the presidency in 1800 by throwing his weight behind Jefferson, now foiled Burr a second time by allowing publication of his "despicable opinion" of Burr. Defeated in the election for New York's governor, Burr challenged Hamilton to a duel and mortally wounded him at Weehawken, New Jersey, on July 11, 1804.

Indicted in two states for his murder of Hamilton, Burr, still vice president, now hatched a scheme so bold that not even his political opponents could believe that he was capable of such treachery. He allied himself with the unsavory military governor of the Louisiana Territory, General James Wilkinson. Wilkinson had been on Spain's payroll intermittently as a secret agent since the 1780s. Together, Burr and Wilkinson conspired to separate the western states south of the Ohio River into an independent confederacy. In addition, Wilkinson had long entertained the idea of an American conquest of Mexico, and Burr now added West Florida as a possible target. They presented these ideas to westerners as having the covert support of the administration, to the British as a way to attack Spanish-owned Mexico and West Florida, and to the Spanish (not naming Mexico and West Florida as targets) as a way to divide up the United States.

By the fall of 1806, Burr and about sixty followers were making their way down the Ohio and Mississippi Rivers to join Wilkinson at Natchez. In October 1806, Jefferson, who described Burr as a crooked gun that never shot straight, denounced the conspiracy. Wilkinson abandoned the conspiracy and proclaimed himself the most loyal of Jefferson's followers. Burr tried to escape to West Florida but was intercepted. Brought back to Richmond, he was put on trial for treason. Chief Justice Marshall presided at the trial and instructed the jury that the prosecution had to prove not merely that Burr had treasonable intentions but also that he had committed treasonable acts, a virtually impossible task inasmuch as the

Technology (and) *Culture*

Mapping America

We take maps for granted, but in Jefferson's day few Americans knew what their nation looked like. Writing to Congress in 1777, George Washington had complained that "the want of accurate maps of the Country" placed him at "a great disadvantage." Treating mapmaking as a public expense, the British government staffed its army with surveyors, whose skills were indispensable to making maps. As a result, the British often had a better knowledge of the American countryside than did Washington's army.

Washington himself was a surveyor, but American surveyors had been employed by land-seeking clients, not governments. This approach to mapping yielded local maps, some of which were biased since the clients had an interest in the outcome. Existing maps of entire colonies were compilations of local maps, subject to all the errors that had crept into local surveys and lacking any common geographic frame of reference.

The accurate mapping of large areas that Washington desired required government funding of many survey parties. A typical survey party included several axemen to clear trees,

two chain bearers, two or three staff carriers, an instrument carrier, and the surveyor. Surveyors used several basic instruments, including a table equipped with paper, a compass, a telescope for measuring direction and heights, and an instrument for measuring angles called a theodolite. A surveyor first measured a baseline from one point to another, as marked by the chain bearers. Next he commenced a process known as triangulation by picking a landmark in the distance, like a hilltop, and measuring its angle from the baseline. A staff man might be standing on the hilltop with a flag attached to his staff. Finally, the surveyor employed trigonometry to calculate the length of each side of the triangle, one of which would serve as the next baseline. For every hour spent walking a plot of land, the survey party would spend three hours recording their measurements on paper.

Washington's complaint about inadequate maps led to the appointment of Scottish-born Robert Erskine as surveyor general of the Continental Army and to government funding of his workers. After the war, the Land Ordinance of 1785, which specified that public lands be surveyed and divided into townships six miles square before auction, again led the national government to employ survey parties. The Land

Map of Lewis and Clark Track
Drawn by Meriwether Lewis's traveling mate on the famous expedition and combining Clark's own observations with those of Indians and explorers, this 1814 map gave Americans their first view of the vast territory purchased in 1803. Clark's depiction of the Rockies was substantially accurate, his description of the Southwest less so.

Ordinance applied only to land lying outside any state. The national government did not take responsibility for mapping the states.

Jefferson's purchase of Louisiana in 1803 pricked a new popular interest in geography. Mapping the Purchase presented several obstacles. Early explorers had surveyed small portions of it, but the territory's vastness ruled out surveys of the entire Purchase. Spain discouraged even local surveys, lest information about this valuable possession leak out. Jefferson and others had to rely on maps compiled from the accounts of travelers who relied on a mixture of their own observations, hearsay accounts of fur traders, and wishful thinking.

Wishful thinking took the form of the belief, embraced by Jefferson, that the sources of the major North American rivers were near each other. If this were true, it would be possible to find a great water highway linking the Pacific to American settlements on the Mississippi. Such a highway would turn America into a commercial link between the riches of the East—Persian silks, Arabian perfumes, the wealth of China—and Europe. It would also facilitate the export of American agricultural produce.

Eager to ensure the profitability of agriculture, Jefferson warmed to this idea. He knew more about geography than anyone else in the American government, and he collected maps, most of which supported the water-highway theory. For example, one map published in Britain in 1778 showed the major American rivers—the Mississippi, Missouri, Colorado, and Columbia—all originating in a small pyramid of high land in present-day South Dakota.

By the time Jefferson launched the Lewis and Clark expedition to explore the Louisiana Purchase, better maps were available. Jefferson saw to it that Lewis and Clark carried a recent map by an Englishman, Aaron Arrowsmith. Arrowsmith's map showed the Rocky Mountains, which were often omitted by other maps. But when Lewis and Clark reached the source of the Missouri River in June 1805, they found no sign of the Columbia, whose source the Arrowsmith map portrayed as a stone's throw from the source of the Missouri, just "an immense range of high mountains."

Their expedition established Lewis and Clark as authorities on the West and stimulated the public's and states' interest in geography. During their expedition, Lewis and Clark had benefited from accurate charts of local geography drawn by Indians on the ground with sticks or on hides with charcoal. Settled in St. Louis after the expedition, Clark received a stream of explorers and traders who brought him more information about the geography of the Purchase, enough to

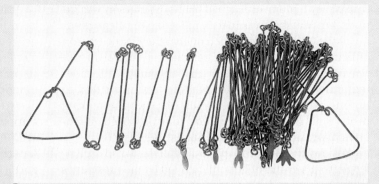

Surveyors' Chain and Pins
The standard surveyor's chain contained 66 links and was 100 feet in length. Eighty lengths of chain equaled one mile, and ten square chains a square mile (640 acres). Surveyors used wooden pins tied at the ends with bright red cloth to mark the chain's position as it was moved.

enable him to draw a manuscript map of the territory. When finally published in 1814, this map gave ordinary Americans their first picture of what Jefferson had bought in 1803. In 1816, John Melish, drawing on Clark's map and his own travels, published by far the most accurate map yet of the United States.

By enabling ordinary Americans to see the vastness of their nation, Melish's map subtly reinforced their sense that the West rightfully belonged to them, not to the Indians or anyone else. The negotiators of the Transcontinental Treaty of 1819, which gave the United States a claim to part of the Pacific coast, relied exclusively on the 1818 edition of Melish's map. Melish's example also spurred state legislatures to subsidize the drawing of accurate state maps.

Hiring Melish in 1816, Pennsylvania became the first state to finance construction of a state map based wholly on "actual survey." Melish was delighted. He had been insisting that "every state should have its own map" and that such maps should be state property, "subject to the control of no individual whatever." Taking six years to complete, the project cost Pennsylvania $30,000 and exhausted Melish, who died shortly after the map's publication. But other states were quick to follow Pennsylvania's lead.

Question for Analysis

Early maps contained many inaccuracies, resulting not just from limits of technology and finance but also from widely held beliefs about what America should look like. Since Americans acted on the basis of their beliefs, how much did maps actually shape events in the age of Jefferson?

conspiracy had never reached fruition. Jefferson was furious, but Marshall was merely following the clear wording of the Constitution, which deliberately made treason difficult to prove. The jury returned a verdict of not proved, which Marshall entered as "not guilty." Still under indictment for his murder of Hamilton, Burr fled to Europe, where he tried to interest Napoleon in making peace with Britain as a prelude to a proposed Anglo-French invasion of the United States and Mexico.

Besides the Burr conspiracy, Jefferson faced a challenge from a group of Republicans led by the president's fellow Virginian, John Randolph, a man of abounding eccentricities and acerbic wit. Like many propertied Americans of the 1770s, Randolph believed that governments always menaced popular liberty. Jefferson had originally shared this view, but he recognized it as an ideology of opposition, not power; once in office, he compromised. In contrast, Randolph remained frozen in the 1770s, denouncing every change as decline and proclaiming that he would throw all politicians to the dogs except that he had too much respect for dogs.

Not surprisingly, Randolph turned on Jefferson, most notably for backing a compromise in the Yazoo land scandal. In 1795, the Georgia legislature had sold the huge Yazoo tract (35 million acres comprising most of present-day Alabama and Mississippi) for a fraction of its value to land companies that had bribed virtually the entire legislature. The next legislature canceled the sale, but many investors, knowing nothing of the bribery, had already bought land in good faith. The scandal posed a moral challenge to Jefferson because of these good-faith purchases, and a political dilemma as well, for some purchasers were northerners whom Jefferson hoped to woo to the Republican Party. In 1803 a federal commission compromised with an award of 5 million acres to Yazoo investors. For Randolph, the compromise was itself a scandal—further evidence of the decay of republican virtue.

The Suppression of American Trade and Impressment

Burr's acquittal and Randolph's taunts shattered the aura of invincibility that had surrounded Jefferson. Now foreign affairs posed an even sharper challenge. As Britain and France resumed their war in Europe, American commerce prospered. American ships carried sugar and coffee from the French and Spanish Caribbean to Europe. This trade not only provided Napoleon with supplies but also drove down the price of sugar and coffee from Britain's colonies by adding to the glut of these commodities on the world market.

Britain insisted that the American carrying trade violated its Rule of 1756, which stated that trade closed in peacetime could not be reopened during war. For example, France usually restricted its sugar trade to French ships during peace and thus could not reopen it to American ships in wartime, when French ships were likely to be seized by Britain's powerful navy. American shippers responded to this rule with the "broken voyage." American vessels would carry French sugar to an American port, pass it through customs, and then reexport it as American produce. Britain tolerated this dodge for nearly a decade but in 1805 initiated a policy of total war against France, including the strangulation of French trade. In 1805, a British court declared the broken voyage illegal.

Next came a series of British trade decrees, known as "Orders in Council," which established a blockade of French-controlled ports on the coast of Europe. Napoleon responded with his so-called Continental System, a series of counterproclamations that ships obeying British regulations would be subject to seizure by France. In effect, this Anglo-French war of decrees outlawed virtually all U.S. trade; if an American ship complied with British regulations, it became a French target, and vice versa.

Both Britain and France seized American ships, but British seizures were far more humiliating to Americans. France was a weaker naval power than Britain; much of the French fleet had been destroyed by the British at the Battle of Trafalgar in October 1805. Accordingly, most of France's seizures of American ships occurred in European ports where American ships had been lured by Napoleon's often inconsistent enforcement of his Continental System. In contrast, British warships hovered just beyond the American coast. The Royal Navy stopped and searched virtually every American vessel off New York, for example. At times, U.S. ships had to line up a few miles from the American coast to be searched by the Royal Navy.

To these provocations the British added **impressment**. For centuries, Royal Navy press gangs had scoured the docks and taverns of British ports and forced ("pressed") civilians into service. As war with France intensified Britain's need for sailors, Britain increasingly extended the practice to seizing alleged Royal Navy deserters on American merchant ships. British sailors had good reason to be discontented with their navy. Discipline on the Royal Navy's "floating hells" was often brutal and the pay low; sailors on American ships made up to five times more than those on British ships. Consequently, the Royal Navy suffered a high rate of desertion to American ships. In 1807, for example, 149 of the 419 sailors on the American warship *Constitution* were British subjects.

Impressment was galling to American pride, since the United States was unable to prevent the seizure even of U.S.-born seamen who could prove their American birth. Between 1803 and 1812, six thousand Americans were impressed. Although impressment did less damage to the American economy than the seizure of ships, it was more offensive.

Any doubts Americans had about British arrogance evaporated in June 1807. A British warship, HMS *Leopard*, patrolling off Hampton Roads, Virginia, attacked an unsuspecting American frigate, USS *Chesapeake*, and forced it to surrender. The British then boarded the vessel and seized four supposed deserters. One, a genuine deserter, was later hanged; the other three, former Britons, had "deserted" only from impressments and were now American citizens. Even the British had never before asserted their right to seize deserters off U.S. navy ships. The so-called *Chesapeake-Leopard* Affair enraged the country. Jefferson remarked that he had not seen so belligerent a spirit in America since 1775.

The Embargo Act of 1807

Yet while making some preparations for war, the president sought peace, first by conducting fruitless negotiations with Britain to gain redress for the *Chesapeake* outrage, and second by steering the Embargo Act through Congress in December 1807. By far the most controversial

Boarding and Taking of the American Ship *Chesapeake*
The loss of the frigate *Chesapeake* to HMS *Leopard* in 1807 and the dying words of its commander, James Lawrence, inspired the motto "Don't Give Up the Ship," which was emblazoned on the battle flag of Captain Oliver Hazard Perry.

legislation of either of Jefferson's administrations, the **Embargo Act of 1807** prohibited vessels from leaving American ports for foreign ports. Technically, it prohibited only exports, but its practical effect was to stop imports as well, for few foreign ships would venture into American ports if they had to leave without cargo. Amazed by the boldness of the act, a British newspaper described the embargo as "little short of an absolute secession from the rest of the civilized world."

Jefferson advocated the embargo as a means of "peaceable coercion." By restricting French and especially British trade with the United States, he hoped to pressure both nations into respecting American neutrality. But the embargo did not have the intended effect. Although British sales to the United States dropped 50 percent between 1807 and 1808, the British quickly found new markets in South America, where rebellions against Spanish rule had flared up, and in Spain itself, where a revolt against Napoleon had opened trade to British shipping. Furthermore, the Embargo Act contained some loopholes. For example, it allowed American ships blown off course to put in at European ports if necessary; suddenly, many captains were reporting that adverse winds had forced them across the Atlantic. Treating the embargo as a joke, Napoleon seized any American ships he could lay hands on and then informed the United States that he was only helping to enforce the embargo. The British were less amused, but the embargo confirmed their view that Jefferson was an ineffectual philosopher, an impotent challenger compared with Napoleon.

The harshest effects of the embargo were felt not in Europe but in the United States. Some thirty thousand American seamen found themselves out of work. Hundreds of merchants went into bankruptcy, and jails swelled with debtors. A New York City newspaper noted that the only activity still flourishing in the city was prosecution for debt. Farmers were devastated. Unable to export their produce or sell it at a decent price to hard-pressed urban dwellers, many farmers could not pay their debts. In desperation, one farmer in Schoharie County, New York, sold his cattle, horses, and farm implements, worth eight hundred dollars before the embargo, for fifty-five dollars. Speculators who had purchased land, expecting to sell it later at a higher price, also took a beating because cash-starved farmers stopped buying land. "I live and that is all," wrote one New York speculator. "I am doing no business, cannot sell anybody property, nor collect any money."

The embargo fell hardest on New England and particularly on Massachusetts, which in 1807 had twice the ship tonnage per capita of any other state and more than a third of the entire nation's ship tonnage in foreign trade. For a state so dependent on foreign trade, the embargo was a calamity. Wits reversed the letters of embargo to form the phrase "O grab me."

The situation was not entirely bleak. The embargo forced a diversion of merchants' capital into manufacturing. In short, unable to export produce, Americans began to make products. Before 1808, the United States had only fifteen mills for fashioning cotton into textiles; by the end of 1809, an additional eighty-seven mills had been constructed (see Chapter 9). But none of this comforted merchants already ruined or mariners driven to soup kitchens. Nor could New Englanders forget that the source of their misery was a policy initiated by one of the "Virginia lordlings," "Mad Tom" Jefferson, who knew little about New England and who had a dogmatic loathing of cities, the very foundations of New England's prosperity. A Massachusetts poet wrote,

Our ships all in motion once whitened the ocean,
They sailed and returned with a cargo;
Now doomed to decay they have fallen a prey
To Jefferson, worms, and embargo.

James Madison and the Failure of Peaceable Coercion

Even before the Embargo Act, Jefferson had announced that he would not be a candidate for reelection. With his blessing, the Republican congressional caucus nominated **James Madison** and George Clinton for the presidency and vice presidency. The Federalists countered with Charles C. Pinckney and Rufus King, the same ticket that had made a negligible showing in 1804. In 1808, the Federalists staged a modest comeback, gaining twenty-four congressional seats. Still, Madison won 122 of 175 electoral votes for president, and the Republicans retained control of Congress.

The Federalist revival, modest as it was, rested on two factors. First, the Embargo Act gave the party the national issue it long had lacked. Second, younger Federalists had abandoned their elders' gentlemanly disdain for campaigning and deliberately imitated vote-winning techniques such as barbecues and mass meetings that had worked for the Republicans.

To some contemporaries, "Little Jemmy" Madison, five feet, four inches tall, seemed a weak and shadowy figure compared to the commanding presence of Jefferson. But in fact, Madison brought to the presidency an intelligence and a capacity for systematic thought that matched Jefferson's. He had the added advantage of being married to Dolley Madison. A striking figure in her turbans and colorful dresses, Dolley arranged Wednesday night receptions at the White House in which she charmed Republicans, and even some Federalists, into sympathy with her husband's policies.

Like Jefferson, Madison believed that American liberty had to rest on the virtue of the people, which he saw as being critically tied to the growth and prosperity of agriculture. More clearly than Jefferson, Madison also recognized that agricultural prosperity depended on trade—farmers needed markets. In particular, the British West Indies, dependent on the United States for much of their lumber and grain, struck Madison as a natural trading partner. Britain alone could not fully supply the West Indies. Therefore, if the United States embargoed its own trade with the West Indies, Madison reasoned, the British, who imported sugar from the West Indies, would be forced to their knees before Americans could suffer severe losses from the embargo. Britain, he wrote, was "more vulnerable in her commerce than in her armies."

The American embargo, however, was coercing no one. Increased trade between Canada and the West Indies made a shambles of Madison's plan to pressure Britain. On March 1, 1809, Congress replaced the Embargo Act with the weaker, face-saving Non-Intercourse Act. The act opened trade to all nations except Britain and France and then authorized Congress to restore trade with those nations if they stopped violating neutral rights. But neither complied. In May 1810, Congress substituted a new measure, Macon's Bill No. 2, for the Non-Intercourse Act. This legislation opened trade with Britain and France, and then offered each a clumsy bribe: if either nation repealed its restrictions on neutral shipping, the United States would halt trade with the other.

None of these steps had the desired effect. While Jefferson and Madison lashed out at France and Britain as moral demons ("The one is a den of robbers and the other of pirates," snapped Jefferson), the belligerents saw the world as composed of a few great powers and many weak ones. When great powers went to war, there were no neutrals. Weak nations like the United States should logically seek the protection of a great power and stop babbling about moral ideals and neutral rights. Despite occasional hints to the contrary, neither Napoleon nor the British intended to accommodate the Americans.

As peaceable coercion became a fiasco, Madison came under fire from militant Republicans, known as **war hawks**, who demanded more aggressive policies. Coming mainly from the South and West, regions where "honor" was a sacred word, the militants were infuriated by insults to the American flag. In addition, economic recession between 1808 and 1810 had convinced the firebrands that British policies were wrecking their regions' economies. The election of 1810 brought several war hawks to Congress. Led by thirty-four-year-old Henry Clay of Kentucky, who preferred war to the "putrescent pool of ignominious peace," the war hawks included John C. Calhoun of South Carolina, Richard M. Johnson of Kentucky, and William King of North Carolina, all future vice presidents. Clay was elected Speaker of the House.

Tecumseh and the Prophet

Voicing a more emotional and pugnacious nationalism than Jefferson and Madison, the war hawks called for the expulsion of the British from Canada and the Spanish from the Floridas. Their demands merged with western settlers' fears that the British in Canada were actively recruiting the Indians to halt the march of American settlement. In reality, American policy, not meddling by the British, was the source of bloodshed on the frontier.

In contrast to his views about blacks, Jefferson believed that Indians and whites could live peacefully together if the Indians abandoned their hunting and nomadic ways and took up farming. If they farmed, they would need less land. Jefferson and Madison insisted that the Indians be compensated fairly for ceded land and that only those Indians with a claim to the land they were ceding be allowed to conclude treaties with whites. Reality conflicted with Jefferson's ideals (see Chapter 7). The march of white settlement was steadily shrinking Indian hunting grounds, while some Indians themselves were becoming more willing to sign away land in payment to whites for blankets, guns, and the liquor that transported them into a daze even as their culture collapsed.

In 1809, no American was more eager to acquire Indian lands than William Henry Harrison, the governor of the Indiana Territory. The federal government had just divided Indiana, splitting off the present states of Illinois and Wisconsin into a separate Illinois Territory. Harrison recognized that, shorn of Illinois, Indiana would not achieve statehood unless it could attract more settlers and that the territory would not gain such settlers without offering them land currently owned by Indians. Disregarding instructions from Washington to negotiate only with Indians who claimed the land they were ceding, Harrison rounded up a delegation of half-starved Indians, none of whom lived on the rich lands along the Wabash River that he craved. By the Treaty of Fort Wayne in September 1809, these Indians ceded millions of acres along the Wabash at a price of two cents an acre.

This treaty outraged the numerous tribes that had not been party to it, and no one more than **Tecumseh**, the Shawnee chief, and his brother, Lalawéthica. Late in 1805 Lalawéthica had had a spiritual experience after a frightening dream in which he saw Indians who drank or beat their wives tormented for eternity. Until then, the Shawnees had looked down on Lalawéthica as a

Tecumseh and William Henry Harrison at Vincennes, August 1810 This portrait of a personal duel between Tecumseh and Indiana governor William Henry Harrison is fanciful. But the confrontation between the two at Vincennes nearly erupted into violence. Tecumseh told Harrison that Indians could never trust whites because "when Jesus Christ came upon the earth you kill'd him and nail'd him on a cross."

drunken misfit, a pale reflection of his handsome brother, Tecumseh. Overnight, Lalawéthica changed. He gave up liquor and began tearful preaching to surrounding tribes to return to their old ways and to avoid contact with whites. He quickly became known as the Prophet. Soon, he would take a new name, **Tenskwatawa**, styling himself the "Open Door" through which all Indians could revitalize their culture. Demoralized by the continuing loss of Native American lands to the whites and by the ravages of their society by alcoholism, Shawnees listened to his message. Meanwhile, Tecumseh sought to unite several tribes in Ohio and the Indiana Territory against American settlers.

The Treaty of Fort Wayne infuriated Tecumseh, who insisted that Indian lands belonged collectively to all the tribes and hence could not be sold by needy splinter groups. He held a conference with Harrison that nearly erupted into violence and that led Harrison to conclude that it was time to attack the Indians. His target was a Shawnee encampment called Prophetstown near the mouth of the Tippecanoe River. With Tecumseh away recruiting southern Indians to his cause, Tenskwatawa ordered an attack on Harrison's encampment, a mile from Prophetstown, in the predawn hours of November 7, 1811. Outnumbered two to one and short of ammunition, Tenskwatawa's force was beaten off after inflicting heavy casualties.

Although it was a small engagement, the Battle of Tippecanoe had several large effects. It made Harrison a national hero, and the memory of the battle would contribute to his election as president three decades later. It discredited Tenskwatawa, whose conduct during the battle drew criticism from his followers. It elevated Tecumseh into a position of recognized leadership among the western tribes. Finally, it persuaded Tecumseh, who long had distrusted the British as much as the Americans, that alliance with the British was the only hope to stop the spread of American settlement.

Congress Votes for War

By spring 1812, President Madison had reached the decision that war with Britain was inevitable. On June 1, he sent his war message to Congress. Meanwhile, an economic depression struck Britain, partly because the American policy of restricting trade with that country had finally started to work. Under pressure from its merchants, Britain suspended the Orders in Council on June 23. But Congress had already passed the declaration of war. Further, Britain's suspension was contingent on France's conduct toward neutrals and failed to meet Madison's demand that Britain unilaterally pledge to respect the rights of neutrals.

Neither war hawks nor westerners held the key to the vote in favor of war. The war hawks comprised a minority within the Republican Party; the West was still too sparsely settled to have many representatives in Congress. Rather, the votes of Republicans in populous states like Pennsylvania, Maryland, and Virginia were the main force propelling the war declaration through

Congress. Opposition to war came mostly from Federalist strongholds in Massachusetts, Connecticut, and New York. Because Federalists were so much stronger in the Northeast than elsewhere, congressional opposition to war revealed a sectional as well as a party split. In general, however, southern Federalists opposed the war declaration, and northern Republicans supported it. In other words, the vote for war followed party lines more closely than sectional lines. Much like James Madison himself, the typical Republican advocate of war had not wanted war in 1810, or even in 1811, but had been led by the accumulation of grievances to demand it in 1812.

In his war message, Madison had listed impressment, the continued presence of British ships in American waters, and British violations of neutral rights as grievances that justified war. None of these complaints were new. Taken together, they do not fully explain why Americans went to war in 1812 rather than earlier—for example, in 1807 after the *Chesapeake-Leopard* Affair. Madison also listed British incitement of the Indians as a stimulus for war. This grievance of recent origin contributed to war feeling in the West. But the West had too few American inhabitants to drive the nation into war. A more important underlying cause was the economic recession that affected the South and West after 1808, as well as the conviction, held by John C. Calhoun and others, that British policy was damaging America's economy.

Finally, the fact that Madison rather than Jefferson was president in 1812 was of major importance. Jefferson had believed that the only motive behind British seizures of American ships was Britain's desire to block American trade with Napoleon. Hence Jefferson had concluded that time was on America's side; the seizures would stop as soon as the war in Europe ceased. In contrast, Madison had become persuaded that Britain's real motive was to strangle American trade once and for all and thereby eliminate the United States as a trading rival. War or no war in Europe, Madison saw Britain as a menace to America. In his war message, he stated flatly that Britain was meddling with American trade not because that trade interfered with Britain's "belligerent rights" but because it "frustrated the monopoly which she covets for her own commerce and navigation."

The War of 1812

Maritime issues had dominated Madison's war message, but the United States lacked a navy strong enough to challenge Britain at sea. American cruisers, notably the *Constitution*, would win a few sensational duels with British warships, but the Americans would prove unable to prevent the British from clamping a naval blockade on the American coast. Canada, which Madison viewed as a key prop of the British Empire, became the principal target. With their vastly larger population and resources, few Americans expected a long or difficult struggle. To Jefferson, the conquest of Canada seemed "a mere matter of marching."

Little justified this optimism. Although many Canadians were immigrants from the United States, to the Americans' surprise they fought to repel the invaders. Many of the best British troops were in Europe fighting Napoleon, but the British in Canada had an invaluable ally in the Indians, who struck fear by dangling scalps from their belts. The British played on this fear, in some cases forcing Americans to surrender by hinting that the Indians might be uncontrollable in battle. Too, the American state militias were filled with Sunday soldiers who "hollered for water half the time, and whiskey the other." Few militiamen understood the goals of the war. In fact, outside Congress there was not much blood lust in 1812. Opposition to the war ran strong in New England; and even in Kentucky, the home of war hawk Henry Clay, only four hundred answered the first call to arms. For many Americans, local attachments were still stronger than national ones.

On to Canada

From the summer of 1812 to the spring of 1814, the Americans launched a series of unsuccessful attacks on Canada (see Map 8.2). In July 1812, General William Hull led an American army from Detroit into Canada, quickly returned when Tecumseh cut his supply line, and surrendered Detroit and two thousand men to thirteen hundred British and Indian troops. In the fall of 1812, a force of American regulars was crushed by the British at the Battle of Queenston, near Niagara Falls, while New York militiamen, contending that they had volunteered only to protect their homes and not to invade Canada, looked on from the New York side of the border. A third American offensive in 1812, a projected attack on Montreal from Plattsburgh, New York, via Lake Champlain, fell apart when the militia again refused to advance into Canada.

The Americans renewed their offensive in 1813 when General William Henry Harrison tried to retake Detroit. A succession of reverses convinced Harrison that offensive operations were futile as long as the British controlled Lake Erie. During the winter of 1812–1813, Captain Oliver H. Perry constructed a little fleet of vessels; on September 10, 1813, he destroyed a British squadron at Put-in-Bay on the western end of the lake. "We have met the enemy, and they are ours," Perry triumphantly reported. Losing control of Lake Erie, the British pulled back from Detroit, but Harrison overtook

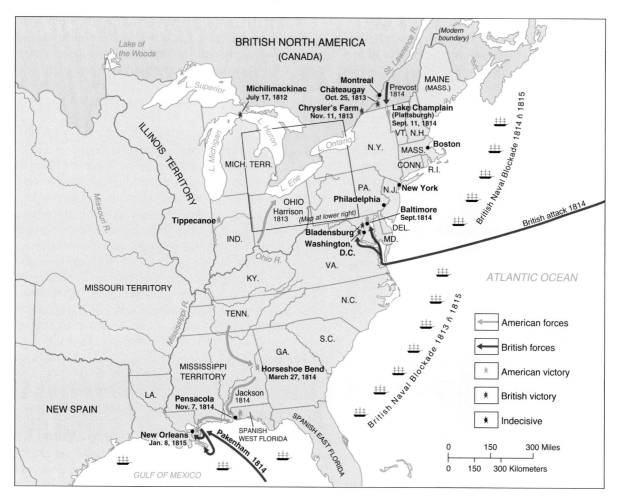

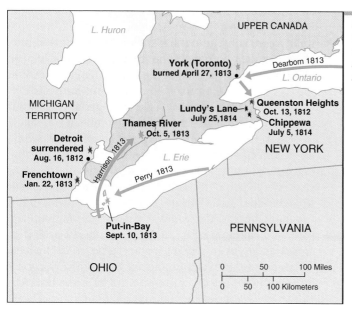

Map 8.2 Major Battles of the War of 1812
Most of the war's major engagements occurred on or near the northern frontier of the United States; but the Royal Navy blockaded the entire Atlantic coast, and the British army penetrated as far south as Washington and New Orleans.

and defeated a combined British and Indian force at the Battle of the Thames on October 5. Tecumseh died in the battle; Colonel Richard Johnson's claim, never proved, to have killed Tecumseh later contributed to Johnson's election as vice president. These victories by Perry and Harrison cheered Americans, but efforts to invade Canada continued to falter. In June 1814, American troops crossed into Canada on the Niagara front but withdrew after fighting two bloody but inconclusive battles at Chippewa (July 5) and Lundy's Lane (July 25).

The British Offensive

With fresh reinforcements from Europe, where Napoleon had abdicated as emperor after his disastrous invasion of Russia, the British took the offensive in the summer of 1814. General Sir George Prevost led a force of ten thousand British veterans in an offensive meant to split the New England states, where opposition to the war was strong, from the rest of the country. The British advanced down Lake Champlain until meeting the well-entrenched American forces at Plattsburgh. After his fleet met defeat on September 11, Prevost abandoned the campaign.

Dolley Madison by Gilbert Stuart, 1804
As the attractive young wife of Secretary of State James Madison, Dolley Madison acted virtually as the nation's First Lady during the administration of Jefferson, a widower. Friendly, tactful, and blessed with an unfailing memory for names and events, she added to her reputation as an elegant hostess after her husband became president.

Ironically, the British achieved a far more spectacular success in an operation originally designed as a diversion from their main thrust down Lake Champlain. In 1814, a British army sailed from Bermuda for Chesapeake Bay, landed near Washington, and met a larger American force, composed mainly of militia, at Bladensburg, Maryland, on August 24. The Battle of Bladensburg quickly became the "Bladensburg races" as the American militia fled, almost without firing a shot. The British then descended on Washington. Madison, who had witnessed the Bladensburg fiasco, escaped into the Virginia hills. His wife, Dolley, pausing only long enough to load her silver, a bed, and a portrait of George Washington onto her carriage, hastened to join her husband, while British troops ate the supper prepared for the Madisons at the presidential mansion. Then they burned the mansion and other public buildings in Washington. A few weeks later, the British attacked Baltimore, but after failing to crack its defenses, they broke off the operation.

The Treaty of Ghent, 1814

In August 1814, negotiations to end the war commenced between British and American commissioners at Ghent, Belgium. Initially, the British demanded territorial concessions from the United States. News of the American naval victory at Plattsburgh and Prevost's retreat to Canada, however, brought home to the British the fact that after two years of fighting, they controlled neither the Great Lakes nor Lake Champlain. Similarly, the spectacular raid on Washington had no strategic significance, so the British gave way on the issue of territorial concessions.

The final **Treaty of Ghent**, signed on Christmas Eve 1814, restored the *status quo ante bellum* (the state of things before the war); the United States neither gained nor lost territory. Several additional issues, including fixing a boundary between the United States and Canada, were referred to joint commissions for future settlement. Nothing was done about impressment, but the end of the war in Europe made neutral rights a dead issue.

Ironically, the most dramatic American victory of the war came after the conclusion of the peace negotiations. In December 1814, a British army, composed of veterans of the Napoleonic Wars and commanded by General Sir Edward Pakenham, descended on New Orleans. On January 8, 1815, two weeks after the signing of the Treaty of Ghent but before word reached America, Pakenham's force attacked an American army under General **Andrew** ("Old Hickory") **Jackson**. Although a legend for his ferocity as an Indian fighter, Jackson inspired little fear among the British, who advanced into the Battle of New Orleans far too confidently, but he did strike enough terror in his own men to prevent another American rout. In

Washingtonians Fleeing the City as the British Invade on August 24, 1814 As the British approached Washington, Margaret Bayard Smith wrote, "a universal confidence reign'd among our citizens. Few doubted our conquering." When American resistance crumbled, she was stunned. After viewing the blackened ruins of the Capitol and the president's mansion, she concluded that Americans must "learn the dreadful[,] horrid trade of war."

an hour of gruesome carnage, Jackson's troops shredded the line of advancing redcoats, killing Pakenham and inflicting more than two thousand casualties while losing only thirteen Americans.

The Hartford Convention

Because the Treaty of Ghent had already concluded the war, the Battle of New Orleans had little significance for diplomats. Indirectly, however, it had an effect on domestic politics by eroding Federalist strength.

The Federalist comeback in the election of 1808 had continued into the 1812 campaign. Buoyed by hostility to the war in the Northeast, the Federalists had thrown their support to DeWitt Clinton, an antiwar Republican. Although Madison won the electoral vote 128 to 89, Clinton carried all of New England except Vermont, as well as New York and New Jersey. American military setbacks in the war intensified Federalist disdain for the Madison administration. Federalists saw a nation misruled for over a decade by Republican bunglers. Jefferson's attack on the judiciary had seemed to threaten the rule of law. His purchase of Louisiana, a measure of doubtful constitutionality, had enhanced Republican

strength and reduced the relative importance of Federalist New England in the Union. The Embargo Act had severely damaged New England's commerce. Now "Mr. Madison's War" was bringing fresh misery to New England in the form of the British blockade. A few Federalists began to talk of New England's secession from the Union. Most, however, rejected the idea, believing that they would soon benefit from popular exhaustion with the war and spring back into power.

In late 1814, a Federalist convention met in Hartford, Connecticut. Although some advocates of secession were present, moderates took control and passed a series of resolutions summarizing New England's grievances. At the root of these grievances lay the belief that New Englanders were becoming a permanent minority in a nation dominated by southern Republicans who failed to understand New England's commercial interests. The convention proposed to amend the Constitution to abolish the three-fifths clause (which gave the South a disproportionate share of votes in Congress by allowing it to count slaves as a basis of representation), to require a two-thirds vote of Congress to declare war and admit new states into the Union, to limit the president to a single term, to prohibit the election of two successive presidents from the same state, and to bar embargoes lasting more than sixty days.

The timing of these proposals was disastrous for the Federalists. News of the Treaty of Ghent and Jackson's victory at New Orleans dashed the Federalists' hopes of gaining broad popular support. The goal of the Hartford Convention had been to assert states' rights rather than disunion, but to many the proceedings smelled of a traitorous plot. The restoration of peace, moreover, stripped the Federalists of the primary grievance that had fueled the convention. In the election of 1816, Republican James Monroe, Madison's hand-picked successor and a fellow Virginian, swept the nation over negligible Federalist opposition. He would win reelection in 1820 with only a single dissenting electoral vote. As a force in national politics, the Federalists were finished.

The Awakening of American Nationalism

The United States emerged from the War of 1812 bruised but intact. In its first major war since the Revolution, the Republic had demonstrated not only that it could fight on even terms against a major power but also that republics could fight wars without turning to despotism. The war produced more than its share of symbols of American nationalism. Whitewash cleared the smoke damage to the presidential mansion; thereafter, it became known as the White House. The British attack on Fort McHenry, guarding Baltimore, prompted a young observer, Francis Scott Key, to compose "The Star-Spangled Banner."

The Battle of New Orleans boosted Andrew Jackson onto the stage of national politics and became a source of legends about American military prowess. It appears to most contemporary scholars that the British lost because Pakenham's men, advancing within range of Jackson's riflemen and cannon, unaccountably paused and became sitting ducks. But in the wake of the battle, Americans spun a different tale. The legend arose that Jackson owed his victory not to Pakenham's blundering tactics but to hawk-eyed Kentucky frontiersmen whose rifles picked off the British with unerring accuracy. In fact, many frontiersmen in Jackson's army had not carried rifles; even if they had, gunpowder smoke would have obscured the enemy. But none of this mattered at the time. Just as Americans preferred militia to professional soldiers, they chose to believe that their greatest victory of the war had been the handiwork of amateurs.

Two Ottawa Chiefs
These two Ottawa chiefs proudly wear the medals bestowed on them by the British. Expecting British support for their land claims at the war's end, they instead were abandoned by the British.

Madison's Nationalism and the Era of Good Feelings, 1817–1824

The War of 1812 had three major political consequences. First, it eliminated the Federalists as a national political force. Second, it went a long way toward convincing the Republicans that the nation was strong and resilient, capable of fighting a war while maintaining the liberty of its people. Third, with the Federalists tainted by suspicion of disloyalty and no longer a force, and with fears about the fragility of republics fading, Republicans increasingly embraced doctrines long associated with the Federalists.

In a message to Congress in December 1815, Madison called for federal support for internal improvements such as roads and canals, tariff protection for the new industries that had sprung up during the embargo, and the creation of a new national bank. (The charter of the first Bank of the United States had expired in 1811.) In Congress, another Republican, Henry Clay of Kentucky, proposed similar measures, which he called the American System, with the aim of making the young nation economically self-sufficient and free from dependence on Europe. In 1816, Congress chartered the Second Bank of the United States and enacted a moderate tariff. Federal support for internal improvements proved to be a thornier problem. Madison favored federal aid in principle but believed that a constitutional amendment was necessary to authorize it. Accordingly, just before leaving office in 1817, he vetoed an internal-improvements bill.

As Republicans adopted positions that they had once disdained, an "**Era of Good Feelings**" dawned on American politics. A Boston newspaper, impressed by the warm reception accorded President James Monroe while touring New England, coined the phrase in 1817. It has stuck as a description of Monroe's two administrations from 1817 to 1825. Compared with Jefferson and Madison, Monroe was not brilliant, polished, or wealthy, but he keenly desired to heal the political divisions that a stronger intellect and personality might have inflamed. The phrase "Era of Good Feelings" reflects not only the war's elimination of some divisive issues but also Monroe's conscious effort to avoid political controversies.

But the good feelings were paper-thin. Madison's 1817 veto of the internal-improvements bill revealed the persistence of disagreements about the role of the federal government under the Constitution. Furthermore, the continuation of slavery was arousing sectional animosities that a journalist's phrase about good feelings could not dispel. Not surprisingly, the postwar consensus began to unravel almost as soon as Americans recognized its existence.

John Marshall and the Supreme Court

In 1819, Jefferson's old antagonist John Marshall, who was still chief justice, issued two opinions that stunned Republicans. The first case, *Dartmouth College* v. *Woodward,* centered on the question of whether New Hampshire could transform a private corporation, Dartmouth College, into a state university. Marshall concluded that the college's original charter, granted to its trustees by George III in 1769, was a contract. Since the Constitution specifically forbade states to interfere with contracts, New Hampshire's effort to turn Dartmouth into a state university was unconstitutional. The implications of Marshall's ruling were far-reaching. Charters or acts of incorporation provided their beneficiaries with various legal privileges and were sought by businesses as well as by colleges. In effect, Marshall said that once a state had chartered a college or a business, it surrendered both its power to alter the charter and, in large measure, its authority to regulate the beneficiary.

A few weeks later, the chief justice handed down an even more momentous decision in **McCulloch v. Maryland**. The issue here was whether the state of Maryland had the power to tax a national corporation, specifically the Baltimore branch of the Second Bank of the United States. Although the bank was a national corporation chartered by Congress, most of the stockholders were private citizens who reaped the profits the bank made. Speaking for a unanimous Court, Marshall ignored these private features of the bank and concentrated instead on two issues. First, did Congress have the power to charter a national bank? Nothing in the Constitution, Marshall conceded, explicitly granted this power. But the broad sweep of enumerated powers, he reasoned, implied the power to charter a bank. Marshall was clearly engaging in a broad, or "loose," rather than strict, construction (interpretation) of the Constitution. The second issue was whether a state could tax an agency of the federal government that lay within its borders. Marshall argued that any power of the national government, enumerated or implied, was supreme within its sphere. States could not interfere with the exercise of federal powers. A tax by Maryland on the Baltimore branch was such an interference. Since "the power to tax involves the power to destroy," Maryland's tax was plainly unconstitutional.

Marshall's decision in the *McCulloch* case dismayed many Republicans. Although Madison and Monroe had supported the establishment of the Second Bank of the United States, the bank had made itself unpopular by tightening its loan policies during the summer of 1818. This contraction of credit triggered the Panic of 1819, a severe depression that gave rise to considerable distress

John Marshall
In his first three decades as chief justice of
the Supreme Court, Marshall greatly
strengthened the power of the Court and
the national government, each of which he
thought vital to preserving the intrinsic
rights of life, liberty, and property.

throughout the country, especially among western farmers. At a time when the bank was widely blamed for the
panic, Marshall's ruling stirred controversy by placing the
bank beyond the regulatory power of any state government. His decision, indeed, was as much an attack on
state sovereignty as it was a defense of the bank. The
Constitution, Marshall argued, was the creation not of
state governments but of the people of all the states, and
thus was more fundamental than state laws. His reasoning assailed the Republican theory, best expressed in the
Virginia and Kentucky Resolutions of 1798–1799 (see
Chapter 7), that the Union was essentially a compact
among states. Republicans had continued to view state
governments as more immediately responsive to the
people's will than the federal government, and they regarded the compact theory of the Union as a guarantor of
popular liberty. As Republicans saw it, Marshall's *McCulloch* decision, along with his decision in the *Dartmouth
College* case, stripped state governments of the power to
impose the will of their people on corporations.

The Missouri Compromise, 1820–1821

The fragility of the Era of Good Feelings became even
more apparent in the two-year-long controversy over
statehood for Missouri. Carved from the Louisiana Purchase, Missouri attracted slaveholders. In 1819, when the

House of Representatives was considering a bill to admit
Missouri as a state, 16 percent of the territory's inhabitants were slaves. Then a New York Republican offered an
amendment that prohibited the further introduction of
slaves and provided for the emancipation, at age twenty-
five, of all slave offspring born after Missouri's admission
as a state. Following rancorous debate, the House accepted the amendment, and the Senate rejected it. Both
chambers voted along sectional lines.

Prior to 1819, slavery had not been the primary source
of the nation's sectional divisions. For example, Federalists' opposition to the embargo and the War of 1812 had
sprung from their fear that the dominant Republicans
were sacrificing New England's commercial interests to
those of the South and West—not from hostility to slavery. The Missouri question, which Jefferson compared to
"a fire bell in the night, [which] awakened me and filled
me with terror," now thrust slavery into the center of
long-standing sectional divisions.

The slavery issue surfaced at this time for several reasons. In 1819, the Union had eleven free and eleven slave
states. The admission of Missouri as a slave state would
upset this balance to the advantage of the South. Equally
important, northerners worried that admitting Missouri as
a slave state would set a precedent for the extension of slavery into the northern part of the Purchase. The slave states
of Alabama, Mississippi, and Louisiana, all carved from the
Purchase before 1819 with little controversy, were south of
Missouri, which was on the same latitude as the free states
of Ohio, Indiana, and Illinois. Finally, the disintegration of
the Federalists as a national force reduced the need for
unity among Republicans, and they increasingly heeded
sectional pressures more than calls for party loyalty.

Virtually every issue that was to wrack the Union during the next forty years was present in the controversy
over Missouri: southern charges that the North was conspiring to destroy the Union and end slavery; accusations
by northerners that southerners were conspiring to extend the institution. Southerners openly proclaimed that
antislavery northerners were kindling fires that only "seas
of blood" could extinguish. Such threats of civil war persuaded some northern congressmen who had originally
supported the restriction of slavery in Missouri to back
down. A series of congressional agreements known collectively as the **Missouri Compromise** resolved the crisis.

To balance the number of free and slave states,
Congress in 1820 admitted Maine as a free state and
Missouri as a slave state; to forestall a further crisis,
it also prohibited slavery in the remainder of the
Louisiana Purchase north of 36°30′—the southern
boundary of Missouri (see Map 8.3). But compromise

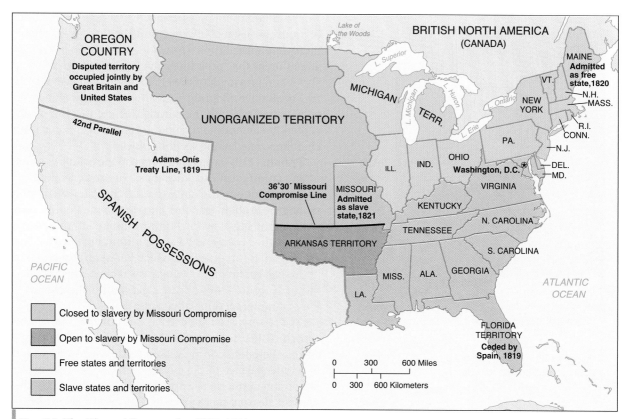

Map 8.3 The Missouri Compromise, 1820–1821
The Missouri Compromise temporarily quelled controversy over slavery by admitting Maine as a free state and Missouri as a slave state, and by prohibiting slavery in the remainder of the Louisiana Purchase north of 36°30′.

did not come easily. The individual components of the eventual compromise passed by close and ominously sectional votes.

No sooner had the compromise been forged than it nearly fell apart. As a prelude to statehood, Missourians drafted a constitution that prohibited free blacks, whom some eastern states viewed as citizens, from entering their territory. This provision clashed with the federal Constitution's provision that citizens of one state were entitled to the same rights as citizens of other states. Balking at Missourians' exclusion of free blacks, antislavery northerners barred Missouri's admission into the Union until 1821, when Henry Clay engineered a new agreement. This second Missouri Compromise prohibited Missouri from discriminating against citizens of other states but left open the issue of whether free blacks were citizens.

The Missouri Compromise was widely viewed as a southern victory. The South had gained admission of Missouri, whose acceptance of slavery was controversial, while the North had merely gained Maine, whose rejection of slavery inspired no controversy. Yet the South had conceded to freedom a vast block of territory north of 36°30′.

Although much of this territory was unorganized Indian country that some viewed as unfit for white habitation, the states of Iowa, Minnesota, Wisconsin, the Dakotas, Nebraska, and Kansas eventually would be formed out of it. Also, the Missouri Compromise reinforced the principle, originally set down by the Northwest Ordinance of 1787, that Congress had the right to prohibit slavery in some territories. Southerners had implicitly accepted the argument that slaves were not like other forms of property that could be moved from place to place at will.

Foreign Policy Under Monroe

American foreign policy between 1816 and 1824 reflected more consensus than conflict. The end of the Napoleonic Wars and the signing of the Treaty of Ghent had removed most of the foreign-policy disagreements between Federalists and Republicans. Moreover, Monroe was fortunate to have as his secretary of state an extraordinary diplomat, **John Quincy Adams**. The son of the last Federalist president, Adams had been the only Federalist in the Senate to support the Louisiana Purchase, and he later became an ardent Republican. An austere and scholarly man whose library equaled his house in monetary value, Adams was a tough negotiator and a fervent nationalist.

As secretary of state, Adams moved quickly to strengthen the peace with Great Britain. During his tenure, the United States and Britain signed the Rush-Bagot Treaty of 1817, which effectively demilitarized the Great Lakes by severely restricting the number of ships that the two powers could maintain there. Next the British-American Convention of 1818 restored to Americans the same fishing rights off Newfoundland that they had enjoyed before the War of 1812 and fixed the boundary between the United States and Canada from the Lake of the Woods west to the Rockies. Beyond the Rockies, the vast country known as Oregon was declared "free and open" to both American and British citizens. As a result of these two agreements, the United States had a secure border with British-controlled Canada for the first time since independence, and a claim to the Pacific.

The nation now turned its attention to dealing with Spain, which still owned East Florida and claimed West Florida. No one was certain whether the Louisiana Purchase included West Florida. Acting as if it did, the United States in 1812 had simply added a slice of West Florida to the state of Louisiana and another slice to the Mississippi Territory. Using the pretext that it was a base for Seminole Indian raids and a refuge for fugitive slaves, Andrew Jackson, now the military commander in the South, invaded East Florida in 1818. He hanged two British subjects and captured Spanish forts. Jackson had acted without explicit orders, but Adams supported the raid, guessing correctly that it would panic the Spanish into further concessions.

In 1819, Spain agreed to the **Adams-Onís (Transcontinental) Treaty**. By its terms, Spain ceded East Florida to the United States, renounced its claims to West Florida, and agreed to a southern border of the United States west of the Mississippi that ran north along the Sabine River (separating Texas from Louisiana) and then westward along the Red and Arkansas Rivers to the Rocky Mountains, finally following the forty-second parallel to the Pacific (see Map 8.3). In effect, the United States conceded that Texas was not part of the Louisiana Purchase, while Spain agreed to a northern limit to its claims to the West Coast. It thereby left the United States free to pursue its interests in Oregon.

The Monroe Doctrine, 1823

John Quincy Adams had long believed that God and nature had ordained that the United States would eventually span the entire continent of North America. Throughout his negotiations leading up to the Adams-Onís Treaty, he made it clear to Spain that, if the Spanish did not concede some of their territory in North America, the United States might seize all of it, including Texas and even Mexico. Americans were fast acquiring a reputation as an aggressive people. Yet Spain was concerned with larger issues than American encroachment. Its primary objective was to suppress the revolutions against Spanish rule that had broken out in South America. To accomplish this goal, Spain sought support from the European monarchs who had organized the Holy Alliance in 1815. The brainchild of the tsar of Russia, the Holy Alliance aimed to quash revolutions everywhere in the name of Christian and monarchist principles. By 1822, its members talked of helping Spain suppress the South American revolutions. But Britain, whose trading interests in South America were hampered by Spanish restrictions, refused to join the Holy Alliance. British foreign minister George Canning proposed that the United States and Britain issue a joint statement opposing any European interference in South America, while pledging that neither would annex any part of Spain's old empire in the New World.

While sharing Canning's opposition to European intervention in the New World, Adams preferred that the United States make a declaration of policy on its own rather than "come in as a cock-boat in the wake of the British man-of-war." Adams flatly rejected Canning's insistence on a joint Anglo-American pledge never to annex any part of Spain's former territories, for Adams wanted the freedom to annex Texas or Cuba, should their inhabitants one day "solicit a union with us."

This was the background of the **Monroe Doctrine**, as President Monroe's message to Congress on December 2, 1823, later came to be called. The message, written largely by Adams, announced three key principles: that unless American interests were involved, U.S. policy was to abstain from European wars; that the "American continents" were not "subjects for future colonization by any European power"; and that the United States would construe any attempt at European colonization in the New World as an "unfriendly act."

Europeans widely derided the Monroe Doctrine as an empty pronouncement. Fear of the British navy, not the Monroe Doctrine, prevented the Holy Alliance from intervening in South America. With hindsight, however, the Europeans might have taken the doctrine more seriously, for it had important implications. First, by pledging itself not to interfere in European wars, the United States was excluding the possibility that it would support revolutionary movements in Europe. For example, Adams opposed U.S. recognition of Greek patriots fighting for independence from the Ottoman Turks. Second, by keeping open its options to annex territory in the Americas, the United States was using the Monroe Doctrine to claim a preeminent position in the New World.

Chronology, 1801–1824

1801	Thomas Jefferson's inauguration.
1802	Repeal of the Judiciary Act of 1801. Yazoo land compromise.
1803	*Marbury* v. *Madison*. Conclusion of the Louisiana Purchase.
1804	Impeachment of Justice Samuel Chase. Aaron Burr kills Alexander Hamilton in a duel. Jefferson elected to a second term.
1804–1806	Lewis and Clark expedition.
1805	British court declares the broken voyage illegal.
1807	*Chesapeake* Affair. Embargo Act passed.
1808	James Madison elected president.
1809	Non-Intercourse Act passed. Embargo Act repealed.
1810	Macon's Bill No. 2.
1811	Battle of Tippecanoe.
1812	United States declares war on Britain. Madison reelected to a second term.

	General William Hull surrenders at Detroit. Battle of Queenston.
1813	Battle of the Thames.
1814	British burn Washington, D.C. Hartford Convention. Treaty of Ghent signed.
1815	Battle of New Orleans.
1816	James Monroe elected president. Second Bank of the United States chartered.
1817	Rush-Bagot Treaty.
1818	British-American Convention of 1818 sets U.S.-Canada border in West. Andrew Jackson invades East Florida.
1819	Adams-Onís (Transcontinental) Treaty. *Dartmouth College* v. *Woodward*. *McCulloch* v. *Maryland*.
1820	Monroe elected to a second term.
1820–1821	Missouri Compromise.
1823	Monroe Doctrine.

Conclusion

Jefferson's philosophy left a strong imprint on his age. Seeking to make the federal government more responsive to the people's will, Jefferson moved quickly to slash public expenditures and to contest Federalist control of the judiciary. His purchase of the Louisiana Territory in 1803 reflected his view that American liberty depended on the perpetuation of agriculture, and it would bring new states, dominated by Republicans, into the Union. As the Federalist Party waned, Jefferson had to face down challenges from within his own party, notably from the mischief of Aaron Burr and from die-hard old Republicans like John Randolph, who charged that Jefferson was abandoning pure Republican doctrines.

Key Terms

John Marshall
Marbury v. *Madison*
Louisiana Purchase
Lewis and Clark expedition
Sacajawea
impressment
Embargo Act of 1807
James Madison
war hawks
Tecumseh

Tenskwatawa
Treaty of Ghent
Andrew Jackson
Era of Good Feelings
McCulloch v. *Maryland*
Missouri Compromise
John Quincy Adams
Adams-Onís (Transcontinental) Treaty
Monroe Doctrine

The outbreak of war between Napoleon's France and Britain, and the threat it posed to American neutrality, preoccupied Jefferson's second term and both terms of his successor, James Madison. The failure of the embargo and peaceable coercion to force Europeans to respect American neutrality led the United States into war with Britain in 1812. The war destroyed the Federalists, who committed political suicide at the Hartford Convention. It also led Madison to jettison part of Jefferson's legacy by calling for a new national bank, federal support for internal improvements, and protective tariffs. The Transcontinental Treaty of 1819 and the Monroe Doctrine's bold pronouncement that European powers must not meddle in the affairs of the Western Hemisphere expressed America's increasingly assertive nationalism.

Conflict was never far below the surface of the apparent consensus of the Era of Good Feelings. In the absence of Federalist opposition, Republicans began to fragment into sectional factions, most notably in the conflict over Missouri's admission to the Union as a slave state.

For Further Reference

Catherine Allgor, *Parlor Politics* (2000). An innovative account of the influence of women in Washington's politics.

Stephen Ambrose, *Undaunted Courage* (1997). Fine study of the Lewis and Clark expedition.

Joseph J. Ellis, *American Sphinx: The Character of Thomas Jefferson* (1997). A prize-winning attempt to unravel Jefferson's complex character.

Jon Kukla, *A Wilderness So Immense: The Louisiana Purchase and the Destiny of America* (2003). The story of the Purchase told on a grand scale.

Drew R. McCoy, *The Last of the Fathers: James Madison and the Republican Legacy* (1989). The best recent book on Madison.

James Ronda, *Lewis and Clark Among the Indians* (1984). A splendid account of Lewis and Clark's negotiations with different tribes.

J. C. A. Stagg, *Mr. Madison's War: Politics, Diplomacy and Warfare in the Early Republic* (1983). An important reinterpretation of the causes of the War of 1812.

G. Edward White, *The Marshall Court and Cultural Change, 1815–1835* (1991). A seminal reinterpretation of the Supreme Court under John Marshall.

Chapter 9

Middlesex Company Woolen Mills, Lowell, Massachusetts, About 1840
By 1840 the earliest "mill villages" with their pastoral settings and reliance on waterpower were giving way to textile mills like these, which occupied large buildings and, as the smokestack indicates, were relying on steam power.

The Transformation of American Society, 1815–1840

Alexis de Tocqueville

In December 1831 two young French aristocrats, **Alexis de Tocqueville** and Gustave de Beaumont, arrived in the small town of Memphis, Tennessee, after a harrowing journey from Cincinnati. They had planned to take a steamboat down the Ohio and Mississippi Rivers to New Orleans, but the early freezing of the Ohio had necessitated an overland trip through Kentucky and Tennessee to reach the Mississippi. Now they were exhausted and, worse, faced the prospect of spending the winter in Memphis.

On Christmas Day, they saw a puff of smoke on the river, the sign of an approaching steamboat. Unfortunately, the steamboat was bound for Louisville, the wrong direction. The young Frenchmen sought to persuade the captain that ice had made an upriver passage impossible and that the only sensible course was to turn around and head south. The steamboat's passengers pleaded with the captain to keep going north. The captain hesitated.

A large group of Choctaw Indians supervised by a federal agent was gathering on the river's bank. Evicted from their homes in Georgia and Alabama, the Choctaws were being resettled on reservations west of the Mississippi. The federal agent accompanying them offered cash to the captain to head south. The captain turned the boat, discharged his passengers, who were forced to wait in Memphis for a thaw, and took on Tocqueville, Beaumont, and the Choctaws.

Before coming to America, Tocqueville and Beaumont had read James Fenimore Cooper's *The Last of the Mohicans*. These dispirited Choctaws were nothing like the proud Indians of Cooper's fiction. "In this whole scene," Tocqueville wrote, "there was an air of ruin and destruction, something which betrayed a final and irrevocable adieu; one couldn't watch without feeling one's heart wrung." Unlike the Spanish, he wrote, the Americans did not massacre the Indians; instead white Americans believed that "whenever a square mile could nourish ten times as many civilized men as savages," the "savages would have to move away."

The two Frenchmen had arrived in the United States seven months earlier with the stated purpose of reporting on American prisons to the French government, but with the real intent of learning more about the sprawling American republic. Tocqueville eventually would weave his impressions of this "half-civilized, half-wild" nation into his two-volume masterpiece, *Democracy in America* (1835, 1840), still considered the most insightful analysis of the American character by a foreigner. From the start, Tocqueville had been struck by the "restless temper" of the Americans, who appeared to live in the middle of "an always moving stream."

Tocqueville came at a time when everything seemed to be changing: where Americans lived, how they worked, and how they related to each other. Improvements in transportation in the form of new roads, canals, and steamboats were stimulating interregional trade and migration to the trans-Appalachian West, encouraging an unprecedented development of towns and cities, and transforming social relationships. Increasingly, farmers raised crops for sale in distant markets rather than merely for their families' consumption. The new urban dwellers formed a market not only for farm products but also for those of new factories springing up in the industrializing East.

To Tocqueville, Americans seemed to have just one goal: "that of getting rich." In some respects, he admired this attitude. White Americans were an industrious and democratic people with little tolerance for restraints based on tradition or privilege. Yet whites treated nonwhites harshly. In Baltimore, an amazed Beaumont described how, when a black man entered a race track along with whites, "one of them gave him a volley of blows with his cane without this deed appearing to surprise either the crowd or the negro himself." Both Frenchmen recognized slavery as a great blot on the American character. Still, whites treated each other as equals. Indeed, they all seemed alike to Tocqueville, animated by the same passion for getting ahead.

Focus Questions

- What caused the upsurge of westward migration after the War of 1812?

- How did the rise of the market economy affect where Americans lived and how they made their living?

- What caused the rise of industrialization?

- What caused urban poverty in this period?

- How did the rise of the market economy and industrialization influence relationships within families and communities?

Westward Expansion

In 1790 the vast majority of the non-Indian population of the United States, nearly 4 million people, lived east of the Appalachian Mountains and within a few hundred miles of the Atlantic Ocean. But by 1840 one-third of the non-Indian population of just over 17 million were living between the Appalachians and the Mississippi River, the area that Americans of the time referred to as the West but that historians call the **Old Northwest** and **Old Southwest**. Migrants brought traditional values and customs with them, but in adapting to the West they gradually developed new values and customs. In short, they became westerners, men and women with a distinctive culture.

Only a few Americans moved west to seek adventure, and these few usually headed into the half-known region west of the Rocky Mountains, the present Far West. Most migrants desired and expected a better version of the life they had known in the East: more land and more bountiful crops. Several factors nurtured this expectation: the growing power of the federal government; its often ruthless removal of the Indians from the path of white settlement; and a boom in the prices of agricultural commodities after the War of 1812.

The Sweep West

Americans moved west in a series of bursts. Americans leapfrogged the Appalachians after 1791 to bring four new states into the Union by 1803: Vermont, Kentucky, Tennessee, and Ohio. The second burst occurred between 1816 and 1821, when six states entered the Union: Indiana, Mississippi, Illinois, Alabama, Maine, and Missouri.

Even as Indiana and Illinois were gaining statehood, settlers were pouring farther west into Michigan. Ohio's population jumped from 45,000 in 1800 to 581,000 by 1820 and 1,519,000 by 1840; Michigan's from 5,000 in 1810 to 212,000 by 1840.

Seeking security, pioneers usually migrated as families rather than as individuals. To reach markets with their produce, most settlers clustered near the navigable rivers of the West, especially the magnificent water system created by the Ohio and Mississippi Rivers. Only with the spread of canals in the 1820s and 1830s, and later of railroads, did westerners feel free to venture far from rivers. In addition, westerners often clustered with people who hailed from the same region back east. For instance, in 1836 a group of farmers from nearby towns met at Castleton, Vermont, listened to a minister intone from the Bible, "And Moses sent them to spy out the land of Canaan," and soon established the town of Vermontville in Michigan. Other migrants to the West were less organized than these latter-day descendants of the Puritans, but most hoped to settle among familiar faces in the West. When they found that southerners already were well entrenched in Indiana, for example, New Englanders tended to prefer Michigan.

Western Society and Customs

Most westerners craved sociability. Even before towns sprang up, rural families joined with their neighbors in group sports and festivities. Men met for games that, with a few exceptions like marbles (popular among all ages), were tests of strength or agility. These included wrestling, weightlifting, pole jumping (for distance rather than height), and a variant of the modern hammer toss. Some of these games were brutal. In gander pulling, horseback riders competed to pull the head off a male duck whose neck had been stripped of feathers and greased. Women usually combined work and play in quilting and sewing parties, carpet tackings, and even chicken and goose pluckings. Social activities brought the genders together. Group corn huskings usually ended with dances; and in a variety of "hoedowns" and "frolics," even westerners who in principle might disapprove of dancing promenaded to singing and a fiddler's tune.

Within western families, there was usually a clear division of labor between men and women. Men performed most of the heaviest labor such as cutting down trees and plowing fields. Women usually rose first in the morning because they were responsible for milking the

Border Settlers in Ohio Around 1840
Before settlers could farm, they had to construct dwellings and clear the land of trees. Large families like this one, in which children and adults alike were expected to work, were an advantage.

cows and preparing breakfast. As they had always done, women fashioned the coverlets that warmed beds in un-heated rooms, and spun yarn and wove the fabrics to make their family's shirts, coats, pants, and dresses. Farmwomen often helped butcher hogs. They knew that the best way to bleed a hog was to slit its throat while it was still alive, and after the bleeding, they were adept at scooping out the innards, washing the heart and liver, and hanging them to dry. There was nothing dainty about the work of pioneer women.

Most western sports and customs had been trans-planted from the East, but the West developed a character of its own. Before 1840, few westerners could afford ele-gant living. Arriving on the Michigan frontier from New York City in 1835, the well-bred Caroline Kirkland quickly discovered that her neighbors thought that they had a right to borrow anything she owned with no more than a blunt declaration that "you've got plenty." "For my own part," Caroline related, "I have lent my broom, my thread, my tape, my spoons, my cat, my thimble, my scissors, my shawl, my shoes, and have been asked for my comb and brushes." Their relative lack of refinement made western-ers easy targets for easterners' contemptuous jibes.

Criticisms of westerners as yokels provoked western-ers to assert that they lived in a land of honest democracy and that the East was soft and decadent. This exchange of insults fostered a regional identity among westerners that further shaped their behavior. Priding themselves on their simple manners, some westerners were intolerant of other westerners who had pretensions to gentility. On one occasion, a traveler who hung up a blanket in a tav-ern to shield his bed from public gaze had it promptly ripped down. On another, a woman who improvised a screen behind which to retire in a crowded room was dis-missed as "stuck up." A politician who rode to a public meeting in a buggy instead of on horseback lost votes.

The Far West

The great majority of pioneers sought stability and pros-perity in the area between the Appalachians and the Mississippi River, the region today known as the Mid-west. By contrast, an adventuring spirit carried a few Americans far beyond the Mississippi. On an exploring expedition in the Southwest in 1806, Zebulon Pike sighted the Colorado peak that was later named after him. The Lewis and Clark expedition whetted interest in the Far West. In 1811, a New York merchant, John Jacob Astor, founded the fur-trading post of Astoria at the mouth of the Columbia River in the Oregon Country. In the 1820s and 1830s, fur traders also operated along the Missouri River from St. Louis to the Rocky Mountains

and beyond. At first, whites relied on Native Americans to bring them furs, but during the 1820s white trappers or "mountain men"—among them, Kit Carson, Jedediah Smith, and the mulatto Jim Beckwourth—gathered furs on their own while performing astounding feats of sur-vival in harsh surroundings.

Jedediah Smith was representative of these men. Born in the Susquehanna Valley of New York in 1799, Smith moved west with his family to Pennsylvania and Illinois and signed on with an expedition bound for the upper Missouri River in 1822. In the course of this and subsequent explorations, he was almost killed by a griz-zly bear in the Black Hills of South Dakota, learned from the Native Americans to trap beaver and kill buffalo, crossed the Mojave Desert into California, explored California's San Joaquin Valley, and hiked back across the Sierras and the primeval Great Basin to the Great Salt Lake, a trip so forbidding that even Native Americans avoided it. The exploits of Smith and the other mountain men were popularized in biographies, and they became legends in their own day.

The Federal Government and the West

Of the various causes of expansion to the Mississippi from 1790 to 1840, the one that operated most generally and uniformly throughout the period was the growing strength of the federal government. Even before the Con-stitution's ratification, several states had ceded their west-ern land claims to the national government, thereby creating the bountiful public domain. The Land Ordi-nance of 1785 had provided for the survey and sale of these lands, and the Northwest Ordinance of 1787 had established procedures for transforming them into states. The Louisiana Purchase of 1803 brought the en-tire Mississippi River under American control, and the Transcontinental Treaty of 1819 wiped out the last ves-tiges of Spanish power east of the Mississippi.

The federal government directly stimulated settle-ment of the West by promising land to men who enlisted during the War of 1812. With 6 million acres allotted to these so-called military bounties, many former soldiers and their families pulled up roots and settled in the West. To facilitate westward migration, Congress author-ized funds in 1816 for the extension of the National Road, a highway begun in 1811 that reached Wheeling, Virginia, on the Ohio River in 1818 and Vandalia, Illinois, by 1838. Soon settlers thronged the road. "Old America seems to be breaking up," a traveler on the National Road wrote in 1817. "We are seldom out of sight, as we travel on this grand track towards the Ohio, of family groups before and behind us."

The same government strength that aided whites brought misery to the Indians. Virtually all the foreign-policy successes during the Jefferson, Madison, and Monroe administrations worked to Native Americans' disadvantage. The Louisiana Purchase and the Transcontinental Treaty stripped them of Spanish protection. In the wake of the Louisiana Purchase, Lewis and Clark bluntly told the Indians that they must "shut their ears to the counsels of bad birds" and listen henceforth only to the "Great Father" in Washington. The outcome of the War of 1812 also worked against the Native Americans; indeed, the Indians were the only real losers of the war. Early in the negotiations leading to the Treaty of Ghent, the British had insisted on the creation of an Indian buffer state between the United States and Canada in the Old Northwest. But after the American victory at the Battle of Plattsburgh, the British dropped the demand and essentially abandoned the Indians to the Americans.

The Removal of the Indians

Westward-moving white settlers found sizable numbers of Native Americans in their paths, particularly in the South, home to the so-called **Five Civilized Tribes**: the Cherokees, Choctaws, Creeks, Chickasaws, and Seminoles. Years of commercial dealings and intermarriage with whites had created in these tribes, especially the Cherokees, an influential minority of mixed-bloods who embraced Christianity, practiced agriculture, built gristmills, and even owned slaves. One of their chiefs, Sequoyah, devised a written form of their language; other Cherokees published a bilingual newspaper, the *Cherokee Phoenix.*

The "civilization" of the southern Indians impressed New England missionaries more than southern whites, who viewed the Civilized Tribes with contempt and their land with envy. Presidents James Monroe and John Quincy Adams had concluded several treaties with Indian tribes providing for their voluntary removal to public lands west of the Mississippi River. Although some assimilated mixed-bloods sold their tribal lands to the government, other mixed-bloods resisted because their prosperity depended on trade with close-by whites. In addition, full-bloods, the majority even in the "civilized" tribes, clung to their land and customs. They wanted to remain near the burial grounds of their ancestors and condemned mixed-bloods who bartered away tribal lands to whites. When the Creek mixed-blood chief William McIntosh sold all Creek lands in Georgia and two-thirds of Creek lands in Alabama to the government in the Treaty of Indian Springs (1825), a Creek tribal council executed him.

During the 1820s, whites in Alabama, Georgia, and Mississippi intensified pressure on the Indians by surveying tribal lands and squatting on them. Southern legislatures, loath to restrain white settlers, passed laws that threatened to expropriate Indian lands unless the Indians moved west. Other laws extended state jurisdiction over the tribes (which effectively outlawed tribal government) and declared that no Indian could be a witness in a court case involving whites (which made it difficult for Indians to collect debts owed them by whites).

These measures delighted President Andrew Jackson. Reared on the frontier and sharing its contempt for Indians, Jackson believed that it was ridiculous to treat the Indians as independent nations; rather, they should be subject to the laws of the states where they lived. This position spelled doom for the Indians, who could not vote or hold state office. In 1834, Cherokee chief John

Political Cartoon of Jackson and Native Americans
This cartoon, which depicts Native Americans as children or dolls subject to father Andrew Jackson, was intended as a satire on Jackson's policy of forcibly removing the Indians to reservations. The painting in the upper right corner pointedly depicts the goddess Liberty trampling a tyrant.

Ross got a taste of what state jurisdiction meant; Georgia, without consulting him, put his house up as a prize in the state lottery.

In 1830, Jackson secured passage of the **Indian Removal Act**, which authorized him to exchange public lands in the West for Indian territories in the East and appropriated $500,000 to cover the expenses of removal. But the real costs of removal, human and monetary, were vastly greater. During Jackson's eight years in office, the federal government forced Indians to exchange 100 million acres of their lands for 32 million acres of public lands. In the late 1820s and early 1830s the Choctaws (whom Tocqueville had observed near Memphis), Creeks, and Chickasaws started their "voluntary" removal to the West. In 1836, Creeks who clung to their homes were forcibly removed, many in chains. Most Seminoles were removed from Florida, but only after a bitter war between 1835 and 1842 that cost the federal government $20 million.

Ironically, the Cherokees, whose leaders were the most accommodating to American political institutions, suffered the worst fate. In 1827, the Cherokees proclaimed themselves an independent republic within Georgia. When the Georgia legislature subsequently extended the state's jurisdiction over this "nation," the Cherokees petitioned the U.S. Supreme Court for an injunction to halt Georgia's action. In the case of *Cherokee Nation* v. *Georgia* (1831), Chief Justice John Marshall denied the Cherokees' claim to status as a republic within Georgia; rather, they were a "domestic dependent nation," a kind of ward of the United States. Marshall added that prolonged occupancy had given the Cherokees a claim to their lands within Georgia. A year later, he clarified the Cherokees' legal position in *Worcester* v. *Georgia* by holding that they were a "distinct" political community entitled to federal protection from tampering by Georgia.

Reportedly sneering, "John Marshall has made his decision; now let him enforce it," President Jackson ignored it. Next, federal agents persuaded some minor Cherokee chiefs to sign the Treaty of New Echota (1835), which ceded all Cherokee lands in the United States for $5.6 million and free passage west. Congress ratified this treaty (by one vote), but the vast majority of Cherokees denounced it. In 1839, a Cherokee party took revenge by murdering its three principal signers, including a former editor of the *Cherokee Phoenix*.

The end of the story was simple and tragic. In 1838 the Cherokees were forcibly removed to the new Indian Territory in what is now Oklahoma. They traveled west along what became known as the "**Trail of Tears**" (see Map 9.1). As a youth, a man who later became a colonel in the Confederate Army had participated in the forced removal of some sixteen thousand Cherokees from their lands east of the Mississippi River, where North Carolina, Georgia, Alabama, and Tennessee more or less converge. He recollected: "I fought through the civil war and have seen men shot to pieces and slaughtered by the thousands, but the Cherokees removal was the cruelest work I ever knew." Perhaps as many as eight thousand Cherokees, more than one-third of the entire nation, died during and just after the removal.

Indians living in the Northwest Territory fared no better. A series of treaties extinguished their land titles, and most moved west of the Mississippi. The removal of the northwestern Indians was notable for two uprisings. The first, led by Red Bird, a Winnebago chief, began in 1827 but was quickly crushed. The second, led by a Sac and Fox chief, Black Hawk, raged along the Illinois frontier until 1832, when federal troops and Illinois militia virtually annihilated Black Hawk's followers. Black Hawk's downfall persuaded the other Old Northwest tribes to cede their lands. Between 1832 and 1837, the United States acquired nearly 190 million acres of Indian land in the Northwest for $70 million in gifts and annual payments.

The Agricultural Boom

In pushing Indians from the paths of white settlers, the federal government was responding to whites' demands for more land. After the War of 1812, the rising prices of agricultural commodities such as wheat, corn, and cotton drew settlers westward in search of better farmland. Several factors accounted for the skyrocketing farm prices. During the Napoleonic Wars, the United States had quickly captured former British markets in the West Indies and former Spanish markets in South America. With the conclusion of the wars, American farmers found brisk demand for their wheat and corn in Britain and France, both exhausted by two decades of warfare. In addition, demand within the United States for western farm commodities intensified after 1815 as the quickening pace of industrialization and urbanization in the East spurred a shift of workers toward nonagricultural employment. Finally, the West's splendid river systems made it possible for farmers in Ohio to ship wheat and corn down the Ohio River to the Mississippi and down the Mississippi to New Orleans. There, wheat and corn were either sold or transshipped to the East, the West Indies, South America, or Europe. Just as government policies made farming in the West possible, high prices for foodstuffs made it attractive.

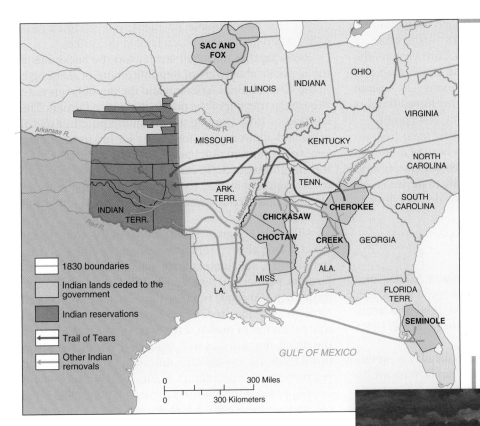

Map 9.1 The Removal of the Native Americans to the West, 1820–1840
The so-called Trail of Tears, followed by the Cherokees, was one of several routes along which various tribes migrated on their forced removal to reservations west of the Mississippi.

SAC AND FOX

OHIO

ILLINOIS   INDIANA

VIRGINIA

Arkansas R.   Missouri R.   Ohio R.

MISSOURI   KENTUCKY

NORTH CAROLINA

ARK. TERR.   TENN.

Tennessee R.

SOUTH CAROLINA

INDIAN TERR.   CHEROKEE

Red R.   Mississippi R.

CHICKASAW

CHOCTAW   CREEK   GEORGIA

1830 boundaries

Indian lands ceded to the government

ALA.

MISS.

LA.

FLORIDA TERR.

Indian reservations

Trail of Tears

SEMINOLE

Other Indian removals

GULF OF MEXICO

0 — 300 Miles
0 — 300 Kilometers

Trail of Tears, **by Robert Lindneux**

As the prospect of raising wheat and corn pulled farmers toward the Old Northwest, Eli Whitney's invention of the cotton gin in 1793 (see Chapter 7) cleared the path for settlement of the Old Southwest, particularly the states of Alabama and Mississippi. As cotton clothing came into fashion around 1815, the British textile industry provided seemingly bottomless demand for raw cotton. By 1820, Alabama and Mississippi were producing nearly half of the nation's cotton. With its warm climate, wet springs and summers, and relatively dry autumns, the Old Southwest was especially suited to cotton cultivation. The explosive thrust of small farmers and planters from the seaboard South into the Old Southwest resembled a gold rush. By 1817, "Alabama fever" gripped the South; settlers bid the price of good land up to thirty to fifty dollars an acre. Accounting for less than a quarter of all American exports between 1802 and 1807, cotton comprised just over half by 1830, and nearly two-thirds by 1836.

The Growth of the Market Economy

Many farmers traditionally had grown only enough food to feed their families (subsistence agriculture). With agricultural commodities like wheat and cotton commanding

high prices, a growing number of farmers added a cash crop (called commercial agriculture, or the **market economy**). In the South, slaves increasingly became a valuable commodity; the sale of slaves from declining agricultural states in the Southeast to planters and farmers migrating to Alabama and Mississippi grew into a huge business after 1815. "Virginia," an observer stated in 1832, "is, in fact, a *negro* raising State for other States; she produces enough for her own supply and six thousand a year for sale."

The unprecedented scale of commercial agriculture after 1815 exposed farmers to new risks. Farmers had no control over prices in distant markets. Furthermore, the often long interval between harvesting a cash crop and selling it forced farmers to borrow money to sustain their families. Thus the market economy forced farmers into short-term debt in the hope of long-term profit.

The debt was frequently worse than most had expected. Many western farmers had to borrow money to buy their land. The roots of this indebtedness for land lay in the federal government's inability to devise an effective policy for transferring the public domain directly into the hands of small farmers.

Federal Land Policy

Partisan and sectional pressures buffeted federal land policy like a kite in a March wind. The result was a succession of land laws passed between 1796 and 1820, each of which sought to undo the damage caused by its predecessors.

At the root of early federal land policy lay a preference for the orderly settlement of the public domain. To this end, the Ordinance of 1785 divided public lands into sections of 640 acres (see Chapter 6). The architects of the ordinance did not expect that ordinary farmers could afford such large lots; rather, they assumed that farmers who shared ties based on religion or region of origin would band together to purchase sections. This outcome would ensure that compatible settlers would live on adjoining lots in what amounted to rural neighborhoods, and it would make the task of government much easier than if settlers were to live in isolation on widely scattered homesteads.

Political developments in the 1790s undermined the expectations of the ordinance's framers. Because their political bases lay in the East, the Federalists were reluctant to encourage headlong settlement of the West, but at the same time they were eager to raise revenue for the federal government from land sales. They reconciled the goals of retarding actual settlement while gaining revenue by encouraging the sale of huge tracts of land to wealthy speculators who had no intention of farming the land themselves. The speculators held onto the land until its value rose and then sold off parcels to farmers. For example, in the 1790s the Holland Land Company, composed mainly of Dutch investors, bought up much of western New York and western Pennsylvania. A federal land law passed in 1796 reflected Federalist aims by maintaining the minimum purchase at 640 acres at a minimum price of two dollars an acre, and by allowing

only a year for complete payment. Few small farmers could afford to buy that much land at that price.

Believing that the small farmer was the backbone of the Republic and aware of Republican political strength in the West, Thomas Jefferson and the Republicans tried to ease the transfer of the public domain to farmers. The land law of 1800 dropped the minimum purchase to 320 acres and allowed up to four years for full payment but kept the minimum purchase price at $2 an acre. In 1804, the minimum purchase came down to 160 acres, in 1820 to 80 acres, and in 1832 to 40 acres. The minimum price also declined from $2 an acre in 1800 to $1.64 in 1804 and $1.25 in 1820.

Although Congress steadily liberalized land policy, speculators always remained one step ahead. Long before 1832, speculators were selling forty-acre lots to farmers. Farmers preferred small lots (and rarely bought more than 160 acres) because the farms they purchased typically were forested. A new landowner could clear no more than ten to twelve acres of trees a year. All land in the public domain was sold at auction, usually for much more than the two-dollar minimum. With agricultural prices soaring, speculators assumed that land would continue to rise in value and accordingly were willing to bid high on new land, which they resold to farmers at hefty prices.

After the War of 1812, speculators found it increasingly easy to borrow money. The chartering of the Second Bank of the United States in 1816 had the dual effect of increasing the amount of money in circulation and stimulating the chartering of private banks within individual states (state banks). The circulation of all banks grew from $45 million in bank notes in 1812 to $100 million in 1817. Many state banks were founded primarily to lend their directors money for land speculation. The result was an orgy of land speculation between 1815 and 1819. In 1819, the dollar value of sales of public land was over 1,000 percent greater than the average between 1800 and 1814.

The Speculator and the Squatter

Nevertheless, most of the public domain eventually found its way into the hands of small farmers. Because speculators gained nothing by holding land for prolonged periods, they were only too happy to sell it when the price was right. In addition, a familiar frontier type, the squatter, exerted a restraining influence on the speculator.

Even before the creation of the public domain, **squatters** had helped themselves to western land. George Washington himself had been unable to drive squatters off lands he owned in the West. Squatters were an independent and proud lot, scornful of their fellow citizens who were "softened by Ease, enervated by Affluence and Luxurious Plenty, & unaccustomed to Fatigues, Hardships, Difficulties or dangers." Disdaining land speculators above all, squatters formed claims associations to police land auctions and prevent speculators from bidding up the price of land. Squatters also pressured Congress to allow them preemption rights—that is, the right to purchase at the minimum price land that they had already settled on and improved. Seeking to undo the damaging effects of its own laws, Congress responded by passing special preemption laws for squatters in specific areas and finally, in 1841, acknowledged a general right of preemption.

Preemption laws were of no use to farmers who arrived after speculators had already bought up land. Having spent their small savings on livestock, seed, and tools, these settlers had to buy land from speculators on credit at interest rates that ranged as high as 40 percent. Many western farmers, drowning in debt, had to skimp on subsistence crops while expanding cash crops in the hope of paying off their creditors.

Countless farmers who had carried basically conservative expectations to the West quickly became economic adventurers. Forced to raise cash crops in a hurry, many worked their acreage to exhaustion and thus had to keep moving in search of new land. The phrase "the moving frontier" refers not only to the obvious fact that the line of settlement shifted farther west with each passing decade, but also to the fact that the same people kept moving. The experience of Abraham Lincoln's parents, who migrated from the East through several farms in Kentucky and then to Indiana, was representative of the westward trek.

The Panic of 1819

The land boom collapsed in the financial **Panic of 1819**. The state banks' loose practices contributed mightily to the panic. Like the Bank of the United States, these banks issued their own bank notes. A bank note was just a piece of paper with a printed promise from the bank's directors to pay the bearer ("redeem") a certain amount of specie (gold or silver coinage) on demand. State banks had long issued far more bank notes than they could redeem, and these notes had fueled the economic boom after 1815. With credit so readily available, farmers borrowed money to buy more land and to plant more crops, confident that they could repay their loans when they sold their crops. After 1817, however, the combination

of bumper crops in Europe and a recession in Britain trimmed foreign demand for U.S. wheat, flour, and cotton at the very time when American farmers were becoming more dependent on exports to pay their debts.

In the summer of 1818, reacting to the flood of state bank notes, the Bank of the United States began to insist that state banks redeem in specie their notes that were held by the Bank of the United States. Because the Bank of the United States had more branches than any state bank, notes of state banks were often presented by their holders to branches of the Bank of the United States for redemption. Whenever the Bank of the United States redeemed a state bank note in specie, it became a creditor of the state bank. To pay their debts to the Bank of the United States, the state banks had no choice but to force farmers and land speculators to repay loans. The result was a general curtailment of credit throughout the nation, particularly in the West.

The biggest losers were the land speculators. Land that had once sold for as much as sixty-nine dollars an acre dropped to two dollars an acre. Land prices fell because the credit squeeze drove down the market prices of staples like wheat, corn, cotton, and tobacco. Cotton, which sold for thirty-two cents a pound in 1818, sank as low as seventeen cents a pound in 1820. Since farmers could not get much cash for their crops, they could not pay the debts that they had incurred to buy land. Since speculators could not collect money owed them by farmers, the value of land that they still held for sale collapsed.

The Panic left a bitter taste about banks, particularly the Bank of the United States, which was widely blamed for the hard times. Further, plummeting prices for cash crops demonstrated how much farmers were coming to depend on distant markets. In effect, it took a severe business reversal to show farmers the extent to which they had become entrepreneurs. The fall in the prices of cash crops accelerated the search for better forms of transportation to reach faraway markets. If the cost of transporting crops could be cut, farmers could keep a larger share of the value of their crops and thereby adjust to falling prices.

The Transportation Revolution: Steamboats, Canals, and Railroads

The transportation system linking Americans in 1820 had severe weaknesses. The great rivers west of the Appalachians flowed north to south and hence could not by themselves connect western farmers to eastern markets. Roads were expensive to maintain, and horse-drawn wagons could carry only limited produce. Consequently, after 1820 attention and investment shifted to improving transportation on waterways, thus initiating the **transportation revolution**.

In 1807, Robert R. Livingston and Robert Fulton introduced the steamboat *Clermont* on the Hudson River. They soon gained a monopoly from the New York legislature to run a New York–New Jersey ferry service. Spectacular profits lured competitors, who secured a license from Congress and then filed suit to break the Livingston-Fulton monopoly. After a long court battle, the Supreme Court decided against the monopoly in 1824 in the famous case of ***Gibbons* v. *Ogden***. Speaking for a unanimous court, Chief Justice John Marshall ruled that Congress's constitutional power to regulate interstate commerce applied to navigation and thus had to prevail over New York's power to license the Livingston-Fulton monopoly. In the aftermath of this decision, other state-granted monopolies collapsed, and steamboat traffic increased rapidly. The number of steamboats operating on western rivers jumped from 17 in 1817 to 727 by 1855.

Steamboats assumed a vital role along the Mississippi–Ohio River system. They were vastly superior to keelboats (covered flatboats pushed by oars or poles). It took a keelboat three or four months to complete the 1,350-mile voyage from New Orleans to Louisville; in 1817 a steamboat could make the trip in twenty-five days. The development of long, shallow hulls permitted the navigation of the Mississippi-Ohio system even when hot, dry summers lowered the river level. Steamboats became more ornate as well as practical. To compete for passengers, they began to offer luxurious cabins and lounges, called saloons. The saloon of the *Eclipse,* a Mississippi River steamboat, was the length of a football field and featured skylights, chandeliers, a ceiling crisscrossed with Gothic arches, and velvet-upholstered mahogany furniture.

The Paddle Steamer *Ouishita* on the Red River in the Louisiana Territory, 1836
With its several smokestacks and enclosed deck, the *Ouishita* was typical of the second generation of steamboats. Large interior rooms made for a comfortable passage.

Once steamboats had demonstrated the feasibility of upriver navigation, the interest of farmers, merchants, and their elected representatives shifted away from turnpikes and toward canals. Although the cost of canal construction was mind-boggling—Jefferson dismissed the idea as little short of madness—canals offered the prospect of connecting the Mississippi–Ohio River system with the Great Lakes, and the Great Lakes with eastern markets.

Constructed between 1817 and 1825, New York's **Erie Canal**, connecting the Hudson River with Lake Erie, enabled produce from Ohio to reach New York City by a continuous stretch of waterways (see Map 9.2; also see Technology and Culture: Building the Erie Canal). Completion of the Erie Canal started a canal boom during the late 1820s and 1830s. Ohio constructed a network of canals that allowed its farmers to send their wheat by water to Lake Erie. After transport across Lake Erie, the wheat would be milled into flour in Rochester, New York, then shipped on the Erie Canal to Albany and down the Hudson River to New York City. Throughout the nation, canals reduced shipping costs from twenty to thirty cents a ton per mile in 1815 to two to three cents a ton per mile by 1830.

When another economic depression hit in the late 1830s, states found themselves overcommitted to costly canal projects and ultimately scrapped many. As the canal boom was ending, the railroad, an entirely new form of transportation, was being introduced. In 1825, the world's first commercial railroad began operation in England, and by 1840 some three thousand miles of track had been laid in America, about the same as the total canal mileage in 1840. During the 1830s, investment in American railroads exceeded that in canals. Cities like Baltimore and Boston, which lacked major inland waterway connections, turned to railroads to enlarge their share of the western market. The Baltimore and Ohio Railroad, chartered in 1828, took business away from the Chesapeake and Ohio Canal farther south. Blocked by the Berkshire Mountains from building a canal to the Erie, Massachusetts chartered the Boston and Worcester Railroad in 1831 and the Western Railroad (from Worcester to Albany) in 1833.

Cheaper to build, faster, and able to reach more places, railroads had obvious advantages over canals. But railroads' potential was only slowly realized. Most early railroads ran between cities in the East, rather than from east to west, and carried more passengers than freight. Not until 1849 did freight revenues exceed passenger revenues, and not until 1850 was the East Coast connected by rail to the Great Lakes.

Two factors explain the relatively slow spread of interregional railroads. First, unlike canals, which were built by state governments, most railroads were constructed by private corporations seeking quick profits. To minimize their original investment, railroad companies commonly resorted to cost-cutting measures such as covering wooden rails with iron bars. As a result, although relatively cheap to build, American railroads needed constant repairs. In contrast, although expensive to construct, canals needed relatively little maintenance and were kept in operation for decades after railroads appeared. Second, it remained much cheaper to ship bulky commodities such as iron ore, coal, and nonperishable agricultural produce by canal.

The Growth of the Cities

The transportation revolution speeded the growth of towns and cities. Canals and railroads vastly increased opportunities for city businesses: banks to lend money, insurers to cover risks of transport, warehouses and brokers to store and sell goods. In relative terms, the most rapid urbanization in American history occurred between 1820 and 1860. The Erie Canal turned New York City into the nation's largest city; its population rose from 124,000 in 1820 to 800,000 by 1860. An even more revealing change was the transformation of sleepy villages of a few hundred people into thriving towns of several thousand. For example, the Erie Canal turned Rochester, New York, from home to a few hundred villagers in 1817 into the Flour City with nine thousand residents by 1830.

City and town growth occurred with dramatic suddenness, especially in the West (see Map 9.3). Pittsburgh, Cincinnati, and St. Louis were little more than hamlets in 1800. The War of 1812 stimulated the growth of Pittsburgh, whose iron forges provided shot and weapons for American soldiers, and Cincinnati, which became a staging ground for attacks on the British in the Old Northwest. Meanwhile, St. Louis acquired some importance as a fur-trading center. Then, between 1815 and 1819, the agricultural boom and the introduction of the steamboat transformed all three places from outposts with transient populations of hunters, traders, and soldiers into bustling cities. Cincinnati's population nearly quadrupled between 1810 and 1820, then doubled in the 1820s.

With the exception of Lexington, Kentucky, whose lack of access to water forced it into relative stagnation after 1820, all the prominent western cities were river ports: Pittsburgh, Cincinnati, and Louisville on the Ohio; St. Louis

Building the Erie Canal

The building of canals was the most expensive, difficult, and dramatic feature of the transportation revolution upon which the market economy depended. Water highways that followed the lay of the land, crossing rivers and ascending hills, canals called forth stupendous feats of engineering and numbing labor. Parts of the Erie Canal ran through a virtual wilderness. Trees had to be felled, stumps uprooted, earth excavated to several feet of depth, and solid rock, two miles of it toward the western end of the Erie, blasted through. The builders were aided by a superior type of blasting powder manufactured in Delaware by a French immigrant, E. I. du Pont, and by a clever machine devised in 1819 by one of the canal workers that made it possible to pull down a tree, however tall, by running a cable secured to a screw and crank up the tree and then turning the crank till the tree dropped.

Like other canals, the Erie also required locks and aqueducts, arched causeways whose wooden troughs carried canal boats over natural bodies of water in the path of construction.

The Erie's eighty-three locks were watertight compartments that acted as steps to overcome natural rises and falls in the terrain. At Lockport, side-by-side locks carried traffic up a rise of seventy-three feet. The locks themselves were anywhere from ninety to one hundred feet high by fifteen to eighteen feet wide. Their sides were built of cut stone, with foot-thick timbers as floors and two layers of planks on top of the timber. Huge wooden lock gates were fitted with smaller gates (wickets) for releasing water from a lock while the main gates remained closed.

Although a few short canals had been constructed in the 1790s, nothing on the scale of the Erie had ever been attempted. France and Britain had several canals with locks and aqueducts, but European experience had not been written down, and, in any event, the techniques for building canals in Europe were of limited application to New York. The short canals of Europe relied more on stone than was feasible in New York, where wood was abundant and quarries distant from the canal site. Building a canal

Erie Canal, by John William Hill, 1831
Construction of the Erie Canal was a remarkable feat, all the more so because the United States did not possess a single school of engineering at the time. The project's heroes were lawyers and merchants who taught themselves engineering, and brawny workmen, often Irish immigrants, who hacked a waterway through the forests and valleys of New York.

363 miles long required thousands of workers, hundreds of supervisors, and several engineers. When construction of the Erie commenced in 1817, New York had no public work force, no employees who had ever supervised the building of even a short canal, and virtually no trained engineers. (Aside from the trickle of graduates of the military academy at West Point, the United States had no engineering students and no schools devoted to training them.) By occupation, the prominent engineers on the Erie were judges, merchants, and surveyors; none had formal training in engineering.

Building the canal required endless adaptations to circumstances. Since the state had no public work force, laborers, often Irish immigrants, were engaged and paid by private contractors, usually local artisans or farmers, each of whom contracted with the state to build up to a mile of the canal. Engineering problems were solved by trial and error. For example, one of the most difficult tasks in building the Erie was to find a way to seal its banks so that the earth would not absorb the four feet of water that marked the canal's depth and thus leave canal barges stranded on mud. In the 1790s an English immigrant had introduced Americans to a process called "puddling," forming a cement sealant out of soil or rock, but the Erie builders needed to find a form of soil or stone that would make a good sealant and also be abundant in New York. The very length of the canal ruled out transporting substances over long distances. After repeated experiments with different kinds of limestone, in 1818 canal engineer Canvass White discovered a type that, when heated to a high temperature, reduced to a powder and, when mixed with water and sand, became a cement with the great virtue of hardening under water. The Erie served as a great school of engineering, educating a generation of Americans in the principles and practices of canal building. After its completion, its "graduates" moved to other states to oversee the construction of new canals.

When the Erie Canal opened in 1825, it was not without defects. Its banks sometimes collapsed. Lines of barges piled up in front of each lock, creating colossal traffic jams. In December, the freezing of the Erie made it unusable until April. But the opening of the canal dazzled the imaginations of Americans. Not only had technology removed an obstacle placed by nature in the path of progress; it also conveyed small luxuries to unlikely places. Now farmers in the West marveled at the availability of oysters from Long Island.

Operation of a Canal Lock

Locks made it possible for canal traffic to follow the rises and falls of the land. To lower a boat, the lock was filled by opening the upper gates (shown on the right, already opened) and letting in water. After the water level had risen, the upper gates were closed, and the lower gates (shown here on the left, still closed) were opened to drain the lock and to allow the water to fall to the level of the canal below. Once the boat had dropped to the lower level, it proceeded on its way, pulled by the two mules shown on the boat's right. These steps were repeated in reverse to raise the boat.

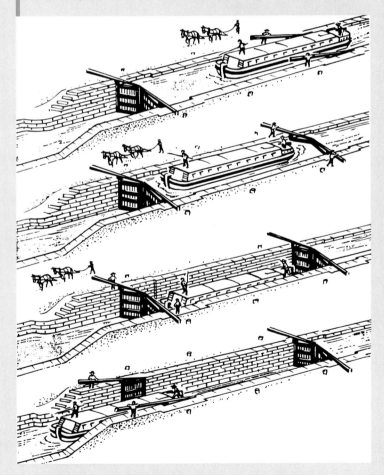

Question for Analysis

- Canals were hugely expensive to build, and railroads were just around the corner. Reviewing the material in this chapter and in Chapter 11, what do you see as the advantages and disadvantages of investment in canals?

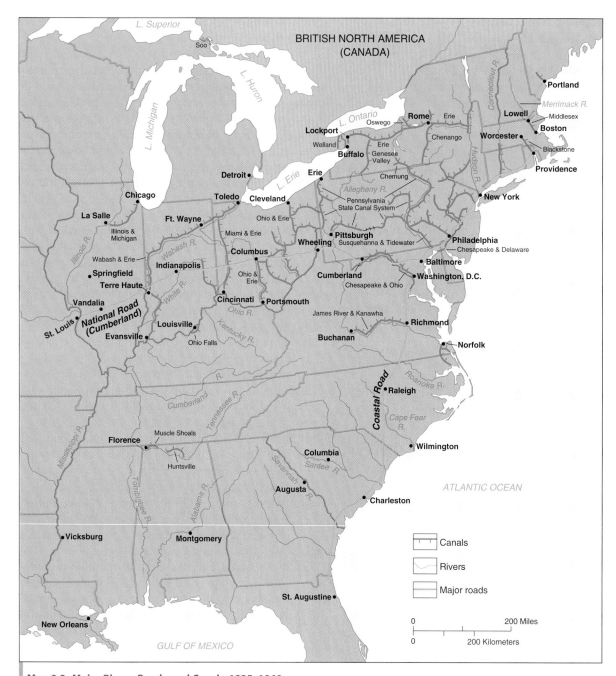

Map 9.2 Major Rivers, Roads, and Canals, 1825–1860
Railroads and canals increasingly tied the economy of the Midwest to that of the Northeast.

and New Orleans on the Mississippi (see Map 9.4). Except for Pittsburgh, all were essentially commercial hubs rather than manufacturing centers and were flooded by individuals eager to make money. In 1819, land speculators in St. Louis were bidding as much as a thousand dollars an acre for lots that had sold for thirty dollars an acre in

1815. Waterfronts endowed with natural beauty were swiftly overrun by stores and docks.

The transportation revolution acted like a fickle god, selecting some cities for growth while sentencing others to relative decline. Just as the steamboat had elevated the river cities over landlocked Lexington, the completion

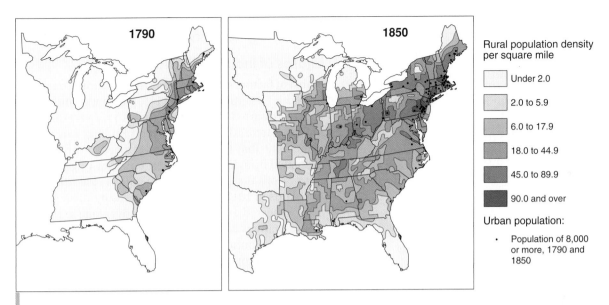

Map 9.3 Population Distribution, 1790 and 1850
By 1850, high population density characterized parts of the Midwest as well as the Northeast.
Source: 1900 Census of Population, Statistical Atlas, plates 2 and 8.

of the Erie Canal shifted the center of western economic activity toward the Great Lakes. The result was a gradual decline in the importance of river cities such as Cincinnati and Louisville and a rise in the importance of lake cities such as Buffalo, Cleveland, Detroit, Chicago, and Milwaukee. In 1830, nearly 75 percent of all western city-dwellers lived in the river ports of New Orleans, Louisville, Cincinnati, and Pittsburgh; by 1840 the proportion had dropped to 20 percent.

Industrial Beginnings

Spurred initially by the transportation revolution and the development of interregional trade, the growth of cities and towns received an added boost from the development of industrialization. The United States lagged a generation behind Britain in building factories. Eager to keep the lead, Britain banned the emigration of its skilled mechanics. Passing himself off as a farm laborer, one of these mechanics, Samuel Slater, came to the United States in 1789 and helped design and build the first cotton mill in the United States at Pawtucket, Rhode Island, the following year. The mill spun yarn by using Slater's adaptation of the spinning frame invented by the Englishman Richard Arkwright. Slater's work force quickly grew from nine to one hundred, and his mills multiplied. From these beginnings, the pace of industrialization

quickened in the 1810s and 1820s, especially in the production of cotton textiles and shoes.

Industrialization varied widely from region to region. There was very little in the South, whose economy was based on cash crops, especially cotton (see Chapter 12). Cold economic calculations led wealthy southerners to invest in land and slaves rather than machines. In contrast, New England's poor soil stimulated investment in factories instead of agriculture. Industrialization itself was a gradual process, with several distinct components. It always involved the subdivision of tasks, with each worker now fabricating only a part of the final product. Often, but not always, it led to the gathering of workers in large factories. Finally, high-speed machines replaced skilled handwork. In some industries, these elements arrived simultaneously, but more often their timing was spread out over several years.

Industrialization changed lives. Most workers in the early factories were recruited from farms. On farms, men and women had worked hard from sunrise to sunset, but they had set their own pace and taken breaks after completing tasks. Factory workers, operating machines that ran continuously, encountered the new discipline of industrial time, regulated by clocks rather than tasks and signaled by the ringing of bells. Industrialization also changed the lives of those outside of factories by encouraging specialization. During the colonial era, most farm families had made their own clothes and often their shoes.

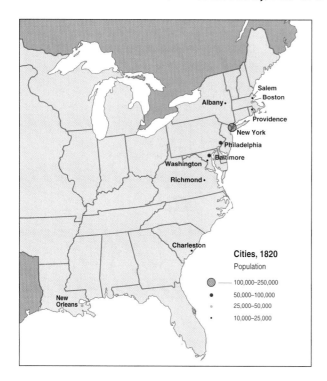

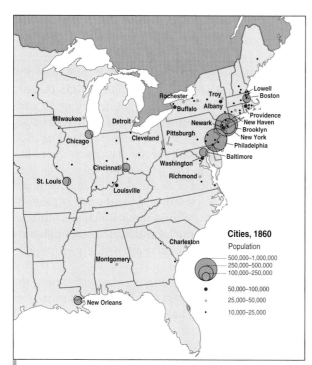

Map 9.4 American Cities, 1820 and 1860
In 1820, most cities were seaports. By 1860, however, cities dotted the nation's interior and included San Francisco on the West Coast. This change occurred in large measure because of the transportation revolution.
Source: Statistical Abstract of the United States.

With industrialization, they concentrated on farming, while purchasing factory-made clothes and shoes.

Causes of Industrialization

A host of factors stimulated industrialization. Some were political. The Embargo Act of 1807 persuaded merchants who were barred from foreign trade to redirect their capital into factories. The Era of Good Feelings saw general agreement that the United States needed tariffs. Once protected from foreign competition, New England's output of cloth that was spun from cotton rose from 4 million yards in 1817 to 323 million yards by 1840. America also possessed an environmental advantage in the form of the many cascading rivers that flowed from the Appalachian Mountains to the Atlantic Ocean and that provided abundant waterpower for mills. The transportation revolution also played a key role by bringing eastern manufacturers closer to markets in the South and West.

Industrialization also sprang from tensions in the rural economy, especially in New England, where in the late eighteenth century population grew beyond the available land to support it. Farm families adopted new strategies to survive. For example, a farmer would decide to grow flax, which his wife and daughters would make into linen for sale; or he would choose to plant broomcorn (used for making broom whisks), and he and his sons would spend the winter months making brooms for local sale. In time, he would form a partnership with other broom makers to manufacture brooms on a larger scale and for more-distant markets. At some point, he would cease to be a farmer; instead, he would purchase his broomcorn from farmers and, with hired help, concentrate on manufacturing brooms. By now, his contacts with merchants, who would provide him with broom handles and twine and who would purchase and sell all the brooms he could make, had become extensive.

In contrast to broom making, some industries, like textiles, depended on new technologies. Although Britain had a head start in developing the technology relevant to industrialization, Americans had a strong incentive to close the gap. With a larger population and far less land, Britain contained a class of landless laborers who would work cheaply in factories. In contrast, the comparatively high wages paid unskilled laborers in the United States spurred the search for labor-saving machines. In some instances, Americans simply copied British designs. Ostensibly on vacation, a wealthy Boston merchant, Francis Cabot Lowell, used his visit to England in 1811 to charm information about British textile machinery out of his hosts; later he engaged an American mechanic to construct machines from drawings he had made each night in his hotel room.

The United States also benefited from the fact that, unlike Britain, America had no craft organizations (called guilds) that tied artisans to a single trade. As a result, American artisans freely experimented with machines outside their crafts. In the 1790s, Oliver Evans, a wagon-maker from Delaware, built an automated flour mill that required only a single supervisor to watch as the grain poured in on one side and was discharged from the other as flour.

Even in the absence of new technology, Americans searched for new methods of production to cut costs. After inventing the cotton gin, **Eli Whitney** won a government contract in 1798 to produce ten thousand muskets by 1800. Whitney's idea was to meet this seemingly impossible deadline by using unskilled workers to make interchangeable parts that could be used in any of his factory's muskets. Whitney promised much more than he could deliver (see Chapter 11), and he missed his deadline by nearly a decade. But his idea captured the imagination of prominent Americans, including Thomas Jefferson.

Textile Towns in New England

New England became America's first industrial region (see Map 9.5). The trade wars leading up to the War of 1812 had devastated its commercial economy and persuaded its wealthy merchants to invest in manufacturing. The many swift rivers were ideal sources of waterpower for mills. The westward migration of many of New England's young men left a surplus of young women, who supplied cheap industrial labor.

Cotton textiles led the way. In 1813, a group of Boston merchants, known as the Boston Associates and including Francis Cabot Lowell, incorporated the Boston Manufacturing Company. With ten times the capital of any previous American cotton mill, this company quickly built textile mills in the Massachusetts towns of Waltham and Lowell. By 1836, the Boston Associates controlled eight companies employing more than six thousand workers.

The **Waltham and Lowell textile mills** differed in two ways from the earlier Rhode Island mills established by

Map 9.5 U.S. Manufacturing Employment, 1820 and 1850

In 1820, manufacturing employment was concentrated mostly in the Northeast, where the first textile mills appeared. By 1850, the density of manufacturing in the Northeast had increased, but new manufacturing centers arose in Baltimore, Pittsburgh, and Cincinnati.

Source: Historical Atlas of the United States, 2nd ed. (Washington, D.C.: National Geographic Society, 1993), p. 148. Reprinted by permission of National Geographic Maps/National Geographic Society Image Collection.

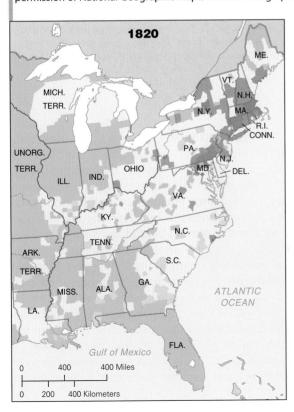

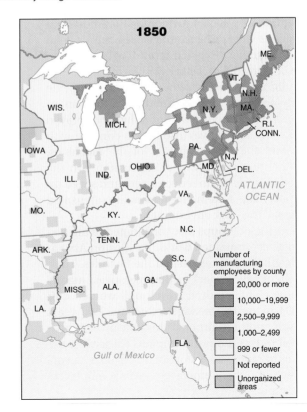

Samuel Slater. Slater's mills performed only two of the operations needed to turn raw cotton into clothing: carding (separating batches of cotton into fine strands) and spinning these strands into yarn. In what was essentially cottage manufacturing, he contracted the weaving to women working in their homes. Unlike Slater's mills, the Waltham and Lowell mills turned out finished fabrics that required only one additional step, stitching into clothes. In addition, the Waltham and Lowell mills upset the traditional order of New England society to a degree that Slater had never contemplated. Slater had sought to preserve tradition not only by contracting weaving to farm families but also by hiring entire families for carding and spinning in his mill complexes. Men raised crops on nearby company lands, while women and children tended the machines inside. In contrast, 80 percent of the workers in Waltham and Lowell, places that had not even existed in the eighteenth century, were young unmarried women who had been lured from farms by the promise of wages. Mary Paul, a Vermont teenager, settled her doubts about leaving home for Lowell by concluding that "I . . . must work where I can get more pay."

In place of traditional family discipline, the workers ("operatives") experienced new restraints. They had to live either in company boardinghouses or in licensed private dwellings, attend church on the Sabbath, observe a 10:00 P.M. curfew, and accept the company's "moral police." Regulations were designed to give the mills a good reputation so that New England farm daughters would continue to be attracted to factory work.

Mill conditions were far from attractive. To provide the humidity necessary to keep the threads from snapping, overseers nailed factory windows shut and sprayed the air with water. Operatives also had to contend with flying dust and the deafening roar of the machines. Keener competition and a worsening economy in the late 1830s led mill owners to reduce wages and speed up work schedules. The system's impersonality intensified the harshness of the work environment.

Each of the major groups that contributed to the system lived in a self-contained world. The Boston Associates raised capital but rarely visited the factories. Their agents, all men, gave orders to the operatives, mainly women. Some eight hundred Lowell mill women quit work in 1834 to protest a wage reduction. Two years later, there was another "turnout," this time involving fifteen hundred to two thousand women. These were the largest strikes in American history to that date, noteworthy as strikes not only of employees against employers but also of women against men.

Mill Girl Around 1850
This girl mostly likely worked in a Massachusetts textile mill, at either Lowell or Waltham. Her swollen and rough hands suggest that she was a "warper," one of the jobs usually given to children. Warpers were responsible for constantly straightening out the strands of cotton or wool as they entered the loom.

The Waltham and Lowell mills were the most conspicuous examples of industrialization before 1840, but they were not typical of industrial development. Outside of textiles, many industries continued to depend on industrial "**outwork.**" In contrast to the farmer who planted flax for fabrication into linen by his wife and daughters, the key movers behind outwork were merchants who provided households with raw materials and paid wages. For example, more than fifty thousand New England farmwomen, mainly daughters and widows, earned wages in their homes during the 1830s by making hats out of straw and palm leaves. Similarly, before the introduction of the sewing machine led to the concentration of all aspects of shoe manufacture in large factories in the 1850s, women often sewed parts of shoes at home and sent the piecework to factories for finishing.

Artisans and Workers in Mid-Atlantic Cities

Manufacturing in cities like New York and Philadelphia also depended on outwork. These cities lacked the fast-flowing rivers that powered machines in New England, and their high population densities made it unnecessary to gather workers into large factories. Nonetheless, they became industrial centers. Lured by the prospect of distant markets, some urban artisans and merchants started to scour the country for orders for consumer goods. They hired unskilled workers, often women, to work in small shops or homes fashioning parts of shoes or saddles or dresses. A New York reporter wrote,

We have been in some fifty cellars in different parts of the city, each inhabited by a shoemaker and his family. The floor is made of rough plank laid loosely down, and the ceiling is not quite so high as a tall man. The walls are dark and damp and . . . the miserable room is lighted only by . . . the little light that struggles from the steep and rotting stairs. In this apartment often lives the man and his work-bench, the wife, and five or six children of all ages; and perhaps a palsied grandfather or grandmother and often both. . . . Here they work, here they cook, they eat, they sleep, they pray.

New York and Philadelphia were home to artisans with proud craft traditions and independence. Those with highly marketable skills like cutting leather or clothing patterns continued to earn good wages. Others grew rich by turning themselves into businessmen who spent less time making products than making trips to obtain orders. But artisans lacking the capital to become businessmen found themselves on the downslide in the face of competition from cheap, unskilled labor.

In the late 1820s, skilled male artisans in New York, Philadelphia, and other cities began to form trade unions and workingmen's political parties to protect their interests. Disdaining association with unskilled workers, most of these groups initially sought to restore privileges and working conditions that artisans had once enjoyed rather than to act as leaders of unskilled workers. But the steady deterioration of working conditions in the early 1830s tended to throw skilled and unskilled workers into the same boat. When coal haulers in Philadelphia struck for a ten-hour day in 1835, they were quickly joined by carpenters, cigar makers, shoemakers, leatherworkers, and other artisans in the United States' first general strike.

The emergence of organized worker protest underscored the mixed blessings of economic development. Although some benefited from the new commercial and

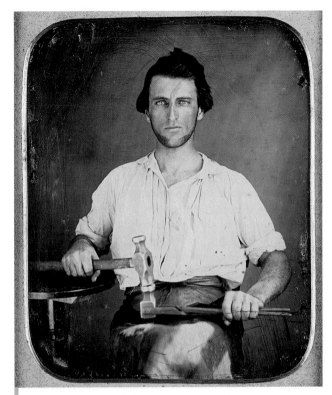

Dageurrotype of Skilled Artisan
This photograph of a Pennsylvania toolmaker, taken around 1850, omits the furnace in which he heated metal for molding but reveals the pride that he brought to his craft.

industrial economy, others found their economic position worsening. By the 1830s, many white Americans wondered whether their nation was truly a land of equality.

Equality and Inequality

That one (white) man was as good as another became the national creed in antebellum (pre–Civil War) America. For example, servants insisted on being called the "help" and on being viewed as neighbors invited to assist in running the household rather than as permanent subordinates. Merchants, held in disdain in Europe by the nobility, refused in America to bow to anyone. Politicians never lost an opportunity to celebrate artisans and farmers as every bit the equal of lawyers and bankers. Tocqueville observed that the wealthiest Americans pretended to respect equality by riding in public in ordinary rather than luxurious carriages.

The market and transportation revolutions, however, were placing new pressure on the ideal of equality between 1815 and 1840. Improved transportation enabled eastern farmers to migrate to the richer soils of the West, but also made it difficult for eastern farmers who lacked the means or the desire to move west to compete with the cheaper grains now carried east by canals and railroads. Unable to compete with western grains, many eastern farmers had to move to cities, where they took whatever work they could find, sometimes in factories but more often as casual day laborers on the docks or in small workshops where their willingness to work for low wages undercut the position of skilled artisans. Tocqueville thought that the wide distribution of land in America and the individual American's insistence on being treated as an equal created more equality in America than in France. But he worried that the lower classes in the major cities were becoming "a rabble more dangerous even than that of European towns."

Urban Inequality: The Rich and the Poor

A few large cities provided the most striking examples of growing inequality. In Boston, for example, the richest 10 percent of the population had owned a little over half of the city's real estate and personal property in 1771. By 1833, the richest 4 percent owned 59 percent of the wealth, and by 1848 nearly two-thirds. In New York City, the richest 4 percent owned nearly half the wealth in 1828 and more than two-thirds by 1845. Splendid residences and social clubs set the rich apart. In 1828, over half of the five hundred wealthiest families in New York City lived on just eight of its more than 250 streets. By the late 1820s the city had a club so exclusive that it was called simply The Club.

Although commentators celebrated the self-made American who rose from poverty to wealth, the vast majority of those who became extremely rich started out with considerable wealth. Fewer than five of every hundred wealthy individuals started poor, and close to ninety of every hundred started rich. The usual way to wealth was to inherit it, marry into more, and then invest wisely. There were just enough instances of fabulously successful poor boys like John Jacob Astor, who built a fur-trading empire, to sustain popular belief in the rags-to-riches myth, but not enough to turn that myth into a reality.

At the opposite end of the social ladder were the poor. By today's standards, most antebellum Americans were poor. They lived close to the edge of misery, depended heavily on their children's labor to meet expenses, and had little money to spend on medical care or recreation. But when antebellum Americans spoke of poverty, they

were not thinking of the hardships that affected most people. Instead, they were referring to "pauperism," a state of dependency or inability to fend for oneself that affected some people. Epidemics of yellow fever and cholera could devastate families. A frozen canal, river, or harbor spelled unemployment for boatmen and dock workers, and for workers in factories that depended on waterpower. The absence of health insurance and old-age pensions condemned many infirm and aged people to pauperism.

Contemporaries usually classified all such people as the "deserving" poor and contrasted them with the "undeserving" poor, such as indolent loafers and drunkards whose poverty was seen as being self-willed. Most moralists assumed that since pauperism resulted either from circumstances beyond anyone's control, such as old age and disease, or from voluntary decisions to squander money on liquor, it could not afflict entire groups generation after generation.

This assumption was comforting but also misleading. A class of people who could not escape poverty was emerging in the major cities during the first half of the nineteenth century. One source was immigration. As early as 1801, a New York newspaper called attention to the arrival of boatloads of immigrants with large families, without money or health, and "expiring from the want of sustenance."

The poorest white immigrants were from Ireland, where English landlords had evicted peasants from the land and converted it to commercial use in the eighteenth century. Severed from the land, the Irish increasingly became a nation of wanderers, scrounging for wages wherever they could. "The poor Irishman," it was said, "the wheelbarrow is his country." By the early 1830s, the great majority of canal workers in the North were Irish immigrants. Without the backbreaking labor of the Irish, the Erie Canal would never have been built. Other Irish congregated in New York's infamous Five Points district. Starting with the conversion of a brewery into housing for hundreds of people in 1837, Five Points became the worst slum in America.

The Irish were not only poor but were also Catholics, a faith despised by the Protestant majority in the United States. In short, they were different and had little claim on the kindly impulses of most Protestants. But even the Protestant poor came in for rough treatment in the years between 1815 and 1840. The more that Americans convinced themselves that success was within everyone's grasp, the less they accepted the traditional doctrine that poverty was ordained by God, and the more they were inclined to hold the poor responsible for their own misery.

Ironically, even as many Americans blamed the poor for being poor, they practiced discrimination that kept some groups mired in enduring poverty. Nowhere was this more true than in the case of northern free blacks.

Free Blacks in the North

Prejudice against blacks was deeply ingrained in white society throughout the nation. Although slavery had largely disappeared in the North by 1820, laws penalized blacks in many ways. One form of discrimination was to restrict their right to vote. In New York State, for example, a constitutional revision of 1821 eliminated property requirements for white voters but kept them for blacks. Rhode Island banned blacks from voting in 1822; Pennsylvania did the same in 1837. Throughout the half-century after 1800, blacks could vote on equal terms with whites in only one of the nation's major cities, Boston.

Laws frequently barred free blacks from migrating to other states and cities. Missouri's original constitution authorized the state legislature to prevent blacks from entering the state "under any pretext whatsoever." Municipal ordinances often barred free blacks from public conveyances and facilities and either excluded them from public schools or forced them into segregated schools. Segregation was the rule in northern jails, almshouses, and hospitals.

Of all restrictions on free blacks, the most damaging was the social pressure that forced them into the least-skilled and lowest-paying occupations throughout the northern cities. Recollecting his youthful days in Providence, Rhode Island, in the early 1830s, the free black William J. Brown wrote: "To drive carriages, carry a market basket after the boss, and brush his boots, or saw wood and run errands was as high as a colored man could rise." Although a few free blacks became successful entrepreneurs and grew moderately wealthy, urban free blacks were only half as likely as city-dwellers in general to own real estate.

One important black response to discrimination was to establish their own churches. White churches confined blacks to separate benches or galleries. When black worshipers mistakenly sat in a gallery designated for whites at a Methodist church in Philadelphia, they were ejected from the church. Their leader, former slave and future bishop **Richard Allen**, related, "we all went out of the church in a body, and they were no longer plagued by us." Allen initiated a movement that resulted in the organization of the **African Methodist Episcopal Church**, the first black-run Protestant denomination, in 1816. By 1822, the A.M.E. Church had

Portrait of a Black Man
At a time when job opportunities for African-Americans were limited, the attire of this black man and the presence of the steamboat *New Philadelphia* in the background make it likely that he was the ship's steward or head waiter. The *New Philadelphia* was the first Hudson River steamboat to introduce "colored waiters." Its reputation for speed and innovation was a source of great pride to its officers and crew.

active congregations in Washington, D.C., Pittsburgh, New York City, and throughout the mid-Atlantic states. Its members campaigned against slavery, in part by refusing to purchase produce grown by slaves.

Just as northern African-Americans seceded from white churches to form their own, free blacks gradually acquired some control over the education of their children at a time when northern city governments made negligible provision for the education of free persons of color. Initially, northern blacks had to depend on the philanthropy of sympathetic whites to educate their children. For example, an antislavery society in New

York launched the African Free School in 1787 with white teachers. But the 1820s and 1830s witnessed an explosion of black self-help societies like New York City's Phoenixonian Literary Society, devoted to encouraging black education and run by such black graduates of the African Free School as Samuel Cornish and Henry Garnett.

The "Middling Classes"

The majority of antebellum Americans lived neither in splendid wealth nor in grinding poverty. Most belonged to what men and women of the time called the middling classes. Even though the wealthy owned an increasing proportion of all wealth, most people's standard of living rose between 1800 and 1860, particularly between 1840 and 1860 when per capita income grew at an annual rate of around 1.5 percent.

Americans applied the term *middling classes* to families headed by professionals, small merchants and manufacturers, landowning farmers, and self-employed artisans. Commentators portrayed these people as living stable and secure lives. In reality, life in the middle often was unpredictable. The increasingly commercial economy of antebellum America created greater opportunities for success and for failure. An enterprising import merchant, Alan Melville, the father of novelist Herman Melville, had an abounding faith in his nation, in "our national Eagle, 'with an eye that never winks and a wing that never tires,' " and in the inevitable triumph of honesty and prudence. The Melvilles lived comfortably in Albany and New York City, but Melville's business sagged in the late 1820s. In 1830, he begged his father for a loan of five hundred dollars, proclaiming, "I am destitute of resources and without a shilling—without immediate assistance I know not what will become of me." He got the five hundred dollars plus an additional three thousand dollars, but the downward spiral continued. In 1832 he died, broken in spirit and nearly insane.

In the emerging market economy, even such seemingly crisp occupational descriptions as farmer and artisan often proved misleading. Asa G. Sheldon, born in Massachusetts in 1788, described himself in his autobiography as a farmer, offered advice on growing corn and cranberries, and gave speeches about the glories of farming. Although Sheldon undoubtedly knew a great deal about farming, he actually spent very little time tilling the soil. In 1812, he began to transport hops from New England to brewers in New York City, and he soon extended this business to Philadelphia and Baltimore. He invested his profits in land, but

rather than farm the land, he made money selling its timber. When a business setback forced him to sell his property, he was soon back in operation "through the disinterested kindness of friends" who lent him money with which he purchased carts and oxen. These he used to get contracts for filling in swamps in Boston and for clearing and grading land for railroads. From all this and from the backbreaking labor of the Irish immigrants he hired to do the shoveling, Sheldon the "farmer" grew prosperous.

The emerging market economy also transformed the lives of artisans. During the colonial period, artisans had formed a proud and cohesive group whose members often attained the goal of self-employment. They owned their own tools, made their own products on order from customers, boarded their apprentices and journeymen in their homes, and passed their skills on to their children. By 1840, in contrast, artisans had entered a new world of economic relationships. This was true even of a craft like carpentry that did not experience any industrial or technological change. Town and city growth in the wake of the transportation revolution created a demand for housing. Some carpenters, usually those with access to capital, became contractors. They took orders for more houses than they could build themselves and hired large numbers of journeymen to do the construction work. Likewise, as we have seen, in the early industrialization of shoe manufacturing during the 1820s, some shoemakers spent less time crafting shoes than making trips to obtain orders for their products, then hired workers to fashion parts of shoes. In effect, the old class of artisans was splitting into two new groupings. On one side were artisans who had become entrepreneurs; on the other, journeymen with little prospect of self-employment.

An additional characteristic of the middling classes, one they shared with the poor, was a high degree of transience, or spatial mobility. The transportation revolution made it easier for Americans to purchase services as well as goods and spurred many young men to abandon farming for the professions. For example, the number of medical schools rose from one in 1765 to twenty in 1830 and sixty-five in 1860. Frequently, the new men who crowded into medicine and into the ministry and law were forced into incessant motion. Physicians rode from town to town looking for patients. The itinerant clergyman mounted on an old nag and riding the countryside to visit the faithful or to conduct revivals became a familiar figure in newly settled areas. Even well-established lawyers and judges spent part of each year riding from one county courthouse to another, to plead and decide cases, bunking (usually two to a bed) in rough country inns.

Transience affected the lives of most Americans. Farmers who cultivated land intensively in order to raise a cash crop, and so pay their debts, exhausted the land quickly and had to move on. For skilled and unskilled workers alike, work was often seasonal; workers had to move from job to job to survive. Canal workers and boatmen had to secure new work when waterways froze. Even city-dwellers who shifted jobs often had to change residences, for the cities were spreading out at a much faster rate than was public transportation. Some idea of the degree of transience can be gained from a survey by the Boston police on Saturday, September 6, 1851. At a time when Boston's population was 145,000, the survey showed that from 6:30 A.M. to 7:30 P.M., 41,729 people entered the city and 42,313 left. At a time when there were few suburbs, it is safe to say that these people were not commuters. Most likely, they were moving in search of work, as much a necessity for many in the middling classes as for the poor.

The Revolution in Social Relationships

Following the War of 1812, the growth of interregional trade, commercial agriculture, and manufacturing changed not only the lives of individuals but also the ways in which they related to each other. Two broad generalizations encompass these changes. First, many Americans questioned authority to an unprecedented degree. In 1775, they had rebelled against their king. Now, it seemed, they were rebelling as well against their lawyers, their physicians, their ministers, and even their parents. An attitude of individualism sprouted and took firm root in antebellum America. Once individualism had meant nothing more than selfishness, but now Americans used the word to signify positive qualities: self-reliance and the conviction that each person was the best judge of his or her own true interests. Ordinary Americans might still agree with the opinions of their leaders, but only after they had thought matters through on their own. Those with superior wealth, education, or social position could no longer expect the automatic deference of the common people.

Second, even as Americans widely proclaimed themselves a nation of self-reliant individualists and questioned the traditional basis of authority, they sought to construct new foundations for authority. For example, middle-class men and women came to embrace the idea that women possessed a "separate sphere" of authority in the home. In addition, individuals increasingly joined with others in these years to form voluntary associations through which they might influence the direction that their society would take.

The Attack on the Professions

In the swiftly changing antebellum society, claims to social superiority were questioned as never before. As a writer put it in 1836, "Everywhere the disposition is found among those who live in the valleys to ask those who live on the hills, 'How came we here and you there?'"

Intense criticism of lawyers, physicians, and ministers exemplified this assault on authority. As far back as the 1780s, Benjamin Austin, a radical Boston artisan, had complained that lawyers needlessly prolonged and confused court cases so that they could charge high fees. Between 1800 and 1840, a wave of religious revivals known as the Second Great Awakening (see Chapter 10) sparked new attacks on the professions. Some revivalists blasted the clergy for creating complicated theologies that ordinary men and women could not comprehend, for drinking expensive wines, and for fleecing the people. One religious revivalist, Elias Smith, extended the criticism to physicians, whom he accused of inventing Latin and Greek names for diseases in order to disguise their own ignorance of how to cure them.

These jabs at the learned professions peaked between 1820 and 1850. In medicine, a movement arose under the leadership of Samuel Thomson, a farmer's son with little formal education, to eliminate all barriers to entry into the medical profession. Thomson believed that anyone could understand the principles of medicine and become a physician. His crusade was remarkably successful. By 1845, every state had repealed laws that required licenses and education to practice medicine. Meanwhile, attacks on lawyers sharpened, and relations between ministers and their parishioners grew tense and acrimonious. In colonial New England, ministers had usually served a single parish for life, but by the 1830s a rapid turnover of ministers was becoming the norm as finicky parishioners commonly dismissed clergymen whose theology displeased them. Ministers themselves were becoming more ambitious—more inclined to leave small, poor congregations for large, wealthy ones.

The increasing commercialization of the economy contributed both to the growing number of professionals and to the attacks on them. Like so many other antebellum Americans, freshly minted lawyers and doctors often were transients without deep roots in the towns that they served and without convincing claims to social superiority. Describing lawyers and physicians, a contemporary observer wrote, "Men dropped down into their places as from clouds. Nobody knew who or what they were, except as they claimed, or as a surface view of their character indicated." A horse doctor one day would the next day hang up his sign as "Physician and Surgeon" and "fire at random a box of his pills into your bowels, with a vague chance of hitting some disease unknown to him, but with a better prospect of killing the patient, whom or whose administrator he charged some ten dollars a trial for his marksmanship."

The questioning of authority was particularly sharp on the frontier. Here, to eastern and foreign visitors, it seemed that every man they met was a "judge," "general," "colonel," or "squire." In a society in which everyone was new, such titles were easily adopted and just as easily challenged. Where neither law nor custom sanctioned claims of superiority, would-be gentlemen substituted an exaggerated sense of personal honor. Obsessed with their fragile status, many reacted testily to the slightest insult. Dueling became a widespread frontier practice. At a Kentucky militia parade in 1819, an officer's dog jogged onto the field and sat at his master's knee. Enraged by this breach of military decorum, another officer ran the dog through with his sword. A week later, both officers met with pistols at ten paces. One was killed; the other maimed for life.

The Challenge to Family Authority

In contrast to adults' public philosophical attacks on the learned professions, children engaged in a quiet questioning of parental authority. Economic change created new opportunities that forced young people to choose between staying at home to help their parents and venturing out on their own. Writing to her parents in Vermont shortly before taking a job in a Lowell textile mill, eighteen-year-old Sally Rice quickly got to the point. "I must of course have something of my own before many more years have passed over my head and where is that something coming from if I go home and earn nothing. You may think me unkind but how can you blame me if I want to stay here. I have but one life to live and I want to enjoy myself as I can while I live."

A similar desire for independence tempted young men to leave home at earlier ages than in the past. Although the great migration to the West was primarily a movement of entire families, movement from farms to towns and cities within regions was frequently spear-

headed by restless and single young people. Two young men in Virginia put it succinctly. "All the promise of life seemed to us to be at the other end of the rainbow—somewhere else—anywhere else but on the farm. . . . And so all our youthful plans had as their chief object the getting away from the farm."

Antebellum Americans also widely wished to be free of close parental supervision, and their changing attitudes influenced courtship and marriage. Many young people who no longer depended on their parents for land insisted on privacy in courting and wanted to decide for themselves when and whom to marry. Whereas seventeenth-century Puritans had advised young people to choose marriage partners whom they could learn to love, by the early 1800s young men and women viewed romantic love as indispensable to a successful marriage. "In affairs of love," a young lawyer in Maine wrote, "young people's hearts are generally much wiser than old people's heads."

One sign of young people's growing control over courtship and marriage was the declining likelihood that the young women of a family would marry in their exact birth order. Traditionally, fathers had wanted their daughters to marry in the order of their birth to avoid planting the suspicion that there was something wrong with one or more of them. Toward the end of the eighteenth century, however, daughters were making their own marital decisions, and the practice ceased to be customary. Another mark of the times was the growing number of long engagements. Having made the decision to marry, some young women were reluctant to tie the knot, fearing that marriage would snuff out their independence. For example, New Yorkers Caroline and William Kirkland were engaged for seven years before their marriage in 1828. Equally striking was the increasing number of young women who chose not to marry. **Catharine Beecher**, a leading author and the daughter of the prominent minister Lyman Beecher, broke off her engagement to a young man during the 1820s despite her father's pressure to marry him. She later renewed the engagement, but after her fiancé's death in a shipwreck, she remained single for the rest of her life.

Moralists reacted with alarm to signs that young people were living in a world of their own. They flooded the country with books of advice to youth, such as William Alcott's *The Young Man's Guide,* which went through thirty-one editions between 1833 and 1858. The vast number of such advice books sold in antebellum America all said the same thing. They did not advise young men and women to return to farms, and they assumed that parents had little control over them. Rather, the authors exhorted youths to develop habitual rectitude, self-control, and "character." It was an age not just of the self-made adult but also of the self-made youth.

Wives and Husbands

Another class of advice books pouring from the antebellum presses counseled wives and husbands on their rights and duties. These were a sign that relations between spouses, too, were changing. Young men and women who had grown accustomed to making decisions on their own as teenagers were more likely than their ancestors to approach wedlock as a compact between equals. Of course, wives remained unequal to their husbands in many ways. With few exceptions, the law did not allow married women to own property. But relations between wives and husbands were changing during the 1820s and 1830s toward a form of equality.

One source of the change, zealously advocated by Catharine Beecher, lay in the doctrine of **separate spheres**. Traditionally, women had been viewed as subordinate to men in all spheres of life. Now middle-class men and women developed a kind of separate-but-equal doctrine that portrayed men as superior in making money and governing the world, and women as superior for their moral influence on family members.

One of the most important duties assigned to the sphere of women was raising children. During the eighteenth century, church sermons reminded fathers of their duty to govern the family; by the 1830s child-rearing manuals were addressed to mothers rather than fathers. "How entire and perfect is this dominion over the unformed character of your infant," the popular writer Lydia Sigourney proclaimed in her *Letters to Mothers* (1838). Advice books instructed mothers to discipline their children by loving them and withdrawing affection when they misbehaved rather than by using corporal punishment. A whipped child might become more obedient but would remain sullen and bitter; gentler methods would penetrate the child's heart, making the child want to do the right thing.

The idea of a separate women's sphere blended with a related image of the family and home as refuges secluded from a society marked by commotion and disorder. The popular culture of the 1830s and 1840s painted an alluring portrait of the pleasures of home life through

The Country Parson Disturbed at Breakfast
This young couple's decision to wed seems to have been on the spur of the moment. As young men and women became more independent of parental control, they gave their impulses freer play.

songs like "Home, Sweet Home" and poems such as Henry Wadsworth Longfellow's "The Children's Hour" and Clement Moore's "A Visit from St. Nicholas." The publication of Moore's poem coincided with the growing popularity of Christmas as a holiday season in which family members gathered to exchange warm affection. Even the physical appearance of houses changed. The prominent architect Andrew Jackson Downing published plans for peaceful single-family homes that he hoped would offset the "spirit of unrest" and the feverish pace of American life. He wrote of the ideal home, "There should be something to love. There must be nooks about it, where one would love to linger; windows, where one can enjoy the quiet landscape at his leisure; cozy rooms, where all fireside joys are invited to dwell."

Downing deserves high marks as a prophet, because one of the motives that impelled many Americans to flee cities for suburbs in the twentieth century was the desire to own their own homes. In the 1820s and 1830s, this ideal was beyond the reach of most people—not only blacks, immigrants, and sweatshop workers, but also most members of the middle class. In the countryside, although middle-class farmers still managed productive households, these were anything but tranquil; wives milked cows and bled hogs, and children fetched wood, drove cows to pasture, and chased blackbirds from cornfields. In the cities, middle-class families often had to sacrifice their privacy by taking in boarders to supplement family income.

Despite their distortions, the doctrine of separate spheres and the image of the home as a refuge from a harsh world intersected with reality at some points. The rising number of urban families headed by lawyers and merchants (who worked away from home) gave mothers time to spend on child rearing. Above all, even if they could not afford to live in a Downing-designed house, married women found that they could capitalize on these notions to gain new power within their families. A subtle implication of the doctrine of separate spheres was that women should have control not only over the discipline of children but also over the more fundamental issue of how many children they would bear.

In 1800, the United States had one of the highest birthrates ever recorded. The average American woman bore 7.04 children. It is safe to say that married women had become pregnant as often as possible. In the prevailing farm economy, children carried out essential

tasks and, as time passed, took care of their aging parents. Most parents had assumed that the more children, the better. The spread of a commercial economy raised troublesome questions about children's economic value. Unlike a farmer, a merchant or lawyer could not send his children to work at the age of seven or eight. The average woman was bearing only 5.02 children by 1850, and 3.98 by 1900. The birthrate remained high among blacks and many immigrant groups, but it fell drastically among native-born whites, particularly in towns and cities. The birthrate also declined in rural areas, but more sharply in rural villages than on farms, and more sharply in the East, where land was scarce, than in the West, where abundant land created continued incentives for parents to have many children.

For the most part, the decline in the birthrate was accomplished by abstinence from sexual intercourse, by *coitus interruptus* (withdrawal before ejaculation), or by abortion. By the 1840s, abortionists advertised remedies for "female irregularities," a common euphemism for unwanted pregnancies. There were no foolproof birth-control devices, and as much misinformation as information circulated about techniques of birth control. Nonetheless, interest in birth-control devices was intensifying. In 1832, Charles Knowlton, a Massachusetts physician, described the procedure for vaginal douching in his book *Fruits of Philosophy*. Although Knowlton was frequently prosecuted and once jailed for obscenity, efforts to suppress his ideas publicized them even more. By 1865, popular tracts had familiarized Americans with a wide range of birth-control methods, including the condom and the diaphragm. The decision to limit family size was usually reached jointly by wives and husbands. Economic and ideological considerations blended together. Husbands could note that the economic value of children was declining; wives, that having fewer children would give them more time to nurture each one and thereby carry out domestic duties.

Supporters of the ideal of separate spheres did not advocate full legal equality for women. Indeed, the idea of separate spheres was an explicit alternative to legal equality. But the concept did enhance women's power within marriage by justifying their demands for influence over such vital issues as child rearing and the frequency of pregnancies. In addition, it allowed some women a measure of independence from the home. For example, it sanctioned the travels of Catharine Beecher, a leading advocate of separate spheres, to lecture women on better ways to raise children and manage their households.

Horizontal Allegiances and the Rise of Voluntary Associations

As some forms of authority, such as the authority of parents over their children and husbands over their wives, were weakening, Americans devised new ways for individuals to extend their influence over others. The pre–Civil War period witnessed the widespread substitution of **horizontal allegiances** for **vertical allegiances**. In vertical allegiances, authority flows from the top down. Subordinates identify their interests with those of their superiors rather than with others in the same subordinate role. The traditional patriarchal family was an example of a vertical allegiance: the wife and children looked up to the father for leadership. Another example occurred in the small eighteenth-century workshop, where apprentices and journeymen took direction from the master craftsman and even lived in the craftsman's house, subject to his authority.

Although vertical relationships did not disappear, they became less important in people's lives. Increasingly, relationships were more likely to be marked by horizontal allegiances that linked those in a similar position. For example, in large textile mills, operatives discovered that they had more in common with one another than with their managers and overseers. Similarly, married women formed maternal associations to exchange advice about child rearing. Young men formed debating societies to sharpen their wits and to bring themselves to the attention of influential older men. Maternal and debating societies exemplified the American zeal for **voluntary associations**—associations that arose apart from government and sought to accomplish some goal of value to their members. Tocqueville observed that the government stood at the head of every enterprise in France, but that in America "you will be sure to find an association."

Voluntary associations encouraged sociability. As transients and newcomers flocked into towns and cities, they tended to join others with similar characteristics, experiences, or interests. Gender was the basis of many voluntary societies. Of twenty-six religious and charitable associations in Utica, New York, in 1832, for instance, one-third were exclusively for women. Race was still another basis for voluntary associations. Although their names did not indicate it, Boston's Thompson Literary and Debating Society and its Philomathean Adelphic Union for the Promotion of Literature and Science were organizations for free blacks.

Voluntary associations also enhanced their members' public influence. At a time when state legislatures had little interest in regulating the sale of alcoholic beverages, men and women joined in temperance societies to promote voluntary abstinence. To combat prostitution, women formed moral-reform societies, which sought to shame men into chastity by publishing the names of brothel patrons in newspapers. Aiming to suppress an ancient vice, moral-reform societies also tended to enhance women's power over men. Moral reformers attributed the prevalence of prostitution to the lustfulness of men who, unable to control their passions, exploited poor and vulnerable girls. Just as strikes in Lowell in the 1830s were a form of collective action by working women, moral-reform societies represented collective action by middle-class women to increase their influence in society. Here, as elsewhere, the tendency of the times was to forge new forms of horizontal allegiance between like-minded Americans.

Conclusion

European demand for American cotton and other agricultural products, federal policies that eased the sale of public lands and encouraged the removal of Indians from the path of white settlement, and the availability of loose-lending banks and paper money all contributed to the flow of population into the area between the Appalachians and the Mississippi River after 1815. The collapse of the boom in 1819 reminded farmers of how dependent they had become on distant markets and prompted improvements in transportation during the 1820s and 1830s. The introduction of steamboats, the building of canals, and the gradual spread of railroads—the transportation revolution—encouraged a turn to commercial occupations and the growth of towns and cities. Now able to reach distant

Chronology, 1815–1840

1790	Samuel Slater opens his first Rhode Island mill for the production of cotton yarn.
1793	Eli Whitney invents the cotton gin.
1807	Robert R. Livingston and Robert Fulton introduce the steamboat *Clermont* on the Hudson River.
1811	Construction of the National Road begins at Cumberland, Maryland.
1813	Incorporation of the Boston Manufacturing Company.
1816	Second Bank of the United States chartered.
1817–1825	Construction of the Erie Canal started.
	Mississippi enters the Union.
1819	Economic panic, ushering in four-year depression.
	Alabama enters the Union.
1820–1850	Growth of female moral-reform societies.

1820s	Expansion of New England textile mills.
1824	*Gibbons* v. *Ogden*.
1828	Baltimore and Ohio Railroad chartered.
1830	Indian Removal Act passed by Congress.
1831	*Cherokee Nation* v. *Georgia*.
	Alexis de Tocqueville begins visit to the United States to study American penitentiaries.
1832	*Worcester* v. *Georgia*.
1834	First strike at the Lowell mills.
1835	Treaty of New Echota.
1837	Economic panic begins a depression that lasts until 1843.
1838	The Trail of Tears.
1840	System of production by interchangeable parts perfected.

consumers, merchants plunged capital into manufacturing enterprises. Ranging from the great textile mills of Lowell and Waltham to rural cottages that performed outwork to urban sweatshops, early industrialization laid the foundations for America's emergence a half-century later as a major industrial power.

The changes associated with the market economy and early industrialization carved new avenues to prosperity for some—and to penury for others. They challenged traditional hierarchies and created new forms of social alignment based on voluntary associations. By joining voluntary associations based on shared interests or opinions, footloose Americans forged new identities that paralleled and often supplanted older allegiances to their parents or places of birth.

Key Terms

Alexis de Tocqueville	Eli Whitney
Old Northwest	Waltham and Lowell textile mills
Old Southwest	mills
Five Civilized Tribes	outwork
Indian Removal Act, 1830	Richard Allen
Trail of Tears	African Methodist Episcopal Church
market economy	Church
squatters	Catharine Beecher
Panic of 1819	separate spheres
Transportation revolution	horizontal allegiances
Gibbons v. *Ogden*	vertical allegiances
Erie Canal	voluntary associations

For Further Reference

Edward J. Balleisen, *Navigating Failure: Bankruptcy and Commercial Society in Antebellum America* (2001). An important study of the risks spawned by the market economy.

Thomas Dublin, *Women at Work: The Transformation of Work and Community in Lowell, Massachusetts, 1826–1860* (1979). Traces the origins, work experiences, and eventual destinations of the Lowell mill girls.

Eddie S. Glaude, *Exodus! Religion, Race, and Nation in Early Nineteenth-Century Black America* (2000). A fascinating account of the impact of the biblical Book of Exodus on black Christians.

John Lauritz Larson, *Internal Improvement: National Public Works and the Promise of Popular Government in the Early United States* (2001). An overview of road and canal projects that shows how local and regional rivalries frustrated plans for a nationally integrated system of improvements.

Harry N. Scheiber, *The Ohio Canal Era: A Case Study of Government and the Economy, 1820–1861* (1969). An analysis that speaks volumes about economic growth in the early Republic.

Alan Taylor, *William Cooper's Town* (1995). A compelling portrait of the New York frontier in the late eighteenth and early nineteenth centuries.

Peter Way, *Common Labour* (1993). Insightful book on the lives of canal workers.

Chapter 10

First State Election in Michigan
Michigan's early elections were rowdy. Here, Detroit voters cast ballots in Michigan's first state gubernatorial election in 1837. Democrat candidate Stevens Mason, shown on the left soliciting a vote and backed by the "no monopoly" banner on the right (partial view), defeated the Whig candidate.

Democratic Politics, Religious Revival, and Reform,

1824–1840

Frances Wright

New Yorkers who greeted the ship *Amity* when it arrived from Liverpool in September 1818 caught their first glimpse of Frances Wright, a tall twenty-two-year-old Scotswoman with piercing blue eyes.

The well-educated daughter of a wealthy linen merchant, Wright was not one of those European snobs who came to complain about America. Rather, she warmly admired the American Revolution, in her eyes the dawn of a new age of equality. She would continue to applaud equality. But her insistence that Americans live up to her interpretation of that ideal led her to champion causes that clashed with the conservative realities of American society.

Wright made a second trip to the United States in 1825, this time accompanying the Marquis de Lafayette, the Revolutionary War hero with whom she was rumored to be having a love affair. Now bent on undermining slavery, Wright decided to establish her own utopian experiment on the frontier.

With lukewarm support from Thomas Jefferson, she purchased property near present-day Memphis, Tennessee, and cleared land for a small plantation, "Nashoba." She bought about thirty slaves and set them to work on crops so they could earn back their purchase price and buy their freedom. But Nashoba's crops were meager and its debts chronic. Worse, Nashoba was a public-relations disaster. Her overseer took a mulatto mistress, and Wright called for a blending of the races. Wright contributed to undermining the idea of gradual emancipation, still acceptable to many southerners in the 1820s, by linking it to racial mixing.

By 1830, Wright had shifted her focus to urban workers and become a public lecturer in the cities. Blessed with a "rich and thrilling" voice and clothed in a draped garment of white muslin that made her look like an ancient goddess, she always appeared on stage carrying a copy of the Declaration of Independence. In her lectures, she condemned organized religion for encouraging ignorance and superstition and attacked capital punishment. She called for equal education for women, the right for married women to own property, liberalized divorce laws, and birth control. She proposed a system of state-supported boarding schools for all children aged two to sixteen that would protect them from both religious indoctrination by their parents and the vicious influences of the city streets.

After a trip to France, she returned to the United States in 1835, now championing the Democratic Party by attacking the Bank of the United States as an institution that enriched the wealthy and blighted the poor. Urban workers were drawn to her message that the new Republic had failed to deliver the equality promised by the American Revolution. Even denouncers of Wright's more radical ideas recognized that something had gone wrong. Few could overlook the widening gap between the rich and poor, rising crime, and sharpening clashes between the North, the South, and the West. The Era of Good Feelings would disappear within a decade as new parties—the Democrats and Whigs—replaced the Federalists and Republicans. More was at work than a change of names. The new parties took advantage of the transportation revolution to arouse voters in every corner of the nation with inflammatory rhetoric. To Democrats, the Bank of the United States was a "monster." To Whigs, Andrew Jackson, the Democratic leader, had become a dictator with a trail of blood behind him.

Wright had hoped to revitalize American democracy by appealing to secular revolutionary principles. She failed to grasp the importance of Christianity in American life. America was swept in the 1820s and 1830s by intense religious revivals, called the Second Great Awakening. Although Wright viewed religion as the enemy of social improvement, the revivals contributed to the great wave of reform movements during the era between 1820 and 1840, including banning alcohol and freeing slaves. Revivalists justified reform, not as enacting the principles of 1776, but as a way to achieve the Kingdom of God on earth. In the eyes of revivalists, drunkards and slaveholders were sinners in need of reformation. Ironically, Americans drawn to reform movements often started with a loathing of the rough-and-tumble of mass politics, only to discover that the success of their reforms depended on their ability to influence the political process.

During the 1820s and 1830s, the political and reform agendas of Americans diverged increasingly from those of the Founders. The Founders had feared popular participation in politics, enjoyed their wine and rum, left an ambiguous legacy on slavery, and displayed only occasional interest in women's rights. Yet even as Americans shifted their political and social priorities, they continued to venerate the Founders, who were revered in death even more than in life. Histories of the United States, biographies of Revolutionary patriots, and torchlight parades that bore portraits of Washington and Jefferson alongside those of Andrew Jackson all helped reassure the citizens of the young nation that they were remaining loyal to their republican heritage.

Focus Questions

- How did the democratization of American politics contribute to the rise of Andrew Jackson?

- How did Jackson's policies and the Panic of 1837 help launch and solidify the Whig Party?

- What new assumptions about human nature lay behind the religious movements of the period?

- Did the reform movements primarily aim at making Americans more equal or just more orderly?

The Rise of Democratic Politics, 1824–1832

In 1824, Andrew Jackson and Martin Van Buren, who would guide the Democratic Party in the 1830s, and Henry Clay and John Quincy Adams, who would become that decade's leading Whigs, all belonged to the Republican Party of Thomas Jefferson. Yet by 1824 the Republican Party was coming apart under pressures generated by industrialization in New England, the spread of cotton cultivation in the South, and westward expansion. These forces sparked issues that would become the basis for the new political division between Democrats and Whigs. In general, Republicans who retained Jefferson's preference for states' rights became Democrats; Republicans who believed that the national government should actively encourage economic development, the so-called National Republicans, became Whigs.

Regardless of which path a politician chose, all leaders in the 1820s and 1830s had to adapt to the rising democratic idea of politics as a forum for the expression of the will of the common people rather than as an activity that gentlemen conducted for the people. Gentlemen could still be elected to office, but their success now depended less on their education and wealth than on their ability to identify and follow the will of the majority. Americans still looked up to their political leaders, but the leaders could no longer look down on the people.

Democratic Ferment

Political democratization took several forms. One of the most common was the abolition of the requirement that voters own property. None of the new western states required property ownership for voting, and eastern states gradually liberalized their laws. Moreover, written ballots replaced the custom of voting aloud, which had enabled superiors to influence their inferiors at the polls. Appointive office increasingly became elective. The Electoral College survived, but the choice of presidential electors by state legislatures gave way to their direct election by the voters. In 1800, rather than voting for Thomas Jefferson or John Adams, most Americans could do no more than vote for the men who would vote for the men who would vote for Jefferson or Adams. By 1824, however, legislatures chose electors in only six states, and by 1832 only in South Carolina.

The fierce tug of war between the Republicans and the Federalists in the 1790s and early 1800s had taught both parties to court voters. At grand party-run barbecues from Maine to Maryland, potential voters washed down free clams and oysters with free beer and whiskey. Republicans sought to expand suffrage in the North, and Federalists did likewise in the South, each in the hope of becoming the majority party in that section.

Political democratization developed at an uneven pace. In 1820, both the Federalists and Republicans were still organized from the top down. To nominate candidates, for example, both parties relied on the caucus (a conference of party members in the legislature) rather than on popularly elected nominating conventions. Nor was political democracy extended to all. Women continued to be excluded from voting. Free blacks in the North found that the same popular conventions that extended voting rights to nearly all whites effectively disfranchised African-Americans. Yet no one could mistake the tendency of the times: to oppose the people or democracy had become a formula for political suicide. The people, a Federalist moaned, "have become too saucy and are really beginning to fancy themselves equal to their betters."

The Election of 1824

Sectional tensions brought the Era of Good Feelings to an end in 1824 when five candidates, all Republicans, vied for the presidency. John Quincy Adams emerged as New England's favorite. South Carolina's brilliant John C. Calhoun contended with Georgia's William Crawford, an old-school Jeffersonian, for southern support. Out of the West marched **Henry Clay** of Kentucky, ambitious, crafty, and confident that his American System of protective tariffs and federally supported internal improvements would endear him to manufacturing interests in the East as well as to the West.

Clay's belief that he was holding a solid block of western states was punctured by the rise of a fifth candidate, Andrew Jackson of Tennessee. At first, none of the other candidates took Jackson seriously. But he was popular on the frontier and in the South and stunned his rivals by gaining the support of opponents of the American System from Pennsylvania and other northern states.

Although the Republican congressional caucus chose Crawford as the party's official candidate early in 1824, the caucus could no longer unify the party. Three-fourths of the Republicans in Congress had refused to attend the caucus. Crawford's already diminished prospects evaporated when he suffered a paralyzing stroke. Impressed by Jackson's support, Calhoun withdrew from the race and ran unopposed for the vice presidency.

In the election, Jackson won more popular and electoral votes than any other candidate (Adams, Crawford, and Clay) but failed to gain the majority required by the Constitution (see Table 10.1). Thus the election was thrown into the House of Representatives, whose members had to choose from the three top candidates—Jackson, Adams, and Crawford. Hoping to forge an alliance between the West and Northeast in a future bid for the presidency, Clay gave his support to Adams. Clay's action secured the presidency for Adams, but when Adams promptly appointed Clay his secretary of state, Jackson's supporters raged that a "corrupt bargain" had cheated Jackson of the presidency. Although there is no evidence that Adams had traded Clay's support for an explicit agreement to appoint Clay his secretary of state (an office from which Jefferson, Madison, Monroe, and Adams himself had risen to the presidency), the allegation of a corrupt bargain was widely believed. It formed a cloud that hung over Adams's presidency.

John Quincy Adams as President

Failing to understand the changing political climate, Adams made several other miscalculations that would cloak his presidency in controversy. For example, in 1825 he proposed a program of federal aid for internal improvements. Strict Jeffersonians had always opposed such aid as unconstitutional, but now they were joined by pragmatists like New York's governor and, later, U.S. senator Martin Van Buren. Aware that New York had just completed construction of the Erie Canal with its own

Table 10.1   The Election of 1824

Candidates	Parties	Electoral Vote	Popular Vote	Percentage of Popular Vote
John Quincy Adams	Democratic-Republican	84	108,740	30.5
Andrew Jackson	Democratic-Republican	99	153,544	43.1
William H. Crawford	Democratic-Republican	41	46,618	13.1
Henry Clay	Democratic-Republican	37	47,136	13.2

funds, Van Buren opposed federal aid to improvements on the grounds that it would enable other states to build rival canals. Adams next proposed sending American delegates to a conference of newly independent Latin American nations, a proposal that infuriated southerners because it would imply U.S. recognition of Haiti, the black republic created by slave revolutionaries.

Instead of seeking new bases of support, Adams clung to the increasingly obsolete notion of the president as custodian of the public good, aloof from partisan politics. He alienated his supporters by appointing his opponents to high office and wrote loftily, "I have no wish to fortify myself by the support of any party whatever." Idealistic as his view was, it guaranteed him a single-term presidency.

The Rise of Andrew Jackson

As Adams's popularity declined, Andrew Jackson's rose. Although Jackson's victory over the British in the Battle of New Orleans had made him a hero, veteran politicians distrusted his notoriously hot temper and his penchant for duels. (Jackson had once challenged an opposing lawyer to a duel for ridiculing his legal arguments in a court case.) But as the only presidential candidate in the election of 1824 not linked to the Monroe administration, Jackson benefited from discontent after the Panic of 1819, which, in Calhoun's words, left people with "a general mass of disaffection to the Government" and "looking out anywhere for a leader." To many Americans, Jackson, who as a boy had fought in the Revolution, seemed like a living link to a more virtuous past.

Jackson's supporters swiftly established committees throughout the country. Two years before the election of 1828, towns and villages across the United States buzzed with furious but unfocused political activity. With the exception of the few remaining Federalists, almost everyone called himself a Republican. Because supporters of Jackson, Adams, and Clay still styled themselves Republicans, few realized that a new political system was being born. The man most alert to the signs of the times was Martin Van Buren, who was to become vice president during Jackson's second term and president upon Jackson's retirement.

Van Buren exemplified a new breed of politician. A tavernkeeper's son, he had started his political career in county politics. As governor, he built a powerful political machine, the Albany Regency, composed mainly of men like himself from the lower and middling ranks. His archrival in New York politics, DeWitt Clinton, was all that Van Buren was not—tall, handsome, and aristocratic. But Van Buren had a geniality that made ordinary people feel comfortable and an uncanny ability to sense the direction in which the political winds were about to blow. Van Buren loved politics, which he viewed as a wonderful game. He was one of the first prominent American politicians to make personal friends from among his political enemies.

The election of 1824 convinced Van Buren of the need for renewed two-party competition. Without the discipline imposed by a strong opposition party, the Republicans had splintered into sectional pieces. No candidate had secured an electoral majority, and the House of Representatives had decided the outcome amid charges of intrigue and corruption. It would be better, Van Buren concluded, to let all the shades of opinion in the nation be reduced to two. Then the parties would clash, and a clear popular winner would emerge. Jackson's strong showing in the election persuaded Van Buren that "Old Hickory" could lead a new political party. In the election of 1828, this party, which gradually became known as the **Democratic Party**, put up Jackson for president and Calhoun for vice president. Its opponents, calling themselves the National Republicans, rallied behind Adams and his running mate, treasury secretary Richard Rush. Slowly but surely, the second American party system was taking shape.

The Election of 1828

The 1828 campaign was a vicious, mudslinging affair. The National Republicans attacked Jackson as a gambler, an adulterer, and a murderer. He was directly responsible for several men's deaths in duels and military executions; and in 1791 he had married Rachel Robards, erroneously believing that her divorce from her first husband had become final. "Ought a convicted adulteress and her

"Cinque" by Nathaniel Joselyn
In 1839, fifty-three Africans who had been illegally transported to
Cuba as slaves rose up and seized control of the Cuban schooner
Amistad. After an American revenue schooner intercepted the
Amistad off Long Island, the slaves were imprisoned in New
Haven, Connecticut, while the courts considered the claims of
their Cuban owners to restitution. After an impassioned plea for
their freedom by former president John Quincy Adams, the U.S.
Supreme Court ruled in favor of their leader, Joseph Cinque, and
his men and ordered them returned to Africa as free people.

paramour husband," the Adams men taunted, "be placed
in the highest office of this free and Christian land?"
Jackson's supporters replied in kind. They accused Adams
of wearing silk underwear, being rich, being in debt, and
having gained favor with the tsar of Russia by trying to
provide him with a beautiful American prostitute.

Although both sides engaged in tossing barbs, Jackson's
men had better aim. Charges by Adams's supporters that
Jackson was an illiterate backwoodsman added to Jackson's popular appeal by making him seem like an ordinary citizen. Jackson's supporters portrayed the clash as
one between "the democracy of the country, on the one
hand, and a lordly purse-proud aristocracy on the other."
Jackson, they said, was the common man incarnate, his
mind unclouded by learning, his morals simple and true,
his will fierce and resolute. In contrast, Jackson's men

represented Adams as an aristocrat, a dry scholar whose
learning obscured the truth, a man who could write but
not fight. Much of this, of course, was wild exaggeration.
Jackson was a wealthy planter, not a simple frontiersman. But it was what people wanted to hear. Jackson was
presented as the common man's image of his better self
as uncorrupt, natural, and plain.

The election swept Jackson into office with more
than twice the electoral vote of Adams (see Map 10.1).
Yet the popular vote, much closer, made it clear that the
people were not simply responding to the personalities
or images of the candidates. The vote also reflected the
strongly sectional bases of the new parties. The popular
vote was close only in the middle states and the Northwest. Adams gained double Jackson's vote in New England; Jackson received double Adams's vote in the South
and nearly triple Adams's vote in the Southwest.

Jackson in Office

Riding to office on a wave of opposition to corruption and
privilege, Jackson made the federal civil service his first
target. Many officeholders, he thought, were treating their
jobs as personal possessions to which their long service
entitled them. Jackson disagreed. Believing that the duties
of most officeholders were simple, he supported "rotation
in office" so that as many plain people as possible would
have a chance to work for the government. He did not
invent rotation, but he applied it more harshly than his
predecessors by firing nearly half of the higher civil service, especially postmasters and customs officers.

Map 10.1 The Election of 1828

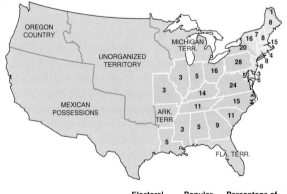

		Electoral Vote	Popular Vote	Percentage of Popular Vote
Democratic Andrew Jackson		178	642,553	56
National Republican John Q. Adams		83	500,897	44
Divided	5 6			

Andrew Jackson, by Ralph Earl
Jackson during the nullification crisis, looking serene in the uniform of a major-general and determined to face down the greatest challenge to his presidency.

Although Jackson defended his removals on the democratically flavored grounds of rotation, he also had a partisan motive. His removals were concentrated in the Northeast, the stronghold of John Quincy Adams. In their place he appointed his supporters, including Samuel Swartwout. Appointed the chief customs officer for the port of New York, Swartwout caused Jackson embarrassment by running off with millions of dollars of customs receipts. Critics dubbed the practice of basing appointments on party loyalty the "**spoils system**."

At least to its victims, Jackson's application of rotation seemed arbitrary because he refused to offer any reasons to justify individual removals. His stand on internal improvements and tariffs sparked even more intense controversy. Although not opposed to all federal aid for internal improvements, Jackson was sure that public officials used such aid to woo supporters by handing out favors to special interests. To end this lavish and corrupt giveaway, he flatly rejected federal support for roads within states. Accordingly, in 1830 he vetoed a bill providing federal money for a road in Kentucky between Maysville and Lexington for its "purely local character."

Jackson's strongest support lay in the South. The Indian Removal Act of 1830 (see Chapter 9) enhanced his popularity there. The tariff issue, however, would test the South's loyalty to Jackson. In 1828, while Adams was still president, some of Jackson's supporters in Congress had contributed to the passage of a high protective tariff that was as favorable to western agriculture and New England manufacturing as it was unfavorable to southerners, who had few industries to protect and who now would have to pay more for manufactured goods. Taking for granted the South's support for Jackson in the coming election, Jackson's supporters had calculated that southerners would blame the Adams administration for this "Tariff of Abominations." In reality, Jackson, not Adams, bore the South's fury over the tariff.

Nullification

The tariff of 1828 laid the basis for a rift between Jackson and his vice president, John C. Calhoun, that was to shake the foundations of the Republic. Early in his career, Calhoun had been an ardent nationalist. He had entered Congress in 1811 as a war hawk, supported the protectionist tariff of 1816, and dismissed strict construction of the Constitution as refined philosophical nonsense. During the late 1820s, however, Calhoun the nationalist gradually became Calhoun the states' rights sectionalist. The reasons for his shift were complex. He had supported the tariff of 1816 as a measure conducive to national defense in the wake of the War of 1812. By encouraging fledgling industries, he had reasoned, the tariff would free the United States from dependence on Britain and provide revenue for military preparedness. By 1826, however, few Americans perceived national defense as a priority. Furthermore, the infant industries of 1816 had grown into troublesome adolescents that demanded higher and higher tariffs.

Calhoun also burned with ambition to be president. Jackson had stated that he would only serve one term, and Calhoun assumed that he would succeed Jackson. To do so, however, he had to maintain the support of the South, which was increasingly taking an antitariff stance. As the center of cotton production had shifted to Alabama and Mississippi in the Southwest, Calhoun's home state, South Carolina, had suffered an economic decline throughout the 1820s, which its voters blamed on high tariffs. Tariffs not only drove up the price of manufactured goods but also threatened to reduce the sale of British textile products in the United States. Such a reduction might eventually lower the British demand for southern cotton and cut cotton prices. The more New England industrialized, the clearer it became that tariff laws were pieces of sectional legislation. New Englanders like Massachusetts's eloquent Daniel Webster swung toward protectionism; southerners responded with militant hostility.

Calhoun followed the Virginia and Kentucky Resolutions of 1798–1799 in viewing the Union as a compact by which the states had conferred limited and specified powers on the federal government. Although the Constitution

John C. Calhoun, **by Charles Bird King, c. 1825**
Jackson, defeated in the presidential election of 1824, won handily
four years later. The magnetic Calhoun, Jackson's vice president,
broke with Jackson over nullification and the Peggy Eaton affair
and resigned the vice presidency in 1832.

did empower Congress to levy tariffs, Calhoun insisted
that only tariffs that raised revenue for such common purposes as defense were constitutional. Set so high that it deterred foreign exporters from shipping their products to
the United States, the tariff of 1828 could raise little revenue, and hence it failed to meet Calhoun's criterion
of constitutionality: that federal laws benefit everyone
equally. In 1828, Calhoun anonymously wrote the widely
circulated *South Carolina Exposition and Protest,* in which
he spelled out his argument that the tariff of 1828 was unconstitutional and that aggrieved states therefore had the
right to nullify, or override, the law within their borders.

Vehement opposition to tariffs in the South, and especially in South Carolina, rested on more than economic considerations, however. Southerners feared that
a federal government that passed tariff laws favoring one
section over another might also pass laws meddling with
slavery. Because Jackson himself was a slaveholder, the
fear of federal interference with slavery was perhaps far-
fetched. But South Carolinians, long apprehensive of
assaults on their crucial institution of slavery, had many

reasons for concern. South Carolina was one of only two
states in which blacks comprised a majority of the population in 1830. Moreover, in 1831 a bloody slave revolt
led by Nat Turner boiled up in Virginia. That same year in
Massachusetts, William Lloyd Garrison established *The
Liberator,* an abolitionist newspaper. These developments were enough to convince many troubled South
Carolinians that a line had to be drawn against tariffs
and possible future interference with slavery.

Like Calhoun, Jackson was strong-willed and proud.
Unlike Calhoun, he was already president and the leader
of a national party that included supporters in protariff
states like Pennsylvania (which had gone for Jackson in
the election of 1828). Thus to retain key northern support
while soothing the South, Jackson devised two policies.

The first was to distribute surplus federal revenue to the
states. Tariff schedules kept some goods out of the United
States but let many others in for a price. The price, in the
form of duties on imports, became federal revenue. In the
years before federal income taxes, tariffs were a major
source of federal revenue. Jackson hoped that this revenue,
fairly distributed among the states, would remove the taint
of sectional injustice from the tariff and force the federal
government to restrict its own expenditures. All of this was
good Jeffersonianism. Second, Jackson hoped to ease tariffs down from the sky-high level of 1828.

Calhoun disliked the idea of distributing federal revenue to the states because he believed that such a policy
could become an excuse to maintain tariffs forever. But
he was loath to break openly with Jackson. Between 1828
and 1831, Calhoun muffled his protest, hoping that
Jackson would lower the tariff and that he, Calhoun,
would retain both Jackson's favor and his chances for the
presidency. Congress did pass new, slightly reduced tariff rates in 1832, but these did not come close to satisfying South Carolinians.

Before passage of the tariff of 1832, however, two personal issues had ruptured relations between Calhoun
and Jackson. In 1829, Jackson's secretary of war, John H.
Eaton, married the widowed daughter of a Washington
tavernkeeper. By her own account, Peggy O'Neale Tim-
berlake was "frivolous, wayward, [and] passionate." While
still married to a naval officer away on duty, Peggy had
acquired the reputation of flirting with Eaton, who
boarded at her father's tavern. After her husband's death
and her marriage to Eaton, she and Eaton were snubbed
socially by Calhoun's wife and by his friends in the cabinet. Jackson, still angry about how his own wife had
been wounded by slander during the campaign of 1828,
not only befriended the Eatons but concluded that Calhoun had initiated the snubbing to discredit him and to
advance Calhoun's own presidential aspirations.

To make matters worse, in 1830 Jackson received convincing documentation of his suspicion that in 1818 Calhoun, as secretary of war under President Monroe, had urged that Jackson be punished for his unauthorized raid into Spanish Florida. The revelation that Calhoun had tried to stab him in the back in 1818, combined with the spurning of the Eatons, convinced Jackson that he had to "destroy [Calhoun] regardless of what injury it might do me or my administration." A symbolic confrontation occurred between Jackson and Calhoun at a Jefferson Day dinner in April 1830. Jackson proposed the toast, "Our Union: It must be preserved." Calhoun responded: "The Union next to Liberty the most dear. May we always remember that it can only be preserved by distributing equally the benefits and burdens of the Union."

The stage was now set for the **Nullification crisis**, a direct clash between the president and his vice president. In 1831, Calhoun acknowledged his authorship of the *South Carolina Exposition and Protest.* In November 1832, a South Carolina convention nullified the tariffs of 1828 and 1832 and forbade the collection of customs duties within the state. Jackson reacted quickly. He despised nullification, calling it an "abominable doctrine" that would reduce the government to anarchy, and he berated the South Carolina nullifiers as "unprincipled men who would rather rule in hell, than be subordinate in heaven." Jackson even began to send arms to loyal Unionists in South Carolina. In December 1832, he issued a proclamation that, while promising South Carolinians further tariff reductions, lambasted nullification as itself unconstitutional. The Constitution, he emphasized, had established "a single nation," not a league of states.

The crisis eased in March 1833 when Jackson signed into law two measures—"the olive branch and the sword," in one historian's words. The olive branch was the tariff of 1833 (also called the Compromise Tariff), which provided for a gradual but significant lowering of duties between 1833 and 1842. The sword was the Force Bill, authorizing the president to use arms to collect customs duties in South Carolina. Although South Carolina did not abandon nullification in principle—in fact, it nullified the Force Bill—it construed the Compromise Tariff as a concession and rescinded its nullification of the tariffs of 1828 and 1832.

Like most of the accommodations by which the Union lurched from one sectional crisis to the next before the Civil War, the Compromise of 1833 grew out of a mixture of partisanship and statesmanship. The moving spirit behind the Compromise Tariff was Kentucky's senator Henry Clay, who had long favored high tariffs. A combination of motives brought Clay and the nullifiers together in favor of tariff reduction. Clay feared that without concessions to South Carolina on tariffs, the Force Bill would produce civil war. Furthermore, he was apprehensive that without compromise, the principle of protective tariffs would disappear under the wave of Jackson's immense popularity. In short, Clay would rather take responsibility for lowering tariffs than allow the initiative on tariff questions to pass to the Jacksonians.

For their part, the nullifiers hated Jackson and defiantly toasted "Andrew Jackson: On the soil of South Carolina he received an humble birthplace. May he not find in it a traitor's grave!" Although recognizing that South Carolina had failed to gain support for nullification from other southern states and that they would have to bow to pressure, the nullifiers preferred that Clay, not Jackson, be the hero of the hour. So they supported Clay's Compromise Tariff. Everywhere Americans now hailed Clay as the Great Compromiser. Even Martin Van Buren frankly stated that Clay had "saved the country."

The Bank Veto and the Election of 1832

Jackson recognized that the gap between the rich and the poor was widening during the 1820s and 1830s (see Chapter 9). He did not object to the rich gaining wealth by hard work. But he believed that the wealthy often grew even richer by securing favors, "privileges," from corrupt legislatures. In addition, his disastrous financial speculations early in his career led him to suspect all banks, paper money, and monopolies. On each count, the Bank of the United States was guilty.

The **second Bank of the United States** had received a twenty-year charter from Congress in 1816. As a creditor of state banks, the Bank of the United States restrained their printing and lending of money by its ability to demand the redemption of state bank notes in specie (gold or silver coinage). The bank's power enabled it to check the excesses of state banks, but also provoked hostility. In fact, it was widely blamed for precipitating the Panic of 1819. Further, at a time of mounting attacks on privilege, the bank was undeniably privileged. As the official depository for federal revenue, its capacity to lend money vastly exceeded that of any state bank. Its capital of $35 million amounted to more than double the annual expenditures of the federal government. Yet this institution, more powerful than any bank today, was only remotely controlled by the government. Its stockholders were private citizens—a "few monied capitalists" in Jackson's words. Although chartered by Congress, the bank was located in Philadelphia, not Washington, and its directors enjoyed considerable independence. Its president, the aristocratic Nicholas Biddle, viewed himself as a public servant, duty-bound to keep the bank above politics.

Urged on by Henry Clay, who hoped to ride a probank bandwagon into the White House in 1832, Biddle secured congressional passage of a bill to recharter the bank. In vetoing the recharter bill, Jackson denounced the bank as a private and privileged monopoly that drained the West of specie, was immune to taxation by the states, and made "the rich richer and the potent more powerful." Failing to persuade Congress to override Jackson's veto, Clay now pinned his hopes on gaining the presidency himself.

By 1832, Jackson had made his views on major issues clear. He was simultaneously a staunch defender of states' rights and a staunch Unionist. Although he cherished the Union, he believed that the states were far too diverse to accept strong direction from Washington. The safest course was to allow the states considerable freedom so that they would remain content within the Union and reject dangerous doctrines like nullification.

Throwing aside earlier promises to retire, Jackson again ran for the presidency in 1832, with Martin Van Buren as his running mate. Henry Clay ran on the National Republican ticket, touting his American System of protective tariffs, national banking, and federal support for internal improvements. Jackson's overwhelming personal popularity swamped Clay. Secure in office for another four years, Jackson was ready to finish dismantling the Bank of the United States.

The Bank Controversy and the Second Party System, 1833–1840

Jackson's veto of the recharter of the Bank of the United States ignited a searing controversy. Following the veto, Jackson took steps to destroy the Bank of the United States so that it could never be revived. His banking policies spurred the rise of the opposition Whig Party, mightily stimulated popular interest in politics, and contributed to the severe economic downturn, known as the Panic of 1837, that greeted his successor, Martin Van Buren. By 1840, the Whig and Democratic parties divided crisply over a fundamental issue: banks or no banks.

In part, tempers flared over banking because the U.S. government did not issue paper currency of its own; there were no "official" dollar bills as we know them today. Paper currency consisted of notes (promises to redeem in specie) dispensed by banks. These IOUs fueled economic development by making it easier for businesses and farmers to acquire loans to build factories or buy land. But if a note depreciated after its issuance because of public doubts about a bank's solvency, wage

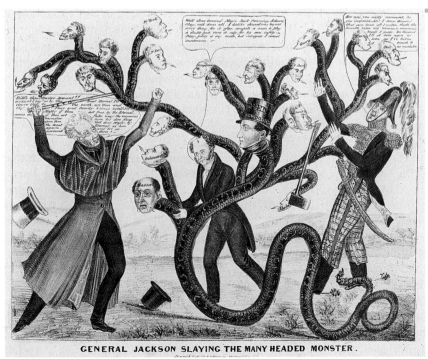

GENERAL JACKSON SLAYING THE MANY HEADED MONSTER.

Jackson Versus the Bank
Andrew Jackson, aided by Martin Van Buren (center), attacks the Bank of the United States, which, like the many-headed serpent Hydra of Greek mythology, keeps sprouting new heads. The largest head belongs to Nicholas Biddle, the bank's president.

earners who had been paid in paper rather than specie would suffer. Further, paper money encouraged a speculative economy, one that raised profits and risks. For example, paper money encouraged farmers to buy land on credit in the expectation that its price would rise, but a sudden drop in agricultural prices would leave them mired in debt. Would the United States embrace swift economic development at the price of allowing some to get rich quickly off investments while others languished? Or would it opt for more modest growth within traditional channels that were based on "honest" manual work and frugality? Between 1833 and 1840 these questions would dominate American politics.

The War on the Bank

Jackson could have allowed the bank to die a natural death when its charter ran out in 1836. But Jackson and several of his rabid followers viewed the bank as a kind of dragon that would grow new limbs as soon as old ones were cut off. When Biddle, anticipating further moves against the bank by Jackson, began to call in the bank's loans and contract credit during the winter of 1832–1833, Jacksonians saw their darkest fears confirmed. The bank, Jackson assured Van Buren, "is trying to kill me, but I will kill it." Accordingly, Jackson embarked on a controversial policy of removing federal deposits from the Bank of the United States and placing them in state banks, called "pet banks" by their critics because they were usually selected for their loyalty to the Democratic Party.

Jackson himself opposed paper money and easy credit for encouraging ordinary Americans to embark on get-rich-quick schemes. But as state banks became depositories for federal revenue, they were able to print more paper money and extend more loans to farmers who were eager to buy public lands in the West and to speculators who bought land in the expectation of reselling it at a profit. Government land sales rose from $6 million in 1834 to $25 million in 1836. The policy of removal seemed a formula for producing exactly the kind of economy that Jackson wanted to abolish.

Jackson recognized the danger and hoped to sharply limit the number of state banks that would become depositories for federal revenue. But as state banks increasingly clamored for federal revenue, the number of state-bank depositories soon multiplied beyond Jackson's expectations. There were twenty-three by the end of 1833. Jackson found himself caught between crosswinds. On the one hand, many Democrats resented the Bank of the United States because it periodically contracted credit and restricted lending by state banks. Western Democrats, in particular, had long viewed the Cincinnati branch of the Bank of the United States as inadequate to supply their need for credit and favored an expansion of banking activity. Advocating soft money (paper), these Democrats in 1836 pressured a reluctant Jackson to sign the Deposit Act, which increased the number of deposit banks and loosened federal control over them. On the other hand, Jackson believed that paper money sapped "public virtue," and "robbed honest labour of its earnings to make knaves rich, powerful and dangerous." Seeking to reverse the damaging effects of the Deposit Act, Jackson issued a proclamation in 1836 called the Specie Circular, which provided that only specie could be accepted in payment for public lands.

Prior to 1837, when a depression struck, most Democrats favored soft money. The rival hard-money (specie) view was warmly advocated within Jackson's inner circle of advisers and from a faction of the New York Democratic Party called the Locofocos. The Locofocos, who had the ardent support of Frances Wright, grew out of various "workingmen's" parties that had sprouted during the late 1820s in northern cities and that called for free public education, the abolition of imprisonment for debt, and a ten-hour workday. Most of these parties had collapsed within a few years, but in New York the "workies" had gradually been absorbed by the Democratic Party. Once in the party, they were hard to keep in line. A mixture of intellectuals and small artisans and journeymen threatened by economic change, they worried about inflation, preferred to be paid in specie, and distrusted banks and paper money. In 1835, a faction of workingmen had broken away from Tammany Hall, the main Democratic Party organization in New York City, and held a dissident meeting in a hall whose candles were illuminated by a newfangled invention, the "loco foco," or match. Thereafter, these radical workingmen were known as Locofocos.

The Rise of Whig Opposition

During Jackson's second term, the opposition National Republican Party gave way to the new **Whig Party**, which developed a broader base in both the South and the North than had the National Republicans. Jackson's magnetic personality had swept him to victory in 1828 and 1832. But as Jackson's vague Jeffersonianism was replaced by suspicion of federal aid for internal improvements and protective tariffs, and by hard-and-fast positions against the Bank of the United States and nullification, more of those alienated by Jackson's policies joined the opposition.

Jackson's crushing of nullification, for example, led some of its southern supporters into the Whig Party, not because the Whigs favored nullification but because they opposed Jackson. Jackson's war on the Bank of the United States produced the same result. His policy of removing deposits from the bank pleased some southerners but dismayed others who had been satisfied with the bank and who did not share westerners' mania for cheaper and easier credit. Jackson's suspicion of federal aid for internal improvements also alienated some southerners who feared that the South would languish behind the North unless it began to push ahead with improvements. Because so much southern capital was tied up in slavery, pro-improvement southerners looked to the federal government for aid, and when they were met with a cold shoulder, they drifted into the Whig Party. None of this added up to an overturning of the Democratic Party in the South; the South was still the Democrats' firmest base. But the Whigs were making significant inroads, particularly in southern market towns and among planters who had close ties to southern bankers and merchants.

Meanwhile, social reformers in the North were infusing new vitality into the opposition to Jackson. These reformers wanted to improve American society by ending slavery and the sale of liquor, improving public education, and elevating public morality. Most opponents of liquor (temperance reformers) and most public-school reformers gravitated to the Whigs. Whig philosophy was more compatible with their goals than were Democratic ideals. Where Democrats maintained that the government should not impose a uniform standard of conduct on a diverse society, the Whigs' commitment to Clay's American System implied an acceptance of active intervention by the government to change society. Reformers wanted the government to play a positive role by suppressing the liquor trade and by establishing centralized systems of public education. Thus a shared sympathy for active government programs tended to unite Whigs and reformers.

Reformers also indirectly stimulated new support for the Whigs from native-born Protestant workers. The reformers, themselves almost all Protestants, widely distrusted immigrants, especially the Irish, who viewed drinking as a normal recreation and who, as Catholics, suspected (correctly) that the public schools favored by reformers would teach Protestant doctrines. The rise of reform agitation and its frequent association with the Whigs drove the Irish into the arms of the Democrats—but, by the same token, gained support for the Whigs from many native-born Protestant workers who were contemptuous of the Irish.

No source of Whig strength, however, was more remarkable than Anti-Masonry, a protest movement against the secrecy and exclusiveness of the Masonic lodges,

which had long provided prominent men, including George Washington, with fraternal fellowship and exotic rituals. The spark that set off the Anti-Masonic crusade was the abduction and disappearance in 1826 of William Morgan, a New York stonemason, who had threatened to expose Masonic secrets. Every effort to solve the mystery of Morgan's disappearance ran into a stone wall because local officials were themselves Masons, seemingly bent on obstructing the investigation. Throughout the Northeast, the public became increasingly aroused against the Masonic order, and rumors spread that Masonry was a powerful, anti-Christian conspiracy of the rich to suppress popular liberty and an exclusive retreat for drunkards. Anti-Masonry brought intensely moralistic small farmers and artisans from the Northeast into the Whig Party.

By 1836, the Whigs had become a national party with widespread appeal. In both the North and South, they attracted those with close ties to the market economy—commercial farmers, planters, merchants, and bankers. In the North, they also gained support from reformers, evangelical clergymen (especially Presbyterians and Congregationalists), Anti-Masons, and manufacturers. In the South they appealed to some former nullificationists; Calhoun himself briefly became a Whig. Everywhere the Whigs assailed Jackson as an imperious dictator, "King Andrew I"; indeed, they had taken the name "Whigs" to associate their cause with that of the American patriots who had opposed King George III in 1776.

The Election of 1836

When it came to popularity, Jackson was a hard act to follow. In 1836, the Democrats ran Martin Van Buren for the presidency, a politician whose star had risen as Calhoun's had fallen. Party rhetoric reminded everyone that Van Buren was Jackson's favorite, and then contended that the Democratic Party itself, with Van Buren as its mere agent, was the real heir to Jackson, the perfect embodiment of the popular will. Less cohesive than the Democrats, the Whigs could not unite on a single candidate. Rather, four anti–Van Buren candidates emerged in different parts of the country. These included three Whigs—William Henry Harrison of Ohio, Daniel Webster of Massachusetts, and W. P. Mangum of North Carolina—and one Democrat, Hugh Lawson White of Tennessee, who distrusted Van Buren and who would defect to the Whigs after the election.

Democrats accused the Whigs of a plot to so divide the vote that no candidate would receive the required majority of votes in the Electoral College. That would

Russia
Oregon Country
British North America
United States
Texas
Mexico

 BEYOND AMERICA—GLOBAL INTERACTIONS

The Panic of 1837

Historians long blamed Andrew Jackson's policies for the Panic of 1837. Jackson's veto of the recharter of the Bank of the United States in 1832, their argument ran, led to the destruction of a valuable institution that policed the responsible state banks. His policy of transferring deposits from the Bank of the United States to state banks expanded the state banks' reserves and led them recklessly to print paper money and extend loans. Finally, his Specie Circular of 1836 drastically reduced the amount of money in circulation. This deflation—the money supply fell by 34 percent from 1838 to 1842—had a catastrophic effect on commodity prices. In a nation of small producers in which most people depended on farming for their living, collapsing commodity prices spelled personal misery. But farmers were not the only victims. Half of the skilled workers in New York City reportedly lost their jobs in the immediate wake of the Panic, and those fortunate enough to find work saw

The Times
Panicked depositors crowd a bank, a pawnbroker has a lot of customers, drunks stagger, and beggars plead for charity in this ironic depiction of the Fourth of July, 1837.

their wage rates drop by one-third between 1836 1842.

In the late 1960s, however, economic historians trained in new techniques of precise measurement started to chip away at this interpretation. If the Specie Circular had really drained specie from banks, we would expect to find major flows of specie from eastern banks, which had the largest specie reserves, to banks in the West, where land was being purchased. But only slight specie flows occurred. Finding little evidence to support the traditional interpretation of the Panic, historians began to look for causes beyond the borders of the United States. This approach made sense, for the American economy was comparatively small in the 1830s, heavily dependent on foreign investment to build its canals, and increasingly reliant on a single export, cotton.

It now appears that developments in Mexico, China, and Britain played a far more important role than Jackson's policies in triggering the collapse. During the 1820s, the United States imported freshly mined silver from Mexico, which Americans then used to pay for silk and tea from China. Next, in the 1830s the Chinese increasingly developed a taste for opium, which was grown in India. Since India was then under British control, the Chinese used silver acquired from the United States to pay the British merchants who managed the opium trade. As long as silver was flowing into Britain, the Bank of England did not worry that specie was simultaneously flowing *out* of Britain in the form of investment in canals and other projects in the United States. However, in 1836, the Bank of England, worried that British investors were overextending themselves in loans to America, raised interest rates in order to keep specie at home. To continue to attract foreign investment, American banks raised their interest rates, so credit became much harder to obtain on both sides of the Atlantic.

Making a bad situation worse, the price of raw cotton plummeted early in 1837. Since loans in the United States, especially in the South, were often secured by cotton, the collapsing price of cotton wiped out many lenders. Once again, the causes lay beyond America's borders. Raw cotton had commanded high prices from 1832 to 1835 because bumper wheat harvests in England had cut the cost of food and made it possible for British workers to spend more on goods spun from American cotton. But poor harvests from 1836 through 1838 drove up the cost of food in Britain, leaving workers there with less money to spend on

The Bank of England, 1833
The Bank of England moved to this impressive neo-classical building in 1833. At the time, Britain was the world's leading industrial nation. The bank's influence over interest rates and financial markets gave it enormous global influence.

clothing. British demand for American raw cotton declined. To top it off, the U.S. cotton crop of 1839 was among the best ever, driving down the price of cotton even more.

When British wheat harvests declined, Britain had to import wheat to feed its people. To pay for these imports, the Bank of England had to attract capital from abroad by raising interest rates. Interest rates in Britain more than doubled from mid 1838 to mid-1839. Soaring interest rates spelled disaster for Americans, who had started a new round of canal building with the expectation that British investors would lend the money. But British investors could now get a higher return keeping their money at home than investing in American canals. As British investment dried up, the United States was left with quarter- and half-built canals that went nowhere.

So, who was to blame for the American collapse? No one in particular. The Whigs and the Democrats raged at each other for causing the depression, but its roots lay in transatlantic events over which the United States, with its undeveloped economy and dependence on cotton exports, had little control. When Britain caught a cold, the United States came down with the flu.

Question for Analysis

- In what way did the reliance of the American economy on cotton as its main export make it vulnerable to poor wheat harvests in Britain?

throw the election into the House of Representatives, where, as in 1824, deals and bargains would be struck. In reality, the Whigs had no overall strategy, and Van Buren won a clear majority of the electoral votes. But there were signs of trouble ahead for the Democrats. The popular vote was close, notably in the South, where the Democrats had won two-thirds of the votes in 1832 but barely half in 1836.

The Panic of 1837

Jackson left office in a burst of glory and returned to his Nashville home in a triumphal procession. But the public's mood quickly became less festive, for no sooner was Van Buren in office than a severe depression, called the **Panic of 1837**, struck. (See Beyond America—Global Interactions: The Panic of 1837.)

In the speculative boom of 1835 and 1836 that was born of Jackson's policy of removing federal deposits from the Bank of the United States and placing them in state banks, the total number of banks doubled, the value of bank notes in circulation nearly tripled, and both commodity and land prices soared. Encouraged by easy money and high commodity prices, states made new commitments to build canals. Then in May 1837, prices began to tumble, and bank after bank suspended specie payments. After a short rally, the economy crashed again in 1839. The Bank of the United States, which had continued to operate as a state bank with a Pennsylvania charter, failed. Nicholas Biddle was charged with fraud and theft. Banks throughout the nation once again suspended specie payments.

The ensuing depression was far more severe and prolonged than the economic downturn of 1819. Those lucky enough to find work saw their wage rates drop by roughly one-third between 1836 and 1842. In despair, many workers turned to the teachings of William Miller, a New England religious enthusiast whose reading of the Bible convinced him that the end of the world was imminent. Dressed in black coats and stovepipe hats, Miller's followers roamed urban sidewalks and rural villages in search of converts. Many Millerites sold their possessions and purchased white robes to ascend into heaven on October 22, 1843, the date on which Millerite leaders calculated the world would end. Ironically, by then the worst of the depression was over; but at its depths in the late 1830s and early 1840s, the economic slump fed the gloom that made despairing people receptive to Miller's predictions.

Called the "sly fox" and the "little magician" for his political craftiness, Van Buren would need these skills to confront the depression that was causing misery not only for ordinary citizens but also for the Democratic Party.

Railing against "Martin Van Ruin," in 1838 the Whigs swept the governorship and most of the legislative seats in Van Buren's own New York.

To seize the initiative, Van Buren called for the creation of an independent Treasury. The idea was simple: instead of depositing its money in banks, which would then use federal funds as the basis for speculative loans, the government would hold its revenues and keep them from the grasp of corporations. When Van Buren finally signed the Independent Treasury Bill into law on July 4, 1840, his supporters hailed it as America's second Declaration of Independence.

The independent Treasury reflected the deep Jacksonian suspicion of an alliance between government and banking. But the Independent Treasury Act failed to address the banking issue on the state level, where newly chartered state banks—of which there were more than nine hundred by 1840—lent money to farmers and businessmen. Blaming the depression on Jackson's Specie Circular rather than on the banks, Whigs continued to encourage the chartering of banks as a way to spur economic development. In contrast, a growing number of Democrats blamed the depression on banks and on paper money and swung toward the hard-money stance long favored by Jackson and his inner circle. In Louisiana and Arkansas, Democrats successfully prohibited banks altogether, and elsewhere they imposed severe restrictions on banks—for example, by banning the issuing of paper money in small denominations. In sum, after 1837 the Democrats became an antibank, hard-money party.

The Election of 1840

Despite the depression, Van Buren gained his party's renomination. Avoiding their mistake of 1836, the Whigs settled on a single candidate, Ohio's William Henry Harrison, and ran former Virginia Senator John Tyler as vice president. Harrison, who was sixty-seven years old and barely eking out a living on a farm, was picked because he had few enemies. Early in the campaign, the Democrats made a fatal mistake by ridiculing Harrison as "Old Granny," a man who desired only to spend his declining years in a log cabin sipping cider. Without knowing it, the Democrats had handed the Whigs the most famous campaign symbol in American history. The Whigs immediately reminded the public that Harrison had been a rugged frontiersman, the hero of the Battle of Tippecanoe, and a defender of all frontier people who lived in log cabins.

Refusing to publish a platform, the Whigs ran a "hurrah" campaign. They used log cabins for headquarters, sang log-cabin songs, gave out log-cabin cider, and called their newspaper *Log Cabin*. For a slogan, they trumpeted

"Tippecanoe and Tyler too." When not celebrating log cabins, they attacked Van Buren as a soft aristocrat who lived in "regal splendor." Whereas Harrison was content to drink hard cider from a plain mug, the Whigs observed, Van Buren had turned the White House into a palace fit for an oriental despot and drank fine wines from silver goblets while he watched people go hungry in the streets.

Map 10.2 The Election of 1840

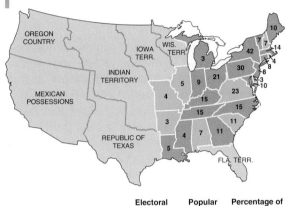

	Electoral Vote	Popular Vote	Percentage of Popular Vote
Whig William H. Harrison	234	1,274,624	53.1
Democratic Martin Van Buren	60	1,127,781	46.9

The election results gave Harrison a clear victory (see Map 10.2). Van Buren carried only seven states and even failed to hold his own state of New York. The depression would have made it difficult, if not impossible, for any Democrat to have triumphed in 1840, but Van Buren had other disabilities besides the economic collapse. Unlike Harrison and Jackson, he had no halo of military glory. Moreover, Van Buren ran a surprisingly sluggish campaign. Prior to 1840, the Whigs had been slower than the Democrats to mobilize voters by new techniques. But in 1840, it was Van Buren who directed his campaign the old-fashioned way by writing encouraging letters to key supporters, whereas Harrison broke with tradition and went around the country (often on railroads) campaigning. Ironically, Van Buren, the master politician, was beaten at his own game.

The Second Party System Matures

In losing the presidency in 1840, Van Buren actually received four hundred thousand more popular votes than any previous presidential candidate. The total number

"The New Era Whig Trap Sprung," New York, 1840 This Whig cartoon from the election of 1840 shows Democrat Martin Van Buren trapped inside the Whig campaign symbol, a log cabin. Andrew Jackson is desperately trying to pry him out.

THE NEW ERA WHIG TRAP SPRUNG

of votes cast in presidential elections had risen from 1.2 million in 1828 to 1.5 million in 1836 to 2.4 million in 1840. The 60 percent leap in the size of the popular vote between 1836 and 1840 is the greatest proportional jump between consecutive elections in American history. Neither lower suffrage requirements nor population growth was the main cause of this increase. Rather, it resulted from a jump in the percentage of eligible voters who chose to vote. In the three elections before 1840, the proportion of white males who voted had fluctuated between 55 percent and 58 percent; in 1840 it rose to 80 percent.

Both the depression and the frenzy of the log-cabin campaign had brought voters to the polls. Yet voter turnout stayed up even after prosperity returned in the 1840s. The second party system, which had been developing slowly since 1828, reached a high plateau in 1840 and remained there for more than a decade. Politicians increasingly presented clear alternatives to voters. The gradual hardening of the line between the two parties stimulated enduring popular interest in politics.

No less than the tariff and banking issues, reform also aroused partisan passions by 1840. Yet the seeds of many of the reform movements that burst upon the national scene in the 1830s were initially sown in the field of religion rather than politics.

The Rise of Popular Religion

In *Democracy in America,* Alexis de Tocqueville pointed out an important difference between France and the United States. "In France I had almost always seen the spirit of religion and the spirit of freedom pursuing courses diametrically opposed to each other; but in America I found that they were intimately united, and that they reigned in common over the same country." From this assertion Tocqueville drew a startling conclusion: religion was "the foremost of the political institutions" of the United States.

In calling religion a political institution, Tocqueville did not mean that Americans gave special political privileges to any particular denomination. Rather, he was referring to the way in which religious impulses reinforced American democracy and liberty. Just as Americans demanded that politics be made accessible to the average person, they insisted that ministers preach doctrines that appealed to ordinary people. The most successful ministers were those who used plain words to move the heart, not those who tried to dazzle their listeners with theological complexities. Increasingly, too, Americans

demanded theological doctrines that put individuals in charge of their own religious destiny. They thrust aside the Calvinist creed that God had arbitrarily selected some people for salvation and others for damnation, and substituted the belief that anyone could attain heaven.

Thus heaven as well as politics became democratized in these years. The harmony between religious and democratic impulses owed much to a series of religious revivals known as the Second Great Awakening.

The Second Great Awakening

The **Second Great Awakening** had begun in Connecticut during the 1790s and set ablaze one section of the nation after another during the following half-century. At first, educated Congregationalists and Presbyterians such as Yale University's president Timothy Dwight had dominated the revivals. But as they spread from Connecticut to frontier states like Tennessee and Kentucky, revivals had undergone striking changes that were typified by the rise of camp meetings. These were gigantic revivals in which members of several denominations gathered together in sprawling open-air camps for up to a week to hear revivalists proclaim that the Second Coming of Jesus was near and that the time for repentance was now.

The most famous camp meeting occurred at Cane Ridge, Kentucky, in August 1801, when a huge crowd came together on a hillside to listen to thunderous sermons and to sing hymns and experience the influx of divine grace. One eyewitness described the meeting:

At night, the whole scene was awfully sublime. The ranges of tents, the fires, reflecting light amidst the branches of the towering trees; the candles and lamps illuminating the encampment; hundreds moving to and fro, with lights or torches, like Gideon's army; the preaching, praying, singing, and shouting, all heard at once, rushing from different parts of the ground, like the sound of many waters, was enough to swallow up all the powers of contemplation.

The Cane Ridge revival was an episode of the larger Great Kentucky Revival of 1800–1801. Among the distinguishing features of these frontier revivals was the appearance of "exercises" in which men and women rolled around like logs, jerked their heads furiously (a phenomenon known simply as "the jerks"), and grunted like animals (the "barking exercise"). Observing the apparent pandemonium that had broken loose, critics had blasted the frontier frenzy for encouraging fleshly lust more than spirituality and complained that "more souls were begot than saved" in revivals. In fact, the early frontier revivals had challenged traditional religious customs. The most successful frontier revivalist preachers were not college graduates but ordinary farmers and artisans who had experienced powerful religious conversions and who had contempt for learned ministers with their dry expositions of orthodoxy.

No religious denomination had been more successful on the frontier than the Methodists. With fewer than seventy thousand members in 1800, the Methodists had become America's largest Protestant denomination by 1844, claiming a little over a million members. In contrast to New England Congregationalists and Presbyterians, Methodists emphasized that religion was primarily a matter of the heart rather than the head. The frontier Methodists disdained "settled" ministers tied to fixed parishes. Instead, they preferred itinerant circuit riders—young, unmarried men who moved on horseback from place to place and preached in houses, open fields, or wherever else listeners gathered.

Although the frontier revivals disrupted religious custom, they also promoted law, order, and morality on the frontier. Drunken rowdies who tried to invade camp

meetings met their match in brawny itinerants like the Methodist Peter Cartwright. It was not only in camp meetings that Cartwright and his peers sought to raise the moral standard of the frontier. After Methodist circuit riders left, their converts formed weekly "classes" to provide mutual encouragement and to chastise one another for drunkenness, fighting, fornication, gossiping, and even sharp business practices.

Eastern Revivals

By the 1820s, the Second Great Awakening had begun to shift back to the East. The hottest revival fires blazed in an area of western New York known as the "Burned-Over District." No longer a frontier, western New York teemed with descendants of Puritans who hungered for religious experience and with people drawn by the hope of wealth after the completion of the Erie Canal. It was a fertile field of high expectations and bitter discontent.

The man who harnessed these anxieties to religion was **Charles G. Finney**. Finney began his career as a lawyer, but after a religious conversion in 1821, which he described as a "retainer from the Lord Jesus Christ to plead his cause," he became a Presbyterian minister and conducted revivals in towns like Rome and Utica along the canal. Although he also found time for trips to New York and Boston, his greatest "harvest" came in the thriving canal city of Rochester in 1830–1831.

The Rochester revival had several features that justify Finney's reputation as the "father of modern revivalism." First, it was a citywide revival in which all denominations participated. Finney was a pioneer of cooperation among Protestant denominations. In addition, in Rochester and elsewhere, Finney introduced devices for speeding conversions, such as the "anxious seat," a bench to which those ready for conversion were led so that they could be made objects of special prayer, and the "protracted meeting," which went on nightly for up to a week.

Finney's emphasis on special revival techniques sharply distinguished him from eighteenth-century revivalists, such as Jonathan Edwards. Whereas Edwards had portrayed revivals as the miraculous work of God, Finney made them out to be human creations. The divine spirit flowed in revivals, but humans made them happen. Although a Presbyterian, Finney flatly rejected the Calvinist belief that humans had a natural and nearly irresistible inclination to sin (the doctrine of "human depravity"). Rather, he affirmed, sin was purely a voluntary act; no one had to sin. Men and women could will themselves out of sin just as readily as they had willed themselves into it. Indeed, he declared, it was theoretically possible for men and women to will

Charles and Elizabeth Finney
Finney had an active career after his New York revivals. He served as president of Oberlin College from 1851 to 1866. This photograph of Finney and his second wife, Elizabeth Atkinson, was taken while they were on an evangelistic tour of Great Britain in 1850.

themselves free of all sin—to live perfectly. Those who heard Finney and similar revivalists came away convinced that they had experienced the washing away of all past guilt and the beginning of a new life. "I have been born again," a young convert wrote. "I am three days old when I write this letter."

Originally controversial, Finney's ideas came to dominate "evangelical" Protestantism—forms of Protestantism that focused on the need for an emotional religious conversion. He was successful because he told people what they wanted to hear: that their destinies were in their own hands. A society that celebrated the "self-made" individual embraced Finney's assertion that, even in religion, people could make of themselves what they chose. Moreover, compared to most frontier revivalists, Finney had an unusually dignified style. Taken together, these factors gave him a potent appeal to merchants, lawyers, and small manufacturers in the towns and cities of the North.

More than most revivalists, Finney recognized that few revivals would have gotten off the ground without the mass participation of women. During the Second Great Awakening, female converts outnumbered male converts by about two to one. Finney encouraged women to give public testimonies of their religious experiences in church, and he often converted husbands by first converting their wives and daughters. After a visit by Finney, Melania Smith, the wife of a Rochester physician who had little time for religion, greeted her husband with a reminder of "the woe which is denounced against the families which call not on the Name of the Lord." Soon Dr. Smith heeded his wife's pleading and joined one of Rochester's Presbyterian churches.

Critics of Revivals: The Unitarians

Whereas some praised revivals for saving souls, others doubted that they produced permanent changes in behavior and condemned them for encouraging "such extravagant and incoherent expressions, and such enthusiastic fervor, as puts common sense and modesty to the blush."

One small but influential group of revival critics was the Unitarians. The basic doctrine of Unitarianism—that Jesus Christ was less than fully divine—had gained quiet acceptance among religious liberals during the eighteenth century. However, it was not until the early nineteenth century that Unitarianism emerged as a formal denomination with its own churches, ministry, and national organization. In New England, hundreds of Congregational churches were torn apart by the withdrawal of socially prominent families who had embraced Unitarianism and by legal battles over which group—Congregationalists or Unitarians—could occupy church property. Although Unitarians won relatively few converts outside New England, their tendency to attract the wealthy and educated gave them influence beyond their numbers.

Unitarians criticized revivals as uncouth emotional exhibitions and argued that moral goodness should be cultivated by a gradual process of "character building" in which the individual learned to model his or her behavior on that of Jesus rather than by a sudden emotional conversion as in a revival. Yet Unitarians and revivalists shared the belief that human behavior could be changed for the better. Both rejected the Calvinist emphasis on innate human wickedness. William Ellery Channing, a Unitarian leader, claimed that Christianity had but one purpose: "the perfection of human nature, the elevation of men into nobler beings."

The Rise of Mormonism

The Unitarians' assertion that Jesus Christ was more human than divine challenged a basic doctrine of orthodox Christianity. Yet Unitarianism proved far less controversial than another of the new denominations of the 1820s and 1830s—the Church of Jesus Christ of Latter-day Saints, or **Mormons**. Its founder, Joseph Smith, grew to manhood in one of those families that seemed to be in constant motion to and fro, but never up. After moving his family nearly twenty times in ten years, Smith's ne'er-do-well father settled in Palmyra, New York, in the heart of the Burned-Over District. As a boy, Smith dreamed of finding buried treasure, while his religious views were convulsed by the conflicting claims of the denominations that thrived in the region. "Some were contending for the Methodist faith, some for the Presbyterian, and some for the Baptists," Smith later wrote. He wondered who was right and who wrong, or whether they were "all wrong together."

The sort of perplexity that Smith experienced was widespread in the Burned-Over District, but his resolution of the confusion was unique. Smith claimed that an angel led him to a buried book of revelation and to special seer stones for use in translating it. He completed his translation of this Book of Mormon in 1827. The Book of Mormon tells the story of an ancient Hebrew prophet, Lehi, whose descendants came to America and created a prosperous civilization that looked forward to the appearance of Jesus as its savior. Jesus had actually appeared and performed miracles in the New World, the book claimed, but the American descendants of Lehi had departed from the Lord's ways and quarreled among themselves. God had cursed some with dark skin; these were the American Indians, who, when later discovered by Columbus, had forgotten their history.

Despite his astonishing claims, Smith quickly gathered followers. The appeal of Mormonism lay partly in its positioning of America at the center of Christian history and partly in Smith's assertion that he had discovered a new revelation. The idea of an additional revelation beyond the Bible appeared to some to resolve the turmoil created by the Protestant denominations' inability to agree on what the Bible said or meant.

Smith and his followers steadily moved west from New York to Ohio and Missouri. Then they migrated to Illinois, where they built a model city, Nauvoo, and a magnificent temple supported by thirty huge pillars (see Map 10.3). By moving to these areas, the Mormons hoped to draw closer to the Indians, whose conversion was one of their goals, and to escape persecution. Smith's claim to have received a new revelation virtually guaranteed a hostile reception for the Mormons wherever they went because Smith had seemingly undermined the authority of the Bible, one of the two documents (the other being the Constitution) upon which the ideals of the American Republic rested.

Smith added fuel to the fire when he reported in 1843 that he had received still another revelation, this one sanctioning the Mormon practice of having multiple wives, or polygyny. Although Smith did not publicly proclaim polygyny as a doctrine, its practice among Mormons was a poorly kept secret. Smith's self-image also intensified the controversy that boiled around Mormonism. He refused to view himself merely as the founder of another denomination; instead, he saw himself as a prophet of the kingdom of God and was called a "Second Mohammed." Mormonism would be to Christianity what Christianity had been to Judaism: an all-encompassing, higher form of religion. In 1844, Smith announced his candidacy for the presidency of the United States. But the state of Illinois was already moving against him. Charged with treason, he was jailed in Carthage, Illinois, and along with his brother was murdered there by a mob in June 1844.

Mormonism is one of the few religions to have originated in the United States, and Smith initially had hoped that Americans would respond to his call. Some did, especially among the poor and downtrodden, but the hostility of the "Gentiles" (non-Mormons) gradually persuaded Smith that the future of Mormons lay in their separation from society. In this respect, Mormonism mirrored the efforts of several religious communal societies whose members resolutely set themselves apart from society. In general, these religious communitarians were less numerous, controversial, and long-lasting than

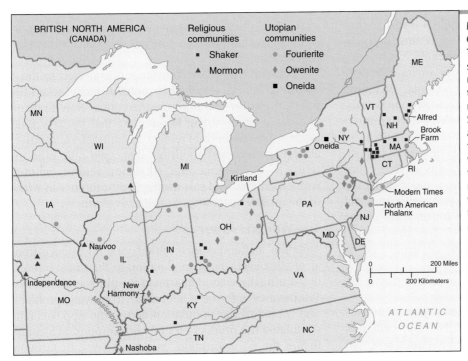

Map 10.3 Religious and Utopian Communities, 1800–1845
The desire to construct a perfect society influenced the founding of a number of communities, especially in the period from 1800 to 1845. Religious motives dominated the founding of Shaker and Mormon communities. In addition to the ideas of Robert Owen, those of the Frenchman Charles Fourier, who sought to cure the evils of competitive society by establishing a harmonious world in which men and women worked at "attractive" labor, influenced the founding of communities like Modern Times on Long Island and the North American Phalanx at Red Bank, New Jersey. Brook Farm was, for a period, a Fourierite community. John Humphrey Noyes's Oneida mingled religious and secular motives in ways hard to disentangle.

the Mormons, but one group among them, the Shakers, has continued to fascinate Americans.

The Shakers

Mother Ann Lee, the illiterate daughter of an English blacksmith, founded the Shakers, a name that came from a convulsive religious dance that was part of their ceremony. Lee and her followers established several tightly knit agricultural-artisan communities after her arrival in America in 1774. Shaker furniture became renowned for its beauty and strength, and Shakers invented such conveniences as the clothespin and the circular saw.

For all their achievements as artisans, the Shakers were fundamentally otherworldly and hostile to materialism. Having watched four of her children die in infancy, Mother Lee claimed to have seen a vision in which God expelled Adam and Eve from the Garden of Eden for having engaged in sexual intercourse. Shaker communities banned marriage and rigidly separated the sleeping quarters and workshops of men and women to discourage casual contacts. To maintain their membership—at their peak in the 1830s and 1840s the Shakers numbered about six thousand in eight states—Shakers relied on converts and adopting orphans.

To avoid becoming dependent on the evil ways of the outside world, Shakers pooled their land and implements, and they created remarkably prosperous villages. A journalist exclaimed that the lawns of Shaker villages would arouse the envy of a monarch. Even their road dust seemed pure, said another, while a British visitor concluded that "the earth does not show more flourishing fields, gardens, and orchards than theirs."

Shakers chose to live apart from society. But the message of most evangelical Protestants, including Charles G. Finney, was that religion and economic individualism—a person's pursuit of wealth—were compatible. Most revivalists told people that getting ahead in the world was acceptable as long as they were honest, temperate, and bound by the dictates of their consciences. By encouraging assimilation into rather than retreat from society, evangelicalism provided a powerful stimulus to the numerous reform movements of the 1820s and 1830s.

The Age of Reform

Democratic ferment was not confined to politics and religion. During the 1820s and 1830s, unprecedented numbers of men and women joined organizations that aimed to improve society. The abolition of slavery, women's rights, temperance, better treatment of criminals and the insane, public education, and even the establishment of utopian communities were high on various reformers' agendas.

At a time when women were not allowed to vote, free people of color increasingly were excluded from politics, and the major parties usually avoided controversial issues like slavery and women's rights, participation in reform movements offered women and blacks an opportunity to influence public issues. The white males drawn to reform movements viewed politics as a sorry spectacle that allowed a man like Andrew Jackson, a duelist who had married a divorcee, to become president and that routinely rewarded persons who would sacrifice any principle for victory at the polls. Although they occasionally cooperated with political parties, especially the Whigs, reformers gave their loyalty to their causes, not to parties.

Inclined to view all social problems as clashes between good and evil, reformers believed that they were on God's side on every issue. Religious revivalism contributed to their intense moralism. Virtually all prominent temperance reformers of the 1820s and 1830s, for example, had initially been inspired by revivals. But revivalism and reform were not always intimately linked. Influential school reformers and women's rights advocates were frequently religious liberals—either hostile or indifferent to revivals. Abolitionists criticized the churches for condoning slavery. Yet abolitionists borrowed the evangelical preachers' language and psychology by portraying slaveholding as a sin that called for immediate repentance.

Although the reform movements appealed to those excluded from or repelled by politics, most lacked the political parties' national organizations. New England and those parts of the Midwest settled by New Englanders were hotbeds of reform. In contrast, southerners actively suppressed abolition, displayed only mild interest in temperance and education reform, ignored women's rights, and saw utopian communities as proof of the mental instability of northern reformers.

The War on Liquor

Agitation for temperance (either total abstinence from alcoholic beverages or moderation in their use) intensified during the second quarter of the nineteenth century. Temperance reformers addressed a growing problem. The spread of the population across the Appalachians stimulated the production and consumption of alcohol. Before the transportation revolution, western farmers,

Signing the Pledge, 1840s
Pressured by his determined wife and pleading child, this reluctant tippler is about to submit to "moral suasion" and sign the pledge to abstain from alcohol.

unable to get their grain to markets, commonly distilled it into spirits. Annual per capita consumption of rum, whiskey, gin, and brandy rose until it exceeded seven gallons by 1830, nearly triple today's rate. By the late 1820s, the average adult male drank a half-pint of liquor a day. With some justification, reformers saw alcoholic excess as a male indulgence whose bitter consequences (spending wages on liquor instead of food) fell on women and children.

There had been agitation against intemperance before 1825, but the Connecticut revivalist Lyman Beecher ushered in a new phase that year. In six widely acclaimed lectures, he thundered against all use of alcohol. A year later, evangelical Protestants created the **American Temperance Society**, the first national temperance organization. By 1834, some five thousand state and local temperance societies were loosely affiliated with the American Temperance Society. Although these societies were nearly always headed by men, from

one-third to one-half of their members were women, who found in temperance agitation a public outlet for their moral energies. Whereas previous temperance supporters had advised moderation in the use of spirits, the American Temperance Society followed Beecher in demanding total abstinence. The society flooded the country with tracts denouncing the "amazing evil" of strong drink and urged churches to expel any members who condoned alcohol.

Among the main targets of the evangelical temperance reformers were moderate drinkers in the laboring classes. In the small shops where a handful of journeymen and apprentices worked informally, passing the jug every few hours was a time-honored way to relieve fatigue and monotony. But large factories demanded a more disciplined, sober work force, and evangelical temperance reformers quickly gained manufacturers' support. In East Dudley, Massachusetts, for example, three factory owners refused to sell liquor in factory stores, calculating that any profits from the sale would be more than offset by lost working time and "the scenes of riot and wickedness thus produced."

Workers showed little interest in temperance before the late 1830s. But after the Panic of 1837, a new stage of temperance agitation sprang up in the form of the Washington Temperance Societies. Starting in Baltimore in 1840, the Washingtonians were more likely to be mechanics (workingmen) and laborers than ministers and manufacturers. Many were reformed drunkards, and most had concluded that their survival in the harsh climate of depression depended on their commitment to sobriety and frugality. For example, Charles T. Woodman, a baker, had been forced by the collapse of his business to flee Boston for Philadelphia to escape his creditors. Like most Washingtonians, Woodman blamed his ruin on a relapse into his "old habit" of drink. The forces dislocating workers in the late 1830s were often far beyond their control. Part of the appeal of temperance was that it lay within their control. Take care of temperance, a Washingtonian assured a Baltimore audience, and the Lord would take care of the economy.

For all their differences from earlier temperance associations, the Washingtonians reflected the impact of revivals even more than did the American Temperance Society. Viewing drinking as sinful, they held "experience meetings" in which members described their "salvation" from liquor and their "regeneration" through abstinence or "teetotalism" (an emphatic form of the

The Antislavery Alphabet
Viewing children as morally pure and hence as natural opponents of slavery, abolitionists produced antislavery toys, games, and, as we see here, alphabet books.

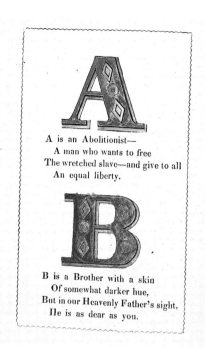

A is an Abolitionist—
A man who wants to free
The wretched slave—and give to all
An equal liberty.

B is a Brother with a skin
Of somewhat darker hue,
But in our Heavenly Father's sight,
He is as dear as you.

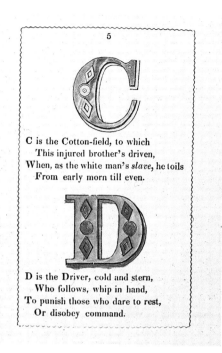

C is the Cotton-field, to which
This injured brother's driven,
When, as the white man's *slave*, he toils
From early morn till even.

D is the Driver, cold and stern,
Who follows, whip in hand,
To punish those who dare to rest,
Or disobey command.

word *total*). Their wives joined "Martha Washington" societies in which they pledged to smell their husbands' breath each night and paraded with banners that read "Teetotal or No Husband." The Washingtonians spread farther and faster than any other antebellum temperance organization.

As temperance won new supporters, the crusaders gradually shifted from calls for individuals to abstain to demands that towns and even states ban all traffic in liquor. This shift from moral suasion to legal prohibition was controversial, even within the movement. But by the late 1830s, prohibition was scoring victories. In 1838, Massachusetts prohibited the sale of distilled spirits in amounts less than fifteen gallons, thereby restricting small purchases by individual drinkers; in 1851 Maine banned the manufacture and sale of all intoxicating beverages. Controversial though these laws were, the temperance movement won a measure of success. After rising steadily between 1800 and 1830, per capita consumption of distilled spirits began to fall during the 1830s. The rate of consumption during the 1840s was less than half that in the 1820s.

Public-School Reform

Like temperance reformers, school reformers encouraged orderliness and thrift in the common people. Rural America's "district" schools became a main target. Here students

ranging in age from three to twenty or more crowded into a single room and learned to read and count, but little more. Students never forgot the primitive conditions and harsh discipline of these schools, especially the floggings until "the youngster vomited or wet his breeches."

Expecting little from education, rural parents were content with these schools. But reformers, who insisted that schools equip students for the emerging competitive and industrial economy, saw them in a different light. **Horace Mann**, who in 1837 became the first secretary of the newly created Massachusetts board of education, presided over sweeping reforms to transform schools into institutions that occupied most of a child's time and energy. Mann's goals included shifting financial support from parents to the state, extending the school term from two or three to as many as ten months, standardizing textbooks, classifying students into grades based on their age and attainment, and compelling attendance.

School reformers sought to spread uniform cultural values as well as to combat ignorance. Requiring students to arrive at a set time would teach punctuality, and matching students against their peers would stimulate the competitiveness required by an industrialized society. Children would read the same books and absorb such lessons as "Idleness is the nest in which mischief lays its eggs." The McGuffey readers, which sold 50 million copies between 1836 and 1870, preached industry, honesty, sobriety, and patriotism.

Although school reform made few gains in the South (see Chapter 12), much of the North remodeled its schools along the lines advocated by Mann, and in 1852 Massachusetts passed the nation's first compulsory school law. Success did not come easily. Educational reformers faced challenges from farmers, who were satisfied with the informality of the district schools, and from urban Catholics, led by New York City's Bishop John Hughes, who pointed out that the textbooks used in public schools dispensed anti-Catholic and anti-Irish barbs. And in both rural and urban areas, the laboring poor opposed compulsory education as a menace to parents who depended on their children's wages.

Yet school reformers prevailed, in part because their opponents, rural Protestants and urban Catholics, were incapable of cooperating with each other. In part, too, reformers succeeded by gaining influential allies. For example, their stress on free, tax-supported schools won the backing of the urban workingmen's parties that arose in the late 1820s; and their emphasis on punctuality appealed to manufacturers who needed a disciplined work force. The new ideas also attracted reform-minded women who recognized that the grading of schools would ease women's entry into teaching. Many people doubted that a woman could control a one-room school with pupils of widely variant ages, but managing a class of eight-year-olds was different. Catharine Beecher accurately predicted that school reform would render teaching a suitable profession for women. By 1900, about 70 percent of the nation's schoolteachers were women.

School reform also appealed to native-born Americans alarmed by the swelling tide of immigration. The public school emerged as the favorite device by which reformers forged a common American culture out of an increasingly diverse society. "We must decompose and cleanse the impurities which rush into our midst" through the "one infallible filter—the SCHOOL."

School reformers were eager to assimilate immigrants into the mainstream, but few stressed the integration of black and white children. When black children were fortunate enough to get any schooling, it was usually in segregated schools. Black children who entered integrated public schools met with such virulent prejudice that black leaders in northern cities frequently preferred segregated schools.

Abolition

Antislavery sentiment among whites flourished in the Revolutionary era but declined in the early nineteenth century. The main antislavery organization founded between 1800 and 1830 was the American Colonization Society (1816), which displayed little moral outrage against slavery. The society proposed a plan for gradual emancipation, with compensation to the slave owner, and the shipment of freed blacks to what became the nation of Liberia in Africa. This proposal attracted support from some slaveholders in the Upper South who would never have dreamed of a general emancipation.

At its core, colonization was hard-hearted and soft-headed. Its proponents assumed that blacks were a degraded race that did not belong in American society, and they underestimated the growing dependence of the South's economy on slavery. Confronted by a soaring demand for cotton and other commodities, few southerners were willing to free their slaves, even if compensated. In any event, the American Colonization Society never had enough funds to buy freedom for more than a fraction of slaves. Between 1820 and 1830, only 1,400 blacks migrated to Liberia, and most were already free. In striking contrast, the American slave population, fed by natural increase (the excess of births over deaths), rose from 1,191,000 in 1810 to more than 2,000,000 in 1830.

During the 1820s, the main source of radical opposition to slavery was blacks themselves. Blacks had little enthusiasm for colonization. Most American blacks were native-born rather than African-born. How, they asked, could they be sent back to a continent that they had never left? "We are natives of this country," a black pastor in New York proclaimed. "We only ask that we be treated as well as foreigners." In opposition to colonization, blacks formed scores of abolition societies. David Walker, a Boston free black who opened a used clothing store in 1827, smuggled antislavery tracts into the South by stuffing them into the pockets of clothes he shipped to the South. In 1829, Walker published an *Appeal . . . to the Colored Citizens of the World,* which urged slaves to murder their masters if necessary to gain their freedom.

Not all whites acquiesced to the continuance of slavery. In 1821, the Quaker Benjamin Lundy began a newspaper, the *Genius of Universal Emancipation,* and put forth proposals that no new slave states be admitted to the Union, that the internal slave trade be outlawed, that the three-fifths clause of the Constitution be repealed, and that Congress abolish slavery wherever it had the authority to do so. In 1828, Lundy hired a young New Englander, **William Lloyd Garrison**, as an assistant editor. Prematurely bald, wearing steel-rimmed glasses, and typically donning a black suit and black cravat, Garrison looked more like a schoolmaster than a rebel. But in 1831, when he launched his own newspaper, *The Liberator*, he quickly established himself as the most famous and controversial white abolitionist. "I am in earnest," Garrison wrote. "I will not equivocate—I will not excuse—I will not retreat a single inch—AND I WILL BE HEARD."

Garrison's battle cry was "immediate emancipation." In place of exiling blacks to Africa, he substituted the truly radical notion that blacks should enjoy civil (or legal) equality with whites. He greeted slaves as "a Man and a Brother," "a Woman and a Sister." Even Garrison, however, did not think that all slaves could be freed overnight. "Immediate emancipation" meant that all people had to realize that slavery was sinful and its continued existence intolerable.

Garrison quickly gained support from the growing number of black abolitionists. A black barber in Pittsburgh sent Garrison sixty dollars to help with *The Liberator*. Black agents sold subscriptions, and three-fourths of *The Liberator*'s subscribers in the early years were black.

The escaped slave Frederick Douglass and a remarkable freed slave who named herself Sojourner Truth proved eloquent lecturers against slavery. Douglass could rivet an audience with an opening line. "I appear before the immense assembly this evening as a thief and a robber," he gibed. "I stole this head, these limbs, this body from my master, and ran off with them."

Relations between black and white abolitionists were not always harmonious. White abolitionists called for legal equality for blacks but not necessarily for social equality. Not without racial prejudice, they preferred light-skinned to dark-skinned Negroes and, with the exception of Garrison, were hesitant to admit blacks to antislavery societies. Yet the prejudices of white abolitionists were mild compared to those of most whites. A white man or woman could do few things less popular in the 1830s than become an abolitionist. Mobs, often including people in favor of colonization, repeatedly attacked abolitionists. For example, a Boston mob, searching for a British abolitionist in 1835, found Garrison instead and dragged him through town on the end of a rope. An abolitionist editor, Elijah Lovejoy, was murdered by a mob in Alton, Illinois, in 1837.

Abolitionists drew on the language of revivals and described slavery as sin, but the Protestant churches did not rally behind abolition as strongly as they rallied behind temperance. Lyman Beecher roared against the evils of strong drink but whimpered about those of slavery, and in 1834 he tried to suppress abolitionists at Cincinnati's Lane Theological Seminary. In response, Theodore Dwight Weld, an idealistic follower of Charles G. Finney, led a mass withdrawal of students. These "Lane rebels" formed the nucleus of abolitionist activity at antislavery Oberlin College.

As if external hostility were not enough, abolitionists argued continually with each other. The American Anti-Slavery Society, founded in 1833, was the scene of several battles between Garrison and prominent New York and midwestern abolitionists such as the Lewis brothers and Arthur Tappan, Theodore Dwight Weld, and James G. Birney. One of the issues between the two sides was whether abolitionists should enter politics as a distinct party. In 1840, Garrison's opponents ran Birney for president on the ticket of the newly formed Liberty Party. As for Garrison himself, he was increasingly rejecting all laws and governments, as well as political parties, as part of his doctrine of "nonresistance." In 1838, he and his followers had founded the New England Non-Resistance Society. Their starting point was the fact that slavery depended on force. Garrison then added that all governments ultimately rested on force; even laws passed by elected legislatures needed police enforcement. Because Garrison viewed force as the opposite of Christian love, he concluded that Christians should refuse to vote, hold office, or have anything to do with government. It is a small wonder that many abolitionists thought of Garrison as extreme, or "ultra."

The second issue that divided the American Anti-Slavery Society concerned the role of women in the abolitionist movement. In 1837 **Angelina and Sarah Grimké**, daughters of a South Carolina slaveholder, embarked on an antislavery lecture tour of New England. Women had become deeply involved in antislavery societies during the 1830s, but always in female auxiliaries affiliated with organizations run by men. What made the Grimké sisters so controversial was that they drew mixed audiences of men and women to their lectures at a time when it was thought indelicate for women to speak before male audiences. Clergymen chastised the Grimké sisters for lecturing men rather than obeying them.

Such criticism backfired, however, because the Grimkés increasingly took up the cause of women's rights. In 1838, each wrote a classic of American feminism. Sarah produced *Letters on the Condition of Women and the Equality of the Sexes*, and Angelina contributed *Letters to Catharine E. Beecher* (Lyman Beecher's daughter, a militant opponent of female equality). Some abolitionists tried to dampen the feminist flames. Abolitionist poet John Greenleaf Whittier dismissed women's grievances as "paltry" compared to the "great and dreadful wrongs of the slave." Even Theodore Dwight Weld, who had married Angelina Grimké, wanted to subordinate women's rights to antislavery. But the fiery passions would not be extinguished. Garrison, welcoming the controversy, promptly espoused women's rights and urged that women be given positions equal to men in the American Anti-Slavery Society. In 1840, the election of a woman, Abby Kelley, to a previously all-male committee split the American Anti-Slavery Society wide open. A substantial minority of profeminist delegates left— some to join the Liberty Party, others to follow Lewis Tappan into the new American and Foreign Anti-Slavery Society.

The disruption of the American Anti-Slavery Society did not greatly damage abolitionism. The national society had never had much control over the local societies that had grown swiftly during the mid-1830s. By 1840, there were more than fifteen hundred local societies, principally in Massachusetts, New York, and Ohio. By circulating abolitionist tracts, newspapers, and even chocolates with antislavery messages on their wrappers, these local societies kept the country ablaze with agitation.

One of the most disruptive abolitionist techniques was to flood Congress with petitions calling for an end to slavery in the District of Columbia. Congress had no time to consider all the petitions, but to refuse to address them meant depriving citizens of their right to have petitions heard. In 1836, southerners secured congressional adoption of the "gag rule," which automatically tabled abolitionist petitions and thus prevented discussion of them in Congress. Former president John Quincy Adams, then a representative from Massachusetts, led the struggle against the gag rule and finally secured its repeal in 1845.

The debate over the gag rule subtly shifted the issue from the abolition of slavery to the constitutional rights of free expression and petitioning Congress. Members of Congress with little sympathy for abolitionists found themselves attacking the South for suppressing the right of petition. In a way, the gag-rule episode vindicated Garrison's tactic of stirring up emotions on the slavery issue. By holding passions over slavery at the boiling point, Garrison kept the South on the defensive. The less secure southerners felt, the more they were tempted into clumsy overreactions like the gag rule.

Women's Rights

The position of American women in the 1830s contained many contradictions. Women could not vote. If married, they had no right to own property (even inherited property) or to retain their own earnings. Yet the spread of reform movements provided women with unprecedented opportunities for public activity without challenging the prevailing belief that their proper sphere was the home. By suppressing liquor, for example, women could claim that they were transforming wretched homes into nurseries of happiness.

The argument that women were natural guardians of the family was double-edged. It justified reform activities on behalf of the family, but it undercut women's demands for legal equality. Let women attend to their sphere, the counterargument ran, and leave politics and finance to men. So deeply ingrained was sexual inequality that most feminists did not start out intending to attack it. Instead, their experiences in other reform movements, notably abolition, led them to the issue of women's rights.

Among the early women's rights advocates who started their reform careers as abolitionists were the Grimké sisters, the Philadelphia Quaker **Lucretia Mott**, Lucy Stone, and Abby Kelley. Like abolition, the cause of women's rights revolved around the conviction that differences of race and gender were unimportant and incidental. "Men and women," Sarah Grimké wrote, "are CREATED EQUAL! They are both moral and accountable beings, and whatever is right for man to do, is right for woman." The most articulate and aggressive advocates of women's rights, moreover, tended to gravitate to William Lloyd Garrison rather than to more moderate abolitionists. Garrison, himself a vigorous feminist, repeatedly stressed the special degradation of women under slavery. The early issues of *The Liberator* contained a "Ladies' Department" headed by a picture of a kneeling slave woman imploring, "Am I Not a Woman and a Sister?" It was common knowledge that slave women were vulnerable to the sexual demands of white masters. Garrison denounced the South as a vast brothel and described slave women as "treated with more indelicacy and cruelty than cattle."

Although their involvement in abolition aroused advocates of women's rights, the discrimination they encountered within the abolition movement infuriated them and impelled them to make women's rights

Elizabeth Cady Stanton with Sons, 1848
This daguerreotype shows Elizabeth Cady Stanton as she looked in 1848, the year of the Seneca Falls Convention. When she was eleven, her brother died, and her grieving father said to her, "Oh, my daughter, I wish you were a boy." The young Stanton resolved to prove to him that a daughter was as valuable as a son. Her career as a reformer, which carried her into temperance, anti-slavery, and women's rights, did not deter her from raising seven children.

a separate cause. In the 1840s, Lucy Stone became the first abolitionist to lecture solely on women's rights. When Lucretia Mott and other American women tried to be seated at the World's Anti-Slavery Convention in London in 1840, they were relegated to a screened-off section. The incident made a sharp impression not only on Mott but also on **Elizabeth Cady Stanton**, who had chosen to accompany her abolitionist husband to the meeting as a honeymoon trip. In 1848, Mott and Stanton organized a women's rights convention at Seneca Falls, New York. The **Seneca Falls convention**'s Declaration of Sentiments, modeled on the Declaration of Independence, began with the assertion that "all men and women are created equal." The convention passed twelve resolutions, and only one, a call for the right of women to vote, failed to pass

unanimously; but it did pass. Ironically, after the Civil War, the call for woman suffrage became the main demand of women's rights advocates for the rest of the century.

Women's rights advocates won a few notable victories. For example, in 1860 Stanton's lobbying helped secure passage of a New York law allowing married women to own property. This was not the first such law, but it was the most comprehensive to date, and it helped meet the demand of the early feminists for greater equality within marriage. But women's rights had less impact than most other reforms. Temperance and school reform were far more popular, and abolitionism created more commotion. Women would not secure the right to vote throughout the nation until 1920, fifty-five years after the Thirteenth Amendment abolished slavery. One reason for the relatively slow advance of women's rights was that piecemeal gains—such as married women's securing the right to own property in several states by the time of the Civil War—satisfied many women. The cause of women's rights also suffered from a close association with abolitionism, which was unpopular. In addition, the advance of feminism was slowed by the competition that it faced from the alternative ideal of separate spheres (see Chapter 9). By sanctioning activities in reforms such as temperance and education, the doctrine of separate spheres provided many women with worthwhile pursuits beyond the family. In this way, it blunted the edge of female demands for full equality.

Penitentiaries and Asylums

Beginning in the 1820s, reformers tried to combat poverty, crime, and insanity by establishing highly regimented institutions, which were products of striking new assumptions about the causes of deviancy. As poverty and crime had increased and grown more visible in early-nineteenth-century cities, alarmed investigators concluded that indigence and deviant behavior resulted not from defects in human nature, as colonial Americans had thought, but from drunken fathers and broken homes. The failure of parental discipline, not the will of God or the wickedness of human nature, lay at the root of evil. Both religious revivalists and secular reformers increasingly concluded that human nature could be altered by the right combination of moral influences. Most grasped the optimistic logic voiced by William Ellery Channing: "The study of the causes of crime may lead us to its cure."

To cure crime, reformers created substitutes for parental discipline, most notably the penitentiary. Penitentiaries were prisons marked by an unprecedented degree of order and discipline. Of course, colonial Americans had incarcerated criminal offenders, but jails had been used mainly to hold prisoners awaiting trial or to lock up debtors. For much of the eighteenth century, the threat of the gallows rather than of imprisonment had deterred wrongdoers. In contrast, nineteenth-century reformers believed that, rightly managed, penitentiaries would bring about the sincere reformation of offenders.

To purge offenders' violent habits, reformers usually insisted on solitary confinement. Between 1819 and 1825, New York built penitentiaries at Auburn and Ossining ("Sing Sing") in which prisoners were confined in small, windowless cells at night. By day, they could work together but never speak and rarely even look at each other. Some reformers criticized this "Auburn system" for allowing too much contact and preferred the rival "Pennsylvania system," in which each prisoner spent all of his or her time in a single cell with a walled courtyard for exercise and received no news or visits from the outside.

Antebellum America also witnessed a remarkable transformation in the treatment of poor people. The prevailing colonial practice of offering relief to the poor by supporting them in a household ("outdoor relief") gradually gave way to the construction of almshouses for the infirm poor and workhouses for the able-bodied poor ("indoor relief"). The argument for indoor relief was much the same as the rationale for penitentiaries: plucking the poor from their demoralizing surroundings and exposing them to a highly regimented institution could change them into virtuous, productive citizens. However lofty the motives behind workhouses and almshouses, the results were often abysmal. In 1833, a legislative committee found that the inmates of the Boston House of Industry were packed seven to a room and included unwed mothers, the sick, and the insane as well as the poor.

As for insane people, those living in a workhouse such as the Boston House of Industry were relatively well off, for many experienced even worse treatment by confinement in prisons. In 1841, **Dorothea Dix**, an idealistic Unitarian schoolteacher, was teaching a Sunday school class in a jail in East Cambridge, Massachusetts, and discovered insane people kept in an unheated room. Dix then investigated jails and almshouses across the state. In 1843, she presented a memorial to the state legislature that described the insane confined "in cages, closets, cellars, stalls, pens! Chained, naked, beaten with rods, and lashed into obedience." With the support of Horace Mann and Boston reformer Samuel G. Howe, she encouraged legislatures to build insane asylums. By the time of the Civil War, twenty-eight states, four cities, and the federal government had constructed public mental institutions.

Penitentiaries, workhouses, and insane asylums all reflected the same optimistic belief that deviancy could be erased by resettling deviants in the right environment. But what was the "right" environment? Part of the answer was clear-cut. Heated rooms were better than frigid ones, and sober parents preferable to drunkards. But reformers demanded much more than warm rooms and responsible parents. They were convinced that the unfettered freedom and individualism of American society were themselves defects in the environment and that the poor, criminal, and insane needed extraordinary regimentation if they were to change.

Pennsylvania's Eastern State Penitentiary
Begun in 1822 in Philadelphia, this penitentiary was the showcase of the so-called Pennsylvania or "separate" system of prison discipline. Each inmate occupied a single cell and at all times was kept from contact with other inmates. This sketch was done by inmate 2954 in 1855.

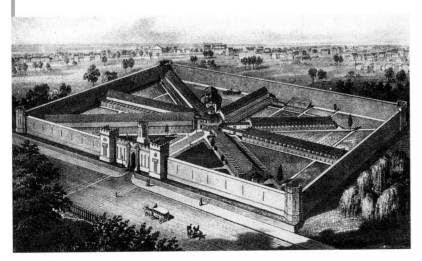

Prison inmates were to march around in lockstep; in workhouses the poor, treated much like prisoners, were often forbidden to leave or receive visitors without permission. The idealism behind such institutions was genuine, but later generations would question reformers' underlying assumptions.

Utopian Communities

The belief that individuals could live perfectly took its most extreme form in the **utopian communities** that flourished during the reform years. Most of them, founded by intellectuals, were intended as alternatives to the prevailing competitive economy and as models whose success would inspire others.

American interest in utopian communities first surfaced during the 1820s. In 1825, the British industrialist and philanthropist Robert Owen founded the New Harmony community in Indiana. Owen had already acquired a formidable reputation (and a fortune) from his management of cotton mills at New Lanark, Scotland. His innovations at New Lanark had substantially improved his workers' educational opportunities and living conditions, and had left him convinced that similar changes could transform the lives of working people everywhere. He saw the problem of the early industrial age as social rather than political. If social arrangements could be perfected, all vice and misery would disappear; human character was formed, "without exception," by people's surroundings or environment. The key to perfecting social arrangements lay, in turn, in the creation of small, planned communities— "Villages of Unity and Mutual Cooperation" containing a perfect balance of occupational, religious, and political groups.

Lured to the United States by cheap land and by Americans' receptivity to experiments, Owen confidently predicted that by 1827 the northern states would embrace the principles embodied in New Harmony. By 1827, there was little left to embrace, for the community, a magnet for idlers and fanatics, had quickly fallen apart. Owen had clashed with clergymen, who still believed that original sin, not environment, shaped human character. Yet Owenism survived the wreckage of New Harmony. The notions that human character was formed by environment and that cooperation was superior to competition had a potent impact on urban workers for the next half-century. Owen's ideas, for example, impelled workingmen's leaders to support educational reform during the late 1820s.

Experimental communities with names like Hopedale, Fruitlands, and Brook Farm proliferated amid the economic chaos of the late 1830s and 1840s. Brook Farm, near Boston, was the creation of a group of religious philosophers called transcendentalists. Most transcendentalists, including Ralph Waldo Emerson, had started as Unitarians but then sought to revitalize Christianity by proclaiming the infinite spiritual capacities of ordinary men and women. Like other utopias, Brook Farm was both a retreat and a model. Certain that the competitive commercial life of the cities was unnatural, philosophers spent their evenings in lofty musings after a day perspiring in the cabbage patch. Brook Farm attracted several renowned writers, including Emerson and Nathaniel Hawthorne, and its literary magazine, *The Dial*, became a forum for transcendentalist ideas about philosophy, art, and literature (also see Chapter 11).

The most controversial of the antebellum utopian communities, the Oneida community established in 1848 in New York state by John Humphrey Noyes, challenged conventional notions of religion, property, gender roles, sex, dress, and motherhood. Renouncing private property, Oneidans practiced communism. Noyes insisted that men perform kitchen duties, and allowed women to work in the community's stores and factories. But what most upset outsiders was Noyes's application of communism to marriage. After exchanging wives with one of his followers, Noyes proclaimed that at Oneida all women would be married to all men and all men to all women. A committee of elders headed by "Father" Noyes decided on sexual pairings for procreation.

Contemporaries dismissed Noyes, who was also an abolitionist, as a licentious crackpot. Southerners cited him to prove that antislavery ideals threatened civilization itself. Yet Oneida achieved considerable economic prosperity and attracted new members long after less-radical utopias like Brook Farm had collapsed. By embracing communism in marriage, Oneidans had burned their bridges to society and had little choice but to stay together.

Widely derided as fit only for eccentrics, antebellum utopias nevertheless exemplified in extreme form the idealism and hopefulness that permeated nearly all reform in the Age of Jackson.

Chronology, 1824–1840

1824	John Quincy Adams elected president by the House of Representatives.
1826	American Temperance Society organized.
1828	Andrew Jackson elected president. "Tariff of Abominations." John Calhoun anonymously writes *South Carolina Exposition and Protest.*
1830	Jackson's Maysville Road Bill veto. Indian Removal Act.
1830–1831	Charles G. Finney's Rochester revival.
1831	William Lloyd Garrison starts *The Liberator.*
1832	Jackson vetoes recharter of the Bank of the United States. Jackson reelected president. South Carolina Nullification Proclamation.
1833	Force Bill. Compromise Tariff. American Anti-Slavery Society founded. South Carolina nullifies the Force Bill.
1834	Whig Party organized.
1836	Specie Circular. Martin Van Buren elected president.
1837	Horace Mann becomes secretary of the Massachusetts Board of Education. Elijah Lovejoy murdered by proslavery mob. Grimké sisters set out on lecture tour of New England.
1837–1843	Economic depression.
1838	Garrison's New England Non-Resistance Society founded. Sarah Grimké's *Letters on the Condition of Women and the Equality of the Sexes* and Angelina Grimké's *Letters to Catharine E. Beecher.*
1840	Independent Treasury Act passed. William Henry Harrison elected president. First Washington Temperance Society started.
1841	Dorothea Dix begins exposé of prison conditions. Brook Farm community founded.
1848	Seneca Falls convention.

Conclusion

The voice of the common people resounded through politics during the 1820s and 1830s. As barriers to the direct expression of the popular will such as property requirements for voting and the indirect election of presidential electors collapsed, the gentlemanly leadership and surface harmony of the Era of Good Feelings gave way to the raucous huzzahs of mass political parties. A similar development transformed American religion. Mass revivals swelled the numbers of Methodists and Baptists—denominations that de-emphasized an educated ministry—while Presbyterians and Congregationalists who insisted on an educated clergy declined in relative numbers. Calvinist clergymen found their doctrine of human depravity hammered by popular revivalists' stress on Americans' capacity to remake themselves.

The louder the people spoke, the less unified they became. The cries of "foul" that had enveloped the election of 1824 later catapulted Andrew Jackson into office as the embodiment of the popular will. But

Jackson's seemingly dictatorial manner and his stands on internal improvements, tariffs, nullification, and banking divided the electorate and contributed to the emergence of the Whig Party. The Panic of 1837 deepened party divisions by shoving wavering Democrats toward a hard-money, antibank position. Similarly, revivals, which aimed to unite Americans in a religion of the heart, spawned critics of religious excess (Unitarians) and indirectly gave rise to hotly controversial religious groups (Mormons).

Seeded in part by religious revivals, a variety of reform movements also sprouted in the 1820s and 1830s. Such causes as women's rights and the abolition of slavery promised legal equality for groups excluded from participation in politics. Other reforms, such as temperance, public-school reform, prison reform, and the establishment of utopian communities, rested on the view that human nature could be improved and even perfected by a combination of individual effort and the right environment. Yet for all of their optimism about improving human nature, reformers were gripped by profound anxieties about the direction of American society. Reformers did not hesitate to coerce people into change by calling for the legal prohibition of liquor and for compulsory education. For criminals they devised

Key Terms

political democratization	Mormons
Henry Clay	American Temperance Society
Democratic Party	Horace Mann
spoils system	William Lloyd Garrison
nullification crisis	Angelina and Sarah Grimké
second Bank of the United States	Lucretia Mott
	Elizabeth Cady Stanton
Whig Party	Seneca Falls convention
Panic of 1837	Dorothea Dix
Second Great Awakening	utopian communities
Charles G. Finney	

highly repressive institutions designed to bring out the basic goodness of human nature. Both reformers and politicians sought to slay the demons that threatened the Republic. Often disdaining politics as corrupt, reformers blasted liquor, ignorance, and slavery with the same fervor that Jacksonians directed at banks and monopolies. Yet reformers who called for the legal prohibition of liquor and the reform of public education or who organized an abolitionist political party were reluctantly acknowledging that in a mass democracy everything sooner or later became political.

For Further Reference

Lee Benson, *The Concept of Jacksonian Democracy: New York as a Test Case* (1961). A major revisionist interpretation of the period.

Catherine A. Brekus, *Strangers and Pilgrims: Female Preaching in America, 1740–1845* (1998). An informative overview of how female preachers shaped religious practices in early America.

Donald B. Cole, *The Presidency of Andrew Jackson* (1993). Fine brief account.

William W. Freehling, *Prelude to Civil War* (1966). A major study of the nullification crisis.

Michael F. Holt, *The Rise and Fall of the American Whig Party* (1999). A comprehensive and masterful study.

Richard R. John, *Spreading the News: The American Postal System from Franklin to Morse* (1995). Provides excellent insight into the role of communications in the public life of American democracy.

Paul Johnson, *A Shopkeeper's Millennium: Society and Revivals in Rochester, New York, 1815–1837* (1978). A lively account of the relationship between

Finney's revivals and social, economic, and political change.

Steven Mintz, *Moralists and Modernizers* (1995). A clearly written overview that stresses the modernizing features of antebellum reform movements.

Robert V. Remini, *Henry Clay: Statesman for the Union* (1991). An important biography of the leading Whig statesman of the period.

Sean Wilentz, *The Rise of American Democracy: Jefferson to Lincoln* (2005). A very detailed account of the development of democratic institutions and attitudes in the United States.

First State Election in Michigan

Chapter 11

Steam Locomotive Crossing the Niagara Railway Suspension Bridge, 1860s
Suspension bridges like this one were developed in the 1850s to bear the great weight of locomotives and railroad cars.

Technology, Culture, and Everyday Life,

1840–1860

Isaac Singer

Isaac M. Singer's life was not going well. Thirty-nine in 1850 and often penniless, he had been an unsuccessful actor, stage hand, ticket seller, carpenter, and inventor. His early inventions had been clever, but not much in demand. Having deserted his wife and children, he promised marriage to lure Mary Ann Sponslor into living with him. Sponslor tried to please him, nursing him when he was sick and even taking up acting, but to no avail. Instead of marrying her, Singer often beat her, and he would have affairs with several other women during the 1850s. But by 1860 Singer had grown fabulously wealthy. In 1850 he had come upon and quickly improved a sewing machine similar to one patented in 1846 by Elias Howe, Jr.

Here was a machine that everyone wanted; sewing-machine designers were practically bumping into each other at the patent office. The rise of the New England textile industry in the 1820s had spurred the development of the ready-made clothing industry, but the textile factories did not stitch pieces of fabric together to make clothes. Rather, factories contracted sewing out to young women who stitched fabric by hand in their homes. Sewing was both a business that employed women and a social activity that women cherished. Even fashionable ladies with no need to earn cash formed sewing circles to finish or mend their families' wardrobes, to make garments for the poor, and to chat.

Stitching by hand took as long as three hours for a pair of pants and seven hours for a calico dress. In contrast, a pair of pants could be stitched by machine in thirty-eight minutes, and a calico dress in fifty-seven minutes. But the early sewing machines, themselves hand-made, were expensive; in 1851 the largest sewing machine company could turn out only 700 to 800 sewing machines a year. The number jumped to 21,000 by 1859 and to 174,000 by 1872. What made this huge increase possible was the adaptation to sewing-machine manufacturing of machine tools that had recently been devised for the manufacture of pistols and revolvers.

Contemporaries could not praise sewing machines enough. Most of the machines were sold to factories. By saving time, they made clothing cheaper, and they gave a terrific boost to the ready-made clothing industry. The *New York Tribune* predicted that, with the spread of sewing machines, people "will dress better, change oftener, and altogether grow better looking." This upbeat response to technological change was typical of the 1850s. Many Americans believed that *technology*, a word coined in 1829 to describe the application of science to improving the conveniences of life, was God's chosen instrument of progress. Just as the *Tribune* predicted that sewing machines would create a nation "without spot or blemish," others forecast that the telegraph, another invention of the age, would usher in world peace.

Yet progress had a darker side. Revolvers were useless for hunting and of little value in battle, but excellent for the violent settling of private scores. The farmwomen who had traditionally earned money sewing by hand in their homes gradually gave way to women who sewed by machine in small urban factories that came to be labeled sweatshops for their gruesome conditions. Philosophers and artists began to worry about the despoliation of the landscape by the very factories that made guns and sewing machines, and conservationists launched conscious efforts to preserve enclaves of nature as parks and retreats safe from progress.

Focus Questions

- What technological improvements increased industrial productivity between 1840 and 1860?

- How did technology transform the daily lives of middle-class Americans between 1840 and 1860?

- How did American pastimes and entertainment change between 1840 and 1860?

- How did Americans express their distinctiveness in their literature and art?

Technology and Economic Growth

Widely hailed as democratic, the benefits of technology drew praise from all sides. Conservatives like Daniel Webster praised machines for doing the work of ten people without consuming food or clothing, while Sarah Bagley, a Lowell mill operative and labor organizer, traced the improvement of society to the development of technology.

The technology that transformed life in antebellum America included the steam engine, the cotton gin, the reaper, the sewing machine, and the telegraph. Some of these originated in Europe, but Americans had a flair for investing in others' inventions and perfecting their own. Improvements in Eli Whitney's cotton gin between 1793 and 1860, for example, led to an eightfold increase in the amount of cotton that could be ginned in a day. Of course, technology did not benefit everyone. For example, the cotton gin riveted slavery more firmly in place by intensifying southern dependence on cotton. Technology also rendered many traditional skills obsolete and so undercut the position of artisans. But technology contributed to improvements in transportation and increases in productivity, which in turn lowered commodity prices and raised the living standards of a sizable body of free Americans between 1840 and 1860.

Agricultural Advancement

Although few settlers ventured onto the treeless, semi-arid Great Plains before the Civil War, settlements edged westward after 1830 from the woodlands of Ohio and Kentucky into parts of Indiana, Michigan, Illinois, and Missouri, where flat grasslands (prairies) alternated with forests. The prairie's matted soil was difficult to break for planting, but in 1837 John Deere invented a steel-tipped plow that halved the labor to clear acres to till. Timber for housing and fencing was available in nearby woods, and settlements spread rapidly.

Wheat became to midwestern farmers what cotton was to their southern counterparts. "The wheat crop is the great crop of the North-west, for exchange purposes," an agricultural journal noted in 1850. "It pays debts, buys groceries, clothing and lands, and answers more emphatically the purposes of trade among farmers than any other crop." Technological advances sped the harvesting as well as the planting of wheat on the midwestern prairies. Using the traditional hand sickle consumed huge amounts of time and labor, all the more so because cut wheat had to be picked up and bound. Experiments with horse-drawn machines to replace sickles had failed until Cyrus McCormick of Virginia developed the mechanical reaper. In 1834, he patented his machine; in 1847 he opened a factory in Chicago, and by 1860 he had sold 80,000 reapers. During the Civil War, McCormick made immense profits by selling more than 250,000 reapers. The mechanical reaper, which harvested grain seven times faster than traditional methods with half the work force, guaranteed that wheat would dominate the midwestern prairies.

Ironically, just as a Connecticut Yankee, Eli Whitney, had stimulated the foundation of the Old South's economy by inventing the cotton gin, Cyrus McCormick, a proslavery southern Democrat, would help the North win the Civil War. The North provided the main market for the **McCormick reaper** and for the models of his many competitors; the South, with its reliance on unpaid slave labor, had little incentive to invest in labor-saving agricultural machinery. The reaper would keep northern agricultural production high at a time when labor shortages caused by troop mobilization might otherwise have slashed production.

Although Americans proved resourceful at inventing and marketing machines to speed planting and harvesting, they farmed wastefully. With land abundant, farmers were more inclined to look for virgin soil than to improve "worn out" soil. But a movement for agricultural improvement in the form of more efficient use of the soil did develop before 1860, mainly in the East.

Confronted by the superior fertility of western soil, easterners who did not move west or take jobs in factories increasingly experimented with new agricultural techniques. In Orange County, New York, for example, farmers fed their cows the best clover and bluegrass and emphasized cleanliness in the processing of dairy products. Through these practices, they produced a superior butter that commanded more than double the price of ordinary butter. Still other eastern farmers turned to fertilizers to keep their wheat production competitive with that of the bountiful midwestern prairies. By fertilizing their fields with plaster left over from the construction of the James River Canal, Virginia wheat growers raised their average yield per acre to fifteen bushels by the 1850s, up from only six bushels in 1800. Similarly, during the 1840s American cotton planters began to import guano, left by the droppings of sea birds on islands off Peru, for use as fertilizer. Fertilizer helped eastern cotton farmers close the gap created by the superior fertility of soil in the Old Southwest.

Technology and Industrial Progress

Industrial advances between 1840 and 1860 owed an immense debt to the nearly simultaneous development of effective machine tools, power-driven machines that cut and shaped metal. In the early 1800s, Eli Whitney's plan to manufacture muskets by using interchangeable parts

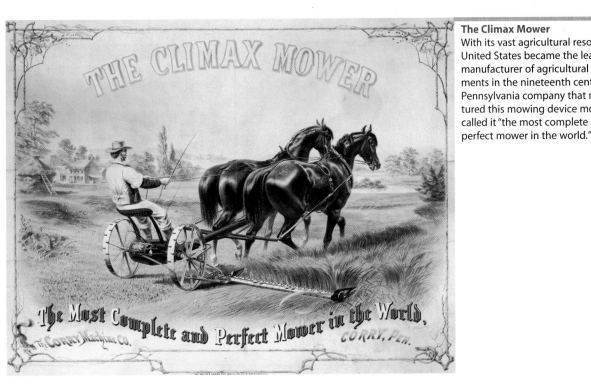

The Climax Mower
With its vast agricultural resources, the United States became the leading manufacturer of agricultural implements in the nineteenth century. The Pennsylvania company that manufactured this mowing device modestly called it "the most complete and perfect mower in the world."

Technology (and) *Culture*

Guns and Gun Culture

Even in the early 1800s, some Americans painted an image of their countrymen as expert marksmen. A popular song attributed the American victory at the Battle of New Orleans in 1815 to the sharpshooting skills of the Kentucky militia. Yet Andrew Jackson, who commanded American forces in the battle, thought otherwise, and historians have agreed with him. Accurate guns were the exception in 1815 and for decades afterward. Balls exited smooth-bore muskets at unpredictable angles and started to tumble after fifty or sixty yards. In 1835, Jackson himself, now president, became a beneficiary of another feature of guns: their unreliability. A would-be assassin fired two single-shot pistols at Jackson at point-blank range. Both misfired.

Guns were not only inaccurate and unreliable; they were also expensive. A gunsmith would count himself fortunate if

he could turn out twenty a year; at the Battle of New Orleans, less than one-third of the Kentucky militiamen had any guns, let alone guns that worked.

Believing that the safety of the Republic depended on a well-armed militia, Thomas Jefferson was keenly interested in finding ways to manufacture guns more rapidly. As president-elect in 1801, he witnessed a demonstration by Eli Whitney, the inventor of the cotton gin, of guns manufactured on the new principle of interchangeable parts. If each part of a gun could be machine-made and then fitted smoothly into the final product, there would be no need for the laborious methods of the skilled gunsmith. In Jefferson's presence, Whitney successfully fitted ten different gunlocks, one after another, to one musket, using only a screwdriver.

Eager to stave off the impending bankruptcy of his cotton-gin business, Whitney had already accepted a federal

Gun Machinery
During the 1850s, machinery greatly accelerated the production of guns. Shown here are a machine for making gun stocks and a jigging machine. The jigging machine had a large revolving wheel, to which were attached different cutting tools used to shape the gunlock frames.

contract to manufacture ten thousand muskets by 1800. His demonstration persuaded Jefferson that, although Whitney had yet to deliver any muskets, he could do the job. What Jefferson did not know was that Whitney cheated on the test: he already had hand-filed each lock so that it would fit. It would be another eight years before Whitney finally delivered the muskets.

Whitney's problem was that as late as 1820 no machines existed that could make gun parts with sufficient precision to be interchangeable. During the 1820s and 1830s, however, John Hall, a Maine gunsmith, began to construct such machines at the federal arsenal at Harpers Ferry, Virginia. Hall devised new machines for drilling cast-steel gun barrels, a variety of large and small drop hammers for pounding pieces of metal into shape, and new tools for cutting metal (called milling machines). With improvements by others during the 1840s and 1850s, these machine tools made it possible to achieve near uniformity, and hence interchangeability, in the parts of guns.

At first, Hall's innovations had little effect, since the army was scaling back its demand for guns in the 1830s. The outbreak of war with Mexico in 1846 marked a turning point. Ten years earlier, a Connecticut inventor, Samuel Colt, had secured a patent for a repeating pistol with a rotating-chambered breech, usually called a revolver. At the start of the Mexican-American War, Colt won a federal contract to provide the army with one thousand revolvers. These proved to be of negligible value during the war, but Colt, a masterful publicist, was soon traveling the globe and telling all that his revolvers had won the war.

Eager to heighten the revolver's appeal to Americans, Colt made use of a recent invention, called a grammagraph, that engraved the same design repeatedly on steel. On the cylinders of his revolvers he impressed images of frontiersmen using their Colt pistols to heroically protect their wives and children from savage Indians.

In contrast to Hall, a man more interested in making than selling guns, Colt had a genius for popularizing gun ownership, not just on the frontier but also among respectable citizens in the East. He gave away scores of specially engraved revolvers to politicians and War Department officials, and he invited western heroes to dine at his Hartford, Connecticut, mansion. New England quickly became the center of a flourishing American gun industry. By 1860, nearly 85 percent of all American guns were manufactured there. By 1859, Colt had cut the price of a new revolver from fifty dollars to nineteen.

As guns became less expensive, they became the weapon of choice for both the military and street toughs. At the Astor Place Riot in 1849 (discussed later), soldiers from New York's Seventh Regiment fired a volley that killed twenty-two people, the first time that militia fired on unarmed citizens. Murderers, who traditionally had gone about their business with knives and clubs, increasingly turned to guns. In the 1850s a surge in urban homicides, usually caused by gun, led to calls for gun control. In 1857, Baltimore became the first city to allow its police to use firearms. Confronted with an outbreak of gang warfare the same year, some New York police captains authorized their men to carry guns. No longer a luxury, guns could be purchased by ordinary citizens in new stores that sold only guns and accessories, forerunners of the modern gun supermarket.

Most states had laws barring blacks from owning guns. Women rarely purchased them. But for white American men, owning guns and knowing how to use them increasingly became a mark of manly self-reliance. Samuel Colt did all he could to encourage this attitude. When the home of a Hartford clergyman was burglarized in 1861, Colt promptly sent the clergyman "a copy of my latest work on 'Moral Reform,'" a Colt revolver. Two years earlier Dan Sickles, a New York congressman, had created a sensation by waylaying his wife's lover, Philip Barton Key (the son of the author of the "Star-Spangled Banner"), across the street from the White House. Armed with two pistols and shouting that Key was a "scoundrel" who had dishonored Sickles's marriage bed, Sickles shot the unarmed Key four times in front of several witnesses, killing him with the final shot. A notorious womanizer, Sickles had repeatedly cheated on his wife, but his behavior struck many men as justifiable. President James Buchanan, a political ally, paid one witness to disappear. Eventually, Sickles was acquitted of murder on the grounds of "temporary insanity." He continued to climb the ladder of politics, and in 1863 he led a regiment at the Battle of Gettysburg.

Question for Analysis

- Historians of technology remind us that innovations have often been linked, that an invention in one sphere gives rise to inventions in related spheres. How did this principle operate in the history of gun manufacture?

Model of McCormick's Reaper, 1850s
Horse-drawn, McCormick's reaper was a relatively simple device. A cutting bar separated the wheat from the chaff. Reels then pushed the cut grain onto the platform for collection and tying into shocks.

made by unskilled workers was stalled by the absence of machine tools. (See Technology and Culture: Guns and Gun Culture). Such tools were being developed in Britain in Whitney's day, but Americans were near strangers to them until the 1830s. By the 1840s, precise machine tools had greatly reduced the need to hand-file parts to make them fit, and they were applied to the manufacture of firearms, clocks, and sewing machines. By 1851, Europeans had started to refer to manufacture by interchangeable parts as the "**American System of Manufacturing**." In 1853, a small-arms factory in England re-equipped itself with machine tools manufactured by two firms in the backwoods of Vermont. After touring American factories in 1854, a British engineer concluded that Americans "universally and willingly" resorted to machines as a substitute for manual labor.

The American manufacturing system had several distinctive advantages. Traditionally, damage to any part of a mechanical contrivance had rendered the whole useless, for no new part would fit. With the perfection of manufacturing by interchangeable parts, however, replacement parts could be obtained. In addition, the improved machine tools upon which the American System depended enabled entrepreneurs to push inventions swiftly into mass production. The likelihood that inventions would quickly enter production attracted investors. By the 1850s, Connecticut firms like Smith and Wesson were mass-producing the revolving pistol, which Samuel Colt had invented in 1836. Sophisticated machine tools

made it possible, a manufacturer wrote, to increase production "by confining a worker to one particular limb of a pistol until he had made two thousand."

After the transmission of the first telegraph message in 1844, Americans also seized enthusiastically on the telegraph's promise to eliminate the constraints of time and space (see Chapter 13, Technology and Culture: The Telegraph). The speed with which Americans formed telegraph companies and strung lines stunned a British engineer, who noted in 1854 that "no private interests can oppose the passage of a line through any property." Although telegraph lines usually transmitted political and commercial messages, some cities adapted them for reporting fires. By the early 1850s, Boston had an elaborate system of telegraph stations that could alert fire companies throughout the city to a blaze in any neighborhood. By 1852, more than fifteen thousand miles of lines connected cities as distant as Quebec, New Orleans, and St. Louis.

The Railroad Boom

Even more than the telegraph, railroad expansion dramatized technology's democratic promise. In 1790, even European royalty could travel no faster than fourteen miles an hour and that only with frequent changes of horses. By 1850, an ordinary American could travel three times as fast on a train, and in considerable comfort. American railroads offered only one class of travel, in contrast to the several classes on European railroads.

With the introduction of adjustable upholstered seats that could serve as couches at night, Americans in effect traveled first class except for African-Americans, who often were forced to sit separately.

Americans loved railroads "as a lover loves his mistress," one Frenchman wrote, but there was little to love about the earliest railroads. Sparks from locomotives showered passengers riding in open cars, which were common. In the absence of brakes, passengers often had to get out and pull trains to stop them. Lacking lights, trains rarely ran at night. Before the introduction of standard time zones in 1883, scheduling was a nightmare; at noon in Boston it was twelve minutes before noon in New York City. Delays were frequent, for trains on single-track lines had to wait on sidings for oncoming trains to pass. Because a train's location was a mystery once it left the station, these waits could seem endless. Between 1840 and 1860, the size of the rail network and the power and convenience of trains underwent a stunning transformation. Railroads extended track from three thousand to thirty thousand miles; flat-roofed coaches replaced open cars; kerosene lamps made night travel possible; and increasingly powerful engines let trains climb steep hills. Fifty thousand miles of telegraph wire enabled dispatchers to communicate with trains en route and thus to reduce delays.

Nonetheless, problems lingered. Sleeping accommodations remained crude, and schedules erratic. Because individual railroads used different gauge track, frequent changes of train were necessary; eight changes interrupted a journey from Charleston to Philadelphia in the 1850s. Yet nothing slowed the advance of railroads or cured Americans' mania for them. By 1860, the United States had more track than all the rest of the world.

Railroads spearheaded the second phase of the transportation revolution. Canals remained in use; the

Steam Locomotive Above Altoona, Pennsylvania, 1860s
Railways were more than a means of transportation. They also inspired the imaginations of Americans. This photograph appeared in a series entitled "The Picturesque on the Pennsylvania Central R.R."

Erie Canal, for example, did not reach its peak volume until 1880. But railroads, faster and less vulnerable to winter freezes, gradually overtook them, first in passengers and then in freight. By 1860, the value of goods transported by railroads greatly surpassed that carried by canals.

As late as 1860, few rail lines extended west of the Mississippi, but railroads had spread like spider webs east of the great river. The railroads turned southern cities like Atlanta and Chattanooga into thriving commercial hubs. Most important, the railroads linked the East and the Midwest. The New York Central and the Erie Railroads joined New York City to Buffalo; the Pennsylvania Railroad connected Philadelphia to Pittsburgh; and the Baltimore and Ohio linked Baltimore to Wheeling, Virginia (now West Virginia). Simultaneously, intense construction in Ohio, Indiana, and Illinois created trunk lines that tied these routes to cities farther west. By 1860 rail lines ran from Buffalo to Cleveland, Toledo, and Chicago; from Pittsburgh to Fort Wayne; and from Wheeling to Cincinnati and St. Louis (see Map 11.1).

Map 11.1 Railroad Growth, 1850–1860
Rail ties between the East and the Midwest greatly increased during the railroad "boom" of the 1850s.

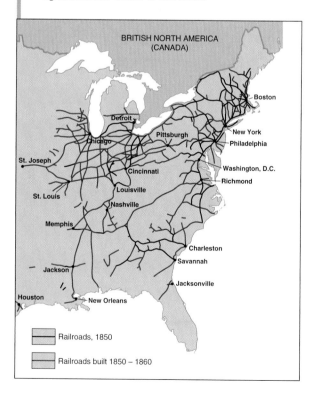

Railroads, 1850

Railroads built 1850 – 1860

Chicago's growth illustrates the impact of these rail links. In 1849, it was a village of a few hundred people with virtually no rail service. By 1860, it had become a city of one hundred thousand served by eleven railroads. Farmers in the Upper Midwest no longer had to ship their grain, livestock, and dairy products down the Mississippi to New Orleans; they could now send products directly east. Chicago supplanted New Orleans as the interior's main commercial hub.

The east-west rail lines stimulated the settlement and agricultural development of the Midwest. By 1860, Illinois, Indiana, and Wisconsin had replaced Ohio, Pennsylvania, and New York as the leading wheat-growing states. Enabling farmers to speed their products to the East, railroads increased the value of farmland and promoted additional settlement. In turn, population growth triggered industrial development in cities such as Chicago; Davenport, Iowa; and Minneapolis, for the new settlers needed lumber for fences and houses and mills to grind wheat into flour.

Railroads also propelled the growth of small towns along their routes. The Illinois Central Railroad, which had more track than any other railroad in 1855, made money not only from its traffic but also from real estate speculation. Purchasing land for stations along its path, the Illinois Central then laid out towns around the stations. The selection of Manteno, Illinois, as a stop on the Illinois Central, for example, transformed the site from a crossroads without a single house in 1854 into a bustling town of nearly a thousand in 1860, replete with hotels, lumberyards, grain elevators, and gristmills. (The Illinois Central even dictated the naming of streets. Those running east and west were always named after trees, and those running north and south were numbered. Soon one rail town looked much like the next.) By the Civil War, few thought of the railroad-linked Midwest as a frontier region or viewed its inhabitants as pioneers.

As the nation's first big business, the railroads transformed the conduct of business. During the early 1830s, railroads, like canals, depended on financial aid from state governments. With the onset of depression in the late 1830s, however, state governments scrapped overly ambitious railroad projects. Convinced that railroads burdened them with high taxes and blasted hopes, voters turned against state aid, and in the early 1840s, several states amended their constitutions to bar state funding for railroads and canals. Federal aid would not become widely available until the Civil War. Although local and county governments tried to fill the void, the dramatic expansion of the railroad network in the 1850s encouraged a shift toward private investment. Well aware of the economic benefits of railroads, individuals living near them had long purchased railroad securities issued by governments and had directly bought stock in railroads, often paying by contributing their labor to building the railroads. But the large railroads of the 1850s needed more capital than such small investors could generate.

Gradually, the center of railroad financing shifted to New York City. In fact, it was the railroad boom of the 1850s that helped make Wall Street the nation's greatest capital market. The securities of all the leading railroads were traded on the floor of the **New York Stock Exchange** during the 1850s. In addition, the growth of railroads turned New York City into the center of modern investment firms. The investment firms evaluated the securities of railroads in Toledo or Davenport or Chattanooga and then found purchasers for these securities in New York, Philadelphia, Paris, London, Amsterdam, and Hamburg. Controlling the flow of funds to railroads, investment bankers began to exert influence over the railroads' internal affairs by supervising administrative reorganizations in times of trouble. A Wall Street analyst noted in 1851 that railroad men seeking financing "must remember that money is power, and that the [financier] can dictate to a great extent his own terms."

Rising Prosperity

Technological advances also improved the lives of consumers by bringing down the prices of many commodities. For example, clocks that cost $50 to fabricate by hand in 1800 could be produced by machine for fifty cents by 1850. In addition, the widening use of steam power contributed to a 25 percent rise in the average worker's real income (actual purchasing power) between 1840 and 1860. Early-nineteenth-century factories, which had depended on water wheels to propel their machines, had to shut down when the rivers or streams froze. With the spread of steam engines, however, factories could stay open longer, and workers could increase their annual wages by working more hours. Cotton textile workers were among those who benefited: although their hourly wages showed little gain, their average annual wages rose from $163 in 1830 to $176 in 1849 to $201 by 1859.

The growth of towns and cities also contributed to an increase in average annual wages. Farmers experienced the same seasonal fluctuations as laborers in the early factories. In sparsely settled rural areas, the onset of winter traditionally brought hard times. As demand for agricultural labor slumped, few alternatives existed to take up the slack. "A year in some farming states such as Pennsylvania," a traveler commented in 1823, "is only of eight months duration, four months being lost to the laborer, who is turned away as a useless animal." In contrast, densely populated towns and cities offered more opportunities for year-round work. The urban dockworker thrown out of his job as a result of frozen waterways might find work as a hotel porter or an unskilled indoor laborer.

Towns and cities also provided women and children with new opportunities for paid work. (Women and children had long performed many vital tasks on farms, but rarely for pay.) The wages of children between the ages of ten and eighteen came to play an integral role in the nineteenth-century family economy. Family heads who earned more than six hundred dollars a year might have been able to afford the luxury of keeping their children in school, but most breadwinners were fortunate if they made three hundred dollars a year. Although the cost of many basic commodities fell between 1815 and 1860 (another consequence of the transportation revolution), most families lived close to the margin. Budgets of working-class families in New York City and Philadelphia during the early 1850s reveal annual expenditures of five hundred to six hundred dollars, with more than 40 percent spent on food, 25 to 30 percent on rent, and most of the remainder on clothing and fuel. Such a family could not survive on the annual wages of the average male head of the household. It needed the wages of the children and, at times, those of the wife as well.

Life in urban wage-earning families was not necessarily superior to life in farming communities. A farmer who owned land, livestock, and a house did not have to worry about paying rent or buying fuel for cooking and heating, and rarely ran short of food. Many Americans continued to aspire to farming as the best of all occupations. But to purchase, clear, and stock a farm involved a considerable capital outlay that could easily amount to five hundred dollars, and the effort promised no rewards for a few years. The majority of workers in agricultural areas did not own farms and were exposed to seasonal fluctuations in demand for agricultural labor. In many respects, they were worse off than urban wage earners.

The economic advantages that attended living in cities help explain why so many Americans moved to urban areas during the first half of the nineteenth century. During the 1840s and 1850s cities also provided their residents with an unprecedented range of comforts and conveniences.

The Quality of Life

"Think of the numberless contrivances and inventions for our comfort and luxury," the poet Walt Whitman exclaimed, "and you will bless your star that Fate has cast your lot in the year of Our Lord 1857." Changes in the quality of daily life occurred within the home and affected such daily activities as eating, drinking, and washing. The patent office in Washington was flooded with sketches of reclining seats, beds convertible into chairs, street-sweeping machines, and fly traps. Machine-made furniture began to transform the interiors of houses. Stoves revolutionized heating and cooking. Railroads brought fresh vegetables to city-dwellers.

Yet change occurred unevenly. Technology enabled the middle class to enjoy luxuries formerly reserved for the rich, but it widened the distance between the middle class and the poor. As middle-class homes became increasingly lavish, the urban poor congregated in cramped tenements. Some critical elements such as medicine lagged far behind the changes wrought by the railroad and the telegraph. Still, the benefits of progress impressed Americans more than its limitations. Lacking medical advances, Americans turned to popular health movements that stressed diet and regimen over doctors.

Dwellings

During the early 1800s, the unattached wood-frame houses, all pointing in different directions, that dotted colonial cities yielded to uniform-looking brick row houses. Typically narrow and long, row houses were practical responses to rising urban land values (as much as 750 percent in Manhattan between 1785 and 1815), and they drew criticism for their "extreme uniformity." But they were not all alike. Middle-class row houses, with cast-iron balconies, elegant doors, curved staircases, and rooms with odd shapes that emphasized their occupants' individuality and taste, were larger and more elaborate than working-class row houses, and less likely to be subdivided for occupancy by several families. The

Family Group
This daguerreotype, taken about 1852, reveals the little things so important to etching a middle-class family's social status: curtains; a wall hanging; a piano with scrolled legs; a small desk with elegantly curved legs; a pet; ladies posed in nonproductive but "improving" activities (music, reading); and a young man seemingly staring into space—and perhaps pondering how to pay for it all.

worst of these subdivided row houses were called tenements and became the usual habitats of Irish immigrants and free blacks.

Furniture also revealed the widening gap between the prosperous and the poor. Families in the middle and upper classes increasingly preferred an ornate furniture style known as rococo. The heavily upholstered backs of sofas were often trimmed with floral designs topped with carved medallions; vines, leaves, and flowers covered both wooden and upholstered surfaces. Mirrors with intricate gilded moldings weighed so much that they threatened to tumble from the walls. The rise of mass production in such furniture centers as Grand Rapids, Michigan, and Cincinnati between 1840 and 1860 reduced the cost of rococo furniture and tended to level taste between the middle and upper classes, while setting those classes off from everyone else.

In rural areas, the quality of housing depended as much on the date of settlement as on social class. In recently settled areas, the standard dwelling was a rude one-room log cabin with planked floors, crude clay chimneys, and windows covered by oiled paper or cloth. As rural communities matured, log cabins gave way to frame houses of two or more rooms and better insulation. Most of these were balloon-frame houses. In place of foot-thick posts and beams laboriously fitted together, a balloon-frame house had a skeleton of thin-sawn timbers nailed together in such a way that every strain ran against the grain of the wood. The simplicity and cheapness of such houses endeared them to western builders who had neither the time nor the skill to cut and fit heavy beams.

Conveniences and Inconveniences

By today's standards, everyday life in the 1840s and 1850s was primitive, but contemporaries were struck by how much better it was becoming. The transportation and industrial revolutions were affecting heating, cooking, and diet. In urban areas where wood was expensive, coal-burning stoves were rapidly displacing open hearths for heating and cooking. Stoves made it possible to cook several dishes at once and thus contributed to the growing variety of the American diet, while railroads brought in fresh vegetables, which in the eighteenth century had been absent from even lavish banquet tables.

Too, contemporaries were struck by the construction of urban waterworks—systems of pipes and aqueducts that brought fresh water from rivers or reservoirs to street hydrants. In the 1840s New York City completed the Croton aqueduct, which carried water into the city from reservoirs to the north, and by 1860 sixty-eight public water systems operated in the United States.

Despite these improvements, newly acquired elegance still bumped shoulders with squalor. Coal burned longer and hotter than wood, but it left a dirty residue that polluted the air and blackened the snow, and a faulty coal stove could fill the air with poisonous carbon monoxide. Seasonal fluctuations continued to affect diets. Only the rich could afford fruit out of season, since they alone could afford to use sugar to preserve it. Indeed, preserving almost any kind of food presented problems. Home iceboxes were rare before 1860, so salt remained the most widely used preservative. One reason antebellum Americans ate more pork than beef was that salt pork didn't taste quite as bad as salt beef.

Although public waterworks were among the most impressive engineering feats of the age, their impact is easily exaggerated. Since the incoming water usually ended its trip at a street hydrant, and only a fraction of the urban population lived near hydrants, houses rarely had running water. Taking a bath required first heating the water, pot by pot, on a stove. A New England physician claimed that not one in five of his patients took one bath a year.

Infrequent baths meant pungent body odors, which mingled with a multitude of strong scents. In the absence of municipal sanitation departments, street cleaning was let to private contractors who gained a reputation for slack performance, so people in cities relied on hogs, which they allowed to roam freely and scavenge. (Hogs that turned down the wrong street often made tasty dinners for the poor.) Stables backed by mounds of manure and outdoor privies added to the stench. Flush toilets were rare outside cities, and within cities sewer systems lagged behind water systems. Boston had only five thousand flush toilets in 1860 for a population of 178,000, a far higher ratio of toilets to people than most cities. Expensive conveniences like running water and flush toilets became another of the ways in which progress set the upper and middle classes apart from the poor. Conveniences also sharpened gender differences. In her widely popular *Treatise on Domestic Economy* (1841), Catharine Beecher told women that technological advances made it their duty to make every house a "glorious temple" by utilizing space more efficiently. Women who no longer made articles for home consumption were now expected to achieve fulfillment by obsessively sweeping floors and polishing furniture. Home, a writer proclaimed, had become woman's "royal court," where she "sways her queenly authority." Skeptical of this trend toward fastidiousness, another writer cautioned women in 1857 against "ultra-housewifery."

Disease and Health

Despite their improving standard of living, Americans remained vulnerable to disease. **Epidemics** swept through antebellum cities and felled thousands. Yellow fever and cholera killed one-fifth of New Orleans's population in 1832–1833, and cholera alone carried off 10 percent of St. Louis's population in 1849. Life expectancy for newborns in New York and Philadelphia during the 1830s and 1840s averaged only twenty-four years.

Ironically, the transportation revolution increased the peril from epidemics. The cholera epidemic of 1832, the first truly national epidemic, followed shipping routes: one branch of the epidemic ran from New York City up the Hudson River, across the Erie Canal to Ohio, and then down the Ohio River to the Mississippi and south to New Orleans; the other branch followed shipping up and down the East Coast from New York City.

The inability of physicians to explain epidemic diseases reinforced hostility toward the profession and made public health a low priority. No one understood that bacteria cause cholera and yellow fever. Physicians clashed over whether epidemic diseases were contagious, spread by touch, or resulted from "miasmas," air-carried gases from rotten vegetation or dead animals. But neither theory worked. Quarantines failed to prevent the spread of epidemics (an argument against the contagionist theory), and many residents of swampy areas contracted neither yellow fever nor cholera (a refutation of the miasma theory). Understandably, municipal leaders declined to delegate more than advisory powers to boards of health, which were dominated by physicians. Although most epidemic diseases baffled antebellum physicians, a basis for forward strides in surgery was laid during the 1840s by the discovery of anesthetics. Prior to 1840, young people often entertained themselves at parties by inhaling nitrous oxide, or "laughing gas," which produced sensations of giddiness and painlessness; and semicomical demonstrations of laughing gas became a form of popular entertainment. (Samuel Colt, the inventor of the revolver, had begun his career as a traveling exhibitor of laughing gas.) But nitrous oxide had to be carried around in bladders, which were difficult to handle, and in any case, few recognized its surgical possibilities. Then in 1842 Crawford Long, a Georgia physician who had attended laughing-gas frolics in his youth, employed sulfuric ether (an easily transportable liquid with the same properties as nitrous oxide) during a surgical operation. Long failed to follow up on his discovery, but four years later William T. G. Morton, a dentist, successfully employed sulfuric ether during an operation at Massachusetts General Hospital in Boston. Within a few years, ether came into wide use in American surgery.

The discovery of anesthesia improved the public image of surgeons, long viewed as brutes who hacked away at agonized patients. It also permitted longer and hence more careful operations. Nevertheless, the failure of most surgeons to recognize the importance of clean hands and sterilized instruments partially offset the benefits of anesthesia before 1860. In 1843, Boston physician and poet Oliver Wendell Holmes, Sr., published an influential paper on how the failure of obstetricians to disinfect their hands often spread a disease called puerperal fever among mothers giving birth in hospitals. Still, the medical profession only gradually accepted the importance of disinfection. Operations remained as dangerous as the diseases or wounds they tried to heal. The mortality rate for amputations hovered around 40 percent. During the Civil War, 87 percent of soldiers who suffered abdominal wounds died from them.

Popular Health Movements

Doubtful of orthodox medicine, antebellum Americans turned to a variety of therapies and regimens that promised longer and healthier lives. One popular response to disease was hydropathy, or the "water cure," which filtered into the United States from Europe during the 1840s. By the mid-1850s the United States had twenty-seven hydropathic sanatoriums, which used cold baths and wet packs to provide "an abundance of water of dewy softness and crystal transparency, to cleanse, renovate, and rejuvenate the disease-worn and dilapidated system." The water cure held a special attraction for well-off women, partly because hydropathics professed to relieve the pain associated with childbirth and menstruation, and partly because hydropathic sanatoriums were congenial gathering places in which middle-class women could relax and exercise in private.

In contrast to the water cure, which required the time and expense of a trip to a sanatorium, Sylvester Graham propounded a health system that anyone could adopt. Alarmed by the 1832 cholera epidemic, Graham counseled changes in diet and regimen as well as total abstinence from alcohol. He urged Americans to substitute vegetables, fruits, and coarse, whole-grain bread (called Graham bread) for meat and to abstain from spices, coffee, and tea as well as from alcohol. Soon Graham added sexual "excess" (by which he meant most sex) to his list of forbidden indulgences. Many of Graham's disciples were reformers. Grahamites had a special table at the Brook Farm community. Until forced out by indignant parents and hungry students, one of Graham's followers ran the student dining room at Oberlin College. Much like Graham, reformers traced the evils of American society to the unnatural cravings of its people. Abolitionists, for example, contended that slavery intensified white men's lust and contributed to the violent behavior of white southerners. Similarly, Graham believed that eating meat stimulated lust and other aggressive impulses.

Graham's doctrines attracted a broad audience. Many towns and cities had boarding houses whose tables were set according to his principles. His books sold well, and his public lectures were thronged. Grahamism addressed the popular desire for better health at a time when orthodox medicine seemed to do more damage than good.

"The Illustrated Phrenological Almanac, 1859"
By dividing the brain into a large number of "faculties," phrenologists like Lorenzo Fowler, editor of the *Phrenological Almanac* for 1859, made the point that each person, regardless of whether born high or low, had an abundance of improvable talents.

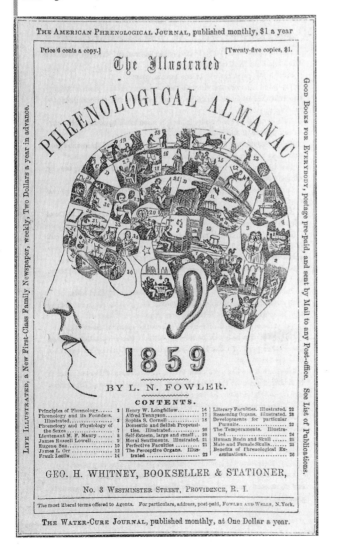

Phrenology

The belief that each person was master of his or her own destiny underlay not only evangelical religion and popular health movements but also the most popular of the antebellum scientific fads: **phrenology**. Imported from Europe, phrenology rested on the idea that the human mind comprised thirty-seven distinct faculties, or "organs," each located in a different part of the brain. Phrenologists thought that the degree of each organ's development determined skull shape, so that they could analyze a person's character by examining the bumps and depressions of the skull.

In the United States two brothers, Orson and Lorenzo Fowler, became the chief promoters of phrenology in the 1840s. Originally intending to become a Protestant missionary, Orson Fowler became instead a missionary for phrenology and opened a publishing house in New York City (Fowler and Wells) that mass-marketed books on the subject. The Fowlers replied to criticism that phrenology was godless by pointing to a huge organ called "Veneration" to prove that people were naturally religious, and they answered charges that phrenology was pessimistic by claiming that exercise could improve every desirable mental organ. Lorenzo Fowler reported that several of his skull bumps had actually grown. Orson Fowler wrapped it all into a tidy slogan: "Self-Made, or Never-Made."

Phrenology appealed to Americans as a "practical" science. In a mobile, individualistic society, it promised practitioners a quick way to assess other people. Some merchants used phrenological charts to pick suitable clerks, and some women even induced their fiancés to undergo phrenological analysis before tying the knot.

Unlike hydropathy, phrenology required no money; unlike Grahamism, it required no abstinence. Easily understood and practiced, and filled with the promise of universal improvement, phrenology was ideal for antebellum America. Just as Americans had invented machines to better their lives, so did they invent "sciences" that promised human betterment.

Democratic Pastimes

Between 1830 and 1860, technology increasingly transformed leisure by making free Americans more dependent on recreation that could be manufactured and sold. People purchased this commodity in the form of cheap newspapers and novels as well as affordable tickets to plays, museums, and lectures.

Just as the Boston Associates had daringly capitalized on new technology to produce textiles at Lowell and Waltham, imaginative entrepreneurs utilized technology to make and sell entertainment. Men like James Gordon Bennett, one of the founders of the penny press in America, and P. T. Barnum, the greatest showman of the nineteenth century, amassed fortunes by making the public want what they had to sell.

Technology also ignited the process by which individuals became spectators rather than creators of their own amusements. Americans had long found ways to enjoy themselves. Even the gloomiest Puritans had indulged in games and sports. After 1830, however, the burden of providing entertainment began to shift from individuals to entrepreneurs who supplied ways to entertain the public.

Newspapers

In 1830, the typical American newspaper was a mere four pages long, with the front and back pages devoted almost wholly to advertisements. The second and third pages contained editorials, details of ship arrivals and cargoes, reprints of political speeches, and notices of political events. Few papers depended on their circulation for profit; even the most prominent papers had a daily circulation of only one or two thousand. Rather, papers often relied on subsidies from political parties or factions. When a party gained power, it inserted paid political notices only in papers loyal to it. "Journalists," a contemporary wrote, "were usually little more than secretaries dependent upon cliques of politicians, merchants, brokers, and office seekers for their prosperity and bread."

As a result, newspapers could be profitable without being popular. Because of their potential for profit, new papers were constantly being established. But most had limited appeal. The typical paper sold for six cents at a time when the average daily wage was less than a dollar. Papers often seemed little more than published bulletin boards. They typically lacked the exciting news stories and eye-catching illustrations that later generations would take for granted.

The 1830s witnessed the beginnings of a stunning transformation. Technological changes, most of which originated in Europe, vastly increased both the supply of paper (still made from rags) and the speed of printing presses. The substitution of steam-driven cylindrical presses for flatbed hand presses led to a tenfold increase in the number of printed pages that could be produced in an hour. Enterprising journalists, among them the Scottish-born James Gordon Bennett, applied the new technology to introduce the **penny press**. Newspapers could now rely on vast circulation rather than on political subsidies to turn a profit. In 1833, the *New York Sun* became America's first penny newspaper, and Bennett's *New York Herald* followed in 1835. By June 1835, the combined

daily circulation of New York's three penny papers reached 44,000; in contrast, the city's eleven dailies had a combined daily circulation of only 26,500 before the dawn of the penny press in 1833. Spearheaded by the penny papers, the combined daily circulation of newspapers throughout the nation rose from roughly 78,000 in 1830 to 300,000 by 1840. The number of weekly newspapers spurted from 65 in 1830 to 138 in 1840.

The penny press also revolutionized the marketing and format of papers. Where single copies of the six-cent papers were usually available only at the printer's office, newsboys hawked the penny papers on busy street corners. Moreover, the penny papers subordinated the recording of political and commercial events to human-interest stories of robberies, murders, rapes, and abandoned children. They dispatched reporters to police courts and printed transcripts of trials. As sociologist Michael Schudson observes, "The penny press invented the modern concept of 'news.'" Rather than merely recording events, the penny papers wove events into gripping stories. They invented not only news but also news reporting. Relying on party stalwarts to dispatch copies of speeches and platforms, and reprinting news items from other papers, the older six-cent papers did little, if any, reporting. In contrast, the penny papers employed their own correspondents and were the first papers to use the telegraph to speed news into print.

Some penny papers were little more than scandal sheets, but the best, like Bennett's *New York Herald* and Horace Greeley's *New York Tribune* (1841), pioneered modern financial and political reporting. From its inception, the *Herald* contained a daily "money article" that analyzed and interpreted financial events. "The spirit, pith, and philosophy of commercial affairs is what men of business want," Bennett wrote. The relentless snooping of the *Tribune*'s Washington reporters outraged politicians. In 1848, *Tribune* correspondents were temporarily barred from the House floor for reporting that Representative Sawyer of Ohio ate his lunch (sausage and bread) each day in the House chamber, picked his teeth with a jackknife, and wiped his greasy hands on his pants and coat.

The Theater

Like newspapers, theaters increasingly appealed to a mass audience. Antebellum theaters were large (twenty-five hundred to four thousand seats in some cities) and crowded by all classes. With seats as cheap as twelve cents and rarely more than fifty cents, the typical theater audience included lawyers and merchants and their wives, artisans and clerks, sailors and noisy boys, and a sizable body of prostitutes. Prostitutes usually sat in the top gallery, called the third tier, "that dark, horrible, guilty" place. The presence of prostitutes in theaters was taken for granted; the only annoyance came when they left the third tier to solicit customers in the more expensive seats.

The prostitutes in attendance were not the only factor that made the antebellum theater vaguely disreputable. Theater audiences were notoriously rowdy. They stamped their feet, hooted at villains, and threw potatoes and garbage at the stage when they disliked the characters or the acting. Individual actors developed huge followings, and the public displayed at least as much interest in the actors as in the plays. In 1849, a long-running feud between the leading American actor, Edwin Forrest, and popular British actor William Macready ended with the Astor Place riot in New York City, which left twenty-two people dead.

The Astor Place riot demonstrated the broad popularity of the theater. Forrest's supporters included Irish workers who loathed the British and appealed to the "working men" to rally against the "aristocrat" Macready. Macready, who projected a more polished and intellectual image than Forrest, attracted the better-educated classes. Had not all classes patronized the theater, the deadly riot would probably never have occurred.

The plays themselves were as diverse as the audiences. Most often performed were melodramas in which virtue was rewarded, vice punished, and the heroine married the hero. Yet the single most popular dramatist was William Shakespeare. In 1835, audiences in Philadelphia witnessed sixty-five performances of Shakespeare's plays. Americans who may never have read a line of Shakespeare grew familiar with Othello, King Lear, Desdemona, and Shylock. Theatrical managers adapted Shakespeare to a popular audience. They highlighted the sword fights and assassinations, cut some speeches, omitted minor characters, and pruned words or references that might have offended the audience's sense of propriety. For example, they substituted *pottels* for *urinals* and quietly advanced Juliet's age at the time that she falls in love with Romeo from fourteen to eighteen. They occasionally changed sad endings to happy ones.

The producers even arranged for short performances between acts. During such an interlude, the audience might have observed a brief impersonation of Tecumseh or Aaron Burr, jugglers and acrobats, a drummer beating twelve drums at once, or a three-year-old who weighed a hundred pounds.

Minstrel Shows

The Yankee or "Brother Jonathan" figure who served as a stock character in many antebellum plays helped audiences form an image of the ideal American as rustic, clever, patriotic, and more than a match for city slickers and decadent European blue bloods. In a different way, the minstrel shows that Americans thronged to see in the 1840s and 1850s forged enduring stereotypes that buttressed white Americans' sense of superiority by diminishing black people.

Minstrel shows arose in northern cities in the 1840s when white men in blackface took to the stage to present an evening of songs, dances, and humorous sketches. Minstrelsy borrowed some authentic elements of African-American culture, especially dances characterized by the sliding, shuffling step of southern blacks, but most of the songs had origins in white culture. Such familiar American songs as Stephen Foster's "Camptown Races" and "Massa's in the Cold Ground," which first aired in minstrel shows, reflected white Americans' notions of how blacks sang more than it represented authentic black music.

In addition, the images of blacks projected by minstrelsy both catered to and reinforced the prejudices of the working-class whites who dominated the audience. Minstrel troupes usually depicted blacks as stupid, clumsy, and obsessively musical, and emphasized the Africanness of blacks by giving their characters names like the Ethiopian Serenaders and their acts titles like the "Nubian Jungle Dance" and the "African Fling." At a time of intensifying political conflict over slavery, minstrel shows planted images and expectations about blacks' behavior through stock characters. These included Uncle Ned, the tattered, humble, and docile slave, and Zip Coon, the arrogant urban free black who paraded around in a high hat, long-tailed coat, and green vest and who lived off his girlfriends' money. Minstrels lampooned blacks who assumed public roles by portraying them as incompetent stump speakers who called Patrick Henry "Henry Patrick," referred to John Hancock as "Boobcock," and confused the word *statute* with *statue*.

By the 1850s, major cities from New York to San Francisco had several minstrel theaters. Touring professional troupes and local amateur talent even brought minstrelsy to small towns and villages. Mark Twain recalled how minstrelsy had burst upon Hannibal, Missouri, in the early 1840s as "a glad and stunning surprise." So popular was the craze that minstrels appeared at the White House and entertained presidents.

P. T. Barnum

P. T. Barnum understood how to turn the antebellum public's craving for entertainment into a profitable business. As a young man in Bethel, Connecticut, he started a newspaper, the *Herald of Freedom*, that assailed wrongdoing in high places. Throughout his life, he thought of himself as a public benefactor and pointed to his profits as proof that he gave people what they wanted. Yet honesty was never his strong suit. As a small-town grocer in Connecticut, he regularly cheated his customers on the principle that they were trying to cheat him. Barnum, in short, was a hustler raised in the land of the Puritans, a cynic and an idealist rolled into one.

After moving to New York City in 1834, Barnum started a new career as an entrepreneur of popular entertainment. His first venture exhibited a black woman, Joice Heth, whom Barnum billed as the 169-year-old former slave nurse of George Washington. Barnum neither knew nor cared how old Joice was (in fact, she was probably around 80); it was enough that people would pay to see her. Strictly speaking, he cheated the public, but he knew that many of his customers shared his doubts about Joice's age. Determined to expose Barnum's gimmick, some poked her to see whether she was really a machine rather than a person. He was playing a game with the public, and the public with him.

In 1841, Barnum purchased a run-down museum in New York City, rechristened it the American Museum, and opened a new chapter in the history of popular entertainment. The founders of most earlier museums had educational purposes. They exhibited stuffed birds and animals, specimens of rock, and portraits. Most of these museums had languished for want of public interest. Barnum, in contrast, made pricking public curiosity the main goal. To attract people, he added collections of curiosities and faked exhibits. Visitors to the American Museum could see ventriloquists, magicians, albinos, a five-year-old person of short stature whom Barnum named General Tom Thumb and later took on a tour of Europe, and the "Feejee Mermaid," a shrunken oddity that Barnum billed as "positively asserted by its owner to have been taken alive in the Feejee Islands." By 1850, the American Museum had become the best-known museum in the nation and a model for popular museums in other cities.

Blessed with a genius for publicity, Barnum recognized that newspapers could invent as well as report news. One of his favorite tactics was to puff his exhibits by writing letters (under various names) to newspapers in which he would hint that the scientific world was agog over some astonishing curiosity of nature that the public could soon see for itself at the American Museum. But Barnum's success rested on more than publicity. A staunch temperance advocate, he provided regular lectures at the American Museum on the evils of alcohol and soon gave the place a reputation as a center for safe family amusement. By marketing his museum as family

Tom Thumb
Barnum helped to arrange the 1863 wedding of "General" Tom Thumb and Lavinia Warren, another person of short stature in his employ. On their wedding tour, Tom and Lavinia visited President Abraham Lincoln in the White House.

entertainment, Barnum helped break down barriers that had long divided the pastimes of husbands from those of their wives.

Finally, Barnum tapped the public's insatiable curiosity about natural wonders. In 1835, the editor of the *New York Sun* had boosted his circulation by claiming that a famous astronomer had discovered pelicans and winged men on the moon. At a time when each passing year brought new technological wonders, the public was ready to believe in anything, even the Feejee Mermaid.

The Quest for Nationality in Literature and Art

Europeans took little notice of American poetry or fiction before the 1820s. "Who ever reads an American book?" a British literary critic taunted in 1820. Americans responded by pointing to Washington Irving, whose

Sketch Book (1820) contained two famous stories, "Rip Van Winkle" and "The Legend of Sleepy Hollow." Naming hotels and steamboats after Irving, Americans soaked him in applause, but they had to concede that Irving had done much of his best writing, including the *Sketch Book*, while living in England.

After 1820, the United States experienced a flowering of literature called the **American Renaissance**. The leading figures of this Renaissance included James Fenimore Cooper, Ralph Waldo Emerson, Henry David Thoreau, Margaret Fuller, Walt Whitman, Nathaniel Hawthorne, Herman Melville, and Edgar Allan Poe. In 1800, American authors accounted for a negligible proportion of the output of American publishers. By 1830, 40 percent of the books published in the United States were written by Americans; by 1850 this had increased to 75 percent.

Not only were Americans writing more books; increasingly, they sought to depict the features of their nation in literature and art. The quest for a distinctively American literature especially shaped the writings of Cooper, Emerson, and Whitman. It also revealed itself in the majestic paintings of the so-called Hudson River school, the first homegrown American movement in painting, and in the landscape architecture of Frederick Law Olmsted.

Roots of the American Renaissance

Two broad developments, one economic and the other philosophical, contributed to this development. First, the transportation revolution created a national market for books, especially fiction. Initially, this worked to the advantage of British authors, especially Sir Walter Scott. With the publication of *Waverley* (1814), a historical novel set in Britain of the 1740s, Scott's star began its spectacular ascent on the American horizon. Americans named more than a dozen towns Waverley; advertisements for Scott's subsequent novels bore the simple caption, "By the author of *Waverley*." Scott's success demonstrated that the public wanted to read fiction. Although American publishers continued to pirate British novels (reprinting them without paying copyright fees), Scott's success prompted Americans like James Fenimore Cooper to write fiction for sale.

Second, the American Renaissance reflected the rise of a philosophical movement known as romanticism. By insisting that literature reveal the longings of an individual author's soul, romanticism challenged the eighteenth-century view, known as classicism, that standards of beauty were universal. For the classicist, the ideal author was an educated gentleman who wrote elegant poetry and essays that displayed learning and refinement and that conformed to timeless standards of taste and excellence. In contrast, romantics expected a literary work to be emotionally charged, a unique reflection of its creator's inner feelings.

The emergence of a national market for books and the influence of romanticism combined to democratize literature. The conventions of classicism led writers to view literature as a pastime of gentlemen. They were to write only for one another (and never for profit) and use literature as a vehicle for displaying their learning, especially their knowledge of ancient Greek and Roman civilization. In contrast, the emerging national market for books tended to elevate the importance of fiction—a comparatively democratic form of literature—more than poetry and essays. Writing (and reading) fiction did not require knowledge of Latin and Greek or a familiarity with ancient history and mythology. Significantly, many of the best-selling novels of the antebellum period—for example, Harriet Beecher Stowe's *Uncle Tom's Cabin*—were written by women, who were still barred from higher education. In addition, fiction had a subversive quality that contributed to its popularity. Authors could create unconventional characters, situations, and outcomes. The essay usually had an unmistakable conclusion. In contrast, the novel left more room for interpretation by the reader. A novel might well have a lesson to teach, but the reader's interest was likely to be aroused less by the moral than by the development of characters and plot.

Cooper, Emerson, Thoreau, Fuller, and Whitman

James Fenimore Cooper was the first important figure in this literary upsurge. His most significant innovation was to introduce a distinctively American fictional character, the frontiersman Natty Bumppo ("Leatherstocking"). In *The Pioneers* (1823), Natty appears as an old man settled on the shores of Lake Otsego in upstate New York. A hunter, Natty blames farmers for the wanton destruction of game and for turning the majestic forests into deserts of tree stumps. As a spokesman for nature against the march of civilization, Natty immediately became a popular figure, and in subsequent novels such as *The Last of the Mohicans* (1826), *The Pathfinder* (1840), and *The Deerslayer* (1841), Cooper unfolded Natty's earlier life for an appreciative reading public.

Although he disliked fiction, **Ralph Waldo Emerson** emerged in the late 1830s as the most influential spokesman for American literary nationalism. As the leading light of the movement known as transcendentalism, an American offshoot of romanticism, Emerson contended that our ideas of God and freedom are inborn; knowledge resembles sight—an instantaneous and direct perception of truth. That being so, Emerson concluded, learned people enjoy no special advantage in pursuing truth. All persons can glimpse the truth if only they trust the promptings of their hearts.

Transcendentalist doctrine pointed to the exhilarating conclusion that the United States, a young and democratic society, could produce as noble a literature and art as the more traditional societies of Europe. "Our day of dependence, our long apprenticeship to the learning of other lands draws to a close," Emerson announced in his address "The American Scholar" (1837). The time had come for Americans to trust themselves. Let "the single man plant himself indomitably on his instincts and there abide," he proclaimed, and "the huge world will come around to him."

Emerson admired Cooper's fiction, but his own version of American literary nationalism was expressed mainly in his essays, which mixed broad themes—"Beauty," "Wealth," and "Representative Men"—with pungent and vivid language. For example, he wrote in praise of independent thinking that the scholar should not "quit his belief that a popgun is a popgun, though the ancient and honorable of the earth affirm it to be the crack of doom." Equally remarkable was Emerson's way of developing his subjects. A contemporary compared listening to Emerson to trying to see the sun in a fog; one could see light but never the sun itself. Believing that knowledge reflected God's voice within each person and that truth was intuitive and individual, he never amassed persuasive evidence or presented systematic arguments to prove his point. Rather, he relied on a sequence of vivid if unconnected assertions whose truth the reader would instantly see. (They did not always see it; one reader complained that she might have understood Emerson better if she had stood on her head.)

Emerson had a magnetic attraction for intellectually inclined young men and women who did not fit neatly into American society. In the 1830s, several of them gathered in Concord, Massachusetts, to share Emerson's intellectual pursuits. **Henry David Thoreau** was representative of the younger Emersonians. A crucial difference separated the two men. Adventurous in thought, Emerson was not adventurous in action. Thoreau was more of a doer. At one point he went to jail rather than pay his poll tax. This revenue, he knew, would support

Margaret Fuller
Disappointed that his first child was a girl, Margaret Fuller's father decided to educate her as if she were a boy. As a child, she wrecked her health studying Latin, English, and French classics. She joined Ralph Waldo Emerson's circle of transcendentalists. In 1846, Horace Greeley sent her to Europe as the *Tribune*'s foreign correspondent. There she met artists and writers, observed the Revolutions of 1848, and married an Italian nobleman. On her return to America in 1850, she, her husband, and infant son died in a shipwreck off Long Island.

the war with Mexico, which he viewed as part of a southern conspiracy to extend slavery. The experience led Thoreau to write "Civil Disobedience" (1849), in which he defended a citizen's right to disobey unjust laws.

In the spring of 1845, Thoreau moved a few miles from Concord to the woods near Walden Pond. There he constructed a cabin on land owned by Emerson and spent parts of the next two years providing for his wants away from civilization. His stated purpose in retreating to Walden was to write a description (later published) of a canoe trip that he and his brother had taken in 1839. During his stay in the woods, however, he conceived and wrote a much more important book, *Walden* (1854). A contemporary described *Walden* as "the logbook of his woodland cruise," and indeed, Thoreau filled its pages with descriptions of hawks and wild pigeons, his invention of raisin bread, his trapping of the woodchucks that ate his vegetable garden, and his construction of a cabin for exactly $28.50. But true to transcendentalism, Thoreau had a larger message. His rustic retreat taught him that he (and by implication, others) could satisfy material wants with only a few weeks' work each year and thereby leave more time for reexamining life's purpose. The problem with Americans, he said, was that they turned themselves into "mere machines" to acquire wealth without asking why. Thoreau bore the uncomfortable truth that material and moral progress were not as intimately related as Americans liked to think.

Among the most remarkable figures in Emerson's circle was **Margaret Fuller**, whose status as an intellectual woman distanced her from conventional society. Disappointed that his first child was not a boy, her Harvard-educated father, a prominent Massachusetts politician, determined to give Margaret the sort of education young men would have acquired at Harvard. Drilled by her father in Latin and Greek, her reading branched into modern German romantics and the English literary classics. Her exposure to Emerson's ideas during a sojourn in Concord in 1836 pushed her toward transcendentalism, with its vindication of the free life of the spirit over formal doctrines and of the need for each person to discover truth on his or her own.

Ingeniously, Fuller turned transcendentalism into an occupation of sorts. Between 1839 and 1844 she supported herself by presiding over "Conversations" for fee-paying participants drawn from Boston's elite men and women. Transcendentalism also influenced her classic of American feminism, *Woman in the Nineteenth Century* (1845). Breaking with the prevailing notion of separate spheres for men and women, Fuller contended that no woman could achieve the kind of personal fulfillment lauded by Emerson unless she developed her intellectual abilities and overcame her fear of being called masculine.

One of Emerson's qualities was an ability to sympathize with such dissimilar people as the reclusive and critical Thoreau, the scholarly and aloof Fuller, and the outgoing and earthy **Walt Whitman**. Self-taught and in love with virtually everything about America except slavery, Whitman left school at eleven and became a printer's apprentice and later a journalist and editor for various newspapers in Brooklyn, Manhattan, and New Orleans. A familiar figure at Democratic Party functions, he marched in party parades and put his pen to the service of its antislavery wing.

Journalism and politics gave Whitman an intimate knowledge of ordinary Americans; the more he knew them, the more he liked them. His reading of Emerson nurtured his belief that America was to be the cradle of a new citizen in whom natural virtue would flourish unimpeded by European corruption, a man like Andrew Jackson, that "massive, yet most sweet and plain character." The threads of Whitman's early career came together in his major work *Leaves of Grass*, a book of poems first published in 1855 and reissued with voluminous additions in subsequent years.

Leaves of Grass shattered most existing poetic conventions. Not only did Whitman write in free verse (that is, most of his poems had neither rhyme nor meter), but the poems were also lusty and blunt at a time when delicacy reigned in the literary world. Whitman wrote of "the scent of these armpits finer than prayer" and "winds whose soft-tickling genitals rub against me." No less remarkably, Whitman intruded himself into his poems, one of which he titled "Song of Walt Whitman" (later retitled "Song of Myself"). It was not egotism that moved him to sing of himself. Rather, he viewed himself—crude, plain, self-taught, and passionately democratic—as the personification of the American people. He was

Comrade of raftsmen and coalmen, comrade of all who shake hands and welcome to drink and meat,

A learner with the simplest, a teacher of the thoughtfullest.

By 1860, Whitman had acquired a considerable reputation as a poet. Nevertheless, the original edition of *Leaves* (a run of only about eight hundred copies) was ignored or derided as a "heterogeneous mass of bombast, egotism, vulgarity, and nonsense." One reviewer suggested that it was the work of an escaped lunatic. Only Emerson and a few others reacted enthusiastically. Within two weeks of publication, Emerson, never having met Whitman, wrote, "I find it the most extraordinary piece of wit and wisdom that America has yet contributed." Emerson had long called for the appearance of "the poet of America" and knew in a flash that Whitman was that poet.

Hawthorne, Melville, and Poe

Emerson, Fuller, Thoreau, and Whitman expressed themselves in essays and poetry. In contrast, two major writers of the 1840s and 1850s—**Nathaniel Hawthorne** and **Herman Melville**—primarily wrote fiction, and another, **Edgar Allan Poe**, wrote both fiction and poetry. Although they were major contributors to the American Renaissance, Hawthorne, Melville, and Poe paid little heed to Emerson's call for a literature that would comprehend the everyday experiences of ordinary Americans. Hawthorne, for example, set *The Scarlet Letter* (1850) in New England's Puritan past, *The House of the*

Seven Gables (1851) in a mansion haunted not by ghosts but by memories of the past, and *The Marble Faun* (1859) in Rome. Poe set several of his short stories such as "The Murders in the Rue Morgue" (1841) and "The Cask of Amontillado" (1846) in Europe; as one critic has noted, "His art could have been produced as easily had he been born in Europe." Melville did draw materials and themes from his own experiences as a sailor and from the lore of the New England whaling industry, but for his novels *Typee* (1846), *Omoo* (1847), and *Mardi* (1849), he picked the exotic setting of islands in the South Seas; and for his masterpiece *Moby-Dick* (1851) the ill-fated whaler *Pequod*. If the only surviving documents from the 1840s and 1850s were its major novels, historians would face an impossible task in describing the appearance of antebellum American society.

The unusual settings favored by these three writers partly reflected their view that American life lacked the materials for great fiction. Hawthorne, for example, bemoaned the difficulty of writing about a country "where there is no shadow, no antiquity, no mystery, no picturesque and gloomy wrong, nor anything but a commonplace prosperity in broad and simple daylight, as is happily the case with my dear native land." In addition, psychology rather than society fascinated the three writers; each probed the depths of the human mind rather than the intricacies of social relationships. Their preoccupation with analyzing the mental states of their characters grew out of their underlying pessimism about the human condition. Emerson, Whitman, and (to a degree) Thoreau optimistically believed that human conflicts could be resolved if only individuals followed the promptings of their better selves. In contrast, Hawthorne, Melville, and Poe saw individuals as bundles of conflicting forces that, despite the best intentions, might never be reconciled.

Their pessimism led them to create characters obsessed by pride, guilt, a desire for revenge, or a quest for perfection, and then to set their stories along the byways of society, where they would be free to explore the complexities of human motivation without the jarring intrusion of everyday life. For example, in *The Scarlet Letter* Hawthorne turned to the Puritan past in order to examine the psychological and moral consequences of the adultery committed by Hester Prynne and the minister Arthur Dimmesdale. So completely did Hawthorne focus on the moral dilemmas of his central characters that he conveyed little sense of the social life of the Puritan village in which the novel is set. Melville, who dedicated *Moby-Dick* to Hawthorne, shared the latter's pessimism. In the novel's Captain Ahab, Melville created

Nathaniel Hawthorne
This photograph shows Hawthorne as he appeared in 1850, the publication year of *The Scarlet Letter*. *The House of the Seven Gables* was published in the following year.

a frightening character whose relentless and futile pursuit of the white whale fails to fill the chasm in his soul and brings death to all of his mates save the narrator, Ishmael. Poe also channeled his pessimism into creative achievements. In perhaps his finest short story, "The Fall of the House of Usher" (1839), he demonstrated an uncanny ability to weave the symbol of a crumbling mansion with the mental agony of a crumbling family.

Hawthorne, Melville, and Poe ignored Emerson's call to write about the everyday experiences of their fellow Americans. Nor did they follow Cooper's lead by creating distinctively American heroes. Yet each contributed to an indisputably American literature. Ironically, their conviction that the lives of ordinary Americans provided inadequate materials for fiction led them to create a uniquely

American fiction marked less by the description of the complex social relationships of ordinary life than by the analysis of moral dilemmas and psychological states. In this way, they unintentionally fulfilled a prediction made by Alexis de Tocqueville that writers in democratic nations, while rejecting many of the traditional sources of fiction, would explore the abstract and universal questions of human nature.

Literature in the Marketplace

Few eighteenth-century gentleman-authors imagined that they were writing for the public or that they would make money from their literary productions. That suspicion that commercialism corrupted art did not disappear during the American Renaissance. The shy and reclusive poet Emily Dickinson, who lived all of her fifty-six years on the same street in Amherst, Massachusetts ("I do not go from home," she wrote with characteristic pithiness) and who wrote exquisite poems that examined, in her words, every splinter in the groove of the brain, refused to publish her work. But in an age lacking university professorships or foundation fellowships for creative writers, authors were both tempted and often compelled to write for profit. For example, Poe, a heavy drinker always pressed for cash, scratched out a meager living writing short stories for popular magazines. Despite his reputation for aloof self-reliance, Thoreau craved recognition by the public and in 1843 tried, unsuccessfully, to market his poems in New York City. Only after meeting disappointment as a poet did he turn to detailed narratives of nature, and these did prove popular.

Emerson, too, wanted to reach a broader public, and after abandoning his first vocation as a Unitarian minister he virtually invented a new one, that of "lyceum" lecturer. Lyceums, local organizations for sponsoring lectures, spread throughout the northern tier of states between the late 1820s and 1860; by 1840 thirty-five hundred towns had lyceums. Most of Emerson's published essays originated as lectures before lyceums in the Northeast and Midwest. He delivered some sixty speeches in Ohio alone between 1850 and 1867, and lecture fees provided him with his main form of income. Thanks to newly built railroads and cheap newspapers that announced their comings and goings, others followed in his path. Thoreau presented a digest of *Walden* as a lyceum lecture before the book itself was published. One stalwart of the lyceum circuit said that he did it for "F-A-M-E—Fifty and My Expenses," and Herman Melville pledged, "If they will pay my expenses and give a reasonable fee, I am ready to lecture in Labrador or on the Isle of Desolation off Patagonia."

The age offered women few opportunities for public speaking, and most lyceum lecturers were men. But women discovered ways to tap into the growing market for literature. Writing fiction was the most lucrative occupation open to women before the Civil War. For example, the popular novelist Susan Warner had been brought up in luxury and then tossed into poverty by the financial ruin of her father in the Panic of 1837. Writing fiction supplied her with cash as well as pleasure.

Warner and others benefited from advances in the technology of printing that brought down the price of books. Before 1830, the novels of Sir Walter Scott had been issued in three-volume sets that retailed for as much as thirty dollars. As canals and railroads opened crossroads stores to the latest fiction, publishers in New York and Philadelphia vied to deliver inexpensive novels to the shelves. By the 1840s, cheap paperbacks that sold for as little as seven cents began to flood the market. Those who chose not to purchase books could read fiction in so-called story newspapers such as the *New York Ledger*, which was devoted mainly to serializing novels and which had an astonishing weekly circulation of four hundred thousand by 1860. In addition, the spread of (usually) coeducational public schools and academies contributed to higher literacy and a widening audience, especially among women, for fiction.

The most popular form of fiction in the 1840s and 1850s was the sentimental novel, a kind of women's fiction written by women about women and mainly for women. In the typical plot, a female orphan or spoiled rich girl thrown on hard times by a drunken father learned to master every situation. The moral of Warner's *The Wide, Wide World* (1850) was that women had what it took to clean up the messes left by men. Not all popular fiction was sentimental. More expressive of the rage felt by some women were novels like Ned Buntline's *The G'hals of New York* (1850), where a woman becomes the mistress of a criminal but, after years of maltreatment, plots his downfall and turns him over to the police. In George Thompson's *The Countess* (1849), wealthy New York women use their sexual charms to entrap and manipulate men, whom they deride as "self-styled Emperors."

Such authors as Emerson, Hawthorne, Poe, and Melville, who now are recognized as major figures, had to swim in the sea of popular culture represented by the story newspapers and sentimental novels. Emerson, the intellectual, competed on the lecture circuit with P. T. Barnum, the showman. Hawthorne complained about the popularity of the "female scribblers." Poe thought that the public's judgment of a writer's merits was nearly always wrong. Indeed, the public did fail to see Melville's genius; the qualities of

Moby-Dick were not widely recognized until the twentieth century. By and large, however, the major writers were not ignored by their society. Emerson's lectures made him famous. Hawthorne's *The Scarlet Letter* enjoyed respectable sales. Poe's poem "The Raven" (1844) was so popular that some suggested substituting the raven for the eagle as the national bird. What these writers discovered, sometimes the hard way, was that to make a living as authors they had to meet certain popular expectations. For example, *The Scarlet Letter* had greater popular appeal than *Moby-Dick* in part because the former told a love story while the latter, with its all-male cast and high-seas exploits, was simply not what the public looked for in a novel.

American Landscape Painting

American painters also sought to develop nationality in art between 1820 and 1860. Lacking the mythic past that European artists drew on—the legendary gods and goddesses of ancient Greece and Rome—Americans subordinated history and figure painting to landscape painting. Just as Hawthorne had complained about the flat, dull character of American society, so had the painters of the Hudson River school recognized that the American landscape lacked the European landscape's "poetry of decay" in the form of ruined castles and crumbling temples. Like everything else in the United States, the landscape was fresh, relatively untouched by the human imprint. This fact posed a challenge to the Hudson River school painters.

The **Hudson River school** flourished from the 1820s to the 1870s. Numbering more than fifty painters, it was best represented by Thomas Cole, Asher Durand, and Frederick Church. All three men painted scenes of the region around the Hudson River, a waterway that Americans compared in majesty to the Rhine. But none was exclusively a landscapist. Some of Cole's most popular paintings were allegories, including *The Course of Empire*, a sequence of five canvases depicting the rise and fall of an ancient city and clearly implying that luxury doomed republican virtue. Nor did these artists paint only the Hudson. Church, a student of Cole and internationally the best known of the three, painted the Andes Mountains during an extended trip to South America in 1853. After the Civil War, the German-born Albert Bierstadt applied many Hudson River school techniques in his monumental canvases of the Rocky Mountains.

Cotopaxi
Frederick Church made extended trips in 1853 and 1857 to the Andean Mountains of Colombia and Ecuador. Majesty and tranquillity mingle in this painting, considered Church's masterpiece, of smoke pouring from the massive volcano, Cotopaxi, and nearly obliterating the sinking sun.

The works of Washington Irving and the opening of the Erie Canal had sparked artistic interest in the Hudson during the 1820s. After 1830, the writings of Emerson and Thoreau popularized a new view of nature. Intent on cultivating land, the pioneers of Kentucky and Ohio had deforested a vast area. One traveler complained that Americans would rather view a wheat field or a cabbage patch than a virgin forest. But Emerson, Thoreau, and landscape architects like Frederick Law Olmsted glorified nature; "in wildness is the preservation of the world," Thoreau wrote. Their outlook blended with growing popular fears that, as one contemporary expressed it in 1847, "The axe of civilization is busy with our old forests." As the "wild and picturesque haunts of the Red Man" became "the abodes of commerce and the seats of civilization," he concluded, "it behooves our artists to rescue from its grasp the little that is left before it is too late."

The Hudson River painters wanted to do more than preserve a passing wilderness. Their special contribution

Tchow-ee-put-o-kaw, 1834

Rainmaking Among the Mandan, 1837–1839
George Catlin's paintings preserved the faces, customs, and habitats of the Indian tribes whose civilization was collapsing in the face of white advance.

to American art was to emphasize emotional effect over accuracy. Cole's use of rich coloring, billowing clouds, massive gnarled trees, towering peaks, and deep chasms so heightened the dramatic impact of his paintings that the poet and editor William Cullen Bryant compared them to "acts of religion." Similar motifs marked Church's paintings of the Andes Mountains, which used erupting volcanoes and thunderstorms to evoke dread and a sense of majesty. Lacking the poignant antiquities that dotted European landscapes, the Americans strove to capture the natural grandeur of their own landscape.

Like Cole, the painter **George Catlin** also tried to preserve a vanishing America. Observing a delegation of Indians passing through Philadelphia in 1824, Catlin resolved on his life's work: to paint as many Native Americans as possible in their pure and "savage" state. Journeying up the Missouri River in 1832, he sketched at a feverish pace, and in 1837 he first exhibited his "Indian gallery" of 437 oil paintings and thousands of sketches of faces and customs from nearly fifty tribes.

Catlin's Indian paintings made him famous, but his romantic view of Indians as noble savages ("the Indian mind is a beautiful blank") was a double-edged sword. Catlin's admirers delighted in his portrayals of dignified Indians but shared his view that such noble creatures were "doomed" to oblivion by the march of progress.

By the 1830s, sprawling urban growth was prompting landscape architects to create little enclaves of nature that might serve as sources of spiritual refreshment to harried city-dwellers. Starting with the opening of Mount Auburn Cemetery near Boston in 1831, "rural" cemeteries with pastoral names such as "Harmony Grove" and "Greenwood" sprang up near major cities and quickly became tourist attractions, so much so that one orator described them as designed for the living rather than the dead. In 1858, New York City chose a plan drawn by **Frederick Law Olmsted** and Calvert Vaux for its proposed Central Park. Olmsted (who became the park's chief architect) and Vaux wanted the park to look as much like the countryside as possible, showing nothing of the surrounding city. A bordering line of trees screened out buildings, drainage pipes were dug to create lakes, and four sunken thoroughfares were cut across the park to carry traffic. The effect was to make Central Park an idealized version of nature, "picturesque" in that it would remind visitors of the landscapes that they had seen in pictures. Thus nature was made to mirror art.

Conclusion

Technological advances transformed the lives of millions of Americans between 1840 and 1860. The mechanical reaper increased wheat production and enabled agriculture to keep pace with the growing population. The development of machine tools, first in gun manufacture and next in the manufacturing of sewing machines, helped Americans achieve Eli Whitney's ideal of production by interchangeable parts and made a range of luxuries affordable for the middle class. Steam power reduced the vulnerability of factories to the vagaries of the weather, stretched out the employment season, and increased productivity and income. The spread of railroads and the invention of the telegraph shrunk the barriers of space and time.

Many of these developments unified Americans. Railroad tracks threaded the nation together. The telegraph speeded communication and made it possible for Americans in widely scattered areas to read about the same current events in their newspapers. The advances in printing that gave birth to the penny press and the inexpensive novel contributed to a widening of the reading public. Not only were Americans now more able to read the same news items; increasingly, they read the same best sellers, just as they flocked to the commercial amusements marketed by P. T. Barnum. Advocates of progress hailed these developments as instruments of ever-rising popular happiness. Even disease came to be seen less as a divine punishment for human depravity than as God's warning to those who ate or drank too much.

Progress carried a price. By bringing commodities once available only to the rich within the financial reach of the middle class, technology narrowed the social distance between these classes. At the same time, though, it set them off more sharply from the poor and intensified the division between the experiences of middle-class men and women. Progress also posed moral and spiritual challenges. The march of progress threatened to devour unspoiled nature. In different ways, writers like James Fenimore Cooper, Ralph Waldo Emerson, and Henry David Thoreau called attention to the conflict between nature and civilization as a distinctive feature of the American experience. Artists of the Hudson River school created majestic paintings of the natural wonders of the New World. For their part, Nathaniel Hawthorne and Herman Melville challenged the easy confidence that technology and democracy could liberate Americans from the dilemmas of the human condition.

Chronology, 1840–1860

1820	Washington Irving, *The Sketch Book*.
1823	Philadelphia completes the first urban water-supply system. James Fenimore Cooper, *The Pioneers*.
1826	Cooper, *The Last of the Mohicans*.
1831	Mount Auburn Cemetery opens.
1832	A cholera epidemic strikes the United States.
1833	The *New York Sun*, the first penny newspaper, is established.
1834	Cyrus McCormick patents the mechanical reaper.
1835	James Gordon Bennett establishes the *New York Herald*.
1837	Ralph Waldo Emerson, "The American Scholar."
1841	P. T. Barnum opens the American Museum. Edgar Allan Poe, "The Murders in the Rue Morgue."
1844	First telegraph message transmitted.
1846	W. T. G. Morton successfully uses anesthesia. Elias Howe, Jr., patents the sewing machine.
1849	Second major cholera epidemic. Astor Place theater riot leaves twenty dead.
1850	Nathaniel Hawthorne, *The Scarlet Letter*.
1851	Hawthorne, *The House of the Seven Gables*. Herman Melville, *Moby-Dick*. Erie Railroad completes its line to the West.
1853	Ten small railroads are consolidated into the New York Central Railroad.
1854	Henry David Thoreau, *Walden*.
1855	Walt Whitman, *Leaves of Grass*.
1856	Pennsylvania Railroad completes Chicago link.
1857	Baltimore–St. Louis rail service completed.
1858	Frederick Law Olmsted is appointed architect in chief for Central Park.

For Further Reference

Richard S. Bushman, *The Refinement of America: Persons, Houses, Cities* (1992). An excellent study of the ideal of "respectability" in middle-class culture.

Mary Kupiec Cayton, *Emerson's Emergence: Self and Society in the Transformation of New England, 1800–1845* (1989). A sensitive interpretation of the major figure in the American Renaissance.

Ruth S. Cowan, *A Social History of American Technology* (1997). An excellent survey.

Judith A. McGaw, ed., *Early American Technology* (1994). A collection of fine essays on technology from the colonial era to 1850.

Meredith L. McGill, *American Literature and the Culture of Reprinting, 1834–1853* (2002). An analysis of the complex relationship between mass production of books, copyright law, and American literary nationalism.

Barbara Novak, *Nature and Culture: American Landscape Painting, 1825–1875* (1982). An insightful study of the relationships between landscape painting and contemporary religious and philosophical currents.

David S. Reynolds, *Beneath the American Renaissance* (1988). A fascinating account of the relationship between the major writers and popular culture.

Gwendolyn Wright, *Building the Dream: A Social History of Housing in America* (1981). An exploration of the ideologies and policies that have shaped American housing since Puritan times.

Key Terms

McCormick reaper
American System of Manufacturing
New York Stock Exchange
epidemics
phrenology
penny press
minstrel shows
P. T. Barnum
American Renaissance
James Fenimore Cooper
Ralph Waldo Emerson
Henry David Thoreau
Margaret Fuller
Walt Whitman
Nathaniel Hawthorne
Herman Melville
Edgar Allan Poe
Hudson River school
George Catlin
Frederick Law Olmsted

Chapter 12

African-American Family Group in Virginia, 1861 or 1862
This photograph was taken by an antislavery New Englander, Larkin Mead, who went south to assist the slaves after the outbreak of the Civil War.

The Old South and Slavery, 1830–1860

Nat Turner

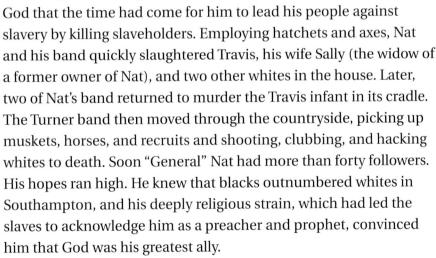

In the early morning hours of August 22, 1831, **Nat Turner** and six other slaves slipped into the house of Joseph Travis in Southampton County, Virginia. Nat had been preparing for this moment since February, when he had interpreted a solar eclipse as a long-awaited sign from God that the time had come for him to lead his people against slavery by killing slaveholders. Employing hatchets and axes, Nat and his band quickly slaughtered Travis, his wife Sally (the widow of a former owner of Nat), and two other whites in the house. Later, two of Nat's band returned to murder the Travis infant in its cradle. The Turner band then moved through the countryside, picking up muskets, horses, and recruits and shooting, clubbing, and hacking whites to death. Soon "General" Nat had more than forty followers. His hopes ran high. He knew that blacks outnumbered whites in Southampton, and his deeply religious strain, which had led the slaves to acknowledge him as a preacher and prophet, convinced him that God was his greatest ally.

By noon Turner's army, now grown to sixty or seventy followers, had murdered about sixty whites. As word of trouble spread, militia and vigilantes, thousands strong, poured into Southampton from across the border in North Carolina and from other counties in Virginia. Following the path of destruction was easy. One farmstead after another revealed dismembered bodies and fresh blood.

337

Now it was the whites' turn for vengeance. Scores of blacks who had no part in the rebellion were killed. Turner's band was overpowered, and those not shot on sight were jailed, to be tried and hanged in due course. Turner himself slipped away and hid in the woods until his capture on October 30. After a trial, he too was hanged.

Revenge was one thing, understanding another. In his subsequently published "Confessions" (recorded by his court-appointed lawyer), Turner did not claim that he had been mistreated by his owners. What they did reveal was an intelligent and deeply religious man who had somehow learned to read and write as a boy, and who claimed to have seen heavenly visions of white and black spirits fighting each other. Turner's mystical streak, well known in the neighborhood, had never before seemed dangerous. White Baptist and Methodist preachers had converted innumerable slaves to Christianity at the turn of the century. Christianity was supposed to make slaves more docile, but Nat Turner's ability to read had enabled him to find passages in the Bible that threatened death to him who "stealeth" a man, a fair description of slavery. Asked by his lawyer if he now found himself mistaken, Turner replied, "Was not Christ crucified?" Small wonder that a niece of George Washington concluded that she and all other white Virginians were now living on a "smothered volcano."

Before Turner, white Virginians had worried little about a slave rebellion. There had been a brief scare in 1800 when a plot led by a slave named Gabriel Prosser was discovered and nipped in the bud. Overall, slavery in Virginia seemed mild to whites living there, a far cry from the harsh regimen of the new cotton-growing areas in Alabama and Mississippi. On hearing of trouble in Southside, many whites had jumped to the conclusion that the British were invading and only gradually absorbed the more menacing thought that the slaves were rebelling.

"What is to be done?" an editorial writer moaned in the *Richmond Enquirer*. "Oh my God, I don't know, but something must be done." In the wake of Turner's insurrection, many Virginians, especially nonslaveholding whites in the western part of the state, urged that Virginia follow the lead of northern states and emancipate its slaves. During the winter of 1831–1832, the Virginia legislature wrangled over emancipation proposals. The narrow defeat of these proposals marked a turning point; thereafter, opposition to slavery steadily weakened not only in Virginia but throughout the region known to history as the Old South.

As late as the Revolution, *south* referred more to a direction than to a place. In 1775, slavery had known no sectional boundaries in America. But as one northern state after another embraced emancipation, slavery became the "peculiar institution" that distinguished the Old South from other sections.

A rift of sorts split the Old South into the **Upper South** (Virginia, North Carolina, Tennessee, and Arkansas) and the **Lower**, or **Deep**, **South** (South Carolina, Georgia, Florida, Alabama, Mississippi, Louisiana, and Texas). With its diversified economy based on raising wheat, tobacco, hemp, vegetables, and livestock, the Upper South relied far less than the Lower South on slavery and cotton, and in 1861 it approached secession more reluctantly than its sister states. Yet in the final analysis slavery forged the Upper South and Lower South into a single **Old South** where it scarred all social relationships: between blacks and whites, among whites, and even among blacks. Without slavery there never would have been an Old South.

Focus Questions

- How did the rise of cotton cultivation affect the society and economy of the Old South?

- What major social divisions segmented the white South?

- Why did nonslaveholding whites feel their futures were tied to the survival of slavery?

- What were the distinctive features of African-American society and culture in the South?

King Cotton

In 1790, the South was essentially stagnant. Tobacco, its primary cash crop, had lost economic vitality even as it had depleted the once-rich southern soils. The growing of alternative cash crops, such as rice and cotton, was confined to coastal areas. Three out of four southerners still lived along the Atlantic seaboard, specifically in the Chesapeake and the Carolinas. One of three resided in Virginia alone.

The contrast between that South and the dynamic South of 1850 was stunning. By 1850, southerners had moved south and west. Now, only one of every seven southerners lived in Virginia, and cotton reigned as king, shaping this new South. The growth of the British textile industry had created a huge demand for cotton, while

Indian removal (see Chapter 9) had made way for southern expansion into the "**Cotton Kingdom**," a broad
swath of territory that stretched from South Carolina,
Georgia, and northern Florida in the east through Alabama, Mississippi, central and western Tennessee, and
Louisiana, and from there on to Arkansas and Texas (see
Map 12.1).

The Lure of Cotton

To a British traveler, it seemed that all southerners could
talk about was cotton. "Every flow of wind from the
shore wafted off the smell of that useful plant; at every

dock or wharf we encountered it in huge piles or pyramids of bales, and our decks were soon choked with it.
All day, and almost all night long, the captain, pilot,
crew, and passengers were talking of nothing else."

A warm climate, wet springs and summers, and relatively dry autumns made the Lower South ideal for cultivating cotton. In contrast to the sugar industry, which
thrived in southeastern Louisiana, cotton required neither expensive irrigation canals nor costly machinery.
Sugar was a rich man's crop that demanded a considerable capital investment to grow and process. But cotton
could be grown profitably on any scale. A cotton farmer

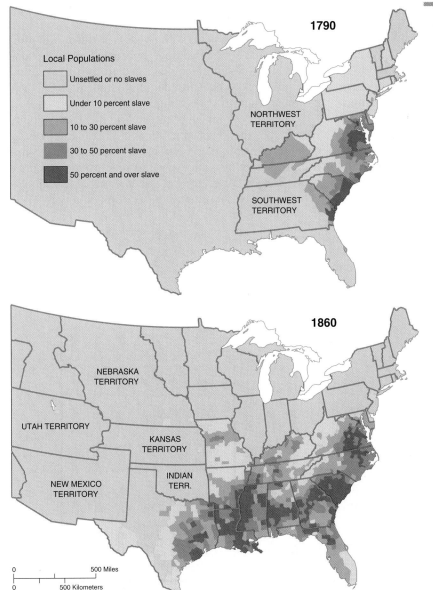

**Map 12.1 Distribution of Slaves, 1790 and
1860**
In 1790 the majority of slaves resided along
the southeastern seaboard. By 1860, however,
slavery had spread throughout the South, and
slaves were most heavily concentrated in the
Deep South states.
Source: Reprinted with permission of
McGraw-Hill, Inc. from *Ordeal by Fire: The Civil
War and Reconstruction* by James M. McPherson.
Copyright 1982 by Alfred A. Knopf, Inc.

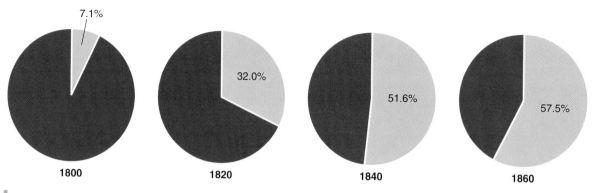

Figure 12.1 Value of Cotton Exports as a Percentage of All U.S. Exports, 1800–1860
By 1840 cotton accounted for more than half of all U.S. exports.

did not even need to own a gin; commercial gins were available. Nor did a cotton farmer have to own slaves; in 1860, 35 to 50 percent of all farmers in the cotton belt owned no slaves. Cotton was profitable for anyone, even nonslaveholders, to grow; it promised to make poor men prosperous and rich men kings (see Figure 12.1).

Although modest cotton cultivation did not require slaves, large-scale cotton growing and slavery grew together (see Figure 12.2). As the southern slave population nearly doubled between 1810 and 1830, cotton employed three-fourths of all southern slaves. Owning

slaves made it possible to harvest vast tracts of cotton speedily, a crucial advantage because a sudden rainstorm at harvest time could pelt cotton to the ground and soil it. Slaveholding planters could increase their cotton acreage and hence their profits.

An added advantage of cotton lay in its compatibility with the production of corn. Corn could be planted earlier or later than cotton and harvested before or after. Since the cost of owning a slave was the same whether or not he or she was working, corn production enabled slaveholders to shift slave labor between corn and cotton. By 1860,

Figure 12.2 Growth of Cotton Production and the Slave Population, 1790–1860
Cotton and slavery rose together in the Old South.

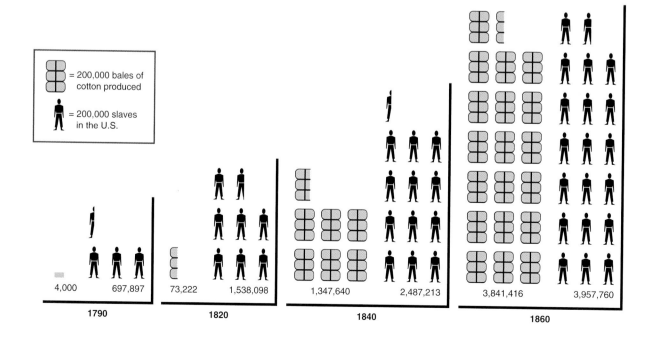

the acreage devoted to corn in the Old South actually exceeded that devoted to cotton. Economically, corn and cotton gave the South the best of two worlds. Fed by intense demand in Britain and New England, cotton prices remained high and money flowed into the South. Because of southern self-sufficiency in growing corn and raising livestock that thrived on corn (in 1860 the region had two-thirds of the nation's hogs), money did not drain away to pay for food. In 1860, the twelve wealthiest counties in the United States were all in the South.

Ties Between the Lower and Upper South

Two giant cash crops, sugar and cotton, dominated agriculture in the Lower South. The Upper South, a region of tobacco, vegetable, hemp, and wheat growers, depended far less on the great cash crops. Yet the Upper South identified with the Lower South rather than with the agricultural regions of the free states.

A range of social, political, and economic factors promoted this unity. First, many settlers in the Lower South had come from the Upper South. Second, all white southerners benefited from the three-fifths clause of the Constitution, which enabled them to count slaves as a basis for congressional representation. Third, all southerners were stung by abolitionist criticisms of slavery, which drew no distinction between the Upper and Lower South. Economic ties also linked the South. The profitability of cotton and sugar increased the value of slaves throughout the entire region and encouraged the **internal slave trade** from the Upper to the Lower South.

New Orleans, 1841
As the South's main port for transporting cotton, New Orleans was the destination of many types of vessels. Here we see a flat boat in the foreground; steamboats, which were used mainly for carrying traffic on the Mississippi River; and sailing ships, used for transport to New England or Europe.

Map 12.2 The Internal Slave Trade, 1810–1860
An internal slave trade developed after the slave trade with Africa ended in 1808. With the growth of cotton production, farmers in the Upper South found it profitable to sell their slaves to planters in the Lower South.

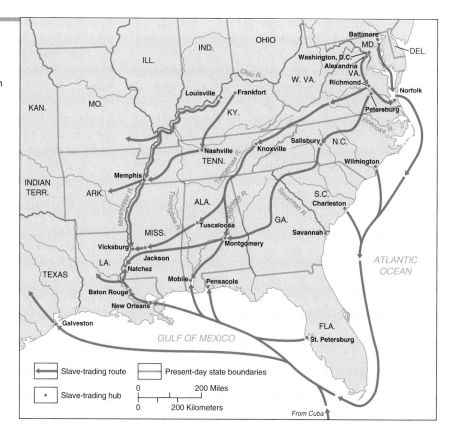

Without the sale of its slaves to the Lower South, an observer wrote, "Virginia will be a desert" (see Map 12.2).

The North and South Diverge

The changes responsible for the dynamic growth of the South widened the distance between it and the North. At a time when the North was rapidly urbanizing, the South remained predominantly rural. In 1860, the proportion of the South's population living in urban areas was only one-third that of New England and the mid-Atlantic states, down from one-half in 1820.

One reason for the rural character of the South was its lack of industries. Although one-third of the American population lived there in 1850, the South accounted for only 10 percent of the nation's manufacturing. The industrial output of the entire South in 1850 was less than that of New Hampshire and only one-third that of Massachusetts.

Some southerners, including J. D. B. De Bow of New Orleans, advocated factories as a way to revive the economies of older states like Virginia and South Carolina, to reduce the South's dependency on northern manufactured products, and to show that the South was not a backwater. After touring northern textile mills,

South Carolina's William Gregg established a company town for textiles at Graniteville in 1845. By 1860, Richmond boasted the nation's fourth-largest producer of iron products, the **Tredegar Iron Works**, which contributed greatly to the Confederate cause during the Civil War. But these were exceptions.

Compared to factories in the North, most southern factories were small, produced for nearby markets, and were closely tied to agriculture. The leading northern factories turned hides into tanned leather and leather into shoes, or cotton into threads and threads into suits. In contrast, southern factories, only a step removed from agriculture, turned grain into flour, corn into meal, and logs into lumber.

Slavery posed a major obstacle to southern industrialization, but not because slaves were unfit for factories. The Tredegar Iron Works employed slaves in skilled positions. But industrial slavery troubled southerners. Slaves who were hired out to factory masters sometimes passed themselves off as free and acted as if they were free by negotiating better working conditions. A Virginia planter who rented slaves to an iron manufacturer complained that they "got the habit of roaming about and *taking care of themselves.*"

The chief brake on southern industrialization was money, not labor. To raise the capital needed to build factories, southerners would have to sell slaves. They had little incentive to do so. Cash crops like cotton and sugar were proven winners, whereas the benefits of industrialization were remote and doubtful. Successful industrialization, further, threatened to disrupt southern social relations by attracting antislavery white immigrants from the North. As long as southerners believed that an economy founded on cash crops would remain profitable, they had little reason to leap into the uncertainties of industrialization.

The South also lagged behind the North in provisions for public education. As was true of southern arguments for industrialization, pro-education arguments were bountiful, but these issued from a small segment of the South's leadership and made little impact. White southerners rejected compulsory education and were reluctant to tax property to support schools. They abhorred the thought of educating slaves, so much so that southern lawmakers made it a crime to teach slaves to read. Some public aid flowed to state universities, but for most whites the only available schools were private. As a result, white illiteracy, which had been declining in the North, remained high in the South. For example, nearly 60 percent of the North Carolinians who enlisted in the U.S. army before the Civil War were illiterate. The comparable proportion for northern enlistees was less than 30 percent.

Agricultural, self-sufficient, and independent, the middling and poor whites of the South remained unconvinced of the need for public education. They had little dependency on the printed word, few complex economic transactions, and infrequent dealings with urban people. Even the large planters, some of whom did support public education, had less commitment to it than did northern manufacturers. Whereas many northern businessmen accepted Horace Mann's argument that public schools would create a more orderly and alert work force, planters had no need for an educated white work force. They already had a black one that they were determined to keep illiterate lest it acquire ideas of freedom.

Because the South diverged so sharply from the North, it is tempting to view the South as backward and lethargic, doomed to be bypassed by the more energetic northern states. Increasingly, northerners associated the spread of cities and factories with progress. Finding few cities and factories in the South, they concluded that the region was a stranger to progress as well. A northern journalist wrote of white southerners in the 1850s that "[t]hey work little, and that little, badly; they earn little, they sell little; they buy little, and they have little—very little—of the common comforts and consolations of civilized life." Visitors to the South sometimes thought that they were traveling backward in time. "It seems as if everything had stopped growing, and was growing backwards," novelist Harriet Beecher Stowe wrote of the region.

Yet the white South did not lack progressive features. In 1840, per capita income in the white South was only slightly below the national average, and by 1860 it exceeded the national average. Although it is true that southerners made few contributions to technology to rival those of northerners, many southerners had a progressive zeal for agricultural improvement. Virginian Edmund Ruffin, who fired the first cannon on Fort Sumter in 1861 and committed suicide in despair at the South's defeat in 1865, was an enthusiastic supporter of crop rotation and of the use of fertilizer, and was an important figure in the history of scientific agriculture. Like northerners, white southerners were restless, eager to make money, skillful at managing complex commercial enterprises, and, when they chose, capable of becoming successful industrialists.

The Social Groups of the White South

Although all agricultural regions of the South contained slaveholders and nonslaveholders, there was considerable diversity within each group. In every southern state, some slaveholders owned vast estates, magnificent homes, and hundreds of slaves, but most lived more modestly. In 1860, one-quarter of all white families in the South owned slaves (see Figure 12.3). Of these, nearly half owned fewer than five slaves, and nearly three-quarters had fewer than ten slaves. Only 12 percent owned twenty or more slaves, and only 1 percent had a hundred or more. Large slaveholders clearly were a minority within a minority. Nonslaveholders also formed a diverse group. Most owned farms and drew on the labor of family members, but others squatted on land in the so-called pine barrens or piney woods and scratched out livelihoods by raising livestock, hunting and fishing, and planting a few acres of corn, oats, or sweet potatoes.

Planters (those owning twenty or more slaves), small slaveholders, yeomen (family farmers), and pine barrens folk composed the South's four main white groups. Lawyers, physicians, merchants, and artisans did not fall into any of these groups, but they tended to identify their interests with one or another of the agricultural groups. Rural artisans and merchants had extensive dealings

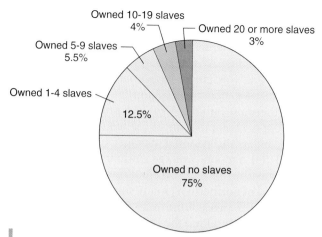

Figure 12.3 Slave Ownership in the South, 1860
In combination with the impact of Hinton R. Helper's *The Impending Crisis of the South* (1857), which called on nonslaveholders to abolish the institution of slavery in their own interest, this decline left slaveholders worried about the loyalty of non-slaveholders to slavery.

H. E. Hayward and Slave Nurse Louisa, 1830
Slavery did not prevent white children and their slave nurses from forming attachments to each other.

with yeomen. Urban merchants and lawyers depended on the planters and adopted their viewpoint on most issues. Similarly, slave traders relied on the plantation economy for their livelihood. Nathan Bedford Forrest, the uneducated son of a humble Tennessee blacksmith, made a fortune as a slave trader in Natchez, Mississippi. When the Civil War broke out, Forrest enlisted in the Confederate army as a private and rose swiftly to become the South's greatest cavalry general. Plantation slavery directed Forrest's allegiances as surely as it did those of planters like Jefferson Davis, the Confederacy's president.

Planters and Plantation Mistresses

With porticoed mansion and fields teeming with slaves, the plantation still stands at the center of the popular image of the Old South. This romanticized view, reinforced by novels and motion pictures like *Gone with the Wind*, is not entirely misleading, for the South contained plantations that travelers found "superb beyond description." Whether devoted to cotton, tobacco, rice, or sugar, **plantation agriculture** was characterized by a high degree of division of labor. In the 1850s, Bellmead, a tobacco plantation on Virginia's James River, was virtually an agricultural equivalent of a factory village. Its more than one hundred slaves were classified into the domestic staff (butlers, waiters, seamstresses, laundresses, maids, and gardeners), the pasture staff (shepherds, cowherds, and hog drivers), outdoor artisans (stonemasons and carpenters), indoor artisans (blacksmiths, carpenters, shoemakers, spinners, and

weavers), and field hands. Such a division of labor was inconceivable without abundant slaves and land. Wade Hampton's cotton plantation near Columbia, South Carolina, encompassed twenty-four hundred acres. With such resources, it is not surprising that large plantations could generate incomes that contemporaries viewed as immense (twenty to thirty thousand dollars a year).

During the first flush of settlement in the Piedmont and trans-Appalachian South in the eighteenth century, most well-off planters had been content to live in simple log cabins. In contrast, between 1810 and 1860, elite planters often vied with one another to build stately mansions. Some, like Lyman Hardy of Mississippi, hired architects. Hardy's Auburn, built in 1812 near Natchez, featured Ionic columns and a portico thirty-one feet long and twelve feet deep. Others copied designs from books like Andrew Jackson Downing's *Architecture of Country Houses* (1850), which sold sixteen thousand copies between 1850 and 1865.

However impressive, these were not typical planters. The wealth of most planters, especially in states like Alabama and Mississippi, consisted primarily in the value of their slaves rather than in expensive furniture or silver plate. In monetary terms, slaves were worth a great deal, as much as seventeen hundred dollars for a field hand in the 1850s. Planters could convert their wealth into cash for purchasing luxuries only by selling slaves. A planter who sold his slaves ceased to be a planter and relinquished the South's most prestigious social status. Not surprisingly, most planters clung to large-scale slaveholding, even if it meant scrimping on their lifestyles. A northern journalist observed that in the Southwest, men worth millions lived as if they were not worth hundreds.

In their constant worry about profit, planters enjoyed neither repose nor security. High fixed costs—housing and feeding slaves, maintaining cotton gins, hiring overseers—led them to search for more and better land, higher efficiency, and greater self-sufficiency. Because cotton prices fluctuated seasonally, planters often assigned their cotton to commercial agents in cities, who held the cotton until the price was right. The agents extended credit so that planters could pay their bills until the cotton was sold. Indebtedness became part of the plantation economy and intensified the planters' quest for profitability.

Plantation agriculture placed psychological strains as well as economic burdens on planters and their wives. Frequent moves disrupted circles of friends and relatives, all the more so because migration to the Old Southwest (Alabama, Mississippi, and eastern Texas) carried families into progressively less settled, more desolate areas. Until 1850, this area was still the frontier.

For plantation women, migration to the Southwest often amounted to a fall from grace, for many of them had grown up in seaboard elegance, only to find themselves in isolated regions, surrounded by slaves and bereft of the companionship of white social peers. "I am

Colonel and Mrs. James A. Whiteside, Son Charles, and Servants, by James A. Cameron, c. 1858–1859
This portrait captures the patriarchy as well as the graciousness that whites associated with the ideal plantation. Not only the slave waiter and nurse but the planter's wife appear overshadowed by the master's presence.

sad tonight, sickness preys on my frame," wrote a bride who moved to Mississippi in 1833. "I am alone and more than 150 miles from any near relative in the wild woods of an Indian nation." At times, wives lacked even their husbands' companionship. Plantation agriculture kept men on the road, scouting new land for purchase, supervising outlying holdings, and transacting business in New Orleans or Memphis.

Planters and their wives found various ways to cope with their isolation from civilized society. Hiring overseers to supervise their plantations, many spent long periods of time in cities. In 1850, fully one-half the planters in the Mississippi Delta were absentees living in or near Natchez or New Orleans rather than on their plantations. Most planters acted as their own overseers, however, and dealt with harsh living conditions by opening their homes to visitors. The responsibility for such hospitality fell heavily on wives, who might have to entertain as many as fifteen people for breakfast and attend to the needs of visitors who stayed for days. Plantation wives bore the burdens of raising their children, supervising house slaves, making clothes and carpets, looking after smokehouses and dairies, planting gardens, and keeping accounts. On the frequent occasions when their husbands were away on business or holding political office, their wives, along with their overseers, ran their plantations.

Among the greatest sorrows of some plantation mistresses was the presence of mulatto children, who stood as daily reminders of their husbands' infidelity. Mary Boykin Chesnut, an astute Charleston woman and famous diarist, commented, "Any lady is ready to tell you who is the father of all the mulatto children in everybody's household but her own. These, she seems to think, drop from clouds." Insisting on sexual purity for white women, southern men followed a looser standard for themselves. After the death of his wife, the brother of the abolitionist sisters Sarah and Angelina Grimké fathered three mulatto children. The gentlemanly code usually tolerated such transgressions as long as they were not paraded in public—and, at times, even if they were. Richard M. Johnson of Kentucky, the man who allegedly killed Tecumseh during the War of 1812, was elected vice president of the United States in 1836 despite having lived openly for years with his black mistress.

The isolation, drudgery, and humiliation that planters' wives experienced turned very few against the system. When the Civil War came, they supported the Confederacy as enthusiastically as any group. However much they might hate living as white islands in a sea of slaves, they recognized no less than their husbands that their wealth and position depended on slavery.

The Small Slaveholders

In 1860, 88 percent of all slaveholders owned fewer than twenty slaves, and most of these possessed fewer than ten. Some slave owners were not even farmers: one out of every five was employed outside of agriculture, usually as a lawyer, physician, merchant, or artisan.

As a large and extremely diverse group, small slaveholders experienced conflicting loyalties and ambitions. In the upland regions, they absorbed the outlook of yeomen (nonslaveholding family farmers), the numerically dominant group. Typically, small upland slaveholders owned only a few slaves and rarely aspired to become large planters. In contrast, in the low country and delta regions, where planters formed the dominant group, small slaveholders often aspired to planter status. In these planter-dominated areas, someone with ten slaves could realistically look forward to the day when he would own thirty. The deltas were thus filled with ambitious and acquisitive individuals who linked success to owning more slaves. Whether one owned ten slaves or fifty, the logic of slaveholding was much the same. The investment in slaves could be justified only by setting them to work on profitable crops. Profitable crops demanded, in turn, more and better land. Much like the planters, the small slaveholders of the low country and delta areas were restless and footloose.

The social structure of the deltas was fluid but not infinitely so. Small slaveholders were usually younger than large slaveholders, and many hoped to become planters in their own right. But as the antebellum period wore on, a clear tendency developed toward the geographical segregation of small slaveholders from planters in the cotton belt.

Small slaveholders led the initial push into the cotton belt in the 1810s and 1820s, whereas the large planters, reluctant to risk transporting their hundreds of slaves into the still turbulent new territory, remained in the seaboard South. Gradually, however, the large planters ventured into Alabama and Mississippi.

Colonel Thomas Dabney, a planter originally from tidewater Virginia, made several scouting tours of the Southwest before moving his family and slaves to the region of Vicksburg, Mississippi, where he started a four-thousand-acre plantation. The small slaveholders already on the scene at first resented Dabney's genteel manners and misguided efforts to win friends. He showed up at house raisings to lend a hand. However, the hands he lent were not his own, which remained gloved, but those of his slaves. The small slaveholders muttered about transplanted Virginia snobs. Dabney responded to complaints by buying up much of the best land in the region. In itself, this was no loss to the small slaveholders. They had been first on the scene, and it was their land that the Dabneys of the South purchased.

Dabney and men like him quickly turned the whole region from Vicksburg to Natchez into large plantations. The small farmers took the proceeds from the sale of their land, bought more slaves, and moved elsewhere to grow cotton. Small slaveholders gradually transformed the region from Vicksburg to Tuscaloosa, Alabama, into a belt of medium-size farms with a dozen or so slaves on each.

The Yeomen

Nonslaveholding family farmers, or yeomen, comprised the largest single group of southern whites. Most were landowners. Landholding yeomen, because they owned no slaves of their own, frequently hired slaves at harvest time to help in the fields. Where the land was poor, as in eastern Tennessee, the landowning yeomen were typically subsistence farmers, but most grew some crops for the market. Whether they engaged in subsistence or commercial agriculture, they controlled landholdings far more modest than those of the planters—more likely in the range of fifty to two hundred acres than five hundred or more acres.

Yeomen could be found anywhere in the South, but they tended to congregate in the upland regions. In the seaboard South, they populated the Piedmont region of Georgia, South Carolina, North Carolina, and Virginia; in the Southwest, they usually lived in the hilly upcountry, far from the rich alluvial soil of the deltas. A minority of yeomen did not own land. Typically young, these men resided with and worked for landowners to whom they were related.

The leading characteristic of the yeomen was the value that they attached to self-sufficiency. As nonslaveholders, they were not carried along by the logic that impelled slaveholders to acquire more land and plant more cash crops. Although most yeomen raised cash crops, they devoted a higher proportion of their acreage to subsistence crops like corn, sweet potatoes, and oats than did planters. The ideal of the planters was profit with modest self-sufficiency; that of the yeomen, self-sufficiency with modest profit.

Yeomen dwelling in the low country and delta regions dominated by planters were often dismissed as "poor white trash." But in the upland areas, where they constituted the dominant group, yeomen were highly respectable. There they coexisted peacefully with the slaveholders, who typically owned only a few slaves (large planters were rare in the upland areas). Both the small slaveholders and the yeomen were essentially family farmers. With or without the aid of a few slaves, fathers and sons cleared the land and plowed, planted, and hoed the fields. Wives and daughters planted and tended vegetable gardens, helped at harvest, occasionally cared for livestock, cooked, and made clothes for the family.

In contrast to the far-flung commercial transactions of the planters, who depended on distant commercial agents to market their crops, the economic transactions of yeomen usually occurred within the neighborhood of their farms. Yeomen often exchanged their cotton, wheat, or tobacco for goods and services from local artisans and merchants. In some areas, they sold their surplus corn to the herdsmen and drovers who made a living in the South's upland regions by specializing in raising hogs. Along the French Broad River in eastern Tennessee, some twenty to thirty thousand hogs were fattened for market each year; at peak season a traveler would see a thousand hogs a mile. When driven to market, the hogs were quartered at night in huge stock stands, veritable hog "hotels," and fed with corn supplied by the local yeomen.

The People of the Pine Barrens

One of the most controversial groups in the Old South was the independent whites of the wooded pine barrens. Making up about 10 percent of southern whites, they usually squatted on the land, put up crude cabins, cleared some acreage on which they planted corn between tree stumps, and grazed hogs and cattle in the woods. They neither raised cash crops nor engaged in the daily routine of orderly work that characterized family farmers. With their ramshackle houses and handful of stump-strewn acres, they appeared lazy and shiftless.

Antislavery northerners cited the **pine barrens people** as proof that slavery degraded poor whites, but southerners shot back that while the pine barrens people were poor, they could at least feed themselves, unlike the paupers of northern cities. In general, the people of the pine barrens were self-reliant and fiercely independent. Pine barrens men were reluctant to hire themselves out as laborers to do "slave" tasks, and the women refused to become servants.

Neither victimized nor oppressed, these people generally lived in the pine barrens by choice. The grandson of a farmer who had migrated from Emanuel County, Georgia, to the Mississippi pine barrens explained his grandfather's decision: "The turpentine smell, the moan of the winds through the pine trees, and nobody within fifty miles of him, [were] too captivating . . . to be resisted, and he rested there."

Social Relations in the White South

Northerners often charged that slavery twisted the entire social structure of the South out of shape. The enslavement of blacks, they alleged, robbed lower-class whites of the incentive to work, reduced them to shiftless misery, and rendered the South a throwback in an otherwise progressive age. Stung by northern allegations that slavery turned the white South into a region of rich planters and poor common folk, southerners retorted that the real center of white inequality was the North, where merchants and financiers paraded in fine silks and never soiled their hands with manual labor.

In reality, a curious mix of aristocratic and democratic, premodern and modern features marked social relations in the white South. Although it contained considerable class inequality, property ownership was widespread. Rich planters occupied seats in state legislatures out of proportion to their numbers in the population, but they did not necessarily get their way, nor did their political agenda always differ from that of other whites.

Not just its social structure but also the behavior of individual white southerners struck northern observers as running to extremes. One minute southerners were hospitable and gracious; the next, savagely violent. "The Americans of the South," Alexis de Tocqueville asserted, "are brave, comparatively ignorant, hospitable, generous, easy to irritate, violent in their resentments, without industry or the spirit of enterprise." The practice of dueling intensified in the Old South at a time when it was dying in the North. Yet there were voices within the South, especially among the clergy, that urged white southerners to turn the other cheek when faced with insults.

Conflict and Consensus in the White South

Planters tangled with yeomen on several issues in the Old South. With their extensive economic dealings and need for credit, planters and their urban commercial allies inclined toward the Whig party, which was generally more sympathetic to banking and economic development. Cherishing their self-sufficiency and economically independent, the yeomen tended to be Democrats.

The occasions for conflict between these groups were minimal, however, and an underlying political unity reigned. Especially in the Lower South, each of the four main social groups—planters, small slaveholders, yeomen, and pine barrens people—tended to cluster in different regions. The delta areas that planters dominated contained relatively small numbers of yeomen. In other regions small slave-owning families with ten to fifteen slaves predominated. In the upland areas far from the deltas, the yeomen congregated. The people of the pine barrens lived in a world of their own. There was more geographical intermingling of groups in the Upper South than in the Lower, but throughout the South each group attained a degree of independence from the others. With widespread landownership and relatively few factories, the Old South was not a place where whites worked for other whites, and this tended to minimize friction.

In addition, the white South's political structure was sufficiently democratic to prevent any one social group from gaining exclusive control over politics. It is true that in both the Upper and the Lower South, the majority of state legislators were planters. Large planters with fifty or more slaves were represented in legislatures far out of proportion to their numbers in the population. Yet these same planters owed their election to the popular vote. The white South was affected by the same democratic currents that swept northern politics between 1815 and 1860, and the newer states of the South had usually entered the Union with democratic constitutions that included universal white manhood suffrage—the right of all adult white males to vote.

Although yeomen often voted for planters, the nonslaveholders did not issue their elected representatives a blank check to govern as they pleased. During the 1830s and 1840s, Whig planters who favored banks faced intense and often successful opposition from Democratic yeomen. These yeomen blamed banks for the Panic of 1837 and pressured southern legislatures to restrict bank operations. On banking issues, nonslaveholders got their way often enough to nurture their belief that they ultimately controlled politics and that slaveholders could not block their goals.

Conflict over Slavery

Nevertheless, there was considerable potential for conflict between the slaveholders and nonslaveholders. The white carpenter who complained in 1849 that "unjust, oppressive, and degrading" competition from slave labor depressed his wages surely had a point. Between 1830 and 1860, slaveholders gained an increasing proportion of the South's wealth while declining as a proportion of its white population. The size of the slaveholding class shrank from 36 percent of the white population in 1831 to 31 percent in 1850 and to 25 percent in 1860. A Louisiana editor warned in 1858 that "the present tendency of supply and demand is to concentrate all the slaves in the hands of the few, and thus excite the envy rather than cultivate the sympathy of the people." Some southerners began to support the idea of Congress's reopening the African slave trade to increase the supply of slaves, bring down their price, and give more whites a stake in the institution.

As the proposed **Virginia emancipation legislation** in 1831–1832 (see this chapter's introduction) attests, slaveholders had good reasons for uncertainty over the allegiance of nonslaveholders to the "peculiar institution" of slavery. The publication in 1857 of Hinton R. Helper's *The Impending Crisis of the South*, which called upon nonslaveholders to abolish slavery in their own interest, revealed the persistence of a degree of white opposition to slavery. On balance, however, slavery did not create profound and lasting divisions between the South's slaveholders and nonslaveholders. Although antagonism to slavery flourished in parts of Virginia up to 1860, proposals for emancipation dropped from the state's political agenda after 1832. In Kentucky, calls for emancipation were revived in 1849 in a popular referendum. But the pro-emancipation forces went down to crushing defeat. Thereafter, the continuation of slavery ceased to be a political issue in Kentucky and elsewhere in the South.

The rise and fall of pro-emancipation sentiment in the South raises a key question. Since the majority of white southerners were not slaveholders, why did they not attack the institution more consistently? To look ahead, why did so many of them fight ferociously and die bravely during the Civil War in defense of an institution in which they appeared not to have had any real stake?

There are various answers to these questions. First, some nonslaveholders hoped to become slaveholders. Second, most simply accepted the racial assumptions upon which slavery rested. Whether slaveholders or nonslaveholders, white southerners dreaded the likelihood that emancipation might encourage "impudent" blacks to entertain ideas of social equality with whites. Blacks might demand the right to sit next to whites in railroad cars and even make advances to white women. "Now suppose they [the slaves] was free," a white southerner told a northern journalist in the 1850s; "you see they'd all think themselves just as good as we; of course they would if they was free. Now just suppose you had a

family of children, how would you like to hev a niggar steppin' up to your darter?" Slavery, in short, appealed to whites as a legal, time-honored, and foolproof way to enforce the social subordination of blacks.

Finally, no one knew where the slaves, if freed, would go or what they would do. Colonizing freed blacks in Africa was unrealistic, southerners concluded, but they also believed that without colonization emancipation would lead to a race war. In 1860, Georgia's governor sent a blunt message to his constituents, many of them nonslaveholders: "So soon as the slaves were at liberty thousands of them would leave the cotton and rice fields . . . and make their way to the healthier climate of the mountain region [where] we should have them plundering and stealing, robbing and killing." There was no mistaking the conclusion. Emancipation would not merely deprive slaveholders of their property; it would also jeopardize the lives of nonslaveholders.

The Proslavery Argument

Between 1830 and 1860, southern writers constructed a defense of slavery as a positive good rather than a necessary evil. Southerners answered northern attacks on slavery as a backward institution by pointing out that the slave society of ancient Athens had produced Plato and Aristotle and that Roman slaveholders had laid the basis of Western civilization. (See Beyond America— Global Interactions: Slavery as a Global Institution.) A Virginian, **George Fitzhugh**, launched another line of attack by contrasting the plight of northern factory workers, "wage slaves" who were callously discarded by their bosses when they were too old or too sick to work, with the southern slaves, who were fed and clothed even when old and ill because they were the property of conscientious masters.

Many proslavery treatises were aimed less at northerners than at skeptics among the South's nonslaveholding yeomanry. Southern clergymen, who wrote roughly half of all proslavery tracts, invoked the Bible, especially St. Paul's order that slaves obey their masters. Too, proslavery writers warned southerners that the real intention of abolitionists, many of whom advocated equal rights for women, was to destroy the family as much as slavery by undermining the "natural" submission of children to parents, wives to husbands, and slaves to masters.

As southerners closed ranks behind slavery, they increasingly suppressed open discussion of the institution within the South. In the 1830s, southerners seized and burned abolitionist literature mailed to the South. In Kentucky, abolitionist editor Cassius Marcellus Clay po-

Slavery as a Global Institution

Defenders of slavery in the Old South, who often pointed to the antiquity and universality of slavery as justifications for keeping what northerners called the "peculiar institution," were right about one thing: slavery was ancient in origin and as late as 1800 it was a global institution, stretching from China and Japan to the Americas. Set within a broad historical context, slavery ranks among the most widespread institutions in history. Few groups today have ancestors who at one time or another were not slaves.

All of the great civilizations in history had sanctioned slavery, and so had the major religions. Slaves built the magnificent stone monuments of ancient Egypt, Greece, and Rome. According to the Hebrew Bible, the Lord told Moses on Mount Sinai that the Hebrews could hold slaves as long as they bought them from other nations. In the New Testament, St. Paul commanded slaves to obey their masters. The early Christians viewed enslavement as a just punishment for sin. Slavery persisted in Europe after the collapse of the Roman empire, though on a smaller scale. The bubonic plague that killed about one-third of the population of Europe in the 1340s intensified European demand for slaves. Because the popes of the Catholic church condemned taking Christians as slaves, slave traders increasingly sought slaves from the non-Christian people of Russia and eastern Europe.

No less than Judaism and Christianity, Islam sanctioned slavery. The prophet Muhammad described an idealized master-slave relationship as the basis of social order. Although Muslims were forbidden to enslave Christians and Jews (Christians thought nothing of enslaving Muslims), non-monotheists were fair game. In the centuries of Islamic expansion following Muhammad's death in 632, Muslim warriors surged across the Arabian peninsula, into the Persian and Byzantine empires, into east Africa, across North Africa and the Mediterranean, and into France, taking slaves from the peoples conquered. In the ninth century, Muslims transported African slaves to Basra in southern Iraq to prepare wetlands for agriculture. From the thirteenth through the fifteenth centuries, the Muslim rulers of Asia Minor and Egypt brought slaves from the Balkans and the Caucasus to serve them.

Ottoman *Devshirme*, Sixteenth Century
To supply their empire with soldiers and administrators the Ottoman Turks developed a system of recruitment called *devshirme*, which bore many characteristics of slavery. Boys were chosen, here by a Janissary officer, from the sultan's Christian subjects, primarily in the Balkans. Once converted to Islam, these youths were sent to Istanbul for training.

After Muslims captured Constantinople (now Istanbul) in 1453, they diverted the flow of slaves from east Europe exclusively to Muslim rulers. Christian rulers turned to sub-Saharan Africa for slaves. European traders did not have to conquer Africa to take slaves, for Africans routinely enslaved other Africans, usually captives taken in war, and sold them to the traders.

The maritime expansion of Portugal and Spain from 1450 to 1660 led to their settling African slaves first on islands in the Atlantic and then in the Caribbean, northeast Brazil, Mexico, and the Andes. The Portuguese also carried slaves to Asia during this period. In the century and a half after 1660, British, Dutch, French, and Brazilian merchants supplanted the Portuguese and the Spanish as the major players in the slave trade. The French carried slaves from Mozambique in Africa to islands in the Indian Ocean; the Dutch settled slaves in what is now Indonesia and in South Africa; and the British used slaves as labor in their valuable sugar colonies in the West Indies and began to ship a significant number of slaves to North America. (See Chapter 2, Technology and Culture: Sugar Production in the Americas.)

Slavery always involved the ownership of one person by another, and in all societies enslavement carried a taint. No one would make a free choice to become a slave. But slavery was not the same everywhere. Slavery in the Americas typically involved back-breaking labor on the sugar plantations of Barbados and Jamaica or in the cotton fields of the Lower South. In contrast, before the sixteenth and seventeenth centuries slaves had played only a limited role in agriculture. For example, the Romans employed slaves as domestic servants, gladiators, teachers, doctors, pharmacists, and administrators. Muslims turned captured boys and young men into slave soldiers, called Mamluks. Mamluks first appeared in Egypt in the ninth century; in the thirteenth century Mamluk officers assassinated the claimant to the Egyptian throne and became the effective rulers of Egypt until the sixteenth century. The crack infantry of the Muslim Ottoman empire, which was founded around 1300 in Asia Minor and which controlled most of southeast Europe by 1520, consisted of military slaves called "janissaries." Sub-Sahara African societies put slaves to work as domestics, soldiers, and officials. Africans also valued slaves as wives and children. By increasing the extent and influence of an African man's lineage, the offspring of slave mothers, although never fully escaping the taint of their slave origins, merged into local tribes and clans and added to the status of their father.

Gaining freedom was also a real possibility in most societies. In ancient Rome, the manumission of slaves was a frequent occurrence. A Roman who freed his slaves, who likely would then become loyal retainers of their former master, would earn the slaves' lasting gratitude without blemishing his own social status. In addition, both Christianity and Islam encouraged the emancipation of converted slaves. Islam required slaveholders to make efforts to convert their slaves, and conversion very often led to freedom. Under Islam, concubinage also provided a route to freedom. Although a Muslim was allowed only four wives, there was no limit on the number of concubines (slave mistresses) he could acquire. A concubine who bore her master's children rose in status and had to be freed upon her master's death. By the mid-fourteenth century, Ottoman rulers had come to prefer concubinage over legal marriage, partly to avoid the political alliances that accompanied the latter. A sultan's concubine became a member of the royal family when she bore him a child. If her son ascended to the throne, she became the queen mother.

By these measures, slavery in the Americas, including the Old South, was extremely harsh, a fact which explains the greater frequency of slave rebellions in the New World than elsewhere. The vast majority of slaves in the Americas worked under disagreeable conditions as members of a despised race.

By 1700, it had become an established legal principle in the American South that conversion to Christianity was no basis for emancipation, and by 1860 manumissions had become rare. Southern defenders of slavery were correct in stating that slavery was an ancient institution and sanctioned by many world religions. But the form of slavery that they were defending differed from the type of slavery that had prevailed throughout much of history.

Question for Analysis

- In what basic ways did slavery in the New World differ from slavery in Europe, Africa, and the Islamic world?

THE NEGRO IN HIS OWN COUNTRY.

THE NEGRO IN AMERICA.

The Negro in His Own Country and the Negro in America
Proslavery propagandists contrasted what they believed to be the black's
African savagery with the blessings of civilization on an American
plantation.

sitioned two cannons and a powder keg to protect his
press, but in 1845 a mob dismantled it anyway. By 1860,
any southerner found with a copy of *The Impending Crisis* had reason to fear for his life.

The rise of the proslavery argument coincided with a
shift in the position of the southern churches on slavery.
During the 1790s and early 1800s, some Protestant ministers had assailed slavery as immoral. By the 1830s,
however, most members of the southern clergy had convinced themselves that slavery was not only compatible

with Christianity but also necessary for the proper
exercise of the Christian religion. Slavery, they proclaimed, provided the opportunity to display Christian responsibility toward one's inferiors, and it
helped blacks develop Christian virtues like humility and self-control. Southerners increasingly attacked antislavery evangelicals in the North for
disrupting the "superior" social arrangement of the
South. In 1837, southerners and conservative northerners had combined to drive the antislavery New
School Presbyterians out of that denomination's
main body. In 1844, the Methodist Episcopal
Church split into northern and southern wings. In
1845, Baptists formed a separate Southern Convention. In effect, southern evangelicals seceded
from national church denominations long before
the South seceded from the Union.

Violence in the Old South

Throughout the colonial and antebellum periods, violence deeply colored the daily lives of white southerners. In the 1760s, a minister described backcountry
Virginians "biting one anothers Lips and Noses off,
and gowging one another—that is, thrusting out anothers Eyes, and kicking one another on the Cods
[genitals], to the Great damage of many a Poor
Woman." In the 1840s, a New York newspaper described a fight between two raftsmen on the Mississippi that started when one accidentally bumped the
other into shallow water. When it was over, one rafts-
man was dead. The other gloated, "I can lick a steamboat. My fingernails is related to a sawmill on my
mother's side, . . . and the brass buttons on my coat
have all been boiled in poison."

Gouging out eyes became a specialty of sorts
among poor whites. On one occasion, a South Carolina judge entered his court to find a plaintiff, a
juror, and two witnesses all missing one eye. Stories
of eye gouging and ear biting lost nothing in the
telling and became part of the folklore of the Old
South. Mike Fink, a legendary southern fighter and
hunter, boasted that he was so mean that, in infancy, he
refused his mother's milk and cried out for a bottle of
whiskey. Yet beneath the folklore lay the reality of violence that gave the South a murder rate as much as ten
times higher than that of the North.

The Code of Honor and Dueling

At the root of most violence in the white South lay intensified feelings of personal pride that themselves reflected
the inescapable presence of slaves. Every day of their

lives, white southerners saw slaves who were degraded, insulted, and powerless to resist. This experience had a searing impact on whites, for it encouraged them to react violently to even trivial insults in order to demonstrate that they had nothing in common with the slaves.

Among gentlemen, this exaggerated pride took the form of a distinctive **southern code of honor**, with honor defined as an extraordinary sensitivity to one's reputation, a belief that one's self-esteem depends on the judgment of others. In the antebellum North, moralists celebrated a rival ideal, character—the quality that enabled an individual to behave in a steady fashion regardless of how others acted toward him or her. A person possessed of character acted out of the prompting of conscience. In contrast, in the honor culture of the Old South, the slightest insult, as long as it was perceived as intentional, could become the basis for a duel.

Formalized by British and French officers during the Revolutionary War, dueling gained a secure niche in the Old South as a means by which gentlemen dealt with affronts to their honor. To outsiders, the incidents that sparked duels seemed trivial: a casual remark accidentally overheard, a harmless brushing against someone at a public event, even a hostile glance. Yet dueling did not necessarily terminate in violence. Dueling constituted part of a complex code of etiquette that governed relations among gentlemen in the Old South and, like all forms of etiquette, called for a curious sort of self-restraint. Gentlemen viewed dueling as a refined alternative to the random violence of lower-class life. The code of dueling did not dictate that the insulted party leap at his antagonist's throat or draw his pistol at the perceived moment of insult. Rather, he was to remain cool, bide his time, settle on a choice of weapons, and agree to a meeting place. In the interval, negotiations between friends of the parties sought to clear up the "misunderstanding" that had evoked the challenge. In this way, most confrontations ended peaceably rather than on the field of honor at dawn.

Although dueling was as much a way of settling disputes peaceably as of ending them violently, the ritual could easily terminate in a death or maiming. Dueling did not allow the resolution of grievances by the courts, a form of redress that would have guaranteed a peaceful outcome. As a way of settling personal disputes that involved honor, recourse to the law struck many southerners as cowardly and shameless. Andrew Jackson's mother told the future president, "The law affords no remedy that can satisfy the feelings of a true man."

In addition, dueling rested on the assumption that a gentleman could recognize another gentleman and hence would know when to respond to a challenge.

Nothing in the code of dueling compelled a gentleman to duel someone beneath his status because such a person's opinion of a gentleman hardly mattered. An insolent porter who insulted a gentleman might get a whipping but did not merit a challenge to a duel. Yet it was often difficult to determine who was a gentleman. The Old South teemed with pretentious would-be gentlemen. A clerk in a country store in Arkansas in the 1850s found it remarkable that ordinary farmers who hung around the store talked of their honor and that the store's proprietor, a German Jew, kept a dueling pistol.

The Southern Evangelicals and White Values

With its emphasis on the personal redress of grievances and its inclination toward violence, the ideal of honor potentially conflicted with the values preached by the southern evangelical churches, notably the Baptists, Methodists, and Presbyterians. These evangelical denominations were on the rise even before the Great Kentucky Revival of 1800–1801 and continued to grow in the wake of the revival. For example, the Methodists grew from forty-eight thousand southern members in 1801 to eighty thousand by 1807. All of the evangelical denominations stressed humility and self-restraint, virtues in contrast to the entire culture of show and display that buttressed the extravagance and violence of the Old South.

Evangelicals continued to rail against dueling, but by the 1830s their values had changed in subtle ways. In the late eighteenth century, evangelical preachers had reached out to the South's subordinate groups: women, slaves, and the poor. They had frequently allowed women and slaves to exhort in churches open to both whites and blacks. By the 1830s, evangelical women were expected to remain silent in church. Pushed to the periphery of white churches, slaves increasingly conducted their own worship services. In addition, Methodists and Baptists increasingly attracted well-to-do converts, and they began to open colleges such as Randolph-Macon (Methodist, 1830) and Wake Forest (Baptist, 1838).

With these developments, the once antagonistic relationship between evangelicals and the gentry became one of cooperation. Evangelical clergymen absorbed some gentry values, including a regard for their honor and reputation that prompted them to throw taunts and threats back at their detractors. In turn, the gentry embraced evangelical virtues. By the 1860s, the South contained many Christian gentlemen like the Bible-quoting Presbyterian general Thomas J. "Stonewall" Jackson, fierce in a righteous war but a sworn opponent of strong drink, the gaming table, and the duel.

Life Under Slavery

As they fashioned the proslavery argument, southern clergymen emphasized the Christian responsibility of masters toward their slaves. "Give your servants that which is just and equal," a Baptist minister advised in 1854, "knowing that you also have a Master in heaven." Some masters were benevolent, and many more liked to think that they were benevolent. But masters bought slaves to make a profit on their labor, not to practice charity toward them. Kind masters might complain about cruel overseers, but the masters hired and paid the overseers to get as much work as possible out of blacks. When the master of one plantation chastised his overseer for "barbarity," the latter replied, "Do you not remember what you told me the time you employed me that [if] I failed to make you good crops I would have to leave?" Indeed, kindness was a double-edged sword, for the benevolent master came to expect grateful affection from his slaves and then interpreted that affection as loyalty to the institution of slavery. In fact, blacks felt little, if any, loyalty to slavery. When northern troops descended upon plantations during the Civil War, masters were dismayed to find many of their most trusted slaves deserting to Union lines.

Although the kindness or cruelty of masters made some difference to slaves, the most important determinants of their experiences under slavery depended on such impersonal factors as the kind of agriculture in which they were engaged, whether they resided in rural or urban areas, and whether they lived in the eighteenth or nineteenth century. The experiences of slaves working on cotton plantations in the 1830s differed drastically from those of slaves in 1700 for reasons unrelated to the kindness or brutality of masters.

The Maturing of the Plantation System

Slavery changed significantly between 1700 and 1830. In 1700, the typical slave was a young man in his twenties who had recently arrived aboard a slave ship from Africa or the Caribbean and worked in the company of other recent arrivals on isolated small farms. Drawn from different African regions and cultures, few such slaves spoke the same language. Because commercial slave ships contained twice as many men as women, and because slaves were widely scattered, blacks had difficulty finding sexual partners and creating a semblance of family life. Furthermore, as a result of severe malnutrition, black women who had been brought to North America on slave ships bore relatively few children. Thus the slave trade had a devastating effect on natural increase among blacks. Without importation, the number of slaves in North America would have declined between 1710 and 1730.

In contrast, by 1830 the typical North American slave was as likely to be female as male, had been born in America, spoke a form of English that made communication with other slaves possible, and worked in the company of numerous other slaves on a plantation. The key to the change lay in the rise of plantation agriculture in the Chesapeake and South Carolina during the eighteenth century. Plantation slaves had an easier time finding mates than those on the remote farms of the early 1700s. As the ratio between slave men and women fell into balance, marriages occurred with increasing

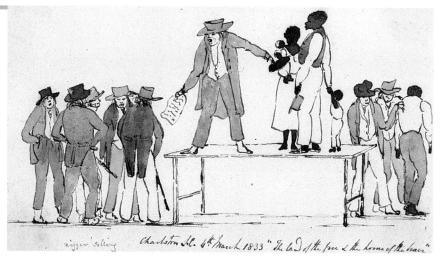

The Land of the Free and the Home of the Brave, by Henry Byam Martin, 1833
White southerners could not escape the fact that much of the Western world loathed their "peculiar institution." In 1833, when a Canadian sketched this Charleston slave auction, Britain was about to abolish slavery in the West Indies.

frequency between slaves on the same or nearby plantations. The native-born slave population rose after 1730 and soared after 1750. Importation of African slaves gradually declined after 1760, and Congress banned it in 1808.

Work and Discipline of Plantation Slaves

In 1850, the typical slave worked on a large farm or plantation with at least ten fellow bond servants. Almost three-quarters of all slaves that year were owned by masters with ten or more slaves, and slightly over one-half lived in units of twenty or more slaves. On smaller units, slaves usually worked under the **task system**. Each slave had a daily or weekly quota of tasks to complete. On the large cotton and sugar plantations, slaves would occasionally work under the task system, but more closely supervised and regimented **gang labor** prevailed.

The day of antebellum plantation slaves usually began an hour before sunrise with the sounding of a horn or bell. After a sparse breakfast, slaves marched to the fields. A traveler in Mississippi described a procession of slaves on their way to work. "First came, led by an old driver carrying a whip, forty of the largest and strongest women I ever saw together; they were all in a simple uniform dress of bluish check stuff, the skirts reaching little below the knee; their legs and feet were bare; they carried themselves loftily, each having a hoe over the shoulder, and walking with a free, powerful swing." Then came the plow hands, "thirty strong, mostly men, but few of them women. . . . A lean and vigilant white overseer, on a brisk pony, brought up the rear."

As this account indicates, slave men and women worked side by side in the fields. Female slaves who did not labor in the fields scarcely idled their hours away. A former slave, John Curry, described how his mother milked cows, cared for the children whose mothers worked in the fields, cooked for field hands, did the ironing and washing for her master's household, and took care of her own seven children. Plantations never lacked tasks for slaves of either gender. As former slave Solomon

Black Women and Men on a Trek Home, South Carolina Much like northern factories, large plantations made it possible to impose discipline and order on their work force. Here black women loaded down with cotton join their men on the march home after a day in the fields.

Northup noted, "ploughing, planting, picking cotton, gathering the corn, and pulling and burning stalks, occupies the whole of the four seasons of the year. Drawing and cutting wood, pressing cotton, fattening and killing hogs, are but incidental labors."

Regardless of the season, the slave's day stretched from dawn to dusk. Touring the South in the 1850s, Frederick Law Olmsted prided himself on rising early and riding late but added, "I always found the negroes in the field when I first looked out, and generally had to wait for the negroes to come from the field to have my horse fed when I stopped for the night." When darkness made fieldwork impossible, slaves transported cotton bales to the gin house, gathered up wood for supper fires, and fed the mules. Weary from their labors, they slept in log cabins on wooden planks. "The softest couches in the world," a former bondsman wryly observed, "are not to be found in the log mansions of a slave."

Although virtually all antebellum Americans worked long hours, no laboring group experienced the same combination of long hours and harsh discipline as did slave field hands. Northern factory workers did not have to put up with drivers who, like one described by Olmsted, walked among the slaves with a whip, "which he often cracked at them, sometimes allowing the lash to fall lightly upon their shoulders." The lash did not always fall lightly. The annals of American slavery contain stories of repulsive brutality. Pregnant slave women were sometimes forced to lie in depressions in the ground and endure whipping on their backs, a practice that supposedly protected the fetus while abusing the mother.

The disciplining and punishment of slaves were often left to white overseers and black drivers rather than to masters. "Dat was de meanest devil dat ever lived on the Lord's green earth," a former Mississippi slave said of his driver. The barbaric discipline meted out by others pricked the conscience of many a master. But even masters who professed Christianity viewed the disciplining of slaves as a priority—indeed, as a Christian duty to ensure the slaves' proper "submissiveness." The black abolitionist **Frederick Douglass**, once a slave, recalled that his worst master had been converted at a Methodist camp meeting. "If religion had any effect on his character at all," Douglass related, "it made him more cruel and hateful in all his ways."

Despite the relentless, often vicious discipline, plantation agriculture gave a minority of slaves opportunities for advancement, not from slavery to freedom but from unskilled and exhausting fieldwork to semiskilled or skilled indoor work. Some slaves developed skills like blacksmithing and carpentry, and learned to operate cotton gins. Others were trained as cooks, butlers, and dining-room attendants. These house slaves became legendary for their arrogant disdain of field hands and poor whites. The legend often distorted the reality, for house slaves were as subject to discipline as field slaves. "I liked the field work better than I did the house work," a female slave recalled. "We could talk and do anything we wanted to, just so we picked the cotton." Such sentiments were typical, but skilled slave artisans and house servants were greatly valued and treated accordingly; they occupied higher rungs than field hands on the social ladder of slavery.

The Slave Family

Masters had an incentive to encourage slave marriages in order to bring new slaves into the world and to discourage slaves from running away. Some masters baked wedding cakes for slaves and even arbitrated marital disputes. Still, the keenest challenge to the slave family came not from the slaves themselves but from slavery. The law did not recognize or protect slave families. Although some slaveholders were reluctant to break slave marriages by sale, economic hardships might force their hand. The reality, one historian has calculated, was that in a lifetime, on average, a slave would witness the sale of eleven family members.

Naturally, the commonplace buying and selling of slaves severely disrupted slaves' attempts to create a stable family life. Poignant testimony to the effects of sale on slave families, and to the desire of slaves to remain near their families, was provided by an advertisement for a runaway slave in North Carolina in 1851. The advertisement described the fugitive as presumed to be "lurking in the neighborhood of E. D. Walker's, at Moore's Creek, who owns most of his relatives, or Nathan Bonham's who owns his mother; or, perhaps, near Fletcher Bell's, at Long Creek, who owns his father." Small wonder that a slave preacher pronounced a slave couple married "until death or *distance* do you part."

Aside from disruption by sale, slave families experienced separations and degradations from other sources. The marriage of a slave woman gave her no protection against the sexual demands of a master nor, indeed, of any white. The slave children of white masters became targets of the wrath of white mistresses at times. Sarah Wilson, the daughter of a slave and her white master, remembered that as a child, she was "picked on" by her mistress until the master ordered his wife to let Sarah alone because she "got big, big blood in her." Slave women who worked in the fields were usually separated from their children by day; young sons and daughters often were cared for by the aged or by the mothers of other children. When slave women took husbands from nearby (rather than their own) plantations, the children usually stayed with the mother. Hannah Chapman remembered that her father tried to visit his family under cover of darkness "because he missed us and us longed for him." But if his master found him, "us would track him the nex' day by de blood stains."

Despite enormous obstacles, the relationships within slave families were often intimate and, where possible, long-lasting. In the absence of legal protection, slaves developed their own standards of family morality. A southern white woman observed that slaves "did not consider it wrong for a girl to have a child before she married, but afterwards were extremely severe upon anything like infidelity on her part." When given the opportunity, slaves sought to solemnize their marriages before clergymen. White clergymen who accompanied the Union army into Mississippi and Louisiana in the closing years of the Civil War conducted thousands of marriage rites for slaves who had long viewed themselves as married and desired a formal ceremony and registration.

On balance, slave families differed profoundly from white families. Even on large plantations where roughly equal numbers of black men and women made marriage a theoretical possibility, planters, including George Washington, often divided their holdings into several dispersed farms and distributed their slaves among them without regard to marriage ties. Conditions on small farms and new plantations discouraged the formation of families, and everywhere spouses were vulnerable to being sold as payment for the master's debts. Slave adults were more likely than whites never to marry or to marry late, and slave children were more likely to live with a single parent (usually the mother) or with neither parent.

In white families, the parent-child bond overrode all others; slaves, in contrast, emphasized ties between children and their grandparents, uncles, and aunts as well as their parents. Such broad kinship ties marked the West African cultures from which many slaves had originally been brought to America, and they were reinforced by the separations between children and one or both parents that routinely occurred under slavery. Frederick Douglass never knew his father and saw his mother infrequently, but he vividly remembered his grandmother, "a good nurse, and a capital hand at making nets for catching shad and herring."

In addition, slaves often created "fictive" kin networks; in the absence of uncles and aunts, they simply called friends their uncles, aunts, brothers, or sisters. In effect, slaves invested nonkin relations with symbolic kin functions. In this way, they helped protect themselves against the involuntary disruption of family ties by forced sale and established a broader community of obligation. When plantation slaves greeted each other as "brudder," they were not making a statement about actual kinship but about kindred obligations they felt for each other. Apologists for slavery liked to argue that a "community of interests" bound masters and slaves together. In truth, the real community of interests was the one that slaves developed among themselves in order to survive.

The Longevity, Diet, and Health of Slaves

In general, slaves in the United States reproduced faster and lived longer than slaves elsewhere in the Western Hemisphere. The evidence comes from a compelling statistic. In 1825, 36 percent of all slaves in the Western Hemisphere lived in the United States, whereas Brazil accounted for 31 percent. Yet of the 10 to 12 million African slaves who had been imported to the New World between the fifteenth and nineteenth centuries, only some 550,000 (about 5 percent) had come to North America, whereas 3.5 million (nearly 33 percent) had been taken to Brazil. Mortality had depleted the slave populations in Brazil and the Caribbean to a far greater extent than in North America.

Several factors account for the different rates. First, the gender ratio among slaves equalized more rapidly in North America, encouraging earlier and longer marriages and more children. Second, because growing corn and raising livestock were compatible with cotton cultivation, the Old South produced plenty of food. The normal ration for a slave was a peck of cornmeal and three to four pounds of fatty pork a week. Slaves often supplemented this nutritionally unbalanced diet with vegetables grown in small plots that masters allowed them to farm and with catfish and game. In the barren winter months, slaves ate less than in the summer; in this respect, however, they did not differ much from most whites.

As for disease, slaves had greater immunities to both malaria and yellow fever than did whites, but they suffered more from cholera, dysentery, and diarrhea. In the absence of privies, slaves usually relieved themselves behind bushes; urine and feces washed into the sources of drinking water and caused many diseases. Yet slaves developed some remedies that, though commonly ridiculed by whites, were effective against stomach ailments. For example, the slaves' belief that eating white clay would cure dysentery and diarrhea rested on a firm basis; we know now that kaolin, an ingredient of white clay, is a remedy for these ailments.

Although slave remedies were often more effective than those of white physicians, slaves experienced higher mortality rates than whites. At any age, a slave could expect a shorter life than a white, most strikingly in infancy. Rates of infant mortality for slaves were at least twice those of whites. Between 1850 and 1860, fewer than two out of three black children survived to the age of ten. Whereas the worst mortality occurred on plantations in disease-ridden, low-lying areas, pregnant, overworked field hands often miscarried or gave birth to weakened infants even in healthier regions. Masters allowed pregnant women to rest, but rarely enough. "Labor is conducive to health," a Mississippi planter told a northern journalist; "a healthy woman will rear most children."

Slaves off Plantations

Although plantation agriculture gave some slaves, especially men and boys, opportunities to acquire specialized skills, it imposed a good deal of supervision on them. The greatest opportunities for slaves were reserved for those who worked off plantations and farms, either as laborers in extractive industries like mining and lumbering or as artisans in towns and cities.

Because lucrative cotton growing attracted so many whites onto small farms, a perennial shortage of white labor plagued almost all the nonagricultural sectors of the southern economy. As a consequence, there was a steady demand for slaves to drive wagons, to work as stevedores (ship-cargo handlers) in port cities, to man river barges, and to perform various tasks in mining and lumbering. In 1860, lumbering employed sixteen thousand workers, most of them slaves who cut trees, hauled them to sawmills, and fashioned them into useful lumber. In sawmills, black engineers fired and fixed the steam engines that provided power. In iron-ore ranges and ironworks, slaves not only served as laborers but occasionally supervised less-skilled white workers. Just as mill girls comprised the labor force of the booming textile industry in New England, so did slave women and children work in the South's fledgling textile mills.

Slave or free, blacks found it easier to pursue skilled occupations in southern cities than in northern ones, partly because southern cities attracted few immigrants to compete for work, and partly because the profitability of southern cash crops long had pulled white laborers out of towns and cities, and left behind opportunities for blacks, slave or free, to acquire craft skills. Slaves who worked in factories, mining, or lumbering usually were hired rather than owned by their employers. If working conditions deteriorated to the point where slaves fell ill or died, masters would refuse to provide employers with more slaves. Consequently, working conditions for slaves

off plantations usually stayed at a tolerable level. Watching workers load cotton onto a steamboat, Frederick Law Olmsted was amazed to see slaves sent to the top of the bank to roll the bales down to Irishmen who stowed them on the ship. Asking the reason for this arrangement, Olmsted was told, "The niggers are worth too much to be risked here; if the Paddies [Irish] are knocked overboard, or get their backs broke, nobody loses anything."

Life on the Margin: Free Blacks in the Old South

Free blacks were more likely than southern blacks in general to live in cities. In 1860, one-third of the free blacks in the Upper South and more than half in the Lower South were urban.

The relatively specialized economies of the cities provided free people of color with opportunities to become carpenters, coopers (barrel makers), barbers, and even small traders. A visitor to an antebellum southern market would find that most of the meat, fish, vegetables, and fruit had been prepared for sale by free blacks. Urban free blacks formed their own fraternal orders and churches; a church run by free blacks was often the largest house of worship in a southern city. In New Orleans, free blacks had their own literary journals and opera. In Natchez, a free black barber, William Tiler Johnson, invested the profits of his shop in real estate, acquired stores that he rented out, purchased slaves and a plantation, and even hired a white overseer.

As Johnson's career suggests, some free blacks were highly successful. But free blacks were always vulnerable in southern society and became more so as the antebellum period wore on. Although free blacks continued to increase in absolute numbers (a little more than a quarter-million free people of color dwelled in the South in 1860), the rate of growth of the free-black population slowed after 1810. Between 1790 and 1810, this population had more than tripled, to 108,265. The reason for the slowdown after 1810 was that fewer southern whites were setting slaves free. Until 1820, masters with doubts about the rightness of slavery frequently manumitted (freed) their black mistresses and mulatto children, and some set free their entire work forces. In the wake of the Nat Turner rebellion in 1831, laws restricting the liberties of free blacks were tightened. During the mid-1830s, for example, most southern states made it a felony to teach blacks to read and write. Every southern state forbade free blacks to enter that state, and in 1859 Arkansas ordered all free blacks to leave.

A Barber's Shop at Richmond, Virginia, 1861
Free blacks dominated the barber's trade in Richmond on the eve of the Civil War. As meeting places for men, barber shops supplied newspapers and political discussion. Black barbers were politically informed and prosperous. As was the custom at the time, barbers also performed medical procedures like drawing blood.

So although a free-black culture flowered in cities like New Orleans and Natchez, that culture did not reflect the conditions under which most free blacks lived. Free blacks were tolerated in New Orleans, in part because there were not too many of them. A much higher percentage of blacks were free in the Upper South than in the Lower South. Furthermore, although a disproportionate number of free blacks lived in cities, the majority lived in rural areas, where whites lumped them together with slaves. Even a successful free black like William Tiler Johnson could never dine or drink with whites. When Johnson attended the theater, he sat in the colored gallery.

The position of free blacks in the Old South contained many contradictions. So did their minds. As the offspring, or the descendants of offspring, of mixed liaisons, a disproportionate number of free blacks had light brown skin. Some of them were as color-conscious as whites and looked down on "darky" field hands and coal-black laborers. Yet as whites' discrimination against free people of color intensified during the late antebellum period, many free blacks realized that whatever future they had was as blacks, not as whites. Feelings of racial solidarity grew stronger among free blacks in the 1850s, and after the Civil War, the leaders of the freed slaves were usually blacks who had been free before the war.

Slave Resistance

The Old South was a seedbed of organized slave insurrections. In the delta areas of the Lower South where blacks outnumbered whites, slaves experienced continuous forced labor on plantations and communicated their bitterness to each other in the slave quarters. Free blacks in the cities could have provided leadership for rebellions. Rumors of slave conspiracies flew around the southern white community, and all whites shuddered over the massive black insurrection that had destroyed French rule in Saint Domingue.

Yet Nat Turner's 1831 insurrection in Virginia was the only slave rebellion that resulted in the deaths of whites. A larger but more obscure uprising occurred in Louisiana in 1811 when some two hundred slaves sought to march on New Orleans. Other, better known, slave insurrections were merely conspiracies that never materialized. In 1800, Virginia slave Gabriel Prosser's planned uprising was betrayed by other slaves, and Gabriel and his followers were executed. That same year, a South Carolina slave, **Denmark Vesey**, won fifteen hundred dollars in a lottery and bought his freedom. Purchasing a carpentry shop in Charleston and becoming a preacher at that city's African Methodist Episcopal Church, Vesey built a cadre of black followers, including a slave of the governor of South Carolina and a black conjurer named Gullah Jack. In 1822, they devised a plan to attack Charleston and seize all the city's arms and ammunition, but other slaves informed authorities, and the conspirators were executed.

For several reasons, the Old South experienced far fewer rebellions than the Caribbean region or South America. Although slaves formed a majority in South Carolina and a few other states, they did not constitute

Fugitives in Flight, **by Roman Thomas Noble**
Growing up in Kentucky, artist Thomas Noble was probably familiar with scenes of slaves fleeing across the Ohio River
to freedom. Although he served in the Confederate army during the Civil War, Noble began to paint antislavery themes
after the war.

a large majority in any state. In contrast to the Caribbean, an area of absentee landlords and sparse white population, the white presence in the Old South was formidable, and the whites had all the guns and soldiers. The rumors of slave conspiracies that periodically swept the white South demonstrated to blacks the promptness with which whites could muster forces and mount slave patrols. The development of family ties among slaves made them reluctant to risk death and leave their children parentless. Finally, blacks who ran away or plotted rebellions had no allies. Southern Indians routinely captured runaway slaves and exchanged them for rewards; some Indians even owned slaves.

Short of rebellion, slaves could try to escape to freedom in the North. Perhaps the most ingenious, Henry Brown, induced a friend to ship him from Richmond to Philadelphia in a box and won immediate fame as "Box" Brown. Some light mulattos passed as whites. More

often, fugitive slaves borrowed, stole, or forged passes from plantations or obtained papers describing themselves as free. Frederick Douglass borrowed a sailor's papers in making his escape from Baltimore to New York City in 1838. Some former slaves, among them **Harriet Tubman** and Josiah Henson, made repeated trips back to the South to help other slaves escape. These sundry methods of escape fed the "**Underground Railroad**," supposedly an organized network of safe houses owned by white abolitionists who spirited blacks to freedom in the North and Canada. In reality, fugitive slaves owed very little to abolitionists. Some white sympathizers in border states did provide safe houses for blacks, but these houses were better known to watchful slave catchers than to most blacks.

Escape to freedom was a dream rather than an alternative for most blacks. Out of millions of slaves, probably fewer than a thousand escaped to the North. Yet slaves often ran away from masters not to escape to freedom but to visit spouses or avoid punishment. Most runaways remained in the South; some returned to kinder former masters. During the eighteenth century, African slaves had often run away in groups to the interior and sought to create self-sufficient colonies or villages of the sort that they had known in Africa. But once the United States acquired Florida, long a haven for runaways, few uninhabited places remained in the South to which slaves could flee.

Despite poor prospects for permanent escape, slaves could disappear for prolonged periods into the free-black communities of southern cities. Because whites in the Old South depended so heavily on black labor, slaves enjoyed a fair degree of practical freedom to drive wagons to market and to come and go when they were off plantations. Slaves hired out or sent to a city might overstay their leave and even pass themselves off as free. The experience of slavery has sometimes been compared to the experience of prisoners in penitentiaries or on chain gangs, but the analogy is misleading. The supervision that slaves experienced was sometimes intense (for example, when working at harvest time under a driver), but often lax; it was irregular rather than consistent.

The fact that antebellum slaves frequently enjoyed some degree of practical freedom did not change the underlying oppressiveness of slavery. But it did give slaves a sense that they had certain rights on a day-to-day basis, and it helped deflect slave resistance into forms that were essentially furtive rather than open and violent. Theft was so common that planters learned to keep their tools, smokehouses, closets, and trunks under lock and key. Overworked field hands might leave valuable tools out to rust, or feign illness, or simply refuse to work. As an institution, slavery was vulnerable to such tactics; unlike free laborers, slaves could not be fired for negligence or malingering. Frederick Law Olmsted found slaveholders in the 1850s afraid to inflict punishment on slaves "lest the slave should abscond, or take a sulky fit and not work, or poison some of the family, or set fire to the dwelling, or have recourse to any other mode of avenging himself."

Olmsted's reference to arson and poisoning reminds us that not all furtive resistance was peaceful. Arson and poisoning, both common in African culture as forms of vengeance, were widespread in the Old South, and the fear of each was even more so. Masters afflicted by dysentery and similar ailments never knew for sure that they had not been poisoned.

Arson, poisoning, work stoppages, and negligence were alternatives to violent rebellion. Yet these furtive forms of resistance differed from rebellion. The goal of rebellion was freedom from slavery. The goal of furtive resistance was to make slavery bearable. The kind of resistance that slaves usually practiced sought to establish customs and rules that would govern the conduct of masters as well as that of slaves without challenging the institution of slavery as such. Most slaves would have preferred freedom but settled for less. "White folks do as they please," an ex-slave said, "and the darkies do as they can."

The Emergence of African-American Culture

A distinctive culture emerged among blacks in the slave quarters of antebellum plantations. This culture drew on both African and American sources, but it was more than a mixture of the two. Enslaved blacks gave a distinctive twist to the American as well as African components of their culture.

The Language of Slaves

Before slaves could develop a common culture, they had to be able to communicate with one another. During the colonial period, verbal communication among slaves had often been difficult, for most slaves had been born in Africa, which contained an abundance of cultures and languages. The captain of a slave ship noted in 1744,

As for the languages of Gambia [in West Africa], they are so many and so different that the Natives on either Side of the River cannot understand each other; which, if rightly consider'd, is no small happiness to the Europeans who go thither to trade for slaves.

In the pens into which they were herded before shipment and on the slave ships themselves, however, Africans developed a "pidgin"—a language that has no native speakers in which people with different native languages can communicate. Pidgin is not unique to black people. Nor is pidgin English the only form of pidgin; slaves who were sent to South America developed Spanish and Portuguese pidgin languages.

Many of the early African-born slaves learned pidgin English poorly or not at all, but as American-born slaves came to comprise an increasingly large proportion of all slaves, pidgin English took root. Indeed, it became the only language most slaves knew. Like all pidgins, it was a simplified language. Slaves usually dropped the verb *to be* (which had no equivalent in African tongues) and either ignored or confused genders. Instead of saying "Mary is in the cabin," they said, "Mary, he in cabin." To negate, they substituted *no* for *not*, saying, "He no wicked." Pidgin English contained several African words. Some, like *banjo*, became part of standard English; others, like *goober* (peanut), became part of southern white slang. Although they picked up pidgin terms, whites ridiculed field hands' speech. Some slaves, particularly house servants and skilled artisans, learned to speak standard English but had no trouble understanding the pidgin of field hands. However strange pidgin sounded to some, it was indispensable for communication among slaves.

African-American Religion

The development of a common language was the first step in forging African-American culture. No less important was the religion of the slaves.

Africa was home to rich and diverse religious customs and beliefs. Some of the early slaves were Muslims; a few had acquired Christian beliefs either in Africa or in the New World. But the majority of the slaves transported from Africa were neither Muslims nor Christians but rather worshipers in one of many native African religions. Most of these religions, which whites lumped together as heathen, drew little distinction between the spiritual and material worlds. Any event or development, from a storm to an earthquake or an illness, was assumed to stem from supernatural forces. These forces were represented by God, by spirits that inhabited the woods and waters, and by the spirits of ancestors. In addition, the religions of West Africa, the region from which most American slaves originally came, attached special significance to water, which symbolized life and hope.

The majority of the slaves brought to America in the seventeenth and eighteenth centuries were young men who may not have absorbed much of this religious heritage before their enslavement. In any case, Africans differed from each other in their specific beliefs and practices. For these reasons, African religions could never have unified blacks in America. Yet some Africans probably clung to their beliefs during the seventeenth and eighteenth centuries, a tendency made easier by the fact that whites undertook few efforts before the 1790s to convert slaves to Christianity.

Dimly remembered African beliefs such as the reverence for water may have predisposed slaves to accept Christianity when they were finally urged to do so, because water has a symbolic significance for Christians, too, in the sacrament of baptism. The Christianity preached to slaves by Methodist and Baptist revivalists during the late eighteenth and nineteenth centuries, moreover, resembled African religions in that it also drew few distinctions between the sacred and the secular. Just as Africans believed that a crop-destroying drought or a plague resulted from supernatural forces, the early revivalists knew in their hearts that every drunkard who fell off his horse and every Sabbath-breaker struck by lightning had experienced a deliberate and direct punishment from God.

By the 1790s, blacks formed about a quarter of the membership of the Methodist and Baptist denominations. Masters continued to fear that a Christianized slave would be a rebellious slave. Converted slaves did in fact play a significant role in each of the three major slave rebellions in the Old South. The leaders of Prosser's rebellion in 1800 used the Bible to prove that slaves, like the ancient Israelites, could prevail against overwhelming numbers. Denmark Vesey read the Bible, and most of the slaves executed for joining his conspiracy belonged to Charleston's African Methodist Church. Nat Turner was both a preacher and a prophet.

Despite the "subversive" effect of Christianity on some slaves, however, these uprisings, particularly the Nat Turner rebellion, actually stimulated Protestant missionaries to intensify their efforts to convert slaves. Missionaries pointed to the self-taught Turner to prove that slaves would hear about Christianity in any event and that organized efforts to convert blacks were the only way to ensure that slaves learned correct versions of Christianity, which emphasized obedience rather than insurgence. Georgia missionary and slaveholder Charles Colcock Jones reassuringly told white planters of the venerable black preacher who, upon receiving some abolitionist tracts in the mail, promptly turned them over to the white authorities for destruction. A Christian slave, the argument ran, would be a better slave. For whites, the clincher was the split of the Methodists, Baptists, and Presbyterians into northern and southern wings by the mid-1840s. Now, they argued, it had finally become safe to convert slaves, for the churches had rid themselves of their antislavery wings. Between 1845 and 1860 the number of black Baptists doubled.

The experiences of Christianized blacks in the Old South illustrate many of the contradictions of life under slavery. Urban blacks often had their own churches, but in the rural South, where the great

Princess Feather Quilt
This quilt was woven by Mississippi slaves.

without telling them about the Chosen People, the ancient Jews whom Moses led from captivity in Pharaoh's Egypt into the Promised Land of Israel. Inevitably, slaves drew parallels between their own condition and the Jews' captivity. Like the Jews, blacks concluded, they themselves were "de people of de Lord." If they kept the faith, then, like the Jews, they too would reach the Promised Land. The themes of the Chosen People and the Promised Land ran through the sacred songs, or "spirituals," that blacks sang, to the point where Moses and Jesus almost merged:

Gwine to write to Massa Jesus,
To send some Valiant Soldier
To turn back Pharaoh's army,
Hallelu!

A listener could interpret a phrase like "the Promised Land" in several ways; it could refer to Israel, to heaven, or to freedom. From the perspective of whites, the only permissible interpretations were Israel and heaven, but some blacks, like Denmark Vesey, thought of freedom as well. The ease with which slaves constructed alternative interpretations of the Bible also reflected the fact that many plantations contained black preachers, slaves trained by white ministers to spread Christianity among blacks. When in the presence of masters or white ministers, these black preachers usually just repeated the familiar biblical command, "Obey your master." Often, however, slaves met for services apart from whites, usually on Sunday evenings but during the week as well. Then the message changed. A black preacher in Texas related how his master would say, "tell them niggers iffen they obeys the master they goes to Heaven." The minister quickly added, "I knowed there's something better for them, but I daren't tell them 'cept on the sly. That I done lots. I tells 'em iffen they keep praying, the Lord will set 'em free."

Some slaves privately interpreted Christianity as a religion of liberation from the oppression of slavery, but most recognized that their prospects for freedom were slight. On the whole, Christianity did not turn them into revolutionaries. Neither did it necessarily turn them

majority of blacks lived, slaves worshiped in the same churches as whites. Although the slaves sat in segregated sections, they heard the same sermons and sang the same hymns as whites. Some black preachers actually developed followings among whites, and Christian masters were sometimes rebuked by biracial churches for abusing Christian slaves in the same congregation. The churches were, in fact, the most interracial institutions in the Old South. Yet none of this meant that Christianity was an acceptable route to black liberation. Ministers went out of their way to remind slaves that spiritual equality was not the same as civil equality. The effort to convert slaves gained momentum only to the extent that it was certain that Christianity would not change the basic inequality of southern society.

Although they listened to the same sermons as whites, slaves did not necessarily draw the same conclusions. It was impossible to Christianize the slaves

Mary Edmonia Lewis and
Forever Free
Named Wildfire by her Chippewa mother and black father, Mary Edmonia Lewis adopted a Christian name upon entering Oberlin College. Later she studied sculpture in Boston and Rome. Her *Forever Free* (1867) commemorated the abolition of slavery.

into model slaves. It did, however, provide slaves with a view of slavery different from their masters' outlook. Where the masters argued that slavery was a benign and divinely ordained institution in blacks' best interests, Christianity told them that slavery was really an affliction, a terrible and unjust institution that God had allowed in order to test their faith. For having endured slavery, he would reward blacks. For having created it, he would punish masters.

Black Music and Dance

Compared to the prevailing cultural patterns among elite whites, the culture of blacks in the Old South was extremely expressive. In religious services, blacks shouted "Amen" and let their bodily movements reflect their feelings long after white religious observances, some of which had once been similarly expressive, had grown sober and sedate. Frederick Law Olmsted recorded how, during a slave service in New Orleans during the 1850s, parishioners "in indescribable expression of ecstasy" exclaimed every few moments: "Glory! oh yes! yes!—sweet Lord! sweet Lord!"

Slaves also expressed their feelings in music and dance. Drawing on their African musical heritage, which used hand clapping to mark rhythm, American slaves made rhythmical hand clapping—called patting juba—an indispensable accompaniment to dancing because southern law forbade them to own "drums, horns, or other loud instruments, which may call together or give sign or notice to one another of their wicked designs and intentions." Slaves also played an African instrument, the banjo, and beat tin buckets as a substitute for drums. Whatever instrument they played, their music was tied to bodily movement. Sometimes, slaves imitated white dances like the minuet, but in a way that ridiculed the high manners of their masters. More often, they expressed themselves in a dance African in origin, emphasizing shuffling steps and bodily contortions rather than the erect precision of whites' dances.

Whether at work or at prayer, slaves liked to sing. Work songs describing slave experiences usually consisted of a leader's chant and a choral response:

I love old Virginny
So ho! boys! so ho!
I love to shuck corn
So ho! boys! so ho!
Now's picking cotton time
So ho! boys! so ho!

Masters encouraged such songs, believing that singing induced the slaves to work harder and that the innocent content of most work songs proved that the slaves were happy. Recalling his own past, Frederick Douglass came closer to the truth when he observed that "slaves sing most when they are most unhappy. The songs of the slave represent the sorrows of his heart; and he is relieved by them, only as an aching heart is relieved by its tears."

Blacks also sang religious songs, later known as **spirituals**. The origin of spirituals is shrouded in obscurity, but it is clear that by 1820 blacks at camp meetings had improvised what one white described as "short scraps of disjointed affirmations, pledges, or prayers lengthened out with long repetition choruses." As this description suggests, whites usually took a dim view of spirituals and tried to make slaves sing "good psalms and hymns" instead of "the extravagant and nonsensical chants, and catches, and hallelujah songs of their own composing." Spirituals reflected the potent emphasis that the slaves' religion put on deliverance from earthly travails. To a degree, the same was true of white hymns, but spirituals were more direct and concrete. Slaves sang, for example,

In that morning, true believers,
In that morning,
We will sit aside of Jesus
In that morning,
If you should go fore I go,
In that morning,
You will sit aside of Jesus
In that morning,
True believers, where your tickets
In that morning,
Master Jesus got your tickets
In that morning.

Another spiritual proclaimed, "We will soon be free, when the Lord will call us home."

Conclusion

The cotton gin revitalized southern agriculture and spurred a redistribution of the South's population, slave and free, from Virginia and other southeastern states to southwestern states like Alabama and Mississippi. As the Old South became more dependent on cotton, it also became more reliant on slave labor.

Slavery left a deep imprint on social relations among the Old South's major white social groups: the planters, the small slaveholders, the yeomen, and the people of the pine barrens. The presence of slaves fed the exaggerated notions of personal honor that made white southerners so violent. Although there was always potential for conflict between slaveholders and nonslaveholders, slavery gave a distinctive unity to the Old South. Most whites did not own any slaves, but the vast majority concluded that their region's prosperity, their ascendancy over blacks, and perhaps even their safety depended on perpetuating slavery. Slavery also shaped the North's perception of the South. Whether northerners believed that the federal government should tamper with slavery or not, they grew convinced that slavery had cut the South off from progress and had turned it into a region of "sterile lands and bankrupt estates."

In contrast, to most white southerners the North, and especially the industrial Northeast, appeared to be the region that deviated from the march of progress. In their eyes, most Americans—indeed, most people throughout the world—practiced agriculture, and agriculture rendered the South a more comfortable place than factories rendered the North. In reaction to northern assaults on slavery, southerners portrayed the institution as a time-honored and benevolent response to the natural inequality of the black and white races. Southerners pointed to the slaves' adequate nutrition, their embrace of Christianity, the affection of some slaves for their masters, and even their work songs as evidence of their contentment.

Chronology, 1830–1860

1790s	Methodists and Baptists start to make major strides in converting slaves to Christianity.	1835	Arkansas admitted to the Union.
1793	Eli Whitney invents the cotton gin.	1837	Economic panic begins, lowering cotton prices.
1800	Gabriel Prosser leads a slave rebellion in Virginia.	1844–1845	Methodist Episcopal and Baptist Churches split into northern and southern wings over slavery.
1808	Congress prohibits external slave trade.		
1812	Louisiana, the first state formed out of the Louisiana Purchase, is admitted to the Union.	1845	Florida and Texas admitted to the Union.
		1849	Sugar production in Louisiana reaches its peak.
1816–1819	Boom in cotton prices stimulates settlement of the Old Southwest.	1849–1860	Period of high cotton prices.
1819–1820	Missouri Compromise.	1857	Hinton R. Helper, *The Impending Crisis of the South*.
1822	Denmark Vesey's conspiracy uncovered in South Carolina.	1859	John Brown's raid on Harpers Ferry.
1831	William Lloyd Garrison starts *The Liberator*.	1860	South Carolina secedes from the Union.
	Nat Turner rebellion in Virginia.		
1832	Virginia legislature narrowly defeats a proposal for gradual emancipation.		
	Virginia's Thomas R. Dew writes an influential defense of slavery.		

These white perceptions of the culture that developed in the slave quarters with the maturing of plantation agriculture were misguided. In reality, few if any slaves accepted slavery. Although slaves rebelled infrequently and had little chance for permanent escape, they often engaged in covert resistance to their bondage. They embraced Christianity, but they understood it differently from whites. Whereas whites heard in the Christian gospel the need to make slaves submissive, slaves learned of the gross injustice of human bondage and the promise of eventual deliverance.

Key Terms

Nat Turner
Upper South
Lower (Deep) South
Old South
Cotton Kingdom
internal slave trade
Tredegar Iron Works
plantation agriculture
pine barrens people
Virginia emancipation legislation
The Impending Crisis of the South
George Fitzhugh
southern code of honor
task system
gang labor
Frederick Douglass
free blacks
Denmark Vesey
Harriet Tubman
Underground Railroad
spirituals

For Further Reference

Orville Vernon Burton, *In My Father's House Are Many Mansions: Family and Community in Edgefield, South Carolina* (1985). An extremely valuable study of the South Carolina upcountry.

Catherine Clinton, *The Plantation Mistress* (1982). Illuminates the world of women in the South.

Bruce Collins, *White Society in the Antebellum South* (1985). A very good, brief synthesis of southern white society and culture.

Robert W. Fogel, *Without Consent or Contract: The Rise and Fall of American Slavery* (1989). A comprehensive reexamination of the slaves' productivity and welfare.

Eugene D. Genovese, *Roll, Jordan, Roll: The World the Slaves Made* (1974). The most influential work on slavery in the Old South written during the last thirty-five years; a penetrating analysis of the paternalistic relationship between masters and their slaves.

Kenneth S. Greenberg, *Honor and Slavery* (1996). An analysis of the role of the Old South's honor culture in male fighting, gambling, sports, and drinking.

Christine Leigh Heyrman, *Southern Cross: The Beginnings of the Bible Belt* (1997). An intriguing account of southern religious culture.

Walter Johnson, *Soul by Soul: Life Inside the Antebellum Slave Market* (1999). An excellent study of the domestic slave trade.

Stephanie McCurry, *Masters of Small Worlds* (1995). An illuminating and influential account of race, class, and gender relations in the South Carolina low country.

Jonathan Daniel Wells, *The Origins of the Southern Middle Class, 1800–1861* (2004). Stresses the compatibility between slavery and modernization in the eyes of southerners.

Emily West, *Chains of Love: Slave Couples in Antebellum South Carolina* (2004). Good description of cross-plantation unions among slaves who sought to create a private world.

Chapter 13

Gold Miners
At first, gold rushers worked individually, each with a shovel and pan. By the 1850s, devices like the one shown here, a "long tom," were making mining a cooperative venture.

Immigration, Expansion, and Sectional Conflict,

1840–1848

José Antonio Navarro

V isitors to Texas will find a thoroughfare named after José Antonio Navarro (1795–1871) in his native San Antonio, an official Navarro Day, and a Navarro County. A monument to him in front of Navarro's county courthouse is inscribed "Lover of Liberty, Foe of Despotism." He was one of two native Texans to have signed the state of Coahuila-Texas's Declaration of Independence from Mexico in 1836, and he became a member of the Congress of the independent Republic of Texas. After Texas was annexed by the United States in 1845, Navarro served as a member of the convention that drew up the state's constitution and served in its senate.

In sum, Navarro is justly remembered as a founder of Texas. But *Tejano* (a native Texan of Mexican descent) was just one of several identities thrust upon him and his father Angel Navarro in the course of their lives. Asked to bestow a name on the seat of Navarro County, he suggested Corsicana (it stuck) to commemorate his father's birthplace, the craggy Mediterranean island of Corsica, also the birthplace of Napoleon. Angel had enlisted in the Spanish army and eventually made his way to Mexico, first to Saltillo and then to San Antonio.

In 1811, three years after Angel's death, Mexicans began the struggle that would lead to independence from Spain in 1821. San Antonio was a center of resistance to Spanish rule, and Navarro, who observed many skirmishes during the war, was now proud to be a Mexican. But in the 1820s other Mexicans began to call him an "Anglicized Mexican." Although Navarro never learned to speak English, he had become friends with American citizens ("Anglos"), including

James Bowie, who married his niece and who would die at the Alamo, and **Stephen F. Austin**.

Austin exemplified the shifting allegiances of many Anglos on the American frontier. Born in Virginia, he had followed his father in 1798 to what is now Missouri but was then Spanish territory. His father became a Spanish citizen. Stephen eventually moved to Texas to fulfill his father's dream of settling American families there. Navarro, who had become a merchant and lawyer, ardently supported this goal, for Texas was underpopulated and vulnerable to Indian raids. Navarro, the Anglicized Mexican, formed an alliance with Austin, the "Mexicanized Anglo," to turn Texas into an agriculturally and ethnically rich province.

Resentment against the centralizing tendencies of the Mexican government and its indifference to the welfare of remote Texas led Navarro and Austin to support Texas's successful battle for independence from Mexico. Then, in 1841, Navarro signed on to an expedition to Santa Fe, still part of Mexico. The expedition's goals—perhaps trade and perhaps liberating Santa Fe from Mexican rule—are less clear than its fate. It became lost in the trackless wilderness that still covered much of Texas and was captured by Mexican troops. To Mexicans, Navarro was a traitor for having signed Texas's Declaration of Independence. Mexican president Antonio López Santa Anna personally saw to it that Navarro was confined to the filthiest prison in Mexico, but then offered him freedom and wealth if he would renounce his allegiance to Texas. "I will never forsake Texas and her cause," Navarro replied. "I am her son."

Navarro made a daring escape from prison and returned to San Antonio, only to find that the now dominant Anglos were forsaking people like him. In their eyes, a *Tejano* was just another Mexican, and no one needed Mexicans. "The continuation of greasers [Mexicans] among us," a resolution drafted by Anglos in Goliad proclaimed, "is an intolerable nuisance." Navarro was starting to realize that the Texas in which he had first entered public life, a place where Anglos and *Tejanos* lived in harmony, was being swallowed by the relentless expansion of the United States. Although urged to run for a vacancy in the U.S. Senate in 1849, Navarro declined and never held public office again.

Many others tried to escape the reach of what Americans called their "Manifest Destiny." To escape persecution after the murder of the Mormon prophet Joseph Smith (see Chapter 10), between 1845 and 1847 Brigham Young led the main body of Mormons on a trek from Illinois to the Great Salt Lake Valley, then part of Mexico, only

to find the land that Mormons called Deseret had been absorbed by the United States at the conclusion of its war with Mexico in 1848. "Americans regard this continent as their birthright," thundered Sam Houston, the first president of the Republic of Texas, in 1847. Indians and Mexicans had to make way for "our mighty march." This was not idle talk. In less than a thousand fevered days during President James K. Polk's administration (1845–1849), the United States increased its land area by 50 percent. It annexed Texas, negotiated Britain out of half of the vast Oregon territory, and fought a war with Mexico that led to the annexation of California and New Mexico. Meanwhile, immigrants poured into the United States, mainly from Europe. The number of immigrants during the 1840s and 1850s exceeded the nation's entire population in 1790.

Immigration and territorial expansion were linked. Most immigrants gravitated to the expansionist Democratic Party. The immigrant vote helped tip the election of 1844 to Polk, an ardent expansionist. Further, tensions flared between immigrants and the native-born, which were reflected in ugly outbursts of anti-immigrant feeling. Influential Democrats concluded that the best solution to intensifying class and ethnic conflicts lay in expanding the national boundaries, bringing more land under cultivation, and recapturing the ideal of America as a nation of self-sufficient farmers.

Democrats also saw expansion as a way to reduce strife between the sections. Oregon would gratify the North; Texas, the South; and California, everyone. In reality, expansion brought sectional antagonisms to the boiling point, split the Democratic Party in the late 1840s, and set the nation on the path to Civil War.

Focus Questions

- How did immigration in the 1840s influence the balance of power between the Whig and Democratic parties?

- What economic and political forces fed westward expansion during the 1840s?

- How did westward expansion threaten war with Britain and Mexico?

- How did the outcome of the Mexican-American War intensify intersectional conflict?

Newcomers and Natives

Between 1815 and 1860, 5 million European immigrants landed in the United States (see Figure 13.1). Of these, 4.2 million arrived between 1840 and 1860; 3 million of them came in the single decade from 1845 to 1854. This ten-year period witnessed the largest immigration proportionate to the total population (then around 20 million) in American history. The Irish led the way as the most numerous immigrants between 1840 and 1860, with the Germans running a close second. Smaller contingents continued to immigrate to the United States from England, Scotland, and Wales, and a growing number came from Norway, Sweden, Switzerland, and Holland. But by 1860 three-fourths of the 4.1 million foreign-born Americans were either Irish or German.

Expectations and Realities

A desire for religious freedom drew some immigrants to the United States. Mormon missionaries actively recruited converts in the slums of English factory towns.

But a far larger number of Europeans sailed for America to better their economic condition. Travelers' accounts and letters from relatives described America as a utopia for poor people. German peasants learned that they could purchase a large farm in America for the price of renting a small one in Germany. Britons were told that enough good peaches and apples were left rotting in the orchards of Ohio to sink the British fleet.

Hoping for the best, emigrants often encountered the worst. Their problems began at ports of embarkation, where hucksters frequently sold them worthless tickets and where ships scheduled to leave in June might not sail until August. Countless emigrants spent precious savings in waterfront slums while awaiting departure. The ocean voyage itself proved terrifying; many emigrants had never set foot on a ship. Most sailed on cargo ships as steerage passengers, where, for six weeks or more, they endured quarters almost as crowded as on slave ships.

For many emigrants, the greatest shock came when they landed. "The folks aboard ship formed great plans for their future, all of which vanished quickly after landing,"

Figure 13.1 German, Irish, and Total Immigration, 1830–1860
Irish and German immigrants led the more than tenfold growth of immigration between 1830 and 1860.
Source: U.S. Bureau of the Census, *Historical Statistics of the United States, Colonial Times to 1970,* Bicentennial Edition (Washington, D.C., 1975.)

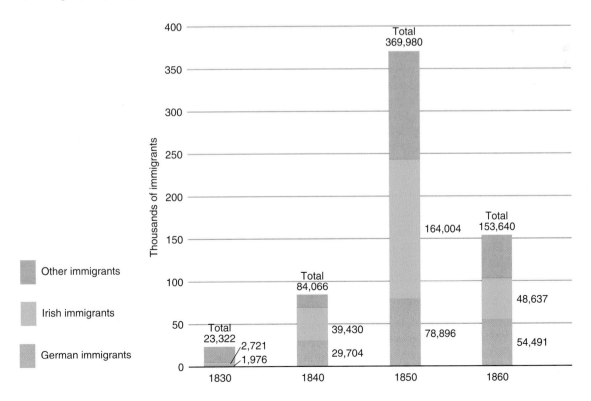

wrote a young German from Frankfurt in 1840. Immigrants quickly discovered that farming in America bore little resemblance to farming in Europe. European farmers' lives revolved around villages that were fringed by the fields that they worked. In contrast, American farmers lived in relative isolation. Farmers on widely scattered plots of land met occasionally at revivals or militia musters. But they lacked the compact village life of European farmers, and they possessed an individualistic psychology that led them to speculate in land and to move frequently.

Clear patterns emerged amid the shocks and dislocations of immigration. Most of the Irish settlers before 1840 departed from Liverpool on sailing ships that carried English manufactures to eastern Canada and New England in return for timber. On arrival in America, few of these Irish had the capital to become farmers, so they crowded into the urban areas of New England, New York, Pennsylvania, and New Jersey, where they could more easily find jobs. In contrast, German emigrants usually left from continental ports on ships engaged in the cotton trade with New Orleans. Deterred from settling in the South by the presence of slavery, the oppressive climate, and the lack of economic opportunity, the Germans congregated in the upper Mississippi and Ohio valleys, especially in Illinois, Ohio, Wisconsin, and Missouri. Geographical concentration also characterized most of the smaller groups of immigrants. More than half of the Norwegian immigrants, for example, settled in Wisconsin, where they typically became farmers.

Cities, rather than farms, attracted most antebellum immigrants. By 1860, **German and Irish immigrants** formed more than 60 percent of the population of St. Louis; nearly half the population of New York City, Chicago, Cincinnati, Milwaukee, Detroit, and San Francisco; and well over a third that of New Orleans, Baltimore, and Boston. These fast-growing cities created an intense demand for the labor of people with strong backs and a willingness to work for low wages. Irish construction gangs built the houses, new streets, and aqueducts that were changing the face of urban America and dug the canals and railroads that threaded together the rapidly developing cities. A popular song recounted the fate of the thousands of Irishmen who died of cholera contracted during the building of a canal in New Orleans:

> *Ten thousand Micks, they swung their picks,*
> *To build the New Canal*
> *But the choleray was stronger 'n they.*
> *An' twice it killed them awl.*

The cities provided the sort of community life that seemed lacking in farming settlements. Immigrant societies like the Friendly Sons of St. Patrick took root in cities and combined with associations like the Hibernian Society for the Relief of Emigrants from Ireland to welcome the newcomers.

The Germans

In the mid-nineteenth century, the Germans were an extremely diverse group. In 1860, Germany was not a unified state but a collection of principalities and small kingdoms. German immigrants thought of themselves as Bavarians, Westphalians, or Saxons rather than as Germans. Moreover, the German immigrants included Catholics, Protestants, and Jews as well as a sprinkling of freethinkers who denounced the ritual, clergy, and doctrines of all religions. Although few in number, these critics were vehement in their attacks on the established churches. A pious Milwaukee Lutheran complained in 1860 that he could not drink a glass of beer in a saloon "without being angered by anti-Christian remarks or raillery against preachers."

German immigrants came from a wide range of social classes and occupations. The majority had engaged in farming, but a sizable minority were professionals, artisans, and tradespeople. Heinrich Steinweg, an obscure piano maker from Lower Saxony, arrived in New York City in 1851, anglicized his name to Henry Steinway, and in 1853 opened the firm of Steinway and Sons, which quickly achieved international acclaim for the quality of its pianos. Levi Strauss, a Jewish tailor from Bavaria, migrated to the United States in 1847. On hearing of the discovery of gold in California in 1848, Strauss gathered rolls of cloth and sailed for San Francisco. When a miner told him of the need for durable work trousers, Strauss fashioned a pair of overalls from canvas. To meet a quickly skyrocketing demand, he opened a factory in San Francisco; his cheap overalls, later known as blue jeans or Levi's, made him rich and famous.

For all their differences, the Germans were bound together by their common language, which strongly induced recent immigrants to the United States to congregate in German neighborhoods. Even prosperous Germans bent on climbing the social ladder usually did so within their ethnic communities. Germans formed their own militia and fire companies, sponsored parochial schools in which German was the language of instruction, started German-language newspapers, and organized their own balls and singing groups. The range of voluntary associations among Germans was almost as broad as among native-born Americans.

Other factors beyond their common language brought unity to the German immigrants. Ironically, the Germans' diversity also promoted their solidarity. For example, because they were able to supply their own doctors, lawyers,

German Winter Gardens
A well-known beer hall on lower Manhattan's Bowery, the German Winter Gardens were famous for music and sociability.

teachers, journalists, merchants, artisans, and clergy, the Germans had little need to go outside their own neighborhoods. Moreover, economic self-sufficiency conspired with the strong bonds of their language to encourage a clannish psychology among the German immigrants. Although they admired the Germans' industriousness, native-born Americans resented their economic success and disdained their clannishness. German refugee Moritz Busch complained that "the great mass of Anglo-Americans" held the Germans in contempt. The Germans responded by becoming even more clannish. Their psychological separateness made it difficult for the Germans to be as politically influential as the Irish immigrants.

The Irish

Between 1815 and the mid-1820s, most Irish immigrants were Protestants, small landowners and merchants in search of better economic opportunity. Many were drawn by enthusiastic veterans of the War of 1812, who had reported that America was a paradise filled with fertile land and abundant game, a place where "all a man wanted was a gun and sufficient ammunition to be able to live like a prince." Compared to Irish immigrants in the mid-1820s, those in the mid-1840s were poorer and more frequently Catholic, primarily comprising tenant farmers whom Protestant landowners had evicted as "superfluous."

Protestant or Catholic, rich or poor, eight hundred thousand to a million Irish immigrants entered the United States between 1815 and 1844. Then, between 1845 and the early 1850s, a blight destroyed every harvest of Ireland's potatoes, virtually the only food of the peasantry, and created one of the most devastating famines in history. The Great Famine inflicted indescribable suffering on the Irish peasantry and killed perhaps a million people. One landlord characterized the surviving tenants on his estate as no more than "famished and ghastly skeletons." To escape the ravages of famine, 1.8 million Irish migrated to the United States in the decade after 1845.

Overwhelmingly poor and Catholic, these newest Irish immigrants usually entered the work force at or near the bottom. The popular image of Paddy with his pickax and Bridget the maid contained a good deal of truth. Irish men in the cities dug cellars and often lived in them; outside the cities, they dug canals and railroad beds. Irish women often became domestic servants. Compared to other immigrant women, a high proportion of Irish women entered the work force, if not as maids then often as textile workers. By the 1840s, Irish women were displacing native-born women in the textile mills of Lowell and Waltham. Poverty drove Irish women to work at an early age, and the outdoor, all-season work performed by their husbands turned many of them into working widows. Winifred Rooney became a nursemaid at the age of seven and an errand girl at eleven. She then learned needlework, a skill that helped her support her family after her husband's early death. The high proportion of employed Irish women reflected more than simply their poverty. Compared to the predominantly male German immigrants, more than half of the Irish immigrants were women, most of whom were single adults. In both Ireland and America, the Irish usually married late, and many never married. For Irish women to become self-supporting was only natural.

The lot of most Irish people was harsh. One immigrant described the life of the average Irish laborer in America as "despicable, humiliating, [and] slavish"; there was "no love for him—no protection of life—[he] can be shot down, run through, kicked, cuffed, spat upon—and no redress, but a response of 'served the damn son of an Irish b____ right, damn him.'" Yet some Irish struggled up the social ladder. In Philadelphia, which had a more varied industrial base than Boston, Irish men made their way into iron foundries, where some became foremen and supervisors. Other Irish rose into the middle class by opening grocery and liquor stores.

The varied occupations pursued by Irish immigrants brought them into conflict with two quite different groups. The poorer Irish who dug canals and cellars, hauled cargo on the docks, washed laundry for others, and served white families competed directly with equally poor free blacks. This competition stirred up Irish animosity toward blacks and a hatred of abolitionists. At the same time, enough Irish men eventually secured skilled or semiskilled jobs that clashes with native-born white workers became unavoidable.

Anti-Catholicism, Nativism, and Labor Protest

The hostility of native-born whites toward the Irish often took the form of anti-Catholicism, a latent impulse among American Protestants since Puritan days. The surge of Irish immigration during the second quarter of the nineteenth century revived anti-Catholic fever. For example, in 1834 a mob, fueled by rumors that a Catholic convent in Charlestown, Massachusetts, contained dungeons and torture chambers, burned the building to the ground. In 1835, the combative evangelical Protestant Lyman Beecher issued *A Plea for the West,* a tract in which he warned faithful Protestants of an alleged Catholic conspiracy to send immigrants to the West in sufficient numbers to dominate the region. A year later, the publication of Maria Monk's best-selling *Awful Disclosures of the Hotel Dieu Nunnery in Montreal* rekindled anti-Catholic hysteria. Although Maria Monk was actually a prostitute who had never lived in a convent, she professed to be a former nun. In her book, she described how the mother superior forced nuns to submit to the lustful advances of priests who entered the convent by a subterranean passage.

As Catholic immigration swelled in the 1840s, Protestants mounted a political counterattack. It took the form of nativist (anti-immigrant) societies with names like the American Republican party and the United Order of Americans. Although usually started as secret or semisecret fraternal orders, most of these societies developed political offshoots. One, the Order of the Star-Spangled Banner, would evolve by 1854 into the "Know-Nothing," or American, party and would become a major political force in the 1850s.

During the 1840s, however, nativist parties enjoyed only brief moments in the sun. These occurred mainly during flare-ups over local issues, such as whether students in predominantly Catholic neighborhoods should be allowed to use the Catholic Douay rather than Protestant King James version of the Bible for the scriptural readings that began each school day. In 1844, for example, after the American Republican party won some offices in Philadelphia elections, fiery Protestant orators mounted soapboxes to denounce "popery," and Protestant mobs descended on Catholic neighborhoods. Before the militia quelled these "Bible Riots," thirty buildings lay in charred ruins, and at least sixteen people had been killed.

Nativism fed on an explosive mixture of fears and discontents. Protestants thought that their doctrine that each individual could interpret the Bible was more democratic than Catholicism, which made doctrine the province of the pope and bishops. In addition, at a time when the wages of native-born artisans and journeymen were depressed by the subdivision of tasks and by the aftermath of the Panic of 1837 (see Chapter 10), many Protestant workers concluded that Catholic immigrants, often desperately poor and willing to work for anything, were threats to their jobs.

Demand for land reform joined nativism as a proposed solution to workers' economic woes. Land reformers argued that workers' true interests could never be reconciled with an economic order in which factory workers sold their labor for wages and became "wage slaves." In 1844, the English-born radical George Henry Evans organized the National Reform Association and rallied supporters with the slogan "Vote Yourself a Farm." Evans advanced neo-Jeffersonian plans for the establishment of "rural republican townships" composed of 160-acre plots for workers. Land reform had some appeal to articulate and self-consciously radical workers, particularly artisans and small masters whose independence was being threatened by factories and who feared that American labor was "fast verging on the servile dependence" common in Europe. But the doctrine offered little to factory operatives and wage-earning journeymen who completely lacked economic independence. In an age when a horse cost the average worker three months' pay and most factory workers dreaded "the horrors of wilderness life," the idea of solving industrial problems by resettling workers on farms seemed a pipe dream.

Labor unions appealed to workers left cold by the promises of land reformers. For example, desperately poor Irish immigrants, refugees from an agricultural society, believed that they could gain more by unions and strikes than by plowing and planting. Even women workers organized unions in these years. The leader of a seamstresses' union proclaimed, "Too long have we been bound down by tyrant employers."

Probably the most important development for workers in the 1840s was a state court decision. In ***Commonwealth v. Hunt*** (1842), the Massachusetts Supreme Judicial Court ruled that labor unions were not illegal monopolies that restrained trade. But because less than 1 percent of the work force belonged to labor unions in the 1840s, this decision initially had little impact. Massachusetts employers brushed aside the *Commonwealth* decision, firing union agitators and replacing them with cheap immigrant labor. "Hundreds of honest laborers," a labor paper reported in 1848, "have been dismissed from employment in the manufactories of New England because they have been suspected of knowing their rights and daring to assert them." This repression effectively blunted demands for a ten-hour workday in an era when the twelve- or fourteen-hour day was typical.

Ethnic and religious tensions also split the working class during the 1830s and 1840s. Friction between native-born and immigrant workers inevitably became intertwined with the political divisions of the second party system.

Immigrant Politics

Few immigrants had ever cast a vote in an election prior to their arrival in America, and only a small fraction were refugees from political persecution. Political upheavals had erupted in Austria and several of the German states in the turbulent year of 1848 (the so-called Revolutions of 1848), but among the million German immigrants to the United States, only about ten thousand were political refugees, or "Forty-Eighters."

Once they had settled in the United States, however, many immigrants became politically active. They quickly found that urban political organizations, some of them dominated by earlier immigrants, would help them find lodging and employment, in return for votes. Both the Irish and the Germans identified overwhelmingly with the Democratic Party. An obituary of 1837 that described a New Yorker as a "warm-hearted Irishman and an unflinching Democrat" could have been written of millions of other Irish. Similarly, the Germans became stalwart supporters of the Democrats in cities like Milwaukee and St. Louis.

Immigrants' fears about jobs partly explain their widespread support of the Democrats. Former president Andrew Jackson had given the Democratic Party an anti-aristocratic coloration, making the Democrats seem more sympathetic than the Whigs to the common people. In addition, antislavery was linked to the Whig party, and the Irish loathed abolitionism because they feared that freed slaves would become their economic competitors. Moreover, the Whigs' moral and religious values seemed to threaten those of the Irish and Germans. Hearty-drinking Irish and German immigrants shunned temperance-crusading Whigs, many of whom were also rabid anti-Catholics. Even public-school reform, championed by the Whigs, was seen as a menace to the Catholicism of Irish children and as a threat to German language and culture.

Although liquor regulations and school laws were city or state concerns rather than federal responsibilities, the Democratic Party schooled immigrants in broad, national principles. It taught them to venerate George Washington, to revere Thomas Jefferson and Andrew Jackson, and to view "monied capitalists" as parasites who would tremble when the people spoke. It introduced immigrants to Democratic newspapers, Democratic picnics, and Democratic parades. The Democrats, by identifying their party with all that they thought best about the United States, helped give immigrants a sense of themselves as Americans. By the same token, the Democratic Party introduced immigrants to national issues. It redirected political loyalties that often had been forged on local issues into the arena of national politics. During the 1830s, the party had persuaded immigrants that national measures like the Bank of the United States and the tariff, seemingly remote from their daily lives, were vital to them. Now, in the 1840s, the Democrats would try to convince immigrants that national expansion likewise advanced their interests.

The West and Beyond

As late as 1840, Americans who referred to the West still meant the area between the Appalachian Mountains

and the Mississippi River or just beyond. West of that lay the inhospitable Great Plains, a semiarid plateau with few trees. Winds sucked the moisture from the soil. Bands of nomadic Indians—including the Pawnees, Kiowas, and Sioux—roamed this territory and gained sustenance mainly from the buffalo. They ate its meat, wore its fur, and covered their dwellings with its hide. Aside from some well-watered sections of northern Missouri and eastern Kansas and Nebraska, the Great Plains presented would-be farmers with massive obstacles.

The formidable barrier of the Great Plains did not stop settlement of the West in the long run. Temporarily, however, it shifted public interest toward the verdant region lying beyond the Rockies, the Far West (see Map 13.1).

Map 13.1 Trails to the West, 1840
By 1840, several trails carried pioneers from Missouri and Illinois to the West.

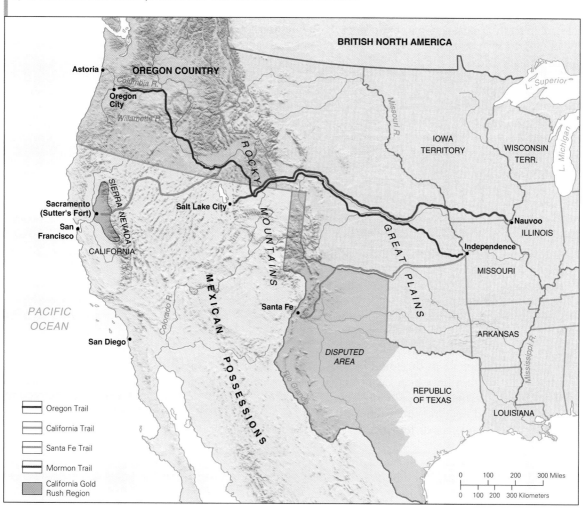

The Far West

By the Transcontinental (or Adams-Onís) Treaty of 1819, the United States had given up its claims to Texas west of the Sabine River. This had left Spain in undisputed possession not only of Texas but also of California and the vast territory of New Mexico. Combined, California and New Mexico included all of present-day California and New Mexico as well as modern Nevada, Utah, and Arizona, and parts of Wyoming and Colorado. Two years later, Mexico won its independence from Spain and took over all North American territory previously claimed by Spain.

The Adams-Onís Treaty also had provided for Spain to cede to the United States its claims to the **Oregon country** north of the forty-second parallel (the northern boundary of California). Then in 1824 and 1825, Russia abandoned its claims to Oregon south of 54°40′ (the southern boundary of Alaska). In 1827, the United States and Britain, each of which had claims to Oregon based on discovery and exploration, revived an agreement (originally signed in 1818) for joint occupation of the territory between 42° and 54°40′, a colossal area that contemporaries could describe no more precisely than the "North West Coast of America, Westward of the Stony [Rocky] Mountains" and that included all of modern Oregon, Washington, and Idaho as well as parts of present-day Wyoming, Montana, and Canada.

Collectively, Texas, New Mexico, California, and Oregon comprised an area larger than Britain, France, and Germany combined. Such a vast region should have tempted them, but during the 1820s Mexico, Britain, and the United States viewed the Far West as a remote and shadowy frontier. By 1820, the American line of settlement had reached only to Missouri, well over two thousand miles (counting detours for mountains) from the West Coast. El Paso on the Rio Grande and Taos in New Mexico lay, respectively, twelve hundred and fifteen hundred miles north of Mexico City. Britain, of course, was many thousands of miles from Oregon.

Far Western Trade

After sailing around South America and up the Pacific, early merchants had established American and British outposts on the West Coast. Between the late 1790s and the 1820s, for example, Boston merchants had built a thriving exchange of coffee, tea, spices, cutlery, clothes, and hardware—indeed, anything that could be bought or manufactured in the eastern United States—for furs (especially those of sea otters), cattle, hides, and tallow (rendered from cattle fat and used for making soap and candles). Between 1826 and 1828 alone, Boston traders took more than 6 million cattle hides out of California; in the otherwise undeveloped California economy, these hides, called "California bank-notes," served as the main medium of exchange. During the 1820s, the British Hudson's Bay Company developed a similar trade in Oregon and northern California.

The California trade created little friction with Mexico. Producing virtually no manufactured goods, Hispanic people born in California (called *Californios*) were as eager to buy as the traders were to sell. Many traders who did settle in California quickly learned to speak Spanish and became assimilated into Mexican culture.

Farther south, trading links developed during the 1820s between St. Louis and Santa Fe along the famed **Santa Fe Trail**. The Panic of 1819 left the American Midwest short of cash and its merchants burdened by unsold goods. Pulling themselves up from adversity, however, plucky midwesterners loaded wagon trains with tools, clothing, and household sundries each spring and rumbled westward to Santa Fe, where they traded their merchandise for mules and New

Indians Dancing Outside the California Mission of San Francisco, 1813
Converting the Indians to Christianity was a major objective of the Franciscan priests who ran the Spanish missions.

Mexican silver. Mexico welcomed this trade. By the 1830s, more than half the goods entering New Mexico by the Santa Fe Trail trickled into the mineral-rich interior provinces of Mexico such as Chihuahua and Sonora, with the result that the Mexican silver peso, which midwestern traders brought back with them, quickly became the principal medium of exchange in Missouri.

The profitability of the beaver trade also prompted Americans to venture west from St. Louis to trap beaver in what is today western Colorado and eastern Utah. There they competed with agents of the Hudson's Bay Company. In 1825, on the Green River in Mexican territory, the St. Louis–based trader William Ashley inaugurated an annual encampment where traders exchanged beaver pelts for supplies, thereby saving themselves the trip to St. Louis. Although silk hats had become more fashionable than beaver hats by 1854, over a half-million beaver pelts were auctioned off in London alone that year.

For the most part, American traders and trappers operating on the northern Mexican frontier in the 1820s and 1830s posed more of a threat to the beaver than to Mexico's provinces. The Mexican people of California and New Mexico depended on the American trade for manufactured goods, and Mexican officials in both provinces relied on customs duties to support their governments. In New Mexico, the government often had to await the arrival of the annual caravan of traders from St. Louis before it could pay its officials and soldiers.

Although the relations between Mexicans and Americans were mutually beneficial during the 1820s, the potential for conflict was always present. Spanish-speaking, Roman Catholic, and accustomed to a more hierarchical society, the Mexicans formed a striking contrast to the largely Protestant, individualistic Americans. And although few American traders themselves became permanent residents of Mexico, many returned with glowing reports of the climate and fertility of Mexico's northern provinces. By the 1820s, American settlers were already moving into eastern Texas. At the same time, the ties that bound the central government of Mexico to its northern frontier provinces were starting to fray.

The American Settlement of Texas to 1835

During the 1820s, Americans began to settle the eastern part of the Mexican state known as Coahuila-Texas, which lacked the deserts and mountains that formed a natural barrier along the boundaries of New Mexico and California. Initially, Mexico encouraged this migration, partly to gain protection against Indian attacks that had intensified with the erosion of the Spanish-Mexican system of missions.

Spain, and later Mexico, recognized that the key to controlling the frontier provinces lay in promoting their settlement by civilized Hispanic people—Spaniards, Mexicans, and Indians who had embraced Catholicism and agriculture. The key instruments of Spain's expansion on the frontier had long been the Spanish missions. Paid by the government, the Franciscan priests who staffed the missions endeavored to convert Native Americans and settle them as farmers on mission lands. To protect the missions, the Spanish often had constructed forts, or presidios, near them. San Francisco was the site of a mission and a presidio founded in 1776, and did not develop as a town until the 1830s.

Dealt a blow by the successful struggle for Mexican independence, Spain's system of missions began to decline in the late 1820s. The Mexican government gradually "secularized" the missions by distributing their lands to ambitious government officials and private ranchers who turned the mission Indians into forced laborers. As many Native Americans fled the missions, returned to their nomadic ways, and joined with Indians who had always resisted the missions, lawlessness surged on the Mexican frontier, and few Mexicans ventured into the undeveloped territory.

In 1824, the Mexican government began to encourage American colonization of Texas by bestowing generous land grants on agents known as *empresarios* to recruit peaceful American settlers for Texas. Initially, most Americans, like the *empresario* Stephen F. Austin, were content to live in Texas as naturalized Mexican citizens. But trouble brewed quickly. Most of the American settlers were southern farmers, often slaveholders. Having emancipated its own slaves in 1829, Mexico closed Texas to further American immigration in 1830 and forbade the introduction of more slaves. But the Americans, white and black, kept coming, and in 1834 Austin secured repeal of the 1830 prohibition on American immigration. Two years later, Mexican general Manuel Mier y Téran ran a sword through his heart in despair over Mexico's inability to stem and control the American advance. By 1836, Texas contained some thirty thousand white Americans, five thousand black slaves, and four thousand Mexicans.

As American immigration swelled, Mexican politics (which Austin compared to the country's volcanic geology) grew increasingly unstable. In 1834, Mexican president Antonio López de Santa Anna instituted a policy of restricting the powers of the regimes in Coahuila-Texas and other Mexican states. His actions ignited a series of rebellions in those regions, the most important of which became known as the Texas Revolution.

Entirro de un Angel **(Funeral of an Angel), by Theodore Gentilz**
Protestant Americans who ventured into Texas came upon a Hispanic culture unlike anything they had seen. Here a San Antonio procession follows the coffin of a baptized infant who, in Catholic belief, will become an angel in heaven.

The Texas Revolution, 1836

Santa Anna's brutality in crushing most of the rebellions alarmed Austin, who initially had hoped to secure greater autonomy for Texas within Mexico, not independence. When Santa Anna invaded Texas in the fall of 1835, however, Austin cast his lot with the more radical Americans who wanted independence.

At first, Santa Anna's army met with success. In late February 1836, his force of 4,000 men laid siege to San Antonio, whose 200 defenders, including some *Tejanos*, retreated into an abandoned mission, the **Alamo.** After repelling repeated attacks, the remaining 187 Texans were overwhelmed on March 6. Most were killed in the final assault. A few, including the famed frontiersman Davy Crockett, surrendered. Crockett then was executed on Santa Anna's orders. A few weeks later, Mexican troops massacred some 350 prisoners taken from an American settlement at Goliad.

Even before these events, Texas delegates had met in a windswept shed in the village of Washington, Texas, and declared the Republic of Texas independent of Mexico. The rebels by then had settled on a military leader, **Sam Houston**, for their president. A giant man who wore leopard-skin vests, Houston retreated east to pick up recruits (mostly Americans who crossed the border to fight Santa Anna). Once reinforced, Houston turned and surprised Santa Anna on a prairie near the San Jacinto River in April. Shouting "Remember the Alamo," Houston's army of eight hundred tore through the Mexican lines, killing nearly half of Santa Anna's men in fifteen minutes and taking Santa Anna himself prisoner. Houston then forced Santa Anna to sign a treaty (which the Mexican government never ratified) recognizing the independence of Texas (see Map 13.2).

American Settlements in California, New Mexico, and Oregon

California and New Mexico, both less accessible than Texas, exerted no more than a mild attraction for American settlers during the 1820s and 1830s. Only a few hundred

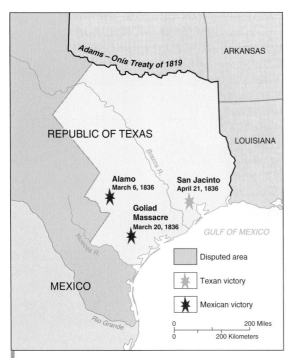

Map 13.2 Major Battles in the Texas Revolution, 1835–1836
Sam Houston's victory at San Jacinto was the decisive action of the war and avenged the massacres at the Alamo and Goliad.

Americans resided in New Mexico in 1840 and perhaps four hundred in California. A contemporary observed that the Americans living in California and New Mexico "are scattered throughout the whole Mexican population, and most of them have Spanish wives. . . . They live in every respect like the Spanish."

Yet the beginnings of change were already evident. During the 1840s, Americans streamed into the Sacramento Valley, welcomed by California's Hispanic population as a way to encourage economic development and lured by favorable reports of the region. One tongue-in-cheek story told of a 250-year-old man who had to leave the idyllic region in order to die. For these land-hungry settlers, no sacrifice seemed too great if it led to California.

To the north, the Oregon country's abundant farmland beckoned settlers from the Mississippi valley. During the 1830s, missionaries like the Methodist Jason Lee moved into Oregon's Willamette valley, and by 1840 the area contained some five hundred Americans. Enthusiastic reports sent back by Lee piqued interest about Oregon. An orator in Missouri described Oregon as a "pioneer's paradise" where "the pigs are running around under the great acorn trees, round and fat and already cooked,

with knives and forks sticking in them so that you can cut off a slice whenever you are hungry." To some, Oregon seemed even more attractive than California. Oregon was already jointly occupied by Britain and the United States, and its prospects for eventual U.S. annexation appeared better than California's.

The Overland Trails

Whether bound for California or Oregon, the pioneers faced a four-month journey across terrain little known in reality but vividly depicted in fiction as an Indian killing ground. Assuming that they would have to fight their way across the Plains, settlers prepared for the trip by buying enough guns for an army from merchants in the rival jump-off towns of Independence and St. Joseph, Missouri. In reality, the pioneers were more likely to shoot themselves or each other by accident than to be shot by the usually cooperative Indians, and much more likely to be scalped by the inflated prices charged by merchants in Independence or "St. Joe."

Once embarked, the emigrants faced new hardships and hazards: kicks from mules, oxen that collapsed from thirst, overloaded wagons that broke down. Trails were difficult to follow—at least until they became littered by the debris of broken wagons and by the bleached bones of oxen. Guidebooks to help emigrants chart their course were more like guessbooks. The Donner party, which set out from Illinois in 1846, lost so much time following the advice of one such book that its members became snowbound in the High Sierras and reached California only after its survivors had turned to cannibalism.

Emigrants responded to the challenges of the overland trails by cooperating closely with one another. Most set out in huge wagon trains rather than as individuals. Reflecting firmly entrenched traditions, husbands depended on their wives to pack and unpack the wagon each day, to milk the cows brought along to stock the new farms in the West, to cook, and to assist with the childbirths that occurred on the trail at about the same frequency as in the nation as a whole. Men yoked and unyoked the oxen, drove the wagons and stock, and formed hunting parties.

Between 1840 and 1848, an estimated 11,500 emigrants followed an overland trail to Oregon, and some 2,700 reached California. These numbers were modest and concentrated in the years from 1844 to 1848. Yet even small numbers could make a huge difference in the Far West, for the British could not effectively settle Oregon at all, and the Mexican population in California was small and scattered. By 1845, California clung to Mexico by the thinnest of threads. The territory's Hispanic population,

Emigrant Train Bedding Down for the Night
Men, women, and children divided the tasks—caring for oxen, feeding horses, drawing water, preparing supper, washing clothes—on the basis of gender and age.

the *Californios*, felt little allegiance to Mexico, which they contemptuously referred to as the "other shore." Nor did they feel any allegiance to the United States. Some *Californios* wanted independence from Mexico; others looked to the day when California might become a protectorate of Britain or perhaps even France. But these *Californios*, with their shaky allegiances, now faced a growing number of American settlers with definite political allegiances.

The Politics of Expansion, 1840–1846

The major issue that arose as a byproduct of westward expansion was whether the United States should annex the independent Texas republic. In the mid-1840s, the Texas-annexation issue generated the kind of political passions that banking questions had ignited in the 1830s, and became entangled with equally unsettling issues relating to California, New Mexico, and Oregon. Between 1846 and 1848, a war with Mexico and a dramatic confrontation with Britain settled all these questions on terms favorable to the United States.

Yet at the start of the 1840s, western issues occupied no more than a tenuous position on the national political agenda. From 1840 to 1842, questions relating to economic recovery—notably, banking, the tariff, and internal improvements—dominated the attention of political

leaders. Only after politicians failed to address the economic issues coherently did opportunistic leaders thrust issues relating to expansion to the top of the political agenda.

The Whig Ascendancy

The election of 1840 brought Whig candidate William Henry Harrison to the presidency and installed Whig majorities in both houses of Congress. The Whigs had raced to power with a program, based on Henry Clay's American System, to stimulate economic recovery, and they had excellent prospects of success. They quickly repealed Van Buren's darling, the Independent Treasury (see Chapter 10). They then planned to establish a national "fiscal agent," which, like the defunct Bank of the United States, would be a private corporation chartered by Congress and charged with regulating the currency. The Whigs also favored a revised tariff that would increase government revenues but remain low enough to permit the importation of foreign goods. According to the Whig plan, the states would then receive tariff-generated revenues for internal improvements, a measure as popular among southern and western Whigs as the tariff was among northeastern Whigs.

The Whig agenda might have breezed into law had it not been for the untimely death of Harrison after only one month in office. With Harrison's demise, Vice President **John Tyler**, an upper-crust Virginian who had been put on the ticket in 1840 to strengthen the Whigs' appeal in the South, assumed the presidency. From virtually every angle, the new president proved a disaster for the Whigs.

A former Democrat, Tyler had broken with Jackson over nullification, but he continued to favor the Democratic philosophy of states' rights. As president, he repeatedly used the veto to shred his new party's program. In August 1841, a Whig bill to create a new national bank fell victim to Tyler's veto, as did a subsequent modification.

Tyler also played havoc with Whig tariff policy. The Compromise Tariff of 1833 had provided for a gradual scaling down of tariff duties, until none was to exceed 20 percent by 1842. Amid the depression of the early 1840s, however, the provision for a 20 percent maximum tariff appeared too low to generate revenue. Without revenue, the Whigs would have no money to distribute among the states for internal improvements and no program with national appeal. In response, the Whig congressional majority passed two bills in the summer of 1842 that simultaneously postponed the final reduction of tariffs to 20 percent and ordered distribution to the states to proceed. Tyler promptly vetoed both bills. Tyler's mounting vetoes infuriated Whig leadership. "Again has the imbecile, into whose hands accident has placed the power, vetoed a bill passed by a majority of those legally authorized to pass it," screamed the *Daily Richmond Whig*. Some Whigs talked of impeaching Tyler. Finally, in August, needing revenue to run the government, Tyler signed a new bill that maintained some tariffs above 20 percent but abandoned distribution to the states.

Tyler's erratic course confounded and disrupted his party. By maintaining some tariffs above 20 percent, the tariff of 1842 satisfied northern manufacturers, but by abandoning distribution, it infuriated many southerners and westerners. Northern Whigs succeeded in passing the bill with the aid of many northern Democrats, particularly protariff Pennsylvanians, whereas large numbers of Whigs in the Upper South and West opposed the tariff of 1842.

In the congressional elections of 1842, the Whigs paid a heavy price for failing to enact their program. Although retaining a slim majority in the Senate, they lost control of the House to the Democrats. Now the nation had one party in control of the Senate, its rival in control of the House, and a president who appeared to belong to neither party.

Tyler and the Annexation of Texas

Although a political maverick disowned by his party, Tyler ardently desired a second term as president. Domestic issues offered him little hope of building a popular following,

but foreign policy was another matter. In 1842, Tyler's secretary of state, Daniel Webster, concluded a treaty with Great Britain, represented by Lord Ashburton, that settled a long-festering dispute over the boundary between Maine and the Canadian province of New Brunswick. Awarding more than half of the disputed territory to the United States, the Webster-Ashburton Treaty was popular in the North. Tyler reasoned that if he could now arrange for the **annexation of Texas**, he would build a national following.

The issue of slavery, however, had long clouded every discussion of Texas. By the late 1830s, antislavery northerners viewed proposals to annex Texas as part of an elaborate southern conspiracy to extend American territory south into Mexico, Cuba, and Central America, thus allowing for an unlimited number of new slave states, while the British presence in Canada would limit the number of free states. In fact, some southerners talked openly of creating as many as four or five slave states out of the vast territory encompassed by Texas.

Nevertheless, in the summer of 1843, Tyler launched a propaganda campaign for Texas annexation. He justified his crusade by reporting that he had learned of certain British designs on Texas, which Americans, he argued, would be prudent to forestall. Tyler's campaign was fed by reports from his unofficial agent in London, Duff Green, a protégé of John C. Calhoun and a man whom John Quincy Adams contemptuously dismissed as an "ambassador of slavery." Green assured Tyler that, as a prelude to undermining slavery in the United States, the British would pressure Mexico to recognize the independence of Texas in return for the abolition of slavery there. Calhoun, who became Tyler's secretary of state early in 1844, embroidered these reports with fanciful theories about British plans to use abolition as a way to destroy rice, sugar, and cotton production in the United States and gain for itself a monopoly on all three staples.

In the spring of 1844, Calhoun and Tyler submitted to the Senate for ratification a treaty, secretly drawn up, annexing Texas to the United States. Among the supporting documents accompanying the treaty was a letter from Calhoun to Richard Pakenham, the British foreign minister in Washington, that defended slavery as beneficial to blacks, the only way to protect them from "vice and pauperism." Antislavery northerners now had evidence that the annexation of Texas was linked to a conspiracy to extend slavery. Both Martin Van Buren, the leading northern Democrat, and Henry Clay, the most powerful Whig, came out against immediate annexation on the grounds that annexation would provoke the kind of sectional conflict that each had sought to bury, and the treaty went down to crushing defeat in the Senate. Decisive as it appeared, however, this vote only postponed the final decision on annexation to the upcoming election of 1844.

The Election of 1844

Tyler's ineptitude turned the presidential campaign into a free-for-all. The president lacked a base in either party, and after testing the waters as an independent, he was forced to drop out of the race.

Henry Clay had a secure grip on the Whig nomination. Martin Van Buren appeared to have an equally firm grasp on the Democratic nomination, but the issue of Texas annexation split his party. Trying to appease all shades of opinion within his party, Van Buren stated that he would abide by whatever Congress might decide on the annexation issue. Van Buren's attempt to evade the issue succeeded only in alienating the modest number of northern annexationists, led by Michigan's former governor Lewis Cass, and the much larger group of

James K. Polk
Lacking charm, Polk bored even his friends, but few presidents could match his record of acquiring land for the United States.

southern annexationists. At the Democratic convention, Van Buren and Cass effectively blocked each other's nomination. The resulting deadlock was broken by the nomination of **James K. Polk** of Tennessee, the first "dark-horse" presidential nominee in American history and a supporter of immediate annexation. (See Technology and Culture: The Telegraph.)

Jeering "Who is James K. Polk?" the Whigs derided the nomination. Polk was little known outside the South, and he had lost successive elections for the governorship of Tennessee. Yet Polk was a wily campaigner, and he persuaded many northerners that annexation of Texas would benefit them. Conjuring an imaginative scenario, Polk and his supporters argued that if Britain succeeded in abolishing slavery in Texas, slavery would not be able to move westward; racial tensions in existing slave states would intensify; and the chances of a race war, which might spill over into the North, would increase. However far-fetched, this argument played effectively on northern racial phobias and helped Polk detach annexation from Calhoun's narrow, prosouthern defense of it.

In contrast to the Democrats, whose position was clear, Clay kept muddying the waters. First he told his followers that he had nothing against annexation as long as it would not disrupt sectional harmony. In September 1844, he came out against annexation. Clay's shifts on annexation alienated his southern supporters and prompted a small but influential body of northern antislavery Whigs to desert to the Liberty party, which had been organized in 1840. Devoted to the abolition of slavery by political action, the Liberty party nominated Ohio's James G. Birney for the presidency.

Annexation was not the sole issue of the campaign. The Whigs infuriated Catholic immigrant voters by nominating Theodore Frelinghuysen as Clay's running mate. A leading Presbyterian layman, Frelinghuysen gave "his head, his hand, and his heart" to temperance and other Protestant causes. His presence on their ticket fixed the image of the Whigs as the orthodox Protestant party and roused the largely Catholic foreign-born voters to turn out in large numbers for the Democrats.

On the eve of the election in New York City, so many Irish marched to the courthouse to be qualified for voting that the windows had to be left open for people to get in and out. "Ireland has reconquered the country which England lost," an embittered Whig moaned. Polk won the electoral vote 170 to 105, but his margin in the popular vote was only 38,000 out of 2.6 million votes cast, and he lost his own state of Tennessee by 113 votes (see Map 13.3). In most states the two main parties contended

Technology and Culture

The Telegraph

In 1837, Samuel F. B. Morse was a forty-six-year-old art professor at New York University trying to get over some disappointments. His talent as a painter was widely recognized, but he was passed over when Congress selected four artists to paint scenes for the rotunda of the Capitol in Washington. He was also well known as a nativist who fiercely opposed Catholic immigration and who had written anti-Catholic tracts. Nativism was on the rise in the 1830s, when more than half a million immigrants arrived in New York City alone. That many of these were Catholics alarmed Morse, who, as an art student in Europe, had been attracted by Italy's beauty but repelled by what he saw as the submissiveness of its people to the pope. In 1836, he had run for mayor of New York City on the ticket of an anti-Catholic nativist party, only to finish last in a field of four.

Since 1832 Morse had been developing one other interest: sending information by electrical currents on wires. That even a crude battery could transmit a shock to a person holding an iron wire had long been known. Benjamin Franklin's kite experiments nearly a century earlier had shown that lightning was a form of electricity. If messages could be sent at the speed of lightning, close to 200,000 miles a second, then the era of instant messaging was at hand.

Fearing needlessly that inventors in France were about to beat him to the punch, Morse moved quickly. He constructed a crude telegraph, which consisted of a battery and a transmitter that sent electrical impulses to an electromagnetic receiver. Once energized, the receiver moved an arm and recorded coded signals on a band of paper. Short impulses appeared as dots, longer ones as dashes. In manifold combinations, these dots and dashes stood for different letters of the alphabet and became known as Morse Code.

With the help of physicists, he improved his device and successfully demonstrated it in a university lecture hall in September 1837. Next, eager to show the public that electrical messaging over long distances was practical, he teamed with Samuel Colt, the inventor of the revolving pistol (see Chapter 11). Colt, whose gun company had gone bankrupt, wanted to persuade Congress that an electrical current could detonate gunpowder. If so, it would be possible to lay mines in the nation's harbors and explode them when hostile warships approached. Morse recognized that if electrical impulses could be transmitted through water, telegraph cables could cross the nation's innumerable rivers. In 1842, before an audience estimated at 40,000 people, including the secretary of war, Colt and Morse ran an electrical cable from one ship in New York harbor to another, aptly named the *Volta,* which had been stripped and mined. The current triggered the mines. "Bang! bang! bang!," reported the *Herald,* "combusti-blowup eruption . . . 1,705,901 pieces."

Six months later Congress approved a grant of $30,000 to build a telegraph line from Washington to Baltimore. Construction went slowly. Morse's plan to bury the cable had to be abandoned because of insulation problems, forcing a resort to lines in the air from wooden post to wooden post. But by May 1844 twenty-two miles had been completed, just in time for news of the Whig national convention, meeting in Baltimore, to be carried by train to Annapolis Junction and then transmitted by wire to dignitaries assembled in the chamber of the Supreme Court in Washington.

Within a few weeks, the line had been completed to Baltimore, where the Democratic national convention was also meeting. Morse asked a friend to send a message of her choice to Baltimore, and she chose (from the Bible) "What hath God wrought?" History books have made this one of the most memorable quotations in American history, but contemporaries were more interested in the next question: "Have you any news?" Much was at stake. The Whig nominee, Henry Clay, had come out against the annexation of Texas. Martin Van Buren, the likely Democratic nominee, had tried to evade the issue. But southern opponents of Van Buren had put in a new rule, requiring a two-thirds majority for nomination. This rule stopped the Van Buren steamroller and eventually led to the nomination of the dark horse, James K. Polk. No less important than the news of Polk's upset victory was its delivery as breaking news. Here was real excitement. "Mr. Brewster is speaking in favor of [James] Buchanan; . . . Mr. Brewster says his delegation will go for V[an] B[uren] but if VB's friends desert him, the delegation will go for Buchanan;" and then "Illinois goes for Polk . . . Mich[igan] goes for Polk . . . Polk is unanimously nom[inated.]"

At first, newspaper editors worried that the telegraph would put them out of business. Since news would arrive instantly, no editor could beat his rivals to a story. Soon they saw their error. With the telegraph, stories could be put out in installments that recorded each new development. Were a story really spicy, newspapers could put out several editions

A Telegrapher, 1853
This young man is clearly proud to be in the technological vanguard of his day. Two illustrious Americans, the steel tycoon Andrew Carnegie and the inventor Thomas A. Edison, started as telegraphers.

a day. Further, the construction of telegraph lines was just starting, with much of the capital coming from newspaper publishers. By 1848, a line ran from Boston all the way to New York City. As yet, no line connected Boston with Halifax in Canada, where steamers from Europe first docked. Newspapers were potentially the most valuable cargo carried by these steamers, for they contained news of prices of European commodity markets. A New Yorker who speculated in wheat futures and who became the first to learn that wheat was up (or down) on the Brussels exchange could make an overnight fortune. Rival newspaper editors hired riders and fast horses to speed news of commodity prices from Halifax to Boston, but they were no match for the ingenious Daniel Craig, who successfully trained carrier pigeons to carry information about European prices over the same route. Craig was so successful that he was hired by the newly formed Associated Press, a consortium of New York City editors who pooled their resources to gain access to news before it reached the telegraph.

In the five years after the opening of the Baltimore-Washington line, the United States expanded to include Texas, the vast Oregon territory, and all or part of the present states of California, Utah, Nevada, New Mexico, Arizona, Wyoming, and Colorado. Morse, who long had feared that European monarchs were conspiring with the pope to infiltrate Catholic immigrants into the sparsely settled West, was confident that his invention would make it possible to protect American liberty against "Catholic plots." The nation would become a lightning-bound network of communities within instant reach of each other. Should European despots threaten invasion, the whole nation could be activated in a moment. Ironically, European monarchs would pose less of a threat than Americans themselves to the safety of the Republic, which would implode in civil war in 1861.

Questions for Analysis

- What obstacles had to be overcome before Morse's invention came into wide use?

- What role did newspapers play in overcoming these obstacles?

Map 13.3 The Election of 1844

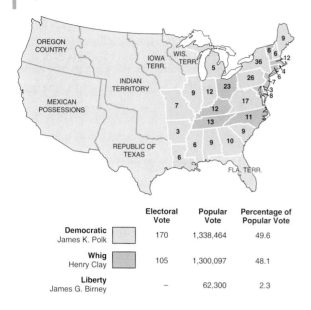

	Electoral Vote	Popular Vote	Percentage of Popular Vote
Democratic James K. Polk	170	1,338,464	49.6
Whig Henry Clay	105	1,300,097	48.1
Liberty James G. Birney	–	62,300	2.3

with each other on close terms, a sign of the maturity of the second party system. A shift of 6,000 votes in New York, where the immigrant vote and Whig defections to the Liberty party hurt Clay, would have given Clay both the state and the presidency.

Manifest Destiny, 1845

The election of 1844 demonstrated one incontestable fact: the annexation of Texas had more national support than Clay had realized. The surging popular sentiment for expansion that made the underdog Polk rather than Clay the man of the hour reflected a growing conviction among the people that America's natural destiny was to expand into Texas and all the way to the Pacific Ocean.

Expansionists emphasized extending the "area of freedom" and talked of "repelling the contaminating proximity of monarchies upon the soil that we have consecrated to the rights of man." For contemporary young Americans like Walt Whitman, such restless expansionism knew few limits. "The more we reflect upon annexation as involving a part of Mexico, the more do doubts and obstacles resolve themselves away," Whitman wrote. "Then there is California, on the way to which lovely tract lies Santa Fe; how long a time will elapse before they shine as two new stars in our mighty firmament?"

Americans awaited only a phrase to capture this ebullient spirit. In 1845, John L. O'Sullivan, a New York Democratic journalist, supplied that phrase when he wrote of "our **manifest destiny** to overspread and to possess the whole of the continent which Providence has given us for the development of the great experiment of liberty and federated self-government entrusted to us."

Advocates of Manifest Destiny used lofty language and invoked God and Nature to sanction expansion. Inasmuch as most proponents of Manifest Destiny were Democrats who favored annexing Texas, northern Whigs frequently dismissed Manifest Destiny as a smoke screen aimed at concealing the evil intent of expanding slavery. In reality, many expansionists were neither supporters of slavery nor zealous annexationists. Most had their eyes not on Texas but on Oregon and California. Despite their flowery phrases, these expansionists rested their case on hard material calculations. Most blamed the post-1837 depression on the failure of the United States to acquire markets for its agricultural surplus and saw the acquisition of Oregon and California as solutions. A Missouri Democrat observed that "the ports of Asia are as convenient to Oregon as the ports of Europe are to the eastern slope of our confederacy, with an infinitely better ocean for navigation." An Alabama Democrat praised California's "safe and capacious harbors," which, he assured, "invite to their bosoms the rich commerce of the East."

Expansionists desired more than profitable trade routes, however. At the heart of their thinking lay an impulse to preserve the predominantly agricultural character of the American people and thereby to safeguard democracy. Fundamentally, most expansionists were Jeffersonians. They equated urbanization and industrialization with social stratification and class strife. After a tour of New England mill towns in 1842, John L. O'Sullivan warned Americans that should they fail to encourage alternatives to factories, the United States would sink to the level of Britain, a nation that the ardent Democratic expansionist James Gordon Bennett described as a land of "bloated wealth" and "terrible misery."

Most Democratic expansionists came to see the acquisition of new territory as a logical complement to their party's policies of low tariffs and decentralized banking. Where tariffs and banks tended to "favor and foster the factory system," expansion would provide farmers with land and with access to foreign markets for their produce. As a consequence, Americans would continue to become farmers, and the foundations of the Republic would remain secure. The acquisition of California and Oregon would provide enough land and harbors to sustain not only the 20 million Americans of 1845 but the 100 million that some expansionists projected for 1900 and the 250 million that O'Sullivan predicted for 1945.

The expansionists' message, especially as delivered by the penny press, made sense to the laboring poor of America's antebellum cities. The *New York Herald,* the nation's largest-selling newspaper in the 1840s, played on the anxieties of its working-class readers by arguing relentlessly for the expulsion of the British from Oregon and for thwarting alleged British plans to abolish slavery in the United States. These readers, many of them fiercely antiblack, anti-British Irish immigrants, welcomed any efforts to open up economic opportunities for the common people. Most also favored the perpetuation of slavery, for the freeing of slaves would throw masses of blacks into the already intense competition for jobs.

The expansionists with whom these laboring-class readers sided drew ideas from Thomas Jefferson, John Quincy Adams, and other leaders of the early Republic who had proclaimed the American people's right to displace both "uncivilized" and European people from the path of their westward movement. Early expansionists, however, had feared that overexpansion might create an ungovernable empire. Jefferson, for example, had proposed an indefinite restriction on the settlement of Louisiana. In contrast, the expansionists of the 1840s, citing the virtues of the telegraph and the railroad, believed that the problem of distance had been "literally annihilated." (See Technology and Culture: The Telegraph.)

Polk and Oregon

The Oregon boundary dispute with Britain grew out of the rising spirit of Manifest Destiny. To soften northern criticism of the still-pending annexation of Texas, the Democrats had included in their 1844 platform the assertion that American title "to the whole of the Territory of Oregon is clear and unquestionable." Taken literally, the platform committed the party to acquire the entire area between California and 54°40′, the southern boundary of Alaska. Since Polk had not yet been elected, the British could safely ignore this extraordinary claim for the moment, and in fact the Oregon issue had aroused far less interest during the campaign than had the annexation of Texas. But in his inaugural address, Polk reasserted the "clear and unquestionable" claim to the "country of Oregon." If by this Polk meant all of Oregon, then the United States, which had never before claimed any part of Oregon north of the forty-ninth parallel, had executed an astounding and belligerent reversal of policy.

Polk's objectives in Oregon were more subtle than his language. He knew that the United States could never obtain all of Oregon without a war with Britain, and he wanted to avoid that. He proposed to use the threat of

hostilities to persuade the British to accept what they had repeatedly rejected in the past—a division of Oregon at the forty-ninth parallel. Such a division, extending the existing boundary between the United States and Canada from the Rockies to the Pacific, would give the United States both the excellent deep-water harbors of Puget Sound and the southern tip of British-controlled Vancouver Island. For their part, the British had long held out for a division along the Columbia River, which entered the Pacific Ocean far south of the forty-ninth parallel (see Map 13.4).

Polk's comments in his inaugural speech roused among westerners a furious interest in acquiring the whole territory. Mass meetings adopted such resolutions as "We are all for Oregon, and *all* Oregon in the West" and "The Whole or None!" Furthermore, each passing year brought new American settlers into Oregon. Even John Quincy Adams, who advocated neither the annexation of Texas nor the 54°40′ boundary for Oregon, believed that the American settlements in Oregon gave the United States a far more reasonable claim to the territory than mere exploration and discovery gave the British. The United States, not Britain, Adams preached, was the nation bound "to make the wilderness blossom as the rose, to establish laws, to increase, multiply, and subdue the earth," all "at the first behest of God Almighty."

Map 13.4 Oregon Boundary Dispute
Although demanding that Britain cede the entire Oregon Territory south of 54°40′, the United States settled for a compromise at the forty-ninth parallel.

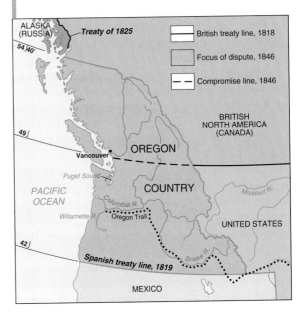

In April 1846, Polk secured from Congress the termination of joint British-American occupation of Oregon and promptly gave Britain the required one-year's notice. With joint occupation abrogated, the British could either go to war over American claims to 54°40′ or negotiate. They chose to negotiate. Although the British raged against "that ill-regulated, overbearing, and aggressive spirit of American democracy," they had too many domestic and foreign problems to welcome a war over what Lord Aberdeen, the British foreign secretary, dismissed as "a few miles of pine swamp." The ensuing treaty provided for a division at the forty-ninth parallel, with some modifications. Britain retained all of Vancouver Island as well as navigation rights on the Columbia River. On June 15, 1846, the Senate ratified the treaty, stipulating that Britain's navigation rights on the Columbia were merely temporary.

The Mexican-American War and Its Aftermath, 1846–1848

Between 1846 and 1848 the United States successfully fought a war with Mexico that led Mexico to renounce all claims to Texas and to cede its provinces of New Mexico and California to the United States. Many Americans rejoiced in the stunning victory. But some recognized that deep divisions over the status of slavery in New Mexico and California boded ill for their nation's future.

The Origins of the Mexican-American War

Even as Polk was challenging Britain over Oregon, the United States and Mexico moved steadily toward war. The impending conflict had both remote and immediate causes. One long-standing grievance lay in the failure of the Mexican government to pay some $2 million in debts owed to American citizens. In addition, bitter memories of the Alamo and the Goliad massacre reinforced American loathing of Mexico. Above all, the issue of Texas embroiled relations between the two nations. Mexico still hoped to regain Texas or at least to keep it independent of the United States.

Behind Mexican anxieties about Texas lay a deeper fear. Mexicans viewed the United States with a mixture of awe and aversion. The United States's political stability contrasted with political chaos in Mexico, where the presidency changed hands twenty times between 1829 and 1844. But Mexicans also saw this "Colossus of the North" as extremely aggressive, prone to trample on anyone in its path and to disguise its intentions with high-sounding phrases like Manifest Destiny. Once in control of Texas, the Mexicans feared, the United States might seize other provinces, perhaps even Mexico itself, and treat the citizens of Mexico much as it treated its slaves.

Unfortunately for Mexico, Polk's election increased the strength of the pro-annexationists, for his campaign had persuaded many northerners that enfolding Texas would bring national benefits. In February 1845, both houses of Congress responded to popular sentiment by passing a resolution annexing Texas. Texans, however, balked, in part because some feared that union with the United States would provoke a Mexican invasion and war on Texas soil.

Confronted by Texan timidity and Mexican belligerence, Polk moved on two fronts. To sweeten the pot for the Texans, he supported their claim to the Rio Grande as the southern boundary of Texas. This claim ran counter to Mexico's view that the Nueces River, a hundred miles northeast of the Rio Grande, bounded Texas. The area between the Nueces and the Rio Grande was largely uninhabited, but the stakes were high. Although only a hundred miles southwest of the Nueces at its mouth on the Gulf of Mexico, the Rio Grande meandered west and then north for nearly two thousand miles and encircled a huge slice of territory, including part of New Mexico. The Texas that Polk proposed to annex thus encompassed far more land than the Texas that had gained independence from Mexico in 1836. On July 4, 1845, reassured by Polk's largesse, a Texas convention overwhelmingly voted to accept annexation. In response to Mexican war preparations, Polk then made a second move, ordering American troops under General **Zachary Taylor** to the edge of the disputed territory. Taylor took up a position at Corpus Christi, a tiny Texas outpost situated just south of the Nueces and hence in territory still claimed by Mexico.

Never far from Polk's thoughts in his insistence on the Rio Grande boundary lay his desire for California and for its fine harbors of San Diego and San Francisco. In fact, Polk had entered the White House with the firm intention of extending American control over California. By the summer of 1845, his followers were openly proclaiming that, if Mexico went to war with the United States over Texas, "the road to California will be open to us." Then in October 1845, Polk received a dispatch from Thomas O. Larkin, the American consul at Monterey, California, that warned darkly of British designs on California but ended with the optimistic assurance that the Mexicans in California would prefer American to British rule. Larkin's message gave Polk the idea that California might be acquired by the same methods as Texas: revolution followed by annexation.

With Texans' acceptance of annexation and Taylor's troops at Corpus Christi, the next move belonged to Mexico. In early 1845, a new Mexican government agreed to negotiate with the United States, and Polk, locked into a war of words with Britain over Oregon, decided to give negotiations a chance. In November 1845, he dispatched John Slidell to Mexico City with instructions to gain Mexican recognition of the annexation of Texas with the Rio Grande border. In exchange, the United States government would assume the debt owed by Mexico to American citizens. Polk also authorized Slidell to offer up to $25 million for California and New Mexico. But by the time Slidell reached Mexico City, the government there had become too weak to make concessions to the United States, and its head, General José Herrera, refused to receive Slidell. Polk then ordered Taylor to move southward to the Rio Grande, hoping to provoke a Mexican attack and unite the American people behind war.

The Mexican government dawdled. Polk was about to send a war message to Congress when word finally arrived that Mexican forces had crossed the Rio Grande and ambushed two companies of Taylor's troops. Now the prowar press had its martyrs. *"American blood has been shed on American soil!"* one of Polk's followers proclaimed. On May 11, Polk informed Congress that war "exists by the act of Mexico herself" and called for a $10 million appropriation to fight the war.

Polk's disarming assertion that the United States was already at war provoked furious opposition in Congress, where antislavery Whigs protested the president's high-handedness. For one thing, the Mexican attack on Taylor's troops had occurred on land never before claimed by the United States. By announcing that war already existed, moreover, Polk seemed to be undercutting Congress's power to declare war and using a mere border incident as a pretext to acquire more slave territory. The pro-Whig *New York Tribune* warned its readers that Polk was "precipitating you into a fathomless abyss of crime and calamity." Antislavery poet James Russell Lowell of Massachusetts wrote of the Polk Democrats,

> *They just want this Californy*
> *So's to lug new slave-states in*
> *To abuse ye, an' to scorn ye,*
> *An' to plunder ye like sin.*

But Polk had maneuvered the Whigs into a corner. Few Whigs could forget that the Federalists' opposition to the War of 1812 had wrecked the Federalist Party, and few

wanted to appear unpatriotic by refusing to support Taylor's beleaguered troops. Swallowing their outrage, most Whigs backed appropriations for war against Mexico.

Polk's single-minded pursuit of his goals had prevailed. A humorless, austere man who banned dancing and liquor at White House receptions, Polk inspired little personal warmth, even among his supporters. But he had clear objectives and pursued them unflinchingly. At every point, he had encountered opposition on the home front: from Whigs who saw him as a reckless adventurer; from northerners of both parties opposed to any expansion of slavery; and from John C. Calhoun, who despised Polk for his high-handedness and fretted that a war with Britain would strip the South of its market for cotton. Yet Polk triumphed over all opposition, in part because of his opponents' fragmentation, in part because of expansion's popular appeal, and in part because of the weakness of his foreign antagonists. Reluctant to fight over Oregon, Britain chose to negotiate. Too weak to negotiate, Mexico chose to fight over territory that it had already lost (Texas) and for territories over which its hold was feeble (California and New Mexico).

The Mexican-American War

Most European observers expected Mexico to win the war. Its regular army was four times the size of the American forces, and it was fighting on home ground. The United States, which had botched its one previous attempt to invade a foreign nation, Canada in 1812, now had to sustain offensive operations in an area remote from American settlements. American expansionists, however, hardly expected the Mexicans to fight at all. A leading Democrat confidently predicted that Mexico would offer only "a slight resistance to the North American race" because its mixed Spanish and Indian population had been degraded by "amalgamation." The newspaper publisher James Gordon Bennett proclaimed that the "imbecile" Mexicans were "as sure to melt away at the approach of [American] energy and enterprise as snow before a southern sun."

In fact, the Mexicans fought bravely and stubbornly, although unsuccessfully. In May 1846, Taylor, "Old Rough and Ready," routed the Mexican army in Texas and pursued it across the Rio Grande, eventually capturing the major city of Monterrey in September. War enthusiasm surged in the United States. Recruiting posters blared, "Here's to old Zach! Glorious Times! Roast Beef, Ice Cream, and Three Months' Advance." Taylor's conspicuously ordinary manner—he went into battle wearing a straw hat and a plain brown coat—endeared him to the public, which kicked up its heels in celebration to the "Rough and Ready Polka" and the "General Taylor Quick Step."

After taking Monterrey, Taylor, starved for supplies, halted and granted Mexico an eight-week armistice. Eager to undercut Taylor's popularity—the Whigs were already touting him as a presidential candidate—Polk stripped him of half his forces and reassigned them to General Winfield Scott. Scott was to mount an amphibious attack on Vera Cruz, far to the south, and proceed to Mexico City, following the path of Cortés and his conquistadors. Events outstripped Polk's scheme, however, when Taylor defeated a far larger Mexican army at the Battle of Buena Vista, on February 22–23, 1847.

While Taylor was winning fame in northern Mexico, and before Scott had launched his attack on Vera Cruz, American forces farther north were dealing decisive blows to the remnants of Mexican rule in New Mexico and California. In the spring of 1846, Colonel Stephen Kearny marched an army from Fort Leavenworth, Kansas, toward Santa Fe. Like the pioneers on the Oregon Trail, Kearny's men faced immense natural obstacles as they marched over barren ground. Finally reaching New Mexico, Kearny took the territory by a combination of bluff, bluster, and perhaps bribery, without firing a shot. The Mexican governor, following his own advice that "it is better to be thought brave than to be so," fled at Kearny's approach. After suppressing a brief rebellion by Mexicans and Indians, Kearny sent a detachment of his army south into Mexico. There, having marched fifteen hundred miles from Fort Leavenworth, these troops joined Taylor in time for the Battle of Buena Vista.

Like New Mexico, California fell easily into American hands. In 1845, Polk had ordered Commodore John D. Sloat and his Pacific Squadron to occupy California's ports in the event of war with Mexico. To ensure victory, Polk also dispatched a courier overland with secret orders for one of the most colorful and important actors in the conquest of California, John C. Frémont. A Georgia-born adventurer, Frémont had married Jesse Benton, the daughter of powerful Senator Thomas Hart Benton of Missouri. Benton used his influence to have accounts of Frémont's explorations in the Northwest (mainly written by Jesse Benton Frémont) published as government documents. All of this earned glory for Frémont as "the Great Pathfinder." Finally overtaken by Polk's courier in Oregon, Frémont was dispatched to California to "watch over the interests of the United States." In June 1846, a small force of American settlers loyal to Frémont seized the village of Sonoma and proclaimed the independent "Bear Flag Republic." The combined efforts of Frémont, Sloat, his successor David Stockton, and Stephen Kearny (who arrived in California after capturing New Mexico) quickly established American control over California.

Patriotism and the Mexican War
U.S. soldiers commonly wore tall hats known as shako caps during the Mexican War. The caps were adorned with decorative plates showing the eagle spreading its wings, the symbol of Manifest Destiny.

The final and most important campaign of the war saw the conquest of Mexico City itself. In March 1847, Winfield Scott landed near Vera Cruz at the head of twelve thousand men and quickly pounded the city into submission. Moving inland, Scott encountered Santa Anna at the seemingly impregnable pass of Cerro Gordo, but a young captain in Scott's command, Robert E. Lee, helped find a trail that led around the Mexican flank to a small peak overlooking the pass. There Scott planted howitzers and, on April 18, stormed the pass and routed the Mexicans. Scott now moved directly on Mexico City. Taking the key fortresses of Churubusco and Chapultepec (where another young captain, Ulysses S. Grant, was cited for bravery), Scott took the city on September 13, 1847 (see Map 13.5).

In virtually all these encounters on Mexican soil, the Mexicans were numerically superior. In the final assault on Mexico City, Scott commanded eleven thousand troops against Santa Anna's twenty-five thousand. But doom stalked the Mexican army. Hampered by Santa Anna's nearly unbroken string of military miscalculations, the Mexicans fell victim to the vastly superior American artillery and to the ability of the Americans to

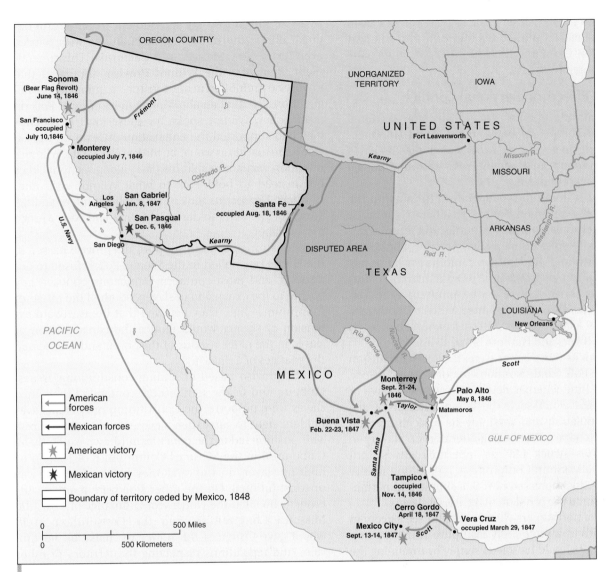

Map 13.5 Major Battles of the Mexican-American War
The Mexican War's decisive campaign began with General Winfield Scott's capture of Vera Cruz and ended with his conquest of Mexico City.

organize massive military movements. The "barbarians of the North" (as Mexicans called the American soldiers) died like flies from yellow fever, and they carried into battle the agonies of venereal disease, which they picked up (and left) in many of the Mexican towns they took. But the Americans benefited from the unprecedented quality of their weapons, supplies, and organization.

By the **Treaty of Guadalupe Hidalgo** (February 2, 1848), Mexico ceded Texas with the Rio Grande boundary, New Mexico, and California to the United States. In return, the United States assumed the claims of American citizens against the Mexican government and paid Mexico $15 million. Although the United States gained

the present states of California, Nevada, New Mexico, Utah, most of Arizona, and parts of Colorado and Wyoming, some rabid expansionists in the Senate denounced the treaty because it failed to include all of Mexico. But the acquisition of California, with its excellent Pacific ports of San Diego and San Francisco, satisfied Polk. Few senators, moreover, wanted to annex the mixed Spanish and Indian population of Mexico. A writer in the *Democratic Review* expressed the prevailing view that "the annexation of the country [Mexico] to the United States would be a calamity," for it would incorporate into the United States "ignorant and indolent half-civilized Indians," not to mention "free negroes and mulattoes" left over from the British slave trade. The virulent racism of American leaders allowed the Mexicans to retain part of their nation. On March 10, 1848, the Senate ratified the treaty by a vote of 38 to 10.

The War's Effects on Sectional Conflict

Wartime patriotic enthusiasm did not stop sectional conflict from sharpening between 1846 and 1848. Questions relating to territorial expansion intensified this conflict, but so too did President Polk's uncompromising and literal Jacksonianism.

Polk had restored the Independent Treasury, to the Whigs' dismay, and had eroded Democratic unity by pursuing Jacksonian policies on tariffs and internal improvements. Despite his campaign promise, applauded by many northern Democrats, to combine a revenue tariff with a measure of protection, his administration's Tariff of 1846 had slashed duties to the minimum necessary for revenue. Polk then disappointed western Democrats, thirsting for federal aid for internal improvements, by vetoing the Rivers and Harbors Bill of 1846.

Important as these issues were, territorial expansion sparked the Polk administration's major battles. To Polk, it mattered little whether new territories were slave or free. Expansion would serve the nation's interests by dispersing population and retaining its agricultural and democratic character. Focusing attention on slavery in the territories struck him as "not only unwise but wicked." The Missouri Compromise, prohibiting slavery north of 36°30′, impressed him as a simple and permanent solution to the problem of territorial slavery.

But many northerners were coming to see slavery in the territories as a profoundly disruptive issue that neither could nor should be solved simply by extending the 36°30′ line westward. Antislavery Whigs who opposed any extension of slavery on moral grounds were still a minority within their party. They posed a lesser threat to Polk than did northern Democrats who feared that expansion of slavery into California and New Mexico (parts of each lay south of 36°30′) would deter free laborers from settling those territories. These Democrats argued that competition with slaves degraded free labor, that the westward extension of slavery would check the westward migration of free labor, and that such a barrier would aggravate the social problems already beginning to plague the East: class strife, social stratification, and labor protest.

The Wilmot Proviso

A young Democratic congressman from Pennsylvania, David Wilmot, became the spokesman for these disaffected northern Democrats. On a sizzling night in August 1846, he introduced an amendment to an appropriations bill for the upcoming negotiations with Mexico over Texas, New Mexico, and California. This amendment, known as the **Wilmot Proviso**, stipulated that slavery be prohibited in any territory acquired by the negotiations. Neither an abolitionist nor a critic of Polk on tariff policy, Wilmot spoke for those loyal Democrats who had supported the annexation of Texas on the assumption that Texas would be the last slave state. Wilmot's intention was not to split his party along sectional lines but instead to hold Polk to what Wilmot and other northern Democrats took as an implicit understanding: Texas for the slaveholders, California and New Mexico for free labor.

With strong northern support, the proviso passed in the House but stalled in the Senate. Polk refused to endorse it, and most southern Democrats opposed any barrier to the expansion of slavery south of the Missouri Compromise line. They believed that the westward extension of slavery would reduce the concentration of slaves in the older regions of the South and thus lessen the chances of a slave revolt.

The proviso raised unsettling constitutional issues. Calhoun and fellow southerners contended that since slaves were property, the Constitution protected slaveholders' right to carry their slaves wherever they chose. This position led to the conclusion (drawn explicitly by Calhoun) that the Missouri Compromise of 1820, prohibiting slavery in the territories north of 36°30′, was unconstitutional. On the other side were many northerners who cited the Northwest Ordinance of 1787, the Missouri Compromise, and the Constitution itself, which gave Congress the power to "make all needful rules and regulations respecting the territory or other property belonging to the United States," as justification for congressional legislation on slavery in the territories. With the election of 1848 approaching, politicians of both sides, eager to hold their parties together and avert civil war, frantically searched for a middle ground.

The Election of 1848

Having asserted that their policies of national banking and high tariffs alone could pull the nation out of the depression, the Whigs had watched in dismay as prosperity returned under Polk's program of an independent treasury and low tariffs. Never before had Clay's American System seemed so irrelevant. But the Wilmot Proviso gave the Whigs a political windfall; originating in the Democratic Party, it enabled the Whigs to portray themselves as the South's only dependable friends.

"Union" Woodcut, by Thomas W. Strong, 1848
This 1848 campaign poster for Zachary Taylor reminded Americans of his military victories, unmilitary bearing (note the civilian dress and straw hat), and deliberately vague promises. As president, Taylor finally took a stand on the issue of slavery in the Mexican cession, but his position angered the South.

These considerations inclined the majority of Whigs toward Zachary Taylor. As a Louisiana slaveholder, he had obvious appeal to the South. As a political newcomer, he had no loyalty to the discredited American System. As a war hero, he had broad national appeal. Nominating Taylor as their presidential candidate in 1848, the Whigs presented him as an ideal man "without regard to creeds or principles" and ran him without any platform.

The Democrats faced a greater challenge because David Wilmot was one of their own. They could not ignore the issue of slavery in the territories, but if they embraced the position of either Wilmot or Calhoun, the party would split along sectional lines. When Polk declined to run for reelection, the Democrats nominated Lewis Cass of Michigan, who solved their dilemma by announcing the doctrine of "squatter sovereignty," or popular sovereignty as it was later called. Cass argued that Congress should let the question of slavery in the territories

be decided by the people who settled there. Squatter sovereignty appealed to many because of its arresting simplicity and vagueness. It neatly dodged the divisive issue of whether Congress had the power to prohibit territorial slavery. In fact, few Democrats wanted a definitive answer to this question. As long as the doctrine remained ambiguous, northern and southern Democrats alike could interpret it to their respective benefit.

In the campaign, both parties tried to ignore the issue of territorial slavery, but neither succeeded. A faction of the Democratic Party in New York that favored the Wilmot Proviso, called the Barnburners, broke away from the party, linked up with former Liberty party abolitionists, and courted antislavery "Conscience" Whigs to create the **Free-Soil party**. Declaring their dedication to "Free Trade, Free Labor, Free Speech, and Free Men," the Free-Soilers nominated Martin Van Buren on a platform opposing any extension of slavery.

Zachary Taylor benefited from the Democrats' alienation of key northern states over the tariff issue, from Democratic disunity over the Wilmot Proviso, and from his war-hero stature. He captured a majority of electoral votes in both North and South. Although failing to carry any state, the Free-Soil party ran well enough in the North to demonstrate the grass-roots popularity of opposition to slavery extension. Defections to the Free-Soilers, for example, probably cost the Whigs Ohio. By showing that opposition to the spread of slavery had far greater appeal than the staunch abolitionism of the old Liberty party, the Free-Soilers sent the Whigs and Democrats a message that they would be unable to ignore in future elections.

The California Gold Rush

When Wilmot announced his proviso, the issue of slavery in the Far West was more abstract than practical because Mexico had yet to cede any territory and relatively few Americans resided in either California or New Mexico. Nine days before the signing of the Treaty of Guadalupe Hidalgo, however, an American carpenter discovered gold in the foothills of California's Sierra Nevada range. The **California gold rush** began within a few months. A San Francisco newspaper complained that "the whole country from San Francisco to Los Angeles, and from the shore to the base of the Sierra Nevada, resounds with the sordid cry to *gold*, GOLD, GOLD! while the field is left half-planted, the house half-built, and everything neglected but the manufacture of shovels and pickaxes."

Shovels and pickaxes to dig gold from crevices in and around streams were enough for most of the early gold prospectors. But as the most accessible deposits of gold were depleted, individual miners increasingly formed combinations to undertake such costly projects as diverting the course of streams and rivers to uncover gold-laden beds or excavating shafts in the earth. "Hydraulic mining," a development of the mid-1850s, involved channeling water from streams through narrow hoses to blast thousands of cubic yards of earth from hillsides and then sifting the earth through sluices to capture the precious particles of gold.

By December 1848, pamphlets with titles like *The Emigrant's Guide to the Gold Mines* had hit the streets of New York City. Arriving by sea and by land, gold-rushers drove up the population of California from around 15,000 in the summer of 1848 to nearly 250,000 by 1852. Miners came from every corner of the world. A female journalist reported walking through a mining camp in the Sierras and hearing English, Italian, French, Spanish, German, and Hawaiian. Conflicts over claims quickly led to violent clashes between Americans and Hispanics (mostly Mexicans, Chileans, and Peruvians). Americans especially resented the Chinese who flooded into California in the 1850s, most as contract laborers for wealthy Chinese merchants, and who struck Americans as slave laborers. Yet rampant prejudice against the Chinese did not stop some American businessmen from hiring them as contract workers for the American mining combinations that were forming in the 1850s.

Within a decade, the gold rush turned the sleepy Hispanic town of Yerba Buena, with 150 people in 1846, into "a pandemonium of a city" of 50,000 known as San Francisco. No other U.S. city contained people from more parts of the world. Many of the immigrants were Irish convicts who arrived by way of Australia, to which they had been exiled for their crimes. All the ethnic and racial tensions of the gold fields were evident in the city. A young clergyman confessed that he carried a harmless-looking cane, which "will be found to contain a sword two-and-a-half feet long." In 1851, San Francisco's merchants organized the first of several Committees of Vigilance, which patrolled the streets, deported undesirables, and tried and hanged alleged thieves and murderers.

With the gold rush, the issue of slavery in the Far West became practical as well as abstract, and immediate rather than remote. The newcomers attracted to California in 1849 included free blacks and slaves brought by planters from the South. White prospectors loathed the thought of competing with either of these groups and wanted to drive all blacks, along with California's Indians, out of the gold fields. Tensions also intensified between the gold-rushers and the *Californios,* whose extensive (if often vaguely worded) land holdings were protected by the terms of the Treaty of Guadalupe Hidalgo. Spawned by disputed claims and prejudice, violence mounted, and demands grew for a strong civilian government to replace the ineffective military government in place in California since the war. Polk began to fear that without a satisfactory congressional solution to the slavery issue, Californians might organize a government independent of the United States. The gold rush thus guaranteed that the question of slavery in the Mexican cession would be the first item on the agenda for Polk's successor and, indeed, for the nation.

Conclusion

The massive immigration of the 1840s changed the face of American politics. Angered by Whig nativism and anti-Catholicism, the new German and Irish immigrants swelled the ranks of the Democratic Party. Meanwhile, the Whigs were unraveling. The untimely death of President Harrison brought John Tyler, a Democrat in Whig's clothing, to the White House. Tyler's vetoes of key Whig measures left the Whig party in disarray. In combination, these developments led to the surprise election of James K. Polk, a Democrat and ardent expansionist, in 1844.

Wrapped in the language of Manifest Destiny, westward expansion appealed to Americans for many reasons. It fit their belief that settlers had more right to the American continent than did the Europeans (who based their claims on centuries-old explorations), the lethargic and Catholic Mexicans, and the nomadic Indians. Expansion promised trade routes to the Pacific, more land for farming, and, in the case of Texas, more slave states. Polk simultaneously rode the wave of national sentiment for Manifest Destiny and gave it direction by annexing Texas, provoking a crisis with Britain over Oregon, and leading the United States into a war with Mexico. Initially, Polk succeeded in uniting broad swaths of public opinion behind expansion. Polk and his followers ingeniously argued that national expansion was in the interests of northern working-class voters, many of them immigrants. By encouraging the spread of slavery to the Southwest, the argument went, the annexation of Texas would reduce the

Chronology, 1840–1848

1822	Stephen F. Austin founds the first American community in Texas.
1830	Mexico closes Texas to further American immigration.
1835	Santa Anna invades Texas.
1836	Texas declares its independence from Mexico.
	Fall of the Alamo.
	Goliad massacre.
	Battle of San Jacinto.
1840	William Henry Harrison elected president.
1841	Harrison dies; John Tyler becomes president.
1842	Webster-Ashburton Treaty.
1844	James K. Polk elected president.
1845	Congress votes joint resolution to annex Texas.
	Mexico rejects Slidell mission.
1846	The United States declares war on Mexico.
	John C. Frémont proclaims the Bear Flag Republic in California.
	Congress votes to accept a settlement of the Oregon boundary issue with Britain.
	Tariff of 1846.
	Colonel Stephen Kearny occupies Santa Fe.
	Wilmot Proviso introduced.
	Taylor takes Monterrey.
1847	Taylor defeats Santa Anna at the Battle of Buena Vista.
	Vera Cruz falls to Winfield Scott.
	Mexico City falls to Scott.
	Lewis Cass's principle of "squatter sovereignty."
1848	Gold discovered in California.
	Treaty of Guadalupe Hidalgo.
	Taylor elected president.

chances of a race war in the Southeast that might spill over into the North.

Yet even as war with Mexico was commencing, cracks in Polk's coalition were starting to show. The Wilmot Proviso exposed deep sectional divisions that had only been papered over by the ideal of Manifest Destiny and that would explode in the secession of Free-Soil Democrats in 1848. Victorious over Mexico and enriched by the discovery of gold in California, Americans counted the blessings of expansion but began to fear its costs.

Key Terms

Tejano
Stephen F. Austin
German and Irish immigrants
nativism
Commonwealth v. *Hunt*
Oregon country
Californios
Santa Fe Trail
Alamo
Sam Houston
John Tyler
annexation of Texas
James K. Polk
Manifest Destiny
Zachary Taylor
Treaty of Guadalupe Hidalgo
Wilmot Proviso
Free-Soil party
California gold rush

For Further Reference

Peter J. Blodgett, *Land of Golden Dreams* (1999). A vivid account of California in the gold rush.

William R. Brock, *Parties and Political Conscience: American Dilemmas, 1840–1850* (1979). An excellent interpretive study of the politics of the 1840s.

William H. Goetzmann, *When the Eagle Screamed: The Romantic Horizon in American Diplomacy, 1800–1860* (1966). A lively overview of antebellum expansionism.

Maldwyn A. Jones, *American Immigration* (1960). An excellent brief introduction to immigration.

David Montejano, *Anglos and Mexicans in the Making of Texas, 1836–1986* (1987). A grand account of an often neglected topic.

Michael A. Morrison, *Slavery and the American West: The Eclipse of Manifest Destiny and the Coming of the Civil War* (1997). An important study of a key issue.

Malcolm J. Rorabaugh, *Days of Gold: The California Gold Rush and the American Nation* (1997). Emphasizes how the discovery of gold in California reaffirmed the American belief that, regardless of family name or education, anyone who worked hard in America could grow rich.

Charles G. Sellers, *James K. Polk: Continentalist, 1843–1846* (1966). An outstanding political biography.

Chapter 14

Members of the Kansas Free State Battery Stand Ready with a Cannon Left Over from the Mexican War, 1856
They were not wearing uniforms, but these Kansans were soldiers fighting to make Kansas a free state.

From Compromise to Secession, 1850–1861

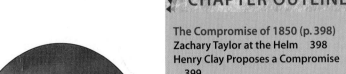

John Brown

I n early July 1859, a man calling himself Isaac Smith and claiming to be a cattle dealer rented a dilapidated farmhouse a few miles from Harpers Ferry, Virginia, the site of a federal arsenal and armory. Before long others arrived, including two young women; soon they were busy unloading boxes of what Smith called "hardware." Although the men seemed reclusive, the women chatted amiably with neighbors, to whom everything appeared normal.

In reality, nothing was normal. "Smith" was **John Brown**, a brooding abolitionist with a price on his head for the massacre of white southerners in Kansas in 1856 and with a conviction that God had ordained him "to purge this land with blood" of the evil of slavery. One of the women was his daughter, the other his daughter-in-law. The "hardware" consisted of rifles and revolvers, which Brown and his recruits—white idealists (including three of Brown's sons), free blacks, and fugitive slaves—intended to use to raid the arsenal and ignite slave insurrections throughout the South.

In some respects, Brown was a marginal figure in the abolitionist movement. Unlike better-known abolitionists, he had written no stirring tracts against slavery. But in Kansas, where civil war between free-staters and slave-staters had broken out in the mid-1850s, Brown had acquired a reputation as someone who could handle the rough stuff. He fascinated many eastern abolitionists, themselves pacifists, who were starting to suspect that only violence would end slavery. Little suspecting his plans for Harpers Ferry, they accepted his disavowal of a role in the Kansas massacre and endorsed, with contributions, his plans to carry on the fight against those who would forcibly turn Kansas into a slave state.

On the moonless evening of October 16, 1859, Brown and eighteen recruits seized the arsenal and armory at Harpers Ferry. Expecting slaves—half of Harpers Ferry's population was enslaved—to rally at once to his cause, Brown then did nothing, while local whites, jumpy about the possibility of a slave insurrection ever since Nat Turner's 1831 rebellion (see Chapter 12), spread the alarm. Soon armed locals—their courage steeled by liquor—militia from surrounding areas, and U.S. Marines dispatched by President James Buchanan and under the command of Colonel Robert E. Lee clogged the streets of Harpers Ferry. On October 18, the Marines stormed the armory where Brown and most of his men had taken refuge, severely wounded and captured Brown, and killed or mortally wounded ten others, including two of Brown's sons. A handful escaped but were eventually captured and executed. Brown himself was speedily tried, convicted, and hanged.

In the immediate wake of Brown's capture, prominent northerners distanced themselves from him. His lawyers contended that he was insane and hence not culpable for his deeds. But Brown himself derided the insanity defense. His conduct during his brief imprisonment was serene, his words eloquent. He told his captors that he had rendered to God the "greatest service man can." Gradually, northern opinion became more sympathetic to Brown, seeing him as a martyr. Ralph Waldo Emerson exulted that Brown's execution would "make the gallows as glorious as the cross." For their part, white southerners came to reject the notion that Brown's plot was the work of an isolated lunatic. A search of the farmhouse after Brown's capture turned up incriminating correspondence between Brown and leading northern abolitionists. To slaveholders, Brown may have botched the raid, but his plan to arm nonslaveholding southern whites with guns and disaffected slaves with pikes (Brown had contracted for the manufacture of a thousand pikes) was plausible. In all the southern states, slaveholding whites were outnumbered by people who did not own slaves (slaves, free blacks, and nonslaveholding whites) by more than three to one. In slaveholders' eyes, Brown was a tool of the abolition movement that would drench the South in blood.

Focus Questions

- How did the Fugitive Slave Act lead to the undoing of the Compromise of 1850?

- Why did the Whig party collapse after the Kansas-Nebraska Act while the Democratic Party survived?

- How did the Republican doctrine of free soil unify northerners against the South?

- Why did southerners conclude that the North was bent on extinguishing slavery in southern states?

The Compromise of 1850

Ralph Waldo Emerson's grim prediction that an American victory in the Mexican-American War would be like swallowing arsenic proved disturbingly accurate. When the war ended in 1848, the United States contained an equal number of free and slave states (fifteen each), but the vast territory acquired by the war threatened to upset this balance. Any solution to the question of slavery in the Mexican cession ensured controversy. The doctrine of **free soil**, which insisted that Congress prohibit slavery in the territories, horrified southerners. The idea of extending the Missouri Compromise line of 36°30' to the Pacific angered free-soilers because it would allow slavery in New Mexico and southern California, while it angered southern proslavery extremists because it conceded that Congress could bar slavery in some territories. A third solution, **popular sovereignty**, which promised to ease the slavery extension issue out of national politics by allowing each territory to decide the question for itself, pleased neither free-soilers nor proslavery extremists.

As the rhetoric escalated, events plunged the nation into crisis. Utah and then California, both acquired from Mexico, sought admission to the Union as free states. Texas, admitted as a slave state in 1845, aggravated matters by claiming the eastern half of New Mexico, where the Mexican government had abolished slavery.

By 1850, these territorial issues had become intertwined with two other concerns. Northerners increasingly attacked slavery in the District of Columbia, within the shadow of the Capitol; southerners complained about lax enforcement of the Fugitive Slave Act of 1793. Any broad compromise would have to take both troublesome matters into account.

Zachary Taylor at the Helm

Although elected president in 1848 without a platform, Zachary Taylor came to office with a clear position on the issue of slavery in the Mexican cession. A slaveholder himself, he took for granted the South's need to defend slavery. Taylor insisted that southerners would best protect slavery if they refrained from rekindling the issue of slavery in the territories. He rejected Calhoun's idea that the protection of slavery in the southern states ultimately depended on the expansion of slavery into the western territories. In Taylor's eyes, neither California nor New Mexico was suited to slavery; in 1849 he told a Pennsylvania audience that "the people of the North need have no apprehension of the further extension of slavery."

Although Taylor looked to the exclusion of slavery from California and New Mexico, his position differed from the one embodied in the Wilmot Proviso, the free-soil measure proposed in 1846 by a northern Democrat. The proviso had insisted that Congress bar slavery in any territories that might be ceded by Mexico. Taylor's plan, in contrast, left the decision to the states. Recognizing that most Californians opposed slavery in their state, Taylor had prompted California to bypass the territorial stage that normally preceded statehood, to draw up its constitution in 1849, and to apply directly for admission as a free state. The president strongly hinted that he expected New Mexico to do the same.

Taylor's strategy appeared to guarantee a quick, practical solution to the problem of slavery extension. It would give the North two new free states. At the same time, it would acknowledge a position upon which all southerners agreed: a state could bar or permit slavery as it chose. This conviction in fact served as the very foundation of the South's defense of slavery, its armor against all the onslaughts of the abolitionists. Nothing in the Constitution forbade a state to act one way or the other on slavery.

Despite its practical features, Taylor's plan dismayed southerners of both parties. Having gored the Democrats in 1848 as the party of the Wilmot Proviso, southern Whigs expected more from the president than a proposal that in effect yielded the proviso's goal—the banning of slavery in the Mexican cession. Many southerners, in addition, questioned Taylor's assumption that slavery could never take root in California or New Mexico. To one observer, who declared that the whole controversy over slavery in the Mexican cession "related to an imaginary negro in an impossible place," southerners pointed out that both areas already contained slaves and that slaves could be employed profitably in mining gold and silver. "California is by nature," a southerner proclaimed, "peculiarly a slaveholding State." Calhoun trembled at the thought of adding more free states. "If this scheme excluding slavery from California and New Mexico should be carried out—if we are to be reduced to a mere handful . . . wo, wo, I say to this Union." Disillusioned with Taylor, nine southern states agreed to send delegations to a southern convention that was scheduled to meet in Nashville in June 1850.

Henry Clay Proposes a Compromise

Taylor might have been able to contain mounting southern opposition if he had held a secure position in the Whig party. But such leading Whigs as Daniel Webster of Massachusetts and Henry Clay of Kentucky, each of whom had presidential aspirations, never reconciled themselves to Taylor, a political novice. Early in 1850, Clay boldly challenged Taylor's leadership by forging a set of compromise proposals to resolve the range of contentious issues. Clay proposed (1) the admission of California as a free state; (2) the division of the remainder of the Mexican cession into two territories, New Mexico and Utah (formerly Deseret), without federal restrictions on slavery; (3) the settlement of the Texas–New Mexico boundary dispute on terms favorable to New Mexico; (4) as an incentive for Texas, an agreement that the federal government would assume the considerable public debt of Texas; (5) the continuance of slavery in the District of Columbia but the abolition of the slave trade; and (6) a more effective fugitive slave law.

Clay rolled all of these proposals into a single "omnibus" bill, which he hoped to steer through Congress. The debates over the omnibus during the late winter and early spring of 1850 witnessed the last major appearances on the public stage of Clay, Webster, and Calhoun—the trio of distinguished senators whose lives had mirrored every public event of note since the War of 1812. Clay played the role of the conciliator, as he had during the controversy over Missouri in 1820 and again during the nullification crisis in the early 1830s. Warning the South against secession, he assured the North that nature would check the spread of slavery more effectively than a thousand Wilmot Provisos. Gaunt and gloomy, a dying Calhoun listened as another senator read his address for him, a repetition of what he had been saying for years: the North's growing power, enhanced by protective tariffs and by the Missouri Compromise's exclusion of slaveholders from the northern part of the Louisiana Purchase, had created an imbalance between the sections. Only a decision by the North to treat the South as an equal could now save the Union. Three days later, Daniel Webster, who believed that slavery, "like the cotton-plant, is confined to certain parallels of climate," delivered his memorable "Seventh of March" speech. Speaking not "as a Massachusetts man, nor as a Northern man, but as an American," Webster chided the North for trying to "reenact the will of God" by legally excluding slavery from the Mexican cession and declared himself a forthright proponent of compromise.

However eloquent, the conciliatory voices of Clay and Webster made few converts. With every call for compromise, some northern or southern speaker would rise and inflame passions. The antislavery New York Whig William Seward, for example, enraged southerners by talking of a "**higher law** than the Constitution"—namely, the will of God against the extension of slavery. Clay's compromise became tied up in a congressional committee. To worsen matters, Clay, who at first had pretended that his proposals were in the spirit of Taylor's plan, broke openly with the president in May, and Taylor attacked Clay as a glory-hunter.

As the Union faced its worst crisis since 1789, a series of events in the summer of 1850 eased the way toward a resolution. When the Nashville convention assembled in June, extremists—called the fire-eaters because of their recklessness—boldly made their presence felt. But their talk of "southern rights" smelled suspiciously like a plot to disrupt the Union. "I would rather sit in council with the six thousand dead who have died of cholera in St. Louis," Senator Thomas Hart Benton of Missouri declared, "than go into convention with such a gang of scamps." Only nine of the fifteen slave states, most in the Lower South, sent delegates to the convention, where moderates took control and isolated the extremists. Then Zachary Taylor, after eating and drinking too much at an Independence Day celebration, fell ill with gastroenteritis and died on July 9.

His successor, Vice President Millard Fillmore, quickly proved to be more favorable than Taylor to the Senate's compromise measure by appointing Daniel Webster as his secretary of state. After the compromise suffered a devastating series of amendments in late July, Illinois Democrat **Stephen A. Douglas** took over the floor leadership from the exhausted Clay. Recognizing that Clay's "omnibus" lacked majority support in Congress, Douglas chopped it into a series of separate measures and sought to secure passage of each bill individually. To secure support from Democrats, he included the principle of popular sovereignty in the bills organizing New Mexico and Utah. By summer's end, Congress had passed each component of the **Compromise of 1850**: statehood for California; territorial status for Utah and New Mexico, allowing popular sovereignty; resolution of the Texas–New Mexico boundary disagreement; federal assumption of the Texas debt; abolition of the slave trade in the District of Columbia; and a new fugitive slave law (see Map 14.1).

Assessing the Compromise

President Fillmore hailed the compromise as a "final settlement" of sectional divisions, and Clay's reputation for conciliation reached new heights. Yet the compromise did not bridge the underlying differences between the two sections. Far from leaping forward to save the Union, Congress had backed into the Compromise of 1850; the majority of congressmen in one or another section opposed virtually all of the specific bills that made up the compromise. Most southerners, for example, voted against the admission of California and the abolition of the slave trade in the District of Columbia; the majority of northerners opposed the Fugitive Slave Act and the organization of New Mexico and Utah without a forthright congressional prohibition of slavery. These measures passed only because the minority of congressmen who genuinely desired compromise combined with the majority in either the North or the South who favored each specific bill.

Each section both gained and lost from the Compromise of 1850. The North won California as a free state, New Mexico and Utah as likely future free states, a favorable settlement of the Texas–New Mexico boundary (most of the disputed area was awarded to New Mexico, a probable free state), and the abolition of the slave trade in the District of Columbia. The South's benefits were cloudier. By stipulating popular sovereignty for New Mexico and Utah, the compromise, to most southerners' relief, had buried the Wilmot Proviso's insistence that Congress formally prohibit slavery in these territories. But to southerners' dismay, the position of the free-soilers remained viable, for the compromise left open the question of whether Congress could prohibit slavery in territories outside of the Mexican cession.

Not surprisingly, southerners reacted ambivalently to the Compromise

Map 14.1 The Compromise of 1850
The Compromise of 1850 admitted California as a free state. Utah and New Mexico were left open to slavery or freedom on the principle of popular sovereignty.

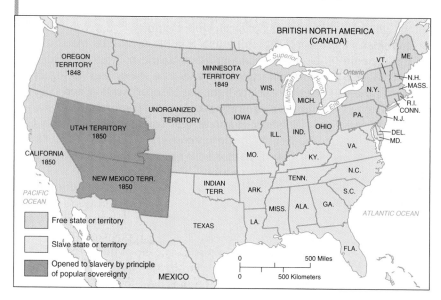

of 1850. In southern state elections during the fall of 1850 and in 1851, procompromise, or Unionist, candidates thrashed anticompromise candidates who talked of southern rights and secession. But even southern Unionists did not dismiss the possibility of secession. Unionists in Georgia, for example, forged the celebrated Georgia Platform, which threatened secession if Congress either prohibited slavery in New Mexico or Utah, or repealed the Fugitive Slave Act.

The one clear advantage gained by the South, a more stringent fugitive slave law, quickly proved a mixed blessing. Because few slaves had been taken into the Mexican cession, the question of slavery there had a hypothetical quality. However, the issues raised by the new fugitive slave law were far from hypothetical; the law authorized real southerners to pursue real fugitives on northern soil. Here was a concrete issue to which the average northerner, who may never have seen a slave and who cared little about slavery a thousand miles away, would respond with fury.

Enforcement of the Fugitive Slave Act

Northern moderates accepted the **Fugitive Slave Act** as the price of saving the Union. But the law contained a string of features distasteful to moderates and outrageous to staunchly antislavery northerners. It denied alleged fugitives the right of trial by jury, did not allow them to testify in their own behalf, permitted their return to slavery merely on the testimony of the claimant, and enabled court-appointed commissioners to collect ten dollars if they ruled for the slaveholder but only five dollars if they ruled for the fugitive. In authorizing federal marshals to raise posses to pursue fugitives on northern soil, the law threatened to turn the North into "one vast hunting ground." In addition, the law targeted not only recent runaways but also those who had fled the South decades earlier. For example, it allowed slave-catchers to wrench a former slave from his family in Indiana in 1851 and return him to the master from whom he had fled in 1832. Above all, the law brought home to northerners the uncomfortable truth that the continuation of slavery depended on their complicity. By legalizing the activities of slave-catchers on northern soil, the law reminded northerners that slavery was a national problem, not merely a peculiar southern institution.

Antislavery northerners assailed the law as the "vilest monument of infamy of the nineteenth century." "Let the President . . . drench our land of freedom in blood," proclaimed Ohio Whig congressman Joshua Giddings, "but he will never make us obey that law." His support for the law turned Senator Daniel Webster of Massachusetts into a villain in the eyes of the very people who for years had revered him as the "godlike Daniel." The abolitionist poet John Greenleaf Whittier wrote of his fallen idol,

All else is gone; from those giant eyes
The soul has fled:
When faith is lost, when honor dies,
The man is dead.

Efforts to catch and return fugitive slaves inflamed feelings in both the North and the South. In 1854, a Boston mob, aroused by antislavery speeches, broke into a courthouse and killed a guard in an abortive effort to rescue the fugitive slave Anthony Burns. Determined to prove that the law could be enforced "even in Boston," President Franklin Pierce sent a detachment of federal troops to escort Burns to the harbor, where a ship carried him back to slavery. No witness would ever forget the scene. As five platoons of troops marched with Burns to the ship, some fifty thousand people lined the streets. As the procession passed, one Bostonian hung from his window a black coffin bearing the words "THE FUNERAL OF LIBERTY." Another draped an American flag upside down as a symbol that "my country is eternally disgraced by this day's proceedings." The Burns incident shattered the complacency of conservative supporters of the Compromise of 1850. "We went to bed one night old fashioned conservative Compromise Union Whigs," the textile manufacturer Amos A. Lawrence wrote, "and waked up stark mad Abolitionists." A Boston committee later successfully purchased Burns's freedom, but other fugitives had worse fates. Margaret Garner, about to be captured and sent back to Kentucky as a slave, slit her daughter's throat and tried to kill her other children rather than witness their return to slavery.

In response to the Fugitive Slave Act, "vigilance" committees spirited endangered blacks to Canada. Lawyers dragged out legal proceedings to raise slave-catchers' expenses, and nine northern states passed **personal-liberty laws**. By such techniques as forbidding the use of state jails to incarcerate alleged fugitives, these laws aimed to preclude state officials from enforcing the law.

The frequent cold stares, obstructive legal tactics, and occasional violence encountered by slaveholders who ventured north to capture runaway slaves helped demonstrate to southerners that opposition to slavery boiled just beneath the surface of northern opinion. In the eyes of most southerners, the South had gained little more from the Compromise of 1850 than the Fugitive Slave Act, and now even that northern concession seemed to be a phantom. After witnessing riots against the Fugitive Slave Act in Boston in 1854, a young Georgian studying law at Harvard wrote to his mother, "Do not be surprised if when I return home you find me a confirmed disunionist."

Uncle Tom's Cabin

The publication in 1852 of Harriet Beecher Stowe's novel **Uncle Tom's Cabin** aroused wide northern sympathy for fugitive slaves. Stowe, the daughter of the famed evangelical Lyman Beecher and the younger sister of Catharine Beecher, the stalwart advocate of domesticity for women, greeted the Fugitive Slave Act with horror and outrage. In a memorable scene from the novel, she depicted the slave Eliza, clutching her infant son, bounding across ice floes on the Ohio River to freedom.

Yet Stowe targeted slavery itself more than merely the slave-catchers who served the institution. Much of her novel's power derives from its view that even good intentions cannot prevail against so evil an institution. Torn from his wife and children by sale and shipped on a steamer for the Lower South, the black slave Uncle Tom rescues little Eva, the daughter of kindly Augustine St. Clare, from drowning. In gratitude, St. Clare purchases Tom from a slave trader and takes him into his home in New Orleans. But after St. Clare dies, his cruel widow sells Tom to the vicious (and northern-born) Simon Legree, who whips Tom to death. Stowe played effectively on the emotions of her audience by demonstrating to an age that revered family life how slavery tore the family apart.

Three hundred thousand copies of *Uncle Tom's Cabin* were sold in 1852, and 1.2 million by the summer of 1853. Stage dramatizations, which added dogs to chase Eliza across the ice, eventually reached perhaps fifty times the number of people as the novel itself. As a play, *Uncle Tom's Cabin* enthralled working-class audiences normally indifferent, if not hostile, to abolitionism. During one stage performance, a reviewer for a New York newspaper observed that the gallery was filled with men "in red woollen shirts, with countenances as hardy and rugged as the implements of industry employed by them in the pursuit of their vocations." Astonished by the silence that fell over these men at the point when Eliza escapes across the river, the reviewer turned to discover that many of them were in tears.

The impact of *Uncle Tom's Cabin* cannot be precisely measured. Although the novel stirred deep feelings, it reflected the prevailing stereotypes of blacks far more than it overturned commonly held views. Stowe portrayed only light-skinned blacks as aggressive and intelligent; she depicted dark-skinned blacks such as Uncle Tom as docile and submissive. In addition, some of the stage dramatizations softened the novel's antislavery message. In one version, which P. T. Barnum produced, Tom was rescued from Legree and happily returned as a slave to his original plantation.

Surgery on the plot, however, could not fully excise the antislavery message of *Uncle Tom's Cabin*. Although the novel hardly lived up to the prediction of a proslavery lawyer that it would convert 2 million people to abolitionism, it did push many waverers toward a more

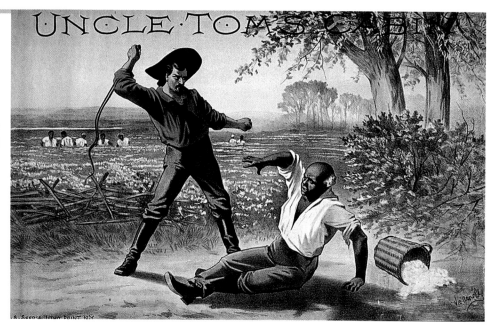

Uncle Tom's Cabin Theater Poster
With its vivid word pictures of slavery, Harriet Beecher Stowe's *Uncle Tom's Cabin* translated well to the stage. Stowe herself was among the many who wrote dramatizations of the novel. Scenes of Eliza crossing the ice of the Ohio River with bloodhounds in pursuit and the evil Simon Legree whipping Uncle Tom outraged northern audiences and turned many against slavery. Southerners damned Mrs. Stowe as a "vile wretch in petticoats."

aggressively antisouthern and antislavery stance. Indeed, fear of its effect inspired a host of southerners to pen anti–Uncle Tom novels. As historian David Potter concluded, the northern attitude toward slavery "was never quite the same after *Uncle Tom's Cabin*."

The Election of 1852

The Fugitive Slave Act fragmented the Whig party. By masterminding defiance of the law, northern Whigs put southern Whigs, who long had come before the southern electorate as the party best able to defend slavery within the Union, on the spot.

Sojourner Truth

Sojourner Truth was born into slavery in upstate New York and named Isabella by her Dutch owner. She was illiterate and a mystic given to hearing messages from God, including one in 1843 that told her to change her name to Sojourner Truth. By then she had joined William Lloyd Garrison's band of abolitionists. In the 1840s and 1850s she traveled from New England to Indiana preaching against slavery. Six feet tall and speaking English with a Dutch accent, she cut a striking figure on the platform, sprinkling humorous asides with vivid gestures, gospel songs, and clever put-downs. In one notable instance, when hecklers questioned her femininity, she bared her breasts to silence them.

In 1852, the Whigs' nomination of Mexican War hero Winfield Scott as their presidential candidate widened the sectional split within the party. Although a Virginian, Scott owed his nomination to the northern free-soil Whigs. His single feeble statement endorsing the Compromise of 1850 undercut southern Whigs trying to portray the Democrats as the party of disunion and themselves as the party of both slavery and the Union.

The Democrats bridged their own sectional division by nominating **Franklin Pierce** of New Hampshire, a dark-horse candidate whose chief attraction was that no faction of the party strongly opposed him. The "ultra men of the South," a friend of Pierce noted, "say they can cheerfully go for him, and none, none, say they cannot." North and South, the Democrats rallied behind both the Compromise and the idea of applying popular sovereignty to all the territories. In the most one-sided election since 1820, Pierce swept to victory. Defeat was especially galling for southern Whigs. In 1848, Zachary Taylor had won 49.8 percent of the South's popular vote; Scott, by comparison, limped home with only 35 percent. In state elections during 1852 and 1853, moreover, the Whigs were devastated in the South; one Whig stalwart lamented "the decisive breaking-up of our party."

The Collapse of the Second Party System, 1853–1856

Franklin Pierce had the dubious distinction of being the last presidential candidate for eighty years to win the popular and electoral vote in both the North and the South. Not until 1932 did another president, Franklin D. Roosevelt, repeat this accomplishment. Pierce was also the last president to hold office under the second party system—Whigs against Democrats. For two decades, the Whigs and the Democrats had battled, often on even terms. Then, within the four years of Pierce's administration, the Whig party disintegrated. In its place two new parties, first the American (Know-Nothing) Party, then the Republican Party, arose.

Unlike the Whig party, the Republican Party was a purely sectional, northern party. Its support came from former northern Whigs and discontented northern Democrats. The Democrats survived as a national party, but with a base so shrunken in the North that the Republican Party, although scarcely a year old, swept two-thirds of the free states in 1856.

For decades, the second party system had kept the conflict over slavery in check by giving Americans other issues—banking, internal improvements, tariffs, and temperance—to argue about. By the 1850s the debate over slavery extension was pushing such issues into the background and exposing raw divisions in each party. Of the two parties, the Whigs had the larger, more aggressive free-soil wing, and hence they were more vulnerable than the Democrats to disruption. When Stephen A. Douglas put forth a proposal in 1854 to organize the vast Nebraska territory without restrictions on slavery, he ignited a firestorm that consumed the Whig party.

The Kansas-Nebraska Act

Signed by President Pierce at the end of May 1854, the **Kansas-Nebraska Act** shattered the already weakened second party system and triggered renewed sectional strife. The origins of the act lay in the seemingly uncontroversial desire of farm families to establish homesteads in the vast prairies west of Iowa and Missouri. Their congressional representatives had repeatedly introduced bills to organize this area so that Native American land titles could be extinguished and a basis for government provided. Also, since the mid-1840s, advocates of national expansion had looked to the day when a railroad would link the Midwest to the Pacific; and St. Louis, Milwaukee, and Chicago had vied to become the eastern end of the projected Pacific railroad.

In January 1854, Senator Stephen A. Douglas of Illinois proposed a bill to organize Nebraska as a territory. An ardent expansionist, Douglas had formed his political ideology in the heady atmosphere of Manifest Destiny during the 1840s. As early as the mid-1840s, he had embraced the ideas of a Pacific railroad and the organization of Nebraska as ways to promote a continuous line of settlement between the Midwest and the Pacific. Although he preferred a railroad from his hometown of Chicago to San Francisco, Douglas dwelled on the national benefits that would attend construction of a railroad from anywhere in the Midwest to the Pacific. Such a railroad would enhance the importance of the Midwest, which could then hold the balance of power between the older sections of the North and South, and guide the nation toward unity rather than disruption. In addition, westward expansion through Nebraska with the aid of a railroad struck Douglas as an issue, comparable to Manifest Destiny, around which the contending factions of the Democratic Party would unite.

Douglas recognized two sources of potential conflict over his Nebraska bill. First, some southerners advocated a rival route for the Pacific railroad that would start at either New Orleans or Memphis. Second, Nebraska lay within the Louisiana Purchase and north of the Missouri Compromise line of 36°30′, a region closed to slavery (see Map 14.2). Unless Douglas made some concessions, southerners would have little incentive to vote for his bill; after all, the organization of Nebraska would simultaneously create a potential free state and increase the chances for a northern, rather than a southern, railroad to the Pacific.

As the floor manager of the Compromise of 1850 in the Senate, Douglas thought that he had an ideal concession to offer to the South. The Compromise of 1850

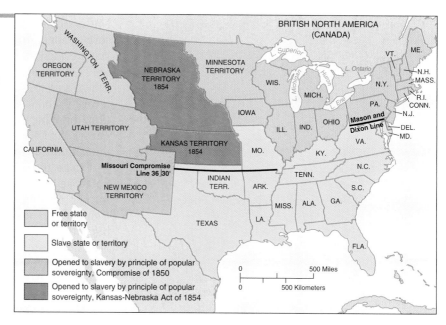

Map 14.2 The Kansas-Nebraska Act, 1854
Kansas and Nebraska lay within the Louisiana Purchase, north of 36°30′, and hence were closed to slavery until Stephen A. Douglas introduced his bills in 1854.

had applied the principle of popular sovereignty to New Mexico and Utah, territories outside of the Louisiana Purchase and hence unaffected by the Missouri Compromise. Why not assume, Douglas reasoned, that the Compromise of 1850 had taken the place of the Missouri Compromise everywhere? Believing that expansion rather than slavery was uppermost in the public's mind, Douglas hoped to avoid controversy over slavery by ignoring the Missouri Compromise. But he quickly came under pressure from southern congressmen, who wanted an explicit repudiation of the Missouri Compromise. Soon they forced Douglas to state publicly that the Nebraska bill "superseded" the Missouri Compromise and rendered it "void." Still under pressure, Douglas next agreed to a division of Nebraska into two territories: Nebraska to the west of Iowa, and Kansas to the west of Missouri. Because Missouri was a slave state, most congressmen assumed that the division aimed to secure Kansas for slavery and Nebraska for free soil.

The modifications of Douglas's original bill set off a storm of protest. Congress quickly tabled the Pacific railroad (which, in the turn of events, would not be built until after the Civil War) and focused on the issue of slavery extension. Antislavery northerners assailed the bill as "an atrocious plot" to violate the "sacred pledge" of the Missouri Compromise and to turn Kansas into a "dreary region of despotism, inhabited by masters and slaves." Their rage electrified southerners, many of whom initially had reacted indifferently to the Nebraska bill. Some southerners had opposed an explicit repeal of the Missouri Compromise, from fear of stimulating sectional discord; others doubted that Kansas would attract many slaveholders. But the furious assault of antislavery northerners united the South behind the Kansas-Nebraska bill by turning the issue into one of sectional pride as much as slavery extension.

Despite the uproar, Douglas successfully guided the Kansas-Nebraska bill through the Senate, where it passed by a vote of 37 to 14. In the House of Representatives, where the bill passed by little more than a whisker, 113 to 100, the true dimensions of the conflict became apparent. Not a single northern Whig representative in the House voted for the bill, whereas the northern Democrats divided evenly, 44 to 44.

The Surge of Free Soil

Amid the clamor over his bill, Douglas ruefully observed that he could now travel to Chicago by the light of his own burning effigies. Neither a fool nor a political novice, he was the victim of a political bombshell—free soil—that exploded under his feet.

Support for free soil united northerners who agreed on little else. Some free-soilers opposed slavery on moral grounds and rejected racist legislation, but others were racists who opposed allowing any African-Americans, slave or free, into the West. An abolitionist traced the free-soil convictions of many westerners to a "perfect, if not supreme" hatred of blacks. Racist free-soilers in Iowa and Illinois secured laws prohibiting settlement by black people.

One opinion shared by free-soilers of all persuasions was that slavery impeded whites' progress. Because a slave worked for nothing, the argument ran, no free laborer could compete with a slave. A territory might contain only a handful of slaves or none at all, but as long as Congress refused to prohibit slavery in the territories, the institution would gain a foothold and free laborers would flee. Wherever slavery appeared, a free-soiler proclaimed, "labor loses its dignity; industry sickens; education finds no schools; religion finds no churches; and the whole land of slavery is impoverished." Free-soilers also blasted the idea that slavery had natural limits. One warned that "slavery is as certain to invade New Mexico and Utah as the sun is to rise"; others predicted that if slavery gained a toehold in Kansas, it would soon invade Minnesota.

To free-soilers, the Kansas-Nebraska Act, with its erasure of the Missouri Compromise, was the last straw, for it revealed, one wrote, "a continuous movement by slaveholders to spread slavery over the entire North." For a Whig congressman from Massachusetts who had voted for the Compromise of 1850 and opposed abolitionists, the Kansas-Nebraska Act, "that most wanton and wicked act, so obviously designed to promote the extension of slavery," was too much to bear. "I now advocate the freedom of Kansas under all circumstances, and the prohibition of slavery in all territories now free."

The Ebbing of Manifest Destiny

The uproar over the Kansas-Nebraska Act embarrassed the Pierce administration. It also doomed Manifest Destiny, the one issue that had held the Democrats together in the 1840s.

Franklin Pierce had come to office championing Manifest Destiny, but increasing sectional rivalries sidetracked his efforts. In 1853, his emissary James Gadsden negotiated the purchase from Mexico of a strip of land south of the Gila River (now southern Arizona and part of southern New Mexico), an acquisition favored by advocates of a southern railroad route to the Pacific. Fierce opposition to the Gadsden Purchase revealed mounting free-soilers' suspicion of expansion, and the Senate approved the treaty only after slashing nine thousand square miles from the parcel. The sectional rivalries beginning to engulf the Nebraska bill clearly threatened any proposal to gain new territory.

Cuba provided even more vivid proof of the change in public attitudes about expansion. In 1854, a former Mississippi governor, John A. Quitman, planned a filibuster (an unofficial military expedition) to seize Cuba from Spain. Eager to acquire Cuba, Pierce may have encouraged Quitman, but Pierce forced Quitman to scuttle the expedition when faced with intense opposition from antislavery northerners who saw filibusters as just another manifestation of the **Slave Power**—the conspiracy of slaveholders and their northern dupes to grab more territory for slavery.

Pierce still hoped to purchase Cuba, but events quickly slipped out of his control. In October 1854, the American ambassadors to Great Britain, France, and Spain, two of them southerners, met in Belgium and issued the unofficial Ostend Manifesto, calling on the United States to acquire Cuba by any means, including force. Beset by the storm over the Kansas-Nebraska Act and the furor over Quitman's proposed filibuster, Pierce rejected the mandate.

Despite Pierce's disavowal of the Ostend Manifesto, the idea of expansion into the Caribbean continued to attract southerners, including the Tennessee-born adventurer William Walker. Slightly built and so unassuming that he usually spoke with his hands in his pockets, Walker seemed an unlikely soldier of fortune. Yet between 1853 and 1860, the year a firing squad in Honduras executed him, Walker led a succession of filibustering expeditions into Central America. Taking advantage of civil chaos in Nicaragua, he made himself the chief political force there, reinstituted slavery, and talked of making Nicaragua a U.S. colony.

For all the proclamations and intrigues that surrounded the movement for southern expansion, its strength and goals remained open to question. With few exceptions, the adventurers were shady characters whom southern politicians might admire but on whom they could never depend. Some southerners were against expansion, among them Louisiana sugar planters who opposed acquiring Cuba because Cuban sugar would compete with their product. But expansionists stirred enough commotion to worry antislavery northerners that the South was conspiring to establish a Caribbean slave empire. Like a card in a poker game, the threat of expansion southward was all the more menacing for not being played. As long as the debate on the extension of slavery focused on the continental United States, prospects for expansion were limited. However, adding Caribbean territory to the pot changed all calculations.

The Whigs Disintegrate, 1854–1855

While straining Democratic unity, the Kansas-Nebraska Act wrecked the Whig party. In the law's immediate aftermath, most northern Whigs hoped to blame the Democrats for the act and to entice free-soil Democrats to their side. In the state and congressional elections of 1854, the Democrats were decisively defeated. But the Whig party failed to benefit from the backlash against the Democrats. However furious at Douglas for initiating the act, free-soil Democrats could not forget that the southern Whigs had supported Douglas. In addition, the northern Whigs themselves were deeply divided between antislavery "Conscience" Whigs, led by Senator William Seward of New York, and conservatives, led by former president Millard Fillmore. The conservatives believed that the Whig party had to adhere to the Compromise of 1850 to maintain itself as a national party.

Divisions within the Whig party repelled antislavery Democrats from affiliating with it and prompted many antislavery Whigs to look for an alternative party. By 1856, the new Republican Party would become the home for most of these northern refugees from the traditional parties; but in 1854 and 1855, when the Republican Party was only starting to organize, the American, or Know-Nothing, party emerged as the principal alternative.

The Rise and Fall of the Know-Nothings, 1853–1856

The **Know-Nothings** evolved out of a secret nativist organization, the Order of the Star-Spangled Banner, founded in 1850. (The party's popular name, Know-Nothing, derived from the standard response of its members to inquiries about its activities: "I know nothing.") This order was one of many such societies that mushroomed in response to the unprecedented immigration of the 1840s. It had sought to rid the United States of immigrant and Catholic political influence by pressuring the existing parties to nominate and appoint only native-born Protestants to office and by advocating an extension of the naturalization period before immigrants could vote.

Throughout the 1840s, nativists usually voted Whig, but their allegiance to the Whigs started to buckle during Winfield Scott's campaign for the presidency in 1852. In an attempt to revitalize his party, which was badly split over slavery, Scott had courted the traditionally Democratic Catholic vote. But Scott's tactic backfired. Most Catholics voted for Franklin Pierce. Nativists, meanwhile, felt betrayed by their party, and after Scott's defeat, many gravitated toward the Know-Nothings. The Kansas-Nebraska Act cemented their allegiance to the Know-Nothings, who in the North opposed both the extension of slavery and

Catholicism. Indeed, an obsessive fear of conspiracies unified the Know-Nothings. They simultaneously denounced a papal conspiracy against the American republic and a Slave Power conspiracy spreading its tentacles throughout the United States.

The Know-Nothings' surge was truly stunning. In 1854, they captured the governorship, all the congressional seats, and almost all the seats in the state legislature in Massachusetts. Know-Nothings were sufficiently strong in the West to retard the emergence of the Republican Party, and so strong in the East that they exploded any hopes that the Whigs had of capitalizing on hostility to the Kansas-Nebraska Act.

After rising spectacularly between 1853 and 1855, the star of Know-Nothingism nevertheless plummeted and gradually disappeared below the horizon after 1856. The Know-Nothings proved as vulnerable as the Whigs to sectional conflicts over slavery. Although primarily a force in the North, the Know-Nothings had a southern wing, comprised mainly of former Whigs who loathed both the antislavery northerners who were abandoning the Whig party and the southern Democrats, whom they viewed as disunionist firebrands. In 1855, these southern Know-Nothings combined with northern conservatives to make acceptance of the Kansas-Nebraska Act part of the Know-Nothing platform, and thus they blurred the attraction of Know-Nothingism to those northern voters who were more antislavery than anti-Catholic.

One such Whig refugee, Illinois congressman Abraham Lincoln, asked pointedly: "How can anyone who abhors the oppression of negroes be in favor of degrading classes of white people?" "We began by declaring," Lincoln continued, "that 'all men are created equal.' We now practically read it 'all men are created equal except negroes.' When the Know-Nothings get control, it will read 'all men are created equal, except Negroes and foreigners and Catholics.'" Finally, even most Know-Nothings eventually came to conclude that, as one observer put it, "neither the Pope nor the foreigners ever can govern the country or endanger its liberties, but the slavebreeders and slavetraders do govern it, and threaten to put an end to all government but theirs." Consequently, the Know-Nothings proved vulnerable to the challenge posed by the emerging Republican Party, which did not officially embrace nativism and which had no southern wing to blunt its antislavery message.

The Republican Party and the Crisis in Kansas, 1855–1856

Born in the chaotic aftermath of the Kansas-Nebraska Act, the **Republican Party** sprang up in several northern states in 1854 and 1855. With the Know-Nothings' demise after 1856, the Republicans would become the main opposition to the Democratic Party, and they would win each presidential election from 1860 until 1884; but in 1855 few would have predicted such a bright future. While united by opposition to the Kansas-Nebraska Act, the party held various shades of opinion in uneasy balance. At one extreme were conservatives who merely wanted to restore the Missouri Compromise; at the other was a small faction of former Liberty Party abolitionists; and the middle held a sizable body of free-soilers.

In addition to bridging these divisions, the Republicans confronted the task of building organizations on the state level, where the Know-Nothings were already well established. Politicians of the day knew that the voters' allegiances were often shaped by state issues, including temperance. Maine's passage of the nation's first statewide prohibition law in 1851 spurred calls elsewhere for liquor regulation. Linking support for temperance with anti-Catholicism and antislavery, the Know-Nothings were well positioned to answer these calls.

Frequently, antislavery voters were also protemperance and anti-Catholic, believing that addiction to alcohol and submission to the pope were both forms of enslavement to be eradicated. Intensely moralistic, such voters viewed the traditional parties as controlled by unprincipled hacks, and they began to search for a new party. In competing with the Know-Nothings on the state level, the Republicans faced a dilemma, stemming from the fact that both parties were targeting many of the same voters. The Republicans had clearer antislavery credentials than did the Know-Nothings, but this fact alone did not guarantee that voters would respond more to antislavery than to anti-Catholicism or temperance. Thus, if the Republicans attacked the Know-Nothings for stressing anti-Catholicism over antislavery, they ran the risk of alienating the very voters whom they had to attract. If they conciliated the Know-Nothings, they might lose their own identity as a party.

Alternately attacking and conciliating, the Republicans had some successes in state elections in 1855; but as popular ire against the Kansas-Nebraska Act cooled, they also suffered setbacks. By the start of 1856, they were organized in only half the northern states and lacked any national organization. The Republicans desperately needed a development that would make voters worry more about the Slave Power than about rum or Catholicism. Salvation for the nascent party came in the form of violence in Kansas, which quickly became known as Bleeding Kansas. This violence united the party around its free-soil center, intensified antislavery feelings, and boosted Republican fortunes.

In the wake of the Kansas-Nebraska Act, Boston-based abolitionists had organized the New England Emigrant Aid Company to send antislavery settlers into Kansas. The abolitionists' aim was to stifle escalating efforts to turn Kansas into a slave state. But antislavery New Englanders arrived slowly in Kansas; the bulk of the territory's early settlers came from Missouri or elsewhere in the Midwest. Very few of these early settlers opposed slavery on moral grounds. Some, in fact, favored slavery; others wanted to keep all blacks, whether slave or free, out of Kansas.

Despite most settlers' racist leanings and utter hatred of abolitionists, Kansas became a battleground between proslavery and antislavery forces. In March 1855, thousands of proslavery Missourian "border ruffians," led by Senator David R. Atchison, crossed into Kansas to vote illegally in the first election for a territorial legislature. Drawing and cocking their revolvers, they quickly silenced any judges who questioned their right to vote in Kansas. These proslavery advocates probably would have won an honest election because they would have been supported by the votes both of slaveholders and of non-slaveholders horrified at rumors that abolitionists planned to use Kansas as a colony for fugitive slaves. But by stealing the election, the proslavery forces committed a grave tactical blunder. A cloud of fraudulence thereafter hung over the proslavery legislature subsequently established at Lecompton, Kansas. "There is not a proslavery man of my acquaintance in Kansas," wrote the wife of an antislavery farmer, "who does not acknowledge that the Bogus Legislature was the result of a gigantic and well planned fraud, that the elections were carried by an invading mob from Missouri." This legislature then further darkened its image by expelling several antislavery legislators and passing a succession of outrageous acts, limiting officeholding to individuals who would swear allegiance to slavery, punishing the harboring of fugitive slaves by ten years' imprisonment, and making the circulation of abolitionist literature a capital offense.

The territorial legislature's actions set off a chain reaction. Free-staters, including a small number of abolitionists and a much larger number of settlers enraged by the proceedings at Lecompton, organized a rival government at Topeka, Kansas, in the summer and fall of 1855. In response, the Lecompton government in May 1856 dispatched a posse to Lawrence, where free-staters, heeding the advice of antislavery minister Henry Ward Beecher that rifles would do more than Bibles to enforce morality in Kansas, had taken up arms and dubbed their guns "Beecher's Bibles." Riding under flags emblazoned "southern rights" and "let yankees tremble and abolitionists fall," the proslavery posse tore through the town like a hell-bent mob, burning several buildings and destroying two free-state presses. There were no deaths, but Republicans immediately dubbed the incident "the sack of Lawrence."

The next move was made by John Brown. The sack of Lawrence convinced Brown that God now beckoned him "to break the jaws of the wicked." In late May, Brown led seven men, including his four sons and his son-in-law, toward the Pottawatomie Creek near Lawrence. Setting upon five men associated with the Lecompton

"Liberty, the Fair Maid of Kansas in the Hands of the 'Border Ruffians'" This cartoon savagely attacks leading northern Democrats for their acquiescence in the murderous actions of proslavery mobs in Kansas. On the left, James Buchanan steals a watch from a corpse. In the center, a tipsy President Franklin Pierce and Lewis Cass leer at the fair maid of Kansas, while on the right Stephen Douglas scalps a victim.

LIBERTY, THE FAIR MAID OF KANSAS—IN THE HANDS OF THE "BORDER RUFFIANS".

government, they shot one to death and hacked the others to pieces with broadswords. Brown's "Pottawatomie massacre" struck terror into the hearts of southerners and completed the transformation of Bleeding Kansas into a battleground between the South and the North (see Map 14.3). A month after the massacre, a South Carolinian living in Kansas wrote to his sister,

I never lie down without taking the precaution to fasten my door and fix it in such a way that if it is forced open, it can be opened only wide enough for one person to come in at a time. I have my rifle, revolver, and old home-stocked pistol where I can lay my hand on them in an instant, besides a hatchet and an axe. I take this precaution to guard against the midnight attacks of the Abolitionists, who never make an attack in open daylight, and no Proslavery man knows when he is safe in this Ter[ritory.]

In Kansas, popular sovereignty flunked its major test. Instead of quickly resolving the issue of slavery extension, popular sovereignty merely institutionalized the division over slavery by creating rival governments in Lecompton and Topeka. The Pierce administration then shot itself in the foot by denouncing the Topeka government and recognizing only its Lecompton rival. Pierce had forced northern Democrats into the awkward position of appearing to ally with the South in support of the "Bogus Legislature" at Lecompton.

Nor did popular sovereignty keep the slavery issue out of national politics. On the day before the sack of Lawrence, Republican senator **Charles Sumner** of Massachusetts delivered a bombastic and wrathful speech, "The Crime Against Kansas," in which he verbally whipped most of the U.S. Senate for complicity in slavery. Sumner singled out Senator Andrew Butler of South Carolina for his choice of "the harlot, slavery" as his mistress and for the "loose expectoration" of his speech (a nasty reference to the aging Butler's tendency to drool). Sumner's oration stunned most senators. Douglas wondered aloud whether Sumner's real aim was "to provoke some of us to kick him as we would a dog in the street." Two days later, a relative of Butler, Democratic representative Preston Brooks of South Carolina, strode into the Senate chamber, found Sumner at his desk, and struck him repeatedly with a cane. The hollow cane broke after five or six blows, but Sumner required stitches, experienced shock, and did not return to the Senate for three years. Brooks became an instant hero in the South, and the fragments of his weapon were "begged as sacred relics." A new cane, presented to Brooks by the city of Charleston, bore the inscription "Hit him again."

Now Bleeding Kansas and Bleeding Sumner united the North. The sack of Lawrence, Pierce's recognition of the proslavery Lecompton government, and Brooks's actions seemed to clinch the Republican argument that an aggressive "slaveocracy" held white northerners in contempt. Abolitionists remained unpopular in northern opinion, but southerners were becoming even less popular. Northern migrants to Kansas coined a name reflecting their feelings about southerners: "the pukes." Other northerners attacked the slaveholding migrants to Kansas as the "Missouri savages." By denouncing Slave Power more than slavery itself, Republican propagandists sidestepped the issue of slavery's morality, which

Map 14.3 Bleeding Kansas
Kansas became a battleground between free-state and slave-state factions in the 1850s.

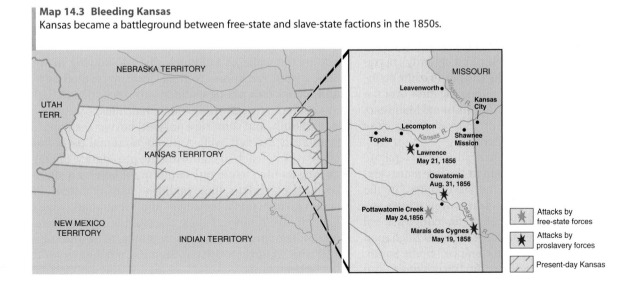

"Southern Chivalry"
Cartoons like this one, showing the beating of antislavery Senator Charles Sumner by Preston "Bully" Brooks, confirmed northern images of white southerners as people who prided themselves on their genteel manners but who behaved like street toughs.

SOUTHERN CHIVALRY — ARGUMENT versus CLUB'S.

divided their followers, and focused on portraying southern planters as arrogant aristocrats and the natural enemies of the laboring people of the North.

The Election of 1856

The election of 1856 revealed the scope of the political realignments of the preceding few years. In this, its first presidential contest, the Republican Party nominated John C. Frémont, the famed "pathfinder" who had played a key role in the conquest of California during the Mexican War. The Republicans then maneuvered the northern Know-Nothings into endorsing Frémont. The southern Know-Nothings picked the last Whig president, Millard Fillmore, as their candidate, and the Democrats dumped Pierce for the seasoned James Buchanan of Pennsylvania. A four-term congressman and long an aspirant to the presidency, Buchanan finally secured his party's nomination because he had the good luck to be out of the country (as minister to Great Britain) during the furor over the Kansas-Nebraska Act. As a signer of the Ostend Manifesto, he was popular in the South: virtually all of his close friends in Washington were southerners.

The campaign quickly turned into two separate races—Frémont versus Buchanan in the free states and Fillmore versus Buchanan in the slave states. In the North, the candidates divided clearly over slavery extension; Frémont's platform called for congressional prohibition of slavery in the territories, whereas Buchanan pledged congressional "non-interference." In the South, Fillmore appealed to traditionally Whig voters and

called for moderation in the face of secessionist threats. But by nominating a well-known moderate in Buchanan, the Democrats undercut some of Fillmore's appeal. Although Fillmore garnered more than 40 percent of the popular vote in ten of the slave states, he carried only Maryland. In the North, Frémont outpolled Buchanan in the popular vote and won eleven of the sixteen free states; if Frémont had carried Pennsylvania and either Illinois, Indiana, or New Jersey, he would have won the election. As it turned out, Buchanan, the only truly national candidate in the race, secured the presidency.

The election yielded three clear conclusions. First, the American party was finished as a major national force. Having worked for the Republican Frémont, most northern Know-Nothings now joined that party, and in the wake of Fillmore's dismal showing in the South, southern Know-Nothings gave up on their party and sought new political affiliations. Second, although in existence scarcely more than a year, lacking any base in the South, and running a political novice, the Republican Party did very well. A purely sectional party had come within reach of capturing the presidency. Finally, as long as the Democrats could unite behind a single national candidate, they would be hard to defeat. To achieve such unity, however, the Democrats would have to find more James Buchanans—"doughface" moderates who would be acceptable to southerners and who would not drive even more northerners into Republican arms.

The Crisis of the Union, 1857–1860

No one ever accused James Buchanan of impulsiveness or fanaticism. Although he disapproved of slavery, he believed that his administration could neither restrict nor end the institution. In 1860, he would pronounce secession a grave wrong, but would affirm that his administration could not stop it. Understandably, contemporaries hailed his election as a victory for moderation. Yet his administration encountered a succession of controversies, first over the famed *Dred Scott* decision of the Supreme Court, then over the proslavery Lecompton constitution in Kansas, next following the raid by John Brown on Harpers Ferry, and finally concerning secession itself. Ironically, a man who sought to avoid controversy presided over one of the most controversy-ridden administrations in American history.

Buchanan's problems arose less from his own actions than from the fact that the forces driving the nation apart were already spinning out of control by 1856. By the time of Buchanan's inauguration, southerners who looked north saw creeping abolitionism in the guise of free soil, whereas northerners who looked south saw an insatiable Slave Power. Once these images had taken hold in the minds of the American people, politicians like James Buchanan had little room to maneuver.

The Dred Scott Case, 1857

Pledged to congressional "non-interference" with slavery in the territories, Buchanan had long looked to the courts for a nonpartisan resolution of the vexatious issue of slavery extension. A case that appeared to promise such a solution had been wending its way through the courts for years; and on March 6, 1857, two days after Buchanan's inauguration, the Supreme Court handed down its decision in **Dred Scott v. Sandford**.

During the 1830s, Dred Scott, a slave, had been taken by his master from the slave state of Missouri into Illinois and the Wisconsin Territory, areas respectively closed to slavery by the Northwest Ordinance of 1787 and the Missouri Compromise. After his master's death, Scott sued for his freedom on the grounds of his residence in free territory. In 1856, the case finally reached the Supreme Court.

The Court faced two key questions. Did Scott's residence in free territory during the 1830s make him free? Regardless of the answer to this question, did Scott, again enslaved in Missouri, have a right to sue in the federal courts? The Court could have resolved the case on narrow grounds by answering the second question in the negative, but Buchanan wanted a far-reaching decision that would deal with the broad issue of slavery in the territories.

In the end, Buchanan got the broad ruling that he sought, but one so controversial that it settled little. In the most important of six separate majority opinions, Chief Justice Roger B. Taney, a seventy-nine-year-old Marylander whom Andrew Jackson had appointed to succeed John Marshall in 1835, began with the narrow conclusion that Scott, a slave, could not sue for his freedom. Then the thunder started. No black, whether a slave or a free person descended from a slave, could become a citizen of the United States, Taney continued. Next Taney whipped the thunderheads into a tornado. Even if Scott had been a legal plaintiff, Taney ruled, his residence in free territory years earlier did not make him free, because the Missouri Compromise, whose provisions prohibited slavery in the Wisconsin Territory, was itself unconstitutional. The compromise, declared Taney, violated the Fifth Amendment's protection of property (including slaves).

Contrary to Buchanan's hopes, the decision touched off a new blast of controversy over slavery in the territories. The antislavery press flayed it as a "willful perversion" filled with "gross historical falsehoods." Taney's ruling gave Republicans more evidence that a fiendish Slave Power conspiracy gripped the nation. Although the Kansas-Nebraska Act had effectively repealed the Missouri Compromise, the Court's majority now rejected even the principle behind the compromise, the idea that Congress could prohibit slavery in the territories. Five of the six justices who rejected this principle were from slave states. The Slave Power, a northern paper bellowed, "has marched over and annihilated the boundaries of the states. We are now one great homogenous slaveholding community."

Like Stephen Douglas after the Kansas-Nebraska Act, President Buchanan now appeared to be a northern dupe of the "slaveocracy." Republicans restrained themselves from open defiance of the decision only by insisting that it did not bind the nation; Taney's comments on the constitutionality of the Missouri Compromise, they contended, amounted merely to *obiter dicta*, opinions superfluous to settling the case.

Reactions to the decision underscored the fact that by 1857 no "judicious" or nonpartisan solution to slavery extension was possible. Anyone who still doubted this needed only to read the fast-breaking news from Kansas.

The Lecompton Constitution, 1857

While the Supreme Court wrestled with the abstract issues raised by the expansion of slavery, Buchanan sought a concrete solution to the gnawing problem of Kansas, where the free-state government at Topeka and the officially recognized proslavery government at Lecompton viewed each other with profound distrust. Buchanan's plan for Kansas looked simple: an elected territorial convention would draw up a constitution that would either permit or prohibit slavery; Buchanan would submit the constitution to Congress; Congress would then admit Kansas as a state.

Unfortunately, the plan exploded in Buchanan's face. Popular sovereignty, the essence of Buchanan's plan, demanded fair play, a scarce quality in Kansas. The territory's history of fraudulent elections left both sides reluctant to commit their fortunes to the polls. An election for a constitutional convention took place in June 1857, but free-staters, by now a majority in Kansas, boycotted the election on the grounds that the proslavery side would rig it. Dominated by proslavery delegates, a constitutional convention then met and drew up a frame of government, the **Lecompton constitution**, that protected the rights of those slaveholders already living in Kansas to their slave property and provided for a referendum in which voters could decide whether to allow in more slaves.

The Lecompton constitution created a dilemma for Buchanan. A supporter of popular sovereignty, he had gone on record in favor of letting the voters in Kansas decide the slavery issue. Now he was confronted by a constitution drawn up by a convention that had been elected by less than 10 percent of the eligible voters, by plans for a referendum that would not allow voters to remove slaves already in Kansas, and by the prospect that the proslavery side would conduct the referendum no more honestly than it had other ballots. Yet Buchanan had compelling reasons to accept the Lecompton constitution as the basis for the admission of Kansas as a state. The South, which had provided him with 112 of his 174 electoral votes in 1856, supported the constitution. Buchanan knew, moreover, that only about two hundred slaves resided in Kansas, and he believed that the prospects for slavery in the remaining territories were slight. The contention over slavery in Kansas struck him as another example of how extremists could turn minor issues into major ones. To accept the constitution and speed the admission of Kansas as either a free state or a slave state seemed the best way to pull the rug from beneath the extremists and quiet the ruckus in Kansas. Accordingly, in December 1857 Buchanan endorsed the Lecompton constitution.

Stephen A. Douglas and other northern Democrats broke with Buchanan. To them, the Lecompton constitution, in allowing voters to decide only whether more slaves could enter Kansas, violated the spirit of popular sovereignty. "I care not whether [slavery] is voted down or voted up," Douglas declared. But to refuse to allow a vote on the constitution itself, with its protection of existing slave property, smacked of a "system of trickery and jugglery to defeat the fair expression of the will of the people."

Even as Douglas broke with Buchanan, events in Kansas took a new turn. A few months after electing delegates to the convention that drew up the Lecompton constitution, Kansans had gone to the polls to elect a territorial legislature. So flagrant was the fraud in this election—one village with thirty eligible voters returned more than sixteen hundred proslavery votes—that the governor disallowed enough proslavery returns to give free-staters a majority in the legislature. This territorial legislature then called for a referendum on the entire document. Whereas the Kansas constitutional convention had restricted the choice of voters to the narrow issue of the future introduction of slaves, the territorial legislature sought a referendum that would allow Kansans to vote against the protection of existing slave property as well.

In December 1857, the referendum called earlier by the constitutional convention was held. Boycotted by free-staters, the constitution with slavery passed overwhelmingly. Two weeks later, in the election called by the territorial legislature, the proslavery side abstained, and the constitution went down to crushing defeat. Buchanan tried to ignore this second election, but when he attempted to bring Kansas into the Union under the Lecompton constitution, Congress blocked him and forced yet another referendum. This time, Kansans were given the choice between accepting or rejecting the entire constitution, with the proviso that rejection would delay statehood. Despite the proviso, Kansans overwhelmingly voted down the constitution.

Buchanan simultaneously had failed to tranquilize Kansas and alienated northerners in his own party. His support for the Lecompton constitution confirmed the suspicion of northern Democrats that the southern Slave Power pulled all the important strings in their party. Douglas became the hero of the hour for northern Democrats. "The bone and sinew of the Northern Democracy are with you," a New Yorker wrote to Douglas. Yet Douglas himself could take little comfort from the Lecompton fiasco, as his cherished formula of popular sovereignty increasingly looked like a prescription for civil strife rather than harmony.

The Lincoln-Douglas Debates, 1858

Despite the acclaim he gained in the North for his stand against the Lecompton constitution, Douglas faced a stiff challenge in Illinois for reelection to the United States Senate. Of his Republican opponent, Abraham Lincoln, Douglas said: "I shall have my hands full. He is the strong man of his party—full of wit, facts, dates—and the best stump speaker with his droll ways and dry jokes, in the West."

Physically as well as ideologically, the two men formed a striking contrast. Tall (6'4'') and gangling, **Abraham Lincoln** once described himself as "a piece of floating drift-wood." Energy, ambition, and a passion for self-education had carried him from the Kentucky log cabin in which he was born in 1809 through a youth filled with various occupations (farm laborer, surveyor, rail-splitter, flatboatman, and storekeeper) into law and politics in his adopted Illinois. There he had capitalized on westerners' support for internal improvements to gain election to Congress in 1846 as a Whig. Having opposed the Mexican-American War and the Kansas-Nebraska Act, he joined the Republican Party in 1856.

Douglas was fully a foot shorter than the towering Lincoln. But his compact frame contained astonishing energy. Born in New England, Douglas appealed primarily to the small farmers of southern origin who populated the Illinois flatlands. To these and others, he was the "little giant," the personification of the Democratic Party in the West. The campaign quickly became more than just another Senate race, for it pitted the Republican Party's rising star against the Senate's leading Democrat and, thanks to the railroad and the telegraph, received unprecedented national attention.

Abraham Lincoln
Clean-shaven at the time of his famous debates with Douglas, Lincoln would soon grow a beard to give himself a more distinguished appearance.

Stephen A. Douglas
Douglas's politics were founded on his unflinching conviction that most Americans favored national expansion and would support popular sovereignty as the fastest and least controversial way to achieve it. Douglas's self-assurance blinded him to rising northern sentiment for free soil.

Although some Republicans extolled Douglas's stand against the Lecompton constitution, to Lincoln nothing had changed. Douglas was still Douglas, the author of the infamous Kansas-Nebraska Act and a man who cared not whether slavery was voted up or down as long as the vote was honest. Opening his campaign with the "House Divided" speech ("this nation cannot exist permanently half slave and half free"), Lincoln reminded his Republican followers of the gulf that still separated his doctrine of free soil from Douglas's popular sovereignty. Douglas dismissed the house-divided doctrine as an invitation to secession. What mattered to him was not slavery, which he viewed as merely an extreme way to subordinate a supposedly inferior race, but the continued expansion of white settlement. Like Lincoln, he wanted to keep slavery out of the path of white settlement. But unlike his rival, Douglas believed that popular sovereignty was the surest way to attain this goal without disrupting the Union.

The high point of the campaign came in a series of seven debates held from August to October 1858. The Lincoln-Douglas debates mixed political drama with the atmosphere of a festival. At the debate in Galesburg, for example, dozens of horse-drawn floats descended on the town from nearby farming communities. One bore thirty-two girls dressed in white, one for each state, and a thirty-third who dressed in black with the label "Kansas" and carried a banner proclaiming "they won't let me in."

Douglas used the debates to portray Lincoln as a virtual abolitionist and advocate of racial equality. Both charges were calculated to doom Lincoln in the eyes of the intensely racist Illinois voters. In response, Lincoln affirmed that Congress had no constitutional authority to abolish slavery in the South, and in one debate he asserted bluntly that "I am not, nor ever have been in favor of bringing about the social and political equality of the white, and black man." However, fending off charges of extremism was getting Lincoln nowhere; so in order to seize the initiative, he tried to maneuver Douglas into a corner.

In view of the *Dred Scott* decision, Lincoln asked in the debate at Freeport, could the people of a territory lawfully exclude slavery? In essence, Lincoln was asking Douglas to reconcile popular sovereignty with the *Dred Scott* decision. Lincoln had long contended that the Court's decision rendered popular sovereignty as thin as soup boiled from the shadow of a pigeon that had starved to death. If, as the Supreme Court's ruling affirmed, Congress had no authority to exclude slavery from a territory, then it seemingly followed that a territorial legislature created by Congress also lacked power to do so. To no one's surprise, Douglas replied that notwithstanding the *Dred Scott* decision, the voters of a territory could effectively exclude slavery simply by refusing to enact laws that gave legal protection to slave property.

Douglas's "Freeport doctrine" salvaged popular sovereignty but did nothing for his reputation among southerners, who preferred the guarantees of the *Dred Scott* ruling to the uncertainties of popular sovereignty. Whereas Douglas's stand against the Lecompton constitution had already tattered his reputation in the South ("he is already dead there," Lincoln affirmed), his Freeport doctrine stiffened southern opposition to his presidential ambitions.

Lincoln faced the problem throughout the debates that free soil and popular sovereignty, although distinguishable in theory, had much the same practical effect. Neither Lincoln nor Douglas doubted that popular sovereignty, if fairly applied, would keep slavery out of the territories. In the closing debates, in order to keep the initiative and sharpen their differences, Lincoln shifted toward attacks on slavery as "a moral, social, and political evil." He argued that Douglas's view of slavery as merely an eccentric and unsavory southern custom would dull the nation's conscience and facilitate the legalization of slavery everywhere. But Lincoln compromised his own position by rejecting both abolition and equality for blacks.

Neither man scored a clear victory in argument, and the senatorial election itself settled no major issues. Douglas's supporters captured a majority of the seats in the state legislature, which at the time was responsible for electing U.S. senators. But despite the racist leanings of most Illinois voters, Republican candidates for the state legislature won a slightly larger share of the popular vote than did their Democratic rivals. Moreover, in its larger significance, the contest solidified the sectional split in the national Democratic Party and made Lincoln famous in the North and infamous in the South.

The Legacy of Harpers Ferry

Although Lincoln rejected abolitionism, he called free soil a step toward the "ultimate extinction" of slavery. Similarly, New York Republican senator William H. Seward spoke of an "irrepressible conflict" between slavery and freedom. Predictably, many white southerners ignored the distinction between free soil and abolition, and concluded that Republicans and abolitionists were joined in an unholy alliance against slavery. To many in the South, the North seemed to be controlled by demented leaders bent on civil war. One southern defender of slavery equated the doctrines of the abolitionists with those of "Socialists, of Free Love and Free Lands, Free Churches, Free Women and Free Negroes-of No-Marriage, No-Religion, No-Private Property, No-Law and No-Government."

Nothing did more to freeze this southern image of the North than the evidence of northern complicity in John Brown's raid on Harpers Ferry and northern sermons that turned Brown into a martyr. In Philadelphia, some 250 outraged southern students left the city's medical schools to enroll in southern schools. True, Lincoln and Seward condemned the raid, but white southerners suspected that they regretted the conspiracy's failure more than the attempt itself.

Brown's abortive raid also rekindled southern fears of a slave insurrection. Rumors flew around the South, and vigilantes turned out to battle conspiracies that existed only in their minds. Volunteers, for example, mobilized to defend northeastern Texas against thousands of abolitionists supposedly on their way to pillage Dallas and its environs. In other incidents, vigilantes rounded up thousands of slaves, tortured some into confessing to nonexistent plots, and then lynched them. The hysteria fed by such rumors played into the hands of the extremists known as fire-eaters, who encouraged the witch-hunt by spreading tales of slave conspiracies in the press so that southern voters would turn to them as alone able to "stem the current of Abolition."

Illustrations of the American Anti-Slavery Almanac for 1840.

"Our Peculiar Domestic Institutions."

Northern Hospitality—New-York nine months law. [The Slave steps out of the Slave State, and his chains fall. A Free State, with another chain, stands ready to re-enslave him.]

Burning of McIntosh at St. Louis, in April, 1836.

Showing how slavery improves the condition of the female sex.

The Negro Pew, or "Free" Seats for black Christians.

Mayor of New-York refusing a Cartman's license to a colored Man.

Servility of the Northern States in arresting and returning fugitive Slaves.

Selling a Mother from her Child.

Hunting Slaves with dogs and guns. A Slave drowned by the dogs.

"Poor things, 'they can't take care of themselves.'"

Mothers with young Children at work in the field.

A Woman chained to a Girl, and a Man in irons at work in the field.

Branding Slaves.

Cutting up a Slave in Kentucky.

Paid. Unpaid.

Illustrations from the *American Anti-Slavery Almanac*

Northern antislavery propagandists indicted the southern way of life, not just slavery. These illustrations depict the South as a region of lynchings, duels, cockfights, and everyday brawls. Even northerners who opposed the abolition of slavery resolved to keep slave-holders out of the western territories.

More and more southerners concluded that the Republican Party itself directed abolitionism and deserved blame for Brown's raid. After all, had not influential Republicans assailed slavery, unconstitutionally tried to ban it, and spoken of an "irrepressible conflict" between slavery and freedom? The Tennessee legislature reflected southern views when it passed resolutions declaring that the Harpers Ferry raid was "the natural fruit of this treasonable 'irrepressible conflict' doctrine put forth by the great head of the Black Republican party and echoed by his subordinates."

The South Contemplates Secession

A pamphlet published in 1860 embodied in its title the growing conviction of southerners that *The South Alone Should Govern the South*. Southerners reached this conclusion gradually and often reluctantly. In 1850, few southerners could have conceived of transferring their allegiance from the United States to some new nation. Relatively insulated from the main tide of immigration, southerners thought of themselves as the most American of Americans. But the events of the 1850s persuaded many southerners that the North had deserted the true principles of the Union. Southerners interpreted northern resistance to the Fugitive Slave Act and to slavery in Kansas as either illegal or unconstitutional, and they viewed headline-grabbing phrases such as "irrepressible conflict" and "a higher law" as virtual declarations of war on the South. To southerners, it was the North, not the South, that had grown peculiar. (See Beyond America—Global Interactions: Slave Emancipation in the Atlantic World.)

To white southerners, the North, not slavery, was the problem. A Mississippi planter, for example, could scarcely believe his eyes when he witnessed a group of northern free blacks refusing to surrender their seats to white women. When assured by northern friends of their support for the South, southerners could only wonder why northerners kept electing Republicans to office. Southerners increasingly described their visits to the North as forays into "enemy territory." More and more, they agreed with a South Carolinian's insistence that the South had to sever itself "from the rotten Northern element."

Viewed as a practical tactic to secure concrete goals, secession did not make a great deal of sense. Some southerners contended that secession would make it easier for the South to acquire more territory for slavery in the Caribbean; yet the South was scarcely united in desiring additional slave territory in Mexico, Cuba, or Central America. States like Alabama, Mississippi, and Texas contained vast tracts of unsettled land that could be converted to cotton cultivation far more easily than the Caribbean. Other southerners continued to complain that the North blocked the access of slaveholders to territories in the continental United States. But if the South were to secede, the remaining continental territories would belong exclusively to the North, which could then legislate for them as it chose. Nor would secession stop future John Browns from infiltrating the South to provoke slave insurrections.

Yet to dwell on the impracticality of secession as a choice for the South is to miss the point. Talk of secession was less a tactic with clear goals than an expression of the South's outrage at what southerners viewed as the irresponsible and unconstitutional course that the Republicans were taking in the North. It was not merely that Republican attacks on slavery sowed the seeds of slave uprisings. More fundamentally, southerners believed that the North was treating the South as its inferior—indeed, as no more than a slave. "Talk of Negro slavery," exclaimed southern proslavery philosopher George Fitzhugh, "is not half so humiliating and disgraceful as the slavery of the South to the North." Having persuaded themselves that slavery made it possible for them to enjoy unprecedented freedom and equality, white southerners took great pride in their homeland. They bitterly dismissed Republican portrayals of the South as a region of arrogant planters and degraded white common folk. Submission to the Republicans, declared Democratic senator Jefferson Davis of Mississippi, "would be intolerable to a proud people."

The Collapse of the Union, 1860–1861

As long as the pliant James Buchanan occupied the White House, southerners did no more than talk about secession. Once aware that Buchanan had declined to seek reelection, however, they approached the election of 1860 with anxiety. Although not all voters realized it, when they cast their ballots in 1860 they were deciding not just the outcome of an election but the fate of the Union. Lincoln's election initiated the process by which the southern states abandoned the United States for a new nation, the Confederate States of America. Initially, the Confederacy consisted only of states in the Lower South. As the Upper South hesitated to embrace secession, moderates searched frantically for a compromise that would save the Union. But they searched in vain. The time for compromise had passed.

The Election of 1860

As a single-issue, free-soil party, the Republicans had done well in the election of 1856. To win in 1860, however, they would have to broaden their appeal in the North, particularly in states like Pennsylvania and Illinois, which they had lost in 1856. To do so, Republican leaders had concluded, they needed to forge an economic program to complement their advocacy of free soil.

A severe economic slump following the so-called Panic of 1857 furnished the Republicans with a fitting opening. The depression shattered more than a decade of American prosperity and thrust economic concerns to the fore. In response, in the late 1850s the Republicans developed an economic program based on support for a protective tariff (popular in Pennsylvania) and on two issues favored in the Midwest, federal aid for internal improvements and the granting to settlers of free 160-acre homesteads out of publicly owned land. By proposing to make these homesteads available to immigrants who were not yet citizens, the Republicans went far in shedding the nativist image that lingered from their early association with the Know-Nothings. Carl Schurz, an 1848 German political refugee who had campaigned for Lincoln against Douglas in 1858, now labored mightily to bring his antislavery countrymen over to the Republican Party.

The Republicans' desire to broaden their appeal also influenced their choice of a candidate. At their convention in Chicago, they nominated Abraham Lincoln over the early front-runner, William H. Seward of New York. Although better known than Lincoln, Seward failed to convince his party that he could carry the key states of Pennsylvania, Illinois, Indiana, and New Jersey. (Rueful Republicans remembered that their presidential candidate John C. Frémont would have won in 1856 if he had carried Pennsylvania and one of the other three states.) Lincoln held the advantage not only of hailing from Illinois but also of projecting a more moderate image than Seward on the slavery issue. Seward's penchant for controversial phrases like "irrepressible conflict" and "higher law" had given him a radical image. Lincoln, in contrast, had repeatedly affirmed that Congress had no constitutional right to interfere with slavery in the South and had explicitly rejected the "higher law" doctrine. The Republicans now needed only to widen their northern appeal.

The Democrats, still claiming to be a national party, had to bridge their own sectional differences. The *Dred Scott* decision and the conflict over the Lecompton constitution had weakened the northern Democrats and strengthened southern Democrats. While Douglas still desperately defended popular sovereignty, southern Democrats stretched *Dred Scott* to conclude that Congress now had to protect slavery in the territories.

The Democratic Party's internal turmoil boiled over at its Charleston convention in the spring of 1860. Failing to force acceptance of a platform guaranteeing federal protection of slavery in the territories, the delegates from the Lower South stalked out. The convention adjourned to Baltimore, where a new fight broke out over the question of seating hastily elected pro-Douglas slates of delegates from the Lower South states that had seceded from the Charleston convention. The decision to seat these pro-Douglas slates led to a walkout by delegates from Virginia and other states in the Upper South. The remaining delegates nominated Douglas; the seceders marched off to another hall in Baltimore and nominated Buchanan's vice president, John C. Breckinridge of Kentucky, on a platform calling for the congressional protection of slavery in the territories. Unable to rally behind a single nominee, the divided Democrats thus ran two candidates, Douglas and Breckinridge. The disruption of the Democratic Party was now complete.

The South still contained an appreciable number of moderates, often former Whigs who had joined with the Know-Nothings behind Fillmore in 1856. In 1860, these moderates, aided by former northern Whigs who opposed both Lincoln and Douglas, forged the new Constitutional Union Party and nominated John Bell, a Tennessee slaveholder who had opposed both the Kansas-Nebraska Act and the Lecompton constitution. Calling for the preservation of the Union, the new party took no stand on the divisive issue of slavery extension.

With four candidates in the field, voters faced a relatively clear choice. Lincoln conceded that the South had a constitutional right to preserve slavery but demanded that Congress prohibit its extension. At the other extreme, Breckinridge insisted that Congress had to protect slavery in any territory that contained slaves. This left the middle ground to Bell and Douglas, the latter still committed to popular sovereignty but in search of a verbal formula that might reconcile it with the *Dred Scott* decision. Lincoln won a clear majority of the electoral vote, 180 to 123 for his three opponents combined. Although Lincoln gained only 39 percent of the popular vote, his popular votes were concentrated in the North, the majority section, and were sufficient to carry every free state. Douglas ran a respectable second to Lincoln in the popular vote but a dismal last in the electoral vote. As the only candidate to campaign in both sections, Douglas suffered from the scattered nature of his votes

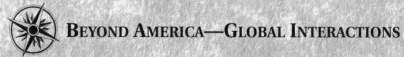
Slave Emancipation in the Atlantic World

Southern defenders of slavery often portrayed northern abolitionists as frenzied extremists who were out of step with the practice of many nations where slavery was still legal. They had a point. In 1860, slavery was lawful in much of Asia and Africa and in nearly all Islamic nations. In forging this argument, however, southerners missed *the* point: slavery in the Americas had been under siege for nearly a century.

After 1760, slavery had come under increasing attack from whites in the United States and Britain. Quakers believed that the "inner light" elevated conscience over tradition, and they provided most of the early recruits for antislavery societies in America and Britain. The principle of natural rights proclaimed by the American revolutionaries of the 1770s also boosted the cause of abolition. All the northern states put slavery on the road to extinction between 1777 and 1804; Congress banned the external slave trade in 1808. American independence also stimulated the antislavery movement in Britain. As long as Britain possessed its American colonies, its government had been reluctant to agitate the slavery issue for fear of arousing the hostility of the southern colonies in America. With American independence, however, antislavery Englishmen like the evangelical Protestants William Wilberforce and Granville Sharp found new listeners in high places in Britain.

The issue in Britain was not slaves on British soil—slaves in Britain had been effectively freed by a judicial decision in 1772—but the international slave trade. Because slave mortality was high in Britain's malaria-ridden sugar colonies like Barbados and Jamaica, the perpetuation of slavery there depended on fresh imports of slaves from Africa. West Indian planters, who formed an influential block in Parliament, staunchly resisted any tampering with the slave trade. But a series of events between 1791 and 1807 undermined their position.

The first of these events occurred in Saint Domingue (now Haiti) in the French West Indies. At the signal of beating drums at 10 P.M. on August 22, 1791, slaves rose against their white masters, burning plantations, killing

Toussaint L'Ouverture
After leading the successful slave insurrection against the French in Saint Domingue in 1791, Toussaint allied in 1794 with the revolutionary French republic, which officially declared an end to slavery. During the next four years his ragged black army prevailed over British and Spanish invaders. When Napoleon Bonaparte tried to re-impose slavery in 1802, Toussaint again turned against the French. At first, his army suffered reverses. Captured and deported to France, Toussaint died in a medieval fortress in April 1803. Within a few months, however, the war in Saint Domingue shifted against the French; victorious blacks established Haiti as an independent nation in 1804.

whites in their beds, and raping their wives on top of their husbands' corpses. The carnage sent shock waves throughout the Atlantic world. Saint Domingue was a very profitable colony. More than twice the size of Jamaica, it produced 30 percent of the world's sugar and more than half of its coffee. With 500,000 black slaves working under oppressive conditions, and 40,000 whites, it was chronically vulnerable to eruption. Further, the insurrection occurred at a time when France itself was in the midst of revolution.

The British government already feared that the ideals of the French Revolution, which had started in 1789, would undermine their monarchy, and they quickly recognized that slaves carried to Jamaica by fleeing French planters were infecting Jamaican slaves with ideas of freedom. When Britain and France went to war in 1793, Britain dispatched an army, larger than any it had sent to crush the American rebellion two decades earlier, to seize Saint Domingue from France and "to prevent a Circulation in the British Colonies of the wild and pernicious Doctrines and Liberty and Equality." But British intervention backfired. Toussaint L'Ouverture, a free black who first joined and then led Saint Domingue's ex-slaves, used guerrilla tactics to inflict heavy casualties on the British army, which had already been decimated by malaria, and in 1798 British troops were forced to evacuate.

Britain's disastrous intervention to preserve West Indian slavery had the unintended effect of enlivening the antislavery movement in Britain. More than half of the nearly 89,000 British troops sent to the West Indies between 1791 and 1801 died of disease or wounds. Even Britons who had no moral objection to slavery found themselves asking whether maintaining colonies based on slave labor was worth the cost.

This practical consideration was soon bolstered by a political argument against slavery. In 1794, the new French Republic had abolished slavery in all French colonies. But in 1802 Napoleon Bonaparte sent an army to crush the rebels in Saint Domingue. Despite savage tactics—one rebel leader's epaulets were nailed to his shoulders before his wife and children, who were then drowned before his eyes—the French army was destroyed by disease and by former slaves desperate to remain free. When the war between France and Britain resumed in 1803, Britain took the moral high ground against Napoleon, the enslaver, by making hostility to slavery a patriotic duty.

In 1807 Parliament banned Britons from engaging in the slave trade. By then, British public opinion had turned against slavery. Because only a small fraction of Britons could vote, West Indian planters continued to have enough influence in Parliament to block the emancipation of slaves. But word of antislavery agitation in Britain reached slaves in Jamaica. In 1831, Christmas fell on a Sunday, and when slaves learned that they would not get an extra day's holiday, they erupted in the largest slave uprising in the history of the British Caribbean. White planters roughed up Protestant missionaries, whom they blamed for seeding the rebellion. Returning to Britain, the missionaries led a renewed onslaught on slavery. In 1833, Parliament decreed the abolition of slavery in all British dependencies. This act, which freed 700,000 slaves in the West Indies and another 60,000 in South Africa, became fully effective on August 1, 1838. Before the Civil War, free American blacks in the North celebrated August 1, not July 4, as their national holiday.

British emancipation breathed new life into the antislavery movement in the United States. John Quincy Adams compared it to an earthquake, and William Lloyd Garrison journeyed to London to study the tactics of British abolitionists. Elsewhere, rebellions against Spanish rule led to laws abolishing slavery in Venezuela (1821), Chile (1823), and Mexico (1829). Although many of these laws had limited effect, once Britain had abolished slavery it had an incentive to undermine slavery everywhere in order to deny its rivals a competitive economic advantage. The argument advanced by southerners in the 1840s that the United States had to annex Texas to prevent Britain from emancipating slaves there was not entirely fanciful. True, Britain was in no position to abolish slavery in Texas, to which it had no claim. But Britain, once the world's leading slave-trading nation and a country with which the United States had already fought two wars, had become the world's leading antislavery nation.

In 1860, slavery survived in the Western Hemisphere only in the American South, Cuba, Puerto Rico, and Brazil. Southerners who had long invoked the universality of slavery as a reason to continue it were now whistling in the dark.

Questions for Analysis

- What factors explain Britain's shift toward antislavery?
- How did this shift affect defenders and opponents of slavery in the United States?

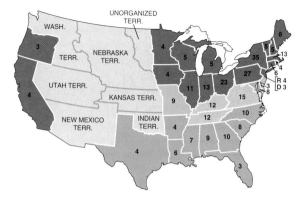

	Electoral Vote	Popular Vote	Percentage of Popular Vote
Republican Abraham Lincoln	180	1,865,593	39.8
Democratic, Southern John C. Breckinridge	72	848,356	18.1
Democratic, Northern Stephen A. Douglas	12	1,382,713	29.5
Constitutional Union John Bell	39	592,906	12.6
Divided			

Map 14.4 The Election of 1860

and carried only Missouri. Bell won Virginia, Kentucky, and Tennessee, and Breckinridge captured Maryland and the Lower South (see Map 14.4).

The Movement for Secession

The president-elect was so unpopular in the South that his name had not even appeared on the ballot in many southern states. Lincoln's election struck most of the white South as a calculated northern insult. The North, a South Carolina planter told a visitor from England, "has got so far toward being abolitionized as to elect a man avowedly hostile to our institutions."

Few southerners believed that Lincoln would fulfill his promise to protect slavery in the South, and most feared that he would act as a mere front man for more John Browns. "Now that the black radical Republicans have the power I suppose they will Brown us all," a South Carolinian lamented. An uneducated Mississippian residing in Illinois expressed his reaction to the election more bluntly:

It seems the north wants the south to raise cotton and sugar rice tobacco for the northern states, also to pay taxes and fight her battles and get territory for the purpose of the north to send her greasy Dutch and free niggers into the territory to get rid of them. At any rate that was what elected old Abe President. Some professed conservative Republicans Think and say that Lincoln will be conservative also but sir my opinion is that Lincoln will deceive

them. [He] will undoubtedly please the abolitionists for at his election they nearly all went into fits with Joy.

Some southerners had threatened secession at the prospect of Lincoln's election. Now the moment of decision had arrived. On December 20, 1860, a South Carolina convention voted unanimously for secession; in short order Alabama, Mississippi, Florida, Georgia, Louisiana, and Texas followed. On February 4, delegates from these seven states met in Montgomery, Alabama, and established the **Confederate States of America**.

Despite the abruptness of southern withdrawal from the Union, the movement for secession was laced with uncertainty. Many southerners had resisted calls for immediate secession. Even after Lincoln's election, fire-eating secessionists had met fierce opposition in the Lower South from so-called cooperationists, who called upon the South to act in unison or not at all. Many cooperationists had hoped to delay secession in order to wring concessions from the North that might remove the need for secession. Jefferson Davis, inaugurated in February 1861 as president of the Confederacy, was a reluctant secessionist who remained in the United States Senate two weeks after his own state of Mississippi had seceded. Even zealous advocates of secession had a hard time reconciling themselves to secession and believing that they were no longer citizens of the United States. "How do you feel now, dear Mother," a Georgian wrote, "that *we* are in a foreign land?"

At first, the Upper South states of Virginia, North Carolina, Tennessee, and Arkansas flatly rejected secession (see Map 14.5). In contrast to the Lower South, which had a guaranteed export market for its cotton, the Upper South depended heavily on economic ties to the North that would be severed by secession. Furthermore, with proportionately far fewer slaves than the Lower South, the states of the Upper South doubted the loyalty of their sizable nonslaveholding populations to the idea of secession. Virginia, for example, had every reason to question the allegiance to secession of its nonslaveholding western counties, which would soon break away to form Unionist West Virginia. Few in the Upper South could forget the raw nerve touched by the publication in 1857 of Hinton R. Helper's *The Impending Crisis of the South*. A nonslaveholding North Carolinian, Helper had described slavery as a curse upon poor white southerners and thereby questioned one of the most sacred southern doctrines, the idea that slavery rendered all whites equal. If secession were to spark a war between the states, moreover, the Upper South appeared to be the likeliest battleground. Whatever the exact weight assignable to each of these factors, one point is clear: the secession movement that South Carolina so boldly started in December 1860 seemed to be falling apart by March 1861.

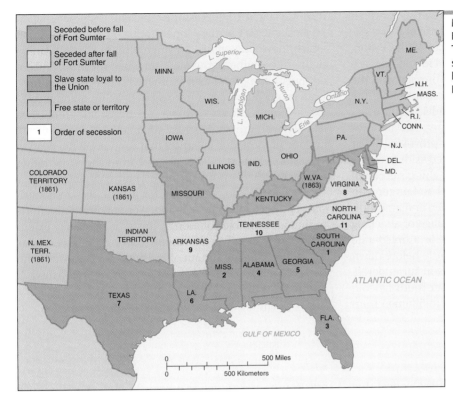

Map 14.5 Secession
Four key states—Virginia, Arkansas, Tennessee, and North Carolina—did not secede until after the fall of Fort Sumter. The border slave states of Maryland, Delaware, Kentucky, and Missouri stayed in the Union.

The Search for Compromise

The lack of southern unity confirmed the view of most Republicans that the secessionists were more bluster than substance. Seward described secession as the work of "a relatively few hotheads," and Lincoln believed that the loyal majority of southerners would soon wrest control from the fire-eating minority.

This perception stiffened Republican resolve to resist compromise. Moderate John J. Crittenden of Kentucky proposed compensation for owners of runaway slaves, repeal of northern personal-liberty laws, a constitutional amendment to prohibit the federal government from interfering with slavery in the southern states, and another amendment to restore the Missouri Compromise line for the remaining territories and protect slavery below it. But in the face of steadfast Republican opposition, the Crittenden plan collapsed.

Lincoln's faith in a "loyal majority" of southerners exaggerated both their numbers and their devotion to the Union. Many southern opponents of the fire-eating secessionists were sitting on the fence and hoping for major concessions from the North; their allegiance to the Union thus was conditional. Lincoln can be faulted for misreading southern opinion, but even if his assessment had been accurate, it is unlikely that he would have

accepted the Crittenden plan. The sticking point was the proposed extension of the Missouri Compromise line. To Republicans this was a surrender, not a compromise, because it hinged on the abandonment of free soil, the founding principle of their party. In addition, Lincoln well knew that some southerners still talked of seizing more territory for slavery in the Caribbean. In proposing to extend the 36°30′ line, the Crittenden plan specifically referred to territories "hereafter acquired." Lincoln feared that it would be only a matter of time "till we shall have to take Cuba as a condition upon which they [the seceding states] will stay in the Union."

Beyond these considerations, the precipitous secession of the Lower South changed the question that Lincoln faced. The issue was no longer slavery extension but secession. The Lower South had left the Union in the face of losing a fair election. For Lincoln to have caved in to such pressure would have violated majority rule, the principle upon which the nation, not just his party, had been founded.

The Coming of War

By the time Lincoln took office in March 1861, little more than a spark was needed to ignite a war. Lincoln pledged in his inaugural address to "hold, occupy, and possess" federal property in the seven states that had seceded, an assertion that committed him to the defense of Fort Pickens in Florida and **Fort Sumter** in the harbor of Charleston, South Carolina. William Seward, whom Lincoln had appointed secretary of state, now became obsessed with the idea of conciliating the Lower South in order to hold the Upper South in the Union. In addition to advising the evacuation of federal forces from Fort Sumter, Seward proposed a scheme to reunify the nation by provoking a war with France and Spain. But Lincoln brushed aside Seward's advice. Instead, the president informed the governor of South Carolina of his intention to supply Fort Sumter with much-needed provisions, but not with men and ammunition. To gain the dubious military advantage of attacking Fort Sumter before the arrival of relief ships, Confederate batteries began to bombard the fort shortly before dawn on April 12. The next day, the fort's garrison surrendered.

Proclaiming an insurrection in the Lower South, Lincoln now appealed for seventy-five thousand militiamen from the loyal states to suppress the rebellion. His proclamation pushed citizens of the Upper South off the fence upon which they had perched for three months. "I am a Union man," one southerner wrote, "but when they [the Lincoln administration] send men south it will change my notions. I can do nothing against my own people." In quick succession, Virginia, North Carolina, Arkansas, and Tennessee leagued with the Confederacy. After acknowledging that "I am one of those dull creatures that cannot see the good of secession," Robert E. Lee resigned from the army rather than lead federal troops against his native Virginia.

The North, too, was ready for a fight, less to abolish slavery than to punish secession. Worn out from his efforts to find a peaceable solution to the issue of slavery extension, and with only a short time to live, Stephen Douglas assaulted "the new system of resistance by the sword and bayonet to the results of the ballot-box" and affirmed: "I deprecate war, but if it must come I am with my country, under all circumstances, and in every contingency."

Conclusion

The expectation of most American political leaders that the Compromise of 1850 would finally resolve the vexing issue of slavery extension had a surface plausibility. In neither 1850 nor 1860 did the great majority of Americans favor the abolition of slavery in the southern states. Rather, they divided over slavery in the territories, an issue seemingly settled by the Compromise. Stephen A. Douglas, its leading architect and a man who assumed that he always had his finger on the popular pulse, was sure that slavery had reached its natural limits, that popular sovereignty would keep it out of the territories, and that the furor over slavery extension would die down.

Douglas believed that only a few hotheads had kept the slavery extension issue alive. He was wrong. The differences between northerners and southerners over slavery extension were grounded on different understandings of liberty, which to northerners meant their freedom to pursue self-interest without competition from slaves, and to southerners their freedom to dispose of their legally acquired property, slaves, as they chose. The Compromise, which had barely scraped through Congress, soon unraveled. Enforcement of the Fugitive Slave Act brought to the surface widespread northern resentment of slaveholders, people who seemingly lived off the work of others, and a determination to exclude the possibility of slavery in the territories. Southern support for Douglas's Kansas-Nebraska bill, with its repeal of the Missouri Compromise and its apparent invitation to southerners to bring slaves into Kansas, persuaded many northerners that the South harbored the design of extending slavery. For their part, southerners, already angered by northern defiance of the Fugitive Slave Act, interpreted northern outrage against Douglas's bill as further evidence of the North's disrespect for the rule of law.

By the mid-1850s, the sectional division was spinning out of the control of politicians. Deep divisions between the Whigs' free-soil northern wing and their proslavery southern wing led to the party's collapse in the wake of the Kansas-Nebraska Act. Divisions between northern and southern Democrats would be papered over as long as the Democratic Party could unite behind Douglas's formula of popular sovereignty. But popular sovereignty failed its test in Kansas. The outbreak of civil strife in Kansas pushed former northern Whigs and many northern Democrats toward the new, purely sectional, Republicans, a party whose very existence southerners interpreted as a mark of northern contempt for them.

The South was not yet ready for secession. Before it took that drastic step, it had to convince itself that the North's real design was not merely to restrict the extension of slavery but to destroy slavery and, with it, the South itself. Northern hostility to the *Dred Scott* decision and sympathy for John Brown struck southerners as proof of just such an intent.

As an expression of principled outrage, secession capped a decade in which each side had clothed itself in

Chronology, 1850–1861

1848	Zachary Taylor elected president.
1849	California seeks admission to the Union as a free state.
1850	Nashville convention assembles to discuss the South's grievances. Compromise of 1850.
1852	Harriet Beecher Stowe, *Uncle Tom's Cabin*. Franklin Pierce elected president.
1853	Gadsden Purchase.
1854	Ostend Manifesto. Kansas-Nebraska Act. William Walker leads filibustering expedition into Nicaragua.
1854–1855	Know-Nothing and Republican parties emerge.
1855	Proslavery forces steal the election for a territorial legislature in Kansas. Proslavery Kansans establish a government in Lecompton. Free-soil government established in Topeka, Kansas.
1856	"The sack of Lawrence." John Brown's Pottawatomie massacre. James Buchanan elected president.
1857	*Dred Scott* decision. President Buchanan endorses the Lecompton constitution in Kansas. Panic of 1857.
1858	Congress refuses to admit Kansas to the Union under the Lecompton constitution. Lincoln-Douglas debates.
1859	John Brown's raid on Harpers Ferry.
1860	Abraham Lincoln elected president. South Carolina secedes from the Union.
1861	The remaining Lower South states secede. Confederate States of America established. Crittenden compromise plan collapses. Lincoln takes office. Firing on Fort Sumter; Civil War begins. Upper South secedes.

principles that were deeply embedded in the nation's political heritage. Both sides subscribed to the rule of law, which each accused the other of deserting. In the end, war broke out between siblings who, although they claimed the same heritage and inheritance, had become virtual strangers to each other.

For Further Reference

Charles B. Dew, *Apostles of Disunion* (2001). A careful analysis of how southerners rationalized secession.

William E. Gienapp, *The Origins of the Republican Party, 1852–1856* (1987). A comprehensive account of the birth of a major party.

Michael F. Holt, *The Political Crisis of the 1850s* (1978). A lively reinterpretation of the politics of the 1850s.

David Potter, *The Impending Crisis, 1848–1861* (1976). The best one-volume overview of the events leading to the Civil War.

Key Terms

John Brown
free soil
popular sovereignty
"higher law"
Stephen A. Douglas
Compromise of 1850
Fugitive Slave Act
personal-liberty laws
Uncle Tom's Cabin
Franklin Pierce

Kansas-Nebraska Act
Slave Power
Know-Nothings
Republican Party
Charles Sumner
Dred Scott v. *Sandford*
Lecompton constitution
Abraham Lincoln
Confederate States of America
Fort Sumter

Leonard L. Richards, *The Slave Power* (2000). An examination of why northerners resented and feared the power of slaveholders to dominate the United States.

Mark Stegmaier, *Texas, New Mexico, and the Compromise of 1850* (1996). A good study of the significance of the Texas–New Mexico boundary dispute for the sectional crisis.

Chapter 15

Soldiers' Photographs, 1861–1865
These photos of Civil War soldiers, made by unknown photographers, ended up at the Dead Letter Office, an agency of the U.S. Postal Service.

Crucible of Freedom: Civil War, 1861–1865

Gertrude Clanton Thomas in the 1850s

"Events transcending in importance anything that has ever happened within the recollection of any living person in *our* country, have occurred since I have written last in my journal," wrote Georgia matron Gertrude Clanton Thomas in July 1861. "*War* has been declared." Fort Sumter in South Carolina had surrendered; Lincoln had called for 75,000 troops; four more southern states—Virginia, North Carolina, Arkansas, and Tennessee—had left the Union; the newly formed Confederate government had moved from Montgomery, Alabama, to Richmond, Virginia; and thousands of troops had passed through Augusta, Georgia, on their way to the front. "So much has taken place," Gertrude Thomas declared, that "I appear to be endeavoring to recall incidents which have occurred many years instead of months ago."

At her marriage in 1852, Gertrude Thomas had become mistress of a small estate, Belmont, about six miles south of Augusta, in Richmond County, Georgia. The estate and thirty thousand dollars' worth of slaves had been part of her dowry. While her husband, Jefferson Thomas, farmed plantation land he had inherited in nearby Burke County, Gertrude Thomas supervised the work force at Belmont and wrestled with her position on slavery. "I will stand to the opinion that the institution of slavery degrades the white man more than the Negro," she had declared in 1858; "all southern women are abolitionists at heart." After secession, her doubts about slavery persisted. "[T]he view has gradually become fixed in my mind that the institution of slavery is not right," she confided to her journal during the war. "I can but think that to hold men and women in *perpetual* bondage is wrong." On other occasions, more practical concerns about slaves emerged. "I do think that if we had the same [amount] invested in something else as a means of support," Gertrude Thomas wrote, "I would willingly, nay gladly, have the responsibility of them taken off my shoulders."

But slavery was the basis of Gertrude Thomas's wealth and social position; she disliked it not because it oppressed the enslaved but because of the problems it posed for the slave-owning elite. When war began, Gertrude and Jefferson Thomas fervently supported the newborn Confederacy. Jefferson Thomas enlisted in a cavalry company, and served until 1862, when, passed over for promotion, he hired a substitute. During the months that he spent with his company in Virginia, Jefferson Thomas longed for swift triumph. "I feel as if I wished this war was over and that I was home and that every Yankee engaged in it was at the bottom of the ocean," he wrote to his wife as 1861 came to a close. Sharing his militance, Gertrude Thomas loyally boosted the Confederate cause. "Our country is invaded—our homes are in danger—We are deprived or they are attempting to deprive us of that glorious liberty for which our Fathers fought and bled and shall we finally submit to this? Never!" she declared. "We are only asking for self-government and freedom to decide our own destinies. We claim nothing of the North but—*to be let alone.*"

As the Civil War raged on, Gertrude Thomas longed for its end. She wrote in her journal on New Year's Day 1862. "God speed the day when our independence shall be achieved, our southern confederacy acknowledged, and peace be with us again." But peace came at a price. In the last year of war, Union invasions damaged the Thomas plantations in Burke County and threatened the property near Augusta as well. The Civil War's end brought further hardship to the Thomas family, which lost a small fortune of fifteen thousand dollars in Confederate bonds and ninety slaves. One by one, the former slaves left the Belmont estate, never to return. "As to the emancipated Negroes," Gertrude Thomas told her journal in May 1865, "while there is of course a natural dislike to the loss of so much property, in my inmost soul, I cannot regret it."

In their determination and belligerence, the Thomases were not alone. When Fort Sumter fell, Union and Confederate volunteers like Jefferson Thomas responded to the rush to arms that engulfed both regions. Partisans on both sides, like Gertrude Thomas, claimed the ideals of liberty, loyalty, and patriotism as their own. Like the

Thomas family, most Americans of 1861 harbored what turned out to be false expectations.

Few volunteers or even politicians anticipated a protracted war. Most northern estimates ranged from one month to a year; rebels, too, counted on a speedy victory. Neither northerners nor southerners anticipated the carnage that the war would bring; one out of every five soldiers who fought in the Civil War died in it. Once it became clear that the war would not end with a few battles, leaders on both sides considered strategies once unpalatable or even unthinkable. The South, where the hand of government had always fallen lightly on the citizenry, found that it had to impose a draft and virtually extort supplies from its civilian population. By the war's end, the Confederacy was even ready to arm its slaves in an ironically desperate effort to save a society founded on slavery. The North, which began the war with the limited objective of overcoming secession and explicitly disclaimed any intention of interfering with slavery, found that in order to win it had to shred the fabric of southern society by destroying slavery. For politicians as well as soldiers, the war defied expectations and turned into a series of surprises. The inseparable connection of Union war goals and the emancipation of slaves was perhaps the most momentous surprise.

Focus Questions

- What advantages did each combatant, Union and Confederate, possess at the start of the Civil War?

- How successfully did the governments and economies of the North and South respond to the pressures of war?

- How did the issue of emancipation transform the war?

- What factors determined the military outcome of the war?

- In what lasting ways did the Civil War change the United States as a nation?

Mobilizing for War

North and South alike were unprepared for war. In April 1861, the Union had only a small army of sixteen thousand men scattered all over the country, mostly in the West. One-third of Union army officers had resigned to join the Confederacy. The nation's new president, Abraham Lincoln, struck many observers as a yokel. That such a government could marshal its people for war seemed a doubtful proposition. The federal government had levied no direct taxes for decades, and it had never imposed a draft. The Confederacy was even less prepared; it had no tax structure, no navy, only two tiny gunpowder factories, and poorly equipped, unconnected railroad lines.

During the first two years of the war, both sides would have to overcome these deficiencies, raise and supply large armies, and finance the heavy costs of war. In each region, mobilization for war expanded the powers of the central government to an extent that few had anticipated.

Recruitment and Conscription

The Civil War armies were the largest organizations ever created in America; by the end of the war, over 2 million men would serve in the Union army and 800,000 in the Confederate army (see Figure 15.1). In the first flush of enthusiasm for war, volunteers rushed to the colors. "I go for wiping them out," a Virginian wrote to his governor. "War! and volunteers are the only topics of conversation or thought," a student at Oberlin College in Ohio told his brother in April 1861. "I cannot study. I cannot sleep. I cannot work, and I don't know as I can write."

At first, the raising of armies depended on local efforts rather than on national or even state direction. Citizens opened recruiting offices in their hometowns, held rallies, and signed up volunteers; regiments were usually composed of soldiers from the same locale. Southern cavalrymen provided their own horses, and uniforms everywhere were left mainly to local option. In both armies, officers up to the rank of colonel were elected by other officers and enlisted men.

This informal and democratic way of raising and organizing soldiers could not long withstand the stress of

Figure 15.1 Opposing Armies of the Civil War
"They sing and whoop, they laugh: they holler to de people on de ground and sing out 'Good-bye,'" remarked a slave watching rebel troops depart. "All going down to die." As this graph shows (see also Figure 15.3), the Civil War had profound human costs. In both the North and South, hardly a family did not grieve for a lost relative or friend. Injured veterans became a common sight in cities, towns, and rural districts well into the twentieth century. This photograph shows Union volunteers with amputations performed by U.S. surgeons during the Civil War.

Union Forces / Confederate Forces

	Union Forces	Confederate Forces
Total size	2,100,000	800,000
Draftees	46,000	120,000
Substitutes	118,000	70,000
Desertions	200,000	104,000
Desertees caught and returned	80,000	21,000
Deaths from battle wounds	110,070	94,000
Deaths from disease	249,930	166,000

war. As early as July 1861, the Union began examinations for officers. Also, as casualties mounted, military demand soon exceeded the supply of volunteers. The Confederacy felt the pinch first and in April 1862 enacted the first **conscription** law in American history. It required all able-bodied white men aged eighteen to thirty-five to serve in the military for three years. Subsequent amendments raised the age limit to forty-five and then to fifty, and lowered it to seventeen.

The Confederacy's Conscription Act antagonized southerners. Opponents charged that the draft was an assault on state sovereignty by a despotic regime and that the law would "do away with all the patriotism we have." Exemptions that applied to many occupations, from religious ministry to shoemaking, angered the nonexempt. So did a loophole, closed in 1863, that allowed the well-off to hire substitutes. One amendment, the so-called 20-Negro law, exempted an owner or overseer of twenty or more slaves from service. Although southerners widely feared that the slave population could not be controlled if all able-bodied white men were away in the army, the 20-Negro law led to complaints about "a rich man's war but a poor man's fight."

Despite opposition, the Confederate draft became increasingly hard to evade, and this fact stimulated volunteering. Only one soldier in five was a draftee, but 70 to 80 percent of eligible white southerners served in the Confederate army. A new conscription law of 1864, which required all soldiers then in the army to stay in for the duration of the war, ensured that a high proportion of Confederate soldiers would be battle-hardened veterans.

Once the army was raised, the Confederacy had to supply it. At first, the South relied on arms and ammunition imported from Europe, weapons confiscated from federal arsenals, and guns captured on the battlefield. These stopgap measures bought time until an industrial base was established. By 1862, southerners had a competent head of ordnance (weaponry), Josiah Gorgas. The Confederacy assigned ordnance contracts to privately owned factories like the Tredegar Iron Works in Richmond, provided loans to establish new factories, and created government-owned industries like the giant Augusta Powder Works in Georgia. The South lost few, if any, battles for want of munitions.

Supplying troops with clothing and food proved more difficult. Southern soldiers frequently went without shoes; during the South's invasion of Maryland in 1862, thousands of Confederate soldiers had to be left behind because they could not march barefoot on Maryland's gravel-surfaced roads. Late in the war, Robert E. Lee's Army of Northern Virginia ran out of food but never out of ammunition. Southern supply problems had several sources: railroads that fell into disrepair or were captured, an economy that relied more heavily on producing tobacco and cotton than growing food, and Union invasions early in the war that overran the livestock and grain-raising districts of central Tennessee and Virginia. Close to desperation, the Confederate Congress in 1863 passed the Impressment Act, which authorized army officers to take food from reluctant farmers at prescribed prices. This unpopular law also empowered agents to impress slaves into labor for the army, a provision that provoked yet more resentment.

The industrial North had fewer problems supplying its troops with arms, clothes, and food. However, recruiting troops was another matter. When the initial tide of enthusiasm for enlistment ebbed, Congress followed the Confederacy's example and turned to conscription with the Enrollment Act of March 1863; every able-bodied white male citizen aged twenty to forty-five now faced the draft.

Like the Confederate conscription law of 1862, the Enrollment Act granted exemptions, although only to high government officials, ministers, and men who were the sole support of widows, orphans, or indigent parents. It also offered two means of escaping the draft: substitution, or paying another man who would serve instead; and commutation, paying a $300 fee to the government. Enrollment districts often competed for volunteers by offering cash payments (bounties); dishonest "bounty jumpers" repeatedly registered and deserted after collecting their payment. Democrats denounced conscription as a violation of individual liberties and states' rights. Ordinary citizens of little means resented the commutation and substitution provision and leveled their own "poor man's fight" charges. Still, as in the Confederacy, the law stimulated volunteering. Only 8 percent of Union soldiers were draftees or substitutes.

Financing the War

The recruitment and supply of huge armies lay far beyond the capacity of American public finance at the start of the war. In the 1840s and 1850s, annual federal spending had averaged only 2 percent of the gross national product. With such meager expenditures, the federal government met its revenue needs from tariff duties and income from the sale of public lands. During the war, however, annual federal expenditures gradually rose, and the need for new sources of revenue became urgent. Yet neither the Union nor the Confederacy initially wished to impose taxes, to which Americans were unaccustomed. In August 1861, the Confederacy enacted a small property tax and the Union an income tax, but neither raised much revenue.

Both sides therefore turned to war bonds; that is, to loans from citizens to be repaid by future generations. Patriotic southerners quickly bought up the Confederacy's first bond issue ($15 million) in 1861. That same year, a financial wizard, Philadelphia banker Jay Cooke, induced the northern public to subscribe to a much larger bond issue ($150 million). But bonds had to be paid for in gold or silver coin (specie), which was in short supply. Soaking up most of its available specie, the South's first bond issue threatened to be its last. In the North, many hoarded their gold rather than spend it on bonds.

Recognizing the limitations of taxation and of bond issues, both sides began to print paper money. Early in 1862, Lincoln signed into law the **Legal Tender Act**, which authorized the issue of $150 million of the so-called greenbacks. Christopher Memminger, the Confederacy's treasury secretary, and Salmon P. Chase, his Union counterpart, shared a distrust of paper money, but as funds dwindled each came around to the idea. The availability of paper money made it easier to pay soldiers, levy taxes, and sell war bonds. Yet doubts about paper money lingered. Unlike gold and silver, which had established market values, the value of paper money depended mainly on the public's confidence in the government that issued it. To bolster that confidence, Union officials made the greenbacks legal tender (that is, acceptable in payment of most public and private debts).

In contrast, the Confederacy never made its paper money legal tender, and suspicions arose that the southern government lacked confidence in its own paper issues. To compound the problem, the Confederacy raised less than 5 percent of its wartime revenue from taxes. (The comparable figure for the North was 21 percent.) The Confederacy did enact a comprehensive tax measure in 1863, but Union invasions and the South's relatively undeveloped system of internal transportation made tax collection a hit-or-miss proposition.

Confidence in the South's paper money quickly evaporated, and the value of Confederate paper in relation to gold plunged. The Confederacy responded by printing more paper money, a billion dollars by 1865, but this action merely accelerated southern inflation. Whereas prices in the North rose about 80 percent during the war, the Confederacy suffered an inflation rate of over 9,000 percent. What cost a southerner one dollar in 1861 cost forty-six dollars by 1864.

By raising taxes, floating bonds, and printing paper money, both the Union and the Confederacy broke with the hard-money, minimal-government traditions of American public finance. For the most part, these changes were unanticipated and often reluctant adaptations to wartime conditions. But in the North, the Republicans took advantage of the departure of the southern Democrats from Congress to push through one measure that they and their Whig predecessors had long advocated, a system of national banking. Passed in February 1863 over the opposition of northern Democrats, the **National Bank Act** established criteria by which a bank could obtain a federal charter and issue national bank notes (notes backed by the federal government). It also gave private bankers an incentive to purchase war bonds. The North's ability to revolutionize its system of public finance reflected both its long experience with complex financial transactions and its political cohesion in wartime.

Political Leadership in Wartime

The Civil War pitted rival political systems as well as armies and economies against each other. The South entered the war with several apparent political advantages. Lincoln's call for militiamen to suppress the rebellion had transformed hesitators in the South into tenacious secessionists. "Never was a people more united or more determined," a New Orleans woman wrote in the spring of 1861. Southerners also claimed a strong leader. A former secretary of war and U.S. senator from Mississippi, President **Jefferson Davis** of the Confederacy possessed experience, honesty, courage, and what one officer described as "a jaw sawed in *steel*."

In contrast, the Union's list of political liabilities appeared lengthy. Loyal but contentious, northern Democrats objected to conscription, the National Bank Act, and the abolition of slavery. Among Republicans, Lincoln had trouble commanding respect. Unlike Davis, he had served in neither the cabinet nor the Senate, and his informal western manners dismayed easterners. Northern setbacks early in the war convinced most Republicans in Congress that Lincoln was an ineffectual leader. Criticism of Lincoln sprang from a group of Republicans who became known as **Radical Republicans** and who included Secretary of the Treasury Salmon P. Chase, Senator Charles Sumner of Massachusetts, and Representative Thaddeus Stevens of Pennsylvania. The Radicals never formed a tightly knit unit; on some issues they cooperated with

Abraham Lincoln
When Lincoln became president in March 1861, he faced more severe problems than any predecessor. Photographer Mathew Brady captured this image of the solemn president-elect on February 23, 1861, a few weeks after the formation of the Confederacy and shortly before Lincoln's inauguration.

Lincoln. But they assailed him early in the war for failing to make emancipation a war goal and later for being too eager to readmit the conquered rebel states into the Union.

Lincoln's distinctive style of leadership at once encouraged and disarmed opposition within the Republican Party. Keeping his counsel to himself until ready to act, he met complaints with homespun anecdotes that caught his opponents off guard. The Radicals frequently concluded that Lincoln was a prisoner of the conservative wing of the party; conservatives complained that he was too close to the Radicals. But Lincoln's cautious reserve had the dual benefit of leaving open his lines of communication with both wings of the party and fragmenting his opposition. He also co-opted some of his critics, including Chase, by bringing them into his cabinet.

In contrast, Jefferson Davis had a knack for making enemies. A West Pointer, he would rather have led the army than the government. His cabinet suffered from frequent resignations; the Confederacy had five secretaries of war in four years, for example. Davis's relations with his vice president, Alexander Stephens of Georgia, bordered on disastrous. A wisp of a man, Stephens weighed less than a hundred pounds and looked like a boy with a withered face. But he compensated for his slight physique with a tongue as acidic as Davis's. Leaving Richmond, the Confederate capital, in 1862, Stephens spent most of the war in Georgia, where he sniped at Davis as "weak and vacillating, timid, petulant, peevish, obstinate."

The clash between Davis and Stephens involved not just personalities but also an ideological division, a rift, in fact, like that at the heart of the Confederacy. The Confederate Constitution, drafted in February 1861, explicitly guaranteed the sovereignty of the Confederate states and prohibited the Confederate Congress from enacting protective tariffs and from supporting internal improvements (measures long opposed by southern voters). For Stephens and other influential Confederate leaders—among them the governors of Georgia and North Carolina—the Confederacy existed not only to protect slavery but, equally important, to enshrine the doctrine of states' rights. In contrast, Davis's main objective was to secure the independence of the South from the North, if necessary at the expense of states' rights.

This difference between Davis and Stephens bore some resemblance to the discord between Lincoln and the northern Democrats. Like Davis, Lincoln believed that winning the war demanded a boost in the central government's power; like Stephens, northern Democrats resisted governmental centralization. But Lincoln could control his foes more skillfully than Davis because, by temperament, he was more suited to conciliation and also because the nature of party politics in the two sections differed.

In the South, the Democrats and the remaining Whigs agreed to suspend party rivalries for the duration of the war. Although intended to promote southern unity, this decision actually encouraged disunity. Without the institutionalization of conflict that party rivalry provided, southern politics disintegrated along personal and factional lines. Lacking a party organization to back him, Davis could not mobilize votes to pass measures that he favored, nor could he depend on the support of party loyalists.

In contrast, in the Union, northern Democrats' organized opposition to Lincoln tended to unify the Republicans. In the 1862 elections, which occurred at a low ebb of Union military fortunes, the Democrats won control of five large states, including Lincoln's own Illinois. Republican leaders learned a lesson: no matter how much they disdained Lincoln, they had to rally behind him or risk losing office. Ultimately, the Union would develop more political cohesion than the Confederacy, not because it had fewer divisions but because it managed its divisions more effectively.

Securing the Union's Borders

Even before large-scale fighting began, Lincoln moved to safeguard Washington, which was bordered by two slave states (Virginia and Maryland) and filled with Confederate sympathizers. A week after Fort Sumter, a Baltimore mob attacked a Massachusetts regiment bound for Washington, but enough troops slipped through to protect the capital. Lincoln then dispatched federal troops to Maryland, where he suspended the writ of *habeas corpus* (a court order requiring that the detainer of a prisoner bring that person to court and show cause for his or her detention); federal troops could now arrest prosecession Marylanders without formally charging them with specific offenses. Cowed by Lincoln's bold moves, the legislatures of Maryland and Delaware (another border slave state) rejected secession.

Next Lincoln authorized the arming of Union sympathizers in Kentucky, a slave state with a Unionist legislature, a secessionist governor, and a thin chance of staying neutral. Lincoln also stationed troops under General Ulysses S. Grant just across the Ohio River from Kentucky, in Illinois. When a Confederate army invaded Kentucky early in 1862, the state's legislature turned to Grant to drive it out. Officially, at least, Kentucky became the third slave state to declare for the Union. The fourth, Missouri, was ravaged by four years of fighting between Union and Confederate troops, and between bands of guerrillas and bushwhackers, a name for Confederate guerrillas who lurked in the underbrush. These included William Quantrill, a rebel desperado, and his murderous apprentices, Frank and Jesse James. Despite savage fighting and the divided loyalties of its people, Missouri never left the Union. West Virginia, admitted to the Union in 1863, would become the last of five border states, or slave states that remained in the Union. (West Virginia was established in 1861, when thirty-five counties in the mainly nonslaveholding region of Virginia

west of the Shenandoah Valley refused to follow the state's leaders into secession.)

By holding the first four border slave states—Maryland, Delaware, Kentucky, and Missouri—in the Union, Lincoln kept open his routes to the free states and gained access to the river systems in Kentucky and Missouri that led into the heart of the Confederacy. Lincoln's firmness, particularly in Maryland, scotched charges that he was weak-willed. The crisis also forced the president to exercise long-dormant powers. In the case *Ex parte* Merryman (1861), Chief Justice Roger B. Taney ruled that Lincoln had exceeded his authority in suspending the writ of *habeas corpus* in Maryland. The president, citing the Constitution's authorization of the writ's suspension in "Cases of Rebellion" (Article I, Section 9), insisted that he, rather than Congress, would determine whether a rebellion existed; and he ignored Taney's ruling.

In Battle, 1861–1862

The Civil War was the first war to rely extensively on railroads, the telegraph, mass-produced weapons, joint army-navy tactics, iron-plated warships, rifled guns and artillery, and trench warfare. All of this lends some justification to its description as the first modern war. But to the participants, slogging through muddy swamps and weighed down with equipment, the war hardly seemed modern. In many ways, the soldiers had the more accurate perspective, for the new weapons did not always work, and both sides employed tactics that were more traditional than modern.

Armies, Weapons, and Strategies

Compared to the Confederacy's 9 million people, one-third of them slaves, the Union had 22 million people in 1861 (see Figure 15.2). The North also had 3.5 times as many white men of military age, 90 percent of all U.S. industrial capacity, and two-thirds of its railroad track. Yet the Union faced a daunting challenge. Its goal was to force the South back into the Union, whereas the South fought merely for its independence. To subdue the Confederacy, the North would have to sustain offensive operations over a vast area.

Measured against this challenge, the Union's advantages in population and technology shrank. The North had more men, but needing to defend long supply lines and occupy captured areas, it could commit a smaller proportion of them to frontline duty. The South, which

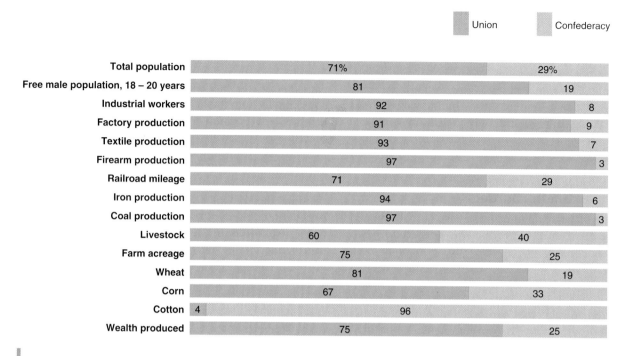

Figure 15.2 Comparative Population and Economic Resources of the Union and the Confederacy, 1861
At the start of the war, the Union enjoyed huge advantages in population, industry, railroad mileage, and wealth, and, as it would soon prove, a superior ability to mobilize its vast resources. The Confederacy, however, enjoyed the many advantages of fighting a defensive war.

relied on slaves for labor, could assign a higher proportion of its white male population to combat. The North required, and possessed, superior railroads, though it had to move troops and supplies huge distances. Fighting defensively on so-called interior lines, the South could shift its troops relatively short distances within its defensive arc without using railroads. Not only could guerrillas easily sabotage northern railroads, but once Union troops moved away from their railroad bases, their supply wagons often bogged down on wretched southern roads that became watery ditches in bad weather. Finally, southerners had an edge in soldiers' morale, for Confederate troops battled on home ground. "No people ever warred for independence," a southern general acknowledged, "with more relative advantages than the Confederates."

The Civil War witnessed experiments with a variety of newly developed weapons, including the submarine, the repeating rifle, and the multibarreled Gatling gun, the forerunner of the machine gun. Yet these innovations had less impact on the war than did the perfection in the 1850s of a bullet whose powder would not clog a rifle's spiraled internal grooves after a few shots.

Like the smoothbore muskets that both armies had employed at the start of the war, most improved rifles had to be reloaded after each shot. But where the smoothbore musket had an effective range of only eighty yards, the Springfield or Enfield rifles widely employed by 1863 could hit targets accurately at up to four hundred yards.

The rifle's development challenged long-accepted military tactics, which identified the mass infantry charge against an opponent's weakest point as the key to victory. Military manuals of the 1840s and 1850s assumed that defenders armed with muskets would be able to fire only a round or two before being overwhelmed. Armed with rifles, however, a defending force could fire several rounds before closing with the enemy. Attackers would now have far greater difficulty getting close enough to thrust bayonets; fewer than 1 percent of the casualties in the Civil War resulted from bayonet wounds.

Thus the rifle produced some changes in tactics. Both sides came to understand the value of trenches, which provided defenders protection against withering rifle fire. By 1865, trenches pockmarked the landscape in Virginia and Georgia. In addition, growing use of the rifle

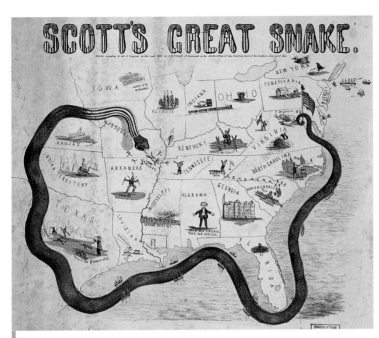

"Scott's Great Snake," 1861
General Winfield Scott's scheme to surround the South and await a seizure of power by southern Unionists drew scorn from critics who called it the Anaconda plan. In this lithograph, the "great snake" prepares to push down the Mississippi, seal off the Confederacy, and crush it.

In the absence of any element of surprise, an attacking army might invite disaster. At the Battle of Fredericksburg in December 1862, Confederate troops inflicted appalling casualties on Union forces attacking uphill over open terrain, and at Gettysburg in July 1863, Union riflemen and artillery shredded charging southerners. But generals might still achieve partial surprise by hitting an enemy before it had concentrated its troops; in fact, this is what the North tried to do at Fredericksburg. Because surprise often proved effective, most generals continued to believe that their best chance of success lay in striking an unwary or weakened enemy with all the troops they could muster rather than in relying on guerrilla or trench warfare.

Much like previous wars, the Civil War was fought basically in a succession of battles during which exposed infantry traded volleys, charged, and countercharged. Whichever side withdrew from the field usually was thought to have lost the battle, but the losing side frequently sustained lighter casualties than the supposed victor. Both sides had trouble exploiting their victories. As a rule, the beaten army moved back a few miles from the field to lick its wounds; the winners stayed in place to lick theirs. Politicians on both sides raged at generals for not pursuing a beaten foe, but it was difficult for a mangled victor to gather horses, mules, supply trains, and exhausted soldiers for a new attack. Not surprisingly, for much of the war, generals on both sides concluded that the best defense was a good offense.

To the extent that the North had a long-range strategy in 1861, it lay in the so-called **Anaconda plan**. Devised by a hero of the Mexican-American War, General Winfield Scott, the plan called for the Union to blockade the southern coastline and to thrust, like a snake, down the Mississippi River. Scott expected that sealing off and severing the Confederacy would make the South recognize the futility of secession and bring southern Unionists to power. But Scott, a southern Unionist, overestimated the strength of Unionist spirit in the South. Furthermore, although Lincoln quickly ordered a blockade of the southern coast, the North hardly had the troops and naval flotillas to seize the Mississippi in 1861. So while the Mississippi remained an objective, northern strategy did not unfold according to any blueprint like the Anaconda plan.

forced generals to rely less on cavalry. Traditionally, the cavalry had ranked among the most prestigious components of an army, in part because cavalry charges were often devastatingly effective and in part because the cavalry helped maintain class distinctions within the army. More accurate rifles reduced the effectiveness of cavalry by increasing the firepower of foot soldiers. As cavalry charges against infantry became more difficult, both sides relegated cavalry to reconnaissance missions and raids on supply trains.

Although the rifle exposed traditional tactics to new hazards, it by no means invalidated those tactics. On the contrary, historians now contend, high casualties reflected the long duration of battles rather than the new efficacy of rifles. The attacking army still stood an excellent chance of success if it achieved surprise. The South's lush forests provided abundant opportunities for an army to sneak up on its opponent. For example, at the Battle of Shiloh in 1862, Confederate attackers surprised and almost defeated a larger Union army despite the rumpus created by green rebel troops en route to the battle, many of whom fired their rifles into the air to see if they would work.

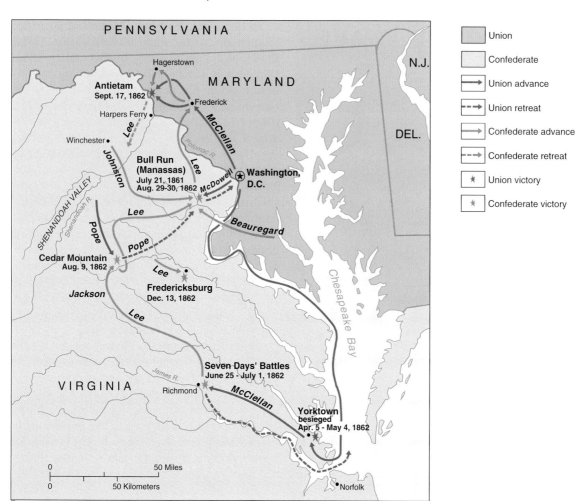

Map 15.1 The War in the East, 1861–1862
Union advances on Richmond were turned back at Fredericksburg and the Seven Days'
Battles, and the Confederacy's invasion of Union territory was stopped at Antietam.

Early in the war, the pressing need to secure the border slave states, particularly Kentucky and Missouri, dictated Union strategy west of the Appalachian Mountains. Once in control of Kentucky, northern troops plunged southward into Tennessee. The Appalachians tended to seal this western theater off from the eastern theater, where major clashes of 1861 occurred.

Stalemate in the East

The Confederacy's decision in May 1861 to move its capital from Montgomery, Alabama, to Richmond, Virginia, shaped Union strategy. "Forward to Richmond" became the Union's first war cry. Before they could reach Richmond, one hundred miles southwest of Washington, Union troops had to dislodge a Confederate army

brazenly encamped at Manassas Junction, Virginia, only twenty-five miles from the Union capital (see Map 15.1). Lincoln ordered General Irvin McDowell to attack his former West Point classmate, Confederate general P. G. T. Beauregard. "You are green, it is true," Lincoln told McDowell, "but they are green also; you are all green alike." In the resulting **First Battle of Bull Run** (or First Manassas), amateur armies clashed in bloody chaos under a blistering July sun. Well-dressed, picnicking Washington dignitaries gathered to view the action. Aided by last-minute reinforcements and by the disorganization of the attacking federals, Beauregard routed the larger Union army.

After Bull Run, Lincoln replaced McDowell with General George B. McClellan as commander of the

Army of the Potomac, the Union's main fighting force in the East. Another West Pointer, McClellan had served with distinction in the Mexican-American War and mastered the art of administration by managing midwestern railroads in the 1850s. Few generals could match his ability to turn a ragtag mob into a disciplined fighting force. His soldiers adored him, but Lincoln quickly became disenchanted. Lincoln believed that the key to a Union victory lay in simultaneous, coordinated attacks on several fronts so that the North could exploit its advantage in manpower and resources. McClellan, a proslavery Democrat, hoped to maneuver the South into a relatively bloodless defeat and then negotiate a peace that would readmit the Confederate states with slavery intact.

In the spring of 1862, McClellan got a chance to implement his strategy. After Bull Run, the Confederates had pulled back to block the Union onslaught against Richmond. Rather than directly attack the Confederate army, McClellan decided to move the Army of the Potomac by water to the tip of the peninsula formed by the York and James Rivers and then move northwestward up the peninsula to Richmond. McClellan's plan had several advantages. Depending on water transport rather than on railroads (which Confederate cavalry could cut), the McClellan strategy reduced the vulnerability of northern supply lines. By dictating an approach to Richmond from the southeast, it threatened the South's supply lines. By aiming for the capital of the Confederacy rather than for the Confederate army stationed to its northeast, McClellan hoped to maneuver the southern troops into a futile attack on his army.

At first the massive Peninsula Campaign unfolded smoothly. Three hundred ships transported seventy thousand men and huge stores of supplies to the tip of the peninsula. Reinforcements swelled McClellan's army to one hundred thousand. By late May, McClellan was within five miles of Richmond. But then he hesitated. Overestimating the Confederates' strength, he refused to launch a final attack without further reinforcements, which were turned back by Confederate general Thomas "Stonewall" Jackson in the Shenandoah Valley.

While McClellan delayed, General **Robert E. Lee** took command of the Confederacy's Army of Northern Virginia. A foe of secession and so courteous that at times he seemed too gentle, Lee possessed the qualities that McClellan most lacked: boldness and a willingness to accept casualties. Seizing the initiative, Lee attacked McClellan in late June 1862. The ensuing Seven Days' Battles, fought in the forests east of Richmond, cost the South nearly twice as many men as the North and ended in a virtual slaughter of Confederates at Malvern Hill. Unnerved by mounting casualties, McClellan sent increasingly panicky reports to Washington. Lincoln, who cared little for McClellan's peninsula strategy, ordered McClellan to call off the campaign and return to Washington.

With McClellan out of the picture, Lee and his lieutenant, Stonewall Jackson, boldly struck north and, at the Second Battle of Bull Run (Second Manassas), routed a Union army under General John Pope. Lee's next stroke was even bolder. Crossing the Potomac River in early September 1862, he invaded western Maryland, where the forthcoming harvest could provide him with desperately needed supplies. By seizing western Maryland, moreover, Lee could threaten Washington, indirectly relieve pressure on Richmond, improve the prospects of peace candidates in the North's upcoming fall elections, and possibly induce Britain and France to recognize the Confederacy as an independent nation. But McClellan met Lee at the **Battle of Antietam** (or Sharpsburg) on September 17. Although a tactical draw, Antietam proved a strategic victory for the North, for Lee subsequently called off his invasion and retreated south of the Potomac.

Heartened by the apparent success of northern arms, Lincoln then issued the Emancipation Proclamation, a war measure that freed all slaves under rebel control. The toll of 24,000 casualties at Antietam, however, made it the bloodiest day of the entire war. A Union veteran recollected that one part of the battlefield contained so many bodies that a man could have walked through it without stepping on the ground.

Complaining that McClellan had "the slows," Lincoln faulted his commander for not pursuing Lee after the battle. McClellan's replacement, General Ambrose Burnside, thought himself and soon proved himself unfit for high command. In December 1862, Burnside led 122,000 federal troops against 78,500 Confederates at the Battle of Fredericksburg. Burnside captured the town of Fredericksburg, northeast of Richmond, but then sacrificed his army in futile charges up the heights west of the town. Even Lee was shaken by the northern casualties. "It is well that war is so terrible, or we should grow too fond of it," he told an aide during the battle. Richmond remained, in the words of a southern song, "a hard road to travel." The war in the East had become a stalemate.

The War in the West

The Union fared better in the West. There, the war ranged over a vast and crucial terrain that provided access to rivers leading directly into the South. The West also

The Battle of Antietam A painting of the Antietam battlefield by James Hope, a Union soldier of the Second Vermont Infantry, shows three brigades of Union troops advancing under Confederate fire. In the photograph of Antietam, dead rebel gunners lie next to the wreckage of their battery. The building in both painting and photograph, a Dunker church, was the scene of furious fighting.

spawned new leadership. During the first year of war, an obscure Union general, **Ulysses S. Grant**, proved his competence. A West Point graduate, Grant had fought in the Mexican-American War and retired from the army in 1854 with a reputation for heavy drinking. He then failed at ventures in farming and in business. When the Civil War began, he gained an army commission through political pressure.

In 1861–1862, Grant retained control of two border states, Missouri and Kentucky. Moving into Tennessee, he captured two strategic forts, Fort Henry on the Tennessee

River and Fort Donelson on the Cumberland. Grant then headed south to attack Corinth, Mississippi, a major railroad junction (see Map 15.2).

In early April 1862, to defend Corinth, Mississippi, Confederate forces under generals Albert Sidney Johnston and P. G. T. Beauregard staged a surprise attack on Grant's army, encamped near a church named Shiloh twenty miles north of the town, in southern Tennessee. Hoping to whip Grant before Union reinforcements arrived, the Confederates exploded from the woods near Shiloh before breakfast and almost drove the federals

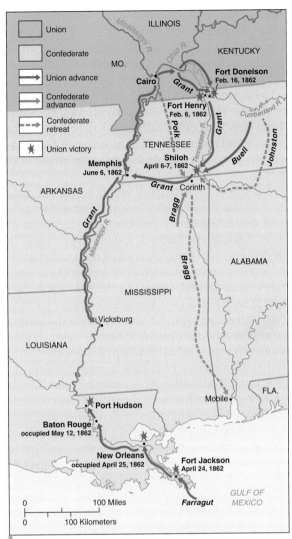

Map 15.2 The War in the West, 1861–1862
By the end of 1862, the North held New Orleans and the entire Mississippi River except for the stretch between Vicksburg and Port Hudson.

twenty-three thousand were killed or wounded, including Confederate general Albert Sidney Johnston, who bled to death from a leg wound. Defeated at Shiloh, the Confederates soon evacuated Corinth.

To attack Grant at Shiloh, the Confederacy had stripped the defenses of New Orleans, leaving only three thousand militia to guard its largest city. A combined Union land-sea force under General Benjamin Butler, a Massachusetts politician, and Admiral David G. Farragut, a Tennessean loyal to the Union, capitalized on the opportunity. Farragut took the city in late April and soon conquered Baton Rouge and Natchez as well. Meanwhile, another Union flotilla moved down the Mississippi and captured Memphis in June. Now the North controlled the entire river, except for a two-hundred-mile stretch between Port Hudson, Louisiana, and Vicksburg, Mississippi.

Union and Confederate forces also clashed in 1862 in the trans-Mississippi West. On the banks of the Rio Grande, Union volunteers, joined by Mexican-American companies, drove a Confederate army from Texas out of New Mexico. A thousand miles to the east, in northern Arkansas and western Missouri, armies vied to secure the Missouri River, a crucial waterway that flowed into the Mississippi. In Pea Ridge, Arkansas, in March 1862, forewarned northern troops scattered a Confederate force of sixteen thousand that included three Cherokee regiments. (Indian units fought on both sides in Missouri, where guerrilla combat raged until the war's end.)

These Union victories changed the nature of the trans-Mississippi war. As the rebel threat faded, regiments of western volunteers that had mobilized to crush Confederates turned to fighting Indians. Conflict between Union forces and Native Americans erupted in Minnesota, Arizona, Nevada, Colorado, and New Mexico, where California volunteers and the New Mexico cavalry, led by Colonel Kit Carson, overwhelmed the Apaches and Navajos. After 1865, federal troops moved west to complete the rout of the Indians that had begun in the Civil War.

The Soldiers' War

Civil War soldiers were typically volunteers who left farms and small towns to join companies of recruits from their locales. Many men who enrolled in 1861 and 1862—those who served at Shiloh and Antietam— reenlisted when their terms expired and became the backbones of their respective armies. Local loyalties spurred enrollment, especially in the South; so did ideals of honor and valor. Soldiers on both sides envisioned

into the Tennessee River. Beauregard cabled Richmond with news of a splendid Confederate victory. But Grant and his lieutenant, **William T. Sherman**—a West Point graduate and Mexican-American war veteran who had most recently run a southern military academy— steadied the Union line. Union reinforcements arrived in the night, and a federal counterattack drove the Confederates from the field the next day. Although Antietam would soon erase the distinction, the **Battle of Shiloh** was the bloodiest in American history to that date. Of the seventy-seven thousand men engaged,

A Union Soldier
Sarah Rosetta Wakeman, alias Private Lyons
Wakeman, served in the Union army disguised as
a man. She joined the 153rd Regiment, New York
State Volunteers.

military life as a transforming experience in which citizens became warriors and boys became men. One New York father who sent two young sons to enlist marveled at how the war provided "so much manhood suddenly achieved." Exultant after a victory, an Alabama volunteer told his father, "With your first shot you become a new man." Thousands of underage volunteers, that is, boys under eighteen, also served in the war; so did at least 250 women disguised as men.

New soldiers moved from recruitment rallies to camps of rendezvous, where local companies were meshed into regiments, and then to camps of instruction. Military training proved notoriously weak, and much of army life was tedious and uncomfortable. Food was one complaint. Union troops ate beans, bacon, salt pork, pickled beef, and a staple called hardtack, square flour-and-water biscuits that were almost impossible to

crack with a blow. Confederate diets featured bacon and cornmeal, and as a southern soldier summed it up, "Our rations is small." Rebel armies often ran out of food, blankets, clothes, socks, and shoes. On both sides, crowded military camps, plagued by poor sanitation and infested with lice, fleas, ticks, flies, and rodents, ensured soaring disease rates and widespread grievances. A sergeant from New York, only partly in jest, described his lot as "laying around in the dirt and mud, living on hardtack, facing death in bullets and shells, eat up by wood-ticks and body-lice."

Expectations of military glory swiftly faded. For most soldiers, Civil War battles meant inuring themselves to the stench of death. Soldiers rapidly grasped the value of caution in combat; you learned, a southerner wrote, "to become cool and deliberate." According to a northern volunteer, "The consuming passion is to get out of the way." Others described the zeal aroused by combat. "[I]t is a terrible sight to see a line of men, two deep, coming up within 300 or 400 yards of you, with bayonets flashing and waving their colors," a New Jersey artilleryman recalled. "[Y]ou know that every shot you fire into them sends some one to eternity, but still you are a prompted by a terrible desire to kill all you can." The deadly cost of battle fell most heavily on the infantry, in which at least three out of four soldiers served. Although repeating rifles were superior weapons, with three or four times the range of the old smoothbore muskets, a combination of inexperience, inadequate training, and barriers of terrain curbed their impact in practice. Instead, large masses of soldiers faced one another at close range for long periods of time, exchanging fire until one side or the other gave up and fell back. The high casualty figures at Shiloh and Antietam reflected not advanced technology but the armies' inability to use it effectively. "Our victories . . . seem to settle nothing; to bring us no nearer to the end of the war," a southern officer wrote in 1862. "It is only so many killed or wounded, leaving the war of blood to go on." Armies gained efficiency in battle through experience, and only late in the war.

In their voluminous letters home (Civil War armies were the most literate armies that had ever existed), volunteers often discussed their motives as soldiers. Some Confederates enlisted to defend slavery, which they paired with liberty. "I choose to fight for southern rights and southern liberty" against the "vandals of the North" who were "determined to destroy slavery," a Kentucky Confederate announced. "A stand must be made for African slavery or it is forever lost," wrote a South Carolinian. A small minority of northern soldiers voiced antislavery sentiments early in the war: "I have no heart in this war if the slaves cannot go free," a

Sailors on the *Monitor*
Union sailors on the deck of the USS *Monitor* in 1862. Typically, when photographers arrived, crew members posed near the turret by themselves, apart from officers.

soldier from Wisconsin declared. Few Union recruits, however, initially shared this antipathy to slavery, and some voiced the opposite view. "I don't want to fire another shot for the negroes and I wish all the abolitionists were in hell," a New York soldier declared. But as the war went on, northern soldiers accepted the need to free the slaves, sometimes for humanitarian reasons. "Since I am down here I have learned and seen more of what the horrors of slavery was than I ever knew before," an Ohio officer wrote from Louisiana. Others had more practical goals. By the summer of 1862, Union soldiers in the South had become agents of liberation; they harbored fugitives who fled behind federal lines. Many who once had damned the "abolitionist war" now endorsed emancipation as part of the Union war effort. As a soldier from Indiana declared, "Every negro we get strengthens us and weakens the rebels."

Ironclads and Cruisers: The Naval War

By plunging its navy into the Confederacy like a dagger, the Union exploited one of its clearest advantages. The North began the war with over forty active warships against none for the South, and by 1865 the United States had the largest navy in the world. Steam-driven ships could penetrate the South's excellent river system from any direction.

Yet the Union navy faced an extraordinary challenge in its efforts to blockade the South's 3,500 miles of coast. Early in the war, small, sleek Confederate blockade-runners darted in and out of southern harbors and inlets with little chance of capture. The North gradually tightened the blockade by outfitting tugs, whalers, excursion steamers, and ferries as well as frigates to patrol southern coasts. The proportion of Confederate blockade-runners that made it through dropped from 90 percent early in the war to 50 percent by 1865. Northern seizure of rebel ports and coastal areas shrank the South's foreign trade even more. In daring amphibious assaults during 1861 and 1862, the Union captured the excellent harbor of Port Royal, South Carolina, the coastal islands off South Carolina, and most of North Carolina's river outlets. Naval patrols and amphibious operations shrank the South's ocean trade to one-third its prewar level.

Despite meager resources, the South strove to offset the North's naval advantage. Early in the war, the Confederacy raised the scuttled Union frigate *Merrimac*, sheathed its sides with an armor of iron plate, rechristened it *Virginia*, and dispatched it to attack wooden Union ships in Hampton Roads, Virginia. The *Merrimac* destroyed two northern warships but met its match in the hastily built Union ironclad the *Monitor*. In the first engagement of ironclads in history, the two ships fought an indecisive battle on March 9, 1862. The South constructed other ironclads and even the first submarine, which dragged a mine through the water to sink a Union ship off Charleston in 1864. Unfortunately, the "fish" failed to resurface and went down with its victim. But the South could never build enough ironclads to overcome the North's supremacy in home waters. The Confederacy had more success on the high seas, where wooden, steam-driven commerce raiders like the *Alabama* and the *Florida* (both built in England) wreaked havoc on the Union's merchant marine. Commerce raiding, however, would not tip the balance of the war in the South's favor because the North, unlike its foe, did not depend on imports for war materials. The South would lose the naval war.

The Diplomatic War

While armies and navies clashed in 1861–1862, conflict developed on a third front, diplomacy. At the outbreak of the war, the Confederacy began a campaign to gain European recognition of its independence. Southern confidence ran high. Planning to establish a colonial empire in Mexico, Napoleon III of France had grounds to welcome the permanent division of the United States. Moreover, the upper classes in France and Britain seemed sympathetic to the aristocratic South and eager for the downfall of the brash Yankee republic. Furthermore, influential southerners had long contended that an embargo of cotton exports would bring Britain to its knees. These southerners reasoned that Britain, dependent on the South for four-fifths of its cotton, would break the Union blockade and provoke a war with the North rather than endure an embargo.

Leaving nothing to chance, the Confederacy in 1861 dispatched emissaries James Mason to Britain and John Slidell to France to lobby for recognition of an independent South. But their ship, the *Trent*, fell into Union hands, and when Mason and Slidell ended up in Boston as prisoners, British tempers exploded. Considering one war at a time enough, President Lincoln released Mason and Slidell.

But settling the *Trent* affair did not eliminate friction between the United States and Britain. Union diplomats protested the construction in British shipyards of two Confederate commerce raiders, the *Florida* and the *Alabama*. In 1863, the U.S. minister to London, Charles Francis Adams (the son of former president John Quincy Adams), threatened war if two British-built ironclads commissioned by the Confederacy, the so-called Laird rams, were turned over to the South. Britain capitulated to Adams's protests and purchased the rams for its own navy.

On balance, the South fell far short of its diplomatic objectives. Although recognizing the Confederacy as a belligerent, neither Britain nor France ever recognized it as a nation. Basically, the Confederacy overestimated the power of its vaunted "**cotton diplomacy**." Southern notions of embargoing cotton exports in order to bring the British to their knees failed. Planters conducted business as usual by raising cotton and trying to slip it through the blockade. Still, the South's share of the British cotton market slumped from 77 percent in 1860 to only 10 percent in 1865. This loss reflected forces beyond southern control. Bumper cotton crops in the late 1850s had glutted the British market by the start of the war and weakened British demand for cotton. In addition, Britain had found new suppliers in Egypt and India, thereby buffering itself from southern pressure. Gradually, too, the North's tightened blockade restricted southern exports.

The South also exaggerated Britain's stake in helping the Confederacy. As a naval power that had frequently blockaded its own enemies, Britain's diplomatic interest lay in supporting the Union blockade in principle; from Britain's standpoint, to help the South break the blockade would set a precedent that could easily boomerang. Finally, although France and Britain often considered recognizing the Confederacy, the timing never seemed quite right. The Union's success at Antietam in 1862 and Lincoln's subsequent issuance of the Emancipation Proclamation dampened Europe's enthusiasm for recognition at a crucial juncture. By transforming the war into a struggle to end slavery, the Emancipation Proclamation produced an upsurge of pro-Union feeling in antislavery Britain, particularly among liberals and the working class. Workingmen in Manchester, England, wrote Lincoln to praise his resolve to free the slaves. The proclamation, declared Henry Adams (diplomat Charles Francis Adams's son) from London, "has done more for us here than all of our former victories and all our diplomacy."

Emancipation Transforms the War, 1863

"I hear old John Brown knocking on the lid of his coffin and shouting 'Let me out! Let me out!'" abolitionist Henry Stanton wrote to his wife after the fall of Fort Sumter. "The Doom of Slavery is at hand." In 1861, this prediction seemed wildly premature. In his inaugural that year, Lincoln had stated bluntly, "I have no purpose, directly or indirectly, to interfere with the institution of slavery in the states where it exists." Yet in two years, the North's priorities shifted. A mix of practical necessity and ideological conviction thrust the emancipation of the slaves to the forefront of northern war goals.

The rise of emancipation as a war goal reflected the changing character of the war. As the struggle dragged on, demands intensified in the North for the prosecution of "total war"—a war that would shatter the social and economic foundations of the Confederacy. Even northerners who saw no moral value in abolishing slavery started to recognize the military value of emancipation as a tactic to cripple the South.

From Confiscation to Emancipation

Union policy on emancipation developed in stages. As soon as northern troops began to invade the South, questions arose about the disposition of captured rebel property, including slaves. Slaves who fled behind the Union lines were sometimes considered "contraband"—enemy property liable to seizure—and were put to work for the Union army. Some northern commanders viewed this practice as a useful tool of war; others did not—especially when they faced the challenge of supervising contingents of former slaves; and the Lincoln administration was evasive. To establish an official policy, Congress in August 1861 passed the first Confiscation Act, which authorized the seizure of all property used in military aid of the rebellion, including slaves. Under this act, slaves who had been employed directly by the armed rebel forces and who later fled to freedom became "captives of war." But nothing in the act actually freed these individuals, nor did the law apply to fugitive slaves who had not worked for the Confederate military.

Several factors underlay the Union's cautious approach to the confiscation of rebel property. Officially maintaining that the South's rebellion lacked any legal basis, Lincoln argued that southerners were still entitled to the Constitution's protection of property. The president also had practical reasons to walk softly. The Union not only contained four slave states but also held a sizable body of proslavery Democrats who strongly opposed turning the war into a crusade against slavery. If the North in any way tampered with slavery, these Democrats feared, southern blacks might come north and compete with white workers. Aware of such fears, Lincoln assured Congress in December 1861 that the war would not become a "remorseless revolutionary struggle."

From the start of the war, however, Radical Republicans pushed Lincoln to adopt a policy of emancipation. Pennsylvanian Thaddeus Stevens urged the Union to "free every slave—slay every traitor—burn every Rebel mansion, if these things be necessary to preserve this temple of freedom." Radicals agreed with black abolitionist Frederick Douglass that "to fight against slaveholders without fighting against slavery, is but a half-hearted business." Each Union defeat, moreover, reminded northerners that the Confederacy, with a slave labor force in place, could commit a higher proportion of its white men to battle. The idea of emancipation as a military measure thus gained increasing favor in the North, and in July 1862 Congress passed the second Confiscation Act. This law authorized the seizure of the property of all persons in rebellion and stipulated that slaves who came within Union lines "shall be forever free." The law also authorized the president to employ blacks as soldiers.

Nevertheless, Lincoln continued to stall, even as pressure for emancipation rose. "My paramount object in this struggle is to save the Union, and is not either to save or destroy slavery," Lincoln told antislavery journalist Horace Greeley. "If I could save the Union without freeing *any* slave, I would do it; and if I could save it by freeing *all* the slaves, I would do it; and if I could do it by freeing some and leaving others alone, I would also do that." Yet Lincoln had always loathed slavery, and by the spring of 1862, he had come around to the Radical position that the war must lead to its abolition. He hesitated principally because he did not want to be stampeded by Congress into a measure that might disrupt northern unity; he was also reluctant to press the issue while Union armies reeled in defeat. After failing to persuade the Union slave states to emancipate slaves in return for federal compensation, Lincoln drafted a proclamation of emancipation, circulated it within his cabinet, and waited for a right moment to announce it. Finally, after the Union victory in September 1862 at Antietam, Lincoln issued the preliminary Emancipation Proclamation, which declared all slaves under rebel control free as of January 1, 1863. Announcing the plan in advance softened the surprise, tested public opinion, and gave the states still in rebellion an opportunity to preserve slavery by returning to the Union—an opportunity that none, however, took. The final **Emancipation Proclamation**, issued on January 1, 1863, declared "forever free" all slaves in areas in rebellion.

The proclamation had limited practical impact. Applying only to rebellious areas where the Union had no authority, it exempted the Union slave states and those parts of the Confederacy then under Union control (Tennessee, West Virginia, southern Louisiana, and sections of Virginia). Moreover, it mainly restated what the second Confiscation Act had already stipulated: if rebels' slaves fell into Union hands, those slaves would be free. Yet the proclamation was a brilliant political stroke. By issuing it as a military measure in his role as commander-in-chief, Lincoln pacified northern conservatives. Its aim, he stressed, was to injure the Confederacy, threaten its property, heighten its dread, sap its morale, and hasten its demise. By issuing the proclamation himself, Lincoln stole the initiative from the Radicals in Congress and mobilized support for the Union among European liberals far more dramatically than could any act of Congress. Furthermore, the declaration pushed the border states toward emancipation: by the end of the war, Maryland and Missouri would abolish slavery. Finally, it increased slaves' incentives to escape as northern troops approached. Fulfilling the

worst of Confederate fears, it enabled blacks to join the Union army.

The Emancipation Proclamation did not end slavery everywhere or free "*all*" the slaves." But it changed the war. From 1863 on, the war for the Union would also be a war against slavery.

Crossing Union Lines

The attacks and counterattacks of the opposing armies turned many slaves into pawns of war. Some slaves became free when Union troops overran their areas. Others fled their plantations as federal troops approached to take refuge behind Union lines. A few were freed by northern assaults, only to be re-enslaved by Confederate counterthrusts. One North Carolina slave celebrated liberation on twelve occasions, as many times as Union soldiers marched through his area. By 1865, about half a million slaves were in Union hands.

In the first year of the war, when the Union had not yet established a policy toward "contrabands" (fugitive slaves), masters were able to retrieve them from the Union army. After 1862, however, the thousands of slaves who crossed Union lines were considered free. Many freedmen served in army camps as cooks, teamsters, and laborers. Some worked for pay on abandoned plantations or were leased out to planters who swore allegiance to the Union. In camps or outside them, freedmen had reason to question the value of their

Fording the Rappahannock River
When federal troops came within reach, those slaves who could do so liberated themselves by fleeing behind Union lines. These Virginia fugitives, lugging all their possessions, move toward freedom in the summer of 1862, after the Second Battle of Bull Run.

liberation. Deductions for clothing, rations, and medicine ate up most, if not all, of their earnings. Labor contracts frequently tied them to their employers for prolonged periods. Moreover, freedmen encountered fierce prejudice among Yankee soldiers, many of whom feared that emancipation would propel blacks north after the war. The best solution to the "question of what to do with the darkies," wrote one northern soldier, "would be to shoot them."

But this was not the whole story. Fugitive slaves who aided the Union army as spies and scouts helped to break down ingrained bigotry. "The sooner we get rid of our foolish prejudice the better for us," a Massachusetts soldier wrote home. Before the end of the war, northern missionary groups and freedmen's aid societies sent agents into the South to work among the freed slaves, distribute relief, and organize schools. In March 1865, just before the hostilities ceased, Congress created the **Freedmen's Bureau**, which had responsibility for the relief, education, and employment of former slaves. The Freedmen's Bureau law also stipulated that forty acres of abandoned or confiscated land could be leased to each freedman or southern Unionist, with an option to buy after three years. This was the first and only time that Congress provided for the redistribution of confiscated Confederate property.

Black Soldiers in the Union Army

During the first year of war, the Union had rejected African-American soldiers. Northern recruiting offices sent black applicants home, and black companies that had been formed in the occupied South were disbanded. After the second Confiscation Act, Union generals formed black regiments in occupied New Orleans and on the Sea Islands off the coasts of South Carolina and Georgia. Only after the Emancipation Proclamation did large-scale enlistment begin. Prominent African-Americans such as Frederick Douglass and Harvard-educated physician Martin Delany worked as recruiting agents in northern cities. Douglass linked black military service to black claims as citizens. "Once let the black man get upon his person the brass letters, U.S.; let him get an eagle on his button, and a musket on his shoulder and bullets in his pocket, and there is no power on earth which can deny that he has earned the right to citizenship." Union drafts now included blacks, recruiting offices appeared in the loyal border states, and freedmen in refugee camps throughout the occupied South were enlisted. By the end of the war, 186,000 African-Americans had served in the Union army, one-tenth of all Union soldiers. Fully half came from the Confederate states.

White Union soldiers commonly objected to the new recruits on racial grounds. But some, including Colonel Thomas Wentworth Higginson, a liberal minister and former John Brown supporter who led a black regiment, welcomed the black soldiers. "Nobody knows anything about these men who has not seen them in battle," Higginson exulted after a successful raid in Florida in 1863. "There is a fierce energy about them beyond anything of which I have ever read, except it be the French Zouaves [French troops in North Africa]." Even Union soldiers who held blacks in contempt came to approve of "anything that will kill a rebel." Furthermore, black recruitment offered new opportunities for whites to secure commissions, for blacks served in separate regiments under white officers. Colonel Robert Gould Shaw of the 54th Massachusetts Infantry, an elite black regiment, died in combat—as did half his troops—in an attack on Fort Wagner in Charleston harbor in July 1863.

Black soldiers suffered a far higher mortality rate than white troops. Typically assigned to labor detachments or garrison duty, blacks were less likely than whites to be killed in action but more likely to die of illness in the disease-ridden garrisons. In addition, the Confederacy refused to treat captured black soldiers as prisoners of war, a policy that prevented their exchange for Confederate prisoners. Instead, Jefferson Davis ordered all blacks taken in battle to be sent back to the states from which they came, where they were re-enslaved or executed. In an especially gruesome incident, when Confederate troops under General Nathan Bedford Forrest captured Fort Pillow, Tennessee, in 1864, they massacred many blacks—an action that provoked outcries but no retaliation from the North.

Well into the war, African-American soldiers faced inequities in pay. White soldiers earned $13 a month plus a $3.50 clothing allowance; black privates received only $10 a month, with clothing deducted. "We have come out like men and we Expected to be Treated as men but we have bin Treated more Like Dogs then men," a black soldier complained to Secretary of War Edwin Stanton. In June 1864, Congress belatedly equalized the earnings of black and white soldiers.

Although fraught with hardships and inequities, military service became a symbol of citizenship for blacks. It proved that "black men can give blows as well as take them," Frederick Douglass declared. "Liberty won by white men would lose half its lustre." Above all, the use of black soldiers, especially former slaves, struck northern generals as a major blow against the

Confederacy. "They will make good soldiers," General Grant wrote to Lincoln in 1863, "and taking them from the enemy weakens him in the same proportion they strengthen us."

Slavery in Wartime

Anxious white southerners on the home front felt perched on a volcano. "We should be practically helpless should the negroes rise," declared a Louisiana planter's daughter, "since there are so few men left at home." When Mary Boykin Chesnut of South Carolina learned of her cousin's murder in bed by two trusted house slaves, she became almost frantic. "The murder," Chesnut wrote, "has clearly driven us all wild." To control 3 million slaves, white southerners tightened slave patrols, moved entire plantations to relative safety from Union troops in Texas or in the upland regions of the coastal South, and spread scare stories among the slaves. "The whites would tell the colored people not to go to the Yankees, for they would harness them to carts . . . in place of horses," reported Susie King Taylor, a black fugitive from Savannah.

Wartime developments affected slaves. Some remained faithful to their owners and helped hide family treasures from marauding Union soldiers. Others were torn between loyalty and lust for freedom: one slave accompanied his master to war, rescued him when he was wounded, and then escaped on his master's horse. Given a viable choice between freedom and bondage, slaves usually chose freedom. Few slaves helped the North as dramatically as Robert Smalls, a hired-out slave boatman who turned over a Confederate steamer to the Union navy, but most who had a chance to flee to Union lines did so. The idea of freedom held irresistible appeal. Upon learning from a Union soldier that he was free, a Virginia coachman dressed in his master's clothes, "put on his best watch and chain, took his stick, and . . . told him [the master] that he might for the future drive his own coach." (Map 15.3)

Most slaves, however, had no escape and remained under the nominal control of their owners. Despite the fears of southern whites, no general uprising of slaves occurred; and the Confederacy continued to impress thousands of slaves to toil in war plants, army camps, and field hospitals. But even slaves with no chance of flight were alert to the opportunity that war provided and swiftly tested the limits of enforced labor. As a Savannah mistress noted as early as 1861, the slaves "show a very different face from what they have had heretofore." Moreover, wartime conditions reduced the slaves' productivity. With most of the white men off at war, the master-slave relationship weakened. The women and boys who remained on plantations complained of their difficulty in controlling slaves, who commonly refused to work, performed their labors inefficiently, or even destroyed property. A Texas wife contended that her slaves were "trying all they can, it seems to me, to aggravate me" by neglecting the stock, breaking plows, and tearing down fences. "You may give your Negroes away," she finally wrote despairingly to her husband in 1864.

Whether southern slaves fled to freedom or merely stopped working, they acted effectively to defy slavery, to liberate themselves from its regulations, and to undermine the plantation system. Thus southern slavery disintegrated even as the Confederacy fought to preserve it. Hard-pressed by Union armies, short of manpower, and unsettled by the erosion of plantation slavery, the Confederate Congress in 1864 considered the drastic step of impressing slaves into its army as soldiers in exchange for their freedom at the war's end. Robert E. Lee favored the use of slaves as soldiers on the grounds that if the Confederacy did not arm its slaves, the Union would. Others were adamantly opposed. "If slaves will make good soldiers," a Georgia general argued, "our whole theory of slavery is wrong." Originally against arming slaves, Jefferson Davis changed his mind in 1865. In March 1865, the Confederate Congress narrowly passed a bill to arm three hundred thousand slave soldiers, although it omitted any mention of emancipation. Since the war ended a few weeks later, however, the plan was never put into effect.

Although the Confederacy's decision to arm the slaves came too late to affect the war, the debate over arming them damaged southern morale. By then, the South's military position had started to deteriorate.

The Turning Point of 1863

In the summer and fall of 1863, Union fortunes dramatically improved in every theater of the war. Yet the year began badly for the North. The slide, which had started with Burnside's defeat at Fredericksburg, Virginia, in December 1862, continued into the spring of 1863. Burnside's successor, General Joseph "Fighting Joe" Hooker, a windbag fond of issuing pompous proclamations to his troops, devised a plan to dislodge the Confederates from Fredericksburg by crossing the Rappahannock River north of the town and descending on the rebel rear. But Lee and Stonewall Jackson routed Hooker at Chancellorsville, Virginia, early in May 1863 (see Map 15.4). The battle proved costly for the South

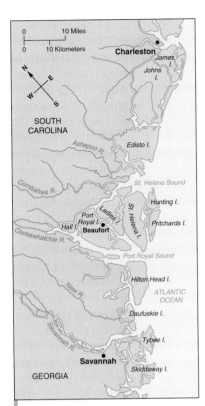

Map 15.3 The Sea Islands
The island chain was the site of unique wartime experiments in new social policies.

Sea Island Teachers and Wage Labor
The arrival of the Union navy on the Sea Islands off the coast of Georgia and South Carolina in November 1861 liberated some ten thousand slaves, the first large group of enslaved people to be freed by the Civil War. The site of pioneer ventures in freedmen's education, black wage labor, and land redistribution, the Sea Islands served as a wartime testing ground for new social policies. Here, teachers and missionaries who worked among ex-slaves gather in front of a stately home in Port Royal (top); the manager of a plantation near Beaufort, South Carolina, also on the island of Port Royal, shares the terms of a labor contract with former slaves, now free laborers, in 1863 (bottom).

because Jackson was accidentally shot by Confederate sentries and died a few days later. Still, Hooker had twice as many men as Lee, so the Union defeat at Chancellorsville humiliated the North. Reports from the West brought no better news. Although repulsed at Shiloh in western Tennessee, the Confederates still had a powerful army in central Tennessee under General Braxton Bragg. Furthermore, despite repeated efforts, Grant was unable to take Vicksburg; the two-hundred-mile stretch of the Mississippi between Vicksburg and Port Hudson remained in rebel hands.

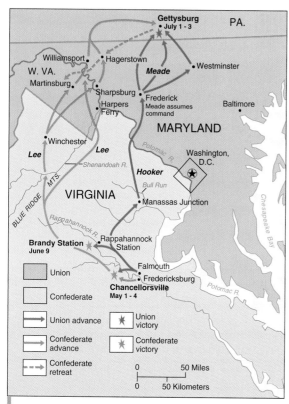

Map 15.4 The War in the East, 1863
Victorious at Chancellorsville in May 1863, Lee again invaded Union territory but was decisively stopped at Gettysburg.

The upswing in Union fortunes began with Lee's decision after Chancellorsville to invade the North. Lee needed supplies that war-wracked Virginia could no longer provide. He also hoped to push Lincoln into sending troops from besieged Vicksburg to the eastern theater. Lee envisioned a major Confederate victory on northern soil that would sway northern sentiment to the pro-peace Democrats and gain European recognition of the Confederacy. Moving his seventy-five thousand men down the Shenandoah Valley, Lee crossed the Potomac into Maryland and pressed forward into southern Pennsylvania. With Lee's army far to the west of Richmond, Hooker recommended a Union stab at the Confederate capital. "Lee's *army,* and not *Richmond,* is your true objective," Lincoln shot back, and he replaced Hooker with the more reliable George G. Meade.

Early in July 1863, Lee's offensive ground to a halt at a Pennsylvania road junction, Gettysburg (see Map 15.5).

Confederates foraging for shoes in the town encountered some Union cavalry. Soon both sides called for reinforcements, and the war's greatest battle, the **Battle of Gettysburg**, began. On July 1, Meade's troops installed themselves in hills south of town along a line that resembled a fishhook: the shank ran along Cemetery Ridge and a northern hook encircled Culp's Hill. By the end of the first day of fighting, most of the troops on both sides had arrived: Meade's army outnumbered the Confederates ninety thousand to seventy-five thousand. On July 2, Lee rejected advice to plant the Confederate army in a defensive position between Meade's forces and Washington and instead attacked the Union flanks, with some success. But because the Confederate assaults were uncoordinated, and some southern generals disregarded orders and struck where they chose, the Union was able to move in reinforcements and regain its earlier losses.

By the afternoon of July 3, believing that the Union flanks had been weakened, Lee attacked Cemetery Ridge in the center of the North's defensive line. After southern cannon shelled the line, a massive infantry force of fifteen thousand Confederates, Pickett's charge, moved in. But as the Confederate cannon sank into the ground and fired a shade too high, and as Union fire wiped out the rebel charge, rifled weapons proved their deadly effectiveness. At the end of the day, Confederate bodies littered the field. "The dead and the dying were lying by the thousands between the two lines," a dazed Louisiana soldier wrote. A little more than half of Pickett's troops were dead, wounded, or captured in the horrible encounter. When Lee withdrew to Virginia on July 4, he had lost seventeen generals and over one-third of his army. Total Union and Confederate casualties numbered almost fifty thousand. Although Meade failed to pursue and destroy the retreating rebels, he had halted Lee's foray into the North, and the Union rejoiced.

Almost simultaneously, the North won a less bloody but more strategic victory in the West, at the **Battle of Vicksburg**; here Grant finally pierced Vicksburg's defenses (see Map 15.6). Situated on a bluff on the east bank of the Mississippi, Vicksburg was protected on the west by the river and on the north by hills, forests, and swamps. It could be attacked only over a thin strip of dry land to its east and south. Positioned to the north of Vicksburg, Grant had to find a way to get his army south of the city and onto the Mississippi's east bank. His solution lay in moving his troops far to the west of the city and down to a point on the river south of Vicksburg. Meanwhile, Union gunboats and supply ships

Gettysburg, 1863
At the end of the three-day Battle of Gettysburg, Lee's army had suffered over 25,000 casualties. These uninjured Confederate captives, who refuse to face the camera and stare off in different directions, may have spent the rest of the war in northern prison camps.

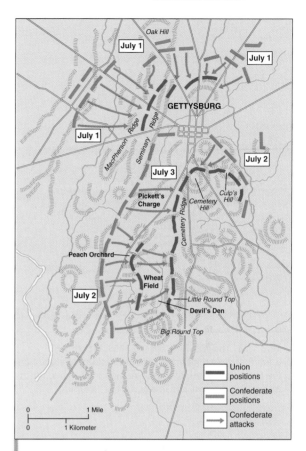

Map 15.5 Gettysburg, 1863
The failure of Pickett's charge against the Union center on July 3 was the decisive action in the war's greatest battle.

ran past the Confederate batteries overlooking the river at Vicksburg (not without sustaining considerable damage) to rendezvous with Grant's army and transport it across to the east bank. Grant then swung in a large semicircle, first northeastward to capture Jackson, the capital of Mississippi, and then westward back to Vicksburg. After a six-week siege, during which famished soldiers and civilians in Vicksburg were reduced to eating mules and even rats, General John C. Pemberton surrendered his thirty-thousand-man garrison to Grant on July 4, the day after Pickett's charge at Gettysburg. Port Hudson, the last Confederate holdout on the Mississippi, soon surrendered to another Union army. "The Father of Waters flows unvexed to the sea," Lincoln declared.

Before the year was out, the Union won another crucial victory in the West. General William S. Rosecrans fought and maneuvered Braxton Bragg's Confederate army out of central Tennessee and into Chattanooga, in the southeastern tip of the state, and then forced Bragg to evacuate Chattanooga. Bragg defeated the pursuing Rosecrans at the Battle of Chickamauga (September 19–20, 1863), one of the bloodiest of the war, and drove him back into Chattanooga. But the arrival of Grant and reinforcements from the Army of the Potomac enabled the North to break Bragg's siege of Chattanooga in November. With Chattanooga secure, the way lay open for a Union strike into Georgia.

Union successes in the second half of 1863 stiffened the North's will to keep fighting and plunged some rebel leaders into despair. Hearing of the fall of Vicksburg, Confederate ordnance chief Josiah Gorgas wrote, "Yesterday we rode the pinnacle of success—today absolute ruin seems our portion. The Confederacy totters to its destruction."

Totter it might, but the South was far from beaten. Although the outcome at Gettysburg quashed southerners' hopes for victory on northern soil, it did not significantly impair Lee's ability to defend Virginia. The loss of Vicksburg and the Mississippi cut off the Confederate states west of the river—Arkansas, Louisiana, and Texas—from those to the east; but these western

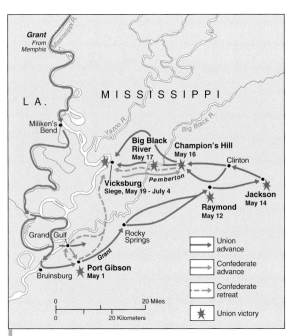

Map 15.6 The War in the West, 1863: Vicksburg
Grant first moved his army west of Vicksburg to a point on the Mississippi south of the town. Then he marched northeast, taking Jackson, and finally west to Vicksburg.

contemporaries thought that the fate of the Confederacy had been sealed.

War and Society, North and South

Extending beyond the battlefields, the Civil War engulfed two economies and societies. By 1863, stark contrasts emerged: with its superior resources, the Union could meet wartime demand as the imperiled Confederacy could not. But both regions experienced labor shortages and inflation. As the conflict dragged on, both societies confronted problems of disunity and dissent, for war issues opened fissures between social classes. In both regions, war encroached on everyday life. Families were disrupted and dislocated, especially in the South. Women on both sides took on new roles at home, in the workplace, and in relief efforts.

The War's Economic Impact: The North

The war affected the Union's economy unevenly. Some industries fared poorly: for instance, a shortage of raw cotton sent the cotton-textile industry into a tailspin. But industries directly related to the war effort, such as the manufacture of arms, shoes, and clothing, profited from huge government contracts; by 1865 the ready-made clothing industry received orders for more than a million uniforms a year. Railroads flourished in wartime. Some privately owned lines, which had overbuilt before the war, doubled their volume of traffic. In

states could still provide soldiers. Even with the loss of Chattanooga, the Confederacy continued to hold most of the Carolinas, Georgia, Florida, and Mississippi. Few

Grant Attacks Vicksburg
An anonymous painting captures the intense activity of Grant's first assault on Vicksburg on May 19, 1863. The Union attack began a six-week siege that did not succeed until July 4, 1863.

1862, the federal government itself went into the railroad business by establishing the United States Military Railroads (USMRR) to carry troops and supplies to the front. By 1865, the USMRR was the largest railroad in the world.

The Republicans in Congress actively promoted business growth during the war. Holding 102 of 146 House seats and 29 of 36 Senate seats in 1861, they overrode Democratic foes and hiked the tariff in 1862 and again in 1864 to protect domestic industries. The Republican-sponsored Pacific Railroad Act of 1862 provided for the development of a transcontinental railroad, an idea that had foundered before the war on feuds over which route such a railroad should follow. With the South out of the picture and no longer able to demand a southern route from New Orleans across the Southwest, Congress chose a northern route from Omaha to San Francisco. Chartering the Union Pacific and Central Railroad corporations, Congress then gave to each large land grants and generous loans. These two corporations combined received more than 60 million acres in land grants and $20 million in government loans. The issuance of greenbacks and the creation of a national banking system, meanwhile, brought a measure of uniformity to the nation's financial system.

The Republicans designed these measures to benefit a variety of social classes, and partially succeeded. The **Homestead Act**, passed in 1862, embodied the party's ideal of "free soil, free labor, free men" by granting 160 acres of public land to settlers after five years of residence on the land. By 1865, twenty thousand homesteaders occupied new land in the West under the Homestead Act. The Republicans also secured passage in 1862 of the **Morrill Land Grant Act**, which gave to the states proceeds of public lands to fund the establishment of universities emphasizing "such branches of learning as are related to agriculture and mechanic arts." The Morrill Act spurred the growth of large state universities, mainly in the Midwest and West. Michigan State, Iowa State, and Purdue universities, among many others, profited from the law.

In general, however, the war benefited the wealthy more than the average citizen. Corrupt contractors grew rich by selling the government substandard merchandise such as the notorious "shoddy" clothing made from compressed rags, which quickly fell apart. Speculators made millions in the gold market. Because the price of gold in relation to greenbacks rose whenever public confidence in the government fell, those who bought gold in the hope that its price would rise gained from Union defeats, and even more from Union disasters. Businessmen with access to scarce commodities also reaped astounding profits. Manpower shortages stimulated wartime demand for the mechanical reaper that Cyrus McCormick had patented in 1834. When paid for reapers in greenbacks, which he distrusted, McCormick immediately reinvested them in pig iron and then watched in glee as wartime demand drove its price from twenty-three dollars to forty dollars a ton.

Ordinary Americans suffered. Higher protective tariffs, wartime excise taxes, and inflation hoisted the prices of finished goods, while wages lagged 20 percent or more behind cost increases for most of the war. Lagging wages became especially severe because boys and women poured into government offices and factories to replace adult male workers who had joined the army. For women employees, entry into government jobs—even at half the pay of male clerks—represented a major advance. Still, employers' threats of hiring more low-paid youths and females undercut the bargaining power of the men who remained in the work force.

Some workers decried their low wages. "We are unable to sustain life for the price offered by contractors who fatten on their contracts," Cincinnati seamstresses declared in a petition to President Lincoln. Cigar makers and locomotive engineers formed national unions, a process that would accelerate after the war. But employers often denounced worker complaints as unpatriotic hindrances to the war effort. In 1864, army troops were diverted from combat to put down protests in war industries from New York to the Midwest.

The War's Economic Impact: The South

The war shattered the South's economy. Indeed, if both regions are considered together, the war retarded *American* economic growth. For example, the commodity output of the American economy, which had registered huge increases of 51 percent and 62 percent in the 1840s and 1850s respectively, rose only 22 percent during the 1860s. This modest gain depended wholly on the North, for in the 1860s commodity output in the South actually *declined* 39 percent.

Multiple factors offset the South's substantial wartime industrial growth. For example, the war wrecked the South's railroads; invading Union troops tore up tracks, twisted rails, and burned railroad cars. Cotton production, once the foundation of the South's prosperity, sank from more than 4 million bales in 1861 to three hundred thousand bales in 1865 as Union invasions

Six North Carolina Women
The departure of most men of military age to serve in the Confederate army reshaped southern households and the experience of family members. The faces of these young North Carolina women, in a portrait entitled "Confederate Belles," reflect hardship, resolution, and no doubt changed expectations.

took their toll on production, particularly in Tennessee and Louisiana.

Invading Union troops also occupied the South's food-growing regions. Moreover, in areas under Confederate control, the drain of manpower into the army decreased the yields per acre of crops like wheat and corn, and scarcities abounded. Agricultural shortages worsened the South's already severe inflation. By 1863, salt selling for $1.25 a sack in New York City cost $60 in the Confederacy. Food riots erupted in 1863 in Mobile, Atlanta, and Richmond; in Richmond the wives of ironworkers paraded to demand lower food prices.

Part of the blame for the South's food shortages rested with the planter class. Despite government pleas to grow more food, many planters continued to raise cotton, with far-reaching consequences. Slave labor, which could have been diverted to army camps, remained essential on cotton plantations. This increased the Confederacy's reliance on its unpopular conscription laws. Moreover, to feed its hungry armies, the Confederacy had to impress food from civilians, a policy that led to resentment and spurred military desertions. Food-impressment agents usually concentrated on the easiest targets—farms run by the wives of active soldiers. "I don't want you to stop fighting them Yankees," wrote the wife of an Alabama soldier, "but try

and get off and come home and fix us all up some and then you can go back." By the end of 1864, half of the Confederacy's soldiers were absent from their units.

The manpower drain that hampered food production reshaped the lives of southern white women. With the enlistment of about three out of four men of military age over the course of the war, Confederate women found their locales "thinned out of men," as a South Carolina woman described her town in 1862. "There is a vacant chair in every house," mourned a Kentucky Confederate girl. Often left in charge of farms and plantations, women faced new challenges and chronic shortages. As factory-made goods became scarce, the southern press urged the revival of home production; one Arkansas woman, a newspaper reported with admiration, not only wove eight yards of cloth a day but had also built her own loom. More commonly, southern homemakers concocted replacements for goods no longer attainable, including inks, dyes, coffee, shoes, and wax candles. "I find myself, every day, doing something I never did before," a Virginia woman declared in 1863. The proximity of war forced many Confederate women into lives as refugees. Property destruction or even the threat of Union invasions drove women and families away from their homes; those with slave property to preserve, in particular, sought to flee before Union forces arrived. Areas remote from military action, especially Texas, were favored destinations. Disorienting and disheartening, the refugee experience sapped morale. "I will never feel like myself again," a Georgia woman who had escaped from the path of Union troops wrote to her husband in 1864.

In one respect, the persistence of cotton growing helped the South because cotton became the basis for the Confederacy's flourishing trade with the enemy. The U.S. Congress virtually legalized this trade in July 1861 by allowing northern commerce with southerners loyal to the Union. In practice, of course, it proved impossible to tell loyalists from disloyalists, and northern traders happily swapped bacon, salt, blankets, and other necessaries for southern cotton. By 1864, traffic through the lines provided enough food to feed Lee's Army of Northern Virginia. To a northern congressman, it seemed that the Union's policy was "to feed an army and fight it at the same time."

Trading with the enemy alleviated the South's food shortages but intensified its morale problems. The prospect of traffic with the Yankees gave planters an incentive to keep growing cotton, and it fattened merchants and middlemen. "Oh! the extortioners," complained a Confederate war-office clerk in Richmond. "Our patriotism is mainly in the army and among the ladies of the South. The avarice and cupidity of men at home could only be exceeded by ravenous wolves."

Dealing with Dissent

Both wartime governments faced mounting dissent and disloyalty. Within the Confederacy, dissent took two basic forms. First, a vocal group of states' rights activists, notably Vice President Alexander Stephens and governors Zebulon Vance of North Carolina and Joseph Brown of Georgia, spent much of the war attacking Jefferson Davis's government as a despotism. Second, loyalty to the Union flourished among a segment of the Confederacy's common people, particularly those living in the Appalachian Mountain region that ran from western North Carolina through eastern Tennessee and into northern Georgia and Alabama. The nonslaveholding small farmers who predominated here saw the Confederate rebellion as a slave owners' conspiracy. Resentful of such measures as the 20-Negro exemption from conscription, they voiced reluctance to fight for what a North Carolinian called "an adored trinity," of cotton, slaves, and "chivalry." "All they want," an Alabama farmer complained of the planters, "is to get you pupt up and to fight for their infurnal negroes

and after you do there fighting you may kiss there hine parts for o they care."

On the whole, the Confederate government responded mildly to popular disaffection. In 1862, the Confederate Congress gave Jefferson Davis the power to suspend the writ of *habeas corpus,* but Davis used his power only sparingly, by occasionally and briefly putting areas under martial law, mainly to aid tax collectors.

Lincoln faced similar challenges in the North, where the Democratic minority opposed both emancipation and the wartime growth of centralized power. Although "War Democrats" conceded that war was necessary to preserve the Union, "Peace Democrats" (called "Copperheads" by their opponents, to suggest a resemblance to a species of easily concealed poisonous snakes) demanded a truce and a peace conference. They charged that administration war policy was intended to "exterminate the South," make reconciliation impossible, and spark "terrible social change and revolution" nationwide.

Strongest in the border states, the Midwest, and the northeastern cities, the Democrats mobilized the support of farmers of southern background in the Ohio Valley and of members of the urban working class, especially recent immigrants, who feared losing their jobs to an influx of free blacks. In 1863, this volatile brew of political, ethnic, racial, and class antagonisms in northern society exploded into antidraft protests in several cities. By far the most violent eruptions were the **New York City draft riots** in July. Enraged by the first drawing of names under the Enrollment Act and by a longshoremen's strike in which blacks had been used as strikebreakers, mobs of Irish working-class men and women roamed the streets for four days until suppressed by federal troops. The city's Irish loathed the idea of being drafted to fight a war on behalf of the slaves who, once emancipated, might migrate north to compete with them for low-paying jobs. They also resented the provision of the draft law that allowed the rich to purchase substitutes. The rioters lynched at least a dozen blacks, injured hundreds more, and burned draft offices, the homes of wealthy Republicans, and the Colored Orphan Asylum.

President Lincoln's dispatch of federal troops to quash these riots typified his forceful response to dissent. Lincoln imposed martial law with far less hesitancy than Davis. After suspending the writ of *habeas corpus* in Maryland in 1861, he barred it nationwide in 1863 and authorized the arrest of rebels, draft resisters, and those engaged in "any disloyal practice." The contrasting responses of Davis and Lincoln to dissent underscored

Technology (and) Culture

The Camera and the Civil War

In October 1862, crowds gathered at photographer Mathew Brady's New York studio to gaze at images of the Civil War, especially at gruesome views of corpses on the battlefield. "Mr. Brady has done something to bring home to us the terrible reality and earnestness of war," declared the *New York Times*. "You will see hushed, reverent groups standing around these weird copies of carnage, bending down to look at the dead . . . . These pictures have a terrible distinctness." Entrepreneurs like Brady and his staff of photographers played an innovative role in the Civil War. Just as new technologies reshaped military strategy, so did the camera transform the image of war. Some fifteen hundred wartime photographers, who took tens of thousands of photos in makeshift studios, in army camps, and in the field, brought visions of military life to people at home. The Civil War became the first heavily photographed war in history.

Invented in 1839, the camera had played a small part in the Mexican-American War (1846–1848) and the Crimean War (1854–1855), but the still-unsophisticated nature of photography limited its influence. Photographs of the 1840s and 1850s were mainly daguerreotypes, reversed images (mirror images) on silver-coated surfaces of copper plates. The daguerreotype process required between fifteen and thirty minutes of exposure and produced only one image. Most daguerreotypes were stiff-looking portraits made in studios. Cheaper versions of daguerreotypes, ambrotypes (negatives on glass) and tintypes (negatives on iron), remained popular for years to come. In the 1850s, a new era of photography opened, with the development of the wet-plate or collodion process and the printing of photographs on paper. In the wet-plate process, the photographer coated a glass plate, or negative, with a chemical solution; exposed the negative (took the photo); and developed it at once in a darkroom. The new process required a short exposure time—a few seconds outdoors and up to a minute indoors—and lent itself to landscapes as well as portraits. Most important, the wet-plate process enabled photographers to generate multiple prints from a single negative. Professional photographers could now mass-produce prints of photos for a wide audience; the wet-plate process made photography not just a craft but a profitable enterprise.

Using new methods and older ones, Civil War photographers churned out many portraits of individual soldiers, often made in temporary tents in army camps; some were ambrotypes or tintypes, and others were cartes-de-visite, or mass-produced portraits mounted on cards (see the first page of this chapter). They disseminated images of political leaders and battle sites; some were stereographs, or two images, each made from the position of one eye, which, fused together, created a sense of spatial depth. Lugging their heavy equipment with them, including portable dark-boxes for developing images, wartime photographers competed both with one another and with sketch artists who also sought to record the war. Wood engravings derived from photographs appeared alongside lithographs in popular magazines such as *Harpers Weekly* and *Frank Leslie's Illustrated Weekly*. Finally,

An etching of Mathew Brady's Photographic Gallery in New York City. Visitors crowded the staircase in the rear, left, to reach an upstairs gallery where Brady exhibited war photos in the fall of 1862.

Two photographers attached to the Army of the Potomac pose in front of their makeshift studio.

and collected hundreds of photos to illustrate case studies and surgical techniques.

Several factors limited the scope of Civil War photography. First, most camera work of the war years was northern; the Union blockade of the South, dwindling photographic supplies, and the sinking Confederate economy curbed southern photography. Photos of the South became part of the record mainly as Union forces invaded the Confederacy.

Second, no Civil War photos showed battles in progress; action photos were not yet possible. Instead, photographers rushed to arrive right after battles had ended, perhaps with cannon and smoke in the distance, to photograph casualties before bodies were removed. But limitations aside, the camera now served, in Mathew Brady's words, as "the eye of history." Americans of the Civil War era appreciated the minute detail of photographs and the apparent truthfulness of the camera. They also responded with emotion to the content of photographs—to the courage of soldiers, to the massive might of the Union army, and to the deadly toll of war.

the Union army used photography for military purposes. Photographers in the army's employ took photos of maps, battle terrain, bridges, armaments, and even medical procedures. The Union army's Surgeon General commissioned

Two postwar publications by photographers George N. Barnard and Alexander Gardner, Brady's large collection of glass negatives, a huge military archive, and thousands of soldiers' portraits remain part of the Civil War's photographic legacy. Only in 1888, when inventor George Eastman introduced roll film (made of celluloid, a synthetic plastic) and a simple box camera, the Kodak, did members of the general public, until then primarily viewers of photography, become photographers themselves.

Northern photographers who traveled south with the Union army were the first to take photos of African-American communities during the Civil War. Photographer Timothy O'Sullivan portrayed these former slaves on a plantation near Beaufort, South Carolina, in January 1863 as they celebrated the first "Emancipation Day," the day that Lincoln issued the Emancipation Proclamation.

Questions for Analysis

- How do photographs affect people's perceptions of the past?

- In what ways does the camera change the historical record?

the differences between the two regions' wartime political systems. As we have seen, Davis lacked the institutionalization of dissent provided by party conflict and thus had to tread warily, lest his opponents brand him a despot. In contrast, Lincoln and other Republicans used dissent to rally patriotic fervor against the Democrats. After the New York City draft riots, the Republicans blamed the violence on New York's antidraft Democratic governor, Horatio Seymour.

Forceful as he was, Lincoln did not unleash a reign of terror against dissent. In general, the North preserved freedom of the press, speech, and assembly. Although some fifteen thousand civilians were arrested during the war, most were quickly released. A few cases, however, aroused widespread concern. In 1864, a military commission sentenced an Indiana man to be hanged for an alleged plot to free Confederate prisoners. The Supreme Court reversed his conviction two years later when it ruled that civilians could not be tried by military courts when the civil courts were open (*Ex parte* Milligan, 1866). Of more concern were the arrests of politicians, notably Clement L. Vallandigham, an Ohio Peace Democrat. Courting arrest, Vallandigham challenged the administration, denounced the suspension of *habeas corpus*, proposed an armistice, and in 1863 was sentenced to jail for the rest of the war by a military commission. When Ohio Democrats then nominated him for governor, Lincoln changed the sentence to banishment. Escorted to enemy lines in Tennessee, Vallandigham was left in the hands of bewildered Confederates and eventually escaped to Canada. The Supreme Court refused to review his case.

The Medical War

Union and Confederacy alike witnessed remarkable wartime patriotism that impelled civilians, especially women, to work tirelessly to alleviate soldiers' suffering. The **United States Sanitary Commission**, formed early in the war by civilians to assist the Union's medical bureau, depended on women volunteers. Described by one woman as a "great artery that bears the people's love to the army," the commission raised funds at "sanitary fairs," bought and distributed supplies, ran special kitchens to supplement army rations, tracked down the missing, and inspected army camps. The volunteers' exploits became legendary. One poor widow, Mary Ann "Mother" Bickerdyke, served sick and wounded Union soldiers as both nurse and surrogate mother. When asked by a doctor by what authority she demanded supplies for the wounded, she shot back, "From the Lord

God Almighty. Do you have anything that ranks higher than that?"

Women also reached out to aid the battlefront through the nursing corps. Some 3,200 women served the Union and the Confederacy as nurses. Already famed for her tireless campaigns on behalf of the insane, Dorothea Dix became the head of the Union's nursing corps. Clara Barton, who began the war as a clerk in the U.S. Patent Office, found ingenious ways to channel medicine to the sick and wounded. Learning of Union movements before Antietam, Barton showed up at the battlefield on the eve of the clash with a wagonload of supplies. When army surgeons ran out of bandages and started to dress wounds with corn husks, she raced forward with lint and bandages. "With what joy," she wrote, "I laid my precious burden down among them." After the war, in 1881, she would found the American Red Cross.

The Confederacy, too, had extraordinary nurses. One, Sally Tompkins, was commissioned a captain for her hospital work; another, Belle Boyd, served the Confederacy as both a nurse and a spy and once dashed through a field, waving her bonnet, to give Stonewall Jackson information. Danger stalked nurses even in hospitals far from the front. Author Louisa May Alcott, a nurse at the Union Hotel Hospital in Washington, D.C., contracted typhoid. Wherever they worked, nurses witnessed haunting, unforgettable sights. "About the amputating table," one reported, "lay large piles of human flesh— legs, arms, feet, and hands . . . the stiffened membranes seemed to be clutching oftentimes at our clothing."

Pioneered by British reformer Florence Nightingale in the 1850s, nursing was a new vocation for women and, in the eyes of many, a brazen departure from women's proper sphere. Male doctors were unsure about how to react to women in the wards. Some saw the potential for mischief, but others viewed nursing and sanitary work as potentially useful. The miasma theory of disease (see Chapter 11) won wide respect among physicians and stimulated some valuable sanitary measures, particularly in hospitals behind the lines. In partial consequence, the ratio of disease to battle deaths was much lower in the Civil War than in the Mexican-American War. Still, for every soldier killed during the Civil War, two died of disease. "These Big Battles is not as Bad as the fever," a North Carolina soldier wrote. The scientific investigations that would lead to the germ theory of disease were only commencing in the 1860s. Arm and leg wounds frequently led to gangrene or tetanus, and typhoid, malaria, diarrhea, and dysentery raged through army camps.

Andersonville Prison
Started in early 1864, the overcrowded Andersonville prison in southwest Georgia provided no shelter for its inmates, who built tentlike structures out of blankets, sticks, or whatever they could find. Exposure, disease, and poor sanitation contributed to a mortality rate almost double that in other Confederate prison camps and made Andersonville a scandal that outlived the war.

Prison camps posed a special problem. Prisoner exchanges between the North and the South, common early in the war, collapsed by midwar, partly because the South refused to exchange black prisoners and partly because the North gradually concluded that exchanges benefited the manpower-short Confederacy more than the Union. As a result, the two sides had far more prisoners than either could handle, and prisoners on both sides suffered gravely. Miserable conditions plagued southern camps. Squalor and insufficient rations turned the Confederate prison camp at Andersonville, Georgia, into a virtual death camp; three thousand prisoners a month (out of a total of thirty-two thousand) were dying there by August 1864. After the war an outraged northern public secured the execution of Andersonville's commandant. Although the commandant was partly to blame, the deterioration of the southern economy had contributed massively to the wretched state of southern prison camps. Union camps were not much better, but had lower fatality rates.

The War and Women's Rights

Female nurses and Sanitary Commission workers were not the only women to serve society in wartime. In both northern and southern government offices and mills, thousands of women took over jobs vacated by men. Moreover, home industry revived at all levels of society. In rural areas, where manpower shortages were most acute, women often did the plowing, planting, and harvesting. "Women were in the field everywhere," an Illinois woman recalled. "No rebuffs could chill their zeal; no reverses repress their ardor."

Few women worked more effectively for their region's cause than Philadelphia-born Anna E. Dickinson. After losing her job in the federal mint (for denouncing General George McClellan as a traitor), Dickinson threw herself into hospital volunteer work and public lecturing. Her lecture "Hospital Life," recounting the soldiers' sufferings, won the attention of Republican politicians. In 1863, hard-pressed by the Democrats, these politicians invited Dickinson, then scarcely twenty-one, to campaign for Republicans in New Hampshire and Connecticut. This decision paid dividends. Articulate and poised, Dickinson captivated her listeners. Soon Republican candidates who had dismissed the offer of aid from a woman begged her to campaign for them.

Northern women's rights advocates hoped that the war would yield equality for women as well as freedom for slaves. Not only should a grateful North reward women for their wartime services, these women reasoned, but it should recognize the link between black rights and women's rights. In 1863, Elizabeth Cady Stanton and Susan B. Anthony organized the **Woman's National Loyal League**. The league's main activity was to gather four hundred thousand signatures on a petition calling for a constitutional amendment to abolish slavery, but Stanton and Anthony used the organization to promote woman suffrage as well.

Despite high expectations, the war did not bring women significantly closer to economic or political equality. Women in government offices and factories continued to be paid less than men. Sanitary Commission workers and most wartime nurses, as volunteers, earned nothing. Nor did the war alter the prevailing definition of woman's sphere. In 1860, that sphere already included charitable and benevolent activities; in wartime the scope of benevolence grew to embrace organized care for the wounded. Yet men continued to dominate the medical profession, and for the rest of the nineteenth century, nurses would be classified in the census as domestic help. The keenest disappointment of women's rights advocates lay in their failure to capitalize on rising sentiment for the abolition of slavery to secure the vote for women. Northern politicians could see little value in woman suffrage. The *New York Herald*, which supported the Loyal League's attack on slavery, dismissed its call for woman suffrage as "nonsense and tomfoolery." Stanton wrote bitterly, "So long as woman labors to second man's endeavors and exalt his sex above her own, her virtues pass unquestioned; but when she dares to demand rights and privileges for herself, her motives, manners, dress, personal appearance, and character are subjects for ridicule and detraction."

The Union Victorious, 1864–1865

Despite successes at Gettysburg and Vicksburg in 1863, the Union stood no closer to taking Richmond at the start of 1864 than in 1861, and most of the Lower South still remained under Confederate control. The Union invasion had taken its toll on the South's home front, but the North's inability to destroy the main Confederate armies had eroded the Union's will to keep attacking. Northern war weariness strengthened the Democrats and jeopardized Lincoln's prospects for reelection in 1864.

The year 1864 proved crucial for the North. While Grant dueled with Lee in the East, a Union army under William T. Sherman attacked from Tennessee into north-

western Georgia and took Atlanta in early September. Atlanta's fall boosted northern morale and helped to reelect Lincoln. Now the curtain rose on the last act of the war. After taking Atlanta, Sherman marched across Georgia to Savannah, devastated the state's resources, and cracked its morale. Pivoting north from Savannah, Sherman moved into South Carolina. Meanwhile, having backed Lee into trenches around Petersburg and Richmond, Grant forced the evacuation of both cities and brought on the Confederacy's collapse.

The Eastern Theater in 1864

Early in 1864, Lincoln made Grant commander of all Union armies and promoted him to lieutenant general. At first glance, the stony-faced Grant seemed an unlikely candidate for so exalted a rank, held previously only by George Washington. Grant's only distinguishing characteristics were his ever-present cigars and a penchant for whittling sticks into chips. "There is no glitter, no parade about him," a contemporary noted. But Grant's success in the West had made him the Union's most popular general. With his promotion, Grant moved his headquarters to the Army of the Potomac in the East and mapped a strategy for final victory.

Like Lincoln, Grant believed that the Union had to coordinate its attacks on all fronts in order to exploit its numerical advantage and prevent the South from shifting troops back and forth between the eastern and western theaters. Accordingly, Grant planned a sustained offensive against Lee in the East while ordering William T. Sherman to attack the rebel army in Georgia. Sherman's mission was to break up the Confederate army and "to get into the interior of the enemy's country . . . inflicting all the damage you can."

The pace of war quickened dramatically. In early May 1864, Grant led 118,000 men against Lee's 64,000 in a forested area near Fredericksburg, Virginia, called the Wilderness. Checked by Lee in a series of bloody engagements (the Battle of the Wilderness, May 5–7), Grant then tried to swing around Lee's right flank, only to suffer new reverses at Spotsylvania on May 12 and Cold Harbor on June 3. These engagements were among the war's fiercest; at Cold Harbor, Grant lost 7,000 men in a single hour. Oliver Wendell Holmes, Jr., a Union lieutenant and later a Supreme Court justice, wrote home how "immense the butcher's bill has been." But Grant refused to interpret repulses as defeats. Rather, he saw these violent engagements as less-than-complete victories. Pressing on, he forced Lee to pull back to the trenches guarding Petersburg and Richmond.

Once entrenched, Lee could no longer swing around to the Union rear, cut Yankee supply lines, or as at Chancellorsville, surprise the Union's main force. Lee did dispatch General Jubal A. Early on raids down the Shenandoah Valley, which the Confederacy had long used both as a granary and as an indirect way to menace Washington. But Grant countered by ordering General Philip Sheridan to march up the valley from the north and devastate it. The time had come, a Union chaplain wrote, "to peel this land." After defeating Early at Winchester, Virginia, in September 1864, Sheridan controlled the Shenandoah Valley.

While Grant and Lee grappled in the Wilderness, Sherman advanced into Georgia at the head of 98,000 men. Opposing him with 53,000 Confederate troops (soon reinforced to 65,000), General Joseph Johnston retreated toward Atlanta. Johnston's plan was to conserve strength for a final defense of Atlanta while forcing Sherman to extend his supply lines. But Jefferson Davis, dismayed by Johnston's defensive strategy, replaced him with the adventurous John B. Hood. Hood, who had lost the use of an arm at Gettysburg and a leg at Chickamauga, had to be strapped to his saddle; but for all his disabilities, he liked to take risks. In a prewar poker game, he had bet $2,500 with "nary a pair in his hand." Hood gave Davis what he wanted, a series of attacks on Sherman's army. The forays, however, failed to dislodge Sherman and severely depleted Hood's army. No longer able to defend Atlanta's supply lines, Hood evacuated the city, which Sherman took on September 2, 1864.

The Election of 1864

Atlanta's fall came at a timely moment for Lincoln, who faced a tough reelection campaign. Lincoln had secured the Republican renomination with difficulty. The Radicals, who had flayed Lincoln for delay in adopting emancipation as a war goal, now dismissed his plans to restore the occupied parts of Tennessee, Louisiana, and Arkansas to the Union. The Radicals insisted that only Congress, not the president, could set the requirements for readmission of conquered states and criticized Lincoln's reconstruction standards as too lenient. The Radicals endorsed Secretary of the Treasury Salmon P. Chase for the nomination. The Democrats, meanwhile, had never forgiven Lincoln for making emancipation a war goal. Now the Peace Democrats demanded an immediate armistice, followed by negotiations between the North and the South to settle outstanding issues.

Facing formidable challenges, Lincoln benefited from both his own resourcefulness and his foes' problems. Chase's challenge failed, and by the time of the Republican convention in July, Lincoln's managers were

firmly in control. To isolate the Peace Democrats and attract prowar Democrats, the Republicans formed a temporary organization, the National Union party, and replaced Lincoln's vice president, Hannibal Hamlin, with a prowar southern Unionist, Democratic Senator Andrew Johnson of Tennessee. This tactic helped exploit the widening division among the Democrats, who nominated George B. McClellan, the former commander of the Army of the Potomac and an advocate of continuing the war until the Confederacy's collapse. But McClellan, saddled with a platform written by the Peace Democrats, spent much of his campaign distancing himself from his party's peace-without-victory plank.

Despite the Democrats' disarray, as late as August 1864, Lincoln seriously doubted that he would be reelected. Leaving little to chance, he arranged for furloughs so that Union soldiers, most of whom supported him, could vote in states lacking absentee ballots. But the timely fall of Atlanta aided him even more. The Confederate defeat punctured the northern antiwar movement and saved Lincoln's presidency. With 55 percent of the popular vote and 212 out of 233 electoral votes, Lincoln swept to victory.

The convention that nominated Lincoln had endorsed a constitutional amendment to abolish slavery, which Congress passed early in 1865. The **Thirteenth Amendment** would be ratified by the end of the year (see Table 15.1).

Sherman's March Through Georgia

Meanwhile, Sherman gave the South a new lesson in total war. After evacuating Atlanta, Hood led his Confederate army north toward Tennessee in the hope of luring Sherman out of Georgia. But Sherman refused to chase Hood around Tennessee and stretch his own supply lines to the breaking point. Rather, Sherman proposed to abandon his supply lines altogether, march his army across Georgia to Savannah, and live off the countryside as he moved along. He would break the South's will to fight, terrify its people, and "make war so terrible . . . that generations would pass before they could appeal again to it."

Sherman began by burning much of Atlanta and forcing the evacuation of most of its civilian population. This harsh measure relieved him of the need to feed and garrison the city. Then, sending enough troops north to ensure the futility of Hood's campaign in Tennessee, he led the bulk of his army, sixty-two thousand men, on a 285-mile trek to Savannah (see Map 15.7). Soon thousands of slaves followed the army. "Dar's de man dat rules the world," a slave cried on seeing Sherman.

Sherman's four columns of infantry, augmented by cavalry screens, moved on a front sixty miles wide and at a pace of ten miles a day. They destroyed everything that

Table 15.1 Emancipation of Slaves in the Atlantic World: A Selective List

HAITI	1794	A series of slave revolts began in St. Domingue in 1791 and 1792, and spread under the leadership of Toussaint L'Ouverture. In 1794 the French Republic abolished slavery in all French colonies. In 1804 St. Domingue became the independent republic of Haiti.
BRITISH WEST INDIES	1834	Parliament in 1833 abolished slavery gradually in all lands under British control, usually with compensation for slave owners. The law affected the entire British Empire, including British colonies in the West Indies such as Barbados and Jamaica. It took effect in 1834.
MARTINIQUE AND GUADELOUPE	1848	Napoleon had restored slavery to these French colonies in 1800; the Second French Republic abolished it in 1848.
UNITED STATES	1865	The Thirteenth Amendment, passed by Congress in January 1865 and ratified in December 1865, freed all slaves in the United States. Prior to that, the second Confiscation Act of 1862 liberated those slaves who came within Union lines, and the Emancipation Proclamation of January 1, 1863, declared free all slaves in areas under Confederate control.
CUBA	1886	In the early 1880s, the Spanish Parliament passed a plan of gradual abolition, which provided an intermediate period of "apprenticeship." In 1886 Spain abolished slavery completely. Cuba remained under Spanish control until the end of the Spanish-American War in 1898.
BRAZIL	1888	Brazil, which had declared its independence from Portugal in 1822, passed a law to effect gradual emancipation in 1871, and in 1888, under the "Golden Law," abolished slavery completely.

could aid southern resistance—arsenals, railroads, munitions plants, cotton gins, cotton stores, crops, and livestock. Railroad destruction was especially thorough; ripping up tracks, Union soldiers heated rails in giant fires and twisted them into "Sherman neckties." Although Sherman's troops were told not to destroy civilian property, foragers carried out their own version of total war, ransacking and sometimes demolishing homes. Indeed, the havoc seemed a vital part of Sherman's strategy. By the time he occupied Savannah, he estimated that his army had destroyed about a hundred million dollars' worth of property.

After taking Savannah in December 1864, Sherman's army wheeled north toward South Carolina, the first state to secede and, in the general's view, one "that deserves all that seems in store for her." Sherman's columns advanced unimpeded to Columbia, South Carolina's capital. After fires set by looters, slaves, soldiers of both sides, and liberated Union prisoners gutted much of the city, Sherman headed for North Carolina. By the spring of 1865, his army had left in its wake over four hundred miles of ruin. Other Union armies moved into Alabama and Georgia and took thousands of prisoners. Northern forces had penetrated the entire Confederacy, except for Texas and Florida, and crushed its wealth. "War is cruelty and you cannot

refine it," Sherman wrote. "Those who brought war into our country deserve all the curses and maledictions a people can pour out."

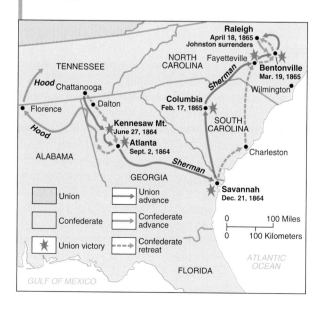

Map 15.7 Sherman's March Through the South, 1864–1865

New Hope Church, Georgia
General Sherman's campaign through Georgia and South Carolina in 1864 turned parts of the landscape into rubble. This scene of devastation in Georgia, captured by northern photographer George N. Barnard in 1866, suggests the impact of war on the southern environment.

Toward Appomattox

While Sherman headed north, Grant renewed his assault on the entrenched Army of Northern Virginia. His objective was Petersburg, a railroad hub south of Richmond (see Map 15.8). Although Grant had failed on several occasions to overwhelm the Confederate defenses in front of Petersburg, the devastation wrought by Sherman's army had taken its toll on Confederate morale. Rebel desertions reached epidemic proportions. Reinforced by Sheridan's army, triumphant from its campaign in the Shenandoah Valley, Grant late in March 1865 swung his forces around the western flank of Petersburg's defenders. Lee could not stop him. On April 2, Sheridan smashed the rebel flank at the Battle of Five Forks. A courier bore the grim news to Jefferson Davis, attending church in Richmond: "General Lee telegraphs that he can hold his position no longer."

Davis left his pew, gathered his government, and fled the city. In the morning of April 3, Union troops entered Richmond, pulled down the Confederate flag, and ran up the Stars and Stripes over the capitol. As white and black regiments entered in triumph, explosions set by retreating Confederates left the city "a sea of flames." "Over all," wrote a Union officer, "hung a canopy of dense smoke lighted up now and then by the bursting shells from the numerous arsenals throughout the city." Fires damaged the Tredegar Iron Works. Union troops liberated the town jail, which housed slaves awaiting sale, and its rejoicing inmates poured into the streets. On April 4, Lincoln toured the city and, for a few minutes, sat at Jefferson Davis's desk with a dreamy expression on his face.

Lee made a last-ditch effort to escape from Grant and reach Lynchburg, sixty miles west of Petersburg. He planned to use rail connections there to join General Joseph Johnston's army, which Sherman had pushed into North Carolina. But Grant and Sheridan swiftly choked off Lee's escape route, and on April 9 Lee bowed to the inevitable. He asked for terms of surrender and met Grant in a private home in the village of **Appomattox Courthouse**, Virginia, east of Lynchburg. While stunned troops gathered outside, Lee appeared in full dress uniform, with a sword. Grant entered in his customary disarray, smoking a cigar. When Union troops began to fire celebratory salutes, Grant put a stop to it. The final surrender of Lee's army occurred four days later. Lee's troops laid down their arms between federal ranks. "On our part," wrote a Union officer, "not a sound of trumpet . . . nor roll of drum; not a cheer . . . but an awed stillness rather." Grant paroled Lee's twenty-six thousand men and sent them home with their horses and mules "to work their little farms." The remnants of Confederate resistance collapsed within a month of Appomattox. Johnston surrendered to Sherman on April 18, and Davis was captured in Georgia on May 10.

Grant returned to a jubilant Washington, and on April 14 he turned down a theater date with the Lincolns. That night at Ford's Theater, an unemployed pro-Confederate actor, John Wilkes Booth, entered Lincoln's box and shot him in the head. Waving a knife, Booth leaped onstage shouting the Virginia state motto, "*Sic semper tyrannis*" ("Such is always the fate of tyrants") and then escaped, despite having broken his leg. That same night, a Booth accomplice stabbed Secretary of State Seward, who later recovered, while a third conspirator, assigned to Vice President Johnson, failed to attack. Union troops hunted down Booth in Virginia within two weeks and shot him to death. Of eight accused accomplices, including a woman boardinghouse keeper, four were hanged and the rest imprisoned. On April 15, when Lincoln died, Andrew Johnson became president. Six days later Lincoln's funeral train departed on a mournful journey from Washington to Springfield, Illinois, with crowds of thousands gathering at stations to weep as it passed.

Map 15.8 The Final Virginia Campaign, 1864–1865
Refusing to abandon his campaign in the face of enormous casualties, Grant finally pushed Lee (below) into defensive fortifications around Petersburg, whose fall doomed Richmond. When Lee tried to escape to the west, Grant cut him off and forced his surrender.

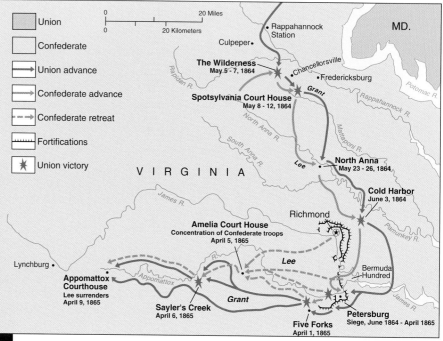

Grant in 1864
Exuding determination and competence, General Ulysses S. Grant posed in front of his tent in 1864. Within a year, Grant's final assault on Petersburg and the Union army's triumphant march into Richmond would bring the war to an end.

The Impact of the War

The Civil War took a larger human toll than any other war in American history. The 620,000 soldiers who lost their lives nearly equaled the number of American soldiers killed in all the nation's earlier and later wars combined (see Figure 15.3). The death count stood at 360,000 Union soldiers and 260,000 Confederates. Most families in the nation suffered losses. Vivid reminders of the price of Union remained beyond the end of the century. For many years, armless and legless veterans gathered at regimental reunions. Citizens erected monuments to the dead in front of town halls and on village greens. Soldiers' widows collected pensions well into the twentieth century.

The economic costs were staggering, but the war did not ruin the national economy, only the southern part of it. Vast Confederate losses, about 60 percent of southern wealth, were offset by northern advances. At the war's end, the North had almost all of the nation's wealth and capacity for production. Spurring economic modernization, the war provided a hospitable climate for industrial development and capital investment. No longer the largest slave-owning power in the world, the United States would now become a major industrial nation.

The war had political as well as economic ramifications. It created a "more perfect Union" in place of the

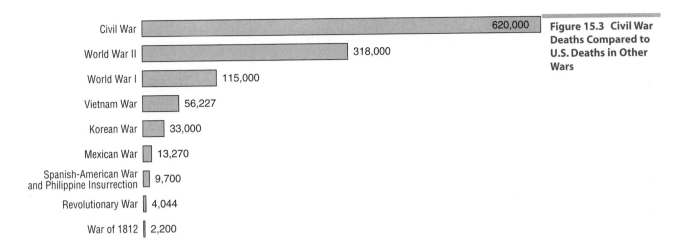

Figure 15.3 Civil War Deaths Compared to U.S. Deaths in Other Wars

prewar federation of states. The doctrine of states' rights did not disappear, but it was shorn of its extreme features. Talk of secession ended; states would never again exercise their antebellum range of powers. The national banking system, created in 1863, gradually supplanted state banks. The greenbacks provided a national currency. The federal government had exercised powers that many in 1860 doubted it possessed. By abolishing slavery and imposing an income tax, it asserted power over kinds of private property once thought untouchable. The war also promoted large-scale organization in both the business world and public life. The giant railroad corporation, with its thousands of employees, and the huge Sanitary Commission, with its thousands of auxiliaries and volunteers, pointed out the road that the nation would take.

Finally, the Civil War fulfilled abolitionist prophecies as well as Unionist goals. Freeing 3.5 million slaves and expediting efforts by slaves to liberate themselves, the war produced the very sort of radical upheaval within southern society that Lincoln had originally said that it would not induce.

Conclusion

When war began in April 1861, both sides were unprepared, but each had distinct strengths. The Union held vast advantages of manpower and resources, including most of the nation's industrial strength and two-thirds of its railroads. The North, however, faced a stiff challenge. To achieve its goal of forcing the rebel states back into the Union, it had to conquer large pieces of southern territory, cripple the South's resources, and destroy its armies. The Union's challenge was the Confederacy's strength. To sustain Confederate independence, the South had to fight a defensive war, far less costly in men and materiel. It had to prevent Union conquest of its territory, preserve its armies from annihilation, and hold out long enough to convince the North that further effort would be pointless. Moreover, southerners expected to be fighting on home ground and to enjoy an advantage in morale. Thus, though its resources were fewer, the Confederacy's task was less daunting.

The start of war challenged governments, North and South, in similar ways: both sides had to raise armies and funds. Within two years, both the Union and the Confederacy had drafted troops, imposed taxes, and printed paper money. As war dragged on, both regions faced political and economic problems. Leaders on each side confronted disunity and dissent. Northern Democrats assailed President Lincoln; in the South, states' rights supporters defied the authority of the Confederate government. The North's two-party system and the skills of its political leaders proved to be assets that the Confederacy lacked. Economically, too, the North held an edge. Both regions endured labor shortages and inflation. But the Union with its far greater resources more handily met the demands of war. In the North, Republicans in Congress enacted innovative laws that enhanced federal might, such as the National Banking Act, the Pacific Railroad Act, and the

Chronology, 1861–1865

1861 President Abraham Lincoln calls for volunteers to suppress the rebellion (April).
Virginia, Arkansas, Tennessee, and North Carolina join the Confederacy (April–May).
Lincoln imposes a naval blockade on the South (April).
U.S. Sanitary Commission formed (June).
First Battle of Bull Run (July).
First Confiscation Act (August).

1862 Legal Tender Act (February).
George B. McClellan's Peninsula Campaign (March–July).
Battle of Shiloh (April).
Confederate Congress passes the Conscription Act (April).
David G. Farragut captures New Orleans (April).
Homestead Act (May).
Seven Days' Battles (June–July).
Pacific Railroad Act (July).
Morrill Land Grant Act (July).
Second Confiscation Act (July).
Second Battle of Bull Run (August).
Battle of Antietam (September).
Preliminary Emancipation Proclamation (September).
Battle of Fredericksburg (December).

1863 Emancipation Proclamation issued (January).
Lincoln suspends writ of *habeas corpus* nationwide (January).
National Bank Act (February).
Congress passes the Enrollment Act (March).
Battle of Chancellorsville (May).
Woman's National Loyal League formed (May).
Battle of Gettysburg (July).
Surrender of Vicksburg (July).
New York City draft riots (July).
Battle of Chickamauga (September).

1864 Ulysses S. Grant given command of all Union armies (March).
Battle of the Wilderness (May).
Battle of Spotsylvania (May).
Battle of Cold Harbor (June).
Surrender of Atlanta (September).
Lincoln reelected (November).
William T. Sherman's march to the sea (November–December).

1865 Congress passes the Thirteenth Amendment (January).
Sherman moves through South Carolina (January–March).
Grant takes Richmond (April).
Robert E. Lee surrenders at Appomattox (April).
Lincoln dies (April).
Joseph Johnston surrenders to Sherman (April).

Homestead Act. The beleaguered South, in contrast, had to cope with food shortages and economic dislocation. Loss of southern manpower to the army took a toll as well; slavery began to disintegrate as a labor system during the war. By 1864, even the Confederate Congress considered measures to free at least some slaves.

Significantly, war itself pressed the North to bring slavery to an end. To deprive the South of resources, the Union began to seize rebel property, including slaves, in 1861. Step by step, Union policy shifted toward emancipation. The second Confiscation Act in 1862 freed slaves who fled behind Union lines. Finally, seizing the initiative from Radical Republicans, Lincoln announced a crucial change in policy. A war

measure, the Emancipation Proclamation of January 1, 1863, served many purposes. The edict freed only slaves behind Confederate lines, those beyond the reach of the Union army. But it won foreign support, outflanked the Radicals, and confounded the Confederates. It also gave Union soldiers the power to liberate slaves, enabled former slaves to serve in the Union army, and vastly strengthened the Union's hand. "Crippling the institution of slavery," as a Union officer declared, meant "striking a blow at the heart of the rebellion." Most important, the proclamation changed the nature of the war. After January 1, 1863, the war to save the Union was also a war to end slavery. Emancipation took effect mainly at the war's end and became permanent with the ratification of the

Thirteenth Amendment in 1865. The proclamation of 1863 was a pivotal turning point in the war.

Historians have long debated the causes of the Union victory. They have weighed many factors, including the North's imposing strengths, or what Robert E. Lee called its "overwhelming numbers and resources." Recently, two competing interpretations have held sway. One focuses on southern shortcomings. Did the South, in the end, lose the will to win? Did the economic dislocations of war undercut southern morale? Were there defects of Confederate nationalism that could not be overcome? Some historians point to internal weaknesses in the Confederacy as a major cause of Union triumph. Other historians stress the utterly unpredictable nature of the conflict. In their view, the two sides were fairly equally matched, and the war was a cliffhanger; that is, the North might have crushed the South much earlier or, alternatively, not at all. The North won the war, these historians contend, because it won a series of crucial contests on the battlefield, including the battles of Antietam, Vicksburg, Gettysburg, and Atlanta, any one of which could have gone the other way. The factors that determined the military outcome of the war continue to be a source of contention.

The impact of the Civil War is more clear-cut than the precise cause of Union triumph. The war gave a massive boost to the northern economy. It left in its wake a stronger national government, with a national banking system, a national currency, and an enfeebled version of states' rights. It confirmed the triumph of the Republican Party, with its commitment to competition, free labor, and industry. Finally, it left a nation of free people, including the millions of African-Americans who had once been slaves. Emancipation and a new sense of nationalism were the war's major legacies. The nation now turned its attention to the restoration of the conquered South to the Union and to deciding the future of the former slaves.

Key Terms

conscription
Legal Tender Act
National Bank Act
Jefferson Davis
Radical Republicans
Anaconda plan
First Battle of Bull Run
Robert E. Lee
Battle of Antietam
Ulysses S. Grant
William T. Sherman
Battle of Shiloh
"cotton diplomacy"
Emancipation Proclamation
Freedmen's Bureau
Battle of Gettysburg
Battle of Vicksburg
Homestead Act
Morrill Land Grant Act
New York City draft riots
United States Sanitary Commission
Woman's National Loyal League
Thirteenth Amendment
Appomattox Courthouse

For Further Reference

Edward L. Ayers, *In the Presence of Mine Enemies: War in the Heart of America, 1859–1863* (2003). Traces the impact of the early years of civil war on Augusta County, Virginia, and Franklin County, Pennsylvania.

Joan E. Cashin, ed., *The War Was You and Me: Civilians in the American Civil War* (2002). Essays on developments on the home fronts, North and South.

David Herbert Donald, *Lincoln* (1995). A compelling biography that reveals connections between Lincoln's private and public lives.

Drew Gilpin Faust, *Mothers of Invention: Women of the Slaveholding South in the American Civil War* (1996). Discusses elite women's relation to slavery, southern culture, and the deprivations of war.

Gary W. Gallagher, *The Confederate War* (1997). Shows how Confederate leaders pursued promising strategies; explores links between morale and the battlefield.

Doris Kearns Goodwin, *Team of Rivals: The Political Genius of Abraham Lincoln* (2005). An analysis of the political figures in Lincoln's cabinet.

James M. McPherson, *Battle Cry of Freedom: The Civil War Era* (1988). An award-winning study of the war years, integrating political, military, and social history.

James M. McPherson, *For Cause and Comrades: Why Men Fought in the Civil War* (1997). Uses soldiers' letters to explore motivation and responses to combat.

George C. Rable, *The Confederate Republic: A Revolt Against Politics* (1994). Discusses the tension between nationalism and individualism in the Confederacy.

Nina Silber, *Daughters of the Union: Northern Women Fight the Civil War* (2002). Explores women's roles in the northern economy, in partisan politics, and as contributors to the Union war effort.

Michael Vorenberg, *Final Freedom: The Civil War, the Abolition of Slavery, and the Thirteenth Amendment* (2001). Considers the framing and ratification of the Thirteenth Amendment and the political context in which emancipation became law.

Chapter 16

The Devastated South
After the Civil War, parts of the devastated Confederacy resembled a wasteland. Homes, crops, and railroads had been destroyed; farming and business had come to a standstill; and uprooted southerners wandered about. Here, ruins of homes in Baton Rouge, Louisiana.

The Crises of Reconstruction, 1865–1877

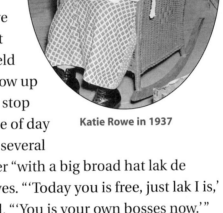

Katie Rowe in 1937

"I never forget de day we was set free," former slave Katie Rowe recalled. "Dat morning we all go to de cotton field early. After a while de old horn blow up at de overseer's house, and we all stop and listen, 'cause it de wrong time of day for de horn." Later that day, after several more blasts of the horn, a stranger "with a big broad hat lak de Yankees wore" addressed the slaves. "'Today you is free, just lak I is,' de man say," Katie Rowe declared. "'You is your own bosses now.'" The date was June 4, 1865.

Born at midcentury, Katie Rowe grew up on a cotton plantation with 200 slaves near Washington, Arkansas. The slaves had "hard traveling" on her plantation, she told an interviewer in 1937. The owner, Dr. Isaac Jones, lived in town, and an overseer ran the place harshly. Dr. Jones was harsh, too. When Union and Confederate forces clashed nearby in 1862 at Pea Ridge, Arkansas, Dr. Jones announced that the enemy would never liberate his slaves because he would shoot them first ("line you up on de bank of Bois d'Arc Creek and free you wid my shotgun"). Soon after, an explosion of the boiler of his steam-powered cotton gin incinerated Dr. Jones. "Later in de war Yankees come in all around and camp, and de overseer git sweet as honey in de comb," Katie Rowe observed. "But we know dey soon be gone."

Emancipation in June 1865 brought an era of transition for the former slaves. "None of us know whar to go," Katie Rowe remembered, "so we all stay and he [the overseer] split up de fields and show us which part we got to work in, and we go on lak we was . . . but dey ain't no horn after dat day." Still, the labor system proved unsatisfactory. "[W]e all gits fooled on dat first go-out," Katie Rowe noted. The overseer "charge us half de crop for de quarter and all de mules and tools and grub." His replacement offered better arrangements: "[W]e all got something left over after dat first go-out." But new changes occurred. The next year the former owner's heirs sold the plantation, "and we scatter off." With her mother, teenage Katie Rowe left for Little Rock to "do work in de town."

Katie eventually married Billy Rowe, a Cherokee, and moved with him to Oklahoma. Interviewed decades later in Tulsa, Oklahoma, where she lived with her youngest daughter, Katie Rowe voiced pride that her children and grandchildren had been educated. She also recalled the days of "hard traveling" and the joyful moment when they ended. "It was the fourth day of June in 1865 that I begins to live," Katie Rowe declared. "I know we living in a better world. . . . I sho' thank de good Lawd I got to see it."

For the nation, as for Katie Rowe, the end of the Civil War was a turning point and an instant of uncharted possibilities. It was also a time of unresolved conflicts. While former slaves exulted over freedom, the postwar mood of ex-Confederates was often as grim as the wasted southern landscape. Unable to face "southern Yankeedom," some planters considered emigrating to the American West or to Europe, Mexico, or Brazil, and a few thousand did. The morale of the vanquished rarely concerns the victors, but the Civil War was a special case, for the Union had sought not merely military triumph but the return of national unity. The federal government in 1865 therefore faced unprecedented questions.

First, how could the Union be restored and the defeated South reintegrated into the nation? Would the Confederate states be treated as conquered territories, or would they quickly rejoin the Union with the same rights as other states? Who would set the standards for readmission—Congress or the president? Most important, what would happen to the more than 3.5 million former slaves? The future of the freedmen constituted the crucial issue of the postwar era, for emancipation had set in motion the most profound upheaval in the nation's history. Before the war, slavery had determined the South's social, economic, and political structure. What would replace it? The end of the Civil War, in short, posed two problems that had to be solved simultaneously: how to readmit the South to the Union and how to define the status of free blacks in American society.

Between 1865 and 1877, the nation met these challenges, but not without discord and turmoil. Conflict prevailed in the halls of Congress as legislators debated plans to readmit the South to the Union; in the former Confederacy, where defeated southerners and newly freed former slaves faced an era of turbulence; and in the postwar North, where economic and political clashes arose. Indeed, the crises of Reconstruction—the restoration of the former Confederate states to the Union—reshaped the legacy of the Civil War.

Focus Questions

- How did Radical Republicans gain control of Reconstruction politics?

- What impact did federal Reconstruction policy have on the former Confederacy and on ex-Confederates?

- How did the newly freed slaves reshape their lives after emancipation?

- What political and economic problems arose in the North during the era of Reconstruction?

- What factors contributed to the end of Reconstruction in 1877?

Reconstruction Politics, 1865–1868

At the end of the Civil War, President Johnson might have exiled, imprisoned, or executed Confederate leaders and imposed martial law indefinitely. Demobilized Confederate soldiers might have continued armed resistance to federal occupation forces. Freed slaves might have taken revenge on former owners and the rest of the white community. But none of these drastic possibilities occurred. Instead, intense *political* conflict dominated the immediate postwar years. In national politics, unparalleled disputes produced new constitutional amendments, a presidential impeachment, and some of the most ambitious domestic legislation ever enacted by Congress, the Reconstruction Acts of 1867–1868. The major outcome of Reconstruction politics was the enfranchisement of black men, a development that few—black or white—had expected when Lee surrendered.

In 1865, only a small group of politicians supported black suffrage. All were Radical Republicans, a minority faction that had emerged during the war. Led by Senator **Charles Sumner** of Massachusetts and Congressman **Thaddeus Stevens** of Pennsylvania, the Radicals had clamored for the abolition of slavery and a demanding reconstruction policy. Any plan to restore the Union, Stevens contended, must "revolutionize Southern institutions, habits, and manners." But the Radicals, outnumbered in Congress by other Republicans and opposed by the Democratic minority, faced long odds. Still, they managed to win broad Republican support for parts of their Reconstruction program, including black male enfranchisement. Just as civil war had led to emancipation, a goal once supported by only a minority of

Americans, so Reconstruction policy became bound to black suffrage, a momentous change that originally had only narrow political backing.

Lincoln's Plan

Conflict over Reconstruction began even before the war ended. In December 1863, President Lincoln issued the Proclamation of Amnesty and Reconstruction, which enabled southern states to rejoin the Union if at least 10 percent of those who had cast ballots in the election of 1860 would take an oath of allegiance to the Union and accept emancipation. This minority could then create a loyal state government. Lincoln's plan excluded some southerners from taking the oath: Confederate government officials, army and naval officers, as well as those military or civil officers who had resigned from Congress or from U.S. commissions in 1861. All such persons would have to apply for presidential pardons. Also excluded, of course, were blacks, who had not been voters in 1860. Lincoln hoped to undermine the Confederacy by establishing pro-Union governments within it; to win the allegiance of southern Unionists (those who had opposed secession), especially former Whigs; and to build a southern Republican party.

Radical Republicans in Congress, however, envisioned a slower readmission process that would bar even more ex-Confederates from political life. The Wade-Davis bill, passed by Congress in July 1864, provided that a military governor would rule each former Confederate state and that after at least half the eligible voters took an oath of allegiance to the Union, delegates could be elected to a state convention that would repeal secession and abolish slavery. To qualify as a voter or delegate, a southerner would have to take a second, "ironclad" oath, swearing that he had never voluntarily supported the Confederacy. Like the 10 percent plan, the congressional plan did not provide for black suffrage, a measure then supported by only some Radicals. Unlike Lincoln's plan, however, the Wade-Davis scheme would have delayed the readmission process almost indefinitely.

Claiming that he did not want to bind himself to any single restoration policy, Lincoln pocket-vetoed the Wade-Davis bill (that is, he failed to sign the bill within ten days of the adjournment of Congress). The bill's sponsors, Senator Benjamin Wade of Ohio and Congressman Henry Winter Davis of Maryland, blasted Lincoln's act as an outrage. By the war's end, the president and Congress had reached an impasse. Arkansas, Louisiana, Tennessee, and parts of Virginia under Union army control moved toward readmission under variants of Lincoln's plan. But Congress refused to seat their delegates, as it had a right to do. Lincoln, meanwhile, hinted that a more rigorous Reconstruction policy might be in store.

Radical Republican Leaders
Charles Sumner, left, senator from Massachusetts, and Thaddeus Stevens, congressman from Pennsylvania, led the Radical Republican faction in Congress.

What Lincoln's ultimate policy would have been remains unknown. But after his assassination, on April 14, 1865, Radical Republicans turned with hope toward his successor, **Andrew Johnson** of Tennessee, in whom they felt they had an ally.

Presidential Reconstruction Under Johnson

The only southern senator to remain in Congress when his state seceded, Andrew Johnson had served as military governor of Tennessee from 1862 to 1864. He had taken a strong anti-Confederate stand, declaring that "treason is a crime and must be made odious." Above all, Johnson had long sought the destruction of the planter aristocracy. A self-educated man of humble North Carolina origins, Johnson had moved to Greenville, Tennessee, in 1826 and became a tailor. His wife, Eliza McCardle, had taught him how to write. He had entered politics in the 1830s as a spokesman for non-slave-owning whites and rose rapidly from local official to congressman to governor to senator. Once the owner of eight slaves, Johnson reversed his position on slavery during the war. When emancipation became Union policy, he supported it. But Johnson neither adopted abolitionist ideals nor challenged racist sentiments. He hoped mainly that the fall of slavery would injure southern aristocrats. Andrew Johnson, in short, had his own political agenda, which, as Republicans would soon learn, did not coincide with theirs. Moreover, he was a lifelong Democrat who had been added to the Republican, or National Union, ticket in 1864 to broaden its appeal and who had become president by accident.

In May 1865, with Congress out of session, Johnson shocked Republicans by announcing in two proclamations his own program to bring back into the Union the seven southern states still without reconstruction governments—Alabama, Florida, Georgia, Mississippi, North Carolina, South Carolina, and Texas. Almost all southerners who took an oath of allegiance would receive a pardon and amnesty, and all their property except slaves would be restored. Oath takers could elect delegates to state conventions, which would provide for regular elections. Each state convention, Johnson later added, would have to proclaim the illegality of secession, repudiate state debts incurred when the state belonged to the Confederacy, and ratify the Thirteenth Amendment, which abolished slavery. (Proposed by an enthusiastic wartime Congress early in 1865, the amendment would be ratified in December of that year.) As under Lincoln's plan, Confederate civil and military officers would still be disqualified, as would well-off ex-Confederates—those with taxable property worth $20,000 or more. This purge of the plantation aristocracy, Johnson said, would benefit "humble men, the peasantry and yeomen of the South, who have been decoyed . . . into rebellion." Poorer whites would now be in control.

Presidential Reconstruction took effect in the summer of 1865, but with unforeseen consequences. Southerners disqualified on the basis of wealth or high Confederate position applied for pardons in droves, and Johnson handed out pardons liberally—some thirteen thousand of them. He also dropped plans for the punishment of treason. By the end of 1865, all seven states had created new civil governments that in effect restored the status quo from before the war. Confederate army officers and large planters assumed state offices. Former Confederate congressmen, state officials, and generals were elected to Congress. Georgia sent Alexander Stephens, the former Confederate vice president, back to Washington as a senator. Some states refused to ratify the Thirteenth Amendment or to repudiate their Confederate debts.

Most infuriating to Radical Republicans, all seven states took steps to ensure a landless, dependent black labor force: they passed **"black codes"** to replace the slave codes, state laws that had regulated slavery. Because Johnson's plan assured the ratification of the Thirteenth Amendment, all states guaranteed the freedmen some basic rights—to marry, own property, make contracts, and testify in court against other blacks—but the codes harshly restricted freedmen's behavior. Some established racial segregation in public places; most prohibited racial intermarriage, jury service by blacks, and court testimony by blacks against whites. All codes included provisions that effectively barred former slaves from leaving the plantations. South Carolina required special licenses for blacks who wished to enter nonagricultural employment. Mississippi prohibited blacks from buying and selling farmland. Most states required annual contracts between landowners and black agricultural workers and provided that blacks without lawful employment would be arrested as vagrants and their labor auctioned off to employers who would pay their fines.

The black codes left freedmen no longer slaves but not really liberated either. Although "free" to sign labor contracts, for instance, those who failed to sign them would be considered in violation of the law and swept back into involuntary servitude. In practice, many clauses in the codes never took effect: the Union army and the Freedmen's Bureau (a federal agency that assisted former slaves) swiftly suspended the enforcement of racially discriminatory provisions of the new laws. But the black codes revealed white southern intentions. They showed what "home rule" would have been like without federal interference.

Many northerners denounced what they saw as southern defiance. "What can be hatched from such an egg but another rebellion?" asked a Boston newspaper. Republicans in Congress agreed. When Congress convened in December 1865, it refused to seat the delegates of the ex-Confederate states. Establishing the Joint (House-Senate) Committee on Reconstruction, Republicans prepared to dismantle the black codes and lock ex-Confederates out of power.

Congress Versus Johnson

Southern blacks' status now became the major issue in Congress. Radical Republicans like Congressman Thaddeus Stevens—who hoped to impose black suffrage on the former Confederacy and delay the readmission of the southern states into the Union—were still a minority in Congress. Conservative Republicans, who tended to favor the Johnson plan, formed a minority too, as did the Democrats, who also supported the president. Moderate Republicans, the largest congressional bloc, agreed with the Radicals that Johnson's plan was too feeble, but they wanted to avoid a dispute with the president. As none of the four congressional blocs could claim the two-thirds majority required to overturn a presidential veto, Johnson's program would prevail unless the moderates and the Radicals joined forces. Ineptly, Johnson alienated a majority of moderates and pushed them into the Radicals' arms.

Two proposals to invalidate the black codes, drafted by a moderate Republican, Senator Lyman Trumbull of Illinois, won wide Republican support. Congress first voted to continue the Freedmen's Bureau, established in 1865, whose term was ending. This federal agency, headed by former Union general O. O. Howard and staffed mainly by army officers, provided relief, rations, and medical care. It also built schools for the freed blacks, put them to work on abandoned or confiscated lands, and tried to protect their rights as laborers. Congress extended the bureau's life for three years and gave it new power: it could run special military courts to settle labor disputes and could invalidate labor contracts forced on freedmen by the black codes. In February 1866, Johnson vetoed the Freedmen's Bureau bill. The Constitution, he declared, did not sanction military trials of civilians in peacetime, nor did it support a system to care for "indigent persons."

In March 1866, Congress passed a second measure proposed by Trumbull, a bill that made blacks U.S. citizens

with the same civil rights as other citizens and authorized federal intervention in the states to ensure black rights in court. Johnson vetoed the civil rights bill also. He argued that it would "operate in favor of the colored and against the white race." In April, Congress overrode his veto; the **Civil Rights Act of 1866** was the first major law ever passed over a presidential veto. In July, Congress enacted the Supplementary Freedmen's Bureau Act over Johnson's veto as well. Johnson's vetoes puzzled many Republicans because the new laws did not undercut presidential Reconstruction. The president insisted, however, that both bills were illegitimate because southerners had been shut out of the Congress that passed them. His stance won support in the South and from northern Democrats. But the president had alienated the moderate Republicans, who began to work with the Radicals against him. Johnson had lost "every friend he has," one moderate declared.

Some historians view Andrew Johnson as a political incompetent who, at this crucial turning point, bungled both his readmission scheme and his political future. Others contend that he was merely trying to forge a coalition of the center, made up of Democrats and non-Radical Republicans. In either case, Johnson underestimated the possibility of Republican unity. Once united, the Republicans took their next step: the passage of a constitutional amendment to prevent the Supreme Court from invalidating the new Civil Rights Act and block Democrats in Congress from repealing it.

The Fourteenth Amendment, 1866

In April 1866, Congress adopted the **Fourteenth Amendment**, which had been proposed by the Joint Committee on Reconstruction. To protect blacks' rights, the amendment declared in its first clause that all persons born or naturalized in the United States were citizens of the nation and citizens of their states and that no state could abridge their rights without due process of law or deny them equal protection of the law. This section nullified the *Dred Scott* decision of 1857, which had declared that blacks were not citizens. Second, the amendment guaranteed that if a state denied suffrage to any of its male citizens, its representation in Congress would be proportionally reduced. This clause did not guarantee black suffrage, but it threatened to deprive southern states of some legislators if black men were denied the vote. This was the first time that the word *male* was written into the Constitution. To the dismay of women's rights advocates, woman suffrage seemed a yet more distant prospect. Third, the amendment disqualified from state and national office *all* prewar officeholders—civil and military, state and federal—who had supported the Confederacy, unless Congress removed their disqualifications by a two-thirds vote. In so providing, Congress intended to invalidate Johnson's wholesale distribution of amnesties and pardons. Finally, the amendment repudiated the Confederate debt and maintained the validity of the federal debt.

The most ambitious step that Congress had yet taken, the Fourteenth Amendment revealed Republican legislators' growing receptivity to Radical demands, including black male enfranchisement. The Fourteenth Amendment was the first national effort to limit state control of civil and political rights, and its passage created a firestorm. Abolitionists decried the second clause as a "swindle" because it did not explicitly ensure black suffrage. Southerners and northern Democrats condemned the third clause as vengeful. Southern legislatures, except for Tennessee's, refused to ratify the amendment, and President Johnson denounced it. His defiance solidified the new alliance between moderate and Radical Republicans, and turned the congressional elections of 1866 into a referendum on the Fourteenth Amendment.

Over the summer, Johnson set off on a whistle-stop train tour from Washington to St. Louis and Chicago and back. But this innovative campaign tactic—the "swing around the circle," as Johnson called it—failed. Humorless and defensive, the president made fresh enemies and doomed his hope of creating a new National Union party that would sink the Fourteenth Amendment. Moderate and Radical Republicans defended the amendment, condemned the president, and branded the

King Andrew
This Thomas Nast cartoon, published in *Harper's Weekly* just before the 1866 congressional elections, conveyed Republican antipathy to Andrew Johnson. The president is depicted as an autocratic tyrant. Radical Republican Thaddeus Stevens, upper right, has his head on the block and is about to lose it. The Republic sits in chains.

Democratic Party "a common sewer . . . into which is emptied every element of treason, North and South."

Republicans carried the congressional elections of 1866 in a landslide, winning almost two-thirds of the House and almost four-fifths of the Senate. They had secured a mandate to overcome southern resistance to the Fourteenth Amendment and to enact their own Reconstruction program, even if the president vetoed every part of it.

Congressional Reconstruction, 1866–1867

The congressional debate over reconstructing the South began in December 1866 and lasted three months. Radical Republican leaders called for black suffrage, federal support for public schools, confiscation of Confederate estates, and an extended period of military occupation in the South. Moderate Republicans, who once would have found such a plan too extreme, now accepted parts of it. In February 1867, after complex legislative maneuvers and many late-night sessions, Congress passed the **Reconstruction Act of 1867**. Johnson vetoed the law, and on March 2 Congress passed it over his veto. Later that year and in 1868, Congress passed three further Reconstruction acts, all enacted over presidential vetoes, to refine and enforce the first (see Table 16.1).

The Reconstruction Act of 1867 invalidated the state governments formed under the Lincoln and Johnson plans. Only Tennessee, which had ratified the Fourteenth Amendment and had been readmitted to the Union, escaped further reconstruction. The new law divided the other ten former Confederate states into five temporary military districts, each run by a Union general (see Map 16.1). Voters—all black men, plus those white men who had not been disqualified by the Fourteenth Amendment—could elect delegates to a state convention that would write a new state constitution granting black suffrage. When eligible voters ratified the new constitution, elections could be held for state officers. Once Congress approved the state constitution, once the state legislature ratified the Fourteenth Amendment, and once the amendment became part of the federal Constitution, Congress would readmit the state into the Union—and Reconstruction, in a constitutional sense, would be complete.

The Reconstruction Act of 1867 was far more radical than the Johnson program because it enfranchised blacks and disfranchised many ex-Confederates. It fulfilled a central goal of the Radical Republicans: to delay the readmission of former Confederate states until Republican governments could be established and thereby prevent an immediate rebel resurgence. But the new law was not as harsh toward ex-Confederates as it might have been. It provided for only temporary military rule, did not prosecute Confederate leaders for treason or permanently bar them from politics, and made no provision for confiscation or redistribution of property.

During the congressional debates, Radical Republican congressman Thaddeus Stevens had argued for the confiscation of large Confederate estates to "humble the proud traitors" and to provide for the former slaves. He had proposed subdividing such confiscated property into forty-acre tracts to be distributed among the freedmen and selling the rest, some 90 percent of it, to pay off war debts. Stevens wanted to crush the planter aristocracy and create a new class of self-sufficient black yeoman farmers. His land-reform bill won the support of other Radicals but never made progress, for most Republicans held property rights sacred. Tampering with such rights in the South, they feared, would jeopardize those rights in the North. Moreover, Stevens's proposal would alienate southern ex-Whigs from the Republican cause, antagonize other white southerners, and thereby endanger the rest of Reconstruction. Thus land reform never came about. The "radical" Reconstruction acts were a compromise.

Congressional Reconstruction took effect in the spring of 1867, but it could not be enforced without military power. Johnson, as Commander in Chief, impeded its implementation by replacing military officers sympathetic to the Radical cause with conservative ones. Republicans seethed. More suspicious than ever of the president, congressional moderates and Radicals once again joined forces to block Johnson from obstructing Reconstruction.

The Impeachment Crisis, 1867–1868

In March 1867, Republicans in Congress passed two laws to limit presidential power. The **Tenure of Office Act** prohibited the president from removing civil officers without Senate consent. Cabinet members, the law stated, were to hold office "during the term of the president by whom they may have been appointed" and could be fired only with the Senate's approval. The goal was to bar Johnson from dismissing Secretary of War Henry Stanton, a Radical ally needed to enforce the Reconstruction acts. The other law, a rider to an army appropriations bill, barred the president from issuing military orders except through the commanding general, Ulysses S. Grant, who could not be removed without the Senate's consent.

The Radicals' enmity toward Johnson, however, would not die until he was out of office. They began to seek grounds on which to impeach him. The House Judiciary Committee, aided by private detectives, could at

Table 16.1   Major Reconstruction Legislation

Law and Date of Congressional Passage	Provisions	Purpose
Civil Rights Act of 1866 (April 1866)*	Declared blacks citizens and guaranteed them equal protection of the laws.	To invalidate the black codes.
Supplementary Freedmen's Bureau Act (July 1866)*	Extended the life of the Freedmen's Aid Bureau and expanded its powers.	To invalidate the black codes.
Reconstruction Act of 1867 (March 1867)*	Invalidated state governments formed under Lincoln and Johnson. Divided the former Confederacy into five military districts. Set forth requirements for readmission of ex-Confederate states to the Union.	To replace presidential Reconstruction with a more stringent plan.
Supplementary Reconstruction Acts		To enforce the First Reconstruction Act.
Second Reconstruction Act (March 1867)*	Required military commanders to initiate voter enrollment.	
Third Reconstruction Act (July 1867)*	Expanded military commanders' powers.	
Fourth Reconstruction Act (March 1868)*	Provided that a majority of voters, however few, could put a new state constitution into force.	
Army Appropriations Act (March 1867)*	Declared in a rider that only the general of the army could issue military orders.	To prevent President Johnson from obstructing Reconstruction.
Tenure of Office Act (March 1867)*	Prohibited the president from removing any federal official without the Senate's consent.	To prevent President Johnson from obstructing Reconstruction.
Omnibus Act (June 1868)†	Readmitted seven ex-Confederate states to the Union.	To restore the Union, under the term of the First Reconstruction Act.
Enforcement Act of 1870 (May 1870)‡	Provided for the protection of black voters.	To enforce the Fifteenth Amendment.
Second Enforcement Act (February 1871)	Provided for federal supervision of southern elections.	To enforce the Fifteenth Amendment.
Third Enforcement Act (Ku Klux Klan Act) (April 1871)	Strengthened sanctions against those who impeded black suffrage.	To combat the Ku Klux Klan and enforce the Fourteenth Amendment.
Amnesty Act (May 1872)	Restored the franchise to almost all ex-Confederates.	Effort by Grant Republicans to deprive Liberal Republicans of a campaign issue.
Civil Rights Act of 1875 (March 1875)§	Outlawed racial segregation in transportation and public accommodations and prevented exclusion of blacks from jury service.	To honor the late senator Charles Sumner.

*Passed over Johnson's veto.

†Georgia was soon returned to military rule. The last four states were readmitted in 1870.

‡Sections of the law declared unconstitutional in 1876.

§Invalidated by the Supreme Court in 1883.

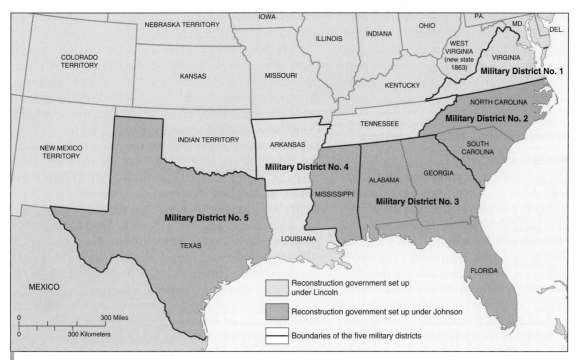

Map 16.1 The Reconstruction of the South
The Reconstruction Act of 1867 divided the former Confederate states, except Tennessee, into five military districts and
set forth the steps by which new state governments could be created.

first uncover no valid charges against Johnson. But Johnson again rescued his foes by providing the charges they needed.

In August 1867, with Congress out of session, Johnson suspended Secretary of War Stanton and replaced him with General Grant. In early 1868, the reconvened Senate refused to approve Stanton's suspension, and Grant, sensing the Republican mood, vacated the office. Johnson then removed Stanton and replaced him with an aged general, Lorenzo Thomas. Johnson's defiance forced Republican moderates, who had at first resisted impeachment, into yet another alliance with the Radicals: the president had "thrown down the gauntlet," a moderate charged. The House approved eleven charges of impeachment, nine of them based on violation of the Tenure of Office Act. The other charges accused Johnson of being "unmindful of the high duties of office," seeking to disgrace Congress, and not enforcing the Reconstruction acts.

Johnson's trial in the Senate, which began in March 1868, riveted public attention for eleven weeks. Seven congressmen, including leading Radical Republicans, served as prosecutors or "managers." Johnson's lawyers maintained that he was merely seeking a court test by violating the Tenure of Office Act, which he thought was unconstitutional. They also contended, somewhat

inconsistently, that the law did not protect Secretary Stanton, an appointee of Lincoln, not Johnson. Finally, they asserted, Johnson was guilty of no crime indictable in a regular court.

The congressional "managers" countered that impeachment was a political process, not a criminal trial, and that Johnson's "abuse of discretionary power" constituted an impeachable offense. Although Senate opinion split along party lines and Republicans held a majority, some of them wavered, fearful that the removal of a president would destroy the balance of power among the three branches of the federal government. They also distrusted Radical Republican Benjamin Wade, the president pro tempore of the Senate, who, because there was no vice president, would become president if Johnson were thrown out.

Intense pressure weighed on the wavering Republicans. Late in May 1868, the Senate voted against Johnson 35 to 19, one vote short of the two-thirds majority needed for conviction. Seven Republicans had risked political suicide and sided with the twelve Senate Democrats in voting against removal. In so doing, they set a precedent. Their vote discouraged impeachment on political grounds for decades to come. But the anti-Johnson forces had also achieved their goal: Andrew

Johnson's career as a national leader would soon end. After serving out the rest of his term, Johnson returned to Tennessee, where he was reelected to the Senate five years later. Republicans in Congress, meanwhile, pursued their last major Reconstruction objective: to guarantee black male suffrage.

The Fifteenth Amendment and the Question of Woman Suffrage, 1869–1870

Black suffrage was the linchpin of congressional Reconstruction. Only with the support of black voters could Republicans secure control of the ex-Confederate states. The Reconstruction Act of 1867 had forced every southern state legislature to enfranchise black men as a prerequisite for readmission to the Union, but much of the North rejected black suffrage at home. Congressional Republicans therefore had two aims. The **Fifteenth Amendment**, drawn up by Republicans and proposed by Congress in 1869, sought to protect black suffrage in the South against future repeal by Congress or the states, and to enfranchise northern and border-state blacks, who would presumably vote Republican. The amendment prohibited the denial of suffrage by the states to any citizen on account of "race, color, or previous condition of servitude."

Democrats argued that the proposed amendment violated states' rights by denying each state the power to determine who would vote. But Democrats did not control enough states to defeat the amendment, and it was ratified in 1870. Four votes came from those ex-Confederate states—Mississippi, Virginia, Georgia, and Texas—that had delayed the Reconstruction process and were therefore forced to approve the Fifteenth Amendment, as well as the Fourteenth, in order to rejoin the Union. Some southerners contended that the new amendment's omissions made it acceptable, for it had, as a Richmond newspaper pointed out, "loopholes through which a coach and four horses can be driven." What were these loopholes? The Fifteenth Amendment neither guaranteed black officeholding nor prohibited voting restrictions such as property requirements and literacy tests. Such restrictions might be used to deny blacks the vote, and indeed, ultimately they were so used.

The debate over black suffrage drew new participants into the political fray. Since the end of the war, a small group of abolitionists, men and women, had sought to revive the cause of women's rights. In 1866, when Congress debated the Fourteenth Amendment, women's rights advocates tried to join forces with their old abolitionist allies to promote both black suffrage and woman suffrage. Most Radical Republicans, however, did not want to be saddled with the woman-suffrage plank; they feared it would impede their primary goal, black enfranchisement.

This defection provoked disputes among women's rights advocates. Some argued that black suffrage would pave the way for the women's vote and that black men deserved priority. "If the elective franchise is not extended to the Negro, he is dead," explained Frederick Douglass, a longtime women's rights supporter. "Woman has a thousand ways by which she can attach herself to the ruling power of the land that we have not." But women's rights leaders Elizabeth Cady Stanton and **Susan B. Anthony** disagreed. In their view, the Fourteenth Amendment had disabled women by including the word *male*, and the Fifteenth Amendment compounded the injury by failing to prohibit the denial of suffrage on account of sex. Instead, Stanton contended, the Fifteenth Amendment established an "aristocracy of sex" and increased women's disadvantages.

The battle over black suffrage and the Fifteenth Amendment split women's rights advocates into two rival suffrage associations, both formed in 1869. The Boston-based American Woman Suffrage Association, endorsed by reformers such as Julia Ward Howe and Lucy Stone, retained an alliance with male abolitionists and campaigned for woman suffrage in the states. The New York–based and more radical National Woman Suffrage Association, led by Stanton and Anthony, condemned its leaders' one-time male allies and promoted a federal woman suffrage amendment.

For the rest of the 1870s, the rival woman suffrage associations vied for constituents. In 1869 and 1870, independent of the suffrage movement, two territories, Wyoming and Utah, enfranchised women. But lacking support, suffragists failed to sway legislators elsewhere. In 1872, Susan B. Anthony mobilized about seventy women to vote nationwide and, as a result, was indicted, convicted, and fined. One of the women who tried to vote in 1872, Missouri suffragist Virginia Minor, brought suit with her husband against the registrar who had excluded her. The Minors based their case on the Fourteenth Amendment, which, they claimed, enfranchised women. In *Minor* v. *Happersett* (1875), however, the Supreme Court declared that a state could constitutionally deny women the vote. Divided and rebuffed, woman-suffrage advocates braced for a long struggle.

By the time the Fifteenth Amendment was ratified in 1870, Congress could look back on five years of momentous achievement. Since the start of 1865, three constitutional amendments had broadened the scope of American democracy by passing three constitutional amendments. The Thirteenth Amendment abolished

Stanton and Anthony, c. 1870
Women's rights advocates Susan B. Anthony and Elizabeth Cady
Stanton began to promote woman suffrage in 1866 when the issue
of black suffrage arose, and subsequently assailed the proposed
Fifteenth Amendment for excluding women. By the end of the
1860s, activists had formed two competing suffragist organizations.

slavery, the Fourteenth expanded civil rights, and the
Fifteenth prohibited the denial of suffrage on the basis
of race (see Table 16.2). Congress had also readmitted
the former Confederate states into the Union. But after
1868 congressional momentum slowed, and in 1869,
when Ulysses S. Grant became president, enmity between Congress and the chief executive ceased. The
theater of action now shifted to the South, where tu-
multuous change was under way.

Reconstruction Governments

During the unstable years of presidential Reconstruction, 1865–1867, the southern states had to create new
governments, revive the war-torn economy, and face the
impact of emancipation. Social and economic crises
abounded. War costs had cut into southern wealth, cities
and factories lay in rubble, plantation-labor systems disintegrated, and racial tensions flared. Beginning in 1865,
freedmen organized black conventions, political meetings at which they protested ill treatment and demanded equal rights. These meetings occurred in a
climate of violence. Race riots erupted in major southern cities, such as Memphis in May 1866 and in New Orleans two months later. Even when Congress imposed
military rule, ex-Confederates did not feel defeated.
"Having reached bottom, there is hope now that we may
rise again," a South Carolina planter wrote in his diary.

Congressional Reconstruction, supervised by federal
troops, took effect in the spring of 1867. The Johnson
regimes were dismantled, state constitutional conventions
met, and voters elected new state governments, which Republicans dominated. In 1868, a majority of the former
Confederate states rejoined the Union, and two years
later, the last four states—Virginia, Mississippi, Georgia,
and Texas—followed.

Readmission to the Union did not end the process
of Reconstruction, for Republicans still held power in
the South. But Republican rule was very brief, lasting
less than a decade in all southern states, far less in
most of them, and on average under five years. Opposition from southern Democrats, the landowning elite,
thousands of vigilantes, and, indeed, most white voters

Table 16.2 The Reconstruction Amendments

Amendment and Date of Congressional Passage	Provisions	Ratification
Thirteenth (January 1865)	Prohibited slavery in the United States.	December 1865.
Fourteenth (June 1866)	Defined citizenship to include all persons born or naturalized in the United States. Provided proportional loss of congressional representation for any state that denied suffrage to any of its male citizens. Disqualified prewar officeholders who supported the Confederacy from state or national office. Repudiated the Confederate debt.	July 1868, after Congress made ratification a prerequisite for readmission of ex-Confederate states to the Union.
Fifteenth (February 1869)	Prohibited the denial of suffrage because of race, color, or previous condition of servitude.	March 1870; ratification required of Virginia, Texas, Mississippi, and Georgia for readmission to the Union.

proved insurmountable. Still, the governments formed under congressional Reconstruction were unique, because black men, including ex-slaves, participated in them. In no other society where slaves had been liberated—neither Haiti, where slaves had revolted in the 1790s, nor the British Caribbean islands, where Parliament had ended slavery in 1833—had freedmen gained democratic political rights.

A New Electorate

The Reconstruction laws of 1867–1868 transformed the southern electorate by temporarily disfranchising 10 to 15 percent of potential white voters and by enfranchising more than seven hundred thousand freedmen. Outnumbering white voters in the South by one hundred thousand, blacks held voting majorities in five states.

The new electorate provided a base for the Republican Party, which had never existed in the South. To scornful Democrats, southern Republicans comprised three types of scoundrels: northern "carpetbaggers," who had allegedly come south seeking wealth and power (with so few possessions that they could be stuffed into traveling bags made of carpet material); southern "scalawags," predominantly poor and ignorant whites, who sought to profit from Republican rule; and hordes of uneducated freedmen, who were ready prey for Republican manipulators. Although the "carpetbag" and "scalawag" labels were derogatory and the stereotypes that they conveyed inaccurate, they remain in use as a form of shorthand. Crossing class and racial lines, the hastily established Republican Party was in fact a loose coalition of diverse factions with often contradictory goals.

To northerners who moved south after the Civil War, the former Confederacy was an undeveloped region, ripe with possibility. The carpetbaggers' ranks included many former Union soldiers who hoped to buy land, open factories, build railroads, or simply enjoy the warmer climate. Albion Tourgee, a young lawyer who had served with the New York and Ohio volunteers, for example, relocated in North Carolina after the war to improve his health; there he worked as a journalist, politician, and Republican judge. Perhaps no more than twenty thousand northern migrants like Tourgee—including veterans, missionaries, teachers, and Freedmen's Bureau agents—headed south immediately after the war, and many returned north by 1867. But those who remained held almost one out of three state offices and wielded disproportionate political power.

Scalawags, white southerners who supported the Republicans, included some entrepreneurs who applauded party policies such as the national banking system and high protective tariffs as well as some prosperous planters, former Whigs who had opposed secession. Their numbers included a few prominent politicians, among them James Orr of South Carolina and Mississippi's governor James Alcorn, who became Republicans in order to retain influence and limit Republican radicalism. Most scalawags, however, were small farmers from the mountain regions of North Carolina, Georgia, Alabama, and Arkansas. Former Unionists who had owned no slaves and felt no loyalty toward the landowning elite, they sought to improve their economic position. Unlike carpetbaggers, they were not committed to black rights or black suffrage; most came from regions with small black populations and cared little whether blacks voted or not. Scalawags held the most political offices during Reconstruction, but they proved the least stable element of the southern Republican coalition: eventually, many drifted back to the Democratic fold.

Freedmen, the backbone of southern Republicanism, provided eight out of ten Republican votes. Republican rule lasted longest in states with the largest black populations—South Carolina, Mississippi, Alabama, and Louisiana. Introduced to politics in the black conventions of 1865–1867, the freedmen sought land, education, civil rights, and political equality, and remained loyal Republicans. As an elderly freedman announced at a Georgia political convention in 1867, "We know our friends." Although Reconstruction governments depended on African-American votes, freedmen held at most one in five political offices. Blacks served in all southern legislatures but constituted a majority only in the legislature of South Carolina, whose population was more than 60 percent black. In the House of Representatives, a mere 6 percent of southern members were black, and almost half of these came from South Carolina. No blacks became governor, and only two served in the U.S. Senate, Hiram Revels and Blanche K. Bruce, both of Mississippi. (Still, the same number of African-Americans served in the Senate during Reconstruction as throughout the entire twentieth century.)

Black officeholders on the state level formed a political elite. They often differed from black voters in background, education, wealth, and complexion. A disproportionate number were literate blacks who had been free before the Civil War. In the South Carolina legislature, for instance, most black members, unlike their constituents, came from large towns and cities; many had spent time in the North; and some were well-off property owners or even former slave owners. Color differences were evident, too: 43 percent of South Carolina's black state legislators were mulattos (mixed race), compared to only 7 percent of the state's black population.

Republicans in the South Carolina Legislature, c. 1868
Only in South Carolina did blacks comprise a majority in the
legislature and dominate the legislative process during
Reconstruction. This photographic collage of "Radical" legislators,
black and white, suggests the extent of black representation. In
1874, blacks won the majority of seats in South Carolina's state
senate as well.

Black officials and black voters often had different
priorities. Most freedmen cared mainly about their economic future, especially about acquiring land, whereas
black officeholders cared most about attaining equal
rights. Still, both groups shared high expectations and
prized enfranchisement. "We'd walk fifteen miles in
wartime to find out about the battle," a Georgia freedman
declared. "We can walk fifteen miles and more to find how
to vote."

Republican Rule

Large numbers of blacks participated in American government for the first time in the state constitutional conventions of 1867–1868. The South Carolina convention
had a black majority, and in Louisiana half the delegates
were freedmen. The conventions forged democratic
changes in their state constitutions. Delegates abolished
property qualifications for officeholding, made many

appointive offices elective, and redistricted state legislatures more equitably. All states established universal
manhood suffrage, and Louisiana and South Carolina
opened public schools to both races. These provisions
integrated the New Orleans public schools as well as
the University of South Carolina, from which whites
withdrew.

But no state instituted land reform. When proposals
for land confiscation and redistribution arose at the
state conventions, they fell to defeat, as they had in Congress. Hoping to attract northern investment to the re-
constructed South, southern Republicans hesitated to
threaten property rights or to adopt land-reform measures that northern Republicans had rejected. South
Carolina did set up a commission to buy land and make
it available to freedmen, and several states changed their
tax structures to force uncultivated land onto the market, but in no case was ex-Confederate land confiscated.

Once civil power shifted from the federal army to the
new state governments, Republican administrations
began ambitious programs of public works. They built
roads, bridges, and public buildings; approved railroad
bonds; and funded institutions to care for orphans, the
insane, and the disabled. Republican regimes also expanded state bureaucracies, raised salaries for government employees, and formed state militia, in which
blacks were often heavily represented. Finally, they created public-school systems, almost nonexistent in the
South until then.

Because rebuilding the devastated South and expanding state government cost millions, taxes skyrock-
eted. State legislatures increased poll taxes or "head"
taxes (levies on individuals); enacted luxury, sales, and
occupation taxes; and imposed new property taxes. Before the war southern states had taxed property in slaves
but had barely taxed landed property. Now state governments assessed even small farmers' holdings, and propertied planters paid what they considered an excessive
burden. Although northern tax rates still exceeded southern rates, southern landowners resented the new levies.
In their view, Reconstruction punished the propertied,
already beset by labor problems and falling land values,
in order to finance the vast expenditures of Republican
legislators.

To Reconstruction's foes, Republican rule was wasteful and corrupt, the "most stupendous system of organized robbery in history." A state like Mississippi, which
had an honest government, provided little basis for such
charges. But critics could justifiably point to Louisiana,
where the governor pocketed thousands of dollars of
state funds and corruption permeated all government

transactions (as indeed it had before the war). Or they could cite South Carolina, where bribery ran rampant. Besides government officials who took bribes, the main postwar profiteers were the railroad promoters who doled them out. Not all were Republicans. Nor did the Republican regimes in the South hold a monopoly on corruption. After the war, bribery pervaded government transactions North and South, and far more money changed hands in the North. But critics assailed Republican rule for additional reasons.

Counterattacks

Ex-Confederates chafed at black enfranchisement and spoke with dread about the "horror of Negro domination." As soon as congressional Reconstruction took effect, former Confederates campaigned to undermine it. Democratic newspapers assailed delegates to North Carolina's constitutional convention as an "Ethiopian minstrelsy . . . baboons, monkeys, mules . . . and other jackasses," and demeaned Louisiana's constitution as "the work of ignorant Negroes cooperating with a gang of white adventurers."

Democrats delayed mobilization until southern states were readmitted to the Union. Then they swung into action, calling themselves Conservatives in order to attract former Whigs. At first, they sought to win the votes of blacks; but when that effort failed, they tried other tactics. In 1868–1869, Georgia Democrats challenged the eligibility of black legislators and expelled them from office. In response, the federal government reestablished military rule in Georgia, but determined Democrats still undercut Republican power. In every southern state, they contested elections, backed dissident Republican factions, elected some Democratic legislators, and lured scalawags away from the Republican Party.

Vigilante efforts to reduce black votes bolstered the Democrats' campaigns to win white ones. Antagonism toward free blacks, long a motif in southern life, had resurged after the war. In 1865, Freedmen's Bureau agents itemized outrages against blacks, including shooting, murder, rape, arson, roasting, and "severe and inhuman beating." Vigilante groups sprang up spontaneously in all parts of the former Confederacy under names like moderators, regulators, and, in Louisiana, Knights of the White Camelia. One group rose to dominance. In the spring of 1866, when the Johnson governments were still in power, six young Confederate war veterans in Tennessee formed a social club, the **Ku Klux Klan**, distinguished by elaborate rituals, hooded costumes, and secret passwords. By the election of 1868, when black men could first vote, Klan dens had spread

to all the southern states. Klansmen embarked on night raids to intimidate black voters. No longer a social club, the Ku Klux Klan was now a widespread terrorist movement and a violent arm of the Democratic Party.

The Klan sought to suppress black voting, reestablish white supremacy, and topple the Reconstruction governments. Its members attacked Freedmen's Bureau officials, white Republicans, black militia units, economically successful blacks, and black voters. Concentrated in areas where the black and white populations were most evenly balanced and racial tensions greatest, Klan dens adapted their tactics and timing to local conditions. In Mississippi the Klan targeted black schools; in Alabama it concentrated on Republican officeholders. In Arkansas terror reigned in

The Ku Klux Klan
The menacing disguise characterized the Ku Klux Klan's campaign of intimidation during Reconstruction. This Mississippi Klansman, black-hooded and carrying a pistol, displays the regalia he used to threaten African-Americans. Captured by federal authorities in 1871, he turned state's witness and revealed to his captors the Klan's secret passwords, signals, and rituals.

1868; in Georgia and Florida Klan strength surged in 1870. Some Democrats denounced Klan members as "cut-throats and riff-raff." But prominent ex-Confederates were also known to be active Klansmen, among them General Nathan Bedford Forrest, the leader of the 1864 Fort Pillow massacre, in which Confederate troops who captured a Union garrison in Tennessee murdered black soldiers after they had surrendered. Vigilantism united southern whites of different social classes and drew on the energy of many Confederate veterans. In areas where the Klan was inactive, other vigilante groups took its place.

Republican legislatures passed laws to outlaw vigilantism, but the state militia could not enforce them. State officials turned to the federal government for help. In response, between May 1870 and February 1871, Congress passed three **Enforcement Acts**, each progressively more stringent. The First Enforcement Act protected black voters, but witnesses to violations were afraid to testify against vigilantes, and local juries refused to convict them. The Second Enforcement Act provided for federal supervision of southern elections, and the Third Enforcement Act, or Ku Klux Klan Act, strengthened punishments for those who prevented blacks from voting. It also empowered the president to use federal troops to enforce the law and to suspend the writ of *habeas corpus* in areas that he declared in insurrection. (The writ of *habeas corpus* is a court order requiring that the detainer of a prisoner bring that person to court and show cause for his or her detention.) The Ku Klux Klan Act generated thousands of arrests; most terrorists, however, escaped conviction.

By 1872, the federal government had effectively suppressed the Klan, but vigilantism had served its purpose. Only a large military presence in the South could have protected black rights, and the government in Washington never provided it. Instead, federal power in the former Confederacy diminished. President Grant steadily reduced troop levels in the South; Congress allowed the Freedmen's Bureau to die in 1869; and the Enforcement acts became dead letters. White southerners, a Georgia politician told congressional investigators in 1871, could not discard "a feeling of bitterness, a feeling that the Negro is a sort of instinctual enemy of ours." The battle over Reconstruction was in essence a battle over the implications of emancipation, and it had begun as soon as the war ended.

The Impact of Emancipation

"The master he says we are all free," a South Carolina slave declared in 1865. "But it don't mean we is white. And it don't mean we is equal." Emancipated slaves faced daunting handicaps. They had no property, tools, or capital and usually possessed meager skills. Only a minority had been trained as artisans, and more than 95 percent were illiterate. Still, the exhilaration of freedom was overwhelming, as slaves realized, "Now I am for myself" and "All that I make is my own." At emancipation, they gained the right to their own labor and a new sense of autonomy. Under Reconstruction the freed blacks struggled to cast off white control and shed the vestiges of slavery.

Confronting Freedom

For the former slaves, liberty meant they could move where they pleased. Some moved out of the slave quarters and set up dwellings elsewhere on their plantations; others left their plantations entirely. Landowners found that one freed slave after another vanished, with house servants and artisans leading the way. "I have never in my life met with such ingratitude," one South Carolina mistress exclaimed when a former slave ran off. Field workers, who had less contact with whites, were more likely to stay behind or more reluctant to leave. Still, flight remained tempting. "The moment they see an opportunity to improve themselves, they will move on," diarist Mary Chesnut observed.

Emancipation stirred waves of migration within the former Confederacy. Some freed slaves left the Upper South for the Deep South and the Southwest—Florida, Mississippi, Arkansas, and Texas—where planters desperately needed labor and paid higher wages. Even more left the countryside for towns and cities, traditional havens of independence for blacks. Urban black populations sometimes doubled or tripled after emancipation. Overall during the 1860s, the urban black population rose by 75 percent, and the number of blacks in small rural towns grew as well. Many migrants eventually returned to their old locales, but they tended to settle on neighboring plantations rather than with their former owners. Freedom was the major goal. "I's wants to be a free man, cum when I please, and nobody say nuffin to me, nor order me roun'," an Alabama freedman told a northern journalist.

Freed blacks' yearnings to find lost family members prompted much movement. "They had a passion, not so much for wandering as for getting together," a Freedmen's Bureau official commented. Parents sought children who had been sold; husbands and wives who had been separated by sale, or who lived on different plantations, reunited; and families reclaimed youngsters from masters' homes. The Freedmen's Bureau helped former slaves get information about missing relatives and travel

Former Slaves on Plantation in Warren County, Mississippi
Emancipation brought the possibility of movement. Some freed people on big plantations (like this one in Warren County, Mississippi) remained where they were; some moved off to find work on other plantations; and others gravitated toward towns and cities. "[R]ight off colored folks started on the move," one former slave recalled. "They seemed to want to get closer to freedom so they'd know what it was—like a place or a city."

to find them. Bureau agents also tried to resolve conflicts that arose when spouses who had been separated under slavery married other people.

Reunification efforts often failed. Some fugitive slaves had died during the war or were untraceable. Other exslaves had formed new relationships and could not revive old ones. "I am married," one husband wrote to a former wife (probably in a dictated letter), "and my wife [and I] have two children, and if you and I meet it would make a very dissatisfied family." But there were success stories, too. "I's hunted an' hunted till I track you up here," one freedman told his wife, whom he found in a refugee camp twenty years after their separation by sale.

Once reunited, freed blacks quickly legalized unions formed under slavery, sometimes in mass ceremonies of up to seventy couples. Legal marriage affected family life. Men asserted themselves as household heads; wives of able-bodied men often withdrew from the labor force to care for homes and families. "When I married my wife, I married her to wait on me and she has got all she can do right here for me and the children," a Tennessee freedman explained.

Black women's desire to secure the privileges of domestic life caused planters severe labor shortages. Before the war at least half of field workers had been women; in 1866, a southern journal claimed, men performed almost all the field labor. Still, by the end of Reconstruction, many black women had returned to agricultural work as part of sharecropper families. Others took paid work in cities, as laundresses, cooks, and domestic servants. (White women often sought employment as well, for the war had incapacitated many white breadwinners, reduced the supply of future husbands, and left families destitute or in diminished circumstances.) However, former slaves continued to view stable, independent domestic life, especially the right to bring up their own children, as a major blessing of freedom. In 1870, eight out of ten black families in the cotton-producing South were two-parent families, about the same proportion as among whites.

African-American Institutions

The freed blacks' desire for independence also led to the postwar growth of black churches. In the late 1860s, some freedmen congregated at churches operated by northern missionaries; others withdrew from white-run churches and formed their own. The African Methodist Episcopal church, founded by Philadelphia blacks in the 1790s, gained thousands of new southern members. Negro Baptist churches sprouted everywhere, often growing out of plantation "praise meetings," religious gatherings organized by slaves.

The black churches offered a fervent, participatory experience. They also provided relief, raised funds for schools, and supported Republican policies. From the outset black ministers assumed leading political roles, first in the black conventions of 1865–1866 and later in the Reconstruction governments. After southern Democrats excluded most freedmen from political life at Re-

construction's end, ministers remained the main pillars of authority in black communities.

Black schools played a crucial role for freedmen as well; exslaves eagerly sought literacy for themselves and even more for their children. At emancipation, blacks organized their own schools, which the Freedmen's Bureau soon supervised. Northern philanthropic societies paid the wages of instructors, about half of them women. In 1869, the bureau reported more than four thousand black schools in the former Confederacy. Within three years, each southern state had a public-school system, at least in principle, generally with separate schools for blacks and whites. Advanced schools for blacks opened as well, to train tradespeople, teachers, and ministers. The Freedmen's Bureau and northern organizations like the American Missionary Association helped found Howard, Atlanta, and Fisk universities (all started in 1866–1867) and Hampton Institute (1868).

Despite these advances, black education remained limited. Few rural blacks could reach the freedmen's schools located in towns. Underfunded black public schools, similarly inaccessible to most rural black children, held classes only for very short seasons and were sometimes the targets of vigilante attacks. At the end of Reconstruction, more than 80 percent of the black population was still illiterate. Still, the proportion of youngsters who could not read and write had declined and would continue to fall (see Table 16.3).

The Freedmen's School
Supported by the Freedmen's Bureau, northern freedmen's aid societies, and black denominations, freedmen's schools reached about 12 percent of school-age black children in the South by 1870. Here, a northern teacher poses with her students at a school in rural North Carolina.

Table 16.3 **Percentage of Persons Unable to Write, by Age Group, 1870–1890, in South Carolina, Georgia, Alabama, Mississippi, and Louisiana**

Age Group	1870	1880	1890
10–14			
Black	78.9	74.1	49.2
White	33.2	34.5	18.7
15–20			
Black	85.3	73.0	54.1
White	24.2	21.0	14.3
Over 20			
Black	90.4	82.3	75.5
White	19.8	17.9	17.1

Source: Roger Ransom and Richard Sutch, *One Kind of Freedom* (Cambridge: Cambridge University Press, 1978), 30.

School segregation and other forms of racial separation were taken for granted. Some black codes of 1865–1866 had segregated public-transit conveyances and public accommodations. Even after the invalidation of the codes, the custom of segregation continued on streetcars, steamboats, and trains as well as in churches, theaters, inns, and restaurants. On railroads, for example, whites could ride in the "ladies' car" or first-class car, whereas blacks had to stay in smoking cars or boxcars with benches. In 1870, Senator Charles Sumner of Massachusetts began promoting a bill to desegregate schools, transportation facilities, juries, and public accommodations. After Sumner's death in 1874, Congress honored him by enacting a new law, the **Civil Rights Act of 1875**, which encompassed many of his proposals, except for the controversial school-integration provision. But in 1883, in the *Civil Rights Cases,* the Supreme Court invalidated the law; the Fourteenth Amendment did not prohibit discrimination by individuals, the Court ruled, only that perpetrated by the state.

White southerners rejected the prospect of racial integration, which they insisted would lead to racial mixing. "If we have social equality, we shall have intermarriage," one white southerner contended, "and if we have intermarriage, we shall degenerate." Urban blacks sometimes challenged segregation practices, and black legislators promoted bills to desegregate public transit. Some black officeholders decried all forms of racial separatism. "The sooner we as a people forget our sable complexion," said a Mobile official, "the better it will be for us as a race." But most freed blacks were less interested in "social equality," in the sense of interracial mingling, than in black liberty and community. The newly formed postwar elite—teachers, ministers, and politicians—served black constituencies and therefore had a vested interest in separate black institutions. Rural blacks, too, widely preferred all-black institutions. They had little desire to mix with whites. On the contrary, they sought freedom from white control. Above all else, they wanted to secure personal independence by acquiring land.

Land, Labor, and Sharecropping

"The sole ambition of the freedman," a New Englander wrote from South Carolina in 1865, "appears to be to become the owner of a little piece of land, there to erect a humble home, and to dwell in peace and security, at his own free will and pleasure." Indeed, to freed blacks everywhere, "forty acres and a mule" (a phrase that originated in 1864 when Union general William T. Sherman set aside land on the South Carolina Sea Islands for black settlement) promised emancipation from plantation labor, from white domination, and from cotton, the "slave crop." Just as garden plots had provided a measure of autonomy under slavery, so did landownership signify economic independence afterward. "We want to be placed on land until we are able to buy it and make it our own," a black minister had told General Sherman in Georgia during the war.

But freedmen's visions of landownership failed to materialize, for, as we have seen, neither Congress nor the southern states imposed large-scale land reform. Some freedmen did obtain land with the help of the Union army or the Freedmen's Bureau, and black soldiers sometimes pooled resources to buy land, as on the Sea Islands of South Carolina and Georgia. The federal government also sought to provide exslaves with land. In 1866, Congress passed the Southern Homestead Act, which set aside 44 million acres of public land in five southern states for freedmen and loyal whites. This acreage contained poor soil, and few former slaves had the resources to survive even until their first harvest. About four thousand blacks resettled on homesteads under the law, but most were unable to establish farms. (White southern homesteaders fared little better.) By the end of Reconstruction, only a small minority of former slaves in each state owned working farms. In Georgia in 1876, for instance, blacks controlled a mere 1.3 percent of total acreage. Without large-scale land reform, the obstacles to black landownership remained overwhelming.

What were these obstacles? First, most freedmen lacked the capital to buy land and the equipment needed to work it. Furthermore, white southerners on the whole opposed selling land to blacks. Most important, planters sought to preserve a black labor force. Freedmen, they insisted, would work only under coercion, and not at all if the possibility of landownership arose. As soon as the war ended, the white South took steps to make sure that black labor would remain available on plantations.

During presidential Reconstruction, southern state legislatures tried to curb black mobility and to preserve a captive labor force through the black codes. Under labor contracts in effect in 1865–1866, freedmen received wages, housing, food, and clothing in exchange for field work. With cash scarce, wages usually took the form of a very small share of the crop, often one-eighth or less, divided among the entire plantation work force. Freedmen's Bureau agents promoted the new labor system; they urged freedmen to sign labor contracts and tried to ensure adequate wages. Imbued with the northern free-labor ideology, which held that wage workers could rise to the status of self-supporting tradesmen and property owners, bureau officials endorsed black wage labor as an interim arrangement that would lead to economic independence. "You must begin at the bottom of the ladder and climb up," Freedmen's Bureau head O. O. Howard exhorted a group of Louisiana freedmen in 1865.

But the freedmen disliked the new wage system, especially the use of gang labor, which resembled the work pattern under slavery. Planters had complaints, too. In some regions the black labor force had shrunk to half its prewar size or less, due to the migration of freedmen and to black women's withdrawal from fieldwork. Once united in defense of slavery, planters now competed for black workers. But the freedmen, whom planters often scorned as lazy or inefficient, did not intend to work as long or as hard as they had labored under slavery. One planter claimed that workers accomplished only "two-fifths of what they did under the old system." As productivity fell, so did land values. To top off the planters' woes, cotton prices plummeted, for during the war northern and foreign buyers had found new sources of cotton in Egypt and India, and the world supply had vastly increased. Finally, the harvests of 1866 and 1867 were extremely poor. By then, an agricultural impasse had been reached: landowners lacked labor, and freedmen lacked land. But free blacks, unlike slaves, had the right to enter into contracts—or to refuse to do so—and thereby gained some leverage.

Planters and freedmen began experimenting with new labor schemes, including the division of plantations into small tenancies (see Map 16.2). **Sharecropping**, the most widespread arrangement, evolved as a compromise.

Under the sharecropping system, landowners subdivided large plantations into farms of thirty to fifty acres, which they rented to freedmen under annual leases for a share of the crop, usually half. Freedmen preferred sharecropping to wage labor because it represented a step toward independence. Heads of households could use the labor of family members. Moreover, a half-share of the crop far exceeded the fraction that freedmen had received as wages under the black codes. Planters often spoke of sharecropping as a concession, but they benefited, too. They retained power over tenants, because annual leases did not have to be renewed; they could expel undesirable tenants at the end of the year. Planters also shared the risk of planting with tenants: if a crop failed, both suffered the loss. Most important, planters retained control of their land and in some cases extended their holdings. The most productive land, therefore, remained in the hands of a small group of owners, as before the war. Sharecropping forced planters to relinquish daily control over the labor of freedmen but helped to preserve the planter elite.

Sharecropping arrangements varied widely. On sugar and rice plantations, the wage system continued; strong markets for sugar and rice meant that planters of those crops could pay their workers in cash—cash that cotton planters lacked. Some freedmen remained independent renters. Some landowners leased areas to white tenants, who then subcontracted with black labor. But by the end of the 1860s, sharecropping prevailed in the cotton South, and the new system continued to expand. A severe depression in 1873 drove many black renters into sharecropping. By then, thousands of independent white farmers had become sharecroppers as well. Stung by wartime losses and by the dismal postwar economy, they sank into debt and lost their land to creditors. Many backcountry residents, no longer able to get by on subsistence farming, shifted to cash crops like cotton and suffered the same fate. At the end of Reconstruction, one-third of the white farmers in Mississippi, for instance, were sharecroppers.

By 1880, 80 percent of the land in the cotton-producing states had been subdivided into tenancies, most of it farmed by sharecroppers, white and black (see Map 16.3). Indeed, white sharecroppers now outnumbered black ones, although a higher proportion of southern blacks, about 75 percent, were involved in the system. Changes in marketing and finance, meanwhile, made the sharecroppers' lot increasingly precarious.

Toward a Crop-Lien Economy

Before the Civil War, planters had depended on factors, or middlemen, who sold them supplies, extended credit, and marketed their crops through urban merchants.

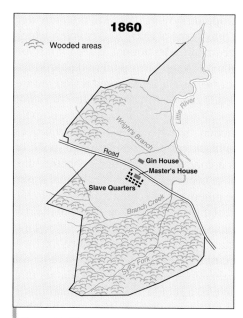

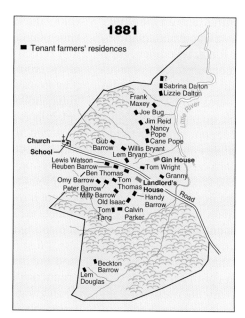

Map 16.2 The Barrow Plantation, 1860 and 1881
The transformation of the Barrow plantation in Oglethorpe County, Georgia, illustrates the striking changes in southern agriculture during Reconstruction. Before the Civil War, about 135 slaves worked on the plantation, supervised by an overseer and a slave foreman. After the war, the former slaves who remained on the plantation signed labor contracts with owner David Crenshaw Barrow. Supervised by a hired foreman, the freedmen grew cotton for wages in competing squads, but they disliked the new arrangement. In the late 1860s, Barrow subdivided his land into tenant farms of twenty-five to thirty acres, and freedmen moved their households from the old slave quarters to their own farms. By 1881, 161 tenants lived on the Barrow plantation, at least half of them children. One out of four families was named Barrow.

These long-distance credit arrangements were backed by the high value and liquidity of slave property. When slavery ended, the factorage system collapsed. The postwar South, with hundreds of thousands of tenants and sharecroppers, needed a far more localized network of credit.

Into the gap stepped the rural merchants (often themselves planters), who advanced supplies to tenants and sharecroppers on credit and sold their crops to wholesalers or textile manufacturers. Because renters had no property to use as collateral, the merchants secured their loans with a lien, or claim, on each farmer's next crop. Exorbitant interest rates of 50 percent or more quickly forced many tenants and sharecroppers into a cycle of indebtedness. Owing part of the crop to a landowner for rent, a sharecropper also owed a rural merchant a large sum (perhaps amounting to the rest of his crop, or more) for supplies. Illiterate tenants who could not keep track of their financial arrangements often fell prey to unscrupulous merchants. "A man that didn't know how to count would always lose," an Arkansas freedman later explained.

Once a tenant's debts or alleged debts exceeded the value of his crop, he was tied to the land, to cotton, and to sharecropping.

By the end of Reconstruction, sharecropping and crop liens had transformed southern agriculture. They bound the region to staple production and prevented crop diversification. Despite plunging cotton prices, creditors—landowners and merchants—insisted that tenants raise only easily marketable cash crops. Short of capital, planters could no longer invest in new equipment or improve their land by such techniques as crop rotation and contour plowing. Soil depletion, land erosion, and agricultural backwardness soon locked much of the South into a cycle of poverty.

Trapped in perpetual debt, tenant farmers became the chief victims of the new agricultural order. Raising cotton for distant markets, for prices over which they had no control, remained the only survival route open to poor farmers, regardless of race. But low income from cotton locked them into sharecropping and crop liens, from which escape was difficult. African-American

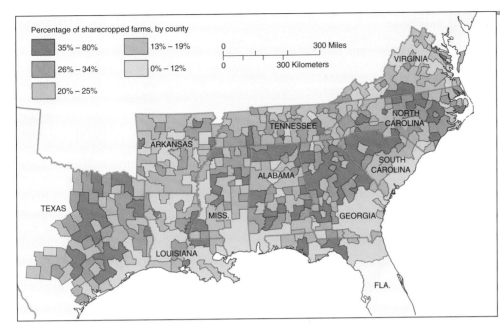

Map 16.3 Southern Sharecropping, 1880
The depressed economy of the late 1870s caused poverty and debt, increased tenancy among white farmers, and forced many renters, black and white, into sharecropping. By 1880, the sharecropping system pervaded most southern counties, with the highest concentrations in the cotton belt from South Carolina to eastern Texas. *Source:* U.S. Census Office, Tenth Census, 1880, *Report of the Production of Agriculture* (Washington, D.C.: Government Printing Office, 1883), Table 5.

tenants, who attained neither landownership nor economic independence, saw their political rights dwindle, too. As one southern regime after another returned to Democratic control, freedmen could no longer look to the state governments for protection. Nor could they turn to the federal government, for northern politicians were preoccupied with their own problems.

New Concerns in the North, 1868–1876

The nomination of Ulysses S. Grant for president in 1868 launched an era of crises in national politics. Grant's two terms in office featured political scandals, a party revolt, a massive depression, and a steady retreat from Reconstruction policies. By the mid-1870s, northern voters cared more about the economic climate, unemployment, labor unrest, and currency problems than about the "southern question." Responsive to the shift in popular mood, Republicans became eager to end sectional conflict and turned their backs on the freedmen of the South.

Grantism

Republicans had good reason to bypass party leaders and nominate the popular Grant to succeed Andrew Johnson. A war hero, Grant was endorsed by Union veterans, widely admired in the North, and unscathed by the bitter feuds of Reconstruction politics. To oppose Grant in 1868, the Democrats nominated New York governor Horatio Seymour, arch-critic of the Lincoln administration

Sharecroppers During Reconstruction
By the end of the 1870s, about three out of four African-Americans in the cotton-producing states had become sharecroppers. Below, sharecroppers pick cotton in Aiken, South Carolina.

Boss Tweed
Thomas Nast's cartoons in *Harper's Weekly* helped topple New York Democratic boss William M. Tweed, who, with his associates, embodied corruption on a large scale. The Tweed Ring had granted lucrative franchises to companies they controlled, padded construction bills, practiced graft and extortion, and exploited every opportunity to plunder the city's funds.

during the war and now a foe of Reconstruction. Grant ran on his personal popularity more than on issues. Although he carried all but eight states, the popular vote was very close; in the South, newly enfranchised freedmen provided Grant's margin of victory.

A strong leader in war, Grant proved a passive president. Although he lacked Johnson's instinct for disaster, he had little political skill. Many of his cabinet appointees were mediocre if not unscrupulous; scandals plagued his administration. In 1869, financier Jay Gould and his partner Jim Fisk tried to corner the gold market with the help of Grant's brother-in-law, a New York speculator. When gold prices tumbled, Gould salvaged his own fortune, but investors were ruined, and Grant's reputation suffered. Then before the president's first term ended, his vice president, Schuyler Colfax, was found to be linked to the Crédit Mobilier, a fraudulent construction company created by the directors of the Union Pacific Railroad to skim off the railroad's profits. Discredited, Colfax was dropped from the Grant ticket in 1872.

More trouble lay ahead. Grant's private secretary, Orville Babcock, was unmasked in 1875 after taking money from the "whiskey ring," a group of distillers who bribed federal agents to avoid paying millions of dollars in whiskey taxes. In 1876, voters learned that Grant's secretary of war, William E. Belknap, had taken bribes to sell lucrative Indian

trading posts in Oklahoma. Impeached and disgraced, Belknap resigned.

Although uninvolved in the scandals, Grant loyally defended his subordinates. To his critics, "Grantism" came to stand for fraud, bribery, and political corruption—evils that spread far beyond Washington. In Pennsylvania, for example, the Standard Oil Company and the Pennsylvania Railroad controlled the legislature. Urban politics also provided rich opportunities for graft and swindles. The New York City press revealed in 1872 that Democratic boss William M. Tweed, the leader of Tammany Hall, led a ring that had looted the city treasury and collected at least $30 million in kickbacks and payoffs. When Mark Twain and coauthor Charles Dudley Warner published their satiric novel *The Gilded Age* (1873), readers recognized the book's speculators, self-promoters, and opportunists as familiar types in public life. (The term "Gilded Age" was subsequently used to refer to the decades from the 1870s to the 1890s.)

Grant had some success in foreign policy. In 1872, his competent secretary of state, Hamilton Fish, engineered the settlement of the *Alabama* claims with Britain. To compensate for damage done by British-built ships sold to the Confederacy during the war, an international tribunal awarded the United States $15.5 million. But the Grant administration faltered when it tried to add nonadjacent territory to the United States, as the Johnson administration had done. In 1867, Johnson's secretary of state, William H. Seward, had negotiated a treaty in which the United States bought Alaska from Russia at the bargain price of $7.2 million. Although the press mocked "Seward's Ice Box," the purchase kindled expansionists' hopes. In 1870, Grant decided to annex the eastern half of the Caribbean island of Santo Domingo. Today called the Dominican Republic, the territory had been passed back and forth since the late eighteenth century among France, Spain, and Haiti. Annexation, Grant believed, would promote Caribbean trade and provide a haven for persecuted southern blacks. American speculators anticipated windfalls from land sales, commerce, and mining. But Congress disliked Grant's plan. Senator Charles Sumner denounced it as an imperialist "dance of blood." The Senate rejected the annexation treaty and further diminished Grant's reputation.

As the election of 1872 approached, dissident Republicans expressed fears that "Grantism" at home and abroad would ruin the party. Even Grant's new running mate, Henry Wilson, referred to the president privately as a burden on his fellow Republicans. The dissidents took action. Led by a combination of former Radicals and other Republicans left out of Grant's "Great Barbecue" (a disparaging reference to profiteers who feasted at the public trough), the president's critics formed their own party, the Liberal Republicans.

The Liberals' Revolt

The Liberal Republican revolt marked a turning point in Reconstruction history. By splitting the Republican Party, **Liberal Republicans** undermined support for Republican southern policy. (The label "liberal" at the time referred to those who endorsed economic doctrines such as free trade, the gold standard, and the law of supply and demand.) Liberals attacked the "regular" Republicans on several issues. Denouncing "Grantism" and "spoilsmen" (political hacks who gained party office), they demanded civil-service reform to bring the "best men" into government. Rejecting the usual Republican high-tariff policy, they espoused free trade. Most important, the Liberals condemned "bayonet rule" in the South. Even some Republicans once known for radicalism now claimed that Reconstruction had achieved its goal: blacks had been enfranchised and could manage for themselves from now on. Corruption in government, North and South, Liberals asserted, posed a greater danger than Confederate resurgence. In the South, indeed, corrupt Republican regimes were *kept* in power, Liberals said, because the "best men"—the most capable politicians—were ex-Confederates who had been barred from officeholding.

For president the new party nominated the editor of the *New York Tribune*, Horace Greeley, who had inconsistently supported both a stringent reconstruction policy and leniency toward former rebels. The Democrats endorsed Greeley as well; their campaign slogan explained their support: "Anything to Beat Grant." Horace Greeley proved so diligent a campaigner that he worked himself to death making speeches from the back of a campaign train. He died a few weeks after the election.

Grant, who won 56 percent of the popular vote, carried all the northern states and most of the sixteen southern and border states. But the division among Republicans affected Reconstruction. To deprive the Liberals of a campaign issue, Grant Republicans in Congress, the "regulars," passed the Amnesty Act, which allowed all but a few hundred ex-Confederate officials to hold office. The flood of private amnesty acts that followed convinced white southerners that any ex-Confederate save Jefferson Davis could rise to power. In Grant's second term, Republican desires to discard the "southern question" mounted as a depression of unprecedented scope gripped the nation.

The Panic of 1873

The postwar years brought accelerated industrialization and rapid economic growth; new businesses, factories, and technological advances transformed the nation's economy in the 1870s (see Technology and Culture: The Sewing Machine) Frantic speculation played a role, too. Investors rushed to profit from rising prices, new markets, high tariffs, and seemingly boundless opportunities. Railroads provided the biggest lure. In May 1869, railroad executives drove a golden spike into the ground at Promontory Point, Utah, joining the Union Pacific and Central Pacific lines. The first transcontinental railroad heralded a new era. By 1873, almost four hundred railroad corporations crisscrossed the Northeast, consuming tons of coal and miles of steel rail from the mines and mills of Pennsylvania and neighboring states. Transforming the economy, the railroad boom led entrepreneurs to overspeculate, with drastic results.

Philadelphia banker Jay Cooke, who had helped finance the Union effort with his wartime bond campaign, had taken over a new transcontinental line, the Northern Pacific, in 1869. Northern Pacific securities sold briskly for several years, but in 1873 the line's construction costs outran new investments. In September of that year, his vaults full of bonds he could no longer sell, Cooke failed to meet his obligations, and his bank, the largest in the nation, shut down. A financial panic began; other firms collapsed, as did the stock market. The Panic of 1873 triggered a five-year depression. Banks closed, farm prices plummeted, steel furnaces stood idle, and one out of four railroads failed. Within two years, eighteen thousand businesses went bankrupt, and 3 million employees were out of jobs by 1878. Those still at work suffered repeated wage cuts; labor protests mounted; and industrial violence spread. The depression of the 1870s revealed that conflicts born of industrialization had replaced sectional divisions.

The depression also fed a dispute over currency that had begun in 1865. During the Civil War, Americans had used both national bank notes, yellow in color, which

Technology (and) *Culture*

The Sewing Machine

"You could scarcely believe ... that such works were necessary for so small a machine," an observer wrote of the Singer Sewing Machine factory that arose in 1873 in Elizabethport, New Jersey. The massive brick building, which occupied a ten-acre plot near railroad lines and New York harbor, produced every part of the sewing machine except the wooden cabinet—made in South Bend, Indiana. Most parts were cast iron; a vast foundry, the size of a football field, had enough molds laid out on its floor to hold thirty tons of pig iron. The factory also housed the forging shop, rumbling room (to wear off the rough edges of metal pieces), drilling room (to put screw holes in product parts), Japanning room (to give machines a black glossy finish), ornamenting room, assembly room, and adjusting room, where inspectors and seamstresses tested machines. According to John Scott, the lawyer for a Singer executive, the new plant was "believed to be the largest establishment in the world devoted to the production of a single article."

The start of the 1873 factory crowned two decades of explosive growth in the sewing machine industry. In 1856, leading manufacturers set up a patent-sharing pool, the Sewing Machine Combination, as a way to avoid costly lawsuits. The patent pool reflected the complexity of sewing machine technology. The sewing machine did not replicate the movement of the human hand. Instead, inventors developed a process that involved a needle with the eye at the head, two threads, feeding devices, thread tension control, and new types of stitches. The lock-stitch machine, first patented in 1846 by its inventor, Elias Howe, was most effective; it used two spools of thread, one above the material and one below. Subsequent inventions refined this machine, and patents accumulated. Entrepreneur Isaac M. Singer, for instance, received patents in the 1850s for a device that sewed curved as well as straight seams and for a foot treadle (power to run the sewing machine came from the operator until the twentieth century).

Sewing machine production presented challenges. Until the late 1850s, skilled mechanics made each machine by hand; parts were not standardized, labor costs were high, and repairs were difficult. To achieve even a modicum of interchangeable parts required factories with special equipment and heavy investment of capital. By the 1870s, three

Singer "New Family" Sewing Machine
The Singer Company began manufacturing sewing machines for home use in 1858. The company's third such model, the "New Family" machine, reigned from 1865 to 1883, when a fourth model, the "Improved Family" machine appeared.

manufacturers dominated the field: Wheeler and Wilson, Grover and Baker, and I. M. Singer. Each company strove for interchangeability of parts, though to varied degrees, and change was gradual, especially at the Singer company. When the New Jersey factory opened in 1873, Singer had fully adopted the "American" system of manufacturing; all parts were made by special machinery, thereby achieving uniformity though not true interchangeability. The company still relied on "fitters" to file parts so that they fit together. Singer's process remained a fusion of European custom-building and the "American" system until the early 1880s.

Heavy and costly, the earliest sewing machines sold only to factories. Ready-made clothing production had previously depended on seamstresses who worked at home; in the 1850s, sewing machines transformed the industry, first in men's clothing, then in cloaks, hats, and other items. Sewing

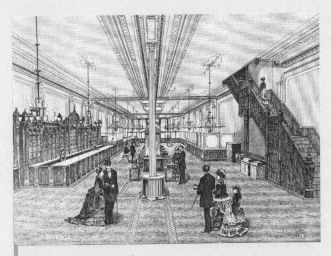

Wheeler and Wilson Salesroom
Sewing machine manufacturers of the 1870s lured customers with imposing and fashionable sales centers. Here, the Wheeler and Wilson Company's salesroom in New York's Union Square in 1874.

machines also affected the making of shoes, sails, flags, trunks, valises, harnesses, mattresses, and umbrellas; producers eagerly adapted the machines to suit industrial demands. The impact of machines on garment production, though uneven, was momentous. In the late 1850s, each machine performed the work of six hand-sewers; seamstresses now competed with machine workers of both sexes and faced displacement. Manufacturers, however, gained a competitive edge. In 1860, a New Haven shirt factory that had once paid 2,000 hand-sewers each $3 a week could hire 400 machine workers at $4 each, cut costs, and hike profits, even while paying off the cost of the machines.

But factories were only part of the sewing machine's clientele: a huge home market beckoned. In 1856, Singer introduced the first machine intended solely for home use—its "family" machine—and other manufacturers followed. To appeal to individual purchasers, Edward Clark, a lawyer for the Singer company and later head of it, introduced the "hire-purchase" plan, or installment buying: by paying a percentage of the price, a buyer could "hire" a machine, make monthly payments (with interest), and eventually own it. Poor seamstresses could not afford the machines, but middle-class women flocked to buy them. Mass production of paper patterns, which began in the 1860s, enabled women at home to make up-to-date fashions; attachments and accessories simplified buttonholing, tucking, pleating, and

other processes, both at the factory and at home. The zigzag stitch machine, for instance, patented by inventor Helen Augusta Blanchard in 1873, sealed the edges of seams and made garments sturdier. In the 1870s, the home sewing machine proved a commercial triumph; profits soared. The machine that sold for $64 in 1870 cost only $12 to produce.

To reach the home market, major producers at first used independent agents who worked mainly on commission. Then they established company-owned-and-run centers in the business districts of major cities, such as New York's Union Square. Elegant stores with carpets, chandeliers, marble facades, and plate glass windows greeted customers, who could watch demonstrations by trained personnel. By the 1870s, manufacturers had developed many marketing tactics that included extensive advertising, door-to-door sales, discounts, and trade-in allowances for older models. The first mass-marketed appliance for home use, the sewing machine symbolized a family's middle-class status. Manufacturers promoted the machine as a labor-saving device that provided, in John Scott's words, "whatever saves the busy housewife's time and increases her opportunities for culture."

In the 1870s, the Singer company surged to preeminence. Its executives strove to improve the production process and reduce prices. Between 1874 and 1880, unscathed by the 1873 depression, Singer doubled its annual production of sewing machines to half a million and six years later doubled it again. In 1877, when the last patents in the patent pool of 1856 expired, Singer became an even more competitive marketer. The company reorganized its sales department, imposed a tight managerial scheme, built factories abroad, and found new markets worldwide. Edward Clark, who became Singer's president in 1876, sought to blanket the globe with regional branch offices; three years later, Singer produced three-quarters of the world's sewing machines. At the 1876 Centennial Exhibition in Philadelphia, thirty American firms exhibited sewing machines in "Machinery Hall," but Singer ruled. "Its system of agencies embraces the civilized world," John Scott boasted in 1880. "On every sea are floating the Singer machines."

Questions for Analysis

- Why were sewing machines a challenge to manufacture?

- How did manufacturers promote sales of sewing machines for home use?

- In what ways did the marketing of sewing machines set patterns for the marketing of consumer goods today?

would eventually be converted into gold, and greenbacks, a paper currency not "backed" by a particular weight in gold. To stabilize the postwar currency, greenbacks would have to be withdrawn from circulation. This "sound-money" policy, favored by investors, won the backing of Congress. But those who depended on easy credit, both indebted farmers and manufacturers, wanted an expanding currency; that is, more greenbacks. Once the depression began, demands for such "easy money" rose. The issue divided both major parties and was compounded by another one: how to repay the federal debt.

In wartime, the Union government had borrowed what were then astronomical sums, on whatever terms it could get, mainly by selling war bonds—in effect, short-term federal IOUs—to private citizens. Bondholders wanted repayment in coin, gold or silver, even though many had paid for bonds in greenbacks. To pacify bondholders, Senator John Sherman of Ohio and other Republican leaders obtained passage of the Public Credit Act of 1869, which promised repayment in coin. With investors reassured by the Public Credit Act, Sherman guided legislation through Congress that swapped the old short-term bonds for new ones payable over the next generation. In 1872, another bill in effect defined "coin" as "gold coin" by dropping the traditional silver dollar from the official coinage. Through a feat of ingenious compromise, which placated investors and debtors, Sherman preserved the public credit, the currency, and Republican unity. In 1875, he engineered the Specie Resumption Act, which promised to put the nation on the gold standard in 1879, while tossing a few bones to Republican voters who wanted "easy money."

But when Democrats gained control of the House in 1875, with the depression in full force, a verbal storm broke out. Many Democrats and some Republicans demanded restoration of the silver dollar in order to expand the currency and relieve the depression. These "free-silver" advocates secured passage of the Bland-Allison Act of 1878, which partially restored silver coinage by requiring the Treasury to buy $2–4 million worth of silver each month and turn it into coin. In 1876, other expansionists formed the **Greenback Party**, which adopted the debtors' cause and fought to keep greenbacks in circulation, though with little success. As the nation emerged from depression in 1879, the clamor for "easy money" subsided, only to resurge in the 1890s. The controversial "money question" of the 1870s, never resolved, gave politicians and voters another reason to forget about the South.

Reconstruction and the Constitution

The Supreme Court of the 1870s also played a role in weakening northern support for Reconstruction. In wartime, few cases of note had come before the Court.

After the war, however, constitutional questions surged into prominence.

First, would the Court support congressional laws to protect freedmen's rights? The decision in *Ex parte* Milligan (1866) suggested not. In *Milligan,* the Court declared that a military commission established by the president or Congress could not try civilians in areas remote from war where the civil courts were functioning. Thus special military courts to enforce the Supplementary Freedmen's Bureau Act were doomed. Second, would the Court sabotage the congressional Reconstruction plan, as Republicans feared? Their qualms were valid, for if the Union was indissoluble, as the North had claimed during the war, then the concept of *restoring* states to the Union would be meaningless. In *Texas* v. *White* (1869), the Court ruled that although the Union was indissoluble and secession was legally impossible, the process of Reconstruction was still constitutional. It was grounded in Congress's power to ensure each state a republican form of government and to recognize the legitimate government in any state.

The 1869 decision protected the Republicans' Reconstruction plan. But in the 1870s, when cases arose involving the Fourteenth and Fifteenth amendments, the Court backed away from Reconstruction policy. In the **Slaughterhouse cases** of 1873, the Supreme Court began to chip away at the Fourteenth Amendment. The cases involved a business monopoly rather than freedmen's rights, but they provided an opportunity to interpret the amendment narrowly. In 1869, the Louisiana legislature had granted a monopoly over the New Orleans slaughterhouse business to one firm and closed down all other slaughterhouses in the interest of public health. The excluded butchers brought suit. The state had deprived them of their lawful occupation without due process of law, they claimed, and such action violated the Fourteenth Amendment, which guaranteed that no state could "abridge the privileges or immunities" of U.S. citizens. The Supreme Court upheld the Louisiana legislature by issuing a doctrine of "dual citizenship." The Fourteenth Amendment, declared the Court, protected only the rights of *national* citizenship, such as the right of interstate travel or the right to federal protection on the high seas. It did not protect those basic civil rights that fell to citizens by virtue of their *state* citizenship. Therefore, the federal government was not obliged to protect such rights against violation by the states. The *Slaughterhouse* decision came close to nullifying the intent of the Fourteenth Amendment—to secure freedmen's rights against state encroachment.

The Supreme Court again backed away from Reconstruction in two cases in 1876 involving the Enforcement

Act of 1870, which had been enacted to protect black suffrage. In *United States v. Reese* and *United States v. Cruikshank*, the Supreme Court undercut the effectiveness of the act. Continuing its retreat from Reconstruction, the Supreme Court in 1883 invalidated both the Civil Rights Act of 1875 and the Ku Klux Klan Act of 1871. These decisions cumulatively dismantled the Reconstruction policies that Republicans had sponsored after the war and confirmed rising northern sentiment that Reconstruction's egalitarian goals could not be enforced.

Republicans in Retreat

The Republicans did not reject Reconstruction suddenly but rather disengaged from it gradually, a process that began with Grant's election to the presidency in 1868. Although not an architect of Reconstruction policy, Grant defended it. But he shared with most Americans a belief in decentralized government and a reluctance to assert federal authority in local and state affairs.

In the 1870s, as the northern military presence shrank in the South, Republican idealism waned in the North. The Liberal Republican revolt of 1872 eroded what remained of radicalism. Although the "regular" Republicans, who backed Grant, continued to defend Reconstruction in the 1872 election, many held ambivalent views. Commercial and industrial interests now dominated both wings of the party, and few Republicans wished to rekindle sectional strife. After the Democrats won control of the House in the 1874 elections, support for Reconstruction became a political liability.

By 1875, the Radical Republicans, so prominent in the 1860s, had vanished from the political scene. Chase, Stevens, and Sumner were dead. Other Radicals had lost office or abandoned their former convictions. "Waving the Bloody Shirt"—defaming Democratic opponents by reviving wartime animosity—now struck many Republicans, including former Radicals, as counterproductive. Party leaders reported that voters were "sick of carpetbag government" and tiring of both the "southern question" and the "Negro question." It seemed pointless to continue the unpopular and expensive policy of military intervention in the South to prop up Republican regimes that even President Grant found corrupt. Finally, few Republicans shared the egalitarian spirit that had animated Stevens and Sumner. Politics aside, Republican leaders and voters generally agreed with southern Democrats that blacks, although worthy of freedom, were inferior to whites. To insist on black equality would be a thankless, divisive, and politically suicidal undertaking. Moreover, it would quash any hope of reunion between the regions. The Republicans' retreat from Reconstruction set the stage for its demise in 1877.

Reconstruction Abandoned, 1876–1877

"We are in a very hot political contest just now," a Mississippi planter wrote to his daughter in 1875, "with a good prospect of turning out the carpetbag thieves by whom we have been robbed for the past six to ten years." Similar contests raged through the South in the 1870s, as the resentment of white majorities grew and Democratic influence surged. By the end of 1872, the Democrats had regained power in Tennessee, Virginia, Georgia, and North Carolina. Within three years, they won control in Texas, Alabama, Arkansas, and Mississippi (see Table 16.4). As the 1876 elections approached, Republican rule survived in only three states—South Carolina, Florida, and Louisiana. Democratic victories in the state elections of 1876 and political bargaining in Washington in 1877 abruptly ended what little remained of Reconstruction.

"Redeeming" the South

Republican collapse in the South accelerated after 1872. Congressional amnesty enabled ex-Confederate officials to regain office; divisions among the Republicans weakened their party's grip on the southern electorate; and attrition diminished Republican ranks. Some carpetbaggers gave up and returned North; others became Democrats. Scalawags deserted in even larger numbers. Southerners who had joined the Republicans to moderate rampant radicalism tired of northern interference; once "home rule" by Democrats seemed possible, staying Republican meant going down with a sinking ship. Scalawag defections ruined Republican prospects. Unable to win new white votes or retain the old ones, the always-precarious Republican coalition crumbled.

Meanwhile, the Democrats mobilized once-apathetic white voters. The resurrected southern Democratic Party was divided: businessmen who envisioned an industrialized "New South" opposed an agrarian faction called the Bourbons, the old planter elite. But all Democrats shared one goal: to oust Republicans from office. Their tactics varied from state to state. Alabama Democrats won by promising to cut taxes and by getting out the white vote. In Louisiana, the "White League," a vigilante organization formed in 1874, undermined the Republicans' hold. Intimidation also proved effective in Mississippi, where violent incidents—like the 1874 slaughter in Vicksburg of about three hundred blacks by rampaging whites—terrorized black voters. In 1875, the "Mississippi plan" took effect: local Democratic clubs armed their members, who dispersed Republican meetings, patrolled voter-registration places, and marched through black areas. "The Republicans are paralyzed

Table 16.4   The Duration of Republican Rule in the Ex-Confederate States

Former Confederate States	Readmission to the Union Under Congressional Reconstruction	Democrats (Conservatives) Gain Control	Duration of Republican Rule
Alabama	June 25, 1868	November 14, 1874	$6\frac{1}{2}$ years
Arkansas	June 22, 1868	November 10, 1874	$6\frac{1}{2}$ years
Florida	June 25, 1868	January 2, 1877	$8\frac{1}{2}$ years
Georgia	July 15, 1870	November 1, 1871	1 year
Louisiana	June 25, 1868	January 2, 1877	$6\frac{1}{2}$ years
Mississippi	February 23, 1870	November 3, 1875	$6\frac{1}{2}$ years
North Carolina	June 25, 1868	November 3, 1870	2 years
South Carolina	June 25, 1868	November 12, 1876	8 years
Tennessee	July 24, 1866*	October 4, 1869	3 years
Texas	March 30, 1870	January 14, 1873	3 years
Virginia	January 26, 1870	October 5, 1869†	0 years

*Admitted before start of congressional Reconstruction.

†Democrats gained control before readmission.

Source: John Hope Franklin, *Reconstruction After the Civil War* (Chicago: University of Chicago Press, 1962), 231.

through fear and will not act," the anguished carpetbag governor of Mississippi wrote to his wife. "Why should I fight a hopeless battle?" In 1876, South Carolina's "Rifle Clubs" and "Red Shirts," armed groups that threatened Republicans, continued the scare tactics that had worked so well in Mississippi.

New outbursts of intimidation did not completely squelch black voting, but Democrats deprived Republicans of enough black votes to win state elections. In some counties, they encouraged freedmen to vote Democratic at supervised polls where voters publicly placed a card with a party label in a box. In other instances, employers and landowners impeded black suffrage. Labor contracts included clauses barring attendance at political meetings; planters used the threat of eviction to keep sharecroppers in line. As the Enforcement acts could not be enforced, intimidation and economic pressure succeeded.

"Redemption," the word Democrats used to describe their return to power, introduced sweeping changes. Some states called constitutional conventions to reverse Republican policies. All cut back expenses, wiped out social programs, lowered taxes, and revised their tax systems to relieve landowners of large burdens. State courts limited the rights of tenants and sharecroppers. Most important, the Democrats, or "redeemers," used the law to ensure a stable black labor force. Legislatures restored vagrancy laws, revised crop-lien statutes to make landowners' claims superior to those of merchants, and rewrote criminal law. Local ordinances in heavily black counties often restricted hunting, fishing, gun carrying, and ownership of dogs and thereby curtailed the everyday activities of freedmen who lived off the land. States passed severe laws against trespassing and theft; stealing livestock or wrongly taking part of a crop became grand larceny with a penalty of up to five years at hard labor. By the end of Reconstruction, a large black convict work force had been leased out to private contractors at low rates.

For the freedmen, whose aspirations had been raised by Republican rule, redemption was devastating. The new laws, Tennessee blacks contended at an 1875 convention, would impose "a condition of servitude scarcely less degrading than that endured before the late civil war." In the late 1870s, as the political climate grew more oppressive, an "exodus" movement spread through Mississippi, Tennessee, Texas, and Louisiana. Some African-Americans decided to become homesteaders in Kansas. After a major outbreak of "Kansas fever" in 1879, four thousand **"exodusters"** from Mississippi and Louisiana joined about ten thousand who had reached Kansas earlier in the decade. But the vast majority of freedmen, devoid of resources, had no migration options or escape route. Mass movement of southern blacks to the North and Midwest would not gain momentum until the twentieth century.

The Election of 1876

By the autumn of 1876, with redemption almost complete, both parties sought to discard the heritage of animosity left by the war and Reconstruction. Republicans

The White League
Alabama's White League, formed in 1874, strove to oust
Republicans from office by intimidating black voters. To political
cartoonist Thomas Nast, such vigilante tactics suggested an
alliance between the White League and the outlawed Ku Klux
Klan.

nominated Rutherford B. Hayes, three times Ohio's
governor, for president. Untainted by the scandals of
the Grant years and popular with all factions in his
party, Hayes presented himself as a "moderate" on
southern policy. He favored "home rule" in the South
and a guarantee of civil and political rights for all—two
planks that were clearly contradictory. The Democrats
nominated Governor Samuel J. Tilden of New York, a
millionaire corporate lawyer and political reformer.
Known for his assaults on the Tweed Ring that had
plundered New York City's treasury, Tilden campaigned
against fraud and waste. Both candidates favored
sound money, endorsed civil-service reform, and decried corruption, an irony since the 1876 election
would be extremely corrupt.

Tilden won the popular vote by a 3 percent margin
and seemed destined to capture the 185 electoral votes
needed for victory (see Map 16.4). But the Republicans
challenged the pro-Tilden returns from South Carolina,
Florida, and Louisiana. If they could deprive the Democrats of these nineteen electoral votes, Hayes would triumph. The Democrats, who needed only one of the
disputed electoral votes for victory, challenged (on a

The Exodus to Kansas
Benjamin "Pap" Singleton, a one-time fugitive slave from Tennessee, returned there to promote
the "exodus" movement of the late 1870s. Forming a real estate company, Singleton traveled
the South recruiting parties of freedmen who were disillusioned with the outcome of
Reconstruction. These emigrants, awaiting a Mississippi River boat, looked forward to political
equality, freedom from violence, and homesteads in Kansas.

technicality) the validity of Oregon's single electoral vote, which the Republicans had won. Twenty electoral votes, therefore, were in contention. But Republicans still controlled the electoral machinery in the three unredeemed southern states, where they threw out enough Democratic ballots to declare Hayes the winner.

The nation now faced an unprecedented dilemma. Each party claimed victory in the contested states, and each accused the other of fraud. In fact, both sets of southern results involved fraud: the Republicans had discarded legitimate Democratic ballots, and the Democrats had illegally prevented freedmen from voting. To resolve the conflict, Congress in January 1877 created a special electoral commission to decide which party would get the contested electoral votes. Made up of senators, representatives, and Supreme Court justices, the commission included seven Democrats, seven Republicans, and one independent, Justice David Davis of Illinois. When Davis resigned to run for the Senate, Congress replaced him with a Republican, and the commission gave Hayes the election by a vote of 8 to 7.

Congress now had to certify the new electoral vote. But since Democrats controlled the House, a new problem loomed. Some Democrats threatened to obstruct debate and delay approval of the electoral vote. Had they done so, the nation would have been without a president on inauguration day, March 4. Room for compromise remained, for many southern Democrats accepted Hayes's election: former scalawags with commercial interests to protect still favored Republican financial policies, and railroad investors hoped that a Republican administration would help them build a southern transcontinental line. Other southerners cared mainly about Democratic state victories and did not mind conceding the presidency as long as the new Republican administration would leave the South alone. Republican leaders, although sure of eventual triumph, were willing to bargain as well, for candidate Hayes desired not merely victory but southern approval.

A series of informal negotiations ensued, at which politicians exchanged promises. Ohio Republicans and southern Democrats, who met at a Washington hotel, reached an agreement that if Hayes won the election, he would remove federal troops from South Carolina and Louisiana, and Democrats could gain control of those states. In other bargaining sessions, southern politicians asked for federal patronage, federal aid to railroads, and federal support for internal improvements. In return, they promised to drop the filibuster, to accept Hayes as president, and

	Uncontested Electoral Vote	Electoral Vote	Popular Vote	Percentage of Popular Vote
Republican Rutherford B. Hayes	165	185	4,034,311	48.0
Democratic Samuel J. Tilden	184	184	4,288,546	51.0
Greenback Peter Cooper	–	–	75,973	1.0
	Disputed			

Map 16.4 The Disputed Election of 1876
Congress resolved the contested electoral vote of 1876 in favor of Republican Rutherford B. Hayes.

to treat freedmen fairly. With the threatened filibuster broken, Congress ratified Hayes's election. Once in office, Hayes fulfilled some of the promises his Republican colleagues had made. He appointed a former Confederate as postmaster general and ordered federal troops who guarded the South Carolina and Louisiana statehouses back to their barracks. Although federal soldiers remained in the South after 1877, they no longer served a political function. The Democrats, meanwhile, took control of state governments in Louisiana, South Carolina, and Florida. When Republican rule toppled in these states, the era of Reconstruction finally ended, though more with a whimper than with a resounding crash.

But some of the bargains struck in the **Compromise of 1877**, such as Democratic promises to treat southern blacks fairly, were forgotten, as were Hayes's pledges to ensure freedmen's rights. "When you turned us loose, you turned us loose to the sky, to the storm, to the whirlwind, and worst of all . . . to the wrath of our infuriated masters," Frederick Douglass had charged at the Republican convention in 1876. "The question now is, do you mean to make good to us the promises in your Constitution?" The answer provided by the 1876 election and the 1877 compromises was "No."

Chronology, 1865–1877

1863	President Abraham Lincoln issues Proclamation of Amnesty and Reconstruction.
1864	Wade-Davis bill passed by Congress and pocket-vetoed by Lincoln.
1865	Freedmen's Bureau established.
	Civil War ends.
	Lincoln assassinated.
	Andrew Johnson becomes president.
	Johnson issues Proclamation of Amnesty and Reconstruction.
	Ex-Confederate states hold constitutional conventions (May–December).
	Black conventions begin in the ex-Confederate states.
	Thirteenth Amendment added to the Constitution.
	Presidential Reconstruction completed.
1866	Congress enacts the Civil Rights Act of 1866 and the Supplementary Freedmen's Bureau Act over Johnson's vetoes.
	Ku Klux Klan founded in Tennessee.
	Tennessee readmitted to the Union.
	Race riots in southern cities.
	Republicans win congressional elections.
1867	Reconstruction Act of 1867.
	William Seward negotiates the purchase of Alaska.
	Constitutional conventions meet in the ex-Confederate states.
	Howard University founded.
1868	President Johnson is impeached, tried, and acquitted.
	Omnibus Act.

	Fourteenth Amendment added to the Constitution.
	Ulysses S. Grant elected president.
1869	Transcontinental railroad completed.
1870	Congress readmits the four remaining southern states to the Union.
	Fifteenth Amendment added to the Constitution.
	Enforcement Act of 1870.
1871	Second Enforcement Act.
	Ku Klux Klan Act.
1872	Liberal Republican party formed.
	Amnesty Act.
	Alabama claims settled.
	Grant reelected president.
1873	Panic of 1873 begins (September–October), setting off a five-year depression.
1874	Democrats gain control of the House of Representatives.
1875	Civil Rights Act of 1875.
	Specie Resumption Act.
1876	Disputed presidential election: Rutherford B. Hayes versus Samuel J. Tilden.
1877	Electoral commission decides election in favor of Hayes.
	The last Republican-controlled governments overthrown in Florida, Louisiana, and South Carolina.
1879	"Exodus" movement spreads through several southern states.

Conclusion

Between 1865 and 1877, the nation experienced a series of crises. In Washington, conflict between President Johnson and Congress led to a stringent Republican plan for restoring the South, a plan that included the radical provision of black male enfranchisement. President Johnson ineptly abetted the triumph of his foes by his defiant stance, which drove moderate Republicans into an alliance against him with Radical Republicans. In the ex-Confederate states, Republicans took over and re-organized state governments. A new electorate, in which recently freed African-Americans were prominent, supported Republican policies. Rebuilding the South cost millions, and state expenditures soared. Objections to taxes, resentment of black suffrage, and fear of "Negro domination" spurred counterattacks on African-Americans by former Confederates.

Emancipation reshaped black communities where former slaves sought new identities as free people. African-Americans reconstituted their families; created black institutions, such as churches and schools; and participated in government for the first time in American history. They also took part in the transformation of southern agriculture. By Reconstruction's end, a new labor system, sharecropping, replaced slavery. Begun as a compromise between freedmen and landowners, sharecropping soon trapped African-Americans and other tenant farmers in a cycle of debt; black political rights waned as well as Republicans lost control of the southern states.

The North, meanwhile, hurtled headlong into an era of industrial growth, labor unrest, and financial crises. The political scandals of the Grant administration and the impact of depression after the Panic of 1873 diverted northern attention from the South. By the mid-1870s, northern politicians were ready to discard the Reconstruction policies that Congress had imposed a decade before. Simultaneously, the southern states returned to Democratic rule, as Republican regimes toppled one by one. Reconstruction's final collapse in 1877 reflected not only a waning of northern resolve but a successful ex-Confederate campaign of violence, intimidation, and protest that had started in the 1860s.

The end of Reconstruction gratified both political parties. Although unable to retain a southern constituency, the Republican Party was no longer burdened by the unpopular "southern question." The Democrats, who had regained power in the former Confederacy, would remain entrenched there for over a century. To be sure, the South was tied to sharecropping and economic backwardness as securely as it had once been tied to slavery. But "home rule" was firmly in place. Reconstruction's end also signified a triumph for nationalism and the spirit of reunion. In the fall of 1877, President Hayes toured the South to champion reconciliation, and similar celebrations continued for decades.

As the nation applauded reunion, Reconstruction's reputation sank. Looking back on the 1860s and 1870s, most late-nineteenth-century Americans dismissed the congressional effort to reconstruct the South as a fiasco—a tragic interlude of "radical rule" or "black reconstruction" fashioned by carpetbaggers, scalawags, and Radical Republicans. With the hindsight of a century, historians continued to regard Reconstruction as a failure, though of a different kind.

No longer viewed as a misguided scheme that collapsed because of radical excess, Reconstruction is now widely seen as a democratic experiment that did not go

Key Terms

Charles Sumner	Susan B. Anthony
Thaddeus Stevens	Ku Klux Klan
Andrew Johnson	Enforcement Acts
presidential Reconstruction	Civil Rights Act of 1875
"black codes"	sharecropping
Civil Rights Act of 1866	Liberal Republicans
Fourteenth Amendment	Greenback Party
Reconstruction Act of 1867	Slaughterhouse Cases
Tenure of Office Act	"exodusters"
Fifteenth Amendment	Compromise of 1877

far enough. Historians cite two main causes. First, Congress did not promote freedmen's independence through land reform; without property of their own, southern blacks lacked the economic power to defend their interests as free citizens. Property ownership, however, does not necessarily ensure political rights, nor does it invariably provide economic security. Considering the depressed state of southern agriculture in the postwar decades, the freedmen's fate as independent farmers would likely have been perilous. Thus the land-reform question, like much else about Reconstruction, remains a subject of debate. A second cause of Reconstruction's collapse is less open to dispute: the federal government neglected to back congressional Reconstruction with military force. Given the choice between protecting blacks' rights at whatever cost and promoting reunion, the government opted for reunion. Reconstruction's failure, therefore, was the federal government's failure to fulfill its own goals and create a biracial democracy in the South. As a result, the nation's adjustment to the consequences of emancipation would continue into the twentieth century.

The Reconstruction era left some significant legacies, including the Fourteenth and Fifteenth amendments. Although neither amendment would be used to protect minority rights for almost a century, they remain monuments to the democratic zeal that swept Congress in the 1860s. The Reconstruction years also hold a significant place in African-American history. The aspirations and achievements of the Reconstruction era left an indelible mark on black citizens. Consigning Reconstruction to history, other Americans turned to their economic futures—to railroads, factories, and mills, and to the exploitation of the country's bountiful natural resources.

For Further Reference

David W. Blight, *Race and Reunion: The Civil War in American Memory* (2001). Explores competing views on the significance of the Civil War in the Reconstruction era and the decades that followed.

Laura F. Edwards, *Gendered Strife and Confusion: The Political Culture of Reconstruction* (1997). Examines the impact of household roles on public affairs and southern lifestyles in a North Carolina county.

Carol F. Faulkner, *Women's Radical Reconstruction: The Freedmen's Aid Movement* (2004). A study of abolitionist teachers and women's rights advocates, their impact on federal policy, and their interactions with former slaves.

Eric Foner, *Reconstruction: America's Unfinished Revolution, 1863–1877* (1988). A thorough exploration of Reconstruction that draws on recent scholarship and stresses the centrality of the black experience.

Steven Hahn, *A Nation Under Our Feet: Black Political Struggles in the Rural South from Slavery to the Great Migration* (2003). How African–American communities shaped politics during and after Reconstruction.

Tera W. Hunter, *To, 'Joy My Freedom: Southern Black Women's Lives and Labors After the Civil War* (1997). Explores the experience of women workers in Atlanta from Reconstruction into the twentieth century.

Leon Litwack, *Been in the Storm So Long: The Aftermath of Slavery* (1979). A comprehensive study of the black response to emancipation in 1865–1866.

Michael Perman, *The Road to Redemption: Southern Politics, 1869–1879* (1984). Examines the impact of Reconstruction on party politics in the post–Civil War South and explains how Reconstruction governments in the southern states collapsed.

Roger L. Ransom and Richard Sutch, *One Kind of Freedom: The Economic Consequences of Emancipation* (1977). Two economists' assessment of the impact of free black labor on the South and explanation of the development of sharecropping and the crop-lien system.

Heather Cox Richardson, *The Death of Reconstruction: Race, Labor, and Politics in the Post–Civil War North, 1865–1901* (2001). Explores northern disenchantment with Reconstruction policies and the dwindling of northern support for freed blacks in the South.

Appendix

Documents

Declaration of Independence

IN CONGRESS, JULY 4, 1776

THE UNANIMOUS DECLARATION OF THE THIRTEEN UNITED STATES OF AMERICA

When, in the course of human events, it becomes necessary for one people to dissolve the political bands which have connected them with another, and to assume, among the powers of the earth, the separate and equal station to which the laws of nature and of nature's God entitle them, a decent respect to the opinions of mankind requires that they should declare the causes which impel them to the separation.

We hold these truths to be self-evident: That all men are created equal; that they are endowed by their Creator with certain unalienable rights; that among these are life, liberty, and the pursuit of happiness; that, to secure these rights, governments are instituted among men, deriving their just powers from the consent of the governed; that whenever any form of government becomes destructive of these ends, it is the right of the people to alter or to abolish it, and to institute new government, laying its foundation on such principles, and organizing its powers in such form, as to them shall seem most likely to effect their safety and happiness. Prudence, indeed, will dictate that governments long established should not be changed for light and transient causes; and accordingly all experience hath shown that mankind are more disposed to suffer, while evils are sufferable, than to right themselves by abolishing the forms to which they are accustomed. But when a long train of abuses and usurpations, pursuing invariably the same object, evinces a design to reduce them under absolute despotism, it is

their right, it is their duty, to throw off such government, and to provide new guards for their future security. Such has been the patient sufferance of these colonies; and such is now the necessity which constrains them to alter their former systems of government. The history of the present King of Great Britain is a history of repeated injuries and usurpations, all having in direct object the establishment of an absolute tyranny over these states. To prove this, let facts be submitted to a candid world.

He has refused his assent to laws, the most wholesome and necessary for the public good.

He has forbidden his governors to pass laws of immediate and pressing importance, unless suspended in their operation till his assent should be obtained; and, when so suspended, he has utterly neglected to attend to them.

He has refused to pass other laws for the accommodation of large districts of people, unless those people would relinquish the right of representation in the legislature, a right inestimable to them, and formidable to tyrants only.

He has called together legislative bodies at places unusual, uncomfortable, and distant from the depository of their public records, for the sole purpose of fatiguing them into compliance with his measures.

He has dissolved representative houses repeatedly, for opposing, with manly firmness, his invasions on the rights of the people.

He has refused for a long time, after such dissolutions, to cause others to be elected; whereby the legislative powers, incapable of annihilation, have returned to the people at large for their exercise; the state remaining, in the mean time, exposed to all the dangers of invasions from without and convulsions within.

He has endeavored to prevent the population of these states; for that purpose obstructing the laws of naturalization of foreigners; refusing to pass others to encourage their migration hither, and raising the conditions of new appropriation of lands.

He has obstructed the administration of justice, by refusing his assent to laws for establishing judiciary powers.

He has made judges dependent on his will alone, for the tenure of their offices, and the amount and payment of their salaries.

He has erected a multitude of new offices, and sent hither swarms of officers to harass our people and eat out their substance.

He has kept among us, in times of peace, standing armies, without the consent of our legislatures.

He has affected to render the military independent of, and superior to, the civil power.

He has combined with others to subject us to a jurisdiction foreign to our constitution, and unacknowledged by our laws, giving his assent to their acts of pretended legislation:

For quartering large bodies of armed troops among us;

For protecting them, by a mock trial, from punishment for any murders which they should commit on the inhabitants of these states;

For cutting off our trade with all parts of the world;

For imposing taxes on us without our consent;

For depriving us, in many cases, of the benefits of trial by jury;

For transporting us beyond seas, to be tried for pretended offenses;

For abolishing the free system of English laws in a neighboring province, establishing therein an arbitrary government, and enlarging its boundaries, so as to render it at once an example and fit instrument for introducing the same absolute rule into these colonies;

For taking away our charters, abolishing our most valuable laws, and altering fundamentally the forms of our governments;

For suspending our own legislatures, and declaring themselves invested with power to legislate for us in all cases whatsoever.

He has abdicated government here, by declaring us out of his protection and waging war against us.

He has plundered our seas, ravaged our coasts, burned our towns, and destroyed the lives of our people.

He is at this time transporting large armies of foreign mercenaries to complete the works of death, desolation,

and tyranny already begun with circumstances of cruelty and perfidy scarcely paralleled in the most barbarous ages, and totally unworthy of the head of a civilized nation.

He has constrained our fellow-citizens, taken captive on the high seas, to bear arms against their country, to become the executioners of their friends and brethren, or to fall themselves by their hands.

He has excited domestic insurrection among us, and has endeavored to bring on the inhabitants of our frontiers the merciless Indian savages, whose known rule of warfare is an undistinguished destruction of all ages, sexes, and conditions.

In every stage of these oppressions we have petitioned for redress in the most humble terms; our repeated petitions have been answered only by repeated injury. A prince, whose character is thus marked by every act which may define a tyrant, is unfit to be the ruler of a free people.

Nor have we been wanting in our attentions to our British brethren. We have warned them, from time to time, of attempts by their legislature to extend an unwarrantable jurisdiction over us. We have reminded them of the circumstances of our emigration and settlement here. We have appealed to their native justice and magnanimity; and we have conjured them by the ties of our common kindred, to disavow these usurpations, which would inevitably interrupt our connections and correspondence. They, too, have been deaf to the voice of justice and of consanguinity. We must, therefore, acquiesce in the necessity which denounces our separation, and hold them, as we hold the rest of mankind, enemies in war, in peace friends.

We, therefore, the representatives of the United States of America, in General Congress assembled, appealing to the Supreme Judge of the world for the rectitude of our intentions, do, in the name and by the authority of the good people of these colonies, solemnly publish and declare, that these United Colonies are, and of right ought to be, FREE AND INDEPENDENT STATES; that they are absolved from all allegiance to the British crown, and that all political connection between them and the state of Great Britain is, and ought to be, totally dissolved; and that, as free and independent states, they have full power to levy war, conclude peace, contract alliances, establish commerce, and do all other acts and things which independent states may of right do. And for the support of this declaration, with a firm reliance on the protection of Divine Providence, we mutually pledge to each other our lives, our fortunes, and our sacred honor.

JOHN HANCOCK [President]
[and fifty-five others]

Constitution of the United States of America

PREAMBLE

We the people of the United States, in order to form a more perfect union, establish justice, insure domestic tranquillity, provide for the common defense, promote the general welfare, and secure the blessings of liberty to ourselves and our posterity, do ordain and establish this CONSTITUTION for the United States of America.

Article I

Section 1.   All legislative powers herein granted shall be vested in a Congress of the United States, which shall consist of a Senate and a House of Representatives.

Section 2.   The House of Representatives shall be composed of members chosen every second year by the people of the several States, and the electors in each State shall have the qualifications requisite for electors of the most numerous branch of the State Legislature.

No person shall be a Representative who shall not have attained to the age of twenty-five years, and been seven years a citizen of the United States, and who shall not, when elected, be an inhabitant of that State in which he shall be chosen.

Representatives and direct taxes shall be apportioned among the several States which may be included within this Union, according to their respective numbers, *which shall be determined by adding to the whole number of free persons, including those bound to service for a term of years and excluding Indians not taxed, three-fifths of all other persons.* The actual enumeration shall be made within three years after the first meeting of the Congress of the United States, and within every subsequent term of ten years, in such manner as they shall by law direct. The number of Representatives shall not exceed one for every thirty thousand, but each State shall have at least one Representative; *and until such enumeration shall be made, the State of New Hampshire shall be entitled to choose three, Massachusetts eight, Rhode Island and Providence Plantations one, Connecticut five, New York six, New Jersey four, Pennsylvania eight, Delaware one, Maryland six, Virginia ten, North Carolina five, South Carolina five, and Georgia three.*

Note: Passages that are no longer in effect are printed in italic type.

When vacancies happen in the representation from any State, the Executive authority thereof shall issue writs of election to fill such vacancies.

The House of Representatives shall choose their Speaker and other officers; and shall have the sole power of impeachment.

Section 3.   The Senate of the United States shall be composed of two Senators from each State, *chosen by the legislature thereof,* for six years; and each Senator shall have one vote.

Immediately after they shall be assembled in consequence of the first election, they shall be divided as equally as may be into three classes. The seats of the Senators of the first class shall be vacated at the expiration of the second year, of the second class at the expiration of the fourth year, and of the third class at the expiration of the sixth year, so that one-third may be chosen every second year; *and if vacancies happen by resignation or otherwise, during the recess of the legislature of any State, the Executive thereof may make temporary appointments until the next meeting of the legislature, which shall then fill such vacancies.*

No person shall be a Senator who shall not have attained to the age of thirty years, and been nine years a citizen of the United States, and who shall not, when elected, be an inhabitant of that State for which he shall be chosen.

The Vice President of the United States shall be President of the Senate, but shall have no vote, unless they be equally divided.

The Senate shall choose their other officers, and also a President *pro tempore*, in the absence of the Vice President, or when he shall exercise the office of the President of the United States.

The Senate shall have the sole power to try all impeachments. When sitting for that purpose, they shall be on oath or affirmation. When the President of the United States is tried, the Chief Justice shall preside: and no person shall be convicted without the concurrence of two-thirds of the members present.

Judgment in cases of impeachment shall not extend further than to removal from the office, and disqualification to hold and enjoy any office of honor, trust or profit under the United States; but the party convicted shall nevertheless be liable and subject to indictment, trial, judgment and punishment, according to law.

Section 4.   The times, places and manner of holding elections for Senators and Representatives shall be prescribed in each State by the legislature thereof; but the Congress may at any time by law make or alter such regulations, except as to the places of choosing Senators.

The Congress shall assemble at least once in every year, and such meeting *shall be on the first Monday in December, unless they shall by law appoint a different day.*

Section 5.   Each house shall be the judge of the elections, returns and qualifications of its own members, and a majority of each shall constitute a quorum to do business; but a smaller number may adjourn from day to day, and may be authorized to compel the attendance of absent members, in such manner, and under such penalties, as each house may provide.

Each house may determine the rules of its proceedings, punish its members for disorderly behavior, and with the concurrence of two-thirds, expel a member.

Each house shall keep a journal of its proceedings, and from time to time publish the same, excepting such parts as may in their judgment require secrecy; and the yeas and nays of the members of either house on any question shall, at the desire of one-fifth of those present, be entered on the journal.

Neither house, during the session of Congress, shall, without the consent of the other, adjourn for more than three days, nor to any other place than that in which the two houses shall be sitting.

Section 6.   The Senators and Representatives shall receive a compensation for their services, to be ascertained by law and paid out of the treasury of the United States. They shall in all cases except treason, felony and breach of the peace, be privileged from arrest during their attendance at the session of their respective houses, and in going to and returning from the same;

and for any speech or debate in either house, they shall not be questioned in any other place.

No Senator or Representative shall, during the time for which he was elected, be appointed to any civil office under the authority of the United States, which shall have been created, or the emoluments whereof shall have been increased, during such time; and no person holding any office under the United States shall be a member of either house during his continuance in office.

Section 7.   All bills for raising revenue shall originate in the House of Representatives; but the Senate may propose or concur with amendments as on other bills.

Every bill which shall have passed the House of Representatives and the Senate, shall, before it become a law, be presented to the President of the United States; if he approve he shall sign it, but if not he shall return it with objections to that house in which it originated, who shall enter the objections at large on their journal, and proceed to reconsider it. If after such reconsideration two-thirds of that house shall agree to pass the bill, it shall be sent, together with the objections, to the other house, by which it shall likewise be reconsidered, and, if approved by two-thirds of that house, it shall become a law. But in all such cases the votes of both houses shall be determined by yeas and nays, and the names of the persons voting for and against the bill shall be entered on the journal of each house respectively. If any bill shall not be returned by the President within ten days (Sundays excepted) after it shall have been presented to him, the same shall be a law, in like manner as if he had signed it, unless the Congress by their adjournment prevent its return, in which case it shall not be a law.

Every order, resolution, or vote to which the concurrence of the Senate and House of Representatives may be necessary (except on a question of adjournment) shall be presented to the President of the United States; and before the same shall take effect, shall be approved by him, or being disapproved by him, shall be repassed by two-thirds of the Senate and House of Representatives, according to the rules and limitations prescribed in the case of a bill.

Section 8.   The Congress shall have power

To lay and collect taxes, duties, imposts, and excises, to pay the debts and provide for the common defense and general welfare of the United States; but all duties, imposts and excises shall be uniform throughout the United States;

To borrow money on the credit of the United States;

To regulate commerce with foreign nations, and among the several States, and with the Indian tribes;

To establish an uniform rule of naturalization, and uniform laws on the subject of bankruptcies throughout the United States;

To coin money, regulate the value thereof, and of foreign coin, and fix the standard of weights and measures;

To provide for the punishment of counterfeiting the securities and current coin of the United States;

To establish post offices and post roads;

To promote the progress of science and useful arts by securing for limited times to authors and inventors the exclusive right to their respective writings and discoveries;

To constitute tribunals inferior to the Supreme Court;

To define and punish piracies and felonies committed on the high seas and offenses against the law of nations;

To declare war, grant letters of marque and reprisal, and make rules concerning captures on land and water;

To raise and support armies, but no appropriation of money to that use shall be for a longer term than two years;

To provide and maintain a navy;

To make rules for the government and regulation of the land and naval forces;

To provide for calling forth the militia to execute the laws of the Union, suppress insurrections, and repel invasions;

To provide for organizing, arming, and disciplining the militia, and for governing such part of them as may be employed in the service of the United States, reserving to the States respectively the appointment of the officers, and the authority of training the militia according to the discipline prescribed by Congress;

To exercise exclusive legislation in all cases whatsoever, over such district (not exceeding ten miles square) as may, by cession of particular States, and the acceptance of Congress, become the seat of government of the United States, and to exercise like authority over all places purchased by the consent of the legislature of the State, in which the same shall be, for erection of forts, magazines, arsenals, dock-yards, and other needful buildings;—and

To make all laws which shall be necessary and proper for carrying into execution the foregoing powers, and all other powers vested by this Constitution in the government of the United States, or in any department or officer thereof.

Section 9.   *The migration or importation of such persons as any of the States now existing shall think proper to admit shall not be prohibited by the Congress prior to the year 1808; but a tax or duty may be imposed on such importation, not exceeding $10 for each person.*

The privilege of the writ of habeas corpus shall not be suspended, unless when in cases of rebellion or invasion the public safety may require it.

No bill of attainder or ex post facto law shall be passed.

No capitation, or other direct, tax shall be laid, unless in proportion to the census or enumeration herein before directed to be taken.

No tax or duty shall be laid on articles exported from any State.

No preference shall be given by any regulation of commerce or revenue to the ports of one State over those of another; nor shall vessels bound to, or from, one State, be obliged to enter, clear, or pay duties in another.

No money shall be drawn from the treasury, but in consequence of appropriations made by law; and a regular statement and account of the receipts and expenditures of all public money shall be published from time to time.

No title of nobility shall be granted by the United States: and no person holding any office of profit or trust under them, shall, without the consent of the Congress, accept of any present, emolument, office, or title, of any kind whatever, from any king, prince, or foreign state.

Section 10.   No State shall enter into any treaty, alliance, or confederation; grant letters of marque and reprisal; coin money; emit bills of credit; make anything but gold and silver coin a tender in payment of debts; pass any bill of attainder, ex post facto law, or law impairing the obligation of contracts, or grant any title of nobility.

No State shall, without the consent of Congress, lay any imposts or duties on imports or exports, except what may be absolutely necessary for executing its inspection laws: and the net produce of all duties and imposts, laid by any State on imports or exports, shall be for the use of the treasury of the United States; and all such laws shall be subject to the revision and control of the Congress.

No State shall, without the consent of Congress, lay any duty of tonnage, keep troops or ships of war in time of peace, enter into any agreement or compact with another State, or with a foreign power, or engage in war, unless actually invaded, or in such imminent danger as will not admit of delay.

Article II

Section 1. The executive power shall be vested in a President of the United States of America. He shall hold his office during the term of four years, and, together with the Vice President, chosen for the same term, be elected as follows:

Each state shall appoint, in such manner as the legislature thereof may direct, a number of electors, equal to the whole number of Senators and Representatives to which the State may be entitled in the Congress; but no Senator or Representative, or person holding an office of trust or profit under the United States, shall be appointed an elector.

The electors shall meet in their respective States, and vote by ballot for two persons, of whom one at least shall not be an inhabitant of the same State with themselves. And they shall make a list of all the persons voted for, and of the number of votes for each; which list they shall sign and certify, and transmit sealed to the seat of government of the United States, directed to the President of the Senate. The President of the Senate shall, in the presence of the Senate and the House of Representatives, open all the certificates, and the votes shall then be counted. The person having the greatest number of votes shall be the President, if such number be a majority of the whole number of electors appointed; and if there be more than one who have such majority, and have an equal number of votes, then the House of Representatives shall immediately choose by ballot one of them for President; and if no person have a majority, then from the five highest on the list said house shall in like manner choose the President. But in choosing the President the votes shall be taken by States, the representation from each State having one vote; a quorum for this purpose shall consist of a member or members from two-thirds of the States, and a majority of all the States shall be necessary to a choice. In every case, after the choice of the President, the person having the greatest number of votes of the electors shall be the Vice President. But if there should remain two or more who have equal votes, the Senate shall choose from them by ballot the Vice President.

The Congress may determine the time of choosing the electors and the day on which they shall give their votes; which day shall be the same throughout the United States.

No person except a natural-born citizen, *or a citizen of the United States at the time of the adoption of this Constitution,* shall be eligible to the office of President; neither shall any person be eligible to that office who shall not have attained to the age of thirty-five years, and been fourteen years a resident within the United States.

In case of the removal of the President from office or of his death, resignation, or inability to discharge the powers and duties of the said office, the same shall devolve on the Vice President, and the Congress may by law provide for the case of removal, death, resignation, or inability, both of the President and Vice President, declaring what officer shall then act as President, and such officer shall act accordingly, until the disability be removed, or a President shall be elected.

The President shall, at stated times, receive for his services a compensation, which shall neither be increased nor diminished during the period for which he shall have been elected, and he shall not receive within that period any other emolument from the United States, or any of them.

Before he enter on the execution of his office, he shall take the following oath or affirmation:—"I do solemnly swear (or affirm) that I will faithfully execute the office of the President of the United States, and will to the best of my ability preserve, protect and defend the Constitution of the United States."

Section 2. The President shall be commander in chief of the army and navy of the United States, and of the militia of the several States, when called into the actual service of the United States; he may require the opinion, in writing, of the principal officer in each of the executive departments, upon any subject relating to the duties of their respective offices, and he shall have power to grant reprieves and pardons for offenses against the United States, except in cases of impeachment.

He shall have power, by and with the advice and consent of the Senate, to make treaties, provided two-thirds of the Senators present concur; and he shall nominate, and by and with the advice and consent of the Senate, shall appoint ambassadors, other public ministers and consuls, judges of the Supreme Court, and all other officers of the United States, whose appointments are not herein otherwise provided for, and which shall be established by law: but Congress may by law vest the appointment of such inferior officers, as they think proper, in the President alone, in the courts of law, or in the heads of departments.

The President shall have power to fill up all vacancies that may happen during the recess of the Senate, by granting commissions which shall expire at the end of their next session.

Section 3. He shall from time to time give to the Congress information of the state of the Union, and recommend to their consideration such measures as he shall judge necessary and expedient; he may, on extraordinary occasions, convene both houses, or either of them, and in case of disagreement between them, with respect to the time of adjournment, he may adjourn them to such time as he shall think proper; he shall receive ambassadors and other public ministers; he shall take care that the laws be faithfully executed, and shall commission all the officers of the United States.

Section 4. The President, Vice President and all civil officers of the United States shall be removed from office on impeachment for, and on conviction of, treason, bribery, or other high crimes and misdemeanors.

Article III

Section 1. The judicial power of the United States shall be vested in one Supreme Court, and in such inferior courts as the Congress may from time to time ordain and establish. The judges, both of the Supreme and inferior courts, shall hold their offices during good behavior, and shall, at stated times, receive for their services a compensation which shall not be diminished during their continuance in office.

Section 2. The judicial power shall extend to all cases, in law and equity, arising under this Constitution, the laws of the United States, and treaties made, or which shall be made, under their authority;—to all cases affecting ambassadors, other public ministers and consuls;—to all cases of admiralty and maritime jurisdiction;—to controversies to which the United States shall be a party;—to controversies between two or more States;—*between a State and citizens of another State;*—between citizens of different States;—between citizens of the same State claiming lands under grants of different States, and between a State, or the citizens thereof, and foreign states, citizens or subjects.

In all cases affecting ambassadors, other public ministers and consuls, and those in which a State shall be party, the Supreme Court shall have original jurisdiction. In all the other cases before mentioned, the Supreme Court shall have appellate jurisdiction, both as to law and fact, with such exceptions, and under such regulations, as the Congress shall make.

The trial of all crimes, except in cases of impeachment, shall be by jury; and such trial shall be held in the State where said crimes shall have been committed; but when not committed within any State, the trial shall be at such place or places as the Congress may by law have directed.

Section 3. Treason against the United States shall consist only in levying war against them, or in adhering to their enemies, giving them aid and comfort. No person shall be convicted of treason unless on the testimony of two witnesses to the same overt act, or on confession in open court.

The Congress shall have power to declare the punishment of treason, but no attainder of treason shall work corruption of blood, or forfeiture except during the life of the person attainted.

Article IV

Section 1. Full faith and credit shall be given in each State to the public acts, records, and judicial proceedings of every other State. And the Congress may by general laws prescribe the manner in which such acts, records, and proceedings shall be proved, and the effect thereof.

Section 2. The citizens of each State shall be entitled to all privileges and immunities of citizens in the several States.

A person charged in any State with treason, felony, or other crime, who shall flee from justice, and be found in another State, shall on demand of the executive authority of the State from which he fled, be delivered up, to be removed to the State having jurisdiction of the crime.

No person held to service or labor in one State, under the laws thereof, escaping into another, shall, in consequence of any law or regulation therein, be discharged from such service or labor, but shall be delivered up on claim of the party to whom such service or labor may be due.

Section 3. New States may be admitted by the Congress into this Union; but no new State shall be formed or erected within the jurisdiction of any other State; nor any State be formed by the junction of two or more States, or parts of States, without the consent of the legislatures of the States concerned as well as of the Congress.

The Congress shall have power to dispose of and make all needful rules and regulations respecting the territory or other property belonging to the United States; and nothing in this Constitution shall be so construed as to prejudice any claims of the United States, or of any particular State.

Section 4. The United States shall guarantee to every State in this Union a republican form of government, and shall protect each of them against invasion; and on application of the legislature, or of the executive (when the legislature cannot be convened), against domestic violence.

Article V

The Congress, whenever two-thirds of both houses shall deem it necessary, shall propose amendments to this Constitution, or, on the application of the legislatures of two-thirds of the several States, shall call a convention for proposing amendments, which, in either case, shall be valid to all intents and purposes, as part of this Constitution, when ratified by the legislatures of three-fourths of the several States, or by conventions in three-fourths thereof, as the one or the other mode of ratification may be proposed by the Congress; provided *that no amendments which may be made prior to the year one thousand eight hundred and eight shall in any manner affect the first and fourth clauses in the ninth section of the first article;* and that no State, without its consent, shall be deprived of its equal suffrage in the Senate.

Article VI

All debts contracted and engagements entered into, before the adoption of this Constitution, shall be as valid against the United States under this Constitution, as under the Confederation.

This Constitution, and the laws of the United States which shall be made in pursuance thereof; and all treaties made, or which shall be made, under the authority of the United States, shall be the supreme law of the land; and the judges in every State shall be bound thereby, anything in the Constitution or laws of any State to the contrary notwithstanding.

The Senators and Representatives before mentioned, and the members of the several State legislatures, and all executive and judicial officers, both of the United States and of the several States, shall be bound by oath or affirmation to support this Constitution; but no religious test shall ever be required as a qualification to any office or public trust under the United States.

Article VII

The ratification of the conventions of nine States shall be sufficient for the establishment of this Constitution between the States so ratifying the same.

Done in Convention by the unanimous consent of the States present, the seventeenth day of September in the year of our Lord one thousand seven hundred and eighty-seven and of the Independence of the United States of America the twelfth. In witness whereof we have hereunto subscribed our names.

[Signed by]
Gº WASHINGTON
Presidt and Deputy from Virginia
[*and thirty-eight others*]

AMENDMENTS TO THE CONSTITUTION

Amendment I*

Congress shall make no law respecting an establishment of religion, or prohibiting the free exercise thereof; or abridging the freedom of speech, or of the press; or the right of the people peaceably to assemble, and to petition the government for a redress of grievances.

Amendment II

A well-regulated militia being necessary to the security of a free State, the right of the people to keep and bear arms shall not be infringed.

Amendment III

No soldier shall, in time of peace, be quartered in any house without the consent of the owner, nor in time of war, but in a manner to be prescribed by law.

Amendment IV

The right of the people to be secure in their persons, houses, papers, and effects, against unreasonable searches and seizures, shall not be violated, and no warrants shall issue but upon probable cause, supported by oath or affirmation, and particularly describing the place to be searched, and the persons or things to be seized.

*The first ten amendments (Bill of Rights) were adopted in 1791.

Amendment V

No person shall be held to answer for a capital, or otherwise infamous crime, unless on a presentment or indictment of a grand jury, except in cases arising in the land or naval forces, or in the militia, when in actual service in time of war or public danger; nor shall any person be subject for the same offense to be twice put in jeopardy of life or limb; nor shall be compelled in any criminal case to be a witness against himself, nor be deprived of life, liberty, or property, without due process of law; nor shall private property be taken for public use without just compensation.

Amendment VI

In all criminal prosecutions, the accused shall enjoy the right to a speedy and public trial, by an impartial jury of the State and district wherein the crime shall have been committed, which district shall have been previously ascertained by law, and to be informed of the nature and cause of the accusation; to be confronted with the witnesses against him; to have compulsory process for obtaining witnesses in his favor, and to have the assistance of counsel for his defense.

Amendment VII

In suits at common law, where the value in controversy shall exceed twenty dollars, the right of trial by jury shall be preserved, and no fact tried by a jury shall be otherwise reexamined in any court of the United States, than according to the rules of the common law.

Amendment VIII

Excessive bail shall not be required, nor excessive fines imposed, nor cruel and unusual punishments inflicted.

Amendment IX

The enumeration in the Constitution, of certain rights, shall not be construed to deny or disparage others retained by the people.

Amendment X

The powers not delegated to the United States by the Constitution, nor prohibited by it to the States, are reserved to the States respectively, or to the people.

Amendment XI
[Adopted 1798]

The judicial power of the United States shall not be construed to extend to any suit in law or equity, commenced or prosecuted against one of the United States by citizens of another State, or by citizens or subjects of any foreign state.

Amendment XII
[Adopted 1804]

The electors shall meet in their respective States, and vote by ballot for President and Vice President, one of whom, at least, shall not be an inhabitant of the same State with themselves; they shall name in their ballots the person voted for as President, and in distinct ballots the person voted for as Vice President, and they shall make distinct lists of all persons voted for as President, and of all persons voted for as Vice President, and of the number of votes for each, which lists they shall sign and certify, and transmit sealed to the seat of government of the United States, directed to the President of the Senate;—the President of the Senate shall, in the presence of the Senate and House of Representatives, open all the certificates and the votes shall then be counted;—the person having the greatest number of votes for President shall be the President, if such number be a majority of the whole number of electors appointed; and if no person have such majority, then from the persons having the highest numbers not exceeding three on the list of those voted for as President, the House of Representatives shall choose immediately, by ballot, the President. But in choosing the President, the votes shall be taken by States, the representation from each State having one vote; a quorum for this purpose shall consist of a member or members from two-thirds of the States, and a majority of all the States shall be necessary to a choice. And if the House of Representatives shall not choose a President whenever the right of choice shall devolve upon them, before *the fourth day of March* next following, then the Vice President shall act as President, as in the case of the death or other constitutional disability of the President.

The person having the greatest number of votes as Vice President shall be the Vice President, if such a number be a majority of the whole number of electors appointed; and if no person have a majority, then from the two highest numbers on the list the Senate shall choose the Vice President; a quorum for the purpose shall consist of two-thirds of the whole number of Senators, and a majority of the whole number shall be necessary to a choice. But no person constitutionally ineligible to the office of President shall be eligible to that of Vice President of the United States.

Amendment XIII
[Adopted 1865]

Section 1.   Neither slavery nor involuntary servitude, except as a punishment for crime whereof the party shall have been duly convicted, shall exist within the United States, or any place subject to their jurisdiction.

Section 2.   Congress shall have power to enforce this article by appropriate legislation.

Amendment XIV
[Adopted 1868]

Section 1.   All persons born or naturalized in the United States, and subject to the jurisdiction thereof, are citizens of the United States and of the State wherein they reside. No State shall make or enforce any law which shall abridge the privileges or immunities of citizens of the United States; nor shall any State deprive any person of life, liberty, or property, without due process of law; nor deny to any person within its jurisdiction the equal protection of the laws.

Section 2.   Representatives shall be apportioned among the several States according to their respective numbers, counting the whole number of persons in each State, excluding Indians not taxed. But when the right to vote at any election for the choice of Electors for President and Vice President of the United States, Representatives in Congress, the executive and judicial officers of a State, or the members of the legislature thereof, is denied to any of the male inhabitants of such State, being twenty-one years of age and citizens of the United States, or in any way abridged, except for participation in rebellion, or other crime, the basis of representation therein shall be reduced in the proportion which the number of such male citizens shall bear to the whole number of male citizens twenty-one years of age in such State.

Section 3.   No person shall be a Senator or Representative in Congress or Elector of President and Vice President, or hold any office, civil or military, under the United States, or under any State, who, having previously taken an oath, as a member of Congress, or as an officer of the United States, or as a member of any State legislature, or as an executive or judicial officer of any State, to support the Constitution of the United States, shall have engaged in insurrection or rebellion against the same, or given aid and comfort to the enemies thereof. Congress may, by a vote of two-thirds of each house, remove such disability.

Section 4.   The validity of the public debt of the United States, authorized by law, including debts incurred for payment of pensions and bounties for services in suppressing insurrection or rebellion, shall not be questioned. But neither the United States nor any State shall assume or pay any debt or obligation incurred in aid of insurrection or rebellion against the United States, or any claim for the loss or emancipation of any slave; but all such debts, obligations, and claims shall be held illegal and void.

Section 5.   The Congress shall have the power to enforce, by appropriate legislation, the provisions of this article.

Amendment XV
[Adopted 1870]

Section 1.   The right of citizens of the United States to vote shall not be denied or abridged by the United States or by any State on account of race, color, or previous condition of servitude.

Section 2.   The Congress shall have power to enforce this article by appropriate legislation.

Amendment XVI
[Adopted 1913]

The Congress shall have power to lay and collect taxes on incomes, from whatever source derived, without apportionment among the several States, and without regard to any census or enumeration.

Amendment XVII
[Adopted 1913]

Section 1.   The Senate of the United States shall be composed of two Senators from each State, elected by the people thereof, for six years; and each Senator shall have one vote. The electors in each State shall have the qualifications requisite for electors of [voters for] the most numerous branch of the State legislatures.

Section 2.   When vacancies happen in the representation of any State in the Senate, the executive authority of such State shall issue writs of election to fill such vacancies: Provided, that the Legislature of any State may empower the executive thereof to make temporary appointments until the people fill the vacancies by election as the Legislature may direct.

Section 3. This amendment shall not be so construed as to affect the election or term of any Senator chosen before it becomes valid as part of the Constitution.

Amendment XVIII
[Adopted 1919; repealed 1933]

Section 1. *After one year from the ratification of this article the manufacture, sale, or transportation of intoxicating liquors within, the importation thereof into, or the exportation thereof from the United States and all territory subject to the jurisdiction thereof, for beverage purposes, is hereby prohibited.*

Section 2. *The Congress and the several States shall have concurrent power to enforce this article by appropriate legislation.*

Section 3. *This article shall be inoperative unless it shall have been ratified as an amendment to the Constitution by the legislatures of the several States, as provided by the Constitution, within seven years from the date of the submission thereof to the States by the Congress.*

Amendment XIX
[Adopted 1920]

Section 1. The right of citizens of the United States to vote shall not be denied or abridged by the United States or by any State on account of sex.

Section 2. The Congress shall have the power to enforce this article by appropriate legislation.

Amendment XX
[Adopted 1933]

Section 1. The terms of the President and Vice President shall end at noon on the 20th day of January, and the terms of Senators and Representatives at noon on the 3d day of January, of the years in which such terms would have ended if this article had not been ratified; and the terms of their successors shall then begin.

Section 2. The Congress shall assemble at least once in every year, and such meeting shall begin at noon on the 3d of January, unless they shall by law appoint a different day.

Section 3. If, at the time fixed for the beginning of the term of the President, the President-elect shall have died, the Vice President-elect shall become President. If a President shall not have been chosen before the time fixed for the beginning of his term, or if the President-elect shall have failed to qualify, then the Vice President-elect shall act as President until a President shall have qualified; and the Congress may by law provide for the case wherein neither a President-elect nor a Vice President-elect shall have qualified, declaring who shall then act as President, or the manner in which one who is to act shall be selected, and such persons shall act accordingly until a President or Vice President shall have qualified.

Section 4. The Congress may by law provide for the case of the death of any of the persons from whom the House of Representatives may choose a President whenever the right of choice shall have devolved upon them, and for the case of the death of any of the persons from whom the Senate may choose a Vice President whenever the right of choice shall have devolved upon them.

Section 5. Sections 1 and 2 shall take effect on the 15th day of October following the ratification of this article.

Section 6. This article shall be inoperative unless it shall have been ratified as an amendment to the Constitution by the Legislatures of three-fourths of the several States within seven years from the date of its submission.

Amendment XXI
[Adopted 1933]

Section 1. The eighteenth article of amendment to the Constitution of the United States is hereby repealed.

Section 2. The transportation or importation into any State, Territory, or Possession of the United States for delivery or use therein of intoxicating liquors, in violation of the laws thereof, is hereby prohibited.

Section 3. This article shall be inoperative unless it shall have been ratified as an amendment to the Constitution by conventions in the several States, as provided in the Constitution, within seven years from the date of submission thereof to the States by the Congress.

Amendment XXII
[Adopted 1951]

Section 1. No person shall be elected to the office of President more than twice, and no person who has held the office of President, or acted as President, for more than two years of a term to which some other person was elected President shall be elected to the office of President more than once. But this article shall not apply to any person holding the office of President when this article was proposed by the Congress, and shall not prevent any person who may be holding the office of President, or acting as President, during the term within which this article becomes operative from holding the office of President or acting as President during the remainder of such term.

Section 2.   This article shall be inoperative unless it shall have been ratified as an amendment to the Constitution by the legislatures of three-fourths of the several States within seven years from the date of its submission to the States by the Congress.

Amendment XXIII
[Adopted 1961]

Section 1.   The District constituting the seat of Government of the United States shall appoint in such manner as the Congress may direct:

A number of electors of President and Vice President equal to the whole number of Senators and Representatives in Congress to which the District would be entitled if it were a State, but in no event more than the least populous State; they shall be in addition to those appointed by the States, but they shall be considered for the purposes of the election of President and Vice President, to be electors appointed by a State; and they shall meet in the District and perform such duties as provided by the twelfth article of amendment.

Section 2.   The Congress shall have the power to enforce this article by appropriate legislation.

Amendment XXIV
[Adopted 1964]

Section 1.   The right of citizens of the United States to vote in any primary or other election for President or Vice President, for electors for President or Vice President, or for Senator or Representative in Congress, shall not be denied or abridged by the United States or any State by reason of failure to pay any poll tax or other tax.

Section 2.   The Congress shall have the power to enforce this article by appropriate legislation.

Amendment XXV
[Adopted 1967]

Section 1.   In case of the removal of the President from office or of his death or resignation, the Vice President shall become President.

Section 2.   Whenever there is a vacancy in the office of the Vice President, the President shall nominate a Vice President who shall take office upon confirmation by a majority vote of both Houses of Congress.

Section 3.   Whenever the President transmits to the President pro tempore of the Senate and the Speaker of the House of Representatives his written declaration that he is unable to discharge the powers and duties of his office, and until he transmits to them a written declaration to the contrary, such powers and duties shall be discharged by the Vice President as Acting President.

Section 4.   Whenever the Vice President and a majority of either the principal officers of the executive departments or of such other body as Congress may by law provide, transmit to the President pro tempore of the Senate and the Speaker of the House of Representatives their written declaration that the President is unable to discharge the powers and duties of his office, the Vice President shall immediately assume the powers and duties of the office as Acting President.

Thereafter, when the President transmits to the President pro tempore of the Senate and the Speaker of the House of Representatives his written declaration that no inability exists, he shall resume the powers and duties of his office unless the Vice President and a majority of either the principal officers of the executive department[s] or of such other body as Congress may by law provide, transmit within four days to the President pro tempore of the Senate and the Speaker of the House of Representatives their written declaration that the President is unable to discharge the powers and duties of his office. Thereupon Congress shall decide the issue, assembling within forty-eight hours for that purpose if not in session. If the Congress, within twenty-one days after receipt of the latter written declaration, or, if Congress is not in session, within twenty-one days after Congress is required to assemble, determines by two-thirds vote of both Houses that the President is unable to discharge the powers and duties of his office, the Vice President shall continue to discharge the same as Acting President; otherwise, the President shall resume the powers and duties of his office.

Amendment XXVI
[Adopted 1971]

Section 1.   The right of citizens of the United States, who are eighteen years of age or older, to vote shall not be denied or abridged by the United States or by any State on account of age.

Section 2.   The Congress shall have power to enforce this article by appropriate legislation.

Amendment XXVII*
[Adopted 1992]

No law, varying the compensation for services of the Senators and Representatives, shall take effect, until an election of Representatives shall have intervened.

---

*Originally proposed in 1789 by James Madison, this amendment failed to win ratification along with the other parts of what became the Bill of Rights. However, the proposed amendment contained no deadline for ratification, and over the years other state legislatures voted to add it to the Constitution; many such ratifications occurred during the 1980s and early 1990s as public frustration with Congress's performance mounted. In May 1992 the Archivist of the United States certified that, with the Michigan legislature's ratification, the article had been approved by three-fourths of the states and thus automatically became part of the Constitution.

The American Land

Admission of States into the Union

State	Date of Admission	State	Date of Admission
1. Delaware	December 7, 1787	26. Michigan	January 26, 1837
2. Pennsylvania	December 12, 1787	27. Florida	March 3, 1845
3. New Jersey	December 18, 1787	28. Texas	December 29, 1845
4. Georgia	January 2, 1788	29. Iowa	December 28, 1846
5. Connecticut	January 9, 1788	30. Wisconsin	May 29, 1848
6. Massachusetts	February 6, 1788	31. California	September 9, 1850
7. Maryland	April 28, 1788	32. Minnesota	May 11, 1858
8. South Carolina	May 23, 1788	33. Oregon	February 14, 1859
9. New Hampshire	June 21, 1788	34. Kansas	January 29, 1861
10. Virginia	June 25, 1788	35. West Virginia	June 20, 1863
11. New York	July 26, 1788	36. Nevada	October 31, 1864
12. North Carolina	November 21, 1789	37. Nebraska	March 1, 1867
13. Rhode Island	May 29, 1790	38. Colorado	August 1, 1876
14. Vermont	March 4, 1791	39. North Dakota	November 2, 1889
15. Kentucky	June 1, 1792	40. South Dakota	November 2, 1889
16. Tennessee	June 1, 1796	41. Montana	November 8, 1889
17. Ohio	March 1, 1803	42. Washington	November 11, 1889
18. Louisiana	April 30, 1812	43. Idaho	July 3, 1890
19. Indiana	December 11, 1816	44. Wyoming	July 10, 1890
20. Mississippi	December 10, 1817	45. Utah	January 4, 1896
21. Illinois	December 3, 1818	46. Oklahoma	November 16, 1907
22. Alabama	December 14, 1819	47. New Mexico	January 6, 1912
23. Maine	March 15, 1820	48. Arizona	February 14, 1912
24. Missouri	August 10, 1821	49. Alaska	January 3, 1959
25. Arkansas	June 15, 1836	50. Hawaii	August 21, 1959

Territorial Expansion

Territory	Date Acquired	Square Miles	How Acquired
Original states and territories	1783	888,685	Treaty of Paris
Louisiana Purchase	1803	827,192	Purchased from France
Florida	1819	72,003	Adams-Onís Treaty
Texas	1845	390,143	Annexation of independent country
Oregon	1846	285,580	Oregon Boundary Treaty
Mexican cession	1848	529,017	Treaty of Guadalupe Hidalgo
Gadsden Purchase	1853	29,640	Purchased from Mexico
Midway Islands	1867	2	Annexation of uninhabited islands
Alaska	1867	589,757	Purchased from Russia
Hawaii	1898	6,450	Annexation of independent country
Wake Island	1898	3	Annexation of uninhabited island
Puerto Rico	1899	3,435	Treaty of Paris
Guam	1899	212	Treaty of Paris
The Philippines	1899–1946	115,600	Treaty of Paris; granted independence
American Samoa	1900	76	Treaty with Germany and Great Britain
Panama Canal Zone	1904–1978	553	Hay-Bunau-Varilla Treaty
U.S. Virgin Islands	1917	133	Purchased from Denmark
Trust Territory of the Pacific Islands*	1947	717	United Nations Trusteeship

*A number of these islands have been granted independence: Federated States of Micronesia, 1990; Marshall Islands, 1991; Palau, 1994.

The American People

Population, Percentage Change, and Racial Composition for the United States, 1790–2004

| Census | Population of United States | Increase over Preceding Census | | Racial Composition, Percent Distribution* | | | |
		Number	Percentage	White	Black	Latino	Asian
1790	3,929,214			80.7	19.3	NA	NA
1800	5,308,483	1,379,269	35.1	81.1	18.9	NA	NA
1810	7,239,881	1,931,398	36.4	81.0	19.0	NA	NA
1820	9,638,453	2,398,572	33.1	81.6	18.4	NA	NA
1830	12,866,020	3,227,567	33.5	81.9	18.1	NA	NA
1840	17,069,453	4,203,433	32.7	83.2	16.8	NA	NA
1850	23,191,876	6,122,423	35.9	84.3	15.7	NA	NA
1860	31,433,321	8,251,445	35.6	85.6	14.1	NA	NA
1870	39,818,449	8,375,128	26.6	86.2	13.5	NA	NA
1880	50,155,783	10,337,334	26.0	86.5	13.1	NA	NA
1890	62,947,714	12,791,931	25.5	87.5	11.9	NA	NA
1900	75,994,575	13,046,861	20.7	87.9	11.6	NA	0.3
1910	91,972,266	15,997,691	21.0	88.9	10.7	NA	0.3
1920	105,710,620	13,738,354	14.9	89.7	9.9	NA	0.3
1930	122,775,046	17,064,426	16.1	89.8	9.7	NA	0.4
1940	131,669,275	8,894,229	7.2	89.8	9.8	NA	0.4
1950	150,697,361	19,028,086	14.5	89.5	10.0	NA	0.4
1960†	179,323,175	28,625,814	19.0	88.6	10.5	NA	0.5
1970	203,235,298	23,912,123	13.3	87.6	11.1	NA	0.7
1980	226,504,825	23,269,527	11.4	85.9	11.8	6.4	1.5
1990	248,709,873	22,205,048	9.8	83.9	12.3	9.0	2.9
2000	281,421,906	32,712,033	13.2	82.2	12.2	11.7	3.8
2004	293,655,400	12,233,494	4.3	80.4	12.8	14.1	4.2

*Not every racial group included (e.g., no Native Americans). Data for 1980, 1990, 2000, and 2004 add up to more than 100% because those who identify themselves as "Latino" may be of any race.
†First year for which figures include Alaska and Hawaii.

Source: Census Bureau, *Historical Statistics of the United States,* updated by relevant *Statistical Abstract of the United States* and http://factfinder.census.gov.

Population Density and Distribution, 1790–2000

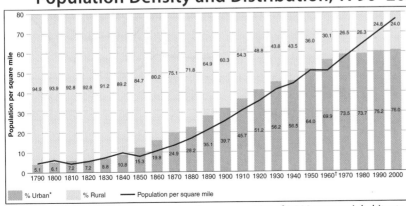

*The Bureau of the Census defines "urban" as communities of 2,500 or more inhabitants.
†First year for which figures include Alaska and Hawaii.
Source: Census Bureau, *Historical Statistics of the United States,* updated by relevant *Statistical Abstract of the United States.*

Changing Characteristics of the U.S. Population

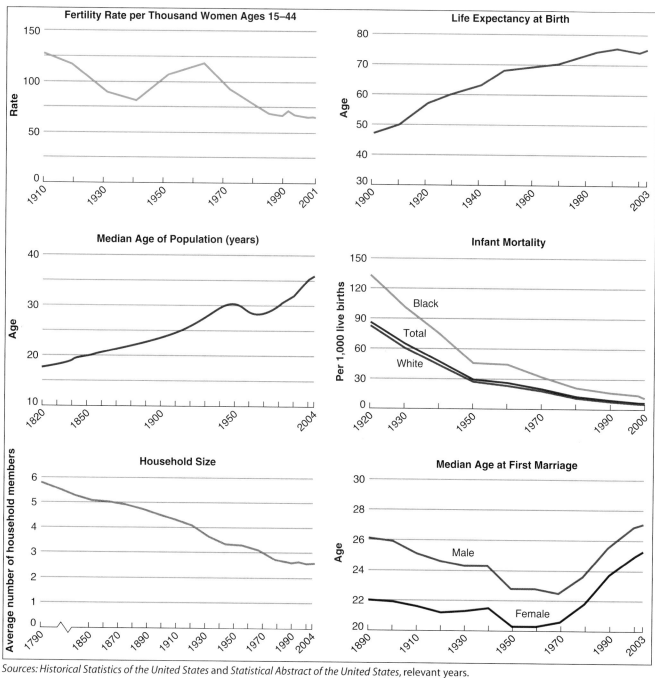

Sources: *Historical Statistics of the United States* and *Statistical Abstract of the United States*, relevant years.

Immigrants to the United States

Immigration Totals by Decade			
Years	*Number*	*Years*	*Number*
1820–1830	151,824	1911–1920	5,735,811
1831–1840	599,125	1921–1930	4,107,209
1841–1850	1,713,251	1931–1940	528,431
1851–1860	2,598,214	1941–1950	1,035,039
1861–1870	2,314,824	1951–1960	2,515,479
1871–1880	2,812,191	1961–1970	3,321,677
1881–1890	5,246,613	1971–1980	4,493,314
1891–1900	3,687,546	1981–1990	7,338,062
1901–1910	8,795,386	1991–2000	9,095,417
		2001-2004	3,780,019

Major Sources of Immigration, 1820–2000

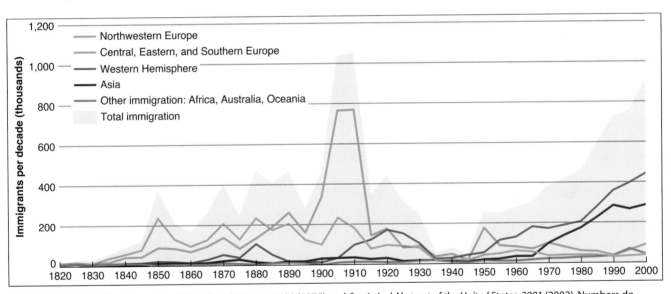

Sources: Historical Statistics of the U.S., Colonial Times to 1970 (1975) and *Statistical Abstract of the United States, 2001* (2002). Numbers do not include undocumented immigrants.

The American Worker

Year	Total Number of Workers	Males as Percent of Total Workers	Females as Percent of Total Workers	Married Women as Percent of Female Workers	Female Workers as Percent of Female Population	Percent of Labor Force Unemployed
1870	12,506,000	85	15	NA	NA	NA
1880	17,392,000	85	15	NA	NA	NA
1890	23,318,000	83	17	14	19	4 (1894 = 18)
1900	29,073,000	82	18	15	21	5
1910	38,167,000	79	21	25	25	6
1920	41,614,000	79	21	23	24	5 (1921 = 12)
1930	48,830,000	78	22	29	25	9 (1933 = 25)
1940	53,011,000	76	24	36	27	15 (1944 = 1)
1950	62,208,000	72	28	52	31	5.3
1960	69,628,000	67	33	55	38	5.5
1970	82,771,000	62	38	59	43	4.9
1980	106,940,000	58	42	55	52	7.1
1990	125,840,000	55	45	54	58	5.6
2000	135,208,000	53	47	55	60	4.0
2004	139,252,000	53.5	46.5	58	59	5.5

NA = Not Available

Source: U. S Census Bureau; Statistical Abstract of the United States (2006).

The American Government

Presidential Elections, 1789–2004

Year	States in the Union	Candidates	Parties	Electoral Vote	Popular Vote	Percentage of Popular Vote
1789	11	GEORGE WASHINGTON	No party designations	69		
		John Adams		34		
		Minor candidates		35		
1792	15	GEORGE WASHINGTON	No party designations	132		
		John Adams		77		
		George Clinton		50		
		Minor candidates		5		
1796	16	JOHN ADAMS	Federalist	71		
		Thomas Jefferson	Democratic-Republican	68		
		Thomas Pinckney	Federalist	59		
		Aaron Burr	Democratic-Republican	30		
		Minor candidates		48		
1800	16	THOMAS JEFFERSON	Democratic-Republican	73		
		Aaron Burr	Democratic-Republican	73		
		John Adams	Federalist	65		
		Charles C. Pinckney	Federalist	64		
		John Jay	Federalist	1		
1804	17	THOMAS JEFFERSON	Democratic-Republican	162		
		Charles C. Pinckney	Federalist	14		
1808	17	JAMES MADISON	Democratic-Republican	122		
		Charles C. Pinckney	Federalist	47		
		George Clinton	Democratic-Republican	6		
1812	18	JAMES MADISON	Democratic-Republican	128		
		DeWitt Clinton	Federalist	89		
1816	19	JAMES MONROE	Democratic-Republican	183		
		Rufus King	Federalist	34		
1820	24	JAMES MONROE	Democratic-Republican	231		
		John Quincy Adams	Independent Republican	1		
1824	24	JOHN QUINCY ADAMS	Democratic-Republican	84	108,740	30.5
		Andrew Jackson	Democratic-Republican	99	153,544	43.1
		William H. Crawford	Democratic-Republican	41	46,618	13.1
		Henry Clay	Democratic-Republican	37	47,136	13.2
1828	24	ANDREW JACKSON	Democratic	178	642,553	56.0
		John Quincy Adams	National Republican	83	500,897	44.0
1832	24	ANDREW JACKSON	Democratic	219	687,502	55.0
		Henry Clay	National Republican	49	530,189	42.4
		William Wirt	Anti-Masonic	7 }	33,108	2.6
		John Floyd	National Republican	11 }		

Because candidates receiving less than 1 percent of the popular vote are omitted, the percentage of popular vote may not total 100 percent. Before the Twelfth Amendment was passed in 1804, the Electoral College voted for two presidential candidates; the runner-up became vice president.

Presidential Elections, 1789–2004 (continued)

Year	States in the Union	Candidates	Parties	Electoral Vote	Popular Vote	Percentage of Popular Vote
1836	26	MARTIN VAN BUREN	Democratic	170	765,483	50.9
		William H. Harrison	Whig	73		
		Hugh L. White	Whig	26		
		Daniel Webster	Whig	14	739,795	49.1
		W. P. Mangum	Whig	11		
1840	26	WILLIAM H. HARRISON	Whig	234	1,274,624	53.1
		Martin Van Buren	Democratic	60	1,127,781	46.9
1844	26	JAMES K. POLK	Democratic	170	1,338,464	49.6
		Henry Clay	Whig	105	1,300,097	48.1
		James G. Birney	Liberty	0	62,300	2.3
1848	30	ZACHARY TAYLOR	Whig	163	1,360,967	47.4
		Lewis Cass	Democratic	127	1,222,342	42.5
		Martin Van Buren	Free Soil	0	291,263	10.1
1852	31	FRANKLIN PIERCE	Democratic	254	1,601,117	50.9
		Winfield Scott	Whig	42	1,385,453	44.1
		John P. Hale	Free Soil	0	155,825	5.0
1856	31	JAMES BUCHANAN	Democratic	174	1,832,955	45.3
		John C. Frémont	Republican	114	1,339,932	33.1
		Millard Fillmore	American	8	871,731	21.6
1860	33	ABRAHAM LINCOLN	Republican	180	1,865,593	39.8
		Stephen A. Douglas	Democratic	12	1,382,713	29.5
		John C. Breckinridge	Democratic	72	848,356	18.1
		John Bell	Constitutional Union	39	592,906	12.6
1864	36	ABRAHAM LINCOLN	Republican	212	2,206,938	55.0
		George B. McClellan	Democratic	21	1,803,787	45.0
1868	37	ULYSSES S. GRANT	Republican	214	3,013,421	52.7
		Horatio Seymour	Democratic	80	2,706,829	47.3
1872	37	ULYSSES S. GRANT	Republican	286	3,596,745	55.6
		Horace Greeley	Democratic	*	2,843,446	43.9
1876	38	RUTHERFORD B. HAYES	Republican	185	4,034,311	48.0
		Samuel J. Tilden	Democratic	184	4,288,546	51.0
		Peter Cooper	Greenback	0	75,973	1.0
1880	38	JAMES A. GARFIELD	Republican	214	4,453,295	48.5
		Winfield S. Hancock	Democratic	155	4,414,082	48.1
		James B. Weaver	Greenback-Labor	0	308,578	3.4
1884	38	GROVER CLEVELAND	Democratic	219	4,879,507	48.5
		James G. Blaine	Republican	182	4,850,293	48.2
		Benjamin F. Butler	Greenback-Labor	0	175,370	1.8
		John P. St. John	Prohibition	0	150,369	1.5
1888	38	BENJAMIN HARRISON	Republican	233	5,477,129	47.9
		Grover Cleveland	Democratic	168	5,537,857	48.6
		Clinton B. Fisk	Prohibition	0	249,506	2.2
		Anson J. Streeter	Union Labor	0	146,935	1.3

*When Greeley died shortly after the election, his supporters divided their votes among the minor candidates.

Because candidates receiving less than 1 percent of the popular vote are omitted, the percentage of popular vote may not total 100 percent.

Presidential Elections, 1789–2004 (continued)

Year	States in the Union	Candidates	Parties	Electoral Vote	Popular Vote	Percentage of Popular Vote
1892	44	GROVER CLEVELAND	Democratic	277	5,555,426	46.1
		Benjamin Harrison	Republican	145	5,182,690	43.0
		James B. Weaver	People's	22	1,029,846	8.5
		John Bidwell	Prohibition	0	264,133	2.2
1896	45	WILLIAM McKINLEY	Republican	271	7,102,246	51.1
		William J. Bryan	Democratic	176	6,492,559	47.7
1900	45	WILLIAM McKINLEY	Republican	292	7,218,491	51.7
		William J. Bryan	Democratic; Populist	155	6,356,734	45.5
		John C. Wooley	Prohibition	0	208,914	1.5
1904	45	THEODORE ROOSEVELT	Republican	336	7,628,461	57.4
		Alton B. Parker	Democratic	140	5,084,223	37.6
		Eugene V. Debs	Socialist	0	402,283	3.0
		Silas C. Swallow	Prohibition	0	258,536	1.9
1908	46	WILLIAM H. TAFT	Republican	321	7,675,320	51.6
		William J. Bryan	Democratic	162	6,412,294	43.1
		Eugene V. Debs	Socialist	0	420,793	2.8
		Eugene W. Chafin	Prohibition	0	253,840	1.7
1912	48	WOODROW WILSON	Democratic	435	6,296,547	41.9
		Theodore Roosevelt	Progressive	88	4,118,571	27.4
		William H. Taft	Republican	8	3,486,720	23.2
		Eugene V. Debs	Socialist	0	900,672	6.0
		Eugene W. Chafin	Prohibition	0	206,275	1.4
1916	48	WOODROW WILSON	Democratic	277	9,127,695	49.4
		Charles E. Hughes	Republican	254	8,533,507	46.2
		A. L. Benson	Socialist	0	585,113	3.2
		J. Frank Hanly	Prohibition	0	220,506	1.2
1920	48	WARREN G. HARDING	Republican	404	16,143,407	60.4
		James N. Cox	Democratic	127	9,130,328	34.2
		Eugene V. Debs	Socialist	0	919,799	3.4
		P. P. Christensen	Farmer-Labor	0	265,411	1.0
1924	48	CALVIN COOLIDGE	Republican	382	15,718,211	54.0
		John W. Davis	Democratic	136	8,385,283	28.8
		Robert M. La Follette	Progressive	13	4,831,289	16.6
1928	48	HERBERT C. HOOVER	Republican	444	21,391,993	58.2
		Alfred E. Smith	Democratic	87	15,016,169	40.9
1932	48	FRANKLIN D. ROOSEVELT	Democratic	472	22,809,638	57.4
		Herbert C. Hoover	Republican	59	15,758,901	39.7
		Norman Thomas	Socialist	0	881,951	2.2
1936	48	FRANKLIN D. ROOSEVELT	Democratic	523	27,752,869	60.8
		Alfred M. Landon	Republican	8	16,674,665	36.5
		William Lemke	Union	0	882,479	1.9

Because candidates receiving less than 1 percent of the popular vote are omitted, the percentage of popular vote may not total 100 percent.

Presidential Elections, 1789–2004 (continued)

Year	States in the Union	Candidates	Parties	Electoral Vote	Popular Vote	Percentage of Popular Vote
1940	48	FRANKLIN D. ROOSEVELT	Democratic	449	27,307,819	54.8
		Wendell L. Willkie	Republican	82	22,321,018	44.8
1944	48	FRANKLIN D. ROOSEVELT	Democratic	432	25,606,585	53.5
		Thomas E. Dewey	Republican	99	22,014,745	46.0
1948	48	HARRY S TRUMAN	Democratic	303	24,105,812	49.5
		Thomas E. Dewey	Republican	189	21,970,065	45.1
		Strom Thurmond	States' Rights	39	1,169,063	2.4
		Henry A. Wallace	Progressive	0	1,157,172	2.4
1952	48	DWIGHT D. EISENHOWER	Republican	442	33,936,234	55.1
		Adlai E. Stevenson	Democratic	89	27,314,992	44.4
1956	48	DWIGHT D. EISENHOWER	Republican	457	35,590,472	57.6
		Adlai E. Stevenson	Democratic	73	26,022,752	42.1
1960	50	JOHN F. KENNEDY	Democratic	303	34,227,096	49.7
		Richard M. Nixon	Republican	219	34,108,546	49.5
		Harry F. Byrd	Independent	15	502,363	0.7
1964	50	LYNDON B. JOHNSON	Democratic	486	43,126,506	61.1
		Barry M. Goldwater	Republican	52	27,176,799	38.5
1968	50	RICHARD M. NIXON	Republican	301	31,770,237	43.4
		Hubert H. Humphrey	Democratic	191	31,270,533	42.7
		George C. Wallace	American Independent	46	9,906,141	13.5
1972	50	RICHARD M. NIXON	Republican	520	47,169,911	60.7
		George S. McGovern	Democratic	17	29,170,383	37.5
1976	50	JIMMY CARTER	Democratic	297	40,827,394	49.9
		Gerald R. Ford	Republican	240	39,145,977	47.9
1980	50	RONALD W. REAGAN	Republican	489	43,899,248	50.8
		Jimmy Carter	Democratic	49	35,481,435	41.0
		John B. Anderson	Independent	0	5,719,437	6.6
		Ed Clark	Libertarian	0	920,859	1.0
1984	50	RONALD W. REAGAN	Republican	525	54,451,521	58.8
		Walter F. Mondale	Democratic	13	37,565,334	40.5
1988	50	GEORGE H. W. BUSH	Republican	426	47,946,422	54.0
		Michael S. Dukakis	Democratic	112	41,016,429	46.0
1992	50	WILLIAM J. CLINTON	Democratic	370	43,728,275	43.2
		George H. W. Bush	Republican	168	38,167,416	37.7
		H. Ross Perot	Independent	0	19,237,247	19.0
1996	50	WILLIAM J. CLINTON	Democratic	379	47,401,185	49.0
		Robert Dole	Republican	159	39,197,469	41.0
		H. Ross Perot	Independent	0	8,085,295	8.0
2000	50	GEORGE W. BUSH	Republican	271	50,456,169	47.9
		Albert Gore, Jr.	Democratic	267	50,996,116	48.4
		Ralph Nader	Green	0	2,783,728	2.7
2004	50	GEORGE W. BUSH	Republican	286	60,693,281	50.7
		John Kerry	Democratic	252	57,355,978	48.3
		Ralph Nader	Independent	0	405,623	0.3

Because candidates receiving less than 1 percent of the popular vote are omitted, the percentage of popular vote may not total 100 percent.

The American Economy

Key Economic Indicators

Year	Gross National Product (GNP) and Gross Domestic Product (GDP)[a] (in $ billions)	Steel Production (in tons)	Corn Production (millions of bushels)	Automobiles Registered	New Housing Starts	Foreign Trade (in $ millions) Exports	Foreign Trade (in $ millions) Imports
1790	NA	NA	NA	NA	NA	20	23
1800	NA	NA	NA	NA	NA	71	91
1810	NA	NA	NA	NA	NA	67	85
1820	NA	NA	NA	NA	NA	70	74
1830	NA	NA	NA	NA	NA	74	71
1840	NA	NA	NA	NA	NA	132	107
1850	NA	NA	592[d]	NA	NA	152	178
1860	NA	13,000	839[e]	NA	NA	400	362
1870	7.4[b]	77,000	1,125	NA	NA	451	462
1880	11.2[c]	1,397,000	1,707	NA	NA	853	761
1890	13.1	4,779,000	1,650	NA	328,000	910	823
1900	18.7	11,227,000	2,662	8,000	189,000	1,499	930
1910	35.3	28,330,000	2,853	458,300	387,000 (1918 = 118,000)	1,919	1,646
1920	91.5	46,183,000	3,071	8,131,500	247,000 (1925 = 937,000)	8,664	5,784
1930	90.7	44,591,000	2,080	23,034,700	330,000 (1933 = 93,000)	4,013	3,500
1940	100.0	66,983,000	2,457	27,465,800	603,000 (1944 = 142,000)	4,030	7,433
1950	286.5	96,836,000	3,075	40,339,000	1,952,000	9,997	8,954
1960	506.5	99,282,000	4,314	61,682,300	1,365,000	19,659	15,093
1970	1,016.0	131,514,000	4,200	89,279,800	1,434,000	42,681	40,356
1980	2,819.5	111,835,000	6,600	121,601,000	1,292,000	220,626	244,871
1990	5,764.9	98,906,000	7,933	133,700,000	1,193,000	394,030	485,453
2000	9,963.1	112,242,000	9,968	133,600,000[f]	1,569,000	781,918	1,218,022

[a]In December 1991 the Bureau of Economic Analysis of the U.S. government began using gross domestic product rather than gross national product as the primary measure of U.S. production.
[b]Figure is average for 1869–1878.
[c]Figure is average for 1879–1888.
[d]Figure for 1849.
[e]Figure for 1859.
[f]Does not include sports utility vehicles (SUVs) and light trucks.

NA = Not available.

A-23

Federal Budget Outlays and Debt

Year	Defense[a]	Veterans Benefits[a]	Income Security[a]	Social Security[a]	Health and Medicare[a]	Education[a,d]	Net Interest Payments[a]	Federal Debt (dollars)
1790	14.9	4.1[b]	NA	NA	NA	NA	55.0	75,463,000[c]
1800	55.7	0.6	NA	NA	NA	NA	31.3	82,976,000
1810	48.4 (1814:79.7)	1.0	NA	NA	NA	NA	34.9	53,173,000
1820	38.4	17.6	NA	NA	NA	NA	28.1	91,016,000
1830	52.9	9.0	NA	NA	NA	NA	12.6	48,565,000
1840	54.3 (1847:80.7)	10.7	NA	NA	NA	NA	0.7	3,573,000
1850	43.8	4.7	NA	NA	NA	NA	1.0	63,453,000
1860	44.2 (1865:88.9)	1.7	NA	NA	NA	NA	5.0	64,844,000
1870	25.7	9.2	NA	NA	NA	NA	41.7	2,436,453,000
1880	19.3	21.2	NA	NA	NA	NA	35.8	2,090,909,000
1890	20.9 (1899:48.6)	33.6	NA	NA	NA	NA	11.4	1,222,397,000
1900	36.6	27.0	NA	NA	NA	NA	7.7	1,263,417,000
1910	45.1 (1919:59.5)	23.2	NA	NA	NA	NA	3.1	1,146,940,000
1920	37.1	3.4	NA	NA	NA	NA	16.0	24,299,321,000
1930	25.3	6.6	NA	NA	NA	NA	19.9	16,185,310,000
1940	17.5 (1945:89.4)	6.0	16.0	0.3	0.5	20.8	9.4	42,967,531,000
1950	32.2	20.3	9.6	1.8	0.6	0.6	11.3	256,853,000,000
1960	52.2	5.9	8.0	12.6	0.9	1.0	7.5	290,525,000,000
1970	41.8	4.4	8.0	15.5	6.2	4.4	7.3	308,921,000,000
1980	22.7	3.6	14.6	20.1	9.4	5.4	8.9	909,050,000,000
1990	23.9	2.3	11.7	19.8	12.4	3.1	14.7	3,266,073,000,000
2000	16.2	2.6	14.1	22.7	19.9	3.5	12.3	5,629,000,000,000

[a]Figures represent percentage of total federal spending for each category. Not included are transportation, commerce, housing, and various other categories.
[b]1789–1791 figure.
[c]1791 figure.
[d]Includes training, employment, and social services.

NA = Not available.

Credits

Historical Society; *p. 261*, National Canal Museum, Hugh Moore Historical Park and Museums, Inc.; *p. 266*, Jack Naylor Collection; *p. 267*, Wm. B. Becker Collection/American Museum of Photography; *p. 269*, "Portrait of a Black Man" artist unknown, Gift of Edgar William and Bernice Chrysler Garbisch, © 2006 Board of Trustees, National Gallery of Art, Washington, D.C.; *p. 273*, Courtesy Childs Gallery, Boston.

Chapter 10   *p. 278*, Gift of Mrs. Samuel T. Carson photograph © 1991 The Detroit Institute of Arts (detail); *p. 279*, Bridgeman Art Library Ltd. © New-York Historical Society, New York, USA; *p. 283*, New Haven Colony Historical Society; *p. 284*, Memphis Brooks Museum of Art, Memphis, TN, Memphis Park Commission Purchase; *p. 285*, National Portrait Gallery/Art Resource, NY; *p. 287*, © Collection of the New-York Historical Society; *p. 290*, Bridgeman Art Library Ltd.; *p. 291*, Guildhall Library, City of London or Guildhall Art Gallery, City of London; *p. 293*, Library of Congress; *p. 295*, Oberlin College Archives, Oberlin, Ohio; *p. 299*, Library of Congress; *p. 300*, Boston Athenaeum; *p. 304*, Coline Jenkins/Elizabeth Cady Stanton Trust; *p. 305*, Rare Book Department, The Free Library of Philadelphia.

Chapter 11   *p. 310*, William B. Becker Collection/American Museum of Photography; *p. 311*, National Portrait Gallery, Smithsonian Institution, Washington, D.C. (Gift of the Singer Company)/Art Resource, NY; *p. 313*, Library of Congress; *p. 314*, "A History of the Colt Revolver from 1836 to 1940" by Charles T. Haven and Frank A. Belden, Courtesy of the Museum of Connecticut History; *p. 316*, National Museum of American History, Smithsonian Institution, Behring Center; *p. 317*, William B. Becker Collection/American Museum of Photography; *p. 320*, George Eastman House; *p. 323*, Historic Cherry Hill, CH 1963.2193, courtesy Albany Institute of History and Art; *p. 326*, Culver Pictures; *p. 328*, Constance Fuller Threinen; *p. 330*, © Hulton-Deutsch Collection/Corbis; *p. 332*, Detroit Institute of Arts, Founders Society Purchase; *p. 333 (top)*, National Museum of American Art/Art Resource, NY; *p. 333 (bottom)*, National Museum of American Art/Art Resource, NYArt.

Chapter 12   *p. 336*, Library of Congress; *p. 337*, Granger Collection; *p. 341*, Miriam and Ira D. Wallach Division of Art, Prints and Photographs, The New York Public Library, Astor, Lenox and Tilden Foundations; *p. 344*, Missouri Historical Society; *p. 345*, Hunter Museum of Art, Chattanooga, TN, Gift of Mr. & Mrs. Thomas B. Whiteside; *p. 350*, Bridgeman Art Library Ltd.; *p. 352 (top)*, Chicago Historical Society; *p. 352 (bottom)*, Chicago Historical Society; *p. 354*, National Archives of Canada; *p. 355*, © Collection of the New-York Historical Society; *p. 359*, Valentine Museum, Cook Collection; *p. 360*, Greenville County Museum of Art, Greenville, SC Museum purchase with funds from the 1994 Museum Antiques Show and the Arthur and Holly Magill Purchase Fund; *p. 363*, Collection of Old Capitol Museum, Mississippi Department of Archives and History; *p. 364 (left)*, Schomburg Center for Research in Black Culture, New York Public Library; *p. 364 (right)*, Moorland-Spingarn Research Center, Howard University, Washington, D.C.

Chapter 13   *p. 368*, The Hallmark Photographic Collection, Hallmark Cards, Inc. Kansas City, Missouri; *p. 369*, Daughters of the Republic of Texas Library; *p. 373*, The Metropolitan Museum of Art, The Edward W. C. Arnold Collection of New York Prints, Maps and Pictures, Bequest of W. C. Arnold, 1954 #54.90.166; *p. 377*, University of California at Berkeley, Bancroft Library; *p. 379*, Daughters of the Republic of Texas Library, Gift of the Tanaguana Society; *p. 381*, The Corcoran Gallery of Art, Washington, D.C.; *p. 383*, James K. Polk Memorial Association, Columbia, Tennessee; *p. 385*, William B. Becker Collection/American Museum of Photography; *p. 390*, Chicago Historical Society; *p. 393*, Library of Congress.

Chapter 14   *p. 396*, Kansas State Historical Society; *p. 397*, Ohio Historical Society; *p. 402*, Smithsonian Institution, Washington, D.C.; *p. 403*, Library of Congress; *p. 408*, Miriam and Ira D. Wallach Division of Art, Prints and Photographs, The New York Public Library, Astor, Lenox and Tilden Foundations; *p. 410*, Library of Congress; *p. 413 (left)*, National Portrait Gallery, Smithsonian Institution, Washington, D.C.//Art Resource, NY; *p. 413 (right)*, Library of Congress; *p. 415*, Library of Congress; *p. 418*, Amistad Research Center, Tulane University.

Chapter 15   *p. 424*, George Eastman House; *p. 425*, Private Collection; *p. 427*, National Library of Medicine; *p. 430*, Library of Congress; *p. 433*, Library of Congress; *p. 436 (top)*, Antietam National Battlefield, Sharpsburg, MD; *p. 436 (bottom)*, Library of Congress; *p. 438*, Courtesy of Jackson K. Doane; *p. 439*, Library of Congress; *p. 442*, Library of Congress; *p. 445 (top)*, Western Reserve Historical Society; *p. 445 (bottom)*, South Carolina Historical Society; *p. 447*, Library of Congress; *p. 448*, Museum of Fine Arts, Boston, Gift of Maxim Karolik for the M. and M. Karolik Collection of American watercolors and Drawings, 1800-1875, 61.362. Photograph © 2007 Museum of Fine Arts, Boston; *p. 450*, Museum of the Confederacy; *p. 452*, Library of Congress; *p. 453 (top)*, US Army Military History Institute; *p. 452 (bottom)*, Collection of the J. Paul Getty Museum; *p. 455*, Library of Congress; *p. 459*, Amon Carter Museum of Western Art; *p. 460 (top)*, Library of Congress; *p. 460 (bottom)*, National Archives.

Chapter 16   *p. 466*, Civil War Photographic Album, Louisiana and Lower Mississippi Valley Collection, LSU Libraries, Louisiana State University; *p.467*, Library of Congress; *p. 469 (left)*, Library of Congress; *p. 469 (right)*, Library of Congress; *p. 472*, *Harper's Weekly*, 1866; *p. 477*, Schlesinger Library; *p. 479*, Museum of the Confederacy; *p. 480*, Private Collection; *p. 482*, Old Court House Museum, Vicksburg, Mississippi; *p. 483*, William Gladstone; *p. 487*, © Collection of the New York Historical Society; *p. 488 (left)*, Brown Brothers; *p. 488 (right)*, *Harper's Weekly*, 1871; *p. 490*, National Museum of American History, Smithsonian Institution; *p. 491*, National Museum of American History, Smithsonian Institution; *p. 495 (top)*, *Harper's Weekly*, October 24, 1874; *p. 495 (bottom left)*, Library of Congress; *p. 495 (bottom right)*, Kansas State Historical Society.

Text Credits

Chapter 3   *p. 58*, From *The Chesapeake in the Seventeenth Century: Essays on Anglo-American Society*, edited by Thad W. Tate and David L. Ammerman. Copyright © 1979 by the University of North Carolina Press. Used by permission of the publisher. *p. 65*, Summer Chilton Powell, Map, "Land Divisions in Sudbury, MA 1639-1656," from *Puritan Village: The Formation of a New England Town*. Copyright © 1970 by Summer Chilton Powell and reprinted with permission of Wesleyan University Press. www.wesleyan.edu/wespress. *p. 67*, Frederick Merk, *History of the Westward Movement*. Copyright © 1979 by Lois Bannister Merk. Used by permission of Alfred A. Knopf, a division of Random House, Inc. *p. 73*, The Geography of Witchcraft, reprinted by permission of the publisher from *Salem Possessed: The Social Origins of Witchcraft* by Paul Boyer and Stephen Nissenbaum, pg. 34, Cambridge, Mass.: Harvard University Press, Copyright © 1974 by the President and Fellows of Harvard College.

Chapter 4   *p. 102*, From Gary B. Nash, *The Urban Crucible: Social Change, Political Consciousness, and the Origins of the American Revolution*. Copyright © 1978 by the President and Fellows of Harvard College. Reprinted with permission.

Chapter 12   *p. 339*, Reprinted with permission of the McGraw-Hill Companies from *Ordeal By Fire: The Civil War And Reconstruction*, Second Edition, by James M. McPherson. Copyright © 1992 by The McGraw-Hill Companies.

Index

352 (illus.); Pueblo Indians and, 83; punishment and, 356; quilt of, 363 (illus.); racism and, 34–35; representation in Congress and, 184–185, 341; Republican party and, 407; during Revolution, 168; rights of free expression and, 303; on Sea Islands, 445 (illus.); in 1776, 172–173; skills and, 356; small slaveholders and, 346–347; society after abolition, 478; in South, 255; South Carolina and, 285; southern conflicts over, 348–349; southern industrialization and, 342; southern proslavery argument and, 349–352; spread of, 73–76; state authority over, 184; state rights to accept or reject, 399; sugar industry and, 38–39; Taylor and, 398–399; in territories, 392–393, 411; in Texas, 378; Thirteenth Amendment and, 457, 470; three-fifths clause and, 185, 240; Truth, Sojourner, and, 403 (illus.); *Uncle Tom's Cabin* and, 402–403; unrest among, 146; uprising in Saint Domingue, 203, 225–226; value of, 344–345; Virginia emancipation legislation and, 349; women and abolition of, 456. *See also* Abolition and abolitionism; Africa; African-Americans; Africans; Antislavery movement; Christianity; Emancipation of slaves; Emancipation Proclamation (1863); Fugitive Slave Act (1850); Fugitive Slave Law (1793); Revolts and rebellions; Thirteenth Amendment

Slave states, 243–244; in Civil War, 431; election of 1856 in, 410; statehood and, 398–401

Slave trade, 33, 34; banning of external, 418; Columbus and, 37; Franklin on, 98; internal, 341–342, 342 (map); Middle Passage and, 98; outlawing of, 216, 301; plantation economy and, 344; Portuguese, 34–35; slave ship and, 100 (illus.); sugar industry and, 39

Sleeping sickness, 26

Slidell, John, 389, 440

Sloat, John D., 390

Smallpox, 40, 41; British-triggered epidemic of, 127; Indians and, 76

Smalls, Robert, 444

Smith, Elias, 271

Smith, Ernest, 6 (illus.)

Smith, Jedediah, 252

Smith, John, 47, 48, 49; on Indians, 19

Smith, Joseph, 296–297, 370

Smith, Margaret Bayard, 221–222, 240 (illus.)

Smith, Melania, 296

Smith, Samuel Harrison, 221

Smith, Venture, 98

Smuggling, 131, 145; after Revolution, 178

Social class, *see* Classes

Social contract, 136

Social mobility, *see* Mobility (social)

Social reform, *see* Reform

Society, 17–19, 18–19, 20; Archaic, 6–7; Aztec, 9; changes in, 210–219; Chesapeake, 54–61; during Civil War, 448–456; colonial, 53–85; conservatism in, 279; in early 1800s, 249–276; in Eastern Woodlands, 13–15; equality and inequality in, 267–271; European, 27–33; immigrant, 372; Indian, 4; in Mesoamerica and South America, 7–9; in New England, 64–66; nonfarming, 15–17; Paleo-Indian, 6; Puritanism and, 33; racial mixing in, 41; reforms in, 298–306; Revolution and, 170–175; revolution in relationships, 271–275; of southern whites, 343–353; in Southwest, 12–13; in West, 251–252. *See also* Cultural diversity; Culture(s); Lifestyle

Society for the Encouragement of Useful Manufactures, 212

Society of Friends, *see* Quakers

Society of Jesus, *see* Jesuits

Society of the Supporters of the Bill of Rights (England), 142

Soft money (paper), 288

Soil: deforestation and, 101–102; fertility improvements for, 313

Soldiers: African-American, 157, 441, 442–443, 443–444; Massacre and, 142; British, as colonists, 159; British in North America, 160; in Civil War, 424 (illus.), 428, 433, 437–439, 438 (illus.); colonial in Seven Years' War, 125; egalitarianism and, 171; military bounties for, 252; quartering of, 137; in Revolution, 161; slaves as, 444. *See also* Armed forces; Military

Somers, Richard, 224 (illus.)

Somerset, James, 146

Songhai empire, 26

"Song of Myself" (Whitman), 329

Sons of Liberty, 134–**135,** 144; nonimportation and, 139; Wilkes and, 141

"Sound money," 492

South: agriculture in, 343; antislavery movement in, 352; Bank of the United States and, 197; blacks and, 481; British expansion in, 108–109; cities in, 103; after Civil War, 466 (illus.); code of honor in, 352–353; Compromise of 1850 and, 400–401; conflicts in society of, 348–353; conflicts over slavery in, 348–349; cotton in, 338–342; crop-lien economy in, 485–487; depression of 1780s and, 182; divisions of, 338; dueling in, 353; education in, 343; election of 1856 in, 410; evangelicals in, 353; fear

of slave insurrection in, 415–416; fears of blacks in, 480–481; freed slaves in, 481–487; French Revolution and, 203; fugitive slaves in, 401; illiteracy in, 484 (illus.); income in, 343; Indians in, 253; industrialization in, 342–343; internal slave trade in, 341–342, 342 (map); Jackson and, 284; Kansas-Nebraska Act and, 404–405; land confiscated during Reconstruction, 473; Missouri as slave state and, 244; North compared with, 342–343; Reconstruction in, 470–471, 475 (map), 477–481; Republican rule in, 479–480, 494 (illus.); Revolution and, 152, 167–168, 169 (map); secession and, 416, 420; sharecropping in, 485–487, 487 (map); slavery and, 98, 173–174, 243, 339 (map), 358, 414–415; tariffs and, 284–286; taxation in, 479; trade in, 178–179; Upper and Lower ties in, 341–342; violence in, 352; Whigs in, 403; white society in, 343–353. *See also* African-Americans; Civil rights; Civil War (U.S.); Confederate States of America; Lower (Deep) South; Reconstruction; Slaves and slavery; Upper South

South Africa: Dutch in, 95

South Alone Should Govern the South, The, 416

South America: cultures of, 7–9; Magellan and, 37; Monroe Doctrine and, 245; revolutions against Spain in, 245; slave rebellions in, 359–360

South Carolina: assembly in, 113; legislature of, 478, 479, 479 (illus.); lifestyle in, 103; Regulators in, 144–145; Republicans in, 478, 479 (illus.); in Revolution, 166, 168; secession and, 420; Sherman in, 458; slaves from, 159–160; tariffs and, 284–286. *See also* Carolina

South Carolina Exposition and Protest (Calhoun), 285, 286

Southeast: Indians in, 181; Spain in, 110

Southern code of honor, 353

Southern Homestead Act (1866), 484

Southwest: agriculture in, 10; cultures of, 12–13; expansion into, 370; Franciscans in, 43, 44; Spain and, 110, 181. *See also* Old Southwest

Southwestern Asia: in 1500, 25 (map)

Sovereignty: Constitution and, 184; Jefferson on state, 209; of states, 178, 243

Spain, 92; during American Revolution, 163, 164–165; American wealth for, 41–42; Armada of, 46; borderlands of, 109–110; borders with, 245; boundary with, 205; Columbus and, 23–24; conquistadors from, 37–40; England and,

The United States of America

Lake Superior
Lake Huron
Lake Michigan
Lake Ontario
Lake Erie

St. Lawrence R.
Connecticut R.
Hudson R.
Delaware R.
Mississippi R.
Cumberland R.
Tennessee R.

MAINE
★ Augusta
• Portland
N.H.
Burlington
• Montpelier
VT.
• Concord
• Manchester
NEW YORK
• Boston
MASS.
Albany
★ Providence
Hartford ★
CONN.
R.I.
• New York
• Trenton
• Philadelphia
Harrisburg ★
NEW JERSEY
PENNSYLVANIA
• Dover
Pittsburgh
DELAWARE
Wheeling
Baltimore
• Annapolis
Washington, D.C.
MARYLAND

WISCONSIN
MICHIGAN
St. Paul
Milwaukee
Madison ★
Lansing
Detroit
Chicago
Cleveland
OHIO
Columbus ★
INDIANA
Indianapolis ★
ILLINOIS
Springfield ★
Cincinnati
WEST VIRGINIA
es Moines
Charleston ★
Frankfort ★
Louisville
KENTUCKY
VIRGINIA
Richmond ★
Norfolk
s City
Jefferson City ★
St. Louis
MISSOURI
Chesapeake Bay

APPALACHIAN MOUNTAINS

Winston-Salem
• Raleigh ★
Knoxville
NORTH CAROLINA
Nashville ★
TENNESSEE
• Charlotte
RKANSAS
Chattanooga
Little Rock ★
Memphis
SOUTH CAROLINA
Columbia ★
ATLANTIC OCEAN

Atlanta ★
Birmingham
MISSISSIPPI
ALABAMA
• Charleston
GEORGIA
hreveport
Montgomery ★
Jackson ★
LOUISIANA
Mobile
Jacksonville
Baton Rouge ★
• New Orleans
Tallahassee ★

GULF OF MEXICO
FLORIDA
Orlando
Tampa
Lake Okeechobee

Land Elevation

Feet		Meters
10,000		3,000
5,000		1,500
2,000		600
1,000		300
500		150
0		0
Below Sea Level		Below Sea Level

Miami

Key West

BAHAMAS

ATLANTIC OCEAN
VIRGIN ISLANDS
San Juan
PUERTO RICO

0   50   100 Miles
0   50   100 Kilometers

0   200   400 Miles
0   200   400 Kilometers

CUBA
DOMINICAN REPUBLIC
HAITI

Albers Equal-Area Projection